Gift of

MENLO MOTHERS' CLUB

*The Young Romantics and
Critical Opinion 1807-1824*

The Young Romantics and Critical Opinion 1807–1824

Poetry of Byron, Shelley, and Keats as seen by their contemporary critics

by

THEODORE REDPATH

Fellow, Senior Lecturer, and Director of English Studies, Trinity College, Cambridge, and Lecturer in English in the University of Cambridge

St. Martin's Press　New York

AFFILIATED PUBLISHERS: Macmillan Limited, London
– also at Bombay, Calcutta, Madras and Melbourne

Printed by Western Printing Services Ltd, Bristol
Made in Great Britain

Preface

This book is intended to provide detailed information about the criticism of the poetry of Byron, Shelley, and Keats, by their contemporaries.

More specifically its aim is twofold—first, to show how the work of these poets appeared to some of the leading or representative critical minds of their time; and secondly, to help to throw light on the poetry itself, by making conveniently available a record of the impressions it made when it had just appeared—impressions which often have a vitality or special character hard for critics writing in later times to recapture or rival, however distinguished in its own way their criticism may be.

It is hoped that the book may reach a public of two kinds: on the one hand, general readers curious to know something more precise and extensive about the reception this poetry received than is generally available in manuals or literary histories; on the other hand, students in universities and other higher educational establishments, and teachers in the upper forms of schools which are studying the work of these poets. In both cases the aim is to help to save readers from forming too simple a picture of the impact which the poems made on the critics of that time.

The criticism is presented here by three means: first, by a general survey of critical opinion on Byron, Shelley, and Keats during the period, especially of the periodical criticism—which constitutes, indeed, almost all the valuable detailed critical work extant; secondly, by an anthology of relevant passages from periodical reviews and articles, correspondence, and diaries; and thirdly, by short accounts of the contemporary criticism of each poet, immediately preceding the selected passages concerning his work. These short accounts are deliberately made to overlap the general survey to some degree, and there is also a certain amount of cross-referencing.

These features are intended to make the book serviceable both to readers primarily interested in a general view and also to those chiefly concerned with the criticism of only one of the three poets.

In the general survey I have started with a brief sketch of the political and ideological situation in the seventeen years 1807–24 that form the total span of time during which the work of the three poets appeared during their lifetimes. The main body of the survey consists of an account of the reception of the chief non-dramatic work of the three poets in eighteen representative periodicals of the time. In this survey I have been concerned to offer accounts of the reviews and articles generally in running form, quoting key words, phrases, and passages, so as to put readers into a direct contact with the critiques which it would be impossible to achieve otherwise, except by wading through the many reviews and articles themselves, which are, in any case, often only accessible with difficulty. Moreover, it would have been out of the question to offer this direct contact with a representative corpus of criticism by reprinting the reviews and articles themselves, since for that a volume far larger than the present would have been required. I would claim that the reader will find here a fuller representation of contemporary criticism of the work of our three poets in one volume than in any other modern work, though for Shelley a distinctly fuller survey and anthology are to be found in Professor Newman Ivey White's excellent book, *The Unextinguished Hearth*.[1] Professor White did not, however, include within his terms of reference criticism of the *Posthumous Poems* (1824), whereas I have done so.

Byron has presented me with an especially hard problem. He was reviewed vastly more than any other writer of his time, in prose or in verse. Hundreds of thousands of words were written about his poems. Even comparatively brief summaries of the periodical criticism would have occupied a volume far larger than the present one. On the other hand, simply to state that his poetry, or one or more of his poems, was received favourably, without indicating the criteria used by the critic, would not be very helpful towards a better understanding either of the criticism or of the poetry. In many cases, indeed, a much fuller account seems to be called for, including indication of passages quoted by the

[1] Published in 1938, by Duke University Press, Durham, North Carolina; reprinted by Octagon Books, New York, 1966, and republished in London by Frank Cass and Co., Ltd, 1966.

critic from the poems, and detailed reference to his remarks about them. The problem is complicated by Byron's creative energy. He poured out more than thirty publications which demanded the attention of the critics. There were several possible solutions to this difficulty, consistent with giving full enough accounts of the criticism. One would have been to limit the number of periodicals referred to to a very small number, say four or five, and to give an account of their critiques of all Byron's poetry. Another would have been to take account of all the periodicals, and to concentrate on their views on selected works. The first of these solutions would not have offered a varied enough spread of critical reactions. It would also have had the disadvantage of directing attention to criticism of many of the works of Byron which are scarcely ever read today, and have no great claim to be. The second solution, however, would still have involved a much longer survey than that which appears below. After careful thought I therefore ultimately decided to select eighteen of the leading periodicals (out of over sixty reviewing periodicals) and to offer an extended survey of their critiques substantially of the poems of Byron which are chiefly read nowadays. This means *English Bards and Scotch Reviewers, Childe Harold's Pilgrimage, The Prisoner of Chillon, Beppo, Don Juan,* and *The Vision of Judgment.* I have, however, included occasional mention of reactions to some of the other poems. I have also included in the anthology Brougham's notorious review of *Hours of Idleness* in the *Edinburgh,* and one other review of that volume, and have mentioned in the survey the poems' reception in some other periodicals. The general solution which I have adopted has one disadvantage—namely, that some of the poems which are little read nowadays had a great vogue in Byron's lifetime—for instance, the so-called 'Eastern Tales'. I have gone a little way towards countering this disadvantage by referring to some facts about this vogue in the short introduction which precedes the selected passages on Byron. I am, however, in any case convinced that the sacrifice was worth making in order to provide a fuller display of contemporary critical reaction to those of Byron's works which still have general interest today. My plan has also involved omitting all but the barest reference to Byron's dramatic works. These works were, however, regarded generally as failures even in Byron's lifetime, and I see no good reason to draw attention to them which would be better bestowed elsewhere.

Shelley has caused me some difficulty of the same kind, but in a far less degree. The reviewers wrote more on *Queen Mab* and *The Cenci* than on any of Shelley's other works. For us, however, these are among the less widely read of Shelley's poetical works. I have therefore adopted for Shelley a similar policy to that followed for Byron.

Keats does not pose a similar problem, and I have, indeed, either surveyed fairly fully, or included in the anthology, a considerable part of the periodical criticism of Keats. A great deal of what Keats wrote seems to interest readers today, and I have included criticism of all three of his volumes in the general survey, in the introduction to the selected passages on Keats, and in the anthology itself. I hope that this plentiful representation of Keats criticism may be a specially welcome feature of this volume.

Since I started work on this project three years ago four important books relevant to the subject have appeared. In 1969 there came out Professor J. O. Hayden's *The Romantic Reviewers, 1802–24*,[1] and in 1970 Professor Andrew Rutherford's *Byron: The Critical Heritage*[2] in the excellent series of that name. Both these books, in their very different ways, are admirable. Both are quite different from the present volume. Professor Hayden's book surveys the historical background and the attitudes, policies, and practice of some sixty reviewing periodicals, and also discusses the critical reception accorded to the work of twelve leading writers of the period in prose and verse. His accounts of the critical reception given to Byron, Shelley, and Keats are thus perforce nowhere near so detailed as those in the present book. Moreover, the scope of Professor Hayden's book does not include criticism outside periodicals, nor is he concerned to offer an anthology. Professor Rutherford's book, on the other hand, is an anthology of criticism, but is confined, of course, to Byron; and, moreover, only about half his book offers criticism written during Byron's lifetime. Further, the criticism cited covers all Byron's poetry, including the Eastern Tales and the dramas, criticism of which, taken together, occupies over a quarter of the anthology. Again, proportionately far more attention is given by Professor Rutherford to the three leading periodicals, the *Edinburgh*, the *Quarterly*, and *Blackwood's*—an entirely legitimate procedure, but different from that adopted here. Finally, Professor Rutherford's

---

[1] London and Chicago, 1969.
[2] London and New York, 1970.

survey of the contemporary criticism consists of about a dozen pages, giving a bird's-eye view, in contrast with the larger-scale map offered in the present volume. More recently there have appeared Mr G. M. Matthews's book *Keats: The Critical Heritage* (1971)[1] and Professor Hayden's anthology of criticism of the work of Wordsworth, Coleridge, Byron, Shelley and Keats, entitled *Romantic Bards and British Reviewers* (also 1971).[2] Mr Matthews's book and mine overlap to a considerable extent. His anthology actually contains more material than mine, though mine does contain a few items not included in his. In my surveys, however, I have included all the reviews which he prints. Part of Mr Matthews's Introduction covers some of the same ground as my surveys, but we have not produced duplicates by any means. Mr Matthews has said a number of interesting things which I have not said, and I can only hope that he will also find some worthwhile points in my own exposition and comments. As to Professor Hayden's anthology, this deals with five poets, and I was moreover delighted to find that, although there is considerable coincidence between the passages we have chosen on Keats, there is rather little between those concerning Shelley, and very little indeed between those on Byron—itself a testimony to the vastness of the corpus of criticism which Byron's contemporaries lavished on his poetry. The surveys in the present volume are also far more extensive and detailed than that in Professor Hayden's book, which is substantially an anthology, with an introduction offering a short but well-informed conspectus of the whole body of criticism of all five poets.

In conclusion I wish to acknowledge the great kindness of my friend and former pupil, Dr Keith Walker, of University College, London, in lending me over a long period his valuable Cambridge Ph.D. Dissertation, *Byron's Readers: A Study of Attitudes towards Byron, 1812–1832*, and other material, and in passing useful information to me from time to time. I also want to acknowledge the loan of Byron material made to me by my old friend and former collaborator, Will Ingram, erstwhile Director of English Studies at Emmanuel College, Cambridge, and now busily retired. I wish also to acknowledge the very great help I have received from Mr Roy Minton, of George G. Harrap and Co. Ltd, in the preparation of this book for the press. Finally, I owe my

[1] London and New York, 1971.
[2] London and Chicago, 1971.

gratitude to my efficient and accurate secretary, Clare Russell, for typing a good deal of the typescript of this book, and for helping me with photographic reproduction; and deep and loving thanks to my wife for every kind of help.

T.R.

Trinity College, Cambridge
January 1973

Contents

List of Abbreviations   19

A General Survey of Critical Opinion

I.   Some Notes on Politics and Ideology in the Years
1807–24   21

II.   Some Leading Literary Periodicals and Reviewers and
their Reception of the Work of Byron, Shelley, and
Keats   24

THE EDINBURGH REVIEW   24
THE QUARTERLY REVIEW   35
BLACKWOOD'S EDINBURGH MAGAZINE   42
THE MONTHLY REVIEW   51
THE BRITISH CRITIC   59
THE CHRISTIAN OBSERVER   69
THE ECLECTIC REVIEW   77
THE BRITISH REVIEW   91
THE LONDON MAGAZINE   108
THE EXAMINER, THE INDICATOR, and THE LITERARY
EXAMINER   116

III.   Other Expressions of Critical Opinion during the Period   134
CONSTABLE'S EDINBURGH MAGAZINE   135
THE MONTHLY MAGAZINE   140
THE NEW MONTHLY MAGAZINE   144
'GOLD'S' LONDON MAGAZINE   151
THE CHAMPION   153
THE LITERARY GAZETTE   157

IV.   Some Generalizations and Comparisons   167

George Gordon, Lord Byron (1788–1824)

A Survey of Contemporary Criticism, 1807–24   179
An Anthology of Contemporary Criticism, 1807–24   207

From the unsigned review by George Edward Griffiths of *Hours of Idleness* (1807) in *The Monthly Review*, November 1807   207

The unsigned review by Henry Brougham of *Hours of Idleness* in *The Edinburgh Review*, January 1808   207

From the review of *English Bards and Scotch Reviewers* (1809) in *The Eclectic Review*, May 1809   212

From Francis Jeffrey's unsigned review of *Childe Harold I and II* (1812) in *The Edinburgh Review*, February 1812   214

A letter about *Childe Harold III* (1816) from John Wilson Croker to John Murray, 18 September 1816   216

From Francis Jeffrey's unsigned review of *Childe Harold III* in *The Edinburgh Review*, December 1816   217

From the review of *Childe Harold III* and *The Prisoner of Chillon and other Poems* (1816) in *The British Critic*, December 1816   222

From William Roberts's unsigned review of *Childe Harold III* in *The British Review*, February 1817   223

From Francis Jeffrey's unsigned review of *Beppo* (1818) in *The Edinburgh Review*, February 1818   224

Hazlitt's brief notice of *Beppo* in *The Yellow Dwarf*, 28 March 1818   226

From William Roberts's unsigned review of *Beppo* in *The British Review*, May 1818   226

From the review of *Childe Harold IV* (1818) in Constable's *Edinburgh Magazine*, May 1818   227

From John Wilson's unsigned review of *Childe Harold IV* in *The Edinburgh Review*, June 1818   229

From William Roberts's unsigned review of *Childe Harold IV* in *The British Review*, August 1818   233

From Walter Scott's unsigned review of *Childe Harold IV* in *The Quarterly Review*, April 1818 (publ. September)   236

From the concluding section of the review of *Childe Harold IV* in *The Monthly Review*, November 1818   246

Diary entries about *Don Juan I and II* (1819) made in 1818–19 by John Cam Hobhouse (later Lord Broughton)   248

From a letter from John Keats to George and Georgiana Keats, 19 February 1819   249

Some remarks about *Don Juan I and II* in a letter from John Wilson Croker to John Murray, 18 July 1819   249

Some remarks on *Don Juan I and II* from a review of
Mazeppa in *The Eclectic Review*, August 1819   250

From the review of *Don Juan I and II* in *The British Critic*,
August 1819   251

Some further remarks on *Don Juan I and II* in a letter
from John Wilson Croker to John Murray, 15 September
1819   254

From a letter from John Keats to George and Georgiana
Keats, 17/27 September 1819   254

From Leigh Hunt's unsigned review of *Don Juan I and II*
in *The Examiner*, 31 October 1819   255

From a letter from Robert Southey to Walter Savage
Landor, 20 February 1820   259

A letter concerning *Don Juan III and IV* (1821) from John
Wilson Croker to John Murray, 26 March 1820   259

From John Scott's unsigned article 'Lord Byron' in the
series 'Living Authors' in *The London Magazine*, January
1821   262

From Robert Southey's Preface to his poem *A Vision of
Judgment*, published 11 April 1821   275

From the anonymous *Letter to the Right Honourable Lord
Byron, by John Bull* (April–May 1821), now known to
have been written by John Gibson Lockhart   276

From the review of *Don Juan III–V* in *The British Critic*,
September 1821   280

From William Roberts's unsigned review of *Don Juan III–
V* in *The British Review*, December 1821   281

From Francis Jeffrey's discussion of *Don Juan* in his
unsigned review of *Sardanapalus, The Two Foscari*, and
Cain in *The Edinburgh Review*, February 1822   286

A summary estimate of *The Vision of Judgment* (1822)
from an article entitled 'Oldmixon's Account of *The
Liberal*' printed in Constable's *Edinburgh Magazine*, November 1822   292

From a letter entitled 'Canting Slander', addressed to
Rev. William Bengo Collyer, printed in *The Examiner*,
10 November 1822   293

From a letter entitled 'Canting Slander', addressed to
Rev. William Bengo Collyer, printed in *The Examiner*, 24
November 1822   293

From the preview of *Don Juan VI–VIII* (1823) in *The Literary Examiner*, 5 July 1823   294

From the preview of *Don Juan IX–XI* (1823) in *The Literary Examiner*, 2, 16 August 1823   296

From the letter to 'Christopher North' signed 'M. ODOHERTY', concerning *Don Juan IX–XI*, printed in *Blackwood's Edinburgh Magazine*, September 1823   297

From the preview of *Don Juan XII–XIV* (1823) in *The Literary Examiner*, 8 November 1823   301

From the review of *Don Juan IX–XI* in *The Monthly Magazine*, December 1823   302

William Hazlitt's critique of *Don Juan*, written in 1824 and published in *The Spirit of the Age*, January 1825   303

Percy Bysshe Shelley (1792–1822)

A Survey of Contemporary Criticism, 1815–22, with an exceptional extension to cover *Posthumous Poems*   304

An Anthology of Contemporary Criticism, 1816–22, with an Exceptional Extension to 1828   327

From Josiah Conder's unsigned review of *Alastor, and other Poems* (1816) in *The Eclectic Review*, October 1816   327

From Leigh Hunt's review of *The Revolt of Islam* (1818) in *The Examiner*, 1, 22 February, and 1 March 1818   329

From the unsigned review (by John Gibson Lockhart and possibly John Wilson) of *The Revolt of Islam* in *Blackwood's Edinburgh Magazine*, January 1819   333

From John Taylor Coleridge's unsigned review of *Laon and Cythna* and of *The Revolt of Islam* in *The Quarterly Review*, April 1819 (publ. September 1819)   337

From the review of *Alastor, and other Poems* in *Blackwood's Edinburgh Magazine*, November 1819   347

From the notice of *Prometheus Unbound* (1819–20) in Baldwin's *London Magazine*, June 1820   350

From a letter from Keats to Shelley, 16 August 1820   350

From the unsigned review (probably mainly or wholly by Lockhart) of *Prometheus Unbound, with other Poems*, in *Blackwood's Edinburgh Magazine*, September 1820   351

From the review of *Prometheus Unbound, with other Poems*, in Gold's *London Magazine*, October 1820   355

From the review of *Prometheus Unbound, with other Poems*, in *The Monthly Review*, February 1821 — 357

From the article 'On the Philosophy and Poetry of Shelley' in Gold's *London Magazine*, February 1821 — 359

From the unsigned review by Rev. Dr W. S. Walker of *Prometheus Unbound, with other Poems*, in *The Quarterly Review*, October 1821 (publ. December) — 362

From the unsigned review (possibly by Rev. George Croly) of *Adonais* (1821) in *Blackwood's Edinburgh Magazine*, December 1821 — 372

The review of *Adonais* in *The Literary Gazette*, 8 December 1821 — 377

From Leigh Hunt's unsigned 'Letters to the readers of *The Examiner* "On the Quarterly Review" ' concerning *Prometheus Unbound* and *Ode to a Skylark*, 9, 16, 23 June 1822 — 381

From Leigh Hunt's unsigned review of *Adonais* in *The Examiner*, 7 July 1822 — 383

From Hazlitt's unsigned review of Shelley's *Posthumous Poems* (1824) in *The Edinburgh Review*, July 1824 — 388

From the review of Shelley's *Posthumous Poems* in Constable's *Edinburgh Magazine*, July 1824 — 396

From the review by 'E. Haselfoot' (W. S. Walker ?) of Shelley's *Posthumous Poems* in *Knight's Quarterly Magazine*, August 1824 — 399

From Leigh Hunt's critique of Shelley's *Posthumous Poems* (apparently written early in 1825, later revised, and printed in this form in *Lord Byron and Some of his Contemporaries*, London, 1828 — 405

John Keats (1795–1821)

A Survey of Contemporary Criticism, 1817–20 — 418

An Anthology of Contemporary Criticism, 1817–20 — 451

From the review of Keats's *Poems* (1817) by John Hamilton Reynolds in *The Champion*, 9 March 1817 — 451

From Leigh Hunt's unsigned review of *Poems* (1817) in *The Examiner*, 6 and 13 July 1817 — 452

From Josiah Conder's unsigned review of *Poems* (1817) in *The Eclectic Review*, September 1817 — 459

From the review of *Poems* (1817) in Constable's *Edinburgh Magazine*, October 1817 — 462

From a letter from Benjamin Bailey to John Taylor,
9 April 1818   465

From the review of *Endymion* (1818) in *The Champion*,
7 June 1818   465

From the article (No. 4) by 'Z' (probably John Gibson
Lockhart and John Wilson) on 'The Cockney School of
Poetry' in *Blackwood's Edinburgh Magazine*, August 1818   467

From a letter from Benjamin Bailey to John Taylor,
29 August 1818   472

John Wilson Croker's unsigned review of *Endymion* in
The Quarterly Review, April 1818 (publ. September 1818)   472

From Richard Woodhouse's 'Notes on the Critiques on
Endymion in *The Quarterly Review* and *Blackwood's
Edinburgh Magazine*', October 1818   476

From the unsigned article by John Hamilton Reynolds in
The Alfred, 6 October 1818, on the treatment of *Endymion*
by *The Quarterly Review*   477

From a letter from Richard Woodhouse to Mary Frogley,
23 October 1818   481

From P. G. Patmore's unsigned review of *Endymion* in
Baldwin's *London Magazine*, April 1820   482

From the review of *Lamia, Isabella, The Eve of St Agnes,
and other Poems* (1820) in *The Monthly Review*, July 1820   488

From the review of *Endymion* in Constable's *Edinburgh
Magazine*, August 1820   490

From Francis Jeffrey's unsigned review of *Endymion* and
of *Lamia, Isabella, The Eve of St Agnes, and other Poems* in
The Edinburgh Review, August 1820   493

From Leigh Hunt's unsigned review of *Lamia, Isabella,
The Eve of St Agnes, and other Poems* in *The Indicator*,
2 and 9 August 1820   497

From the review of *Lamia, Isabella, The Eve of St Agnes,
and other Poems* in *The British Critic*, September 1820   499

From John Scott's unsigned review of *Lamia, Isabella,
The Eve of St Agnes, and other Poems* in *The London Magazine*, September 1820   502

From the review of *Lamia, Isabella, The Eve of St Agnes,
and other Poems* in *The Eclectic Review*, September 1820   505

The review of *Lamia, Isabella, The Eve of St Agnes, and
other Poems* in *The Monthly Magazine*, September 1820   509

16

From John Scott's article 'The Mohock Magazine'
printed in *The London Magazine* for December 1820   510

Select Bibliography   513

Index of Names, Poems, Periodicals, and Criteria   527

List of Abbreviations

(see also the list of abbreviations of the names of modern periodicals at the head of the Select Bibliography)

AJR	*The Anti-Jacobin Review and Magazine*
BC	*The British Critic*
BM	*Blackwood's Edinburgh Magazine*
BR	*The British Review*
Champ	*The Champion*
CO	*The Christian Observer*
CR	*The Critical Review*
D	*The Diary of Henry Crabb Robinson, An Abridgment,* ed. Derek Hudson, London, 1967
DJ	*Don Juan*
Ecl. R	*The Eclectic Review*
Ed. M	*The Edinburgh Magazine* (Constable's)
Eur. M	*The European Magazine*
ER	*The Edinburgh Review*
Exar	*The Examiner*
GM	*The Gentleman's Magazine*
Gold's LM	*The London Magazine and Monthly Critical and Dramatic Review*
HCRBW	*Henry Crabb Robinson on Books and their Writers,* ed. Edith J. Morley, 3 vols., London, 1938
Indicr	*The Indicator*
Investigr	*The Investigator*
JBBJ	*John Bull's British Journal*
KL	*The Letters of John Keats, 1814–1821,* ed. H. J. Rollins, 2 vols. (Cambridge, Mass.; London, 1958)
KQM	*Knight's Quarterly Magazine*
LC	*The Literary Chronicle and Weekly Review*
LG	*The Literary Gazette*

LJ	Byron's *Works: Letters and Journals*, ed. R. E. Prothero, 6 vols., London, 1898–1901
Lit. Exar	*The Literary Examiner*
Lit. J	*The Literary Journal, and General Miscellany*
LM	*The London Magazine* (Baldwin's)
MLN	*Modern Language Notes*
MM	*The Monthly Magazine*
MR	*The Monthly Review*
NMM	*The New Monthly Magazine*
n.s.	new series
P	Byron's *Works: Poetry*, 7 vols., London (1898–1904)
PBSA	*Publications of the Bibliographical Society of America*
PMLA	*Papers of the Modern Language Association of America*
QR	*The Quarterly Review*
SL	*The Letters of Percy Bysshe Shelley*, ed. F. L. Jones, 2 vols. (London, 1964)
SM	*The Scots Magazine*
TLS	*The Times Literary Supplement*
YD	*The Yellow Dwarf*

A General Survey of Critical Opinion
1807–24

I

Some Notes on Politics and Ideology in the Years 1807–24

The literary output of Byron published in his lifetime appeared from 1807 to 1824; that of Shelley from 1810 to 1822 (though the important volume of his *Posthumous Poems* was published in 1824); and that of Keats from 1817 to 1820. In order to understand more fully the contemporary reception of our three poets' work it is worth looking, if only briefly, at the political and ideological background.

During roughly the first half of the period 1807–24—namely, 1807–15—England was at war with Napoleon. Pitt the Younger had died in 1806. George III had got rid of the coalition of Whigs and Tories known as the 'Ministry of All-the-Talents', which had governed the country from 1806 to 1807, and the war was fought out to a successful finish in 1815 under Tory Governments, successively headed by Portland (1807–9), Perceval (1809–12), and Liverpool (1812–27). All these Governments were scared of Jacobinism, and even of milder forms of Radicalism, and a policy of rigid repression of propaganda and public meetings was continued for long after the end of the war. Indeed, it was only after Castlereagh died in 1822, and was succeeded in the Cabinet by Canning, and Sidmouth was replaced at the Home Office by Peel, that more liberal policies began to be introduced.

During the war Napoleon appeared to many Englishmen to embody the spirit of the French Revolution, and he was on that account a hero to some Radicals (for instance, Hazlitt), and a bogey to many people with conservative ideas, such as Wordsworth and Coleridge in this period. To Byron, who was half a Radical, Napoleon was half a hero, and a very fascinating personality, whereas Wellington, as a representative of English conservatism, was rather a sinister personality than a glorious victor.

The war caused considerable economic suffering to the artisan and labouring classes, while the landed class generally throve on improved rents, and contributed less than their just share to its expenses. Over two-thirds of taxation consisted of indirect levy on consumer goods, and less than a quarter was direct. The effect of the war on the merchant classes was mixed; some merchants were bankrupted by the fluctuation in markets, while others made rapid fortunes. Many of the working-class people were very badly off. Trade unions were prohibited, and the policy of guaranteeing minimum wages was deliberately rejected. Byron, Shelley, and Keats were all sympathetic with the poorer classes, and were politically what would now be called 'left of centre', though Shelley was probably the fullest revolutionary in political doctrine.

Another and even more central fact about our three poets is that, in contrast with the major poets of the preceding generation (Crabbe, Blake, Wordsworth, and Coleridge), Byron, Shelley, and Keats were not Christians but freethinkers, both in theology and in morals. Shelley's thought on these important matters was partly rooted in Ancient Greece, and partly in the French freethinking tradition of Voltaire and Condorcet, and in the works of the British freethinkers, Shaftesbury, Hume, and Godwin. He was a more fully developed and more philosophically grounded thinker than the other two poets; and he was certainly more virulently and relentlessly attacked for his speculations. Byron's deviations from Christian doctrine, however, also let him in for some sharp criticism from Christian believers. Criticism of Keats on theological points was rare, partly no doubt because his work did not directly express anti-Christian theological beliefs; but the lax sexual morals which his poetry often seemed to sanction caused him to receive pointed reproof from time to time. Both Byron's and Shelley's matrimonial histories and sexual freedoms caused scandal which affected criticism of their work. Little was known of Keats's private life, and he was not exposed to calumny of that kind. Keats's sexual licences were, in any case, mild in comparison with those of the other two poets.

The dominant religious ideology of that time was, of course, Christian and Anglican, and among Anglicans both High Churchmen and Evangelicals were naturally indisposed to condone serious departures from articles of Christian faith or from Christian morals, and the same was true of the dissenting Methodists and Congregationalists. Fortunately, however, criticism from all these points of view often showed itself capable of recognizing such more specifically 'literary' virtues as energy, command of form, interest of story, insight into character, appropriateness of imagery, accurateness of description, and felicity of diction, even when the work under consideration was unacceptable in point of morals and doctrine. It should, on the other hand, be clearly realized that the ethical and doctrinal strictures of the critics were often perfectly legitimate, for to exclude such considerations wholesale from literary criticism would involve a woeful reduction of its importance. The common criticism of Byron's Eastern Tales, that they presented scoundrels as characters worthy of admiration, was perfectly in place; and an adherent of ecclesiastical Christianity who failed to attack Shelley for his castigation of Christian priestcraft could well have been unfaithful to deep convictions which were far from irrelevant to literary criticism. Again, the question whether a theme is important or unimportant involves appeal to a critical sense of values, and to pass an opinion on such a question might bring into play a critic's whole attitude to life and art. For a Christian the theme of *Paradise Lost* would naturally seem far more important than that of *Endymion*.

Yet although the dominant religious ideology of the time was Christian and Anglican, we need to bear in mind that there were strong currents of freethinking in Britain. Shaftesbury (grandson of Dryden's Achitophel), over a century before, had tried to establish a theory of morals not derived from religion, and Hume had developed such a theory with some subtlety. There had, moreover, been free speculation about doctrinal theology, and non-Christian theism, deism, and even atheism, had been defended by British thinkers. There had also been attacks on the ecclesiastical establishment, not only by Dissenters but also by non-Christians. These native phenomena had been reinforced by the work of French freethinkers, such as Voltaire, the Encyclopaedists, Rousseau, and the ideologists of the French Revolution. There were great variations among freethinkers, but almost all lay outside what would generally have been recognized as the Christian

23

religion. For our specific theme in this book (the contemporary reception of the work of our three poets) the result was that, although freethinking and non-Christian attitudes in poetry were generally received unsympathetically and sometimes rejected with horror, they were not unsupported in the opinion of the time, and were sometimes even explicitly defended in 'advanced' periodicals, such as *The Examiner, The Indicator*, Gold's *London Magazine*, and *John Bull's British Journal*.[1]

Let us now, however, see what the reviewers said about the poems of Byron, Shelley, and Keats.

II

Some Leading Literary Periodicals and Reviewers and their Reception of the Work of Byron, Shelley, and Keats

I shall here survey the reviews of the chief non-dramatic works of Byron and Shelley, and of all the non-dramatic works of Keats, in *The Edinburgh Review, The Quarterly Review, Blackwood's Edinburgh Magazine, The Monthly Review, The British Critic, The Christian Observer, The Eclectic Review, The British Review, The London Magazine* (Baldwin's), *The Examiner, The Indicator*, and *The Literary Examiner*. This represents a wide range of critical opinion.

THE EDINBURGH REVIEW

The Edinburgh Review had been founded in 1802, and was from the start liberal in its political attitudes. Soon afterwards one of its three founders, Francis Jeffrey (1773–1850), had been formally appointed editor. He ran the review until 1829. He had been a struggling lawyer, and was later to become a successful member of the Scottish Bar, later still Lord Advocate, then, after the Reform Act of 1832, M.P. for Edinburgh, and for the last sixteen years of his life a Judge of the Court of Session. Jeffrey was a

---

[1] A Radical periodical, not to be confused with the Tory *John Bull*.

highly intelligent man, of sound Scottish education, and an efficient administrator. He had also a genuine interest in literature, and a fair, though somewhat limited, literary sensibility. He had been brought up on Virgil, Cicero, and Horace, and on Pope, Swift, and Addison, and these writers formed his standards during his early years. Later, however, soon after the turn of the century, he came to be more impressed by the Elizabethans than by either the Roman or the English Augustans, and to consider that the emotional range of poetry had been narrowed at the time of the Restoration, largely under French influence. In his view, Dryden was never 'pathetic', and scarcely ever 'sublime', Swift seemed only vulgar and commonplace, and the serious styles both of Addison and of Swift tame and poor. Jeffrey now thought even of Pope as 'a satirist, and a moralist, and a wit, and a critic, and a fine writer', rather than as a poet.[1] Nevertheless, he did continue to use in his criticism, and to use inexorably, some of the Augustan criteria of literary value. He called, for instance, for polish, good sense, clarity, decorum, and economy; and he condemned homeliness, 'mysticism', obscurity, eccentricity, and wordiness. On the other hand, he had come to admire energy, originality, and strong feeling in poetry. It was natural enough, in view of this combination of attitudes, and of the fact that Jeffrey was politically progressive, that he should have found much in Byron to appeal to him. Nevertheless, as is well known, the *Edinburgh* did not start off with a favourable estimate.

On Byron

The *Edinburgh*'s withering review of Byron's juvenile volume, *Hours of Idleness* (1807), is one of the celebrated *loci* of literary history.[2] Byron thought Jeffrey had written the review, but it was by Henry Brougham, later Lord Brougham, the famous lawyer and Lord Chancellor.[3] *Hours of Idleness* had received some favourable reviews in other periodicals, and Byron was shattered almost to the point of suicide by the appearance in January 1808 of the *Edinburgh*'s contemptuous dismissal. Instead of doing away with himself, however, he very sensibly canalized his hostility by converting a satire which he had ready on contemporary poetry into

[1] 'Weber's *Ford*', *ER*, XVIII, August 1811.
[2] *ER*, XI, January 1808. The whole review is reprinted on pp. 207–13 below.
[3] Satirized by Peacock in *Crotchet Castle* (1831) as the 'learned friend'.

a combined onslaught on his fellow-poets and his adverse reviewers.

The *Edinburgh* did not review the resultant *English Bards and Scotch Reviewers* (1809). Its next review of Byron was of *Childe Harold I and II* (1812).[1] This time Jeffrey was the reviewer, and the review was first in the field. It thought Byron's work had improved 'marvellously', and praised the poem's 'power, spirit, and originality'. Jeffrey thought it surprisingly interesting, considering it had no story or even incident, but was just a series of reflections during travel, without regular order or connexion. He considered the hero 'oddly chosen' and 'imperfectly employed', and also pointed out that though Byron expressly distinguished himself from the Childe, his own reflections had 'a shade of the same gloomy and misanthropic colouring'. He did not believe that such things as the contempt shown for the Portuguese, despondency about Spain, the sarcastic remarks about wars, victories, and military heroes, and the unorthodox religious opinions, lack of respect for priests, and creeds, and dogmas of all kinds, and the doubts about immortality and other fundamental beliefs would be popular with readers. Nevertheless, Jeffrey felt confident that the poem would find favour. Its chief excellence was 'a singular freedom and boldness, both of thought and expression, and a great occasional force and felicity of diction'. Jeffrey considered Byron's 'plain manliness and strength of manner' to be 'infinitely refreshing after the sickly affectations of so many modern writers'. He even wondered whether there was not 'something *piquant* in the very novelty and singularity of that cast of misanthropy and universal scorn'. It excited curiosity to see how objects would appear through so dark a medium, and gave great effect to the flashes of emotion and suppressed sensibility that occasionally burst through the gloom. So, according to Jeffrey (and here he differed from, and was superior to, many of the other critics):

> The best parts of the poem are those which embody those stern and disdainful reflexions, to which the author seems to recur with unfeigned cordiality and eagerness—and through which we think we can sometimes discern the strugglings of a gentler feeling, to which he is afraid to abandon himself.

Jeffrey also found the descriptions 'often exceedingly good', and

[1] *ER*, XIX, February 1812.

he also thought that Byron had availed himself more extensively than any poet since Spenser himself of the great range of tones and manners latent in the Spenserian stanza.

Jeffrey reviewed *The Giaour* (1813),[1] *The Bride of Abydos* (1813),[2] and *The Corsair* (1814).[3] In his review of *The Giaour* he encouraged Byron to continue producing Eastern tales. As we know, Byron did so; and they sold superlatively well. Six thousand copies of *The Bride* were sold in a month, and ten thousand copies of *The Corsair* on the day of publication. Jeffrey thought well of *The Bride*, but still better of *The Corsair*, which he reviewed at great length. He thought Byron now supreme among contemporary poets, and that this was because he depicted 'the stronger and deeper passions' with 'unequalled force and fidelity'. Jeffrey fitted this account into a theory of civilization according to which rude ages were followed, as civilization advanced, by periods in which strong feelings were proscribed, after which powerful spirits eventually arose who wanted strong and natural sensations. This was what was happening now, and so understandably Byron was the reigning favourite. It was natural for such a poet to choose barbaric subjects, and so Byron, in *The Corsair*, had 'adorned a merciless corsair on a rock in the Mediterranean, with every virtue under heaven—except common honesty'. As to other merits of Byron's poetry, Jeffrey enumerates 'unparalleled rapidity of narration, and condensation of thoughts and images—a style always vigorous and original, though sometimes quaint and affected, and more frequently strained, harsh, and abrupt—a diction and versification invariably spirited and almost always harmonious and emphatic'. Nothing was 'diluted . . . or diffused into weakness', but all was

> full of life and nerve, and activity—expanding only in the eloquent expression of strong and favourite affections, and everywhere else concise, energetic, and impetuous—hurrying on with a disdain of little ornaments and accuracies, and not always very solicitous about being comprehended by readers of inferior capacity.

Jeffrey thought *The Corsair* perhaps superior in these respects to all Byron's other work to date. But he wished Byron would offer more sympathetic characters to his readers. 'At present he will

[1] *ER*, XXI, July 1813. [2] *ER*, XXIII, April 1814.
[3] *ER*, XXIII, April 1814.

let us admire nothing but adventurous courage in men, and devoted gentleness in women.' None of his characters had any 'intellect, dignity, or accomplishment'.

The next review of Byron in the *Edinburgh* was a long review by Jeffrey of *Childe Harold III* (1816) and *The Prisoner of Chillon* volume (1816).[1] In this review Jeffrey mentions briefly some of the poems Byron had published since *The Corsair*, but we must concentrate attention on the poems under review. Jeffrey thought *Childe Harold III* perhaps even more forceful and original than *I* and *II*, and that it also contained 'deeper and more matured reflections, and a more intense sensibility to all that is grand and lovely in the external world'. The reflections, moreover, were now clearly the poet's. Jeffrey has high praise for the lines (xxi–xxxv) on the ball before Quatre Bras, the subsequent carnage there and at Ligny and Waterloo,[2] and the broken-hearted families who lost their sons and brothers. He is particularly interesting on the apostrophe to Napoleon and Byron's subsequent reflections. He finds the expression here 'infinitely beautiful and earnest', but sharply criticizes the thoughts for 'breathing the very essence of misanthropical disdain, and embodying opinions which we conceive to be not less erroneous than revolting'. This is the kind of criticism which is hard to find except in reviews by Byron's contemporaries, who took such ideas more seriously than retrospective criticism has generally done. Jeffrey later singles out as 'enchanting' the stanzas characterizing Rousseau (xcix ff.). He is here in marked contrast to a number of other reviewers, who could not stomach the charity towards Rousseau which Jeffrey notices but does not censure. Expecting readers to want 'the relief of a little narrative or description', Jeffrey announces that there is no narrative, and that all the descriptions are blended with deep emotion. Even lovers of pure description, however, would like the lines on the evening calm on Lake Geneva, and the contrasting sketch of the midsummer night's thunderstorm (lxxxv ff.), which Jeffrey thinks 'still more striking and original'. He praises the lines on Voltaire and Gibbon (cv ff.) without any demur, and then comments on some of Byron's concluding reflections (cxi–cxiv). These 'may seem perhaps to savour somewhat of egotism; but this is of the essence of such

---

[1] *ER*, XXVII, December 1816.
[2] The poem runs all together into one great battle.

poetry'. What Jeffrey objects to is the disdainful spirit, yet even so he admires the passage:

> The reckoning, however, is steadily and sternly made; and though he does not spare himself, we must say the world comes off much the worst in comparison. The passage is very singular, and written with much force and dignity.

Jeffrey refuses to publicize the final stanzas despite their beauty. He ends by emphasizing and illustrating the influence on Canto III of the Lake School, with their 'mysticism' and 'unintelligible sublimities'.[1]

This review of Jeffrey's is admirably sensitive and understanding. He picks out unerringly the best passages, describes them vividly and accurately, and goes a long way with the spirit of the poetry. His review has the virtues, but also possibly some of the weaknesses, of balance and poise. He is neither as enthusiastic nor as fanatically condemnatory as some of the other reviewers. On the other hand, he does rightly retain his own scale of moral values, and makes it felt when it seems relevant. How much we value Jeffrey's liberal-minded sanity and balance will depend on our whole attitude to criticism, literature, and, indeed, life.

As to *The Prisoner of Chillon*, Jeffrey found it 'very sweet and touching', words which suggest a rather limited response. The rest of the poems in the volume he thought 'less amiable', most having 'a personal and not very charitable application'. *Darkness* was an exception. It was 'a grand and gloomy sketch', 'executed with great and fearful force', but its conception was 'too oppressive to the imagination, to be contemplated with pleasure, even in the faint reflection of poetry'. *The Dream* was 'written with great beauty—but extremely painful—and abounding with mysteries', into which Jeffrey had no desire to penetrate. He was deeply impressed with the sincerity and force of those poems. Unlike some other reviewers, he saw that it was hopeless to try to preach Byron into philanthropy and cheerfulness. He mourned the prodigal gifts of nature that had been turned to bitterness, but hoped that they might yet 'enter into happier combinations'.

---

[1] Cf. P. Hodgart and T. Redpath, *Romantic Perspectives* (London, 1964; second edition, 1967), pp. 27–31, 163–70, 175–81, and 185–8, for Jeffrey's attacks on the Lake School, and on Wordsworth in particular; and, for an even fuller account, A. Noyes, *Wordsworth and Jeffrey in Controversy* (Bloomington, Indiana, 1941).

Jeffrey's reactions are interesting. He is much more intensely impressed with the dark and terrifying side of Byron than with the 'sweetness' of *The Prisoner* (whose painfulness he misses). Yet, though fascinated, he refuses to succumb, and wistfully and vaguely hopes for some kind of Byron who probably could not have existed.

Jeffrey's review of *Beppo*,[1] which Byron published anonymously in 1818, was favourable. He welcomed the poem, not merely because it was 'extremely clever and amusing', but because it was a specimen of 'a kind of diction and composition of which our English Literature has hitherto afforded very few examples'. Jeffrey took the poem to be a very good instance of *vers de société*, but (unlike some other reviewers) did not notice that it was probably also intended as a criticism of British brashness and clumsiness in dealing with amorous complications of the kind it depicted.

The *Edinburgh* reviewed *Childe Harold IV* (1818) at great length,[2] but the reviewer this time was John Wilson, who had reviewed the canto in *Blackwood's* the month before.[3] Wilson's review is an impassioned and rhetorical performance. It starts with nine pages pointing out resemblances between Byron and Rousseau (a comparison Byron's own mother had made, and which occurs in a number of reviews). Wilson stresses the fact that they expressed their characters to the full, and the fact that they had such wayward and troubled characters to express. Wilson tries to explain how their personalities had come to entrance their readers. He warns that such a fascination could easily fade; but at present he thought the bond between Byron and 'the public mind' was stronger than had ever existed for a poet while alive. He also thought that bond would be 'still more closely rivetted'. The 'ill-sustained misanthropy and disdain' of *Childe Harold I and II* had glimmered more faintly through *III*, and disappeared wholly from *IV*,

> which reflects the high and disturbed visions of earthly glory, as a dark swollen tide images the splendours of the sky in portentous colouring, and broken magnificence.

[1] *ER*, XXIX, February 1818. An extract is printed below on pp. 224–6.
[2] *ER*, XXX, June 1818.
[3] *BM*, III, May 1818. For further details on Wilson see *Romantic Perspectives*, pp. 38–47, 79.

Wilson believed that Byron's mind was 'clearing up, like noon-day, after a stormy and disturbed morning', and that when the change which Wilson anticipated had been fully achieved, the poetry would be 'lofty and pure'. As for the 'dark and sceptical spirit' so far prevalent in Byron's works, Wilson thought it unique in contemporary poetry. Only three great poets of modern times had fully represented 'this restlessness and discomfort of uncertainty as to the government of the world and the future destinies of Man': Goethe, Schiller, and Byron; and Byron alone had made *himself* the tormented spirit. Yet his melancholy was ennobling and elevating, and carried 'its refutation in its grandeur'. Wilson defends Byron against the castigators of his scepticism:

> There is neither philosophy nor religion in those bitter and savage taunts which have been sternly thrown out, from many quarters, against those moods of mind which are involuntary, and will not pass away:—the shadows and spectres which still haunt his imagination, may once have disturbed our own:—through his gloom there are frequent flashes of imagination:—and the sublime sadness which, to him, is breathed from the mysteries of mortal existence, is always joined with a longing after immortality, and expressed in language that is itself divine.

Wilson's own language here (especially when the passage is quoted in isolation) is too heightened for modern taste, but the passage is a generous and, in great measure, an understanding one.

Wilson considers *IV* the finest of the cantos, and *Childe Harold* perhaps the most original poem in English, both in conception and in execution. 'Byron traverses the whole earth, borne along by the whirlwind of his own spirit.' He paints existence in the present, and for the present. When he writes of stirring political events he either gives back to readers their own feelings or tries to displace them with feelings of his own—generally the former! Wilson takes Byron to be the representative of a 'powerful and impassioned people', going out into the world and writing of objects which already command its interest; but he had designs on the public:

> He looks upon them as sentient existences that are important in his poetical existence,—so that he command their feelings and passions, he cares not for their censure or their praise,—for his fame is more than mere literary fame; and he aims in poetry, like the fallen chief whose image is so often before him, at universal

31

dominion, we had almost said, universal tyranny, over the minds of men.

This seems to be a most perceptive comment.

As to detailed criticism, Wilson thought the opening stanzas of *IV* (on Venice) inferior, except for xv–xviii. He was more impressed by the Brenta passage (xxvii–xxix). Byron's descriptions seemed to him now to blend with 'the poet's very life'. Wilson approves of the reflections on Petrarch's house and tomb (xxx ff.), but notes that Byron then suddenly starts away (in xxxiv) 'into one of those terrible fits, which often suddenly appal us in his poetry'. But the pilgrim's admiration of the Greek statues in Florence (xlix–liii) was more 'susceptible' and even more 'learned' than that expressed by any other poet. Wilson even suggests—perhaps somewhat fancifully, as he admits—that Byron was more akin to the Ancient Greek spirit than any other modern poet, in his satisfaction with 'singleness, simplicity, and unity'. Wilson is delighted with the contrast drawn in lxii–lxviii between Trasimene as a battlefield and its modern repose. He also admires the passion of the description of the Cataract of Velino (lxix–lxxii), and the immediately following evocation of mountain scenes. Nor was the commemoration of Rome disappointing. Byron had wisely restrained the subjective pessimism of Harold, and, 'with the genuine submission and reverence natural to a great mind', had disdained 'to be other than passive on such an arena'. Wilson is not so happy about the 'lucubrations' on Cromwell and Napoleon and the French Revolution, and is relieved to be brought back to the pilgrim's own 'gloom and misanthropy' (civ–cv), but he clearly admires more the immediately subsequent passage (cvi–cxii) in which the pilgrim 'blends his spirit' with 'the glorious decay' around him. Wilson is also attracted by the 'full, delicate, and perfect sense of beauty' of the stanzas on the Egerian Grot (cxv–cxix). Soon, however, Byron shies away, and bursts again into 'bitter communings with misery'. Wilson wishes to avoid considering these 'distressing passions', but comments that the passage (cxx–cxxxviii) is 'one of the most awful records of the agonies of man—perhaps the most painful and agitating picture of the misery of the passions, without their degradation, that is to be found in the whole compass of human language'. Wilson is glad to escape from this and look at the 'moonlight and indistinct shadow of the ruins of the Coliseum' (cxliii–cxliv). He is also much impressed by the 'magnificent' ending (clxxvii–end).

Wilson concludes his review with a fine summing-up of the whole of *Childe Harold*, and its change in spirit since 1812, and this part of the review also contains some important reflections on the poetry of the time.[1]

Wilson's review is more passionate than those of Jeffrey, and less securely poised. Its language is at times fantastically oratorical, but it is nevertheless certainly one of the finest contemporary appreciations of *Childe Harold*.

Jeffrey wrote three more reviews of Byron, all of works outside the scope of this book; but at the end of one of these he explains why he disapproves of *Don Juan*, and refuses to review it.[2] In another he shows that he still regards as the chief characteristics of Byron's work features typical of *Childe Harold* and the Eastern Tales, rather than of Byron's satirical poems.[3] These two attitudes go together. Jeffrey refuses to recognize as Byron's major achievement a kind of poetry he finds pernicious because it tends 'to destroy all belief in the reality of virtue'.

Though outside the scope of this book, Macaulay's review in the *Edinburgh* of Moore's *Life of Byron*[4] probably also needs mention. It is masterly in its account of the Byron vogue, and of the change in attitude to Byron's poetry after Byron's separation from his wife in 1816. It is also interesting, though not masterly, in its description of the leading characteristics of Byron's poetry.

On Shelley

The *Edinburgh* never reviewed Shelley in his lifetime. I do not know why. It may have been because Jeffrey did not wish to commit the review either to firm rejection like the *Quarterly*'s, or to championing wild and radical ideas in company with *The Examiner*, or even to aesthetic approval with moral reservations, such as he had given to *Childe Harold* and the Eastern Tales. Jeffrey himself did, however, write in 1828 in a review of a forgotten

[1] The whole of the conclusion of Wilson's review is reprinted on pp. 229–233, below.

[2] *ER*, XXXVI, February 1822 (on *Sardanapalus*, *The Two Foscari*, and *Cain*), pp. 444–52. An extract is reprinted on pp. 286–92 below.

[3] *ER*, XXXV, July 1821 (on *Marino Faliero* and *The Prophecy of Dante*), pp. 271–2.

[4] *ER*, LIII, June 1831. The review is readily accessible in collections of Macaulay's essays. The whole review deserves reading.

poem, *The Fall of Nineveh*, by a forgotten writer, Atherstone:

> Three poets of great promise . . . have been lost 'in the morn and liquid dew of their youth'—in Kirke White, in Keats, and in Pollok; and a powerful, though more uncertain genius extinguished, less prematurely, in Shelley.[1]

There appears to be only one other reference to Shelley by Jeffrey in the *Edinburgh*, in a review in 1829 of Mrs Hemans.[2] There Jeffrey mentions 'the rich melodies of Keats and Shelley' among the 'vast deal of beautiful poetry' which had passed 'into oblivion' since the start of his critical career.

Though the *Edinburgh* did not review Shelley during his lifetime, it did publish a long review of his *Posthumous Poems* (1824) by Hazlitt.[3] Hazlitt praises Shelley's humanity, but criticizes his webs of fancy and metaphysical obscurities, and what Hazlitt believed to be his contradictions of attitude. Shelley's short and least ambitious poems seemed best to Hazlitt: 'give him a larger subject, and time to reflect, and he was sure to get entangled in a system'.

On Keats

As to Keats, it is well known that the *Edinburgh* only reviewed him once, in August 1820. Jeffrey devoted eleven pages to a combined review of *Endymion* (1818) and the 1820 Poems.[4] Seven pages deal with *Endymion*, which Jeffrey says he had not seen before. Keats's publisher, John Taylor, had sent a copy of *Endymion* to Sir James Mackintosh in December 1818, with a high commendation, and Mackintosh was incensed with the kind of adverse criticism Keats had received; but if Taylor thought that a favourable review in the *Edinburgh* might soon follow through Mackintosh's offices he must have been disappointed. Keats himself would have greatly valued a good word from the *Edinburgh*, and was bitter at the silence. In a letter to George and Georgiana Keats in September 1819 he wrote:

> The Edinburgh review are afraid to touch upon my Poem. They do not know what to make of it—they do not like to condemn it and they will not praise it for fear— They are as shy of it as I should be of wearing a Quaker's hat. The fact is they have no real taste—they

[1] *ER*, XLVIII, September 1828. [2] *ER*, L, October 1829.
[3] ER, XL, July 1824. A long extract is printed below on pp. 388–96. See also pp. 322–3 below.
[4] *ER*, XXXIV, August 1820. An extract appears on pp. 493–7 below.

dare not compromise their Judgements on so puzzling a Question. If on my next Publication they should praise me and so lug in Endymion—I will address [them] in a manner they will not at all relish. The Cowardliness of the Edinburgh is worse than the abuse of the Quarterly.

This was precisely what Jeffrey did. Indeed, *Endymion* was 'lugged in' with a vengeance, leaving Jeffrey only four pages for the *Lamia* volume. By then, however, Keats was too ill to carry out his threat even had he wished to. There is no conclusive evidence, however, that Jeffrey was disingenuous. Moreover, the review was highly laudatory, recognizing Keats's work as part of a 'second spring' in English poetry brought on by imitation of Elizabethans, which Jeffrey had helped to promote. Jeffrey did criticize Keats's 'extravagance and irregularity, rash attempts at originality, interminable wanderings, and excessive obscurity', but he took all these as faults of immaturity deserving indulgence.

THE QUARTERLY REVIEW

The Tory *Quarterly Review* was founded in 1809. It was edited by William Gifford (1756–1826) throughout our period. Then John Taylor Coleridge, who was a nephew of the poet, and who had written the scathing review of Shelley's *Revolt of Islam*, became editor for a year, after which John Gibson Lockhart (1794–1854), Sir Walter Scott's son-in-law and biographer, took on the post, and served until 1853. Scott himself, who took a leading part in founding the review, was one of its most important contributors, and wrote some distinguished reviews of Byron. Another important contributor was John Wilson Croker (1780–1857), First Secretary at the Admiralty from 1809 to 1830, whose special province was recent French history, though he has become notorious in literary history as the writer of the slashing review of Keats's *Endymion*. Southey was also a leading contributor, but he wrote no reviews of the main poets and fictional writers of the time. The *Quarterly* occupied a position of authority, with a consequent influence upon the sales of books reviewed or ignored, only matched, if at all, by that of the *Edinburgh*.

On Byron

The *Quarterly* reviewed all the cantos of *Childe Harold*, some of the Eastern Tales and *Lara*, and Byron's plays. Unlike the

Edinburgh, it did not review *Beppo*; but, like its rival, it reviewed no part of *Don Juan*. Since Murray, the publisher of the *Quarterly*, published *Beppo*, and had a hand in the publication of the first five cantos of *Don Juan*, this is understandable. To have joined the abusive reviewers would have been impossible; and equally impossible—because likely to offend many of the *Quarterly's* readers—would have been open defence.

Childe Harold I and II (1812) were reviewed by George Ellis,[1] a friend of Walter Scott, who had helped Scott in the founding of the review, and had reviewed *The Lady of the Lake*. Ellis is uncertain of Byron's plan, and finds Harold otiose, obfuscating, and anachronistic, but praises the work as a poem of travel, comparing it with the *Odyssey*. Ellis dislikes the archaisms, and Byron's mistakes in using them, and also the negligent writing and feeble rhyming. He thought Byron better when he forgot Spenser and used language appropriate to the subject. Ellis misses the humorous effects Byron achieves by his Spenserisms. Ellis also objected to the Childe's opinions, that fame is of small value, and the joys of triumph worthless illusions, and he was disgusted at the libertine's attitude to women, and at Byron's failure to criticize such opinions and attitudes. He also took exception to Byron's own expression of disbelief in immortality, and even to his intrusion of such topics into the poem. This last stricture shows that Ellis had an inadequate conception of the poem, which was not simply descriptive but reflective and philosophical, and had every right to be. Yet Ellis valued the poem highly, praising its 'pleasing versification', 'lively conception', and 'accurate expression'. The review is no masterpiece, but it contains a fair outline of the cantos, and the quotations are well chosen; and the moral and religious objections are, in any case, fairly taken.

Ellis also reviewed *The Giaour* and *The Bride* together in January 1814,[2] and *The Corsair* and *Lara* together in July 1814.[3] He preferred *The Bride* to *The Giaour*, had little to say about *Lara*, and preferred *The Corsair* to all three, even calling it 'the most finished and the most beautiful of Lord Byron's productions'. This was a mistake of poetic scale. His review does, however, make some interesting points, for instance in his praise of Byron for 'detecting' (in 'the most trivial objects') 'what had escaped the observation

[1] *QR*, VII, March 1812.
[2] *QR*, X, January 1814 (publ. March–April 1814).
[3] *QR*, XI, July 1814 (publ. after 20 October 1814).

of all former spectators'—exaggerated, but an unusual and useful exaggeration. Ellis also tries to refute Jeffrey's cyclic theory of civilization and literature.[1] He holds that modern Britons did not crave for strong feelings, and that modern poets probably merely followed 'the impulse of their own studies and habits'. Moreover, Byron was least attractive and popular when he tried to anatomize 'dark bosoms', and this, in any case, was appropriate to philosophy rather than to poetry, which should simply describe the effects of emotion, not analyse its causes. Ellis's refutation is invalid. He does not succeed by his plain contradiction, probably based on a false impression of contemporary Britain. He was also probably wrong about Byron. And his view of the demarcation between poetry and philosophy was unduly restrictive of the scope of poetry.

Ellis died in 1815, and it was Walter Scott who reviewed *Childe Harold III* (1816) and *IV* (1817). He reviewed *III* and *The Prisoner of Chillon* together.[2] The review contains a well-written survey of Byron's poetic career to date, and some account of his social success. Scott thought that posterity would consider it very remarkable that Byron, 'managing his pen with the careless and negligent ease of a man of quality', writing always on the same subjects, and creating the same 'unamiable' characters, should, despite also 'the proverbial fickleness of the public', have maintained the 'ascendency in their favour, which he had acquired by his first matured production'. Scott felt that if Byron's 'empire over the public' had at all diminished, it was through the events of his private life, not through literary decline. This canto was a worthy successor to *I* and *II*. Yet Scott firmly dissents from Byron's slight on Wellington, and from Byron's political opinions, which, however, being the opinions of a poet, he does not take very seriously. He maintains that if Byron himself attached importance to his political views he would need to confess inconsistency between his sympathy with Napoleon on his defeat and his earlier execration of him as a bloated tyrant trying to enslave the Spaniards. At all events, Scott believes and hopes that Byron will some day think better of 'the morals, religion, and constitution of his country'. The point is made with the greatest politeness, and with a notable absence of anything approaching fanaticism, rancour, or superciliousness. The same point, we shall see, was

[1] See p. 27 above.
[2] *QR*, XVI, October 1816 (publ. February 1817).

made in various reviews with one or more of the tones which are conspicuously absent here. Scott has high praise for the passage on the eve of Quatre Bras, and for the lines on Howard; but he jibs at attributing to Napoleon a *just* scorn of mankind. He is much more attracted, in any case, by the non-political parts of the poem, though he does not share Byron's partiality for *La Nouvelle Héloïse* (*III.* lxxix)—'like Lance's pebble-hearted cur, Crab, we remained dry-eyed while all wept around us'. Scott generally seems to prefer the descriptions of natural scenery.

Scott offers an understanding critique of *The Prisoner of Chillon*, noticing acutely that Byron had transformed a story of endurance for the sake of conscience into a study of captivity in the abstract, and its mental and physical effects. He finds the poem 'more powerful than pleasing'. He notes the influence of the Lakers on this and other poems in the volume.

Taking a final, general view of Byron's work, Scott pleads with him, in a very kindly way, to abandon his spirit of defiance, his dark outlook, and his scepticism about the existence of worth, friendship, and sincerity; and to descend from the heights, 'to obtain ease of mind and tranquility'. He offers a recipe in well-intentioned and even noble words; but we may well wonder whether at that time Byron really wanted any more mental tranquillity than was to be gained by expressing the lack of it.

In his review of *Childe Harold IV*[1] Scott first considered what had made the poem so popular. His answer was, first, its originality. Byron was the first poet since Cowper to appear before the public 'an actual living man expressing his own sentiments, thoughts, hopes, and fears'. The Childe was a fancy-dress sketch of Byron drawn by himself. Secondly, feelings expressed in the poem struck awe into its readers. They felt in the presence of a superior being who refused to consult, soothe, flatter, or conciliate them, and even told them that neither they nor anything else was 'worthy the attention of the noble traveller'. This general contempt, if taken seriously, could lead to Epicureanism, which Scott deplored. If not taken seriously, it could be tiresome. Thirdly, however, the poet intimated that he had the talents and genius to win the world if he had thought it worth while. Scott hoped that Byron would deliver himself from 'bad metaphysics and worse politics'. He refused to flatter Byron, or to execrate

[1] *QR*, XIX, April 1818 (publ. September 1818). A long extract is printed on pp. 236–46 below.

him. He criticizes the 'cold and sceptical philosophy which clouds our prospects on earth, and closes those beyond it', but willingly renders to 'this extraordinary poem . . . the full praise that genius in its happiest efforts can demand of us'.

As to *IV* itself, Scott could not accept the rosy picture of Venice at the height of its power, and he rightly saw the best future for Italy in unification, not in the reinforced independence of petty states. But he praises highly later passages in the canto— *e.g.*, that on the Clitumnus (lxvi ff.)—and that on Rome (lxxviii ff.). He admires the 'earnest and energetic force' which renders the Roman scenes real. He finds *IV* markedly different from *I–III*, with 'less of passion, more of deep thought and sentiment, at once collected and general'. 'Terror' was lost, and 'sublimity' gained. This seems a valid insight.

Scott then turns again to the poem as a whole. He believes that its solemnity and gloom derive from introversion, which normally had that effect. Nature has, however, made us social beings, and given us the capacity to derive from relations with other people the happiness which we cannot obtain from preoccupation with ourselves. Yet if we despise or hate other people we are cut off from this. Now, we shall certainly despise or hate them if we think they are nothing but fools and knaves; but if we realize that every individual 'possesses a portion of the ethereal flame, however smothered by unfavourable circumstances', we shall also realize that our better feelings can rightly extend, without degradation, to the 'lowest' of humanity. Scott here maintains a definitely hierarchical view of humanity, but this attitude to people in general is distinctly more friendly than that of Byron. A belief in personal immortality was also, Scott thought, a motive for enduring one's own sufferings and commiserating with those of others. Such beliefs are not, however, to be acquired at will, as Scott seems to imply. Scott ends the review with an appreciation of Byron's 'bold', 'severe', 'Doric' style, and defends his varied use of the Spenserian stanza.

Scott's critiques of Byron are certainly the best the *Quarterly* printed. Heber's attack on four of the plays[1] is, however, a fair-minded critique from the standpoint of a Christian theologian, but it only concerns us for its incidental onslaught on *Don Juan*. On the other hand, there are some interesting remarks about Byron's work in the correspondence of John Wilson Croker, the

[1] *QR*, XXVII, July 1822 (publ. October 1822).

39

Quarterly reviewer who condemned Keats. Croker liked *Childe Harold III*, and writes well about it, but, more important, he defended *Don Juan*. He evidently told Murray from the first that Murray exaggerated the 'danger' of *Don Juan* (to Murray's reputation?), and later he writes to him that if he had published the poem 'without hesitation or asterisks' there would have been 'no outcry either against the publisher or author'.[1] Again, a year later:

> There are levities here and there, more than good taste approves, but nothing to make such a terrible rout about—nothing so bad as 'Tom Jones', nor within a hundred degrees of 'Count Fathom'. . . . If you print and sell 'Tom Jones' and 'Peregrine Pickle', why do you start at 'Don Juan'?[2]

These are cogent points as far as the licentiousness of the poem is concerned; but violent exception was taken to the poem on other grounds also, religious, political, and even moral grounds of a different sort, as we shall see.

On Shelley

The *Quarterly* only reviewed Shelley twice during his life, though it had attacked him incidentally in two earlier numbers.

The Revolt of Islam was reviewed scathingly in an able critique by John Taylor Coleridge, a nephew of the poet.[3] J. T. Coleridge had been a contemporary of Shelley's at Eton. He attacks the doctrines of the poem as pernicious and shallow, while conceding occasional beauty, despite imperfections, to the expression. The poem as a whole, however, he condemns as 'insupportably dull, and laboriously obscure'. Shelley was very angry at this review.

The second review was of the *Prometheus* volume.[4] It was written by William Sidney Walker, a Cambridge don. This was formerly doubted, since Walker has been thought to have written (under the pseudonym 'E. Haselfoot') the very favourable review of Shelley's *Posthumous Poems* in *Knight's Quarterly Magazine* for

[1] *The Croker Papers*, ed. Louis Jennings, 3 vols. (London, 1884), I, 145. I am indebted to Dr Keith Walker, who first drew my attention some years ago to Croker's interesting reactions to *Don Juan*. Some extracts from Croker are reprinted on pp. 249, 254, and 259–62 below.

[2] Samuel Smiles, *A Publisher and his Friends*, 2 vols. (London, 1891), I, 414.

[3] *QR*, XXI, April 1819 (publ. September 1819). A long extract appears below on pp. 337–47.

[4] *QR*, XXVI, October 1821 (publ. December 1821). A long extract appears on pp. 362–72 below.

August 1824,[1] but it is now conclusively established that he was the *Quarterly*'s reviewer.[2] If Walker wrote the later review also, he may have changed his mind about Shelley, or Gifford may have influenced or tinkered with the review in the *Quarterly*. This calls Shelley's poetry all 'brilliance, vacuity, and confusion'. It also criticizes the rhythms as often 'harsh and unmusical', and expresses distaste for the 'new and uncouth words', and the 'awkward and intricate construction of the sentences'. Walker holds that Shelley's 'want of meaning' takes several forms, and he analyses them, referring with ridicule to *The Cloud* and to *Prometheus*. He also accuses Shelley of sometimes descending to doggerel. He asserts, very interestingly, that Shelley never describes a thing directly, but transfers to it the properties of something he takes to resemble it, by language taken partly in a metaphorical meaning, and partly in no meaning at all. *The Sensitive Plant* is cited as an instance where this often occurs. The reviewer also censures Shelley's subjects as remote and uninteresting, and *Prometheus* as undramatic, and filled with 'mere dreaming, shadowy, incoherent abstractions'. Shelley was quite wrong in thinking his work was at all like Greek tragedy. His poems were just bad—exaggerated, verbose, and incoherent. Finally, they offended flagrantly against morality and religion. The review is extreme, but it is well written, and some of the detailed analysis is of considerable interest.

On Keats

The *Quarterly* printed only one review of Keats—the celebrated review of *Endymion* by J. W. Croker.[3] Croker's review upset Keats, but it is doubtful whether it had much share in damaging his health. *Adonais* did much to create the legend, and it is not impossible that Shelley picked on the *Quarterly* rather than *Blackwood's* (which treated Keats far more scurrilously) because it had

[1] *KQM*, III, August 1824.

[2] See H. and H. C. Shine, *The Quarterly Review under William Gifford* (Chapel Hill, University of North Carolina Press, 1949), p. 76. W. S. Walker (1795–1846) was a Fellow of Trinity College, Cambridge (1820–9), and a distinguished classical scholar. He also wrote poems. He is known to have contributed to *Knight's Quarterly Magazine*. He is said to have resigned his Fellowship after nine years because of religious doubts. He is best known today as a considerable Shakespearean scholar, and pioneer of the study of Shakespeare's language and versification.

[3] *QR*, XIX, April 1818 (publ. September 1818). The review is reprinted in full on pp. 472–6 below.

treated Shelley himself roughly, whereas *Blackwood's* had reviewed his work favourably on several occasions. Croker's review has a supercilious tone, but it says some quite reasonable things, from the point of view of a critic who admired the Popean tradition, which Keats had himself derided in *Sleep and Poetry*. Croker's strictures may actually have had some beneficial effect on Keats's poetic development. The review did, however, interfere with sales, and also undermined Keats's self-esteem.[1]

BLACKWOOD'S EDINBURGH MAGAZINE

Blackwood's was established in 1817. After an undistinguished run of six numbers under weak editors, it was entrusted by its founder William Blackwood to a lively triumvirate, John Wilson ('Christopher North') (1785–1854), James Hogg, the 'Ettrick Shepherd' (1770–1835), and John Gibson Lockhart (1794–1854), who has already been mentioned above in connexion with the *Quarterly*. Blackwood himself seems, however, to have retained some measure of moderating control, and to have increased this over the years. Hogg was a rough, homespun genius, whereas Wilson and Lockhart had both been educated at Glasgow University and at Oxford, and were competent classical scholars. Wilson ultimately became Professor of Moral Philosophy at Edinburgh University, and a rum professor he was, especially in later years, even employing a ghost-writer to write his lectures for him.[2] Lockhart became editor of the *Quarterly* in 1825. Both men are of considerable importance in connexion with our three poets.

The spirit which animated the triumvirate was different from that which inspired the two great quarterlies. These buccaneers were out for some fun. Wilson, a remarkably high-spirited but unstable character, was probably the ringleader in the early malpractices of the magazine. *Maga*, as the periodical was soon nicknamed, and is still sub-titled, was ostensibly started to provide a 'nimbler and more familiar' kind of criticism in Edinburgh than that provided by, for instance, *The Edinburgh Review* or Constable's *Scots Magazine*, but from the start of the triumvirate's regime it was evident that to achieve an 'effect' its editors were prepared to go as far as to libel character; and even to ridicule physical defects

[1] A convincing case is made by Harold E. Briggs, 'Keats's Conscious and Unconscious Reactions to Criticisms of *Endymion*', *PMLA*, LX (1945), 1106–29.

[2] For details see Elsie Swann, *Christopher North* (London, 1934).

and infirmities. It was at least ten years before *Maga* thoroughly reformed her ways. Yet her erratic literary criticism even during those years often attained a high standard, and had some remarkably favourable things to say about works whose beliefs were, on central issues in religion, politics, and morality, utterly opposed to her own.

On Byron

Maga reviewed Byron twice in the first year of her existence. Both reviews were by Wilson. They were of *Manfred* (1817) and *The Lament of Tasso* (1817), neither of which falls within our scope. The next year Wilson also reviewed *Childe Harold IV*.[1] The review is less elaborate than his review in the *Quarterly*, but it equally emphasizes Byron's presence in his poetry. Moreover, Wilson even credits Byron with 'deeper passions than probably any other great poet ever had'. Byron had not yet 'soared', however, 'to his utmost pitch'. He had not yet written 'a great poem'. Moreover, much of what he had written was without instruction either for good people or for 'erring or passion-stricken' spirits. Indeed, it was morally dangerous. Wordsworth's influence on Canto III was, however, wholesome, and no danger to Byron's originality. Canto IV itself was perhaps the best of the four, and *Childe Harold* was 'the finest, beyond all comparison, of Byron's poems'. Wilson is sounder here than Jeffrey, who seems not to have seen how much much more important *Childe Harold* was than any of the Eastern Tales.

Shortly afterwards *Blackwood's* published a 'Letter to the Author of *Beppo*'.[2] This may have been Lockhart's work, but was signed PRESBYTER ANGLICANUS.[3] It was accompanied by a covering letter protesting at Jeffrey's favourable reception of *Beppo*, which, in the writer's opinion, represented the 'baseness' of Byron's principles—not, indeed, more openly, but 'infinitely more dangerously' than before. The writer saw the point that Jeffrey had missed, that *Beppo* was not just an example of dexterous *vers de société*. The 'Letter' itself spends most of its time comparing Byron unfavourably with great poets of the past. Unlike them, he was mankind's enemy, who tried to make people

[1] *BM*, III, May 1818.
[2] *BM*, III, June 1818.
[3] This designation suggests the possibility that the writer was Rev. Dr George Croly, on whom see p. 50, n. 2, below.

sympathize with 'all the sickly whims and phantasies of a self-dissatisfied and self-accusing spirit', and to render readers 'devoid of religion, virtue, and happiness'. But his work till now had at least been serious. Now he had cast away his harp, and 'bought, in its stead, a gaudy viol, fit for the fingers of eunuchs, and the ears of courtezans'. How serious the writer of the Letter was is unclear, but if Lockhart wrote it it was simply one of the stunts which *Blackwood's* so often indulged in. For Lockhart, as we shall see, was even an admirer of *Don Juan*.

The next year one or more contributors (not yet satisfactorily identified) wrote some 'Remarks on *Don Juan*' in *Blackwood's*.[1] If Lockhart was involved, these do not fully express his views, as we shall see. They attack the morals of the poem virulently, and they also attack Byron's conduct to his wife. Yet even here there is plenty of praise for certain aspects of the poem—or, rather, of Cantos I and II, which were all that had yet appeared. The reviewer says they contain

> a more thorough and intense infusion of genius and vice—power and profligacy—than in any poem which had ever before been written in the English, or indeed in any other modern language.

He also describes the poem as

> a production . . . which, in spite of all that critics can do or refrain from doing, nothing can possibly prevent from taking a high place in the literature of our country, and remaining to all ages a perpetual monument of the exalted intellect, and the depraved heart, of one of the most remarkable men to whom this country has had the honour and the disgrace of giving birth.

The article quotes 'a few of the passages which can be read without a blush, because the comparative rarity of such passages will, in all probability, operate to the complete exclusion of the work from the libraries of the greater part of my readers'. (Actually it quotes about 480 lines!) The article considers 'the best and the worst part' to be 'without doubt the description of the ship-wreck':

> As a piece of terrible painting, it is as much superior as can be to every description of the kind—not even excepting that in the *Aeneid*—that ever was created. In comparison with the fearful and intense reality of its horrors, every thing that any former poet had thrown together to depict the agonies of the awful scene, appears

[1] *BM*, V, August 1819.

chill and tame. . . . But even here the demon of his depravity does not desert him. We dare not stain our pages with quoting any specimens of the disgusting merriment with which he has interspersed his picture of human suffering. He paints it well, only to shew that he scorns it the more effectually; and of all the fearful sounds which ring in the ears of the dying, the most horrible is the demoniacal laugh with which this unpitying brother exults over the contemplation of their despair. Will our readers believe that the most innocent of all his odious sarcasms is contained in these two lines?

'They grieved for those that perished in the cutter
And also for the biscuit, casks, and butter.'[1]

Whoever wrote these criticisms either did not realize, or deliberately ignored, the fact that Byron was trying *inter alia* to represent realistically the thoughts that might well pass through the minds of the most decent people in those horrible circumstances.

In November 1819 *Blackwood's* printed some rollicking stanzas by William Maginn called 'Don Juan unread',[2] attacking the 'shameless tale' for its 'jests profane' and 'crops of blasphemy'.

Typically, however, the next month *Blackwood's* published 'Remarks on some of our Late Numbers; by a Liberal Whig',[3] in which the writer defends *Don Juan* against the 'very general and total condemnation' it had met with. The 'Remarks' were signed METRODORUS, and were written by J. H. Merivale (1779–1844), a lawyer, and translator from Greek, Italian, and German, who wrote for both *The Monthly Review* and *The Critical Review*. He agreed with the 'Remarks' that *Don Juan* was 'a work of transcendent merit', but repudiated the religious and moral attacks on it.

One of the many pranks of *Blackwood's* was perpetrated in July 1821, when it printed an article written by Wilson[4] on the *Letter to the Right Hon. Lord Byron, by John Bull*, published in London in 1821. The *Letter* itself is far more important than Wilson's article. It is largely an attack on 'cant' and 'humbug' in contemporary literature and criticism; but what concerns us here is its remarkable description of the essential qualities and originality of

[1] *DJ, II.* lxi. The review misquotes. The lines read: 'They grieved for those who perished with the cutter,/And also for the biscuit-casks and butter'.

[2] *BM*, VI, November 1819. Maginn (1793–1842), a brilliant parodist and comic writer, also wrote for the *Literary Gazette* and in 1830 founded *Fraser's Magazine*.

[3] *BM*, VI, December 1819. [4] *BM*, IX, July 1821.

Don Juan, its appreciation of the poem, and its encouragement to Byron to continue writing in that vein.[1] The *Letter* accuses Byron of 'humbug' in much of his serious poetry:

> You are a great poet, but even with your poetry you mix too much of that at present very saleable article against which I am now bestirring myself. The whole of your misanthropy, for example, is humbug.

On the other hand:

> Stick to *Don Juan*: it is the only sincere thing you have ever written; and it will live many years after all your humbug Harolds have ceased to be, in your own words,

'A school-girl's tale—the wonder of an hour'.[2]

Byron found the *Letter* 'diabolically well written, and full of fun and ferocity'.[3] He wanted to find out who wrote it. He suspected one of four people: his friend Hobhouse, Peacock, Isaac d'Israeli, and Washington Irving; but the authorship remained a closely guarded secret. We may also well ask who wrote this remarkable piece. The answer was still uncertain until 1947, when the American scholar Professor Alan Lang Strout proved that the writer was none other than . . . the protean Lockhart![4]

In the light of this fact Wilson's article on the *Letter* seems even more preposterous and amusing than it would otherwise have appeared. Wilson pretends to think the *Letter* was written by Jeremy Bentham in his dotage, and he rates the old man for liking *Don Juan* alone among Byron's works, and for urging Byron 'to continue the "filth" (to use his own word) of that indecent poem, merely to gratify his jaded appetite'. Wilson keeps up the moralistic condemnation of *Don Juan* by *Blackwood's*, and professes to be proud of it.

The next year a letter to 'Christopher North' (Wilson) was printed in *Blackwood's*.[5] It was signed SILURIENSIS, and was written by John Matthews, who also wrote a long poem called *Critique on Lord Byron*, a would-be witty survey of the poet's work

---

[1] See the extracts printed on pp. 276–80 below.

[2] An adaptation of Byron's line, 'A schoolboy's tale, the wonder of an hour' (*Childe Harold II*, ii. 6).

[3] *LJ*, V, 316.

[4] *John Bull's Letter to Lord Byron*, ed. A. L. Strout (Norman, Oklahoma, 1947). [5] *BM*, XI, February 1822.

to date, which *Blackwood's* published later the same year.[1] The letter mostly concerns some of the plays, but it also criticizes obscurity in the poems, especially *Childe Harold*, and, while praising the 'prodigious powers of language' and 'mastership of rhyme' in *Don Juan*, attacks Byron as 'the armed champion of libertinism', and for boasting of 'some of the worst propensities of human nature'.

In January 1823 *Blackwood's* criticized *The Vision of Judgment* in a short section of a long article on *The Liberal No. 1*,[2] in which the poem had been published in October 1822. The critic may have been Wilson. The article gives the poem rough handling; for instance:

> A jest that does not excite a smile, drawled out through nine-and-thirty pages, must be a dull one.

I am afraid I agree with the reviewer, though I am aware that this is not the prevalent view nowadays. The humour seems to me often fourth-form, and far inferior to *Beppo* and to the best parts of *Don Juan*. On a first reading it might still seem funny in places, but it does not, for me at least, stand up to the years. The reviewer is perhaps right, however, in thinking that the object was 'less to amuse than to shock', and the poem did, at least, shock a considerable number of people. The reviewer himself calls it 'a vile composition'. He had thought Southey's poem 'ill-judged', but that that did not excuse the pernicious doctrines in Byron's 'travesty', such as that put into the mouth of Junius:

> I loved my country, and I hated him

i.e., the old King. Loyalty and patriotism were not separable.

Only two other contributions to *Blackwood's* on Byron need mention here.

The first, and more important, is the letter to 'Christopher North' signed M. ODOHERTY on *Don Juan IX–XI*.[3] Lockhart wrote it, and in places it resembles John Bull's *Letter*. It repudiates the 'humbug' in a feeble criticism of *Don Juan* published in *Blackwood's* two months earlier (written by Maginn and Lockhart!)[4] and appeals to 'Tickler' (possibly Maginn and Lockhart) and 'North' (Wilson) to stick to their own 'good old rule—abuse

---

[1] *BM*, XI, April 1822.   [2] *BM*, XIII, January 1823.
[3] *BM*, XIV, September 1823. An extract is printed below on pp. 297–301.
[4] *BM*, XIV, July 1823.

47

wickedness, but acknowledge wit'. It maintains that *Don Juan* is 'without exception, the first of Lord Byron's works'—the most original in point of conception, and that which contained 'the finest specimens of serious poetry' he had ever written (an important point), and 'the finest specimens of ludicrous poetry that our age has witnessed'. This letter is the best of all the accounts of the spirit and status of *Don Juan* printed in any periodical of the time, and is nearly as good as John Bull's *Letter*.

The other contribution is a long article written after Byron's death, defending his personal character, and offering a short conspectus of his poetical achievement.[1] This is beyond our field. Lockhart wrote the article, and his brief judgments of the comparable value of Byron's various poems, once again placing *Don Juan* highest, are of some interest. It is worth noting, however, that when Lockhart came to review Moore's *Life of Byron* in the *Quarterly* in 1831[2] he put *Don Juan* well below *Manfred* and *Sardanapalus*, which he now considered the peak of Byron's achievement—a sad comedown for Lockhart!

On Shelley

The attitude of the Tory *Blackwood's* to the radical Shelley is not altogether what might be expected. In reviewing *The Revolt of Islam*[3] it did, indeed, attack Shelley's 'pernicious' ideas on religion, morals, and politics; but it recognized his 'powerful and vigorous intellect' and poetic 'genius'. As a poet he was 'strong, nervous, original; well entitled to take his place near to the great creative masters' of the age. In particular, he had proved himself a genuine poet by his portrayal of the 'intense, over-mastering, unfearing, unfading love' between Laon and Cythna. The review praises various episodes, including that of the slaughter of the small band of Laon's followers (VI. xi–xviii), which the reviewer considers to be 'painted with a power and energy altogether admirable'. He criticized as weak the plot and arrangement of incidents, but praised Shelley for having 'poured over his narrative a very rare strength and abundance of poetic imagery and feeling', and for 'having steeped every word in the essence of his inspiration'. Until quite recently the evidence favoured the view that Wilson wrote this review, but now there is strong evidence

---

[1] *BM*, XVII, February 1825. [2] *QR*, XLVI, January 1831.
[3] *BM*, IV, January 1819.

that its author may have been Lockhart, or at least that he had a major hand in it.[1]

A similar mixture of philosophical and moral condemnation with aesthetic encouragement characterizes the *Blackwood's* review of *Rosalind and Helen*,[2] which was probably by the same hand, and so, wholly or considerably by Lockhart.

The next full-length review of Shelley in *Blackwood's*[3] was of the *Alastor* volume, published two years before. The reviewer, again probably the same reviewer, thought Shelley 'too fond of allegories'—a species of poetry 'in which the difficulties of the art may be so conveniently blinked, and weakness find so easy a refuge in obscurity'. *Alastor* was 'obscure', even with the Preface, but there was 'the light of poetry even in the darkness of Mr. Shelley's imagination'. Almost all the 'wild poem' had a 'character of extravagance', but it had sublimities, especially in the death scene. Indeed, Shelley loved 'to string his harp among the tombs'. Some of the shorter poems contained 'beauties of no ordinary kind', but they were almost all liable to the charge of 'vagueness or obscurity'.

The review of the *Prometheus* volume[4] (also seemingly by Lockhart in whole or in part) expresses 'deepest pain' at Shelley's gross and miserable use of the Prometheus myth, while praising his 'very extraordinary powers of language and versification'. Shelley had used Jupiter to stand for Religion in general, and clearly considered (as the reviewer also did, 'though with far different feelings'), that with the fall of religion 'every system of human government' would necessarily 'give way and perish'. Shelley looked forward to the extinction of all moral feelings except 'a certain mysterious indefinable *kindliness*' as a further result. Yet

[1] It is attributed to Lockhart by William Blackwood himself in a list of contributors to early numbers of *Blackwood's*. The list is in the National Library of Scotland. See A. L. Strout, 'Lockhart, Champion of Shelley', *TLS*, 12 August 1955, 468. Professor Strout there takes the evidence to be conclusive that the sole author was Lockhart, but, as Professor White rightly pointed out in 1938 (*op. cit.*, 225), even the evidence from Lockhart's letters to William Blackwood does not prove that Lockhart wrote the whole of the review of *Prometheus Unbound*, which is now often attributed solely to him.

[2] *BM*, V, June 1819.   [3] *BM*, VI, November 1819.

[4] *BM*, VII, September 1820. Like the other three reviews, this was formerly ascribed to Wilson, but Miss M. Clive Hildyard in *Lockhart's Literary Criticism* (Oxford, 1931), p. 158, offers evidence which suggests (though not conclusively, I think) that the review may have been wholly or partly Lockhart's.

Prometheus was, in the reviewer's opinion, the best written of all Shelley's works. In places, moreover, one could 'separate the poet from the allegorist' and 'almost fancy that we had recovered some of the lost sublimities of Aeschylus'. Such was the 'magnificent opening scene'. The chorus "The path thro' which that lovely twain . . ." (II. ii. 1 ff.) had 'all the soft and tender gracefulness of Euripides', and breathed at the same time 'the very spirit of one of the grandest odes of Pindar'. And there were many pages just as fine.

From the other poems the reviewer quotes the start of the 'magnificent "Vision of the Sea" ', and he refers to the *Ode to the West Wind* and *Ode to a Skylark* as 'abounding in richest melody of versification, and great tenderness of feeling', but finds *The Sensitive Plant* the most 'affecting' poem of all, and quotes passages 'on a level with the happiest productions of the greatest contemporaries of Mr Shelley'. Later in the review its writer asserts the superiority of Shelley to all the Cockneys, but attacks the principles expressed in his poems, and, in particular, the passages in the *Ode to Liberty* against kings and priests.

In December 1821 *Blackwood's* launched a sharp attack on *Adonais*.[1] The reviewer was Rev. Dr George Croly.[2] The review is, for the most part, inept, intemperate, and even somewhat vulgar. The reviewer sees Shelley, Hunt, Keats, and seemingly also Byron, as revivers of the Della Crusca school of sentiment, prettiness, and egotism which had flourished towards the end of the eighteenth century, and which Gifford had killed by two verse satires.[3] *Adonais* is said to be wholly misplaced, and to consist largely of 'pure nonsense', words flung together 'like pebbles from a sack'.

Wilson struck a further blow at Shelley in a note to a letter to 'C. North' published in *Blackwood's* in February 1822.[4] Wilson described Shelley as a man of genius who had 'no sort of sense or judgment', and dismissed him as merely 'an inspired idiot'.

On Keats

As to Keats, *Blackwood's* treated him abominably, not merely in the notorious article by 'Z' (probably Lockhart and Wilson) on

[1] *BM*, X, December 1821.

[2] George Croly (1780–1860), minor writer in verse and prose. His *Paris in 1815* (1817) was modelled on *Childe Harold* (Byron thought it good). He contributed largely to *Blackwood's* and *The Literary Gazette*.

[3] *The Baviad* (1791) and *The Maeviad* (1795).   [4] *BM*, XI, February 1822.

'The Cockney School of Poetry',[1] in which Keats was advised to go back to 'plasters, pills, and ointment boxes', but in other contemptuous references with which the magazine pursued him till his death, and insulted his memory afterwards.[2] Keats and most of the other Cockneys may well, of course, have seemed highly pretentious to the more conventionally educated classical scholars of Edinburgh, who clearly felt more akin even to the rebellious Shelley, whom they frequently compared with Keats to the latter's disadvantage.[3] Lockhart made some sort of apology for the Cockney School article in the review of Shelley's *Prometheus*,[4] but it is not very convincing, especially in view of the subsequent contempt shown for Keats in 'Tickler's Letter No. 8' in August 1823. What might at first sight appear to be a more or less clear public recantation by the *Quarterly* occurs in its review of Tennyson's 1833 volume, where the reviewer (Croker) asks the publisher of a new edition of Keats to notice the *Quarterly*'s 'conversion' to *Endymion*, which had now achieved 'splendour of fame'.[5] But this turns out to be nothing but a piece of cool and unrepentant irony.

THE MONTHLY REVIEW

The Whig *Monthly Review* (1749–1845) was probably the most important monthly to survive from the eighteenth century. It was in generally better shape in our period than its old rival *The Critical Review* (1736–1817), which, after a number of changes of publisher and editor, and such untoward events as a bankruptcy and a fire, came to an end in 1817. The founder of the *Monthly*, Ralph Griffiths, who had edited it for over fifty years, had, however, died in 1803, and his son, George Edward Griffiths, who conducted the review until 1825, seems not to have had quite the ability or the personality of his father. The *Monthly* was at all events gradually superseded by the *Edinburgh* as the leading review with Whiggish tendencies. Nevertheless, Griffiths had

[1] *BM*, III, August 1818.

[2] See e.g. *BM*, VII, September 1820, 613–17 and 675–9; X, December 1821, 696–700; and XIV, August 1823, 'Letters of Timothy Tickler, Esq., No. 8'.

[3] E.g. *BM*, VI, December 1819, 240, and in 'Tickler's' Letter mentioned in n. 2 above.

[4] *BM*, VII, September 1820, 686–7. That passage was pretty certainly by Lockhart.

[5] *QR*, XCVII, April 1833, 163.

an able team of contributors, and some at least of the literary reviews, especially before 1820, though not so full as those in the quarterlies, are praiseworthy pieces evincing genuine critical perception.

On Byron

The *Monthly* printed nearly thirty reviews of poetry by Byron, starting with *Hours of Idleness* (1807) and ending with *Don Juan XV–XVI* (1824). The *Monthly* was generally favourable, but soon got tired of *Don Juan*.

George Edward Griffiths, the editor, welcomed *Hours of Idleness*.[1] The *Monthly* did not review *English Bards and Scotch Reviewers*, but Thomas Denman (a young barrister, later Lord Chief Justice) wrote a favourable critique of *Childe Harold I and II*.[2] He was puzzled by Byron's calling 'A Romaunt' what was really 'a series of most elegant and correct descriptions, interwoven with reflections full of good sense and shrewdness, but as well styled religious as romantic'. Harold himself seemed functionless. But Denman, like several other critics, thought Byron's use of the Spenserian stanza unrivalled. There was no weakness or wearisomeness in the poem, whose whole effect was 'powerful and elastic'. Denman praised as 'very spirited' the description of the armies on the eve of Talavera (xl–xli), and made no comment on the anti-war sentiments. He thought the tribute to the Maid of Saragoza (liv ff.) 'warm and feeling', and also admired Byron's delineation of the Spanish character and landscape. He found the 'chilling speculations on the future' very powerful, and was struck by the night scene among the Suliotes. Denman thought very highly of Byron's genius, but hoped he would aim at unity of story, connexion of incidents, and distinctiveness, attractiveness, and variety of character. These last restrictive demands reveal that though Denman appreciated much in the poem he missed important features of its overall character. He ends with the uncommon point that the style was too full of classical allusions, and remarks that Byron's great command of graceful and unaffected diction rendered needless the resort to allegory or mythology.

Denman also wrote an overwhelmingly favourable review of *The Giaour*[3]; and *The Bride of Abydos* and *The Corsair* were also favourably reviewed,[4] by John Hodgson, another young lawyer,

[1] *MR*, LIV, November 1807. A short extract appears on p. 207 below.
[2] *MR*, LXVIII, May 1812. [3] *MR*, LXXI, June 1813.
[4] *MR*, LXXIII, January 1814; LXXIII, February 1814.

who had the sense of proportion to wish that Byron would never-theless soon leave these tales and 'resume his suit to the more dignified muse of *Childe Harold*'. It is not known who reviewed *The Siege of Corinth* and *Parisina*,[1] but he summed up Byron's poetic merits and defects, asserting that his greatest merit lay in his skill in dissecting human character, and in drawing and con-trasting the effects of the more violent passions; while his most general faults were want of variety, perpetual gloom, and an unpardonable licence of phraseology and versification.

The *Monthly* thought readers would find *Childe Harold III* somewhat disappointing.[2] This was an unusual view, and it is poorly supported. The reviewer insists that Harold still does nothing but 'think and feel', and that this is 'less redeemed than heretofore by beautiful descriptions and forcible passages'. There was also still 'no plan, unity of story, connection of incidents, attractiveness, and variety of character'. There were still prosaic and unmetrical lines, and unclarity and grammatical licence. Only these last technical points on texture are possibly valid. On the other hand, the review praises the reflections on 'Conquerors and Kings' (xliv–xlv), without making any adverse political comment. It also commends the 'sweet' Drachenfels song, but it condemns the thoughts of such stanzas as lxxiv, evidently on religious grounds. The Rousseau passage (xcix ff.) is praised without demur and also the character-sketches of Gibbon and Voltaire (cv ff.). The review concludes with some detailed criticisms. Stanza xii and the last line of xxxiii are given as cases of the 'prosaic', and a number of examples are offered of deficiency in grammar, syntax, and elegance. Finally, the reviewer hopes that Italy will bring Byron 'happier hours'. He has nothing to say of the magnificent descriptions or of the changes of mood from *I* and *II*. The review itself is disappointing.

The *Monthly* gave little space to the *Chillon* volume,[3] merely noting that Byron had twisted the story of the title poem, and singling out *Darkness* for its 'thoughts that chill and words that freeze'.

The anonymously published *Beppo* elicited a more interesting response from the *Monthly*.[4] The reviewer was delighted with the poem, observing that Byron's satire, 'though at times a little

---

[1] *MR*, LXXIX, February 1816.
[2] *MR*, LXXXI, November 1816.   [3] *MR*, LXXXI, December 1816.
[4] *MR*, LXXXV, March 1818.

tinged with vulgarity', was 'usually good-humoured and often well pointed'; and adding that

> he throws about his observations in a lively strain: and it is very amusing to remark how every thing, of which he speaks or thinks, becomes the immediate thesis of a new episode of playful moralizing.

Praise is given to the 'truth and natural feeling' of the 'sentimentalizing' of xii–xiii, and to the entertaining expressions of Laura when her husband reappears (xci–xcii). The reviewer also quotes with obvious approval the contrasting stanzas on Italy and England (xli–xlvi and xlvii–xlix). He clearly enjoyed his 'very welcome hour of relaxation' over this 'meritoriously droll' poem, but he thought it quite apparent that the author had 'powers for something beyond burlesque', and hoped for 'some more serious specimen' from him, though he was 'inclined to suspect' that the author had already supplied one. The *Monthly* here shows an open-minded attitude about the moral implications of *Beppo*, of which it is apparently well aware.

The *Monthly* found *Childe Harold IV* 'filled with animated descriptions of the scenery and the principal objects of curiosity' of Italy.[1] The description of Venice 'breathed a melancholy grandeur', though part of it was marred by obscurity. The reviewer liked the remarks on Petrarch (xxx ff.), and still more those on the Venus de' Medici (xlix–liii). He was impressed with the lines on the battle of Lake Trasimene (lxii–lxv), and the stanzas on the Clitumnus (lxvi–lxviii), and felt himself 'carried with a frantic impetuosity' by the 'over-wrought, but most earnest and vivid description of Velino' (lxix–lxxii). On the other hand, the reviewer thought Byron's reflections on the first appearance of 'fallen Rome' (xlvi) 'remarkably laboured', and the stanzas on the Palatine Hill (cvi–cvii) 'an accumulation of mere names of external objects . . . heaped together in chaos, following one another too rapidly to suggest any images'. Byron was better on 'the grand relics of antient art', and the stanzas on the Roman father and daughter (cxlviii–cl) were 'very moving'. The reviewer was, however, not much taken with the 'too much dilated' stanzas on the tomb of Caecilia Metella (xcix–civ) or the unconvincing depiction of the feelings of the dying gladiator (cxl–cxli), but he admired the description of the Laocoön (clx), and of the different feelings evoked in a spectator by the simplicity of the Pantheon

[1] *MR*, LXXXVII, November 1818.

(cxlv–cxlvii) and by the magnificence and grandeur of St Peter's (cliii ff.), and he was also impressed by the stanzas on Egeria (cxv–cxix). The lines on the death of Princess Charlotte and her child (clxvii–clxxii) seemed to the reviewer 'beautiful and pathetic', and the stanzas on the ocean he thought were 'written with a vehemence and grandeur of spirit not exceeded by any part of the work'. He intentionally passes over the passages on Byron's 'domestic circumstances'—probably civ–cvi, and certainly the stanzas surrounding the 'moody moping' on Nemesis (cxxxii)—and also various passages in which 'the sentiments expressed' were 'so entirely in discord with the objects delineated' as to make one suspect the 'affectation of singularity'. Byron ought to have got over such peculiarities by now. What was there in the appearance of the Roman daughter to suggest the mention of Cain (cxlix)? How did the Lake of Nemi suggest a snake coiled up in itself, or how does its 'still and placid surface' recall 'the insensibility of settled hate' (clxxiii)? After these detailed observations there follows a good critique of the whole of *Childe Harold*.[1]

When *Don Juan I and II* appeared the *Monthly*[2] was prompted to make this apt comment:

> There *are* master-spirits in the strange history of mind, which, unsatisfied with any partial views, seem to compass in the keenness of their vision those prospects which are distributed among *numbers* of an inferior class; and they are the musicians of nature, who, confined to *no* key, run through the whole scale of harmony from the lowest to the highest note; exhibiting the sublime or the trifling, the witty or the impassioned, the elegant or the impetuous, as the Proteus-god prevails.

The reviewer covered *Mazeppa* as well as *Don Juan*, but he had no great opinion of the former. The *Don* was the thing, a poem which,

> if originality and variety be the surest test of genius, has certainly the highest title to it; and which, we think, would have puzzled Aristotle with all his strength of Poetics to explain, have animated Longinus with some of its passages, have delighted Aristophanes, and have choked Anacreon with joy instead of with a grape.

It seemed to the reviewer almost as if Byron had tried 'to please

---

[1] This is reprinted below on pp. 246–8.   [2] *MR*, LXXXIX, July 1819.

and to displease the world at the same time', but he thought the poem would certainly please some:

> He has here exhibited that wonderful versatility of style and thought which appear almost incompatible within the scope of a single subject; and the familiar and the sentimental, the witty and the sublime, the sarcastic and the pathetic, the gloomy and the droll, are all touched with so happy an art, and mingled together with such a power of union, yet such a discrimination of style, that a perusal of the poem appears more like a pleasing and ludicrous dream, than the sober feeling of reality.

The reviewer is aware of the possible moral objections to the poem, but hopes that readers can by now admire Byron's genius without being in danger from it. He feels bound to condemn (without quoting) certain passages and expressions, but intends to try, like an 'artful chemist', 'to extract an essence from the mass, which, resembling the honey from poisonous flowers, may yet be sweet and pure'. Nevertheless, he hopes that Byron will not carry out his threat to expand the poem to 'twelve, or twenty-four' cantos. That might 'add to his poetic reputation', but could never 'procure for him any moral fame'.

The reviewer quotes Donna Julia's letter (*I.* cxcii–cxcviii) as 'worthy of Ariadne or of Dido', demurs at the 'poetic commandments' (*I.* ccv–ccvi) as disgusting to 'every good feeling of a pious mind', praises the satire of the portrait of Donna Inez (*I.* x–xviii) as 'ridiculously happy', and describes the Don's farewell to Spain (*II.* xviii–xx) as 'a singular mixture of the sentimental and the ludicrous'. 'Real energy and even sublimity of poetry' were, however, always at the poet's command. Yet no part of the poem had 'so much beauty and life of description' as the Haidée episode. The reviewer, though he had 'hair still whiter and years yet graver' than Byron,[1] felt the spell of the 'voluptuous delineation'; yet forced himself to close on a short moral condemnation, of which it is hard to estimate the sincerity.

When two years later *Don Juan III–V* was published the *Monthly*[2] expressed some surprise, since the public, and especially 'masters of families', had seemed against the prolongation of Juan's adventures. Byron had, however, promised 'to write more circumspectly', though he had not altogether fulfilled the promise.

---

[1] Probably an allusion to Byron's reference to his grey hair (*I.* ccxiii).
[2] *MR*, XCV, August 1821.

In any case, his 'narrative' was now 'too much narrative', and his 'excursions' were 'much too excursive', and these became tiresome. The appeal now rested simply on 'occasional passages of beauty, and striking thoughts'. The reviewer was clearly tired of the poem, and expected from its continuation 'the mere repetition of sensual attachment and "casual fruition",—varied in its attendant circumstances but still the same in origin, termination, and tendency'. In *III–V*, however, he does praise 'The Isles of Greece' as 'spirited and feeling', and quotes the scene of Haidée's illness (*IV*. lviii–lxxi) as another example of a 'detached' and 'harmless' passage; but he demurs at Byron's view that 'great names are nothing more than nominal', and censures such rhymes as 'pukes in'–'Euxine', and also the sarcasms against women. The criticisms are thus miscellaneous, but the central change is that the *Monthly* has now taken up a hostile attitude, which seems primarily aesthetic, but also to contain a moral element.

The *Monthly*'s remaining reviews of *Don Juan*[1] show that it had lost interest in the poem, and hoped it would be discontinued. A typical comment is:

> It may be hoped . . . that Lord Byron's present much more noble occupation, in assisting the Greeks during their arduous struggle, may cause Don Juan to experience a long repose.

On Shelley

The *Monthly* condemned the *Alastor* volume for its 'sublime obscurity', while recognizing some 'beautiful imagery' and 'poetical expressions', and suggested that with his next publication Shelley should supply a glossary and copious notes![2]

The *Monthly* saw *The Revolt of Islam* as a product of the French Revolution, a mixture of rhapsodical politics and political rhapsodies, containing 'the strangest vagaries of versification, in answer to the Pindaric flights' of an 'unfledged philosopher in government'. Shelley had poetical talents, and ought to be capable of better things. Here he abused his command of language, and wrote loosely and meaninglessly; and his facility even in the Spenserian stanza led him into 'contemptible' licences of rhythm and rhyme. Moreover, his theories were so extravagant that even extreme Utopians would be unlikely to follow him.[3]

[1] *MR*, CI, July 1823 (on *VI–VIII*); CII, October 1823 (on *IX–XI*); CIII, February 1824 (on *XII–XIV*), April 1824 (on *XV–XVI*).
[2] *MR*, LXXIX, April 1816.   [3] *MR*, LXXXVIII, March 1819.

When the *Monthly* came to review *Rosalind and Helen* it laid more emphasis on the viciousness of Shelley's ideas on free sexual unions, and on the audacity of his attacks on Christianity.[1] But it recognized his 'poetical merits' as 'of no common stamp'.

In its critique of *The Cenci*[2] the *Monthly* attacked the vogue for Elizabethan drama, and the revolting result of its influence in this play. It also attacked Shelley's adhesion to 'the exploded Wordsworthian heresy' of 'familiar language'. That was no language for tragedy, and Shakespeare did not keep to it. Yet Shelley's conduct of this play was plain proof of his powers, and it was to be hoped he would use them for better ends.

In *Prometheus Unbound*, however, the *Monthly* found nothing but 'pure unmixed nonsense'.[3] Detached passages had great merit, but the work as a whole was unintelligible, though some of it was only too plain, and necessarily and intentionally 'most offensive' to every sect of Christians. Yet in some passages there was 'much benevolent feeling, beautiful language, and powerful versification'. The shorter poems bore the same stamp. Shelley was a clever writer, but his talents were pitifully employed.

Thus the *Monthly* was hostile to Shelley's achievement and principles, while admitting his genius and possible promise.

On Keats

Of Keats, the *Monthly* only reviewed the 1820 Poems.[4] It thought the poems displayed 'the ore of true poetic genius, though mingled with dross'. Although often ambiguous and affected, all Keats wrote gave proof of 'deep thought and energetic reflection'. He was a bold originator, and deserved encouragement. Unfortunately, his delineations of the Greek gods only gave a faint idea of the nature the Greek poets attributed to them. Yet *Hyperion* was 'decidedly the best' of Keats's poems, and contained the least conceits. The worst was *Isabella*, which was very affected. There were also too many conceits in the other poems in the volume. Yet Keats was rich in imagination and fancy, and superabundantly fanciful in *To Autumn*, which was a most vivid picture of the reality of nature. The reviewer exhorted Keats to

[1] *MR*, XC, October 1819. [2] *MR*, XCIV, February 1821.
[3] *MR*, XCIV, February 1821.
[2] *MR*, XCII, July 1820. An extract appears on pp. 488–90 below.

58

become 'less strikingly original' and to be 'less fond of the folly of too new or too old phrases'. But he ended by praising the many fine and striking ideas and passages.

THE BRITISH CRITIC

The British Critic was founded in 1793 to represent an anti-revolutionary standpoint in politics and an Anglican orthodoxy in religion. Its early editors were William Beloe (1756–1817) and Robert Nares (1753–1829). Beloe was a fair classical scholar who took Anglican orders. He became for a few years Keeper of Printed Books in the British Museum. Nares was a classical scholar of some distinction, though he is best known today as the compiler of a remarkable glossary of Elizabethan literature. He also took Anglican orders, and eventually became an Archdeacon. He was more moderate in Church matters than Beloe. Nares was Keeper of Manuscripts in the British Museum from 1799 until 1807. He was a Fellow of The Royal Society. The subsequent editors were also clerics. They included the strongly conservative William van Mildert (1765–1836), at one time Regius Professor of Divinity at Oxford, then Bishop of Llandaff and Dean of St Paul's, and later Bishop of Durham, about whom his successor at Oxford said that his knowledge of the exact doctrines of the Church of England was so great that orthodoxy oozed out of his pores, and he would talk of it in his dreams. Other subsequent editors were Thomas Middleton (1769–1822), who became Bishop of Calcutta; and, later still, William Rowe Lyall (1788–1857), who had written a fine review of Wordsworth's *White Doe of Rylstone* in the *Quarterly*, and eventually became Dean of Canterbury. The literary reviewers are, for the most part, yet unidentified, but they included Rev. Francis Wrangham (1769–1852), a man of brilliant academic ability and wide culture, who himself wrote poetry of some merit, and was on friendly terms with Wordsworth and Coleridge even before the publication of *Lyrical Ballads*. Sir John Stoddart (1773–1856), at one time *Times* leader writer, and later Chief Justice of Malta, a *bête noire* of Hazlitt's, who married his sister in 1808, also reviewed for *The British Critic*.

The British Critic maintained a Tory position in politics, and was probably greatly dependent on political support.

The British Critic reviewed Byron's work from *Hours of Idleness* (1807) right through to *The Deformed Transformed* (1824). It started sympathetically, but eventually became extremely hostile.

It commended *Hours of Idleness*,[1] calling it 'very ingenious idleness', which had 'produced some elegant and interesting compositions', and observing that there was 'much taste, and more vigour than would reasonably be expected from a minor'. It singled out the poem 'Oh! had my fate . . .' (entitled '*To—*', but written to Mary Chaworth) 'for even higher praise as to poetry', though the poem told 'some facts' which could not be read 'without regret'.

The British Critic thought very well of *English Bards and Scotch Reviewers*,[2] writing that since the time of Gifford's *Baviad* (1791) it had not met with 'a production combining so much severity with so much genuine wit, humour, and real talent'. It thought one or two people had been unfairly attacked, but that genuine taste had been in danger, and some poor poems vastly overrated. This satire would be 'universally read'.

The review of *Childe Harold I and II*[3] took the poem as 'a descriptive poem', and admired its 'spirit' and 'energy', asserting that 'every page' was 'characterized by genuine poetical feeling, the truest classical taste, and the most correct and mellifluous versification'. It singled out the stanzas on the Spanish women as 'of extraordinary elegance and highly musical', and the opening of Canto II as 'peculiarly spirited and fine'. Its only reservation was on 'the occasional introduction of opinions on religion'. The reviewer also admired the lyrics in the volume.

The British Critic soon tired of the Eastern Tales, and was particularly disappointed with *The Corsair*.[4] Byron's choice of heroes showed a 'very contracted view of human nature'. They were all cast in the same mould; it was 'Mungo here, Mungo there, Mungo everywhere'[5] (a dictum *The British Critic* repeats several times in subsequent reviews). Even female admirers would tire of 'querulous villainy and misanthropic sensibility'. The reviewer of *The Corsair* summed Byron up as 'a very good poet of the second or

[1] *BC*, XXX, October 1807.   [2] *BC*, XXXIII, April 1809.
[3] *BC*, XXXIX, May 1812.   [4] *BC*, I (n.s.), March 1814.
[5] Possibly the likeliest meaning of the peculiar nickname 'Mungo' is the slang sense tentatively offered by the *O.E.D.*, quoting a passage dated 1770: 'a person of position, a swell'.

third order; sometimes pretty, occasionally pathetic, and always intelligible'. *The British Critic* thought more highly of *Lara*,[1] especially for its psychology; though the hero was simply another creation of the same tribe. *The Siege of Corinth* seemed to *The British Critic* either a joke or contemptible, and it objected to *Parisina*, both for the incest theme and for Byron's treatment of it. Moreover, Byron was not a poet 'of feeling'. His creations came from the 'feverish and fretful workings of a confined and selfish sensibility'.[2]

In its review of *Childe Harold III*[3] in April 1816 *The British Critic* makes it quite clear that it thought society had rightly condemned Byron for his matrimonial fiasco, and it expressed surprise that he should again woo the public. His assertion that he had not 'bow'd a patient knee' to 'the idolatries' of 'the world' was false. Every poem he published was a 'living witness' to this. As to *Childe Harold I and II*, which the reviewer states had appeared before he started his 'critical labours', they had been overrated. *Childe Harold III* was 'more likely to find its level'. Its hero was, as usual, Byron himself. The obtrusion of Byron's character on the reader was evidence of poverty of invention and lack of discretion. Byron had boasted of his superior genius, but one only had his word for it. He had written 'a few very fine, and a few very pretty verses' among a heap of 'crude, harsh, unpoetical' strains. That was all the reviewer knew or wished to know of Byron's fame. His style had luckily caught the public taste, but

> The world are now growing tired of their luminary, and wait only for the rise of some new meteor, to transfer their admiration and applause. The noble Lord had talents, which if they had been duly husbanded, might have ensured him a more permanent place in their estimation. His Lordship never could have been a Milton, a Dryden, a Pope, or a Gray, but he would have been a star of the third or fourth magnitude, whose beams would have shone even upon posterity with no contemptible lustre. As the matter stands, he will now be too late convinced that he whose theme is only self, will find at last that self his only audience.

The first sixteen stanzas of this canto were on this 'everlasting theme'. As to Waterloo, Byron, like other poets, was unsuccessful on it, though his description of the Duchess of Richmond's

[1] *BC*, II (n.s.), October 1814. [2] *BC*, V (n.s.), April 1816.
[3] *BC*, VI (n.s.), December 1816.

ball was 'well imagined', and, except for the rugged line xxi. 4, 'happily expressed'. The reviewer disapproved of the lack of patriotism in Byron's reflections on the restoration of 'order, peace, and legitimate society' in Europe. As to xxxvi on Napoleon, if it was 'philosophy' it was 'unintelligible'; if it was 'sentiment' it was 'unbearable'; and if it was 'poetry' it was 'unreadable'. The whole address to Napoleon was 'crude and common place'. As to Wellington, Byron's poetry needed the name of Wellington more than the name of Wellington needed the poetry of Byron. The Rhine scenery (xlvi–lxi) was 'but tamely and ruggedly drawn'. The passages on Switzerland were more successful. The description of the night sail on Lake Geneva (lxxxv–lxxxix) was 'perhaps the most brilliant passage in the poem'. The characters of Voltaire and Gibbon (cv ff.) were drawn 'with more discrimination than we had reason to expect'.

The Prisoner of Chillon is dismissed as not having any passage of enough beauty or originality for quotation, though occasionally pretty, and generally inoffensive. The reviewer is ironical at the expense of the 'sublimity' of *Darkness* and of the 'bathos' of *Churchill's Grave*, and *The Dream* contained 'as usual a long history of "my own magnificent self".' The reviewer thought Byron would gain little credit by the two volumes, though *Childe Harold III* was 'not without a considerable share of poetic merit'.

The British Critic found 'Mungo' again in *Manfred*,[1] and had no high opinion of it. But, somewhat surprisingly, it liked *Beppo*,[2] which it thought morally unexceptionable, and strong satirically, though not a satire. It was, indeed, hard to classify, but was in any case 'a very agreeable composition, written with good humour, and even with gaiety'; and the versification was 'easy', and the language 'correct'.

The British Critic reviewed *Childe Harold IV* at some length.[3] It firmly stated at the outset that, though it admired Byron's poetical talents, it did not think so highly of them as did the world at large. The hostile critic complains again at Byron's egotism, and, somewhat inconsistently, adds that 'the public at large' were now as weary of it as the critic himself. He did not find xi–xvii on Venice up to the magnificence of the subject. They would have done 'well enough for an ordinary prize poem at the University', but were 'unworthy of a matured and real poet with

---

[1] *BC*, VIII (n.s.), July 1817. [2] *BC*, IX (n.s.), March 1818.
[3] *BC*, IX (n.s.), May 1818.

such a theme before him'. Byron was best at description. He was an accurate observer, and 'able to catch the distinguishing traits of each particular climate and country'. Stanzas xxvii–xxix on the moonlit Alpine scene seemed a good instance. The reviewer thought 'classical readers' would be 'much delighted' with the stanzas on the Clitumnus (lxvi–lxviii), but he objected on religious grounds to the use of the term 'Nature's baptism'; and he takes the opportunity of administering a caustic rebuke to Byron for his religious references, and, in particular, for addressing Italy as the 'parent of our religion'—surely a rather insular criticism! As to the many stanzas on Rome, the reviewer thought them uneven in quality. He quotes those on the Coliseum (cxxviii–cxxix) as among the best. The passage on the dying gladiator (cxl–cxli) he thought 'not ill done' but inferior 'in imagination' and 'in point' to some lines on the same subject which he had heard recited in the Sheldonian Theatre at Oxford by a now forgotten Mr Chinnery. He preferred the stanzas on St Peter's (cliii–clix), which he believed Byron had taken more trouble over. They abounded in 'strong and pointed phraseology'; though clix seemed unintelligible, and throughout the passage there was 'too much ponderosity to please'. The reviewer had a higher opinion of the lines on the Apollo Belvedere (clxi–clxii), which he thought among Byron's 'happiest efforts'. He also found the stanza on the Laocoön (clx) able and effective; and he welcomed the 'Epicedium' on Princess Charlotte (clxvii–clxxii)—it was 'well introduced' and 'congenial at once to the taste and to the feelings of every Englishman'. The stanzas on the ocean (clxxviii–clxxxiv) contained 'much to admire, but more to reprobate'. There were 'many well selected, many beautiful, and one or two new ideas', but the 'old leaven' was 'so mixed up with the mass, as to give that colour and flavour to the whole, with which we must ever own ourselves to be highly disgusted'.

Looking back over *Childe Harold* as a whole, the reviewer was not sorry it was completed. The Childe had unmercifully wearied readers with SELF. If the four cantos could be cut down to one-third the size, and all the passages dealing with 'that tiresome theme of his own feelings' were excised, 'enough might remain to stamp the character of his Lordship, as a poet of no inconsiderable merit'. This is perhaps the extremest view of the anti-egoistic type expressed about *Childe Harold* in contemporary periodical criticism.

When it came to review *Don Juan I and II*,[1] *The British Critic*
suggested that Byron had felt that 'some unusual exertion' was
necessary to counteract the cold reception of *Mazeppa*. (The
reception had not really been all that cold.) A satire had accordingly been announced 'in terms so happily mysterious, as to set
the town on the very tiptoe of expectation'. At one time it had
been declared to be 'intolerably severe', at another 'blasphemous';
and it had been whispered that no one dared publish it. After all
this 'portentous parturition' out had crept *Don Juan*—no satire
at all, but a poem which contained very little that was satirical,
and that directed against the Regent and his Ministers and two or
three helpless poets—'the only objects upon which the Noble
Lord could exercise his satirical propensities with security and
effect'. The reviewer's description of the poem is curious (he has
a narrow conception of 'satire'), and the Regent was far from
incapable of protecting himself, as was shown by the imprisonment of Leigh Hunt for a libel on him in 1813. Having denied
that the poem was a satire, however, the reviewer goes on to ask
what it was, and calls that a hard question. He is sure that none of
it could be 'dignified with the name of poetry':

> It has not wit enough to be comic; it has not spirit enough to make
> it lyric; nor is it didactic of any thing but mischief. The versification
> and morality are about upon a par; as far therefore as we are enabled
> to give it any character at all, we should pronounce it a narrative of
> degrading debauchery in doggrel rhyme.

The style was insufferably 'tedious and wearisome'. In over four
hundred 'doggrel' stanzas there were 'not a dozen places that even
in the merriest mood could raise a smile'. The critic may be
suspected of considerable stiffness of mouth! On *I*. viii–xiv he
comments that the Joke is 'rather enigmatical', and that the 'little
touch of blasphemy, at the conclusion', clearly intended as 'a
sharp hit', was really 'neither more nor less than a specimen of
gross impiety, and flippant vulgarity'. Canto I as a whole was
characterized by 'shameless indecency', and the 'apology' at the
end (ccvii–ccviii) was 'trash of the lowest order, and the dullest
species'. We may note here that the critic's objection is both
moral and aesthetic. As for the shipwreck in Canto II, 'the poverty
of a man's wit is never so conspicuous, as when he is driven to
joke upon human misery'. The mixture was 'calculating, vapid,

[1] *BC*, XII (n.s.), August 1819.

and heartless'. It was not 'mad' but 'bad'—'bad in expression, worse in taste, and worst of all in feeling and in heart'. With regard to the 'indecency' and 'blasphemy' of the volume, it was not a 'history' only, but a 'manual' of profligacy, representing vice 'in that alluring and sentimental shape, which at once captivates and corrupts'. But the British nation would not be tricked by this out of 'its national strength, its sturdy and unbending morality'. And as to the 'blasphemous sneers, so liberally scattered through the volume', it was not to be wondered that the man who could 'so laboriously inculcate the breach of one commandment, should furnish a parody of all the ten'. But the 'parody' (*I.* ccv–ccvi) was so 'miserable and poor' that it was really hard to say whether bad principle or bad poetry predominated. The beauties of the poem were, in any case, few. The best stanzas were *I.* cxxii–cxxiii. Though their ideas were ordinary, these stanzas had a 'sweetness' and 'elegance' that even gave them an air of originality. In Canto II the description of the sinking of the ship (lii–liii) rose out of 'the circumambient doggrel'. The reviewer hoped the poem would not be read:

> The good sense, and the good feeling of the English nation must and will banish it from their houses. We should have the worst opinion indeed of any man, upon whose family table this volume were to lie exposed.

Cantos III–V were still more unfavourably received.[1] *The British Critic* became downright abusive:

> The king of birds, in his noble and generous nature, builds his eyrie aloft, under the mid-light of heaven, and gives his callow brood full cognizance of the sun. It is the eft and toad, and lizard on the other hand, the slimy and creeping, and venomous tribes, which shrink from observation, and bring forth in covert. The poem before us is one of those hole and corner deposits; not only begotten but spawned in filth and darkness. Every accoucheur of literature has refused his obstetric aid to the obscure and ditch-delivered foundling; and even its father, though he unblushingly has stamped upon it an image of himself which cannot be mistaken, forbears to give it the full title of avowed legitimacy.

The critic introduces his Mungo quip yet again, and also professes that his appetite fails at the 'ragout' which 'when stripped of its garnish turns out to be garbage'. He thought Byron as salacious as

[1] *BC*, XVI (n.s.), September 1821.

Aretino. His model was not really Pulci, for that poet was only peripherally licentious.

The British Critic's review of Don Juan VI–VIII[1] starts by asserting that though there was a time when 'the friends of literature and virtue mourned over the occasional perversion of Lord Byron's splendid talents', that time was long since past. The 'spell and mystery' which Byron had cast about himself and his adventures had become 'as stale and palpable as most other pieces of solemn charlatanerie'; and 'his tall scornful heroes, all of one family, with hearts as black as their heads, and lips curling as regularly and duly as their whiskers', had ceased to be identified with him. At length he had become 'a contributor to a blasphemous magazine conducted by a knot of refugees and convicted libellers'.[2] As to the present 'shilling's worth of ribaldry', it started with about thirty 'dull twaddling stanzas, spiced with an indecency or two', and went on to the Gulbeyaz episode, which Byron cleverly did not finish, so as to promote the sales of the next instalment. Canto VII started with seven stanzas in Byron's 'most cynical style' to the effect 'that life is not worth a potatoe, that it is difficult to say whether living or dying is the best thing, and that dogs are far our betters'. The reviewer suspects Leigh Hunt's hand in part of the passage on the preparations for the siege of Ismail. He praises, however, the dialogue between Suwarrow and Johnson (lviii–lxii) as possessing 'a great deal of character and terse humour', and finds the last two stanzas of VII 'thrilling', and the start of VIII equally spirited. He suspects the narrative of Juan's conduct at the siege ('in Lord Byron's best and most touching manner') as possibly intended 'to mask some future attack on virtue and good feeling, or to lead to some diabolical conclusion'. There follows an attack on Byron for perverting the character of Don Juan into that of 'a generous but ungovernable boy of 17 . . . artfully enveloped in a constant maze of temptation'; though the reviewer believes that in VI–VIII Byron seems to be more concerned for 'the dull lessons of radicalism' than for indecency. As for the origin of Don Juan, the reviewer offers the theory that Byron started it as a vent from the humiliation he had suffered from the judgment of the public on his private life. He had first, 'with the comprehensive views of a

[1] BC, XX (n.s.), August 1823.
[2] The Liberal, on which see pp. 191–3 below. 'Convicted libellers', of course, refers to the Hunt brothers.

Caligula', attacked 'religion, national spirit, the honour of man, and the virtue of woman'; but, finding this unsuccessful, he then 'bestrode the broken knee'd hobby-horse of Radicalism', and now finally he had sunk 'from the dignity of Milton's fallen angel, to the vulgar horned and tailed devil of a puppet-show'.

The critique of *Don Juan IX–XI*[1] regards Byron as beyond any appeal to conscience, and caustically sets out on the 'nauseous task' of inquiring how far these cantos were likely to serve 'the interests of the firm in which he has thought fit to become an active partner'.[2] The answer was that 'his anxiety in the cause of mischief' had been 'detrimental to his success'. His 'chosen friends' were clearly now regarded as outside the pale both by Tories and by Whigs. He had therefore now started to lash about him at all and sundry 'from the king to the humblest individual of this empire', and at England itself. The story in these cantos was a mere thread, and 'totally destitute, thank Heaven! of those attractions by which vice knows how to recommend himself'. The reviewer professes (in shameless contradiction to the facts) that *The British Critic* had seen Byron's 'muse' in Canto I as 'elegant, highly talented, and graceful', though it had 'lamented her deflection from virtue'. He then traces in a purple passage what he calls 'the history of the vice and progress, the decline and fall, of the tenth, or Juanic muse', simply repeating in florid language the points already made in his review.

Three months later *The British Critic* said its last word on *Don Juan* in its review of *XII–XIV*.[3] It thought that the 'repeated sousings' Byron had received from various quarters had operated in 'disgusting *him* also with his ragged regiment of ex-English associates, and inspired him with the intention of "purging and living cleanly" '. Certainly the circulation of *Don Juan* was now 'chiefly confined to that "operative class", whose wives and daughters are their own housemaids'. Byron now, therefore, seemed to want to return 'to the rose-coloured ottomans and rosewood work tables' from whence his works had been banished. For this reason he had abandoned *The Liberal*, and 'moderated his own cynical growl' into 'somewhat less extravagant cadence' in these cantos. He was, 'for a wonder, neither obtrusively indecent, pointedly blasphemous, nor scurrilously abusive'.

---

[1] *BC*, XX (n.s.), September 1823.
[2] The 'firm' being the publishers of *The Liberal* (see p. 66, n. 2).
[3] *BC*, XX (n.s.), December 1823.

He was still sarcastic about English women, Shakespeare, and the Duke of Wellington, 'but in a more feeble and civil manner'. As to execution, Byron had not 'regained the easy bantering tone of profligacy' which characterized *Beppo*. 'Coarse and bitter feeling' broke out through the whole eighty-three stanzas on the house party at Norman Abbey 'in spite of his efforts to suppress it'. But he was still 'in good humour' with the beauties of nature, and *XIII.* lvi–lviii were a 'green oasis of beautiful description'. Everything else was inferior.

On Shelley

The British Critic had little time for Shelley. It briefly condemned his juvenilia on literary grounds, and dismissed *Alastor*[1] as 'nonsense', ridiculing it as the '*ne plus ultra* of poetical sublimity'. It did not review any of Shelley's other work. We may easily imagine that it could well have continued to find his poems nonsensical, and it is certain that Shelley's ideas would have seemed execrable.

On Keats

Keats received mixed treatment from *The British Critic*. Its review of *Endymion*[2] was a supercilious dismissal of the poem, which it thought would have been '*sui generis*' if Leigh Hunt had never written. The review consists largely of a narration of the story, picking out phrases which the reviewer clearly thinks ridiculous. During his narration of Book II he pauses to administer a moral rebuke to Keats and the Cockneys in general:

> Mr. Keats is not contented with a half initiation into the school he has chosen. And he can strike from unmeaning absurdity into the gross slang of voluptuousness, with as much skill as the worthy prototype whom he has selected. We will assure him, however, that not all the flimsy veil of words in which he would involve immoral images, can atone for their impurity; and we will not disgust our readers by retailing to them the artifices of vicious refinement, by which, under the semblance of "slippery blisses, twinkling eyes, soft complection of faces, and smooth excess of hands", he would palm upon the unsuspicious and the innocent imaginations better adapted to the stews.

The reviewer also notices 'a jacobinical apostrophe' at the start of Book III. He then continues in the moral strain for some time,

[1] *BC*, V (n.s.), May 1816.   [2] *BC*, IX (n.s.), June 1818.

but ends with an ironical reflection on the vast length and fine presentation of the poem, and on the fact that it is written 'for the most part (when there are syllables enough) in the heroic couplet'. The tone of the review resembles that of some of the later reviews of Byron in the same periodical.

The British Critic did, however, do honour to the 1820 volume in a more discriminating review.[1] (A lengthy extract appears on pp. 499–502 below.) Contempt of Hunt is still present, but the review does candidly recognize Keats's poetic powers.

THE CHRISTIAN OBSERVER

The Christian Observer, which ran from 1802 to 1874, was probably the most influential religious periodical in nineteenth-century England. It has, indeed, been said by a modern authority that anyone 'who wishes to study the origins of . . . "Victorianism" cannot afford to neglect this magazine'.[2] *The Christian Observer* was founded as a periodical to represent Anglican but not High Church Christianity. Its supporters and contributors included Hannah More and William Wilberforce and other Evangelicals. Rev. Joseph Pratt was its first editor, but after a few months the editorship was entrusted to Zachary Macaulay, the father of the historian, who held office till 1816, when Rev. J. C. Wilkes took over from him. Zachary Macaulay went on writing for the periodical, and there is no evidence of change of policy.

On Byron

The Christian Observer gave a great deal of attention to Byron, both during his lifetime and for a year or so after his death. Most important for us are its reviews of the first three cantos of *Childe Harold*, though it also reviewed *The Giaour*, *The Corsair*, and *Hebrew Melodies*, and made some general observations, after Byron's death, on his character and writings.[3]

It is not certain who reviewed *Childe Harold I and II*,[4] but he was clearly a writer of some ability. He took his stand on the time-honoured principle that 'the object of poetry is to instruct by

[1] *BC*, XIV (n.s.), September 1820.

[2] F. E. Mineka, *The Dissidence of Dissent* (Chapel Hill, North Carolina, 1944).

[3] These were made in a series of four articles by 'F' entitled 'The Character, Opinions, and Writings of Lord Byron' printed in *CO*, XXV, February, March, April, and May 1825.

[4] *CO*, XI, June 1812.

pleasing'. He announces that he felt an 'eager desire', when a new 'poetic luminary' ascended, 'to find its altitude, to take its bearings, to trace its course, and to calculate its influence upon surrounding bodies', especially when 'a man of rank and notoriety' struck 'his golden harp'. The reviewer had a low opinion of *Hours of Idleness*, and thought *English Bards and Scotch Reviewers* 'too sanguinary'. He had been glad when he heard that Byron was going to travel abroad, as he thought it might soften his temper. Now he had returned, and offered this 'poetical journal' of his travels to the public. The 'Childe' himself was 'a mighty surly fellow', and also 'licentious and sceptical'. Byron rightly disclaimed all connexion with him. Yet, notes the reviewer, curiously enough 'most of the offensive reflections in the poem' were the poet's own. The reviewer praises the powerful description of Lisbon, Cintra, and the surroundings (*I*. xiv–xxvii), which he considers to be 'in the occasionally abrupt manner of Spenser'. The passage on Battle (xxxviii ff.) makes him thankful for the English Channel. He approves of Byron's hostility to war, but not of his failure to distinguish between just and unjust wars, or of his account of the causes of *this* war. He praises the stanzas on the Maid of Saragoza (liv ff.), and the contrast drawn between Sunday customs in Southern Spain and in England (lxviii ff.), though he regrets Byron's omission to mention English church-going. The stanzas on the bullfight (lxxii ff.) he ranks among the best in the volume. As to Canto II, it started finely, but soon there came a stanza (perhaps vii) telling us that 'all religion is gross delusion', and then that the remedy for gloom is to 'pursue what chance or fate proclaimeth best'. The reviewer demurs at all that. On the other hand, he greatly admires the passage on Solitude (xxv–xxvi), and the 'stimulating stanzas on the prostrate cities of Ancient Greece'. As to the ending, where according to the reviewer the poet tells us he must plunge into all the vices, the reviewer's response is one of regret. He goes on to consider the instalment as a whole. He writes at some length of the advantages and disadvantages of the Spenserian stanza. He finds the rhyming couplets of Scott, with occasional deviation into alternate rhymes, 'infinitely preferable'. He holds that 'one of the ends of poetry is to relax', and thinks you cannot do that with Spenserians. Apart from this unfortunate choice of metre, however, Byron, *as a poet*, was to be congratulated. He had 'washed his hands of allegory'. He was far 'briefer' than Spenser. He philosophized and moralized as well as painted

—provided 'food for the mind as well as the eye'—kindled 'the feeling' as well as gratified 'the sense'. On the other hand, his philosophy and morality were 'of a character rather to offend and pollute the mind, than to sooth or to improve it'. This defect was chargeable to the man, or, rather, to his principles. But whatever the cause, the consequences were dreadful. 'The temperament of his mind' was 'the ruin of his poem'. All the best poets had been fine teachers:

> The tendency of the strain of Homer is to transform us for the moment into heroes; of Cowper, into saints; of Milton, into angels; but Lord Byron would almost degrade us into a Thersites or a Caliban; or lodge us as fellow-grumblers, in the stye of Diogenes, or any of his two or four footed snarling or moody posterity.

Until he changed his conceptions Byron could never be a great poet. The reviewer concludes with a moral attack on Byron as a man like Rousseau, confessing the most disgraceful vices. Could Byron conceive that this 'peep into the window of his breast' must not 'revolt every virtuous eye'?

> Can he boldly proclaim his violations of decency and of sobriety; his common contempt for all modifications of religion; his monstrous belief in the universal rest or annihilation of man in a future state; and forget that he is one of those who
>
> > 'Play such tricks before high heaven,
> > As make the angels weep;'
>
> as offend against all moral taste; as attempt to shake the very pillars of domestic happiness and of public security?

Byron had, however, like Rousseau, honestly shown the effect of his creed on his own mind—for instance, the loneliness, and the 'awful uncertainty, or rather the sullen despair' of Claudio's ' "Ay —but to die and go"—alas, . . .' But the reviewer wishes Byron himself would take the hint and find comfort in Christ.

The reviewer of *The Giaour*,[1] J. W. Cunningham,[2] referred to *Childe Harold I and II* as uneven, and as recommended 'to the bad,

[1] *CO*, XII, November 1813.

[2] John William Cunningham (1780–1861) was a Wrangler at Cambridge and subsequently a Fellow of St John's College. He was ordained in 1802. He later wrote a book, from the Evangelical point of view, about the various parties in the Anglican Church since the Reformation. This book, called *The Velvet Cushion*, was published in 1814, and reached its tenth edition two years later. Cunningham became a prominent member of the Evangelical movement, and eventually edited *The Christian Observer* from 1850 to 1858.

by its occasional sensualism; to the good, by its exemplification of the misery of vice, and by certain passages in which lofty truths were conveyed in masculine and elevated language'. He thought that the 'offences against "morality" ' in *The Giaour* were 'innumerable'; and he could not decide 'who is the more shameless offender against all the laws and better feelings and rights of man; the Childe Harold, or the Giaour'. Byron was much impressed by Cunningham's review (which also discussed the literary features of *The Giaour* in detail), and he wrote as much to Zachary Macaulay, who sent a copy of Byron's letter to Cunningham, with a covering letter ending with the common hope of Christian reviewers of the early Byron—'May God touch his heart', which Dr Keith Walker has rightly interpreted as signifying the view that Byron, 'peer and enormously successful poet, was a prominent figure among *those who counted*, those who had to be converted to true Christianity if England was to be saved'.[1]

The Christian Observer's review of *The Corsair*, generally favourable, is far inferior, and for us scarcely of interest except for its general description of Byron as 'a great master of the affections, and a powerful director of their several emotions'. It is worth recalling the opposite opinion expressed by *The British Critic* (p. 61 above).

Far more important is the review of *Childe Harold III*.[2] This reveals that *The Christian Observer* had deliberately refrained from reviewing *Lara*, *The Siege of Corinth*, and *Parisina*, because it thought them poetically inferior, and the *Poems on His Domestic Circumstances* because such an exposure of domestic feuds ought never to have been published. *Childe Harold III*, however, at least had the 'great negative merit' of being free of the 'ruffian tribes' with which Byron had 'peopled his imagination'. It was also 'superior to several of its predecessors in literary merit'. The reviewer takes the opportunity to warn Byron against 'letting off' a poem 'every six months'. The reviewer's detailed comment on Canto III starts by suggesting that the opening, 'though certainly not very musical in its cadences', would appear 'tender and interesting' to those who could 'pardon a little of that egotism' for which the Childe was 'conspicuous'. On the other hand, he regrets that Byron has now identified himself with the Childe, 'a

[1] Keith Walker, *Byron's Readers: A Study of Attitudes, 1812–1832*, unpublished Cambridge Ph.D. dissertation, 1966, p. 32, n. 8.

[2] *CO*, XVI, April 1817.

cold-hearted, sated, sensualist, whose errors are as much those of the understanding as the affections'. The reviewer's regret is an unusual reaction. Most reviewers were glad that the duality had disappeared; but *The Christian Observer* is anxious for Byron's character to be preserved from defilement. The reviewer, indeed, goes on to express the pious hope that, if Byron chooses to be known as Childe Harold, he will publish a further canto, entitled 'The Wandering Childe reclaimed'! The reviewer calls the stanzas in which the Childe recounts his history since his return from his former pilgrimage 'querulous'. He is, however, hopeful of the stanza in which the Childe seems on the verge of repentance. The reviewer refuses, on the other hand, to accept the Childe's despairing "too late", and suggests recourse to Christianity. He declines to inquire into the mystery of ix (on the marriage and its aftermath), but firmly asserts that a man blessed with health, birth, fortune, and a wife and child, 'has only to blame his own headstrong will and wayward passions, if he will remain morbidly discontented and unhappy'. He recognizes, however, that Byron himself admits that it was the Childe's own fault. As to xii–xv in which Byron tells of his preference for solitary wanderings, the reviewer regards xiii–xv as good poetry, but finds the personal feelings expressed painful. A poet should never, in his view, obtrude his melancholy on his readers, unless some 'interesting associations' are connected with it. The reviewer quotes as a contrast some lines by Kirke White, a favourite poet of the Evangelicals. These expressed as morbid feelings as those of the Childe, and the poetry was not as fine as Byron's, but one sympathized unreservedly with the feelings, whereas Byron's 'querulous strains' evoked a 'constant alternation between sympathy and disgust'. To appeal to 'an honest and well-regulated mind' a poet, like an orator, needed moral as well as intellectual qualities. On the other hand, with regard to Waterloo, the reviewer considers that Byron had described best what no poet had yet described well enough. (The reviewer does not seem to notice that Byron does not really *describe* the battle at all.) The battle as reported in the newspapers was so vivid in people's minds that even Homer could not have written anything on it that would not seem flat in comparison. It would not be a good subject till some of its vividness had worn off. The reviewer does, however, praise the contrast Byron offers between the 'revelry' of the ballroom and the 'carnage' of the field, and comments that it 'ought to convey a far more than poetical moral on the uncertainty of human life, and the vanity of worldly pleasures'. The reviewer omits the Bonaparte passage (xxxvi ff.), and goes on to the Rhine stanzas (lvi ff., and the Drachenfels lyric). The contrast between 'the peaceful landscape and the deeds and persons which once animated and adorned its beauties' he considers to be a theme sure of exciting 'a pleasing sympathy', which he interprets in a religious manner. He also hopes that the Drachenfels stanzas referred to a sister:

> England, we trust, is still so old fashioned in her taste and morals, that if a young nobleman should choose to address his amorous ditties to any person except her who ought to be the centre of all his hopes and wishes, he would be obliged, by the voice of public opinion, to select some less conspicuous vehicle for their conveyance.

The reviewer's hope that it might be a sister was something of a contradiction of this proposition, and it would have been even more so had he been better informed as to Byron's relations with Augusta! On the assumption that a sister was referred to, he condescendingly quotes the first two stanzas. He goes on to praise the 'sublime view' of the Alps (lxii); but demurs at the misanthropy of

> Is it not better, then, to be alone,
> And love Earth only for its earthly sake?
>
> [lxxi]

The reviewer contrasts the love of humanity manifested by 'that brother enthusiast to inanimate nature', Bernardin de St Pierre. He also objects to the implication in lxxiv that 'the human soul is grossly material, or that animal life transmigrates from men to brutes'. As to the celebrated question

> Are not the mountains, waves, and skies, a part
> Of me and of my soul, as I of them?
>
> [lxxv]

the reviewer scathingly comments

> We should no more think of answering a man who asks such questions than a child who cries for the moon; and shall, therefore, simply remark, that if this unintelligible rhapsody is meant for poetical sublimity, we had much rather remain among the vulgar herd of men whom Lord Byron characterizes in the same stanza, as
>
> 'Gazing upon the ground with thoughts which dare not glow',

than begin in our old age to 'glow' with a fervour, at once so lawless and irrational.

He regards these thoughts as in any case mere gratuitous ostentation. The lines are, indeed, hard to defend if looked at with Johnsonian scrutiny; though they do have a splendid afflatus. The character of Rousseau (lxxvii ff.) the reviewer considers to be ably drawn, but too partial; and he could not admit that Rousseau's 'lunacy' was of a kind to lessen his moral responsibility, and so 'to render him excusable at that Higher Bar to which he has long since been summoned'. Byron was to be thanked, however, for pointing out (in lxxxii) the 'awful results' of the teaching of Rousseau and 'his compeers' in the 'horrors of the late continental revolutions and disasters'. On the other hand, he was wrong to feel glad, nevertheless, about Rousseau and the rest, that 'mankind' had 'felt their strength, and made it felt'. What their strength had done was to 'overturn, in a moment, the fairest country of Europe', and to 'shake the whole world in its recoil',

> and we fear it will not be till they are again willing to leave the immediate legislation of empires to an intellectual and moral, rather than a numerical and physical, majority, that the repose of nations will be finally secured.

The reviewer is glad to leave the tangle of revolutionary politics for the scene on 'placid Leman' (lxxxv–lxxxvii). He also looks forward to the canto on Italy:

> Lord Byron never treads more nobly than on classic ground; so that, if he can fairly divest himself of ruffians, and egotism, and misanthropy, and scepticism, and will consent to put in their place a little good sense, and good temper, and, above all, (would that the wish were realized) a little Christian feeling, we should hope, even yet, that he might produce a 'pilgrimage to Italy', which, when sufficiently matured, and kept back the suitable Horatian term of years, should eclipse all his former productions, and stamp him with a character far higher, and more desirable, than that of an interesting poet.

The reviewer then quotes the conclusion of Canto III (cxii–cxviii) except for cxvii, which he indignantly refuses to quote, 'since it is impossible to conceive that by any British mother "dull Hate as duty should be taught", to an only child, in reference to one whom, whatever may be his faults or follies, that child is enjoined "to honour and obey" '. The reviewer is sceptical of Byron's

75

assertion that he no longer thirsts for fame (cxii), but is inclined to think Byron's 'I have not loved the world, nor the world me' (cxiii–cxiv) nearer the truth. Possibly, he suggests, the world had not loved Byron because neither his work nor his example had 'done it much service'. In any case, Byron was 'quite even with the world'. This was not, however, for the right reason. There were two ways of not loving the world—St Paul's and Rousseau's —and Byron's seemed to be Rousseau's. It was to be hoped, however, that his feeling of surfeit with the world might lead him, like Solomon, to the 'conclusion that "to fear God, and keep his commandments is the whole duty of man";—his end and his duty, his privilege and reward'. But the reviewer was sorry to say that Byron seemed to admire the 'code of Mohammed' rather than that of Christ. This was exemplified in one of the notes to the poem. Byron had, however, at least admitted 'that there may be still some truth, and reality, and kindness and friendship surviving among men'. If only he had 'extricated himself from the "busy crowd" of idle or sensual flatterers' he would find plenty of this:

> He needed not to have descended from either his political or intellectual rank to have discovered genuine Christianity diffusing her balmy influences in social and domestic life, and leading in her train, though not acknowledging as her equals, all the subordinate graces, and charities, and felicities of human kind.

The reviewer expresses the hope that 'it is not even yet "too late"', and he hopes that Byron will yet enjoy 'the sweets of parental affection', such as were described by 'Mr. Southey' in his Poet's Pilgrimage to Waterloo. In view of the subsequent relations between Byron and Southey it is ironical that the reviewer should have chosen this name to hold up to Byron as the provider of an *exemplum*!

The Christian Observer did not review any more of Byron's poems after this; but there is an incidental comment on *Don Juan I and II* in its review of Crabbe's *Tales of the Hall*.[1] Byron is there referred to as

> that man whose writings display the resources of the finest genius in dark and unnatural connexion with the worst qualities of a perverted heart.

The reviewer asks how long the 'abused British public', and

[1] *CO*, XVIII, October 1819; quoted Keith Walker, *op. cit.*, 40.

especially the women, would 'suffer themselves to be held in the silken chains of a poetical enchantment'. He hopes that by issuing a 'friendly warning' he may have decreased Byron's sales, and speculates that 'the wretched author' might himself perhaps one day thank him for doing so, and for bringing his mind 'to a new position of self-recollection and inquiry'.

There are two adverse mentions of Byron again in 1819, and a caustic note on *The Liberal* in 1823, but then nothing further until after Byron's death, after which *The Christian Observer* printed in 1825 the series of articles by a certain 'F' entitled 'The Character, Opinions, and Writings of Lord Byron'. These fall outside the scope of this book; but they are, in any case, of little value as literary criticism.

On Shelley and Keats

The Christian Observer wasted no time on Shelley. It obviously saw that he was beyond the pale, that there was nothing to be done about him, and that the least said the better. Nor did it review any of Keats's work. It is not so clear why, though it may perhaps have been because he did not seem important enough (*The Christian Observer* was interested in important people), or it may have been because Keats was classed by it with Leigh Hunt, who would have seemed even deeper in the outer darkness than Shelley.

THE ECLECTIC REVIEW

The Eclectic Review (1805–68) was started by a group of men who wished to rescue English literature from 'the dogmatism of superficial writers, and the irreligious influence of a semi-infidel party'.[1] Its avowed object was 'to unite the interests of Religion, Morality, and Literature, giving to each its respective importance, in a candid discussion of the merits of living authors'. After a shaky start the *Eclectic* flourished from 1806 to 1811 under the editorship of a very young man, Daniel Parken, with the able assistance of John Foster, the essayist, and James Montgomery, the poet. These two were both Dissenters, and the *Eclectic* soon became virtually an organ of the Dissenters. After Parken gave up the editorship to practise as a lawyer there was a short period of decline, but in 1814 the *Eclectic* was bought by Josiah Conder (1789–1855), who managed and eventually edited the periodical,

[1] Meaning the Radicals who were not, however, a political 'party' in the strict sense.

retaining control until 1837. Conder was a remarkable personality and an indefatigable worker. Besides editing the *Eclectic* he found time to write many works, including an encyclopaedia of travel, a two-volume work on Protestant Nonconformity, and a number of other Nonconformist works on religion. The reviewers in the *Eclectic*, including Conder himself, often invoke religious and moral criteria of value, but they also pay attention to aesthetic criteria, and they are remarkably free of strong political prejudice.

On Byron

The Eclectic Review gave almost as continual attention to Byron's work as did *The British Critic*. Whereas, however, *The British Critic* assiduously abused *Don Juan*, the *Eclectic* virtually ignored it. Its disapproval is clear enough from its periphrastic reference to the poem in a review of *Mazeppa* as 'a subsequent publication of notorious character',[1] and from the plain statements in the periodical's review of a poem called *Rouge et Noir* (1821) that 'the cold-blooded facetiousness of the Author of Don Juan . . . though less coarse and broad, is, in fact, far more licentious than that of the most exceptionable of our comic writers'; and that, whereas the descriptions of Swift and Smollett 'only quicken the pulse and pollute the memory', those in 'Lord Byron's anonymous poetry' are 'adapted to harden the heart'.[2]

Let us, however, go back to the beginning: the *Eclectic* gave *Hours of Idleness* a mixed reception.[3] The reviewer stoutly declared that he had no intention of kowtowing to a nobleman writing poetry, and went on to assert roundly that these were 'juvenile poems, some of very moderate merit and others of very questionable morality', though the volume was not entirely of exceptionable character or destitute of merit. It showed 'considerable feeling and spirit', and a general 'facility of expression'. Prominence was, however, given to 'voluptuous themes and visions', and the 'licentious manner' in which they were frequently celebrated compelled the reviewer to 'pronounce the volume unsuitable for any refined reader or well-regulated family'. The review ends with an admonition to Byron to declare whether or not he is a Christian.

[1] *Ecl. R*, XII (n.s.), August 1819, 150. An extract appears on pp. 250–1 below.

[2] *Ecl. R*, XVI (n.s.), October 1821, 373–4. I am indebted for this reference to Dr Keith Walker's Cambridge Doctoral Dissertation.

[3] *Ecl. R*, III. ii, November 1807.

English Bards and Scotch Reviewers also elicited a mixed response from the *Eclectic*.[1] The reviewer reports that the poem had already attained a large circulation, 'a circumstance by no means surprising, when we consider its high seasoning of invective and sarcasm, its humour and spirited versification, and the peculiarity of its subject and its occasion, combined with the rank of its reputed author'. The poet and 'the Busby bands of the Edinburgh Reviewers' were pretty fairly matched 'for equitable discrimination, for devotedness to truth, for gentlemanly deportment, and the genuine Christian spirit of candour, amenity, forgiveness of injuries, and reluctance to inflict pain'. The satire belonged to the school of Churchill, and did credit to it; but the 'sheer folly' of jus criticisms of 'many' living poets would defeat the effect of the thet strictures, and the author would be regarded as 'a petulant school-boy', not 'a severe and indignant Censor'. The lavish praise of poetasters was also a blemish. The poem would amuse for a few weeks. Then perhaps Byron would in turn be deflated.

The *Eclectic* received *Childe Harold I and II* on the whole favourably, though with serious reservations.[2] The reviewer thought that Byron's confidence in his talents, which had made him continue as a poet, was justified. The world had now discovered that Byron really was 'a man of genius and a poet', and encomia were heaped upon him. But this was partly because he had shown his opinions as an advocate of Catholic emancipation and 'the adherent of a political party'. Public enthusiasm had, indeed, now gone too far, and would become fainter as the influence of political ideas on readers and critics grew less (a prognostic the reviewer makes without a shred of argument). As to the poem, the title was misleading. Yet there was 'much truth and force' in the depiction of Harold, and 'the moral to be deduced' was 'extremely valuable', though 'a gloomy and painful affair'. It is interesting to find that the *Eclectic* reviewer credits Byron with this moralistic intention, since he goes on to say that Byron 'therefore judiciously introduces himself'. The distribution of roles, however, 'causes inconveniences'. The Childe sometimes forgets his 'heart-struck melancholy', and makes jokes, and Byron sometimes becomes melancholy in his reflections. The reviewer praises the choice of the Spenserian stanza, though he

[1] *Ecl. R*, V. i, May 1809.   [2] *Ecl. R*, VIII. i, June 1812.

79

does not believe it can do all that Beattie had claimed.[1] It was too diffuse for wit, too regular for passion, and too stately for pathos. But Byron had 'no pretension to wit', and was rarely tender or enthusiastic. He was too philosophical, and too disdainful. The reviewer is, however, more concerned for political, and especially for moral, matters. He attacks Byron's treatment of the 'martyrs for the liberty of Spain', and his 'irreverence' towards women, which was 'not very poetical' and was 'misanthropic'. Except for this and for Byron's 'unbelief', however, the reviewer offers his 'warm admiration', praising the 'energy and sublimity' of the reflections, and, still more, the 'distinct and lively' representation of 'national and individual character'. There was 'a keen relish and taste', both for the 'terrific' and for the 'gentler' beauties of nature. Byron's diction, though often 'languid and redundant', and sometimes 'careless and inaccurate', was on the whole 'nervous and idiomatic', displaying the vigour of 'the old English school of poetry'. Byron clearly had a 'strong and argumentative understanding', and 'a disposition to contemplate the pensive and awful rather than the gay and amusing scenes of life'. He was among 'the reasoning class of poets'. He was no satirist (a rash observation, that!). More serious, he denied immortality. Considering the religious background of the *Eclectic*, this review is remarkably open-minded, and takes into account an interestingly wide range of values.

The *Eclectic* reviewed all the Tales, describing *The Giaour*[2] vividly and perceptively, while censuring its moral tendency as 'extremely pernicious'; finding *The Bride* spiritedly told, but not so poetical[3]; and giving its highest praise to *The Corsair* as 'more vigorously conceived, and more carefully elaborated' than the other two poems.[4] Byron excelled almost all his contemporaries in 'delineation of character', and his characters were 'calculated to subserve a highly moral tendency', since they 'deepen our conviction of the miseries inescapably connected with a departure from virtue'. *Childe Harold* exhibited 'the comfortless, hopeless vacuity of the sceptic's heart'. *The Giaour* 'abounded' in passions

[1] James Beattie (1735–1803) had claimed in the Preface to his poem *The Minstrel* (1771–4): 'It admits both simplicity and magnificence of sound and of language, beyond any other stanza that I am acquainted with. It allows the sententiousness of the couplet, as well as the more complex modulation of blank verse.'

[2] *Ecl. R*, X, November 1813.   [3] *Ecl. R*, I (2nd. Ser.), February 1814.

[4] *Ecl. R*, I (2nd. Ser.), April 1814.

of a scarcely less instructive nature. There was nothing in Byron's poetry that displayed any design, or was calculated, to corrupt a virtuous mind, raise a guilty glow of pleasure, or delude the imagination into a love of splendid crime. Moreover, in *The Corsair* there was 'more of virtuous sentiment' than in Byron's former poems, and 'something like an approximation, on some points, to right feeling'. The periodical is evidently somewhat confused, and even contradictory in its observations on these matters. The *Eclectic*'s review of *Lara*[1] was written by Josiah Conder, the editor, who may indeed have written some of the earlier reviews, though that is not known. Conder welcomed the poem as 'a moral picture of still darker features' than *The Corsair*, and 'of instruction still more forcible'. His only stricture was on the 'false taste, to say nothing of inexcusable impiety', of the 'almost atheistical insinuations' by which some of the finest passages were disfigured. It was Conder again who reviewed *The Siege of Corinth* and *Parisina*.[2] He feared that the continual production of tales of this kind would eventually pall on the public. He himself was happy with them if Byron could produce nothing better, such as *Childe Harold*. *The Siege* was, however, one of Byron's best efforts (contrast *The British Critic*'s view). On the other hand, the story of *Parisina* was objectionable 'on ground of taste rather than morality'. The subject (incest) was 'unpleasing', and the treatment did not reconcile one to it. Conder goes on to contend that the fact that Byron had confined himself hitherto to narrating crime and delineating vicious character evinced either great deficiency of taste or very limited powers of conception. The sentiments Byron attributed to his 'personages' did not actually constitute 'characters'. The portraits had no individuality. He described admirably a certain class of emotions, without embodying them in characters, which should have been developed by their actions. But Conder was far from depreciating Byron's genius. In 'energy of expression' and the power of giving to words the life of poetry Byron was unequalled by any contemporary. It was from his use of his powers that Conder concluded they were circumscribed. To go down to posterity there had to be a 'high and holy ambition of legitimate fame'. The 'good', the 'true', and the 'beautiful' had to be the poet's 'ideal archetypes'.

It was Conder again who reviewed *Childe Harold III* and *The*

---

[1] *Ecl. R*, II (2nd. Ser.), October 1814.
[2] *Ecl. R*, V (2nd. Ser.), March 1816.

Prisoner of Chillon volume.[1] He began by applying to Byron his own lines about the 'self-torturing sophist, wild Rousseau' (lxxvii). Whatever opinion a reader might have of Byron's character, he would be 'dazzled even to tears' by this canto. Nevertheless, Conder felt no obligation either to act as Byron's apologist or as his censor (again contrast *The British Critic*). Yet in these poems Byron seemed to be inviting sympathy from 'the impersonal multitude', which he would be too proud to accept personally from an individual:

> The species of egotism, however, which pervades his Lordship's productions, appears less like the display of his own feelings, than the effect of their perpetually haunting him, intercepting and colouring his view of every other object, and rendering it impossible for him to forget
>
> 'the weary dream
> Of selfish grief or gladness'.

This is a far more sympathetic attitude to Byron's 'egotism' than that adopted in most reviews, which consider the 'egotism' to be far more within Byron's power. Which attitude we prefer will, of course, depend on our own view of the puzzling question of the psychological causes of the phenomenon.

With regard to Canto III itself, Conder believed that Byron had probably 'thought too long and darkly' on one real person to be 'capable of giving birth to a purely imaginary being'. All his avatars had 'the same combination of morbid feelings and phrenzied passions, aggravated into various degrees of guilt', and all the subordinate characters were 'shadowy outlines' which served to express 'the objects of passionate emotion and of remembrances real and unreal'. In portraying his principal characters Byron was fixing 'the intent gaze of his imagination' on them; yet 'not like Narcissus, enamoured of the reflection of himself, but losing in the contemplation of that social shadow, the conscious wretchedness of the original'. Conder seems to show considerable insight into Byron's psychology and its poetical results when he goes on to write:

> That very passion for intensity of feeling, which is the unhappy characteristic of Lord Byron's mind, renders him incapable of taking pleasure in the creation of imaginary beings from the purer elements of fancy, and the ordinary materials of humanity. If anything has

[1] *Ecl. R*, VII (2nd. Ser.), March 1817.

power to banish for a moment the ever present thought of self, which like an external presence seems to haunt him, it must be of a nature too horrible, too agonizing to be simply pleasing, or else of that commanding sublimity which suspends, as by physical force, our individual recollections, 'lulling them to sleep amid the music of nobler thoughts'. Of the power of natural scenery to produce this adequate excitement, and to hold the faculties in a trance-like oblivion of the insignificant interests of this world, no one appears to be more deeply susceptible than the Author of these poems; and few have succeeded so well in breathing an intellectual soul into the inanimate forms of grandeur, power, and beauty he describes.

Conder quotes as one instance lxii, and then, as a specimen 'of the very highest order of excellence', lxxxv–lxxxix and xcii–xciii, writing of these seven stanzas that 'Wordsworth, whose strength lies in enduing materiality with intelligence, has nothing finer of the kind'. In these extracts the scenery was 'at once revealed to our inmost feelings, not through the medium of description, as in a picture, but in its effect upon the imagination':

We do not see, we feel, the living landscape, by sympathy with the intense feelings of the poet, who, unable to divest his mind of the individuality of self even amid the conflict of elements, and the infinity of solitude, claims to be 'a portion of the tempest' and of night, and makes Nature itself serve as the expression and voice of his own emotions.

This seems to indicate validly an element in such passages, but I believe Conder underestimates the sensory strength of Byron's descriptions. It is interesting, however, to find him going on to praise

Are not the mountains, waves, and skies, a part
Of me and of my soul, as I of them?

which *The Christian Observer* had found nonsensical. Conder evidently does not take such verses as an expression of pantheism. Otherwise he might have rejected them, as the *Eclectic* repudiated the pantheism of Wordsworth's *Excursion*. Here Conder even sees a very close resemblance between Byron and James Montgomery (who was actually the *Eclectic*'s reviewer of *The Excursion*), who also painted 'from the looking-glass', though his egotism was 'far more amiable' and in itself more 'interesting', though 'less commanding', than Byron's. 'Egotism', to command sympathy, however, had to involve suffering, and this Conder thought it did in the case of both poets. These remarks of Conder's are surely rather penetrating.

As to *The Prisoner of Chillon*, Conder was inclined to think it 'one of the highest efforts of Lord Byron's imagination'. He thought that it formed to some extent an exception to the generalization that Byron could not create characters distinct from himself. Yet the 'vigour of conception' here had no reference to character, but was limited to 'peculiarity of situation', and was employed simply 'in realizing the gradual influence of imprisonment upon the human faculties'. The poem was 'written throughout with exquisite delicacy and pathos' (*The Champion*, in contrast, called the style 'namby-pamby') and in a tone of feeling entirely different from Byron's other poems and closer to the best of Wordsworth's lyrical ballads than any other poetry Conder knew. Returning later to *Childe Harold III*, Conder singles out for praise the reflections on Waterloo, the apostrophe to Howard, and the next stanza as of 'surpassing merit'. With regard to the 'moral sentiments' interspersed through the poems, Conder did not think them likely to 'spread infection', and he believed that the 'radical taint' in Byron's feelings was not medicable by 'sage philosophy'. The misanthropy of "I have not loved the world, nor the world me . . ." must, he thought, be partly affected, or very ungrateful. Byron had mentioned many friends, and not all had forsaken him; and it was his own fault if the world was not his friend,

> for to poets and to peers, especially to one like him, the world is in its disposition most friendly.

And had the 'English Timon's' work been directed to making the world any better? The review's business, however, was not with Byron but with his work and its readers,

> who, we doubt not, will be able to discriminate, at the very height of their admiration, between the brilliant coruscations of sentiment, which flash from his Lordship's genius, and the legitimate evidence of correct principle.

It is hard to be certain whether Conder's confidence was justified, but it may well have been.

The *Eclectic* had little to say of *Beppo*, but gave it reserved approval.[1] It was a 'burlesque poem', and if it were not 'licentious in morality' and 'necessarily vulgar and profane in its expressions',

[1] *Ecl. R*, IX (2nd. Ser.), June 1818.

and 'rather tedious in its narrative', it 'might serve very well to laugh through after dinner'.

The *Eclectic* gave a very fair review to *Childe Harold IV*.[1] The reviewer was Conder, and once again he showed himself an acute and balanced critic. He has some shrewd things to say on Byron's explicit abandonment, in the Preface to this canto, of the distinction between the poet and the Childe. Conder asserts that the Childe had always appeared to be 'nothing more than a pretence . . . for speaking in the third person', and that such a view of him was 'not the fault of the reader'. He concedes that Byron's first thought might have been to make the Childe an imaginary pilgrim, but holds that the poet must have abandoned any such idea very early indeed, 'since the poem has no plan, no action, no dramatic incident which might serve to develop the character of his hero'. Conder goes on to accuse Byron of disingenuousness:

> We cannot imagine that the author was ever honestly solicitous to guard against the mistake which he would fain represent as injurious, claiming, as it should seem, the magnanimity of being '*now*' indifferent to the injury. We apprehend, that by whatever means, or in whatever character, his Lordship might most easily have secured notoriety, that object attained, it would at all times have mattered little in his opinion, that the admiration won from his contemporaries, should have left esteem and sympathy far behind. And if he found that the dark and mysterious fancy portrait, which the public mistook for a real likeness, laid hold of the imagination, and fascinated while it seemed to repel, it is more than probable that the artist was not displeased at having attributed to himself those strong and gloomy traits of character, which his own fancy had pictured in another. There is a species of sublimity of which the *bad* is susceptible, to which in the ideal hero, he might feel to have made some approach, and on this dark elevation he might not be unwilling to seem to stand, shrouded in the indefiniteness of the poetical character. However this may be, the Author by carrying on the poem in his own person, and laying aside entirely his pilgrim-domino, has taken the sure method completely to obliterate in the minds of his readers, the nicely-drawn distinction he in his first canto pretended to support.

Conder does here neglect the possibility that in his Preface to Canto IV Byron, in pretending to have been injured by the identification made by readers and critics, was playing a joke on them; but, all the same, there may well have been a good deal of truth in Conder's analysis.

[1] *Ecl. R*, X (2nd. Ser.), July 1818.

Conder has, nevertheless, high praise for the poem now concluded:

> The poem, completed, may, therefore, as a whole, be considered as a series of descriptive sketches, made during his Lordship's travels, whose pilgrim-ship resolves itself into the plain reality of a philosophical tourist. Assuredly, it demanded no ordinary powers of thought as well as of poetical skill, to impart the charm of continual interest to a long succession of stanzas, cohering together by no other law than that of *juxtaposition*.

Yet Conder, though he considered Byron's 'abilities' to be 'of the highest order', indicated limitations. The chief of these was 'sameness of subject and mode of thinking'; though it was a proof of the poet's 'superlative genius' that he was able to impart to this sameness 'the effect and interest of variety'. Very perceptively, Conder remarks that *Beppo* was no exception to 'sameness'. It showed that Byron had great versatility of *style*, but the thinking was the same. Again, Byron's powers of observation and satire were well known, but he could not 'people the regions of fancy with abstractions wearing the semblance of distinct personality'. Yet Conder is 'not disposed to appreciate slightly the genius which shines out in the present poem'. He quotes the opening of Canto IV, and praises Byron's judgment in taking Rome as the main subject. Not Rome itself, however, could 'make the plaintive egotist forget his griefs and injuries'. Moreover, though the digressions were as well managed as possible, 'the effect of these intrusive passages' was, in Conder's view, 'incongruous with the majesty of the scene'. It was 'an unwelcome interruption to be called off to listen to the oft-told tale' of the Childe's miseries, 'and to hear him denounce upon his unknown enemies "the curse of his forgiveness" '. Conder thought some stanzas in *IV* were 'of a beauty and energy perhaps equal to any passages in the former cantos'. He singles out as especially admirable xxvii–xxix, and, above all, the apostrophe to the Ocean.

The review of *Mazeppa* mentioned above,[1] in which *Don Juan* is obliquely referred to, starts with a long cautionary section on the dangers of a thirst for poetic fame and intellectual dominion. It may ultimately result, warns the reviewer, in a writer's simply taking pleasure in 'the consciousness of exciting vivid sensations in others'; and if the writer be 'a man of depraved feelings', 'the

[1] *Ecl. R*, XII (2nd. Ser.), August 1819.

fable of the Vampyre' will be realized 'in his thus renewing the life of his pleasures from the heart's blood of the principles of his victims'. If it were not for 'the irresistible fascination exerted by a mind of such transcendent faculties', it might be morally instructive to follow the career of such a writer through to the final disgust he would be bound to feel; 'but such a lesson would be dearly purchased at the cost of familiar association with the individual'. The reviewer did not care to follow Byron's career any farther:

> The necessary progress of character as developed in his last *reputed* production [*Don Juan I and II*] has conducted him to a point at which it is no longer safe to follow him even in thought, for fear we should be beguiled of any portion of the detestation due to this bold outrage. Poetry which it is impossible not to read without admiration, yet, which it is equally impossible to admire without losing some degree of self-respect; such as no brother could read aloud to his sister, no husband to his wife;—poetry in which the deliberate purpose of the Author is to corrupt by inflaming the mind, to seduce to the love of evil which he himself has chosen as his good; can be safely dealt with only in one way, by passing it over in silence.

These are strong words. In imputing to Byron a deliberate intention to corrupt they go farther than some of the other reviews which condemned *Don Juan* on moral grounds. On the other hand, the reviewer does honestly and healthily maintain the distinction between the moral and the aesthetic which vanishes in some of the critiques in other periodicals—e.g., *The British Critic*—and this distinction and its resulting tension are still important to us in trying to form an estimate of *Don Juan*. An instance of a typical difficulty is afforded in the short extract from the *Eclectic*'s review printed on pp. 250–1 below.

The review of *Rouge et Noir*, also mentioned above,[1] makes the point that, although John Bull loved a good joke, he had not been 'accustomed to laugh at everything':

> He does not like, and we trust he never will like, to have his best feelings, his most ennobling sentiments, his religious hopes made the fuel of flippant or malignant ridicule. And till he does, he will never relish the polished *diabolism* of Don Juan.

The *Eclectic* kept its word not to review *Don Juan*, but it reviewed

---

[1] *Ecl. R*, XVI (2nd. Ser.), October 1821.

several of Byron's dramas, including *Cain*.[1] The *Eclectic* thought that by publishing *Cain* Byron was intending to test the efficiency of the law, and also to make things awkward for Southey, who had also used sacred names and things for perhaps indictable purposes. Interestingly enough, however, the *Eclectic* regards Southey's *Vision of Judgment* as a 'profane' poem; but *Cain* as not profane. It was not profane to found a drama on Scripture narrative, but it was profane to apply the language of Scripture in a ludicrous connexion, and Southey had done this, though his intentions were undoubtedly far from being irreligious. It is worth adding, however, that later in the review we find the pronouncement that in *Don Juan*, as contrasted with *Cain*, Byron was 'most atrociously and satanically profane'.

The *Eclectic*'s treatment of Byron seems remarkably intelligent and liberal. It goes a long way in sympathy and understanding, without, nevertheless, being false to its basic religious and moral beliefs. In this respect it compares very favourably with *The British Critic*, with its frequently cavalier superciliousness, and its tendency to confound the moral and the aesthetic; and also with *The Christian Observer*, with its fondness for sermonizing, and its propensity to rear at shadows (as shown, for instance, in its strictures upon Byron's supposedly pantheistic lines in *Childe Harold III*).

On Shelley

The only poem of Shelley's reviewed by the *Eclectic* was *Alastor*.[2] The reviewer was Conder, and he thought that even with the Preface ordinary readers would be unable to decipher most of Shelley's allegory. All was 'wild and specious, untangible and incoherent as a dream'. Conder considered that the poem showed the 'utter uselessness of imagination, when wholly undisciplined, and selfishly employed for the mere purposes of intellectual luxury, without reference to those moral ends to which it was designed to be subservient'. Yet a little later in the review Conder appears to believe that the poem was intended to serve a dangerous metaphysical purpose. The two views do not seem consistent. Conder does, however, admit that the work showed 'very considerable talent for descriptive poetry'.

[1] The review of *Cain* is in *Ecl. R*, XVII (2nd. Ser.), May 1822.
[2] *Ecl. R*, VI (2nd. Ser.), October 1816.

The *Eclectic* evidently regarded Shelley thenceforward with some hostility, and did not review him any further. There is, however, a contemptuous reference, in the *Eclectic's* review of Keats's 1820 Poems,[1] to 'the nonsense that Mr. Keats, and Mr. Leigh Hunt, and Mr. Percy Bysshe Shelley, and some other poets about town, have been talking of "the beautiful mythology of Greece"'. Also, in November 1822,[2] the *Eclectic* printed a short note on a very poor poem by one Bernard Barton on Shelley's death. In the course of this note the writer observes that probably none of Shelley's published works had paid for the paper and printing, though everybody had heard of his atheism, and his association with Byron, Hunt, Hazlitt, 'and other apostles of the last and lowest school of infidelity'. His works had remained 'unread and unreadable'. They contained 'beautiful poetry', though he had never, perhaps, excelled that 'wild, fanciful, brilliant, and absurd allegory' *Alastor*:

> But the absence of the sober qualities of common sense and virtuous feeling, the incoherence, savage misanthropy, and daring impiety which disfigure that poem, and which characterize all Mr. Shelley's subsequent productions, deprive his happiest efforts of the power to please, and brand them with worthlessness.

On Keats

The *Eclectic* published two reviews of Keats, one of the 1817 *Poems* and one of the 1820 Poems.

The review of the 1817 *Poems*[3] has the special interest that it was one of the three reviews not written by friends of Keats.[4] The reviewer was Conder. He starts by a theoretical discussion of the relation between poetry and *thought*, in which he opposes what he considers the common practice among 'those who sit down to write verses' of aiming 'at no higher intellectual exertion, than the melodious arrangement of "the cross readings of memory"'. The value of poetry was not in any degree independent of the meaning. Wordsworth, though 'by far the deepest thinker' of modern poets, often expressed thoughts not worth expression.

[1] *Ecl. R*, XIV (2nd. Ser.), September 1820.
[2] *Ecl. R*, XVIII (2nd. Ser.), November 1822.
[3] *Ecl.* R, VIII (2nd Ser.), September 1817. An extract appears at pp. 459–61 below.
[4] The other two independent reviews were those in *The Monthly Magazine* and in Constable's *Edinburgh Magazine*.

Scott, though 'the most exquisite artist' of all, occupied 'the lowest rank in respect to the intellectual quality of his productions'. His best passages were scenic painting. In the lesser poets 'intellect in action' became very faint and rare. In our early poets, by refreshing contrast, the most obvious feature was 'the life and the vividness of thought diffused over their poetry'. This was 'originality', but it did not depend on temporal priority. All that was required to attain originality was that a writer's thoughts 'should bear the stamp of individuality, which is impressed by self-reflective study'. Some of the young poets had been 'making violent efforts to attain originality', and had been seeking with some success new models of imitation in 'the earlier poets' (meaning, no doubt, poets before 1660), but that 'specious sort of originality' lay 'wholly in the turn of expression', and it was 'only the last effort of the cleverness of skill to turn eccentric, when the perfection of correctness' was 'no longer new'. And Conder ends his preliminary discussion with the following challenge:

> We know of no path to legitimate originality, but one, and that is, by restoring poetry to its true dignity as a vehicle for noble thoughts and generous feelings, instead of rendering meaning the mere accident of verse. Let the comparative insignificance of art be duly appreciated, and let the purpose and the meaning be considered as giving the expression all its value; and then, so long as men think and feel for themselves, we shall have poets truly and simply original.

Conder's challenge has much in common with what were to be some of Tolstoy's positions in *What is Art?*

It is not known for certain who wrote the *Eclectic*'s review of the 1820 Poems,[1] but its style suggests Conder. The review is generally astringent, and is even bleak in its view that it was now too late to expect that Keats would 'exhibit any material change as the result of further intellectual growth'. It disappointingly fails to appreciate the greatness of the growth since 1817, and even since *Endymion*, which it dismisses as a 'matchless tissue of sparkling and delicious nonsense'. The review is nevertheless far from worthless. It takes its stand on the same base as the review of the 1817 *Poems*, and finds the new volume wanting according to the criteria there advanced. Moreover, those criteria are worthy of serious respect, and the question on which the soundness of the review must largely be judged is whether the 1820 Poems do or

[1] *Ecl. R*, XIV (2nd. Ser.), September 1820. A long extract appears on pp. 505–9 below.

do not show a mawkish imagination and the lack of a satisfactory sense of values.

THE BRITISH REVIEW

The British Review was a quarterly. It was founded in 1811 by John Weyland, a lawyer, who edited it for one or two issues and then handed it over to William Roberts (1767–1849), also a lawyer, who edited it until 1822. It was an Evangelical periodical. It also supported the Tory Governments. During Roberts's editorship it reviewed many literary works. In 1822 Roberts ceased to be editor, and the review ceased to notice secular works. It was discontinued in 1825.

Many of the reviews of literary works were written by Roberts himself. He was clearly a devout Christian, but he employed literary as well as religious criteria, and some of the reviews evince definite critical ability, and deserve to be better known than they are. According to his son, Roberts wrote all the reviews of Byron, who reacted against some of his strictures by pretending he had bribed *The British Review*, which he called in *Don Juan, I.* ccix (by a name which stuck) 'my Grandmother's Review'.[1] This not only helped to cause Roberts's departure from the editorship, but has contributed to making those who have never read his critiques think of him—quite unjustly, though he was obviously gullible— as nothing but a figure of fun.

Roberts was actually a gifted man. He had won a Scholarship from Eton to Oxford, and had had a very successful academic career there. After travels abroad, during which he met Gibbon, he returned to England, studied, wrote a number of legal textbooks, and practised at the Bar. During his editorship of *The British Review* he was also a Commissioner in Bankruptcy and a Charity Commissioner. He was a thorough Tory and Evangelical, and a friend of Wilberforce and Hannah More. In later life he wrote the *Memoirs of Hannah More*, which had a great sale, and also a number of other literary and historical works.

On Byron

The first review of Byron was of *Childe Harold I and II*.[2] Roberts, in true Evangelical spirit, praised a *nobleman* for engaging in such an edifying activity as writing! He went on, however, to declare

[1] See W. S. Ward, 'Lord Byron and "My Grandmother's Review" ', *MLN*, LXIV (1949), 25–9.   [2] *BR*, III, June 1812.

roundly that *Hours of Idleness* deserved the contempt some reviewers had shown for it, and he regretted that a second edition had appeared. *English Bards*, on the other hand, Roberts admired, and from this poem and passages in *Childe Harold* he inferred that Byron was 'eminently qualified for serious, ethical, and extended satire; according to the Roman model'—that is, aiming at the reformation of society rather than chastisement of an individual. As for *Childe Harold*, its title was puzzling. The poem was 'the narrative of a modern tourist, with little or no incident, but with local descriptions most poetically dressed, and reflections which might occur to a mind like Lord Byron's without the pain or peril of travel'. 'Romaunt' was a misapplied term, and so was 'Childe'. Roberts went into these points at some length. Certainly, Harold was no 'childe' of chivalry. He was 'a mere son of sensuality', who had 'finished a long career of gross and selfish enjoyment with the notable discovery that nothing was good enough for him', and so resolved to travel 'to refresh his jaded appetites, and to see if there be anything new under the sun'. But all was in vain. Roberts found it 'too much to be told by this sort of man that all is vanity'. Though drawn 'with great fidelity and vigour', Harold had no business where he was. He could have been properly used. Presumably Roberts means that Byron could have drawn a moral by criticizing the Childe more severely. As we have seen, this is more or less what the *Eclectic* thought Byron did do. But Roberts makes a rather ingenious point. He argues that, since Byron tells us that Harold had 'no interest' in surrounding objects, the impressions of them must be Byron's own. Harold was a most improper person for Byron to carry about with him in his imagination. He could have used a character like Beattie's Minstrel. It was a pity that he did not imitate Beattie's 'humble religious spirit'. It was a pity also that doubts, if not the denial, of immortality should have 'borrowed the gems of Byron's poetry' to 'captivate the unwary reader'. Those doubts may have been intended to be ascribed to Harold, but that did not appear from the context. Roberts was pleased with the passages where Byron emphasized the unworthiness of the Childe; though, he notes, Byron decides against vice on grounds of expediency alone, without reference to Providence or future retribution. Roberts disapproves of the 'harsh things' said about love, and the sarcasms against women. Harold's 'passion' was 'undistinguishable from what plain men are apt to designate by a coarser appellation'.

It was too much to hear this depraved man hold forth on love and women. Moreover, 'the pains taken in some places to render Harold interesting' tarnished 'the lustre and simplicity of the poem'. Every such attempt had produced glaring inconsistency in the character. As to the texture of the poem, it was deficient in 'many of the characteristics' that gave propriety to the Spenserian stanza. There was certainly 'mellow richness of description', but the subject had put impediments in Byron's way. The stanza had antique associations, and these could not be departed from without detriment. So Byron adopted old words. But then these were inappropriate to the modern theme. Roberts here misses the fun of some of these uses. Roberts also objected to the swearing ('Oh, Christ! it is a goodly sight to see', and so on), and he disliked Byron's compound epithets ('gore-faced', 'lover-loving', and the rest). On the other hand, he admired the rich colouring of the description of the country round Lisbon (*I*. xiv ff.). He also found that the stanzas personifying death and battle (xxxviii ff.) had a 'spirit and vigour' which compelled admiration in spite of judgment, though the personifications were rather overdone. The address to Parnassus (lx ff.) contained many 'spirited and feeling lines', and was on the whole worthy of the theme, but he found the homage 'somewhat too rampant' when it proceeded to 'genuflexion'. Roberts also praised the picture of the lazy luxury of Southern Spain (lxv ff.), though he thought it had too much 'warmth of colouring' to have a 'good moral effect'. The account of the bullfight (lxxii ff.) was finished with great poetical skill, but there were too many epithets crowding impressions on the reader. Stanzas lxxxvii–lxxxviii were too fierce and revengeful, and thus contrary to Christian principles. The lines on religion (*II*. vii ff.), on the other hand, were very beautiful, though they were too despondent, and seemed to deny immortality. Roberts suggests that Byron should read Butler's *Analogy*. He admires 'the lamentations over the prostrate majesty of Greece' (lxxiii ff.), though he thinks that 'the reverence shown for the *religio loci* exceeds ordinary bounds'. Finally, he praises the beauty and originality of the lines on Solitude (xxv ff.), and the 'vivid description' of the palace of Ali Pacha (lvi ff.), which was executed 'under the control of the correctest taste'.

Roberts did not think highly of *The Giaour*, either on aesthetic or on moral grounds.[1] He found *The Bride* better constructed, but

[1] *BR*, V, October 1813.

disapproved of the main character, as, like the Giaour, an un-natural and immoral mixture of deepest criminality and most exalted virtue. Roberts ascribed the type to the influence of Ger-man philosophy.[1] The same sort of objection applied to *The Corsair*, and Roberts professes himself tired of these tales and their heroes.[2]

When *Childe Harold III* appeared Roberts reviewed it at very great length.[3] He opened by suggesting that Byron's literary resources were really 'stinted'. Byron kept repeating himself, and now he wanted his readers 'to undertake another journey with him and his old companion', to hear what they had further to say 'in disparagement of good order and human happiness', and on 'the sacred right of living at large, and doing what one lists'. *The Prisoner of Chillon* volume, since issued, showed 'something of reclaimed nature and the pathos of real sensibility', but it seemed as if Byron 'was at home in his own menagerie', and could find no sufficient excitement outside it. In this canto his descriptive powers did give a new interest to many of the scenes, but the 'colours' of the 'painting' were 'adulterated' by the 'foul admixture' from the personal character of the Childe,

> a moody profligate, who, being destitute of the social principle, supposes himself in love with solitude, and mistakes his quarrel with man whom he has injured, and therefore hates, for a delight in the works of God, whom he has neither loved nor known.

Roberts is indignant at Harold's pretensions:

> We can bear to be the objects of that harmless aversion which is the too frequent result of excess even on the virtuous side, and is wont to be produced by the recoil of too sanguine expectations and ill-requited benevolence; but to be told by an insolent renegade from society, by one who is a professed disciple of Epicurus, and whom the poet represents as 'the outlaw of his own dark mind', that he 'holds little in common with us'; that he cannot 'submit his thoughts to others'; that he has 'a life within himself to breathe without mankind', and, oh exquisite effrontery! that 'disgust has weaned his heart from all worldlings', is too provoking patiently to endure.

After this initial protest Roberts gets down to a very detailed critique of the canto. He protests at the 'hobbling' character of the very first line, which he thinks typical of a modern 'school of

---

[1] *BR*, V, February 1814.   [2] *Ibid.*
[3] *BR*, IX, February 1817 (nearly 10,000 words!).

versifiers, who have ingeniously discovered that cadence, and metre, and musical arrangement, are among the false ornaments and illegitimate arts of poetry'. This is simply Roberts's failure to catch and appreciate the plaintive accents of the line. Nor is Roberts's heavy-handed attack on the opening lines, as dull and insincere, convincing criticism. He is more interesting in his plausible suggestion that Byron may have borrowed the ocean weed simile in st. ii from James Montgomery, whose 'vigorous strains of manly sentiment' Roberts takes the opportunity of recommending to Byron. In iv–vii Byron had given 'a wild and romantic air' to 'a tumultuous assemblage of undisciplined feelings'. Poetry was 'not to be an excuse for every thing'. A man had no right to tell us in verse that after passing "young days of passion" he had "grown aged in *deeds*, not *years*", and "found it a world of woe", unless he would 'also be content to be told by us in return that this is just that conduct which creates the *woe* he laments, and makes a wilderness of the social world'. Roberts's objections become still more violent when he comes to consider xii–xiii, which he calls 'the grand development of Harold's high pretensions, and of what may be called the moral of this laudable production':

> When the hero of Lord Byron's muse, disdaining the enclosures of civilized life and the trammels of domestic order, sighs for a sojourn in caves and forests and gloomy solitudes, the natural wish that rises in our bosoms is only this, that he, and such as he, should go, to return no more, to whatever scene of desolation their angry spirits may conduct them, provided they go far enough from towns and villages, and hamlets and human walks.

And Roberts was very sceptical whether they would find any true satisfaction there, since 'He whose "handy-work" the heavens declare and the firmament showeth' would cause such men 'to see all "through a glass darkly"', and would veil from their view 'the smile that "makes the valleys ring" "and the little hills rejoice"'.

Roberts has also decided views about Byron's comments on Waterloo. He shares Byron's melancholy at the 'harvest of death'; but he has a very different attitude towards Byron's 'political opinions respecting the objects and consequences of the war'. These opinions had 'the same unsoundness of principle and feeling' as characterized the views of too many British people:

> The repose and order of established and legitimate rule are un-

favourable to the dangerous eccentricities of genius and the appetite for vain distinctions. It is in the sentiments and conduct of such men that the subtle connexion between democracy and despotism stands exposed; it is declared and confessed in the cry of Liberty and Bonaparte. We call it subtle because, though we believe it to be manifest to the understanding and consciences of many, or most, of those who profess and promulge these discordant principles, yet in some *young* men, and Lord Byron may be among the number, we suspect these unfriendly dispositions towards the steady tenour of monarchical rule to be rather the result of undisciplined passions, desultory habits of thinking, and a sort of cloudy medium through which men and things are seen by them, than to any systematic hostility towards the government of their country.

In Roberts's view Byron's opinions on the aftermath of Waterloo were self-contradictory. Byron warned against *"praising before we prove"* (in xix), but then at once denounced 'the struggling monarchy of France' as 'a very inferior substitute for the tyranny of that despot of Europe, who was the murderer of her children, the plunderer of her wealth, and "the trampler of her vineyards" '. On the other hand, though all this was 'wretchedly poor and vulgar in point of reasoning and reflection', it was accompanied by 'vigorous and beautiful imagery'. Roberts praises the 'animation, brilliance, and pathos' of the contrast between 'Belgium's capital' the night before, and the grim realities of the battle. But Byron seemed to think that all we had gained by Waterloo was despicable 'military renown'. Roberts begs to differ:

> Not being up to his standard of feeling we shall hold to our prejudices in favour of the importance of national glory; but we must also, with the leave of this sententious poet, consider the blood spilt at Waterloo as the price of our national safety; nor can we deem that victory vain, which has rescued us from the deadly enmity of that man who, in the words of Lord Byron himself, held the world in chains.

And Roberts leaves the topic (though only temporarily) by letting fly at 'tender-hearted mourners for the fate of our enemies' the Parthian shaft that 'the Christian precept commands us to love our enemies, but not out of spite to our friends'.

Roberts next objects to xxxiv with its count of the hours of human enjoyment. Paley and Cowper had formed quite different estimates; but, in any case, Byron was hopelessly unphilosophical in making something 'necessarily relative' the subject of an 'absolute predication'. Nor had he the right to 'hypothecate a certain description of enjoyment as that alone of which man is capable', just because he might know no other. These are all quite reasonable points, even against poetry.

But Roberts returns to the subject of Bonaparte, and attacks the 'shamefully distorted picture' Byron gives of his treatment by his conquerors (xxxix). This attack is a good instance of the un-repeatable freshness which we find in the criticism of these poets by their contemporaries. Roberts willingly affirms that the world had steadily advanced in 'moral dignity', but he believes that 'for compassionate tenderness towards enormous criminality' no age had been 'so distinguished as the present'. People had not given its due to the clemency of the conquerors who had triumphantly entered Paris; whereas 'the undeserving object of that clemency, the author of more misery to man than any of his former oppres-sors' had found in man 'a palliator of his crimes, a commiserator of his too happy lot, and a severe upbraider of his falsely imputed indignities'. Roberts reminds readers of the fate of Toussaint and his sons, and depicts by contrast the courtesies meted out to the strutting Napoleon. But though the moral tendency of this as of most of Byron's poems was 'baneful', it had sadly to be ad-mitted that much of the 'composition' was 'very attractive by its richness of description, vigour of thought, a wild luxuriance of expression, and, in particular, by a certain appearance of genuine seriousness and cordial sincerity, which win an easy entrance into young and unsuspecting bosoms'. For some passages virtue must have been the pattern. How could Byron see so much, and not 'covet the whole', but present us merely with 'dangerous and delusive models of anti-christian virtue and dazzling crimes'?

From all this Roberts gladly turned to pointing out an 'un-tainted' passage (xlvi–xlix), though these stanzas were succeeded by further stanzas about 'Harold's scorn of man, disdain of worldlings, love of babies, his solitary seraphic affection for some one particular female, above what simple matrimony can produce, and other phenomena of this picturesque young gentleman', which to men of Roberts's 'mediocrity and old English habits' seemed nothing but 'vanity and vapour'. The stanzas on Marceau (lvi–lvii) Roberts thought 'very insipid', and he was relieved at the 'short truce from sentiment' in the succeeding passages descriptive of the Rhine scenery, and quotes lx–lxii. As for the 'pathetic' lines on Julia Alpinula (lxvi–lxvii), Roberts questions the rightness of Byron's enthusiasm, for 'the merit of the father . . . was simply that of being a traitor, or of being accused and condemned as such'—a hard-headed but a hard-hitting point by Roberts, who goes on to comment:

> Sickliness sometimes passes for delicacy in the human frame; just so the hectic sensibility of Lord Byron's muse assumes a colour more imposing than the ordinary hue of health itself, while the morbid taint only consumes the core of life, and produces a feverish action of the system, sometimes mistaken for energy, but the real forerunner of exhaustion and death. A 'healthy tenderness' is the inmate of that bosom only where domestic virtue and religious peace direct the feelings to their proper objects, correct their excesses, and consolidate their strength.

Roberts then lays down a moral principle about poetry which deserves serious attention, though it is, I believe, too narrow as it stands:

> No one, through the medium of poetry, has a right to introduce among us a false and nefarious philosophy, calculated to pervert the true ends for which we are born into the world. While poetry confines itself to description, to narration, or to the development of human passion, it has large privileges and a wide domain; but when it undertakes to be the vehicle of preceptive truth, it assumes a responsible office, and its merit must be founded upon other qualities besides the power of charming the ear or delighting the fancy.

Roberts's talk of 'rights' is, in my view, out of court. A poet may do what he wishes. On the other hand, Roberts, and we, have every right to criticize on moral grounds whatever the poet produces. Why Roberts's principle is too narrow—indeed, dangerously too narrow—is that it could easily stifle the growth of poetic works which, though immoral, have other valuable qualities. Whether we believe such works should be stifled depends, of course, on our sense of values. Speaking personally, though—other things being roughly equal—I should generally prefer works which I considered 'moral', I do not think we should banish aesthetic values even when they are conjoined with immoral influences which, if people are moral enough, they ought to be able to resist.

Roberts goes on to suggest that lviii–lxxiii make it clear that Byron's rupture with his fellow-creatures was his own fault. On the other hand, he praises the portrait of Rousseau (lxxvii ff.) as 'vigorous, beautiful, and just', its only fault being 'too much leaning towards apology'. Roberts has an extremely low opinion of Rousseau. After attacking his attitude to women, Roberts makes a summary judgment on his philosophy:

> Perhaps, Voltaire excepted, there has scarcely lived a human being who has sent among mankind so many unextinguishable miseries as this philosophical incendiary.

And Roberts believes that Byron 'much consulted' Rousseau's *Confessions*, and drew 'from that drivelling register of a debauched imagination' the matter of lxxviii and lxxix, with which Roberts 'somewhat doubted whether it would be safe to sully' his page, and which he thought idealized Rousseau's conception of love to an absurd degree.

Once again Roberts is glad to escape to the 'exquisite stanzas' describing 'the night-scene near the sable heights of Jura' (lxxxvi–xc). The references to Voltaire and Gibbon (cv ff.) he finds 'spirited', but cviii ('Yet, peace be with their ashes . . .') he considers 'a strange jumble of doubt and dogma':

> He wishes peace to their ashes because he thinks that, if merited, the penalty is paid. It appears therefore that he has not only settled in his own mind the question whether future punishment will be perpetual or terminable, but has also settled the extent of its duration in the case before him; but this is all subject to the previous question, whether the writers above-mentioned have merited any punishment at all, on which subject he expresses some cautious scepticism. The hour must come, however, he very comfortably concludes, when we shall know how matters are in these respects, or shall all slumber quietly on one pillow in the dust, which we are sure must lie decayed; and when we shall revive, we shall be forgiven or suffer what is just. And thus, having conceived himself to have silenced all disputes, and set conscience at ease, he invites us, with something more of religion than perhaps either Voltaire or Gibbon would have deemed consistent with pure philosophy, to peruse with him the works of our Maker, in that volume which nature opens before our eyes. We shall not stay to comment upon the gentlemanly ease with which these appalling questions are summarily dismissed, but shall content ourselves with surmising that there is an old book of some authority called the Bible, which, if carefully examined, might be found to touch upon some of the topics above adverted to in a manner that might assist the researches of the candid inquirer.

With regard to cxii–cxiv Roberts expresses the wish that Byron, instead of 'reprobating' mankind so severely, 'would try to make us better', and, in particular, diffuse the virtues of 'loyalty, patriotism, charity, and content'.

Stanzas cxv–cxviii puzzled Roberts. He thought them unwisely introduced into the poem. But, as they had been introduced, he feels justified in commenting that it was Byron who had deprived himself of the joys of fatherhood. Roberts also states that he cannot feel much sympathy for Byron in the separation, since the education he would have given the child (cxvi) would have been in most respects 'in direct opposition' to what Roberts himself would have thought advisable.

The execution of the canto, however, Roberts thought quite equal to that of the first two, and greatly superior to that of Byron's smaller poems. He ends with a quite interesting discussion of these more narrowly literary aspects of the poem. (This discussion is reprinted on pp. 223–4 below.)

The British Review[1] dubbed the anonymous *Beppo* 'a very superior performance of the quizzing kind' (incidentally, it mistook the stanzas for Spenserian!). The poem was in one aspect 'a burlesque upon Lord Byron', and in another aspect 'an attack upon the charities and bonds of social life in a spirit of seeming good humour, careless scorn, and gay indecency'. As a burlesque on Byron (so successful that Roberts suspected Byron might be the author!) it was 'harmless and happy', and, indeed, its parody of his profligacy (!) was part of its merit. But in its other aspect it was 'the product of a mind careless, cold, and callous'. Roberts quotes with approval a passage from Madame de Staël's *De l'Allemagne* in which she describes the force of ridicule in undermining virtue. Roberts goes on to point out that Madame de Staël asserts that the only way to resist this corrupting influence consists in 'very decided national habits and character'—an opinion with which Roberts heartily agrees. He was concerned at the deterioration in British national character during the last fifty years, through contamination by Continental ideas and habits. He wanted to regain the 'proud security' of the British national character of half a century before. The poetry of Moore and Byron had been devoted to 'scandalous objects', but it had been censured accordingly by *The British Review*, so that Roberts did not feel it necessary to repeat his attacks. He simply quotes xlvii–lii and

[1] *BR*, XI, May 1818.

lxxxii–lxxxiv, remarking that they can be understood without the story,

> which is, in truth, nothing but a trumpery narrative of a lady and her gallant, and a base acquiescing husband, who, nevertheless, is presented to us as a person of sense and worth.

Roberts, though utterly opposed to Byron's attitude to the affair, has at least seen sharply one of the main points of the poem.

In conclusion Roberts regrets that his critique could not be more favourable, and expresses the hope that the poet was Byron, for he did not 'wish for a duplicate of that eccentric nobleman':

> Such is the value of correct opinion, and a right moral feeling, among Britons at this moment, that we cannot afford to be amused at the expense of decency, and delicacy, and principle.

When *Childe Harold IV* came out Roberts wrote an even longer review than that of Canto III.[1] Many of the points made are the same, but it is interesting to see his reactions to the apparently finished work, which he suspected might not really be finished, since the texture of Byron's plan was so loose that he could always add stanzas or even cantos. Roberts spends a good deal of time on the epistle dedicatory to Byron's friend Hobhouse, especially on Byron's claim to have persistently drawn a line in the earlier cantos between Harold and himself. Roberts considers that claim absurd, since Byron could easily have interwoven a running commentary on Harold's 'sentiments', but had not done so. He could also have displayed a different sort of mind in this last canto, where, according to him, he was speaking almost entirely in his own person; but the mind was the same as the Childe's. Roberts also takes exception to Byron's depreciation of England as contrasted with Italy, and this leads him to a fuller discussion of the degeneration of British character through Continental influence than that in the review of *Beppo*. This discussion is of considerable interest in itself, and of some bearing upon Byron's moral and political attitudes, but space allows only this mere reference to it.[2] Roberts then turns to the canto and begins with a general critique founded on far-reaching principles. His basic point is a religious one, that libertines cannot enjoy solitude and Nature. That point may be in general valid, but it was narrow of him not to admit exceptions, one of which might have been

---

[1] *BR*, XI, August 1818.   [2] *Ibid.*, 6–9.

Byron! Roberts was, indeed, surely a trifle harsh when he wrote this sentence:

> And as far as Lord Byron has identified his own principles and tastes with those of his imaginary companion, so far has he declared his own unfitness to promote or participate in human happiness.

As to Byron's stanzas on his exile (viii–x), Roberts simply asks why Byron could not live in peace at home. If his misfortunes were his own fault, as he seemed to intimate, then he had no right to display them in poetry:

> It is really the first time we have found a writer making a picturesque use of his own faults, covering them with the mantle of the muse, or transforming them into decorations by the magical touch of his genius.

If Byron was suffering anguish through his own fault he ought to make 'a manly effort to follow after that Guide which has conducted so many into the ways of pleasantness and the paths of peace'. But the canto revealed 'no approach to that panacea'. Byron, as so often, treated the 'most solemn and adorable' names with 'profane levity', coupling Jove and Jesus (cxlvi), alluding to the Bethlehem shepherds in the lament for the death of Princess Charlotte (clxx), and introducing religious references gratuitously in xcii and clv.

Roberts goes on to charge Byron with using 'licentious imagery' when describing 'the attractions of the other sex'; though he admits that Canto IV contains less of this than Byron's other poems. There was 'a touch of Orientalism, something Mohammedan, in the descriptions of female excellence' throughout all Byron's poems; and the 'additional colouring of Italian gallantry' in Canto IV did not improve matters. Byron's poems took no account of the 'moral and intellectual capacity and character' of women. The result was that, since his 'warm and impassioned strains' imported no respect for women, so no woman that merited respect could 'peruse them with pleasure', unless she was 'without discernment'.

Roberts then proudly but inaccurately claims that *The British Review* alone had examined Byron's works 'largely, usefully, and impartially', 'in respect to their influence on the heart'. Contemporary poetry, indeed contemporary literature, had become 'the ally of immorality, infidelity, and political disaffection'. 'Iniquity' had its hand on the press. Education, unless it could 'escape the foul inoculation of epidemic vice', would only 'fill the moral world with disease'. Among the 'higher orders' Byron's poetry was universally read, and it was indeed, sad to say, the least objectionable of the most popular poetry in immoral tendency. It was to be hoped that the 'superficial splendour' of the description would 'direct attention from the false sentiments and dangerous character of its dark interior'. Roberts wishes to make clear, in any case, that he does not think Byron wished to make people 'unhappy or unprincipled'. He believed that Byron's was a case of 'undisciplined feeling and disturbed fancy'.

Roberts then quotes a few of the passages in the canto which seemed to him 'to possess the most poetical merit'. He could not 'impartially' exclude xxiii–xxiv, despite their characteristic gloom, but he goes on with relief to cite xxvii–xxix and the description of the Clitumnus and the cataract of Velino (lxvii–lxxi), which he thinks hard to match 'in the whole range of poetry'. Finally, he quotes the opening stanzas on Rome (lxxviii–lxxx), which he writes of as 'full of moral magnificence'.

In conclusion, Roberts offers some impressions of *Childe Harold* as a whole. (These are reprinted on pp. 233–6 below.) Some of the criticisms are simply narrow—for instance, that of the 'lack of plan'—but others—for example, the disgust at egotism, and the strictures on the type of melancholy expressed—raise important issues. The more technical criticisms are also still of interest.

It must already be clear enough that Roberts's reaction to *Don Juan* would be violent. It was. The opening words of his notice (for it is, deliberately, not a review) of Cantos I and II[1] are these:

Of a poem so flagitious that no bookseller has been willing to take upon himself the publication,[2] though most of them disgrace themselves by selling it, what can the critic say? His praise or censure ought to found itself on examples produced from the work itself. For praise, as far as regards the poetry, many passages might be exhibited; for condemnation, as far as regards the morality, all: but none for either purpose can be produced, without insult to the ear of decency, and vexation to the heart that feels for domestic or national happiness.

[1] *BR*, XIV, August 1819.
[2] During this period booksellers were still, of course, often also publishers. Murray had not put his name to the publication of the poem, whose title-page bore no publisher's name, though Murray was the anonymous publisher, and he and a number of other booksellers handled the sales of the book.

Roberts thus refuses to review the cantos, and the rest of the notice consists in claiming the liberty to suppose that Byron was not the author. Roberts rests the claim on two grounds: (i) that the author's name was not on the title-page, and that *The Vampire* (by Byron's doctor, Polidori) had been fathered on Byron, and (ii), and more important, that in Canto I. ccix–ccx the author had alleged that, "for fear some prudish readers should grow skittish", he had sent a bribe to the editor of "the British", who had thanked him by return of post. 'No peer of the British realm could surely be capable of so calumnious a falsehood, refuted', Roberts trusted, 'by the very character and spirit of the journal so defamed'. Roberts goes on to call on Byron for a disclaimer. It is hard to tell for certain whether Roberts was really so humourless as he appears to be in this notice; but he may have been.

When *Don Juan III–V* appeared Roberts did, after all, review them,[1] and this review is the last of those in this periodical that concern us. Roberts starts with a headlong attack against the deliberate ridicule of 'virtue, in her most veracious form'. The work offered 'no proper subject for criticism'—that is, for anything other than *moral* criticism. Roberts does, nevertheless, include some more narrowly 'literary' strictures in his attack against what he calls the 'slip-shod method of versifying'; but the main weight of the onslaught is moral. (The attack is reprinted on pp. 281–5 below.)

Roberts could not recollect anything in English literature 'more utterly reckless of the elements of social union' than the introductory pages of Canto III. The mischief was everywhere, so that expurgation was impossible. Roberts had heard a rumour that the poem was to have a moral ending; but that would be impossible, since it would only seem ironical. The most moral way of ending the poem would be to break it off; though possibly the hero could be hanged for murder, and an expiatory canto added. Roberts was fully aware that Byron would no nothing of the sort; but it would be best for his 'muse' if he did. Wanton details 'must grow dull by repetition'. Moreover, 'the gay critics of the Bond St. or St. James's reading room' might 'pronounce it flat in spite of its profaneness and obscenity'. Let the poet put an end to this poem, and dedicate his talents to the cause of virtue. They would be found 'adequate to the lofty theme'. Some touches in *Don Juan* itself showed that he could *conceive* (and so why not relish?) 'the

[1] *BR*, XVIII, December 1821.

pure, the wholesome, the holy, and the happy'. Roberts quotes *III*. cv–cix by way of example. It was a matter for 'national regret' that a man who could write like this 'should find it the most pleasurable exercise of his faculties to compose a poem which no wise or virtuous parent' could 'tolerate for ten minutes under his roof'. The 'gross indecency' of the poem was not, however, its 'great mischief'. This lay in the 'constant jesting' at 'God's ordinances, and man's relations and duties'. Roberts did not wish to accuse Byron of "a strange design against the creed and morals of the land",[1] but he did wish to accuse him of 'publishing poems' which had 'an obvious tendency to loosen the creed, and corrupt the morals of the land'. Even if the poet should atone by writing in the cause of virtue, much of the mischief already done might be past recalling.

Roberts then writes on 'the most extraordinary part of the character' of the poem, its delight 'in extracting ridicule out of its own pathos'. (The passage is reprinted below on pp. 285–6). Roberts's description of the phenomenon is good. His value-judgments are a matter for discussion. Roberts goes on to suggest that the poet is actually sometimes 'ludicrous against his will', as when he gives his heroine a 'prophet eye' (*IV*. xxii), and writes of 'weaning her eyes back to old thoughts' (lxiv). Again, the whole scene between Lambro and the lovers (xxxv ff.) was 'a remarkable instance of strenuous and blustering insignificance, the result of abortive efforts to be original and extraordinary'. The poet had also bungled the description of the madness of Haidée (lxiii ff.). Canto V was as weak as it was wicked. It was obscene, but its mannerism and monotony encouraged Roberts to hope that the 'period of exhaustion' was approaching. It was 'full of vulgarities of idiom and allusion', and seemed 'to rest its whole interest upon its inflammatory strength, and poisonous efficacy'. Moreover, its humour was 'extremely poor, and of most flimsy texture'.

The poet laid claim to being very devout, and made a solemn confession of faith (*III*. civ). Roberts asks what kind of worship the poet means, and what was 'the Great Whole' whom he prayed to and who had 'produced' and would 'receive' his soul. The poet unjustifiably assumed that it *would* be 'received'. There might be necessary terms, which might be contained 'in a book, which Bacon, and Sir Isaac Newton, and Milton, and Locke, and Pascal,

[1] Alluding to *IV*. v.

and Sir W. Jones'[1] had thought to be 'divinely inspired', and into which 'the devout author of *Don Juan*' had 'never seriously searched'. 'The Great Whole', moreover, might be a mere 'heathen conception, and downright idolatry'; it might be 'hypocrisy'; it might be 'cant'; and Roberts would refuse 'the pious invitation' to kneel down with 'the author of *Don Juan*' and pray to it, until he had 'more certain information as to the nature and objects of this praying'. Let the poet make a sincere confession of abusing his best gifts, and repent, and sacrifice 'upon any altar he pleases' all he could collect of *Don Juan*, and Roberts would willingly 'down with him and pray'. The poet's present form of devotion had confessedly not brought him 'a cheerful mind'. The doubt of immortality hung over the most devout of this sect of Nature-worshippers. In any case, 'his scenic devotion' would do little for Byron at the close of life.

Roberts then makes brief reference to the matter of the alleged bribe, and goes on to praise the genius of the poet, shown both in thought and in expression; but also to urge him to use it fittingly. The writer of such a poem could not fully realize even the beauties of the natural world. And Roberts ends with an expression of despair:

> How should the least of his [God's] works be appreciated by one who opposes him in the greatest? by one who does his endeavour to arrest the moral advancement of the species; and that too at a time when an universal effort of education is adding infinitely to the power of every moral engine; and laying bare and exposed to every impression and every influence, the active energies and irritable fibre of man's immortal part. Charity to themselves and others calls upon such propagators of mischief, for the love of God and of their neighbours, to desist, before the 'iron enters into the soul', and destroys the last hope of sinking humanity; but it calls in vain; the soul's enemy is too loud in their favour for its voice to be heard, and to the encouragement of this cruel instigator is added the clamour of those who 'are inclosed in their own fat', and find their best entertainment in laughing at their own ruin.

On Shelley

The British Review only reviewed one work of Shelley's, *The Cenci*,[2] which it called 'the best, because it is by far the most

[1] Sir William Jones (1746–94), most famous as an Oriental scholar and multilinguist, was also an eminent jurist who served as a judge of the high court at Calcutta. He was a polymath of great ability, and a prodigy of learning.

[2] *BR*, XVII, June 1821.

intelligible, of Mr. Shelley's works'. The reviewer had, however, a very low opinion of the work, both morally and aesthetically. First of all, it was not even dramatic. It was a mere series of dialogues in verse. Again, the subject-matter was 'too disgusting to be moulded into any form capable even of awakening our interest'. Moreover, Shelley had made the story 'infinitely more horrible and more disgusting than he found it'. The depravity of Cenci himself was not even human. No such being ever existed or could exist. Such delineations as these taught nothing, and even if they did, 'knowledge must not be bought at too high a price'. Moreover,

> it is in vain to plead, that the delineations are meant to excite our hatred; they ought not to be presented to the mind at all; still less, pressed upon it long and perseveringly.

The reviewer is making a Platonic point here, and it is far from being an absurd one. He goes on to make more specifically 'literary' objections. The structure of the play was faulty. It took too long to get going; and the fifth Act was 'a mere excrescence'. Again, the language was loose and disjointed, and, when 'ambitious of simplicity', it became 'bald, inelegant, and prosaic'. At other times the language was unintelligible; and there was also a great deal of confused imagery. The reviewer analyses in detail Beatrice's much-admired speech: "How comes this hair undone?",[1] and comes to the conclusion that it is 'the bombast of a declamation, straining to be energetic, and falling into extravagant and unnatural rant'.[2] But, although the reviewer takes account of such 'literary' features, he takes his main stand on moral ground, as he writes in conclusion:

> The moral errors of this book prevent us from quarreling with its literary sins.

On Keats

The British Review offered no review of Keats. It may, like *The Christian Observer*, have considered him not to be among those who counted.

---

[1] *The Cenci*, III. i. 7. ff.

[2] It is interesting to compare this early adverse analysis of a passage in *The Cenci* with the revealing analyses of other passages in *The Cenci* by Dr. F. R. Leavis in *Revaluation* (London, 1936), 223 ff.

The London Magazine (1820–9), at first known as 'Baldwin's *London Magazine*' after its publisher,[1] set out to appreciate the work of the best contemporary writers. John Scott (1783–1821) was appointed editor, and the magazine's heyday was the short period before his death in 1821. This is, indeed, the only part of its existence with which we are here substantially concerned. Scott was an extremely able man, who had turned from a career in the War Office to journalism because of his passionate interest in politics and literature. He had had considerable editorial experience before appointment to *The London Magazine*, including a period as owner and editor of *The Champion*, a liberal weekly with some literary distinction. In 1814–19 he had spent much time on the Continent, and written some admirable accounts of Paris in 1814 and 1815. He was an excellent editor of *The London Magazine*.

The London Magazine had a splendid set of contributors, both under Scott and also for some years afterwards, including Lamb, Hazlitt, De Quincey, Horace Smith, Thomas Noon Talfourd, and P. G. Patmore, the father of Coventry Patmore.

The London Magazine was just as distinguished in its critiques of Byron, Shelley, and Keats as in its appreciation of Wordsworth.

On Byron

John Scott wrote three articles on Byron in 1820, the first year of the magazine's short life (1820–9). The first was on Byron's French critics, the second a brief note on *Manfred*, and the third a general discussion of the relations between the magazine and Byron. The really important article for our purpose, however, is John Scott's article on Byron in the series 'Living Authors',[2] in which Scott had written the excellent appreciation of Wordsworth published in March 1820.[3] This article on Byron came out in January 1821, the month before Scott was killed in a duel with John Christie, a London friend of Lockhart's, as a result of his

---

[1] To distinguish it from Gold's *London Magazine and Monthly Critical and Dramatic Review*, started in January 1820, which was, however, amalgamated with Baldwin's *London Magazine* the following year.

[2] *LM*, II, January 1821. A long extract is printed below on pp. 262–75.

[3] See *Romantic Perspectives*, pp. 74–6.

exposures of the malpractices of the editors of *Blackwood's Magazine*.[1]

Scott's article starts with the firm assertion that Byron's poems did not entitle him to be called the best of contemporary poets, but that his character and life-history had clearly made him the most interesting and remarkable person then writing poetry. Moreover, he would so appear to posterity. But Byron had purchased this very dearly. Notoriety had never been so intimately united with true *fame*. Byron had almost always studiously calculated to make the personal interest in his work more prominent than the poetical. He had barefacedly coupled the histories of his heroes and villains with the incidents of his own life, and mingled their feelings with open disclosures of his own. His creations were 'addressed to the poetical sympathies of his readers, while their main interest' was 'derived from awakening a recollection of some fact' of his life, or a consideration of an analogy to his own character. Scott submits the course of Byron's poetical creation to a very penetrating scrutiny, which needs to be followed in detail in the full article for its complete meaning to be realized.[2] It is a far more subtle indictment than most of those directed against Byron's work.

Scott held that Byron's poetical procedure was doubly unsound, depraving the taste as well as tainting the purity of moral feeling. Moreover, Scott had more than a suspicion that Byron's 'grief' and 'despair' were something of a pose—or, as he puts it, '*feelings of ceremony*'. As to his 'rhymed remorse', Scott conjectures that Byron had probably done 'nothing sufficiently worse than other people' to justify it or even to render it excusable. And presently Scott comes fully into the open:

> To say the truth, then, we long to see Lord Byron once more amongst us, stripped of all the adventitious, and, we must call them, surreptitious advantages, as an author, which he has derived from being considered as too bad for repentance, and too desperate to be pitied.

Though discerning critics could see through Byron's appeals to 'sickly sentimentality', the inexperienced could not. His work was open to condemnation in respect of 'moral tendency, personal

[1] In '*Blackwood's Magazine*', *LM*, I, November 1820; and 'The Mohock Magazine', *LM*, I, December 1820.

[2] The extract printed on pp. 262–75 below should, however, give a fair idea of the nature of Scott's attack.

fairness, and public decency', but 'the worst faults of his style' were traceable to 'looseness of feeling'. Scott does, however, concede that the moral effect of Byron's exposure of 'the ridiculous side of social institutions and domestic observances' might not be so great as some had contended. Considerable freedom had always been allowed to such satire. Scott held the interesting view that Byron's serious poetry was 'of a much more deleterious tendency', through exciting admiration for 'false and hateful qualities'. All the same, Byron had carried his 'levities' too far, and again it looked as if he had adopted this new style just to gain cheap popularity. Fortunately, Byron had also written many noble passages, but his pieces were most certainly 'of a mingled yarn'. Scott then picks out, as 'the features most degrading to the character of the author in his last compositions', 'those . . . calculated to throw doubt altogether on the sincerity of his emotions, and the healthiness of his heart'—in particular the sudden transitions from sublimity or beauty to Satanic laughter. If Byron would reject such a transition in real life he ought also to shun it in his poetry.[1] Nevertheless, despite all this, and despite the unevenness of Byron's work, Scott maintains that he is 'one of the greatest of poets'. Scott praises *Childe Harold* for its lively representation of the essential and peculiar in climes and situations 'which have long fed our dreams of beauty, and of wonders', and for adding 'tenfold efficacy' to them. Scott even finds the inspiringly rendered 'scenery' the 'principal charm' of Byron's poetry:

> What vivacity of observation is apparent in his descriptions, what zeal in his celebrations,—how quick, varied, and bright, the running flame of his allusions!

This is well put, and Scott also coins a useful phrase in this connexion when he calls Byron the '*minstrel of fame*'. Scott does not, however, circumscribe Byron's talent within that boundary. He claims that no living poet had a 'spirit . . . so active' or a 'range of sensibility so wide'. All the same, Scott considers that perhaps 'eloquence, rather than poetry, forms . . . the great charm' of Byron's verses—that his finest passages are generally declamatory. He was best at scenery and 'the exquisite effects of nature',

[1] Scott was not to know that Byron did not 'reject' such 'transitions' in life. He once apologized abjectly to his wife for all his injuries to her, and when she wept forgiveness over him, he started up from her feet, folded his arms, and burst into loud laughter. (Marchand, *Byron*, II. 551.)

and next best at the energetic and earnest expression of 'the bitterness of sceptical emotion'. As a moral philosopher, 'and even as a misanthrope', he was 'childishly inconsistent', so much so as to make us suspect his sincerity.

Scott's survey is clearly the work of a liberal-minded, shrewd, intelligent man, who neither adopts the inflexible standpoint of those critics who would give no licence to satire, nor forgoes moral standards and allows himself to float at the mercy of Byron's manipulation of moods. He is aware of the nihilistic possibilities latent in Byron's dynamic scepticism. He goes more towards Byron than would, say, Roberts, and much more so than the reviewers in *The British Critic*; but he shows greater reserve than Leigh Hunt. These differences of attitude raise acutely the question how far one should respond positively and how far negatively to such features of Byron's work as the rapid alternation of mood in the shipwreck scene in Canto II of *Don Juan*.[1]

Finally, it is perhaps worth briefly mentioning Hazlitt's review of *Marino Faliero*,[2] in which he reaffirmed his opinion that Byron's genius was not dramatic, and dismissed this particular play as 'without a plot, without characters, without fluctuating interest, and without the spirit of dialogue'.

On Shelley

The only substantial review of Shelley in *The London Magazine* is John Scott's review of *The Cenci*.[3] This review also contains some general comments on Shelley's poetry. Scott allows that there is little affectation in Shelley's style, and that his matter 'evinces much real power of intellect, great vivacity of fancy, and a quick, deep, serious feeling, responding readily and harmoniously to every call made on the sensibility by the imagery and incidents of this variegated world'. In *The Cenci* Scott greatly admired the 'vigorous, clear, manly' language; and also 'the most delicate and finished ornaments of sentiment and description, the most touching tenderness, graceful sorrow, and solemn appalling misery'; but

---

[1] It is to Byron's credit that he had a very high opinion of Scott's ability and character. He had known him from early years, when they were both at Marischal College, Aberdeen. After Scott's death he wrote: 'Scott died like a brave man, and he lived an able one. A man of considerable talents and of great acquirements, he had made his way as a literary character with high success and in a few years.'

[2] *LM*, III, May 1821. [3] *LM*, I, May 1820.

he objected that all this was closely connected with the signs of 'a depraved, nay mawkish, or rather emasculated moral taste, craving after trash, filth, and poison, and sickening at wholesome nutriment'. Scott thought that this resulted from vanity and weakness of character. These objections are not far removed from the moral objections Roberts made, but Scott can be seen to be according the play also both literary value and value which he seems to take as literary, but which could well be regarded as moral. Nevertheless, he goes on to emphasize the loathsomeness of the play, while conceding the genius of its author. A man who would do what Count Cenci did would be *mad*, and could not 'properly furnish the principal interest of a dramatic composition, claiming the sympathy of mankind as a representation of human nature'. Shelley in his Preface had informed his readers that 'the person who would treat such a subject must increase the ideal, and diminish the actual horror' of the events, but that was impossible. Moreover, these horrors were utterly different from the horrors of ancient tragedy, which were brought about by destiny, not human will. Shelley thought his play had a moral purpose. He was completely mistaken. 'The radical foulness of moral conception' characterizing the play was 'disgusting and dangerous', though it was 'almost redeemed', 'so far as literary merit [was] concerned, by uncommon force of poetical sentiment, and very considerable purity of poetical style'. The tragedy was 'the production of a man of great genius, and of a most unhappy moral constitution'.

It is interesting to compare Scott's strictures and praise with a passage from a notice of *The Cenci* by Leigh Hunt in *The Examiner*[1]:

> Of Mr. Shelley's Tragedy, called *The Cenci*, which to say the least of it, is undoubtedly the greatest dramatic production of the day, we shall speak at large in a week or two. It is founded on a most terrific family story, which actually took place in Italy: but sentiments of the most amiable, and refreshing, and exalting nature nevertheless breathe in a certain undertone of suggestion through the whole of it, as they always do in the works of this author.

Hunt is praising the play morally in terms not altogether unlike some of those which Scott had classed as literary. But he takes no account, here or elsewhere, of the psychological causes which may have brought Shelley to write his play on such a subject, and

[1] *Exar*, 10 March 1820.

he shows none of Scott's moral horror at the theme, or of Roberts's sense of outrage at Shelley's treatment of it.

On Keats

The London Magazine was consistently kind to Keats. *Endymion* was reviewed by P. G. Patmore,[1] who wrote enthusiastically:

> As a *promise*, we know of nothing like it, except some things of Chatterton.

He gave an ecstatic description of the work, but readily admitted that it was faulty. He contended, however, that the faults went with the beauties, and that the poem would not have had the beauties without them. Patmore also conceded that though the parts were often vivid, the whole was indistinct and confused. He laid stress, however, on the 'freedom, sweetness, and variety' of the versification, maintaining that such features were 'among the most authentic evidences of poetical power'. He also emphasized the richness of the materials, the many exquisite pictures and prospects in which the imagination of the reader could wander about, and the fittingness of the environment for the 'airy and fanciful beings who dwell in it'. He compared some of the scenes to Salvator Rosa, Claude, Poussin, and Titian. In conclusion, he taunted the *Quarterly* for disgracefully pronouncing that it had been unable to discover in the poem anything worthy to redeem it from mere contempt. The *Quarterly* article would have great influence on readers, and, still worse, it would have a baneful effect on the poet himself, by stifling his promise. In view of the *Quarterly*'s critique, Patmore declines to point out the faults of *Endymion*. He also finds it hard to *describe* the beauties 'in any other than general terms', despite the fact that he knows 'of no poetical work which differs from all others more than *Endymion* does'. He suggests that

> its distinguishing feature is perhaps nothing more than the exuberant spirit of youth,—that transport of imagination, fancy, and sensibility—which gushes forth from every part, in a glittering shower of words, and a confused and shadowy pomp of thoughts and images, creating and hurrying each other along like waves of the sea.

[1] *LM*, I, April 1820. An extract appears on pp. 482–7 below. P. G. Patmore was the father of Coventry Patmore. He also wrote for a number of other periodicals, including *The New Monthly Magazine*.

Keats could not yet 'direct the storm', but his promise was rich. Patmore cautions, however, that the promise might not be fulfilled. The times were 'essentially unpoetical', and a spirit had to be 'powerful and resolute' to escape from their influence. This had, states Patmore, been one inducement to write the review, and he urges Keats not to be 'cast down or turned from the course which nature has marked out for him':

> He is and must be a poet—and he may be a great one.

And Patmore ends on the hope and thought that Keats would never disown or attempt to revise *Endymion*, the 'wild and wayward firstling', even should he write maturer poems. Patmore may conceivably have known something of the forthcoming 1820 volume, which was published three months later.

Patmore's review is flowery, but it was encouraging, and, in its way, it hits off some of the features of *Endymion* which were to help to make the poem such a popular one during the decade or two after Keats's death.

Perhaps more important, however, because more critically specific, was John Scott's review of the 1820 Poems.[1] Scott confesses at the outset that he 'opened this volume with considerable anxiety', partly because of the 'unqualified praises' which Keats had received, but more so because of the abuse by which he had been assailed. Scott has some strong things to say about the *Quarterly* and *Blackwood's*, and also, more generally, about the control of literary reviews by political parties. On the other hand, he asserts that Keats, though not a political writer, had expressed in his poetry some impatience with the established order, for instance, in the stanzas in *Isabella* 'tirading against the brothers as "money-bags", "Baalites of pelf", "ledger-men",—and asking "Why, in the name of glory, were they proud?" '—none of which appeared in Boccaccio's story, with his 'larger philosophy' and 'more genial spirit'. These tirades were, in Scott's view,

> no better than extravagant school-boy vituperation of trade and traders; just as if lovers did not trade,—and that, often in stolen goods—or had in general any higher object than a barter of enjoyment!

"Ledger-men" were not to be despised. Lamb's essay on the South-Sea House in *The London Magazine*'s last number was an

[1] *LM*, II, September 1820. An extract is printed below on pp. 502–5.

'elegant reproof' of 'such short-sighted views of character; such idle hostilities against the realities of life'. Scott expresses the wish that Keats would add to his 'picturesque imagination' 'a more pliable, and, at the same time, a more magnanimous sensibility'. Let him anathematize, but let it be, as in Wordsworth's sonnet "The world is too much with us; . . .", 'crawling minds', not 'classes of men'. By his socio-political thoughts Keats had, in any case, incautiously exposed himself to attack from Tory quarters. Nevertheless, his 'delusion' was, at least, 'the offspring of a romantic temperament', whereas 'his maulers' were 'but things of brute matter'.

The injustice done to Keats's work had made Scott hope that the present volume would 'seize fast hold of general sympathy, and thus turn an overwhelming power against the paltry traducers of a talent, more eminently promising in many respects, than any that the present age has been called upon to encourage'. Scott had not found the volume 'quite all that we wished in that respect', but he thought it capable of a more tangible and intelligible appeal to 'common understandings' than Keats's earlier work. Scott cites as evidence the last two stanzas of the *Ode to a Nightingale*, commenting that the passage is 'distinct, noble, pathetic, and true'. He also quotes the description of Madeline preparing for sleep, and falling asleep. He does not know whether to admire most 'the magical delicacy of the hazardous picture', or 'its consummate, irresistible attraction', and observes that 'it has an exquisite moral influence, corresponding with the picturesque effect'. This is well-directed and well-expressed appreciation. Scott is also, however, able to admire the hugeness of *Hyperion*, and his remarks on it show a critical sense which seems to be beyond the range shown in Jeffrey's review of the volume. Scott's enthusiasm about *Hyperion* prompted him to turn on Croker and accuse him of 'cold-blooded conscious dishonesty' in his critique of *Endymion*, since, 'making every allowance for the callousness of a worldly spirit, it is impossible to conceive a total insensibility to the vast beauties scattered profusely over that disordered, ill-digested work'. Yet Scott admits that Keats 'provokes opposition', and that 'not unfrequently he even suggests angry censure':

We cannot help applying the word *insolent*, in a literary sense, to some instances of his neglectfulness, to the random swagger of occasional expressions, to the bravado style of many of his sentiments.

This is all quite just, and it is often conspicuously absent from critiques of Keats. Moreover, it does not blind Scott to the fine qualities of Keats's work. Scott offers, however, some concrete strictures. He takes the chief faults of Keats's work to be: (i) his frequent obscurity and confusion of language; (ii) a too great fondness for 'running out glimmerings of thoughts, and indicating distant shadowy fancies' and 'dwelling on features which are not naturally the most important or prominent'; and (iii) a quaint strangeness of phrase. But Scott ends with a graceful turn:

> But we are by this time tired of criticism; as we hope our readers
> are:—let us then all turn together to the book itself. We have said
> here what we have deemed it our duty to say: we shall there find
> what it will be our delight to enjoy.

Scott's critique must be considered as, on the whole, the most balanced and perceptive of all the contemporary reviews of Keats's last volume.

Scott did not let his defence of Keats rest there. In his article two months later entitled '*Blackwood's Magazine*',[1] he repudiated the assertion by the editors that their attacks on the Cockney School had been restrained within the limits of fair criticism, and he promised to give the matter further attention. This he did in his article 'The Mohock Magazine', published in December.[2] There he objected against Hogg's being drawn in by 'forged papers' as enthusiastically approving of the *Horae Scandicae* which *Blackwood's* had published in the same issue in which the editors had purported to apologize for their treatment of Keats. The purported 'apology', and the references to Keats, will both be found in the extract from Scott's article printed on pp. 502–5 below. It is worth remembering that it was this article that gave rise to the duel in which Scott was killed. Ironically enough, however, there is good evidence that Keats did not like John Scott.[3]

THE EXAMINER, THE INDICATOR, AND
THE LITERARY EXAMINER

The Examiner (1808–81), *The Indicator* (1819–21), and *The Literary Examiner* (1823) are especially notable for their strong support of the work of Byron, Shelley, and Keats. *The Examiner* reviewed all three poets; *The Indicator* reviewed Shelley and Keats; and *The*

[1] *LM*, II, November 1820, 520. [2] *LM*, II, December 1820.
[3] Letter from Charles Brown to Keats, 21 December 1820 (*KL*, II. 364).

Literary Examiner, Byron. Leigh Hunt, the younger partner in *The Examiner*, the editor of the first two periodicals, and at least a contributor to the third, was a friend of all three poets. He was also, within his limits, a fine critic, and certainly understood a good deal of the aims and intentions of each of the writers. *The Examiner* was a very successful weekly mainly devoted to politics, in which it was steadily anti-Tory. *The Indicator* was also a weekly, but entirely concerned with literature. *The Literary Examiner*, another weekly, and a kind of successor to *The Indicator*, was a literary supplement to *The Examiner*.

On Byron

The Examiner offered no review of *Childe Harold*, or of *Beppo*, but it reviewed some of the cantos of *Don Juan*, and defended the poem on several occasions. It also reviewed the first number of *The Liberal*, in which *The Vision of Judgment* appeared, and elsewhere it defended that poem against various attacks. It gave some attention to the plays, and also to the late poems of Byron, *The Age of Bronze* and *The Island*, with none of which we are here concerned. Interestingly enough, it had little to say on the Tales. Leigh Hunt wrote in July 1821[1] that for the most part he did not admire Byron's narratives:

> They are like their heroes, too melodramatic, hasty, and vague. But the passion is sometimes excellent.

Of Byron's dramas he wrote in the same article:

> Whatever good passages such a writer will always put forth, we hold that he has no more qualification than we have, his tendency being to spin everything out of his own perceptions, and colour it with his own eyes.

Again in the same article, when only the first two cantos of *Don Juan* had appeared, Hunt passed the following opinion:

> His *Don Juan* is perhaps his best work, and the one by which he will stand or fall with readers who see beyond times and toilets. It far surpasses, in our opinion, all the Italian models on which it is founded, not excepting the far-famed *Secchia Rapita*.[2] Nor can we see in it the injury to morals and goodness which makes so many

[1] 'In Sketches of Living Poets, No. 2, Lord Byron' in *Exar*, 29 July 1821.
[2] A comedy by Alessandro Tassoni, published in 1624. (*Secchia Rapita* = 'Stolen Pail'.)

people shake their heads, both solid and shallow. Poems of this kind may not be the best things to put abruptly into the hands of young ladies; but people are apt to beg many more questions than they settle about morality; and numbers of such Don Juans as Lord Byron's (not the unfeeling vagabonds in the Italian opera) would be very good and proper, if we would let them. A poet's morals have a natural tendency to recur to first principles, which is a proceeding that others are perpetually making a maxim of, and never observing. If Don Juan is pernicious in anything, it is in that extreme mixture now and then of the piteous and the ludicrous, which tends to put some of our best feelings out of countenance. But if we may judge of its effect on others by ourselves, this kind of despair is accompanied with too much bitterness, in spite of its drollery, and is written in too obvious a spirit of extravagance not to furnish its own contradiction.

The most important of Hunt's reviews of *Don Juan* is that of Cantos I and II.[1] It describes excellently the intermingling of moods in the texture of the work, expresses reservations about some of the changes of feeling, and tries to account for them. Hunt also singles out a few passages 'of the highest order' (all describing Haidée's attentions to the shipwrecked Juan). He goes on to defend the poem against the charge of immorality. The review is sensitive and skilful.

The only other of *The Examiner*'s reviews of *Don Juan* that deserves special mention is that of Cantos III–V.[2] The reviewer writes of *Don Juan* as 'this delightful poem', and states that the continuation 'has excited the smiles of the sincere lovers of nature, and the affected frowns of the canting, full as much as the first part'. Yet he notices that these cantos contain less of 'those deeply impassioned passages, which formed . . . such remarkable and impressive, though often abrupt, contrasts to the gay and satirical manner'. There was now more digression, but it was not so *piquant* and relevant. The review praises, however, the very picturesque description of the Greeks in the gardens of the pirate's house, and the 'powerful sketch' of Lambro. It states that Byron 'in his rambling verses' has 'treated of all things, "past, present, and to come"', and has laid about him among political and poetical contemporaries, in a style exceedingly smart and pleasant, though not always just'; and it finds him 'particularly successful in his

[1] *Exar*, 31 October 1819. A long extract appears on pp. 255–9 below.
[2] *Exar*, 26 August 1821 (mistakenly referred to in the review itself as of 'Cantos II–IV').

careless contempt of the canting moralists who, by the help of their own polluted imaginations, found many hidden indecencies to cry out against in the two former Cantos'.

Further reviews of *Don Juan* appeared in *The Literary Examiner*, which covered Cantos VI–XIV. These reviews will be considered below. Cantos XV and XVI were reviewed in *The Examiner*, but the review is critically negligible.

Besides its reviews of *Don Juan*, *The Examiner*, as we have said, also printed defences of the poem. The most interesting of these is a letter entitled 'Canting Slander',[1] addressed to Rev. William Bengo Collyer, one of the editors of *The Investigator*, a magazine which ran from 1820 to 1824, and was intended, according to its Prospectus, 'to elucidate and establish the agreement and connexion between genuine philosophy and scriptural piety, between sound literature and true religion'. *The Investigator* had attacked *Don Juan* in an article entitled 'Licentious Productions in High Life'.[2] The first part of the letter in *The Examiner* simply points out that invective against *Don Juan* had only increased its sales. In the continuation of the letter the writer undertakes an open defence of the poem, which he alleges no one had yet dared to do. He starts by a firm assertion of his position:

> *Don Juan* appears to me to be a work of extraordinary power and beauty, abounding in passages (to say nothing of the wit and satire) of great sweetness and beauty, and—until you and such as you polluted them by your gross, debasing comments,—innocent and moral.

This is set against what he describes as *The Investigator*'s charge, that *Don Juan* was 'grossly indecent and prophane in its language and allusions—licentious in its descriptions—morose, cynical and brutal in its sentiments'. *The Examiner* dismisses as 'ludicrous' the charge of profanity, based on such lines as

> So Juan wept, as wept the captive Jews
> By Babel's waters, still remembering Sion.
>
> [*II*. xvi]

As to gross indecency, in the whole five published cantos of *Don Juan* there was 'not one idea so gross as may be found in every page of Pope', and 'not so much *plain-speaking*' in them as in *The*

<hr>

[1] *Exar*, 10 November 1822; contd. 24 November 1822. See pp. 293–4 below.

[2] *Investigr*, V, October 1822.

Tatler, *The Spectator*, or even *The Rambler* and *The Guardian*. The writer goes on to counter the accusation that the poet had habitually ridiculed the value of life, and the fear of death, and had jumbled together all that can give distinction to character, beauty to virtue, deformity to vice here, or misery or unhappiness to it hereafter. The writer admits that the poet had often abruptly followed images of pathos or grandeur by ludicrous comparisons and droll conceits. That was, however, characteristic of mixed styles. 'Shakespeare often breaks off in the midst of tragic grief to indulge in a pun.' Whether the poet of *Don Juan* followed this sort of practice to relieve himself from a painful idea, or simply to produce a striking contrast, was open to discussion. The former alternative was supported by the lines

> And if I laugh at any mortal thing,
> 'Tis that I may not weep; and if I weep,
> 'Tis that our nature cannot always bring
> Itself to apathy.

[*IV*. iv]

In any case *Don Juan* was a satirical poem, not a sermon or an essay on The Whole Duty of Man. Again, *The Investigator* had arraigned the poem for the 'brutal inhumanity' of jesting at the shipwrecked wretches who were 'drifting to their watery grave'; but this was only a poem, not a reality. Finally, *Don Juan* did not ridicule every social and amiable feeling. There were many passages of dignity and pathos, and some of 'terrific magnificence'; and certain passages gained in pathos by the introduction of ludicrous images or conceits following them. This last defence is undoubtedly sound; but the attempt to divorce the morality of poetry from the morality of life is more controversial. That attempt was, of course, to be accentuated later in the century.

As to *The Vision of Judgment*, the reviewer (possibly Albany Fonblanque[1]) observed that Southey's poem *A Vision of Judgment*, which had prompted Byron's satire, had excited no horror in pious critics.[2] It had never occurred to them that 'to make free with the presumed attributes of the Deity, and to deal out the judgments of omniscience in propagation of solemn cant, nauseous flattery, and the most interested purpose' was 'in any respect, indecent'. 'The vilest use' of what were regarded as

[1] Later to become editor of *The Examiner*.
[2] *Exar*, 13 October 1822.

sacred images was 'sanctified by a baseness of adulation' which ought to have rendered it 'ten times more odious'. In any case, however, if the Laureate had the right to do that. Quevedo Redivivus[1] (Byron) had a similar right to pass an opposite judgment on George III. 'Mere difference of opinion ought to go for nothing.' The reviewer then gives copious quotations from the poem with brief approving remarks.

Less than a month later *The Examiner* printed a front-page article[2] in the political section entitled 'Odious Cant—George III and Lord Castlereagh', which was a defence of *The Vision of Judgment* against an attack on it in the Tory newspaper *The Courier*. The writer of the *Examiner* article insists that the only point worth discussing is whether the poem was in any way *unfair* to the dead King, and he maintains that it was not. To describe George III as 'an old man, mad, blind, weak, helpless, and a bigot'[3] was not to 'sport with his infirmity', as *The Courier* had alleged. Moreover, far from accusing the old King of tyranny, the poem specifically conceded that he was 'no tyrant', though 'one who shielded tyrants'. What could be fairer than that? Again, the King's domestic virtues had been admitted in the poem. As to his insanity, it was 'mere fatuity and lack of brains'. The shape of his head indicated that he was 'a subject for aberration of mind'. And as to his obstinacy and weakness, it was obvious. But, in any case, the real point was whether or not one had the right to differ from Southey and *The Courier* about the late King's character. The writer thought that, in point of fact, the poet had been fairer to that character than it deserved. George III had caused untold misery to millions of people, especially in the American war. This defence of Byron's poem is not altogether convincing at some points, though the contention that one poet had as much right to attack the old King as had another to adulate him would be valid if one were to regard as nugatory such considerations as *de mortuis* so soon after his death, and that a king might deserve some special respect *per se*.

[1] Byron had published *The Vision of Judgment* under the pseudonym 'Quevedo Redivivus', in reference to the often satirical Spanish poet and prose writer Francisco Gomez de Quevedo y Villegas (1586–1645).

[2] *Exar*, 3 November 1822; contd. 10 November.

[3] As Mr Roy Minton has suggested to me, this phrase will inevitably evoke for the reader the comparable, but more consistently savage, sonnet of Shelley, *England in 1819*, whose first line is so similar to Byron's line xlii. 2, as to suggest that Byron may have borrowed from it.

The Literary Examiner,[1] which ran only from July to December 1823, gave very favourable reviews, or rather previews, of *Don Juan VI–XIV*. It is important to note that Leigh Hunt's brother John was both the publisher of these cantos, and also the initiator of *The Literary Examiner*, which was edited and published by John's son, Henry Leigh Hunt.[2] The previewer or previewers have not been definitely identified, but the style running through the writing seems to me uniform, and not unlike Leigh Hunt's.

The review of *VI–VIII*[3] starts by tilting at the 'grave and fatiguing commonplaces' directed against 'the vagaries of Genius'. The reviewer, however, considers that '*honest* dulness' could not do much harm, and could be 'allowed its unavoidable portion of expletive with great complacency':

> But if the numerous class of innocent and well-intentioned venters of no-meaning are to be thus tolerated, we are not aware of the existence of any species of literary chivalry which demands an equal degree of consideration for the rancour of disappointed venality— the affected horror of alarmed and becloaked hypocrisy—the yell of low political hostility, and the artificial bias of the whole serpentine train of corruption. . . .

As an example of 'low political hostility' the review cites the Constitutional Association's[4] legal proceedings against John Hunt for publishing *The Vision of Judgment* in *The Liberal No. 1*.[5] The reviewer goes on to mention that the real reason for the outcry against Byron's recent works was that 'HE,—a nobleman' had 'burst the enthralment of rank and station; nay more, the stronger

---

[1] Runs of *The Literary Examiner* are hard to come by, and so I have thought it useful to give fairly extended accounts of its treatment of *Don Juan*, the only poem by any of our three poets with which it was directly concerned.

[2] See on this and other matters concerning the Hunts, Professor Louis Landré's comprehensive study, *Leigh Hunt*, 2 vols. (Paris, 1936), I. 162 and *passim*.

[3] *Lit. Exar*, 5, 12 July 1823. Cantos VI–VIII were published on 15 July.

[4] The Constitutional Association was founded in December 1820, 'for opposing the Progress of Disloyal and Seditious Principles'. Its subscribers included the Duke of Wellington, about twenty other peers and nearly forty members of the House of Commons, six English and three Welsh bishops, and nearly a hundred other clergymen. It operated largely by instituting prosecutions against publishers through presenting bills of indictment before Grand Juries. It had rather little success, and by the middle of 1822 its funds, which had amounted to £30,000, were exhausted. For a detailed account see W. H. Wickwar, *The Struggle for the Freedom of the Press, 1819–1832* (London, 1928).

[5] See pp. 191–3 below.

ligatures of an aristocratical bias, and declared for the Many against the Few':

> This it is, which has subjected Lord Byron to the enmity and anger by which, in certain quarters, he is so much honoured; and but for this, he might have written like Rochester, intrigued like Buckingham, and acted all sorts of folly in the manner of Wharton. Nay, his expedition with Satan after the origin of evil, in the person of Cain, would have passed from the Creator of well-fed Rectors, and bowing Deans; a position which has been proved by much kindred matter-of-fact. In a word, the yelpers are a-slip, not for what Lord Byron is, but for what he is not. He might have been all that he is with perfect impunity, save a liberal Lord, which agrees neither with the con-servative principles of the great Holy Alliance, nor the little Con-stitutional Society,—with the confederate interests, nor the pro-prietary Oligarchy, that oppress the British system, all of which, in their several degrees, claim a *vested* right to impede the genial march of society, and make a property of the common rights of mankind.

The reviewer then suggests that what in *Don Juan* had dis-turbed 'the moral prudery of the well-dressed mob' was the poet's exposure of hypocrisy.[1] He also counters the criticism of Byron for taking up 'such dark-featured and reckless heroes' by urging that 'masterless passion' is of the essence of poetry. He continues by pointing out the advantages of the lack of plot in the poem; and then displays some of the wares of *VI*, praising especially the description of Gulbeyaz's agony (cvii–cix). The reviewer calls 'the general complexion' of *VI* '*couleur de rose*, and skittish'; whereas *VII–VIII*, according to him, 'breathe more of fire and sword'. The preview of *VII* is virtually just outline and quotation, but the account of *VIII* clearly shares Byron's anti-war sentiments, and relishes the 'deep incision' he had given Wordsworth (*VIII.* ix) for calling 'Carnage' God's 'daughter'.[2] Otherwise there is not much critical comment in the preview, though it mentions the 'alternation of light and shade, humour and pathos' in the narrative of the Siege of Ismail, and singles out as 'truly characteristic' of Byron the panegyric on General Boon of Ken-tucky, who confined his killing 'a bear or buck' (*VIII.* lxi). The reviewer quotes at length the stanzas on Juan's rescue of

[1] This part of the review is printed below on pp. 294–6.

[2] In a note to the passage in *Don Juan* Byron assigns Wordsworth's assertion to the *Thanksgiving Ode*. It actually occurred in *Ode 1815*, in l. 109, which, with the three preceding lines, was suppressed by Wordsworth in 1845.

Leila from the Cossacks (*VIII.* xc–xcvi), and praises the power of the description of the fate of the Tartar Khan and his sons (*VIII.* civ–cxix). The review ends by emphasizing the 'fertility' of Byron's Muse, and indicating the likelihood of future plenty:

> It is evident, indeed, that the author is bounded by no limits but his own inclination. Juan is scarcely a man at present, and his maturity may be rendered a perfect cornucopia: to say nothing of the great convenience of a medium through which the noble author can with such ease and nonchalance pay off the numerous scores which folly, bigotry, and cant are eternally chalking up to his account—a vehicle in which, with a combination altogether his own, he can mingle rue and wormwood with myrtles and roses—interweave in the same garland, the most delicate blossoms of the spring with the enduring oak and evergreen bay.

To Cantos IX–XI *The Literary Examiner* devoted part of its review section in four numbers,[1] no doubt with the object of building up sales of the cantos. The preview starts by noting that 'in no previous portion of this indescribable production is the sarcasm more caustic, the wit more pungent and volatile, or the general taxing more uncircumscribed'. Juan was now brought to England, 'and introduced to the *haut ton* and *Blues* of London—a field altogether uncultivated by the Society for the Suppression of Vice[2] and therefore peculiarly demanding the attention of an inflexible and *impartial* moralist like the author of *Don Juan*'. The reviewer also observes that the prescription is likely to be taken, since 'there is much reason to fear, that people of quality swallow doses of *Don Juan* with more avidity than religious tracts'. In *IX* the reviewer finds the receipt by the Empress Catherine the Great of the news of the taking of Ismail and Juan's presentation at her Court (lvii ff.) 'in excellent keeping'. There is also high praise for the tribute to Jeffrey, and the nostalgia for Scotland, near the start of *X* (xvi–xix). The reviewer then proceeds to mere outline

---

[1] *Lit. Exar*, 2, 9, 16, 23 August 1823. The Cantos were published on 29 August.

[2] Wilberforce's Society for the Suppression of Vice and Immorality was founded in 1802. It was one of a number of attempts made over the centuries to impose a strict morality on the country. Indeed, its Address to the Public, 1803, shows it to have been consciously a revival of the Society for the Reformation of Manners, founded in 1698 to tighten up moral standards after the laxity of the Restoration period. Wilberforce's society waged a strenuous war against blasphemous and obscene publications, brothels, fortune-tellers, and sabbath-breakers.

and quotation till he reaches the indignant lines, which he clearly approves, on Great Britain's 'political part' after the fall of Napoleon (lxvi–lxviii). He also obviously enjoys the injunction to Mrs Fry (one of the 'Suppressors of Vice') to extend her moral efforts from Newgate to the *grand monde* (lxxxiv–lxxxvii). Canto XI the reviewer considers more typical of Byron than any previous canto.[1] He quotes from the Shooter's Hill passage, praising its originality (viii–xx). He thinks Juan's entry into London by lamplight 'very pleasantly sketched'; and takes delight in Byron's contemptuous stanzas on Ministers and civil servants (xl–xli), and in the satire on the Blues and their attention to the young Spanish bachelor (l–liii). The review goes on to savour Byron's parallels of 'the greatest living poet' with a boxing champion, and with Napoleon (lv–lvi); asserting that 'any assignable' successor to the great poet could only be a 'Louis XVIII'. Byron's traducers, the reviewer urged, should bear in mind that a canto of *Don Juan* would 'at any time lay them prostrate by the score'. The next part of the review has a tilt at the Tory parson poetasters, Milman[2] and Croly,[3] as possible pretenders to the succession; and virulently attacks the anonymous reviewers whom Byron had happily dubbed 'prætorian bands' (lxii). The review then quotes from the description of Juan's 'fashionable life', citing the pointed stanza (lxxv) outlining 'the life and death of young British noblemen'. He appreciates the originality of asking *'où sont les neiges?'* of a world of only eight years before (lxxvi) and the witty turns involved in the passage on that theme (lxxvi–lxxix).

The Literary Examiner followed the same reviewing policy for *XII–XIV*, devoting to them part of the review section of four issues.[4] The review starts by ridiculing the idea of *'The Literary Gazette* and similar high authorities' that Byron's poetic fire was out.[5] Byron was beyond their critical reach. The review goes on to liken the panegyric on Avarice at the start of *XII* (vii–xi) to 'some of the rich soliloquies in the olden comedy'.[6] Then come some quotations from the satire on 'the matronly ladies of the *ton*' and

[1] See the extract from this part of the review on pp. 296–7 below.

[2] Henry Hart Milman (1791–1862), more famous for his historical works, especially for his *History of the Jews* (1829–30).

[3] On Croly, see p. 50, n. 2 above.

[4] *Lit. Exar*, 8, 15, 22, 29 November 1823. The Cantos were published on 17 December.

[5] See the passage from *The Literary Examiner* reprinted on pp. 301–2 below.

[6] Presumably such as in *Volpone*.

the realities of the marriage market (xxvii ff.). The portrait of Lady Pinchbeck is quoted as showing 'an equal acquaintance with human nature and the *beau monde*' (xlii–xlix). The next part of the review takes the opportunity to mention with admiration Byron's departure for Greece, despite what the reviewer takes (possibly wrongly) to be the poet's intellectual fear, shown in the stanzas on Don Quixote (*XIII*. ix ff.), that efforts to redress injury may be laughably futile. The review goes on to advertise the Amundeville 'adventure' (*XIII*. xii ff.), and to quote the 'beautiful description' of Norman Abbey. The third part of the review gives excerpts from the house-party episode (*XIII*. lxxv–end), with little comment except that Byron's quip at Izaak Walton (cvi) would 'mightily enrage the quiet and sapient association of anglers'. This part of the review concludes with approval of some early stanzas of *XIV* (xv–xvii) in which the monotony of the life of the leaders of society is indicated, the reviewer commenting that 'the affections supply the purest sources of human satisfaction', and that in this respect 'it is evident that the two extremes of society are less fortunate than the grades which lie between them'. The fourth and last part of the review opens with mention and quotation of *XIV*. ii–vi, which, with true critical appreciation, it calls 'one of those deep sceptical ponderings which so signally distinguish the poem of *Don Juan* both from its Italian models and from every kindred effort'. Then the reviewer exhibits some stanzas (xxxviii–xlii) from the description of Don Juan in his new milieu, 'a happy sketch of the qualities necessary to a generally agreeable man, and more especially to an *un*coxcombical *homme à bonnes fortunes*' (xxxi ff.). He goes on to praise and quote from the development of the Juan-Adeline *affaire*; and the preview ends abruptly, calling itself 'a slight discursive announcement only', claiming to leave 'more regular and analytical criticism to those to whom, in the present instance, it more formally and properly belongs'; and adding: 'The *most* pious and consistent will of course abuse and extract as usual.'

The previews in *The Literary Examiner* are, indeed, advertisements rather than strictly reviews. There are, however, as we have seen, a number of critical observations strewn through them, and the choice of episodes and passages for mention is in itself of some interest as showing what impressed the critic, as well as what may have seemed particularly likely to attract readers before they saw the poem. Moreover, these previews, if indeed they were written by Leigh Hunt or under his direction, also prompt the question whether Hunt at Pisa may have influenced the direction of *Don Juan* towards the satire on English society which forms the staple of the later cantos of the poem.

The Literary Examiner had ceased publication before Cantos XV–XVI appeared, and these were previewed and reviewed in *The Examiner* itself.[1]

On Shelley

Leigh Hunt's first mention of Shelley in *The Examiner* was in an article 'Young Poets', on 1 December 1816. There Hunt writes that he had so far only seen 'one or two specimens of Shelley's work', and had 'unfortunately mislaid them', but that he would procure what Shelley had published, and if the rest answered to what he had seen he would 'have no hesitation in announcing' Shelley 'for a very striking and original thinker'. The term 'thinker' is of interest, as some indication of what struck Hunt particularly in the work he had seen.

Over a month later *The Examiner* printed Shelley's *Hymn to Intellectual Beauty*, and in November 1817 eight stanzas from *Laon and Cythna*. In January 1818 it printed the Ozymandias sonnet, and an extract from *The Revolt of Islam*, which Hunt reviewed in February and March.[2] Hunt welcomed the poem, but did not anticipate that it would be favourably received. 'Worldly sceptics', 'dull rogues', 'disappointed egotists', 'hypocrites' and 'bigots' would all reject it. Shelley's recommendation of Love as the solution to the world's evils would not be regarded as practicable, though it was also Christ's recommendation. Hunt attacks what he took to be ecclesiastical corruptions of Christian doctrine, and their contradictions. He expresses faith in the power of human beings to increase the sum of happiness, and cites the abolition of the slave trade. Apart from the truth of Shelley's philosophy, the beauties of the poem consisted, in Hunt's view, 'in depth of sentiment, in grandeur of imagery, and a versification remarkably sweet, various, and noble, like the placid playing of a great organ'. Shelley's genius was like that of two opposites, Lucretius

---

[1] *Exar*, 14, 21 March 1824. The Cantos appeared on 16 March. Both the preview and the review are critically negligible.

[2] *Exar*, 1, 22 February, 1 March 1818. A long extract appears on pp. 329–33 below.

and Dante. He was like Lucretius 'in the boldness of his speculations, and in his love of virtue, of external nature, and of love itself'. He was like Dante in 'his gloomier and more imaginative passages'; but contrasted with him in that 'superstition, and pain, and injustice' went hand in hand, 'even in the pleasantest parts of Dante, like the three Furies', while 'philosophy, pleasure, and justice' smiled through 'the most painful passages' of Shelley, like the three Graces. Shelley's defects as a poet were 'obscurity, inartificial and yet not natural economy, violation of costume,[1] and too great a sameness and gratuitousness of image and metaphor'. This poem was 'full of humanity', but would never become popular. This is perceptive criticism, and the philosophical discussion shows that Hunt had entered deeply into Shelley's intentions, and sympathized with them. Whether we accept their point of view depends on our whole attitude to these profound and difficult issues.

The *Quarterly*'s review of *The Revolt of Islam* appeared in September 1819. Hunt at once started a reply, which was published in *The Examiner* on 26 September, and 3 and 10 October. He takes the *Quarterly* to task for using the suppressed *Laon and Cythna*, and then goes on to condemn the review not only for meanness but also for dulness, and for putting its own case badly. The reviewer had stupidly asked how the strictures in the poem on the Moslem religion, law, and government applied to Christians and Englishmen. The application was obvious. Again, the reviewer had alleged that Shelley's abuse of his school, its masters, and his schoolfellows bore evidence against himself as 'an insubordinate, a vain, a mortified spirit'. Hunt counters by quoting 'the pious Cowper's' attacks on public schools. As to the reviewer's recommendation that Shelley should read the Bible, Hunt goes on to assert that Shelley knew 'more of the Bible, than all the Priests who have any thing to do with the Review or its writers'— a sweepingly enthusiastic assertion of very doubtful validity. Hunt next impugns the Christianity of Canning, Croker, and Gifford. As for Shelley's views on sexual freedom, they coincided with those of 'the best and wisest names in philosophy, from Plato down to Condorcet', according to Hunt, who even suggests that Christ may have had similar views. Moreover, the moral spirit of Shelley's philosophy was far closer to Christian benevo-

[1] 'Costume' here meaning appropriateness of any kind of detail to time and place.

lence 'than any the most orthodox dogmas ever published'. The issue of 10 October is devoted to attacking the *Quarterly* for its aspersions on Shelley's private life.

In May 1819 Hunt had favourably reviewed *Rosalind and Helen*,[1] which he thought contained 'for the size, a still finer and more various, as well as a more popular, style of poetry' than *The Revolt of Islam*. The 'humanity' was brought nearer to the reader, while the 'abstractions' remained 'as lofty and noble'. Hunt also has high praise for *Lines written among the Euganean Hills*, which appeared in the same volume. Some of the lines he thought 'among the grandest if not the deepest that Mr. Shelley has produced, with a steady stepping in the measure'.

Hunt wrote a very appreciative review of *The Cenci*, but did not publish it in *The Examiner*. He published it in *The Indicator*,[2] a literary weekly started in 1819 under his editorship. His judgment, usually so discriminating, seems to have lapsed here. Possibly he was influenced by Shelley's dedication of the play to him. At all events, he persisted in his opinion even after Shelley's death, writing of the play as Shelley's most substantial achievement.[3]

The Examiner printed no review of the *Prometheus* volume, but Hunt did write an attack on the *Quarterly*'s review, and his attack was published in the issues of 9, 16, and 23 June 1822. Hunt accuses the review of labouring under the limitation of worldliness, and of judging literary works according to the party of the writers criticized. 'The question is not, "Has he genius?" but "Is he one of us?"' Hunt compares the *Edinburgh* favourably with the *Quarterly* in this respect, and he adds a word in favour of *The Examiner* itself. He goes on to point out that the *Quarterly* reviewer makes no attempt to refute Shelley's doctrines. He thinks it enough to quote a passage against priests to prove it wrong. Hunt takes the opportunity to draw attention to the reviewer's alteration of the four stars into six stars in the passage in the *Ode to Liberty*, one of the poems included in the volume:

> O, that the free would stamp the impious name
> Of * * * * into the dust!

and scouts the idea that the alteration (clearly intended to suggest the gloss 'CHRIST')[4] was accidental, and goes on to indicate what

---

[1] *Exar*, 9 May 1819.   [2] *Indicr*, 26 July 1820.
[3] In *Lord Byron and Some of his Contemporaries* (London, 1828), 218.
[4] The correct gloss would have been 'KING'. See p. 312, n. 3 below.

he considered to be other subterfuges by the reviewer. On the other hand, Hunt concedes to the reviewer that Shelley was 'too apt to draw descriptions of the state of mankind without sufficient light on his canvas', and that his poetry was 'often of too abstract and metaphysical a cast', 'too apt to be too wilful and gratuitous in its metaphors', and that 'it would be better if he did not write metaphysics and polemics in his verse, but kept his poetry for more fitting subjects'. In the third issue Hunt sets out to refute the reviewer's charge of 'nonsense', and his assertion that the whole volume did not contain '*one* original image of nature, *one* simple expression of human feeling, or *one* new association of the appearances of the moral with those of the material world'.[1]

Hunt was in Italy when he wrote his 'letter' on *Adonais* 'to the Readers of *The Examiner*'.[2] He considered the poem as no more likely to be popular than *Prometheus*. It was 'of too subtle and abstract a nature for that purpose', but it would 'delight the few, to whom Mr. Shelley is accustomed to address himself'. It was 'such an elegy as poet might be expected to write on poet'. Shelley's brief acquaintance with Keats had been entirely 'of a poetical character'. But Shelley did not record him as a mere acquaintance:

> It is as the intimate acquaintance of all lovely and lofty thoughts, as the nursling of the Muse, the hope of her coming days, the creator of additional Beauties and Intelligences for the adornment and inhabitation of the material world.

On Keats

Of Keats's poems *The Examiner* only reviewed the 1817 volume,[3] but Hunt also reviewed the 1820 Poems in *The Indicator*.[4] On *Endymion*, however, *The Examiner* only reprinted a paragraph which had appeared in *The Chester Guardian*, and also a long review by Keats's friend John Hamilton Reynolds, which had been published in a West-country newspaper called *The Alfred*.[5] Interestingly enough, Hunt did not approve of *Endymion*. Keats wrote to his brothers that Hunt did not allow it much merit as a

[1] See the extract printed on pp. 381–3 below.
[2] *Exar*, 7 July 1822. [3] *Exar*, 1 June, 6 and 13 July 1817.
[4] *Indicr*, 2, 9 August 1820.
[5] *The Alfred, West of England Journal and General Advertiser*, 6 October 1818. This review and the *Chester Guardian* notice were both reprinted in *Exar*, 11 October 1818.

whole, and said it was unnatural,[1] and Hunt wrote of it years later as 'truly a wilderness'.[2] It evidently offended against Hunt's canon of 'unsuperfluousness'.

Let us go back, however, to earlier days. Hunt first mentioned Keats in *The Examiner* on 1 December 1816 in the article 'Young Poets' already referred to. Hunt there writes of him as one of the three 'young aspirants' (the others being Shelley and Reynolds), who seemed likely to restore the love of 'nature' and of '*thinking* instead of mere *talking*'. Hunt says that a set of Keats's manuscripts had been handed to him, and that they had surprised him 'with the truth of their ambition and ardent grappling with Nature'. He then quotes the sonnet *On first looking into Chapman's Homer*, pointing out one faulty rhyme (which Keats corrected) as a 'peace-offering to the rhyming critics', and interestingly criticizing 'a little vagueness in calling the regions of poetry "the realms of gold" ', but pronouncing the whole to be 'excellent', and especially the sestet, and praising the word "swims" as 'complete', and 'the whole conclusion' as 'equally powerful and quiet'.

Hunt's review of the 1817 *Poems* is admirable criticism.[3] It contains a fascinating survey of the course of English poetry from Restoration times, and then relates Keats's work to recent changes. It is temperate in its praise, conceding that Keats's talent was yet immature, and pointing out with excellent judgment that his main faults were 'a tendency to notice everything too indiscriminately and without an eye to natural proportion and effect', and 'a sense of the proper variety of versification without a due consideration of its principles'. These strictures are amplified and illustrated. Hunt then comes to 'the beauties', which in his view outnumbered the faults 'a hundred-fold', and were 'decidedly opposed to what is false and inharmonious'. They were: 'a fine ear, a fancy and imagination at will, and an intense feeling of external beauty in its most natural and least expressible simplicity'. Hunt attractively exemplifies these 'beauties', laying stress on the truth of the descriptions of nature as well as their grace or fancy, and on the 'natural' character of the descriptions of human sensations and

[1] Letter to George and Tom Keats, 23 January 1818.

[2] *Lord Byron and Some of his Contemporaries*, 257.

[3] *Exar*, 6, 13 July 1817. A long extract appears on pp. 452–9 below. The whole review is reprinted in Edmund Blunden's *Leigh Hunt's 'Examiner' Examined* (London, 1928), and also now in *Keats: The Critical Heritage*, ed. G. M. Matthews (London, 1971).

feelings. He also draws attention to the 'warm and social feelings' in the Epistle to Clarke. Hunt unhesitatingly ranks *Sleep and Poetry* as the best poem in the volume, and expresses approval of its attack on 'the late French school of criticism and monotony'. Hunt also comments on Keats's dissent from the 'morbidity' of some of the work of the Lake Poets, in the passage which concludes by affirming that 'the great end of poesy' is that

it should be a friend
To sooth the cares, and lift the thoughts of man.

(*Sleep and Poetry*, 246–7)

La Belle Dame sans Merci was first printed by Hunt in *The Indicator* for 10 May 1820, with some comments—for instance, that 'the union of imagination and the real is very striking throughout, particularly in the dream', and that 'the mild gentleness of the rest of the thoughts and of the music are alike old, and they are alike young'.

More important, however, though not so impressive as the review of the 1817 *Poems*, is Hunt's critique of the 1820 volume in *The Indicator*.[1] Hunt gives most space to *Lamia*. He quotes the tale as given in Burton, and follows this by narrating Keats's version, with copious quotation of the 'richest passages out of his verse', which would, in Hunt's view, 'leaven a much greater lump', since 'their drops are rich and vital, the essence of a heap of fertile thoughts'. He was clearly impressed by the 'pity and horror' of the description of the serpent, and by the evocation of the atmosphere of the magic palace, and describes the lines on the 'haunting music' (II. 122–4) as 'the very quintessence of the romantic'. Hunt praises Keats's departures in character and moral from the original story ('He would see fair play to the serpent'); but he is not happy at Keats's suggestion that natural history and experimental science destroy the wonder of nature (II. 229–38). As to *Isabella*, Hunt praises the contrast drawn between the happiness of the lovers and the gloom which follows. He singles out the 'masterly anticipation' of Lorenzo's death in the word 'murder'd' (xxvii), which had already been 'justly admired' (by Lamb in *The New Times*, 19 July 1820). On the other hand, he suggests that Keats lapses when he gives the brothers, whom he

[1] *Indicr*, 2, 9 August 1820. An extract is printed below on pp. 497–9. The critique appears in full in Professor Blunden's *Leigh Hunt's 'Examiner' Examined*; and now in *Keats: The Critical Heritage*, ed. G. M. Matthews.

had described as mere 'money-bags' (xviii), the power of uttering
the 'exquisite metaphor' of the sun counting 'his dewy rosary on
the eglantine' (xxiv). But the 'fervid misery' of *Isabella* impresses
Hunt as genuine poetry of the heart, and he admires the expression
'the melodious chuckle in the strings Of her lorn voice' (lxii) as
being 'as true and touching an instance of the effect of a happy
familiar word, as any in all poetry'.[1] With this last point I find it
quite impossible to agree. Hunt calls *The Eve of St Agnes* 'rather a
picture than a story', and praises the portrait of Madeline preparing to go to bed, as 'remarkable for its union of extreme richness
and good taste', commenting that when Keats wrote *Endymion* 'he
could not have resisted doing too much'. Among the lyrics Hunt
singles out the *Ode to a Nightingale*, which he quotes entire. He
found *Hyperion* gigantically impressive. Keats's central idea, that
the empire of the Titans was irrecoverable, because 'intellect . . .
was inevitably displacing a more brute power' seemed to Hunt
the assignment of 'a very grand and deep-thoughted cause'. And
he considered the more imaginative parts of the poem to be
'worthy of this sublime moral'. On the other hand, perhaps unexpectedly, Hunt finds 'something too effeminate and human in
the way in which Apollo receives the exaltation which his wisdom
is giving him'. Hunt was impatient that the poem had been left
as a fragment, but reflected, rather shrewdly, that perhaps Keats
felt that he could not finish it because he could not make his gods
speak greatly enough—'though we may well enough describe
beings greater than ourselves by comparison, unfortunately we
cannot make them speak by comparison'. This passage is an
interesting expression of both Hunt's and Keats's attitudes to the
Greek gods.

Summing up the volume, Hunt refers to the poems as 'solid
stuff', and informs the reader (incorrectly, and probably as a
disingenuous puff) that they were almost all written when Keats
was only twenty. He notes that Keats's blank verse was sometimes like Milton's, and his blank and rhymed verse sometimes like
Chapman's, but asserts that, though Keats shared their 'unearthly
aspirations and abstract yearnings', his 'faculties' were 'altogether his own'. These were 'more social' and more finely 'sensual' than those of the other two poets, and more influenced by
'the modern philosophy of sympathy and natural justice'. Keats's

---

[1] Interestingly enough, Hunt does not notice the parallel with the more
successful image in xxxv.

genius was sometimes energetic, sometimes voluptuous, sometimes both, and in the union these characteristics possessed an
unusually high feeling of humanity. 'Mr. Keats undoubtedly takes
his seat with the oldest and best of our living poets.'

Taken all in all, Hunt's critiques of all our three poets must certainly be reckoned among the best of that time. They were,
indeed, tendentious on matters of religion, politics, and morals,
but a critic has every right to be that: and on aesthetic matters
they were often informed by sensitive and lively perception, and
an intelligent and steadily pervasive sense of values.

III

Other Expressions of Critical Opinion during the Period

The periodicals surveyed above provided most of the best or
most significant reviews of the poetry of our three poets, but
some of the other reviewing periodicals printed at least a few
perceptive or interesting critiques.

Among other monthlies the most notable for our purpose are
probably Constable's *Scots Magazine* (1739–1817), which became
Constable's *Edinburgh Magazine* (1817–26), and was liberal in outlook; *The Monthly Magazine* (1796–1825), a Radical review; *The
New Monthly Magazine* (1814–56), which was originally founded
to counteract the radical tendencies of *The Monthly Magazine*, but
became more liberal from about 1820; and the short-lived Gold's
London Magazine (1820–1), a rival of Baldwin's *London Magazine*,
with which it was amalgamated in July 1821. Among the weeklies
probably the most important for us were *The Champion* (1814–22),
at first mildly liberal under John Scott (later editor of *The London
Magazine*), but eventually more progressive politically under
John Thelwall, the Radical friend of Lamb and Coleridge; and
The Literary Gazette (1817–62), founded by Henry Colburn, who
published *The New Monthly Magazine*, and edited from the middle
of 1817 until 1850 by William Jerdan. *The Literary Gazette* was
substantially a Tory periodical.

CONSTABLE'S EDINBURGH MAGAZINE
On Byron

Constable's *Scots* (later *Edinburgh*) *Magazine* published about a score of reviews of Byron's poetry, from 1813 to 1824.

It found much of *Childe Harold III* 'very fine', a good deal 'pretty middling', and a little 'positively bad'.[1] It was not impressed by Byron's 'powers in describing war scenery', but it found his reflections on Napoleon 'very particularly interesting', not only for their force and truth,

> but because there appears a recognition of some kindred sympathies with the mind which is here painted, and a consciousness within himself, of that impatience of quiet, that eagerness for strong emotions, and proud contempt of the human race which guided that meteor of the moral world to his rise and his fall.

The reviewer admired the stanzas on the reflections and emotions prompted by the Rhine scenery, but did not find the descriptions so happy, and thought the apostrophe to the river in st. l 'almost mawkish', a rare criticism of Byron. The reviewer also objected to the introduction of the mysterious woman to whom the Drachenfels song was addressed, and had no great opinion of the song itself. The Julia Alpinula passage (lxv–lxvi), on the other hand, he found 'very interesting', and greatly admired the stanzas on Lake Geneva at night (lxxxv–lxxxix). The storm scene (xcii–xcvii) he did not like, and he found 'glee, mirth, and dancing' hardly congruous ideas with 'the conflict of such awful forms and elements'. The lengthy passage on Rousseau (xcix–civ) seemed to him not so 'masterly' as the immediately ensuing rapid sketches of Gibbon and Voltaire, which he thought it would be hard to surpass.

The Edinburgh Magazine (as it had now become) received the anonymous *Beppo* with relish,[2] and with the hope that an era of humorous verse was now going to succeed the gloomy productions which had recently held the field.

The Edinburgh Magazine's review of *Childe Harold IV*[3] sensed a change of mood to something more readily accessible to most readers, and also prophesied immortality for the whole poem.

And how did *The Edinburgh Magazine* react to *Don Juan*? It did

---

[1] *SM*, LXXVIII, November 1816.   [2] *Ed. M*, II (2nd. Ser.), April 1818.
[3] *Ed. M*, II (2nd Ser.), May 1818. See the extract on pp. 227–9 below.

not print a review until the first five cantos had appeared, and then the review consisted largely in an amusingly written account of the publication of *I* and *II*, and later of *III–V*.[1] The magazine was, however, definitely shocked. It considered Byron, 'doubtless one of the most extraordinarily gifted intellectual men of the day', to be 'poisoning the current of fine poetry, by the intermixture of ribaldry and blasphemy such as no man of pure taste can read a *second* time, and such as no woman of correct principles can read the *first*'. And the great reviews allowed him to proceed with impunity! The reviewer thought *III–V* lacking in plot, and in execution. He did not respond to the digressions. He considered the specimen of Byron's religious creed offered in *III*. civ 'just such, as a gentleman-highwayman would make'. He wished that 'the fine poetry, which almost redeems the third Canto (the least exceptionable on the ground of immorality) from reprobation, had not been mixed up with very much that is equally frivolous and foolish'. This is rather inflexible criticism, and does not probe deeply enough to make a satisfying case. The critic does, however, pick out 'The Isles of Greece' as 'one of the very finest things (of its kind) in modern poetry', and he ends on the hope that Byron will soon produce something better than his recent work.

So far from being satisfied with what Byron did go on to write, *The Edinburgh Magazine* had some strong things to say about *The Vision of Judgment*[2] and Cantos VI–VIII and IX–XI of *Don Juan*.[3] It was utterly disgusted at Byron's mockery of the blindness and madness of George III:

> Is *blindness* a crime in his eyes? Is *mental estrangement* naturally a subject for patrician mirth and derision? Would Lord Byron seek for subjects of derision in the Bethlem, or would his risible propensities be tickled by observing a blind man walking over a precipice? The extinction or suspension of reason, even in a beggar, is viewed by good men with commiseration, and a feeling approaching to awe: is a venerable and virtuous monarch, then, who, while reason and sight remained to him, was, in the best and noblest sense of the term, the Father of his people, entitled to no portion of human sympathy, or reverence, or even forbearance? The man who described the scene on the raft, and the sordid banquet—more revolting, if possible, than that of Ugolino himself—on the flesh of Pedrillo,

[1] *Ed. M*, IX (2nd. Ser.), August 1821.
[2] *Ed. M*, XI (2nd. Ser.), November 1822. See pp. 292–3 below.
[3] *Ed. M*, XIII (2nd. Ser.), August; September 1823.

would assuredly answer in the negative. But we do not put these queries with the purpose of expostulating with Lord Byron himself. The moral distemper with which he is afflicted is, we fear, long past all chance or hope of cure.

The motive behind the poem was clearly simply desire for revenge upon Southey, but could not that object, mean as it was, have been attained without 'hurling defiance in the face of Heaven, and attempting to assassinate the memory of a good man, merely because he had the misfortune to be a sovereign'? In any case, in the reviewer's opinion, the satire on Southey was far from telling. It was an inferior piece of work.[1]

As for *Don Juan VI–VIII*, the magazine again attacked Byron for his onslaughts on Southey, and it objected to the quotations from Voltaire which Byron had included in the Preface, and to the 'monstrous indecencies' in the poem itself. The reviewer also levelled at Byron a somewhat different kind of attack from those usually made:

All this despicable cant and scurrility about religious, political, and moral hypocrisy, is only a disguise, a cover, a mask, assumed the more effectively to assail, not the abuses of religion or morality, but to sap the very foundations of both.

The reviewer quotes *VI*. xxviii, *VII*. vi, and *VIII*. ix to support his point. Byron's attitudes to religion and morality were, however, too complex and shifting for this criticism to be wholly justified. The reviewer considered *VI*, in any case, to be 'a piece of unredeemed and unrelieved sensuality'. But he had a mixed attitude to *VII* and *VIII*. He thought that they contained some very powerful description, and 'occasional passages of great beauty and strength', 'followed close at the heels, however, by that incessant mockery of human feelings and human sufferings for which this poem, as well as others of the noble bard, are remarkable'. Indeed, 'mockery' was 'the *omne in uno*, the beginning, the middle, and the end of the poem'. This closely corresponds, it may be remembered, with Byron's own description of what he was intending to do in this poem. But the reviewer wholeheartedly praises Byron's 'noble sympathy with liberty', and his 'just abhorrence of the leagued and crowned oppressors of the earth' who were

now occupied in filling up the measure of their crimes against

[1] *Ed. M*, XI (2nd. Ser.), November 1822.

humanity, and in attempting to crush that spirit which they want the skill to guide, as much as the power ultimately to subdue, and which will one day break forth like an overwhelming flood, uprooting their unhallowed thrones, and sweeping away every fragment of despotism from the face of the earth.

Also, though the reviewer could not stomach what he thought 'vile puns and jokes out of place', he considered that 'on the whole' these cantos showed no great diminution of power. Indeed, he believed that *VII* and *VIII* contained as fine passages as any in Byron, and held that

> but for that excess of mockery, of which we have already spoken, the whole description of the assault of Ismail, with its accompaniments, might safely be placed in competition with whatever is most powerful, vigorous, and striking, in English poetry.

When *Don Juan IX–XI* appeared *The Edinburgh Magazine*[1] thought them a great comedown, 'nothing but measured prose, replete with bad puns, stale jests, small wit, indecency, and irreligion', and with 'none of those redeeming bursts of true poetical inspiration, for which their predecessors were remarkable'. They also seemed laboured, and to be animated

> by a spirit generally at war with the world and itself, and apparently susceptible of delight only when it dwells on the follies, miseries, or crimes of mankind.

Byron plainly wanted to become 'the modern Juvenal', and he was certainly 'a keen, and sometimes a powerful satirist'; but he would never 'equal the terseness and vigour of the great original', however much he might 'surpass it in grossness and obscenity'.

The *Edinburgh Magazine* printed no further review of *Don Juan*. In spite of some inflexibility, what it said about the poem seems, on the whole, pretty fair, and it did, as we have seen, eventually seize the essential point that Byron was writing satire—a thing which many of the reviewers were too hot under the collar to realize.

On Shelley

The *Edinburgh Magazine* was no friend to Shelley. It passed an incidental stricture on him in a review of Barry Cornwall's *Marcian*

---

[1] *Ed. M*, XIII (2nd. Ser.), September 1823.

Colonna,[1] compared *Queen Mab* with *Cain* in a review of Byron,[2] and commented briefly on Shelley's translation from Goethe in *The Liberal* No. 1.[3] In other words, it virtually neglected him. Its attitude is, however, clear enough from the last-mentioned comments, in which he is called 'Atheist Shelley', and said to have gone 'to that place where his doubts are already solved, and his state eternally and irrevocably fixed', by which the reviewer can scarcely be thought to be referring to heaven.

On Keats

The Edinburgh Magazine was one of the very few periodicals that reviewed Keats's first volume. It appreciated that he had real talent, but thought that he would need to break away from the Cockneys if the talent were to come to full fruition.[4] *The Edinburgh Magazine* also defended *Endymion*,[5] even going so far as to find it more typical and personal, and as full of 'beauties' as the 1820 volume.

When *The Edinburgh Magazine* came to review the 1820 volume[6] it picked on *Lamia* as the poem 'fullest of fancy', but it also found *Isabella* 'eminently beautiful', though it considered the "ledger-men", "money-bags" touches in bad taste. It quoted some stanzas of *The Eve of St Agnes* without comment, gave the Nightingale Ode entire, inclining to prefer it to any other poem in the book, quoted some lines from *Robin Hood*, and recommended *Fancy* and *To Autumn* as having 'great merit', but confessed that it did not like *Hyperion* as well as some of the other poems, indicating that it seemed to remind one of various other poets as it went along—*e.g.*, of the author of *The Mirror for Magistrates*, of Chaucer, and of Milton. Its final verdict on Keats's volumes was that, though not faultless, they contained 'as much absolute poetry as the works of almost any contemporary writer'. *The Edinburgh Magazine* deserves considerable credit for its friendly yet discriminating attitude to Keats's work.

[1] *Ed. M*, VII (2nd. Ser.), July 1820.
[2] *Ed. M*, X (2nd. Ser.), January 1822.
[3] *Ed. M*, XI, November 1822.
[4] *Ed. M*, I (2nd. Ser.), October 1817. A long extract from this review is reprinted on pp. 462–5 below.
[5] *Ed. M*, VII (2nd. Ser.), August 1820. An extract appears on pp. 490–2 below.
[6] *Ed. M*, VII (2nd. Ser.), October 1820.

THE MONTHLY MAGAZINE
On Byron

The Monthly Magazine also printed some twenty reviews of Byron during his lifetime. Selection is again necessary.

The magazine received *Childe Harold III* very favourably,[1] even sympathizing with the references to Byron's domestic circumstances, and singling out for an especial encomium 'the deep tone of feeling, of philosophy, and of exalted fancy, with which he treats of the themes suggested to him by the scenery he has recently encountered'. This 'tone' the reviewer thought 'always affecting, but sometimes peculiarly grand'. *The Monthly Magazine* was not impressed with *Chillon*, calling it 'little more than a rhapsodical description of the effect of merciless captivity'.[2] On *Childe Harold IV*[3] the magazine remarked that 'whatever Lord Byron touches starts at once from the canvas, and we behold visions like realities before us'. It did not consider *IV* as good as *III* 'in vividness of colouring, and marked delineation of character', yet noted that there was still 'a glowing pencil'. The review goes on, however, to express satisfaction with a patrician's defence of Freedom.

The Monthly Magazine thought that *Beppo* was marked by absence of Byron's usual 'deep intensity of feeling', and commented that this was a bad symptom for a poet, though an excellent one for a man, and expressed the hope that Byron had really begun to be happy.[4] When *Don Juan I and II* appeared *The Monthly Magazine* rated its literary merits high, but its moral qualities very low.[5] It excused Byron on the ground that he had no pretensions to be a moral writer:

> On the contrary he seems to have a wish to be thought otherwise; and it is evident from all his works, that, to the delight which he himself takes in the exercise of his own impressive talents, we are chiefly indebted for the various effusions of his superb poetry.

The reviewer gives high praise to the 'astonishing ease and libertine gaiety' with which the story is managed. He also admires the 'flexibility' of the language, which he believes to have been 'never exhibited so perfectly before'. He has, however, an interesting reservation:

[1] *MM*, XLII, December 1816. [2] *MM*, XLII, January 1817.
[3] *MM*, XLV, June 1818. [4] *MM*, XLV, July 1818.
[5] *MM*, XLVIII, August 1819.

The defect of *Don Juan* is the same which has been objected to in the other works of Lord Byron: much of the interest depends on the incidents; and we are apt to ascribe the emotion with which we are affected in the perusal to the effect of the poetry, while it is, in fact, attributable to the surprise that we feel in seeing such topics so openly treated.

This is an unusual criticism of Byron's work, and it is still food for thought.

I have only space for a brief account of three other reviews of Byron in this periodical: of *Don Juan III–V*, *VI–VIII*, and *IX–XI*. The first of these[1] regards Byron's new cantos as 'a continuation of his serio-comic melo-dramatic harlequinade'. It notes that, as before,

he pours out a singular mixture of pathos, doggrel, wit, and satire, taking a strange and almost malignant delight in dashing the laughter he has raised with tears, and crossing his finest and most affecting passages with burlesque ideas, against which no gravity is proof.

It suggests that 'perhaps this style is the real transcript of his mind'—a remark which is not so platitudinous as it might first appear. The reviewer goes on to notice that there is often a bitter truth lurking under the foolery. There would, for instance, be 'no jocularity in the jingle of his bells' for the Lakers, especially for Southey, and the reviewer defends Byron's attacks on marriage as only shooting at what has 'time out of mind been a legitimate butt', adding:

we have no manner of apprehension that the sarcasms and buffoonery of the noble writer will either disturb the harmony of connubial life, or prevent one Benedick from becoming a married man.

Here, then, we have an extreme of optimism about the possible moral effects of the poem, to contrast with the pessimism of such critics as William Roberts. There is, of course, no chance whatever of our being able to decide which was nearer the truth! Quoting some of the stanzas about love and marriage from *III*. iv onwards, the reviewer pleads that they are no more cynical about human nature than Swift, so why should not Byron have

---

[1] *MM*, LII, September 1821.

his jest? Indeed, in conclusion, the reviewer places the case in a still larger historical perspective:

> We have only to remark, in conclusion, that of the sarcastic wit and poetical talents of this composition, there can be no question; and we must bear in mind that it is framed upon a model, which in all languages has been allowed considerable latitude of subject and expression. Whether the noble author has acted wisely in reviving this style of writing is another matter, but those who are acquainted with the labours of his predecessors in this vineyard, will be inclined to think that he has not exercised his privileges in a very outrageous manner.

The Monthly Magazine's review of *VI–VIII* is another stout defence.[1] It starts by making the point that 'railers and partisans alike' had contributed to the popularity of the poem, with the result that 'scarcely any poem of the present day has been more generally read, or its continuation more eagerly and impatiently awaited'. It goes on to single out for special praise the 'richly poetical' description of Gulbeyaz's 'jealous distress' (*VI*. cv ff.), the opening stanzas of *VIII* on war, and the 'vivid and appalling fidelity' of the description of the horrors of the Siege of Ismail (*VII*. ix ff.). The reviewer concedes that the story moves little in these cantos, but he rightly observes that Byron was far from intending a regular narrative. The whole poem seemed to be the product of an active and powerful mind relaxing. Hence the continual digressions, the irony and sarcastic humour, 'apparent levity which however often serves but as a veil to deep reflection':

> Nor can the talent of the master hand be always concealed; it involuntarily betrays itself in the touches of the pathetic and sublime which frequently present themselves in the course of the poem; in the thoughts 'too big for utterance, and too deep for tears', which are interspersed in various parts of it.

The reviewer did find, however, a smaller proportion of the 'higher class of poetry' in these three cantos—nothing to compare, for instance, with the shipwreck, or the 'mournful end of Haidee', but in 'keen and pervading satire' and 'bitter and biting irony', 'which constitute the peculiar forte of Lord Byron', there seemed to be no falling off. This review here contrasts interestingly with that in *The Literary Gazette*.[2] In the reviewer's opinion there was also just as much of 'playful humour' and 'felicitous transition', 'from grave to gay, from lively to severe'. The

[1] *MM*, LVI, September 1823.   [2] See p. 162 below.

reviewer did think, however, that the generality of readers might find these cantos less amusing, and he also foresaw that 'the canting tribe' would object virulently to a peer expressing the doctrines of liberalism, and 'advocating the cause of the oppressed many against the oppressing few'. The radicalism of this periodical is here seen in full flood. The switches from the terrible to the ludicrous, which deeply shocked some of the reviews, are given soberer names, and regarded as 'felicitous transitions'; and radicalism itself is called by the somewhat milder term 'liberalism'.

The Monthly Magazine also printed a review of Don Juan IX–XI,[1] in which it defends Byron's speed of composition by the argument that 'the best authors in every language have generally written much'. It approves of his attack on tyrants, praises his tribute to Jeffrey, and his onslaught on 'vice sheltered by rank and opulence'. The reviewer thought that these cantos contained more 'of the lofty and pathetic style of poetry' than VI–VIII, and he takes the opportunity to rebuke those who expected an evenness of quality which neither Virgil nor even Homer had supplied. He also includes a short defence of Byron's unorthodox rhymes, which I have reprinted below.[2]

On Shelley

As I mentioned earlier, The Monthly Magazine, despite its left-wing sympathies, had little to say about Shelley. On The Revolt of Islam it commented[3] that the poem proved that 'the age of simplicity' had returned, and it also held that 'the experiment, or affectation, of an almost total neglect of harmonious modulation and quantity' was there 'carried to a very blameable excess'. The reviewer of The Cenci[4] considered it 'unwholesome', and as inspiring not 'terror' but 'horror and disgust'. Yet he writes also of Shelley's 'original and extensive genius' which had 'so frequently favoured the poetical world with productions of no ordinary merit'. What 'productions' he was referring to is quite unclear, since the periodical had not printed any favourable review, and its later critique of the pirated Queen Mab,[5] the only other review it printed, was positively scathing.

[1] MM, LVI, December 1823. [2] On pp. 302–3. [3] MM, XLV, March 1818.
[4] MM, XLIX, April 1820. [5] MM, LI, June 1821.

On the other hand, *The Monthly Magazine* did publish a brief, friendly critique of Keats's 1817 *Poems*,[1] and also a largely favourable one of the 1820 volume.[2]

THE NEW MONTHLY MAGAZINE
On Byron

The New Monthly Magazine printed some twenty pieces on Byron and his work during his lifetime. I am selecting for survey the most important for my purpose.

The first of these is an interesting article called 'Observations on the Poetical Style of Lord Byron'.[3] This starts with the bold claim that no writer since Shakespeare's time had 'surpassed, or even equalled' Byron 'in the force and fidelity' with which he had 'delineated those deep and mysterious emotions, which alternately transport and agonize the souls open to the inroads of the wilder and stormier passions'. Indeed, Byron's works had 'formed a new and splendid era in the history of English poetry'. He had 'drawn characters closer to nature than the "faultless monsters" ' which had 'for so many years occupied the pages of most of our Novelists and Bards'. As we remember, some critics had thought that his mixtures of good and evil were themselves quite *unnatural*. The critic does not argue that point, however, but goes on to consider the common, 'fashionable', stricture that Byron 'regards too frequently the darker shades of human nature'. The critic's answer is thoughtful, and it leads him, as we shall see, into some original and still interesting, though possibly questionable, positions about the relationship between Byron and his characters. The answer the critic gives is that Byron naturally chose to depict characters 'best calculated to display the extent of his genius', just as Salvator Rosa adhered to 'the "horribly sublime", for representation of which he was so exclusively and eminently qualified'. So, continues the critic:

> Why . . . should we seek to prescribe bounds for the imaginative faculties of a Bard, who, aiming at originality, had courage to deviate from the beaten track, and defying the dull and frigid canons

---

[1] *MM*, XLIII, April 1818.
[2] *MM*, L, September 1820. This is reprinted on pp. 509–10 below.
[3] *NMM*, X, September 1818.

of criticism, has genius to conceive, and powers to execute plans upon a far more elevated scale, than precedent is able to afford him.

The critic goes on to discuss another common criticism:

> It has also been observed, and not without some justice, that Lord Byron has infused such noble traits, and such a loftiness of demeanour into the souls of his heroes, as to procure for them infinitely more sympathy, than they ought with propriety to create. But this is an error in which he is by no means single; from the age of Homer to the present; from Achilles to Marmion; our favourable feelings have been excited for persons whose deportment has been by no means exemplary; and who have exhibited as little morality as the Giaour, the Corsair, or Childe Harold.

We are strongly interested in the fate of Milton's Satan. No doubt, says the critic, Milton did not intentionally introduce something 'attractive or fascinating' into the character;

> . . . but certain it is, that men of exalted genius cannot always confine themselves to the limits which prudence may dictate; nor is it fair to imagine, because circumstances may lead the poet to invest his hero with some one feeling which he himself possesses, that he should be made answerable for the vices which are necessary in order to bring about the catastrophe of his story.

The critic's application of this argument to the case of Byron is still worth considering, whether we find it valid or sophistical:

> No writer has ever been so frequently identified with his hero, as Lord Byron; and for this reason: he is not content with representing him, merely as an agent in bringing about a revolution in his drama, but occasionally makes him a vehicle for his own thoughts and sentiments; and that too in such a manner, that it requires no little judgment to separate his Lordship from the 'beings of his mind'.— He cannot avoid enduing them with those deep feelings and lofty aspirations which are so peculiar to himself; and he may be compared to a man who masquerades for a frolic, in the character of an assassin, without a sufficient attention to 'dramatic keeping' to sustain it, and who frequently betrays himself by expressions inconsistent with the disguise he has assumed.

The critic signs himself 'Z.', a teasing initial in view of its use in *Blackwood's*.[1]

The next contribution worth surveying is the notice of *Childe Harold IV*.[2] The writer disclaims the intention of a 'regular

[1] See p. 51 above.   [2] *NMM*, X, September 1818.

review', but he starts with some general observations, and he intersperses his quotations with remarks of some interest. He calls the canto 'this beautiful poem', and agrees with the dedication that it was 'the most thoughtful and comprehensive' of all Byron's works. He detected 'amid the many wild and inextinguishable bursts of energy' which abounded in the canto, 'something like a yearning after the better affections of the heart; a willingness to look forward, with consoling hope, to some end or attainment, over which "Circumstance, that unspiritual god, and miscreator", can have no influence'. Amid the 'utter wretchedness' which occasionally broke forth in this 'immortal lament', there was the appearance of 'passions subdued into mournful resignation':

> ... the soul of the 'wondrous Childe' seems to have been tempered and chastened even by its own fire.

The critic continues:

> No poet was ever gifted with so powerful a talisman for discerning the intenser passions of the heart, as Lord Byron. He reveals to us thoughts and sensations, of which we scarcely believed ourselves capable, and teaches us that we are indeed 'fearfully and wonderfully made'.

He goes on to quote xxiii–xxiv as illustrating 'those mysterious associations by which the mind of man is recalled to a sense of its ills'; praises the 'exquisite burst of patriotism' in viii–ix; claims that Byron, 'the poet of nature', never gave such a fine instance of his 'vividness of perception' as the 'luxurious description of an Italian evening' in xxvii–xxix; notes the 'sense of beauty' shown in the description of the Venus de' Medici (xlix–l); and admires the 'generous tribute' to Tasso (xxxix).

The critic then turns to another aspect of Byron shown in the canto:

> That conflict of wild and terrible emotions which would distract an ordinary mind almost to annihilation, Lord Byron can calmly and fearlessly contemplate, and like the rock which offers its unyielding breast to the ungovernable fury of the world of waters, remain himself 'unhurt amid the war of elements'.

The reviewer quotes some stanzas from the 'address to Time' (cxxx ff.), calling it 'perhaps the finest passage in the whole poem'. And the review concludes by quoting the stanzas on the death of

Princess Charlotte (clxvii–clxxii), and expressing 'infinite satisfaction that we find this tribute to her virtue in a work likely to last for ever'.

Also interesting are some retrospective 'Observations on Lord Byron's Juvenile Poems, with Specimens'.[1] These contain a perceptive comparison of Byron's poetry with that of Scott, which had fallen from public favour. The writer claims that this did not imply that Byron's 'manly, dignified, and nervous poetry' would suffer the same fate. Byron was the 'complete antithesis' to Scott. His work was 'all strength, condensation, and energy'. Scott had 'little energy, and few, if any, of those recondite excellences so peculiar to' Byron's work. Byron was 'the most original writer of the day, and the most condensed and forcible writer of any age'. He did not need to 'wire-draw' his 'beauties'. He was, admittedly, 'sometimes not altogether perspicuous', and ought to remember that 'it is only a lapidary who can estimate the value of an unwrought diamond'. But this was excusable, since he was principally engaged on producing great effects. He used few characters, and excited readers' sympathies not by 'singularity of situation', but by 'intensity of feelings and passions'. His heroes had none of the 'namby-pamby good qualities of Mr. Scott's "gentle knights" '. They were "souls made of fire, and children of the sun", and whilst their 'aberrations' were 'those of an expanded and lofty intellect', their better qualities gained 'such a hold on our attention' that we 'almost forget to regard the darker shades of their characters with that abhorrence, with which, perhaps, they ought sometimes to be contemplated'. 'But', the reviewer argues, in a complex passage,

> this is the fault, not of the poet, but of his genius. He sought to fix upon some theme that would afford ample scope for the display of his powers, and he has succeeded to a miracle; for it may be affirmed, with truth, that there are no heroes, in the whole compass of poetry, so exclusively attractive as his. To tread with safety such slippery ground affords the strongest evidence of the surprising extent of his powers; and that he who appeared to write only for posterity should acquire the immediate and tumultuous approbation of the world, is a fact as honourable to himself as confirmatory of his excellence; more particularly when we recollect the despicable attacks which certain critical drudges of the press—from envy of his talents—have, at various times, made upon his fame.

[1] *NMM*, XI, February 1819.

The writer then attacks the *Edinburgh* for its review of *Hours of Idleness*, but goes on to defend the repulsiveness of the Childe in a novel way:

> Though the hero of this Poem is, as his Lordship himself acknowledges, 'rather a repulsive personage', yet, such a character was needful to express certain opinions and observations, which, from the mouth of a 'Childe', of a less impassioned temperament, would neither have been reasonable nor natural.

The article ends with another attack on the *Edinburgh*, for lyingly asserting its early acceptance of Byron's work; and with five pages of 'specimens' from *Hours of Idleness*.

We may pass over with a bare mention a very laudatory and flowery article 'On the Character and Poetry of Lord Byron', signed 'J. H. Wiffen', and dated from Woburn, 27 February 1819.[1]

More interesting is the reception the *New Monthly* gave to *Don Juan I and II*,[2] which is not altogether unlike that accorded by its rival *The Monthly Magazine*:

> We lament to behold so much fervid genius, elegant literature, and knowledge of the world, united with a spirit of libertinism and infidelity, and employed to corrupt the senses.

On the other hand, the reviewer was much impressed with the portrayal of Julia's struggle against her passion (*I*. lxix ff.):

> We cannot read these passages without being touched by their exquisite beauty, and wishing that a poet so full of the true inspiration had devoted his powers to the cause of virtue. The fire of imagination in these brilliant pictures, and the melody of the versification are worthy of Moore, or Byron,[3] or Scott, or Campbell, or any other poet of the age.

Later the reviewer quotes *II*. li–lii, commenting:

> This scene of horror and destruction is so finely described that our readers will not fail to do it justice. The perusal makes a shuddering chillness run over the frame. . . . The whole course of this disastrous voyage is painted with a surprising force, and a detail of circumstances, which could only have been acquired by one who had often experienced the dangers of the sea.

The reviewer does not, however, care for the 'infidel sneer' in the final couplet of lxxxvi. On the other hand, like many other critics,

[1] *NMM*, XI, May 1819. [2] *NMM*, XII, August 1819.

[3] We need to remember that the cantos were published without their author's name.

he admires the immediately ensuing episode of the two fathers (lxxxvii ff.), as 'told with touches of deep pathos'. The 'unaccountable turn of levity' which 'destroyed' the 'sublime and beautiful description of the rainbow and sun' (xci–xcii), like similar turns elsewhere, is not approved by the reviewer. Haidée, on the other hand, he thinks described 'in terms of exquisite grace, beauty, and sensibility', though the story of the amour has an 'immoral tendency'. The reviewer thinks the style most like Byron's. Haidée was like the Cossack girl in *Mazeppa*. Byron linked his verses. There was the same 'passionate earnestness' in the descriptions of characters, and the same 'burning intensity' and 'utter absorption of every sense in the immediate scene and object'. But though the powers of the writer of *Don Juan* were as 'high' as Byron's, he did not 'so strongly and perfectly identify himself with the principal character' (an interesting point). He 'destroyed the illusion by passing at once from images of pathos, beauty, and grandeur to ludicrous and burlesque similes and expressions'. This showed 'want of judgment and bad taste'—a verdict common to many critics of limited outlook. The review is signed 'W.C.'

Three months later the *New Monthly* lashed out at Byron's work in a lurid article entitled 'Critique on Modern Poets: Lord Byron'.[1] He knew nothing of the passion of love. He never noted or commended 'a single moral or mental quality in the object of his passion'. Byron's muse was characterized by extremes: 'her language is blasphemy, her character misanthropy, her passion hatred, her religion despair'. The end of all poetry was to instruct or please. Byron's did neither. His religious views were pernicious. He was guilty of political 'tergiversations'. Finally:

There is a heartlessness about this man, that is the original sin of his poetry.

Two notes to the article are signed 'H.M.' The writer says he is 'a man advanced in life'.

On Shelley

During Shelley's lifetime the *New Monthly* only reviewed *The Cenci*.[2] It recognized Shelley's 'noble feelings', 'far-reaching

[1] *NMM*, XII, November 1819.

[2] *NMM*, XIII, April 1819. Thomas Noon Talfourd wrote for the *New Monthly* a eulogistic review of *Prometheus*, but Colburn the publisher returned

hopes', and 'high and emphatic imagination', but maintained that he had 'no power of religious truth to balance and rightly to direct his energies':

> Hence a restless activity prompts him to the boldest and most fearful excursions—sometimes almost touching on the portals of heaven, and, at others, sinking a thousand fathoms deep in the cloudy chain of cold fantasy, into regions of chaos and eternal night.

This periodical did, however, print a kindly obituary of Shelley,[1] possibly by Cyrus Redding, one of the liberal forces in the magazine at that time. This claimed that he had 'never been fairly treated as a poet' (which was not completely true), adding:

> His works are full of wild beauties and original ideas, too much intermixed with fanciful theory, but they display a richness of language and imagination rarely surpassed.

On Keats

The only important review or article on Keats in *The New Monthly Magazine* deals with the 1820 Poems.[2] It notes a vast improvement in his poetry:

> These poems are very far superior to any which their author has previously communicated to the press. They have nothing showy, or extravagant, or egocentric about them; but are pieces of calm beauty, or of lone and self-supporting grandeur. There is a fine freeness of touch about them, like that which is manifest in the old marbles, as though the poet played at will his fancies virginal, and produced his most perfect works without toil. We have perused them with the heartiest pleasure—for we feared that their youthful author was suffering his genius to be enthralled in the meshes of sickly affectation—and we rejoice to find these his latest works as

---

it to him because he thought the volume 'full of Jacobinism and blasphemy'. (T. N. Talfourd to James Ollier, 9 September 1820, quoted N. I. White, *Life of Shelley*, II. 301). Thomas Noon Talfourd (1795–1854) pursued concurrently a legal and a literary career. As an advocate he defended Edward Moxon when he was prosecuted for publishing Shelley's *Queen Mab*. He became a judge of the Court of Common Pleas in 1849. As a literary man he was both author and critic. He wrote several tragedies, including *Ion* (1836) which was very successful. He helped Bulwer to edit Hazlitt's literary remains (1836), and he was Lamb's executor and edited his letters (1837) and published memoirs of him (1837). He ran the dramatic department of *The New Monthly Magazine* for several years, and also contributed to *The Retrospective Review*. He was elected M.P. for Reading on three occasions.

[1] *NMM*, VI (n.s.), October 1822. [2] *NMM*, XIV, September 1820.

free from all offensive peculiarities,—as pure, as genuine, and as lofty, as the severest critic could desire.

With regard to particular poems in the collection, the reviewer mentions as an original feature of *Lamia* 'a mingling of Greek majesty with fairy luxuriance which we have not elsewhere seen'. In *Isabella* he considers the description of Isabella's visit with the old nurse to Lorenzo's grave, and their digging for the head, 'as wildly intense as any thing which we can remember'. *The Eve of St Agnes* he calls 'a piece of consecrated fancy', adding that 'a soft religious light is shed over the whole story'. *Hyperion* he notes as being in 'a very different style':

> We do not think any thing exceeds in silent grandeur the opening of this poem, which exhibits Saturn in his solitude.

He quotes I. 1–21, and then accords also very high praise to II. 1–81:

> The picture of the vast abode of Cybele and the Titans—and of its gigantic inhabitants, is in the sublimest style of Æschylus. Lest this praise should be thought extravagant we will make room for the whole.

He concludes with warm encouragement:

> We now take leave of Mr. Keats with wonder at the giant stride which he has taken, and with the good hope that, if he proceeds in the high and pure style which he has now chosen, he will attain an exalted and a lasting station among English poets.

'GOLD'S' LONDON MAGAZINE

Our last monthly is Gold's *London Magazine*—so known in literary circles to distinguish it from *The London Magazine* published by Baldwin, with which it was actually amalgamated after only eighteen months of existence and rivalry. Gold's had very little to say about Byron's poetry, but found a fair amount to discuss in the work of Shelley and Keats.

On Shelley

Gold's printed an extremely understanding review of Shelley's *Prometheus*,[1] in which it recognized that Shelley's drama was no

---

[1] *Gold's LM*, II, September and October 1820. An extract appears below on pp. 355–7.

mere imitation of any of the Greeks, but something new, and concerned with principles of vital importance to the period in which it was written. The magazine followed this up with a fine essay 'On the Philosophy and Poetry of Shelley',[1] in which it views his religion in a liberal spirit, and also places him above all poets of the time, with the possible exception of Wordsworth. This was most unusual. It is a great pity that Shelley does not appear to have seen this review.

On Keats

Gold's *London Magazine* was not so favourable to Keats. It only reviewed the 1820 Poems,[2] but even these it gave short shrift. It pretended to steer a true course between the 'malicious hostility' of the *Quarterly*, and the 'perverted, strange, and affected friendship' of Baldwin's *London Magazine*, exemplified in their treatment of *Endymion*. Actually, however, the review in Gold's was superciliously unfavourable. It did, indeed, early in its course, appear to be stating its objections to Keats's work candidly and fairly:

> We frankly confess our dislike of his rhythm, and his intolerable affectation, and mistaken stringing-together of compound epithets. But still we feel he often *thinks* like a poet. His knowledge of Greek and mythology seems to mystify him on every occasion; and his mode of expression is seldom natural. He does not trust himself to his naturally strong and vital impressions; he says nothing like other men, and appears always on the stretch for words to shew his thoughts are of a different texture from all other writers. He looks as if he mistook affectation for originality—as some men do dirty linen and unreaped chins as proofs of genius. Mr. Keats, however, is young, and may in time learn the folly of so misjudging. His Endymion led us, with all its blemishes, to expect from him higher things; and though disappointed, on this occasion, we are still sanguine of his success. We are sure Leigh Hunt never corrected his exercises in Lamia or the Basil Pot, or else they would have appeared to more advantage.

The reviewer seems, unusually and in sharp contrast with Lockhart, to be crediting Keats with a knowledge of Greek and of mythology, while maintaining that it leads the poet into cloudiness of thought and unnaturalness of expression.

[1] *Gold's LM*, III, February 1821. An extract appears on pp. 359–62 below.
[2] *Gold's LM*, II, August 1820.

It is also very rare to find a critic preferring *Endymion*'s promise to the performance of the 1820 Poems, but the critic's opinion may well have been quite honest. On the other hand, it is hard to say how genuine the touches of general praise really are; for the rest of the review consists simply in running through *Lamia* and *Isabella* with a series of comments designed to show the absurdity of their texture. It must in fairness be added, however, that a few months later Gold's did make some favourable remarks about Keats in an 'Essay on Poetry'.[1]

THE CHAMPION

On Byron

The Champion reviewed a number of Byron's poems. The reviews mainly relevant for us concern *Childe Harold III*, *Beppo*, and *Don Juan I and II*.

The Champion thought *Childe Harold* Byron's best poem up till the time of review (November 1816),[2] and *III* superior to anything he had yet written. The reviewer rejoiced to feel in it a new 'fine vein of humanity', and a new vision of the scenes of nature, 'as though they harmonized' with Byron's 'thoughts'. Byron had 'read Wordsworth to some purpose'. It had 'directed his heart and mind, as well as his eye, to Nature'. Moreover, the 'strength and ardour' of Byron's genius had never been 'more strongly put forth'. And the reviewer went so far as to say that xcvii seemed to him 'one of the grandest in the whole range of English poetry'.

The *Chillon* volume, on the other hand, seemed to *The Champion* expensive, and likely to lessen Byron's popularity.[3] It was generally 'forced, feeble, and imperfect', though there were a few 'spirited and original' passages here and there. Byron had been reading Coleridge's 'mad dreams', and imitated them absurdly in *The Prisoner*. The poem was full of 'namby-pamby stuff'. The lines on the bird were pretty, but unoriginal. The only lines singled out for praise are 73–91.

The Champion favourably reviewed *Manfred* in 1817, but the next critique that concerns us is the short one of *Beppo*.[4] *The Champion* did not think that this poem had 'very high pretensions'; but the review itself is quite inadequate for any pretensions,

[1] *Gold's LM*, III, December 1820.   [2] *Champ*, 24 November 1816.
[3] *Champ*, 1 December 1816.   [4] *Champ*, 29 March 1818.

describing the poem simply as 'generally humorous and satirical with occasional passages of beauty and feeling'.

The Champion's review of Don Juan I and II[1] is somewhat more interesting. It was written by John Thelwall, at that time editor, a Radical, who had been tried in 1794 for treason. The review considers the anonymity of both author and publisher a mere bookseller's trick, since, though 'infinitely more immoral than the publications or the practices prosecuted by the Society for the Suppression of Vice', there seemed nothing in it actionable either by that society or by the Attorney-General. Yet Byron was employing at once 'all the force and energy of his faculties', 'all the powers of poetry and the missiles of wit and ridicule' against everything respectable in morality and religion. Thelwall hoped that, whatever the case with speculative opinions, at least the morals of mankind would withstand the shock. II was perhaps the most powerful thing Byron had written, but it was 'lamentable' to see such powers used for such purposes; for Don Juan was a 'tissue of all immoralities':

> Every sentiment and feeling is sported with that should be sacred to the heart of man; and every tie of social confidence treated as flax to which the flame of his wit and irony is applied to turn the bond into conflagration.

On the other hand, Thelwall admits that the progress of the passion of Juan and Julia is 'traced certainly with great knowledge of the human heart'. Thelwall even makes a further concession, though he hedges it with an important qualification, and the concession itself would have appeared to Byron as mere mealy-mouthed moral casuistry:

> and, but for the seductive colouring with which every incident is embellished, and the air of laxity and perfect contempt of all consequences, with which the delusions of passion and the approaches of crime are treated, it might be put into the hands of youth as a moral warning to guard against the first approaches (the only approaches that can be guarded against) of irregular desires, and that sophistry of sentiment by which our impurest wishes and designs are frequently veiled and disguised even from our very selves, till the moment when their gratification seems within our reach.

[1] Champ, 25 July and 1 August 1819.

Thelwall is deliberately sparing of quotation for fear of ministering to the passion he condemns. On the other hand, he finds the literary critical and the political observations interspersed in the story more to be commended than censured,

> though, in those parts which affect to be critical, the wantonness of wit is sometimes more apparent than the sedateness of impartial judgment; and tho' the politics occasionally savour more of caustic misanthropy than of the ardent patriotic enthusiasm which constitutes, in our estimation, the charm of that subject.

Thelwall ends his review of *I* by admiring the pathos of ccxv ('No more—no more—Oh! never more, my heart, . . .') as a lament over 'the blighted sensibilities of youth'.

Thelwall's review of *II* opens with an interesting passage in which he distinguishes between the 'characteristics' of *I* and *II*, while condemning their common moral 'character'. Both were marked by 'the same unfeeling contempt—we should rather say *indifference*, of all that the social heart should hold in reverence'. The differences were 'complectional and circumstantial'. Canto I exhibited 'the juvenility of the conception, as well as of the hero', and played and sported like a satyr through the 'dawning vices' which it exhibited and almost recommended. In *II* the '*feeling*' became 'deeper and more mature':

> so far, at least, as the term can be considered as applicable to the composition of an author to whom the intensity of power seems a much more darling attribute than the vitality of emotion.

And Thelwall goes on to generalize that it was 'the fault' of all Byron's works that they were 'rather deliberations of the intellect than effusions of the heart' (an unusual point of some interest, somewhat reminiscent of *The British Critic*'s remarks mentioned on p. 61 above), and that they appealed 'to the grosser appetites more than to the passions' (a commoner point, though one which a number of critics would not have accepted). Thelwall supports this last point as follows:

> He has handled subjects, or rather described scenes, repeatedly, and brought them before us in all the vividness of imagination, which in the management of writers very inferior to him in descriptive power would have excited the most affecting sympathies: and yet—who ever shed a tear over the works of Lord Byron?

Thelwall offers a fairly usual explanation of the phenomenon he implies:

> One of the causes of this undoubtedly is that the characters he delineates are never such as can excite any *moral* sympathy:—there is nothing about them which, speaking as moral agents, we can esteem and love.

Thelwall recounts the scene at sea, for the most part without comment, but confesses himself shocked by the 'levity' of the remark on the carpenter's reference (xliii, 7–8) to his having a wife and children—

> Two things for dying people quite bewildering.

It was, Thelwall thought, 'to say the best of it, in deplorably bad taste'; and there was plenty more of the same sort of thing to come. On the other hand, Thelwall much admired the 'rare passage of unmingled pathos' on the two fathers (lxxxvii–xc). Thelwall leaves only little space to refer to the Haidée amour,

> commencing on the side of the heroine, at least, in the most amiable sympathy, indulged, on her part, with the most artless tenderness, and described by the poet with all the seductive voluptuousness in which he so unscrupulously delights to luxuriate.

On Shelley

The Champion printed in December 1821 a short explanation of why Shelley's 'poetical merits' had 'never been duly appreciated by the public'. This was signed 'J.W.', who has not yet been identified. The explanation offered is 'unintelligibility'.[1]

On Keats

It is, however, for its two appreciations of Keats that *The Champion* is most noteworthy. Keats's friend John Hamilton Reynolds ably reviewed the 1817 *Poems*.[2] *The Champion* also reviewed *Endymion*, and the reviewer *may* again have been Reynolds. This is also, in any case, a gifted and appreciative review.[3]

[1] *Champ*, 23 December 1821. This brief article is referred to on p. 312, n. 4 below.
[2] *Champ*, 9 March 1817. An extract appears on pp. 451–2 below.
[3] *Champ*, 7 June 1818. An extract appears below on pp. 465–7.

THE LITERARY GAZETTE
On Byron

The Literary Gazette paid pretty continuous attention to Byron and his work from March 1817 until long after his death in 1824. During his lifetime it printed about forty pieces, mainly about his poems. So rigid selection is here imperative.

A Letter 'On the Poetical Style of Lord Byron'[1] compares him interestingly with Dante:

> Both poets possess the same intensity of passion and force of thought, the same neglect of grace, the same reiteration of stroke upon stroke, which produces in the aggregate, the effect of sublimity, and the same power of conveying all that is horrible and grand, through the medium of emotion rather than of description.

But the writer thought Byron careless about diction. His style failed in 'glowing combinations of words, nervous terseness of sentences, harmony, adequacy, magnificence'. He had clearly the 'mind' of a great poet, but denied himself 'the benefit which he might derive from the art of poetry'.

After a less interesting essay on the general nature of Byron's poetry, and reviews of *Manfred* and *Tasso*, *The Literary Gazette* welcomed *Beppo* warmly.[2] The reviewer thought it by 'our amusing companion *Whistlecraft*[3] again, under a new banner'. The reviewer

---

[1] *LG*, 29 March 1817. [2] *LG*, 14 March 1818.

[3] John Hookham Frere (1769–1846), a very talented literary amateur, who wrote while at Eton for *The Microcosm*, later became a Fellow of Gonville and Caius College, Cambridge, entered the Foreign Office, was elected M.P. for West Looe, and collaborated in *The Anti-Jacobin* with his friend since Eton days, George Canning, whom he succeeded in 1799 as Under-Secretary of State in the Foreign Office. He was British envoy at Lisbon from 1800 to 1802, at Madrid for the next two years, and minister to the Spanish Junta in 1808–9. His meteoric political and diplomatic career came to an abrupt and final end in 1809, when he was recalled for having given what was considered bad advice to Sir John Moore, which resulted in the calamitous retreat to Corunna. Frere married in 1816, and settled in Malta in 1818. He died there in 1846. In *Whistlecraft* Frere was imitating Pulci's *Il Morgante Maggiore* (1481). In *Beppo* Byron was, as he frankly avowed, imitating *Whistlecraft*, though he later not only *read* Pulci's celebrated poem, but eventually translated its first canto. Byron thought of dedicating *Beppo* to Frere, with whom he had been on friendly terms for some years, but he decided against this because of the wide divergence of Frere's outlook on political and social problems from his own. Frere's poem was, of course, a seminal influence on Byron in his adoption of this new style.

calls the poet 'a perfect knight-errant of Parnassus'. He praises the characterization, the description of the office of *Cavalier Servente* (xxxvi–xl), and of the 'soft climate, and language, and females of Italy'; but selects for quotation 'the originally drawn contrast of our native land' (xlvii–xlix). The tale he considered 'nothing but a pretext for the whimsical illustrations appended to it'. He relished the 'vivacity' of the description of the Ridotto (lviii ff.), the satire on 'Christian literary ladies' in contrast with the "poor dear Mussulwomen" (lxx ff.), and the 'deuce of a hit' (lxxv–lxxvi) at the "would-be wits and can't-be gentlemen" (lxxvi. 6) of whom 'so many buz about our great Metropolis'. The dénouement of the 'strange event*less* history' the reviewer found 'as comic as the tale is sprightly', and the poem as a whole 'exquisite of its kind',

> the disporting of a genius which could do more if it wished, but which, even in its careless mood, shews that not only the easy, but the excellent of poetry, is within its scope, and that the most *spirituel* touches may be combined with the shrewdest observation of men and manners.

As 'a mere jeu d'esprit' it was 'admirable', but it stood 'almost at the top of a style of writing with which England is not the most familiar—that of ingenious and playful satire'.

The reviewer of *Childe Harold IV*[1] found the canto bewildering in its transitions from place to place, and from poet to pilgrim, to Hobhouse, to politics, and back to the poet, though his imagination was 'delighted by the sweet medium through which all this confusion' was 'carried on'. He did not care for the 'strange' dedication, with its 'egotism' and 'flattery', and was outraged by its 'abominable slanders' against England. In the poem itself he did not much like the odd intrusions of facetiousness. Unexpectedly, and unlike many critics, however, he apparently admired the poet's digressions on himself (*e.g.*, viii–x), 'a subject on which he is always impassioned and interesting'; though he somewhat narrow-mindedly disapproved of the running-on of stanzas. Italy he thought 'finely painted' in xxvi–xxviii, with 'a freshness' which placed Byron 'by the side of our best descriptive poet' (who, one might ask?) 'in a rather unusual line' (a cryptic phrase). The 'notices' on Tasso and other topics in xxxix–lxv he found too 'desultory', and thought them not 'possessed of that felicity or force which is so often found in Lord Byron's writings'. The

---

[1] *LG*, 2 May 1818.

'apostrophe to the Venus' (li–liii) he even thought partly 'ludicrous'. But he admired the 'spirited' description of the cataract of Velino (lxix–lxxii). He thought the address to Rome (lxxviii ff.) 'among the most beautiful parts of the poem', though it had not 'that extreme depth of pathos' to be found in some of Byron's earlier poems, and which Rome seemed 'so well calculated to have excited'. The review quotes the Napoleon passage (lxxxix–xcii) 'more for the curiosity of the matter than for either poetry or merit'. The reviewer then returns to the question of the comparative value of this and the preceding cantos, and generalizes his impression that this canto was less good. Though 'often poetical', it never offered 'those striking thoughts' and 'sublime effusions which in the author's former works have produced so striking an impression, that, once read, they were never forgotten'. The canto seemed 'more like the unwilling task of winding up, than the strong inspiration of a new passion'. There were not even many remarkably felicitous expressions which one could wish to quote. But the reviewer praises the bold apostrophe to man

> Thou pendulum betwixt a smile and tear (cix. 3)

and stanzas cxix–cxxv on love, and finds 'much poetry, though very unequal' in the lines on the ocean (clxxix–clxxxiv). The lament on Princess Charlotte he also found 'beautiful', though 'misplaced'. Stanzas cxxx–cxxxv contained 'a degree of anguish and asperity' that told 'only too plainly' the 'unenviable state' of Byron's mind. His 'gall and soreness of spirit' were almost obviously 'much the effect of a heated imagination'. On the other hand the reviewer quotes the stanza "There is a pleasure in the pathless woods" (clxxviii) as 'a stanza which breathes as true a poetic feeling as any in the volume'. But he goes on to censure some false quantities, 'as fit for correction in the poem which a Byron holds forth as the most elaborate of his productions'. The reviewer thought that the 'polishing' had not done the canto any good. It had the 'heat' but wanted the 'fire' of its predecessors. It was 'excellent', but no passage bore 'the magic stamp of immortal genius'.

It is interesting, in view of subsequent developments, to find *The Literary Gazette* praising *Don Juan I*[1] as 'an exceedingly clever and entertaining poem', and calling it 'witty if a little licentious, and delightful if not very moral'. The reviewer liked the description of Donna Julia, and the 'charming hit' at Platonic attachments,

[1] *LG*, 17 July 1819.

but objected to the 'profane parody, in which some of our modern bards are *roasted*' (*I.* ccv–ccvi). The poet was evidently loose in religious principles, and social morality, yet 'even when we blame the too great laxity of the poet, we cannot but feel high admiration of his talent'.

The Literary Gazette gave a very full review to *Don Juan II*,[1] which it thought to contain 'more of powerful and genuine poetry' than Canto I. The reviewer makes one of the most perceptive comments of the period on the storm scene:

> In painting the strife of the elements, and the agonies of famine driven by despair to cannibalism, the author puts forth his genius, and commands our souls. We might object to the touches of the ludicrous in these parts, but Voltaire and others, the greatest wits and satirists of all ages have set the example of considering this 'great globe itself', as the theatre of farce, in which human miseries, vices and crimes, are to be laughed at like human follies.

The reviewer also praises the poet's grip on language, and texture:

> Never was English fastened into more luxuriant stanzas than in *Don Juan*. Like the dolphin sporting in its native waves, at every turn, however grotesque, displaying a new hue and a new beauty, the noble author has shown an absolute control over his means, and at every cadence, rhyme or construction, however whimsical, delighted us with novel and magical associations.

After having said that the tale of the shipwreck was 'exquisitely told', however, when the reviewer comes to consider the bleeding to death and eating of Pedrillo (lxxv–lxxviii) he seems to go back somewhat on his generous attitude to the intermixture of pathos and farce. On the other hand, he is strongly impressed by the scene of the two fathers (lxxxvii–xc), and the 'cruel force' with which their afflictions are portrayed. He also praises the description of Haidée's morning visit to Juan (cxlii ff.) as 'one of the finest passages in the poem'; but Byron's treatment of the 'consummation' of this 'amour' contained 'so little of principle' and 'so much of poetry' that the reviewer was at a loss whether to quote. Summing up, he laments the excessive licentiousness of the poem, while praising its interest and power, commenting:

> In ribaldry, he is exceeded, and in drollery (though he is often extremely amusing) surpassed by many writers who have had their

[1] *LG*, 24 July 1819.

day and sunk into oblivion; but in highly-wrought interest, and overwhelming passion, he is himself alone. Here is the basis of his fame, and we could wish that the structure stood uncontaminated with that levity and pruriency which the less scrupulous may laugh at to-day, but which has no claim to the applause of judicious or moral contemporaries, or of impartial posterity.

This review, despite some inconsistency, offers a worth-while, first-hand response to the canto.

Early in 1821 Alaric Watts wrote several interesting articles called 'Lord Byron's Plagiarisms',[1] showing in detail the sources of some of Byron's specific thoughts and lines, in Mme de Staël, Young, Moore, Mrs Radcliffe, Sotheby,[2] Scott, Ossian, and Campbell.

In August 1821 came a review of *Don Juan III–V*.[3] *The Literary Gazette* thought these cantos inferior to *I* and *II*. The 'beauties' were less 'prominent', and the 'obscenity' more 'depraved'— 'devoid of that glow of nature which almost redeemed the earlier loves of the hero'. The reviewer did, however, find the description of Lambro's homecoming (*IV*. xxxv ff.) amusing, and was enchanted by 'The Isles of Greece', which he quotes entire. He also notes the 'mixture of devotion' in the poem, as if Byron had been 'half persuaded to turn Christian' (he cites the Ave Maria passage (*III*. ci–ciii) with high praise). In general, however, *III–V* showed a 'falling-off', 'not only as regards the interest of the tale, but also the poignancy of the humour, and the beauty of the composition'.

When *The Liberal I* appeared (with *The Vision of Judgment* as its pièce de résistance), *The Literary Gazette* gave it a hostile reception.[4] It launched a withering attack on the whole idea of the periodical, and commented particularly on Byron's part in it:

We knew that upon occasion Lord Byron could endite exceedingly stupid tragedies, and even bad poems; but we never imagined he could fall so miserably low as he does in his share of this wretched periodical.

[1] *LG*, 24 February, 3, 10, 17 March 1821.

[2] William Sotheby (1757–1833) was a rich and tolerably gifted literary amateur who wrote a great deal of verse, and who entertained many of the principal authors of the day, and encouraged a number of young writers, including Coleridge. He is remembered chiefly for his translations of Virgil and Wieland, which were highly acclaimed at the time by Jeffrey and Wilson. There is evidence that Keats was much influenced by the translation of Wieland's *Oberon*. See W. W. Beyer, *Keats and the Daemon King* (New York; London, 1947).

[3] *LG*, 11, 18 August 1821.   [4] *LG*, 19, 26 October, 2 November 1822.

The whole review is quite strongly written, and expresses utter disgust and loathing at *The Vision of Judgment*, contempt for its humour (except for a few lines on Southey), and also for the epigrams on Castlereagh published in the same number.

The Literary Gazette regarded *Don Juan VI–VIII* as again poorer than earlier cantos.[1] It took particular exception to *VI*:

> We would even for a moment allow that the theme of *VI* was approachable with any thing like the noble sentiments of a man, instead of being, as it is, the gloating brutality of a wretched debauchee; and then, we would ask, what *man* would choose to wallow in the stye of his own luxury, in words and in description, like a drivelling dotard; and how any one could fancy that the ideas on such affairs were communicable to others, so as to excite a single agreeable emotion? . . . We are thus only arguing the question as a matter of taste: as a moral vomit we shall leave it untouched, between the author and a sickened public. . . .

As a composition the poem was 'seldom above doggrel', and in moral and religious respects it was 'still more offensive' than what had gone before:

> The most obscene allusions are unblushingly hazarded, and indeed defended (on the authority of Voltaire); the most sacred subjects are sedulously sought for profane illustrations; and the whole presents a picture of such gross and grovelling sensuality, as to be more fit for beast than man,—putting civilisation and Christianity, where they are with the author, out of the question.

VII–VIII were mere paraphrases of the French *Histoire de la Nouvelle Russie* in 'indifferent verse'. The subject suited Byron admirably:

> for it admits of that happy jesting with misery, which tends to harden the heart; that hellish laughter amid slaughter and horror, which is so peculiarly the forte of the noble Bard.

On Cantos *IX–XI The Literary Gazette* became more violent than ever.[2] Byron, the plagiarist, had this time borrowed 'the scurrilous trash of the lowest factious newspapers', and he had done it 'so vilely' that, in the reviewer's opinion, he could not really be sane:

> The whole conception is so utterly contemptible and insolent, so disgustingly vulgar and obscene, so wandering in a metaphysical

[1] *LG*, 19 July 1823.   [2] *LG*, 6 September 1823.

162

cloud of scepticism, and so destitute of any thing like a comprehensive or correct idea, so pointless and unpoetical, that it seems impossible that Lord Byron, fallen as we have seen him, can be at the same time in his senses and the author. This opinion is calculated to soften criticism.

The whole production was a 'farrago of vice, of drivelling sensuality, of brutal insensibility and of worthless poetry'. It would 'debase a felon and disgrace a dungeon'. 'Never was there such an insult offered to the understandings and good feelings of mankind.'

On the other hand, Cantos XII–XIV seemed to *The Literary Gazette* to show a distinct improvement.[1] They were not so good as *I–II*, but they were better than the rest, and they certainly exhibited 'a knowledge of life and nature', and were written 'in a sportive, satirical vein' which rendered them 'very entertaining':

> There are many pretty passages, though springing up as it were accidentally, like wallflowers among ruins of rubbish; and the whole smells of the school of Democritus in a pleasant way, laughing not without philosophy, and ridiculing in a spirit which blends playfulness with acute observation. There is thus an absence (ever to be hoped for in his writings!) of those bitter and misanthropic feelings which have made the name of Byron almost a synonyme with Timon. . . .

The reviewer praised the description of Norman Abbey and of those assembled there (*XIII*. lv ff.). These characters were 'from life', for they were 'distinct and peculiar'. Byron's 'flings at England's manners' were 'a little too loose', but 'not offensively so'. There was some poor punning, but the better passages showed his 'talents for raillery and jest in a more advantageous light' than any in which these had recently appeared.

Four months later, however, *The Literary Gazette* condemned the next two Cantos (*XV–XVI*) as so inferior at their best to the worst of the bad cantos that it was inclined to believe them by some imitator.[2] It prints the first ten stanzas as prose, and claims that they absolve the reviewer from 'the task of critical condemnation':

> It is indeed surprising that any person could be so blind as to utter such trash, and that too with an air of unbounded egotistical satisfaction! Vanity, trite reflections upon marriage, his Lady, himself,

[1] *LG*, 6 December 1823. [2] *LG*, 3 April 1824.

—themes of which every one is sick, except the writer,—make up this contemptible publication; in which the versification is worthy of the sense,—if we may prostitute both words, for miserable doggrel and empty nothings.

Yet six weeks later *The Literary Gazette* printed an announcement of Byron's death in handsomely admiring terms.[1]

The Literary Gazette's criticisms, though violent, are by no means wholly unjust. The moral and religious strictures spring from a legitimate point of view, and though the reviews are sometimes blind to the aesthetic merits of the poetry, they are not always so. The reviewer has sometimes been genuinely amused by wit, or moved by pathos. Yet moral and religious considerations generally prevent him from relishing the bitter satire, and, indeed, the reviews show little inclination to grant Byron the privileges of satire in any but the most general form.

On Shelley

The Literary Gazette was throughout deliberately hostile to Shelley. It was outraged by *The Cenci*,[2] describing it as 'the most abominable' 'of all the abominations which intellectual perversion, and poetical atheism, have produced in our times':

> We protest most solemnly, that when we reached the last page of this play, our minds were so impressed with its odious and infernal character, that we could not believe it to be written by a mortal being for the gratification of his fellow-creatures on this earth: it seemed to be the production of a fiend, and calculated for the entertainment of devils in hell.

The Literary Gazette's review of *Prometheus*[3] attacked it as 'unintelligible', and 'little else but absolute raving':

> Were we not assured to the contrary, we should take it for granted that the author was lunatic—as his principles are ludicrously wicked, and his poetry a melange of nonsense, cockneyism, poverty, and pedantry.

Getting down to details, the reviewer ridicules the description of Prometheus as "*nailed*" to an icy rock by "*chains*" of "*burning cold*"; and detects 'the chief secret of Mr Shelley's poetry' to be 'merely opposition of words, phrases, and sentiments, so violent as to be utter nonsense', *e.g.*, in I. 62–9 'the vibrations of stagnant

[1] *LG*, 15 May 1824. [2] *LG*, 1 April 1820. [3] *LG*, 9 September 1820.

springs, and their creeping shuddering;—the swift moveless (*i.e.*, motionless) whirlwinds, on poised wings, which hung mute over a hushed abyss as thunder louder than their own!!' On the last point the reviewer inadvertently or deliberately misrepresents Shelley by leaving out of account the five succeeding words, but there is some justice in the other strictures. Another line of attack here is on Shelley's 'fancy, that by bestowing *colouring* epithets on every thing he mentions, he thereby renders his diction and descriptions vividly poetical'. The reviewer quotes II. i. 13–27 to illustrate 'the ridiculous extent to which the folly is wrought'. 'Surely', he suggests, 'the author looks at nature through a prism instead of spectacles.' 'Next to his colorific powers', the reviewer continues, 'we may rank the author's talent for manufacturing "villainous compounds", as in the description of "Mist" in II. iii. 19–36.' The reviewer goes on to single out II. iv. 2–5, in which Shelley seemed to him to be trying to outdo his admired Milton's 'darkness visible':

> I see a *mighty darkness*
> Filling the seat of power, and *rays* of *gloom*
> Dart round, as *light* from the *meridian sun*
> *Ungazed* upon and *shapeless*—
>
> (reviewer's layout, italics, and punctuation)

The reviewer comments:

> We yield ourselves, miserable hum-drum devils that we are, to this high imaginative faculty of the modern muse. We acknowledge that hyperbola, extravagance, and irreconcileable terms, may be poetry. We admit that common sense has nothing to do with 'the beautiful idealisms' of Mr. Shelley. And we only add, that if this be genuine inspiration, and not the grossest absurdity, then is farce sublime, and maniacal raving the perfection of reasoning: then were all the bards of other times, Homer, Virgil, Horace, drivellers; for their foundations were laid no lower than the capacities of the herd of mankind; and even their noblest elevations were susceptible of appreciation by the very multitude among the Greeks and Romans.

He goes on to dismiss as 'insane stuff' the 'astronomical notions' of IV. iv. 238–61; and the critique continues with 'a sample of the adjectives in this poem to prove the writer's condign abhorrence of any relation between that part of speech and substantives: sleep-unsheltered hours; gentle darkness; horny eyes; keen faint eyes; faint wings; fading waves; crawling glaciers, toads, agony, time, etc.; belated and noontide plumes; milky arms; many-folded mountains; a lake-surrounding flute; veiled lightening asleep (as well as hovering); unbewailing flowers; odour-faded blooms; semi-vital worms; windless pools, windless abodes, and windless air; unerasing waves; unpavilioned skies; rivetted wounds; and void abysms.' Some of these combinations are, indeed, hard to take—*e.g.*, 'sleep-unsheltered hours', 'odour-faded blooms'—but others—*e.g.*, 'crawling glaciers', 'windless pools', 'many-folded mountains'—which would now be readily accepted, demanded a more freely ranging imagination than the reviewer, in common with many other readers of the time, seems to have possessed. The reviewer, however, then fires a summary broadside, and the review is virtually at an end:

> After our quotations, we need not say that the verse is without measure, proportions, or elegance; that the similes are numberless and wholly inapplicable; and that the instances of ludicrous nonsense are not fewer than the pages of the Drama.

The only other important review of Shelley in *The Literary Gazette* is that of *Adonais*.[1] This decries the pretensions of Keats, and castigates the poem as 'fifty-five stanzas, which are, to our seeing, altogether unconnected, interjectional, and nonsensical'. The reviewer also attacks the poem as blasphemous, and as poetically '*contemptible*'; but comments that fortunately it could have 'little circulation in Britain'. Once again the detailed criticisms on aesthetic grounds are of mixed validity, some appealing by their common sense, others unconvincing in their lack of fancy or imagination. As to the religious and moral strictures, our attitude to them will, or should, depend largely on our attitude to life and the world, and so to Shelley's beliefs.

On Keats

As to Keats, *The Literary Gazette* did not review any of his three volumes. Its contemptuous view of his work, however, comes out clearly in the review of *Adonais*.

* * * *

The periodical criticism is far and away the most important record we have of the critical opinions of that time about the work of our three poets. It is only exceptionally that we find in extant cor-

---

[1] *LG*, 8 December 1821. A substantial extract appears on pp. 377–81 below.

respondence, diaries, reminiscences, or records of conversation, anything but the most cursory expressions of critical response. There are one or two sets of lectures or short books in which items of interest occur, but that is all. Reference will be made to some items of this non-periodical criticism in the short accounts of the contemporary criticism of each poet given below.

Despite the absence of recorded critical response, however, it seems quite clear that a good deal of the work of Byron, and of Shelley's work at least *Queen Mab*, had a great number of readers. Apart from Byron's aristocratic and well-to-do middle-class readers, he had evidently a large audience among the poorer classes. A considerable number of pirated editions of most of his poems were printed during our period, and this continued for some time afterwards. Some of his poems, chiefly lyrics, were also printed in *The Mirror of Literature*, which was started in 1823 as a literary periodical for the poorer classes, and which had a regular circulation of 80,000 copies a week.[1] *The Mirror* also occasionally quoted some of Shelley's poetry, but never the radical passages, thus avoiding the Newspaper Stamp Tax, which was designed to discourage political and religious radicalism in working-class journals. Three pirated editions of *Queen Mab* were, however, brought out before 1824, and the radical Press continued to print this and other work by Shelley, and items concerning him, long after our period.[2]

IV

Some Generalizations and Comparisons

In general terms, on the basis of the criticism surveyed and collected in this volume, what can we say that the critics liked and disliked about the work of each of the three poets, and what significant comparisons can be made between the reception which the work of each was accorded?

[1] This and connected matters are treated by Dr Walker, *op. cit.*, 102–13. See also Louis James, *Fiction for the Working Man* (London, 1963).
[2] N. I. White, *Shelley*, II, 405–8.

At the highest level of generality it is probably true to say that the adverse criticisms of Keats were predominantly aesthetic, whereas the adverse criticisms of Byron and Shelley were predominantly extra-aesthetic. Again, Byron was less criticized on aesthetic grounds than was Shelley. This is understandable, since his style was far clearer, and also far closer to the eighteenth-century styles with which the general run of critics were most familiar and most sympathetic. On the other hand, Shelley was criticized almost as much on aesthetic grounds as Keats, though the grounds were different, the stress being chiefly on Shelley's unintelligibility and on Keats's affectation.

Let us now, however, descend a short way from these heights of generality, and consider first, more specifically, the extra-aesthetic grounds on which the three poets were attacked. Byron and Shelley were both assailed on religious, political, and moral grounds, Keats scarcely ever on religious grounds, only occasionally on political grounds (except on account of his known association with Leigh Hunt), but often on moral grounds, especially for the sexual self-indulgence of his poetry—and that even by Byron!

The religious attacks on Byron and Shelley were not, however, wholly similar. Shelley was often attacked for his deliberate and systematic attempt to undermine ecclesiastical Christianity, and also for what was considered to be his atheism, whereas Byron was attacked for what appeared to be lack of faith and sometimes even scepticism on some central points of doctrine, such as immortality, and eternal rewards and punishments, for profanity and jesting blasphemy, and for the pessimistic and even nihilistic attitudes to the world and to sacred human aspirations and feelings which showed him to be devoid of proper religious convictions. The power of his poetry made all this, in the view of his assailants, dangerous for readers.

In the political field the main criticisms of Byron's poetry were directed at his radicalism, his lack of patriotism, his failure to distinguish between just and unjust wars, his scorn for Wellington, his attitude to Napoleon (which to conservatives seemed too favourable, and to Hazlitt not favourable enough), and his vicious onslaughts on George III and Castlereagh after their deaths. Shelley too was attacked for his radicalism, and more fiercely, since he was recognized to be a doctrinaire exponent of such doctrines of the French Revolution as classless equality, world citizenship, and the abolition of private property, monarchy, and ecclesiastical hierarchy.

The greatest array of criticisms of Byron werc, howcvcr, on moral grounds. The characteristics attacked were very various. Against his earlier work one of the chief points urged was that it was misanthropic, and the same kind of criticism was levelled, in other forms, against *Don Juan*. Another criticism of his earlier work (and this was seldom made about the later work) was that it was egotistical. Again, Byron's attempts to make criminal or unsavoury characters attractive through their energy and courage were another subject for moral censure. His criticisms of women and of the marriage tie were also frequently reprehended. And so, though more occasionally, were his parading of personal griefs, and his vicious attacks on his wife. Another recurrent objection to the earlier work, already mentioned—namely, that it expressed too gloomy and despairing a view of life—was some-times given a moral slant, and explained by some critics as an attitude naturally resulting from sated sensuality. Other critics, including such shrewd men as Lockhart and John Scott, thought of it as savouring of 'humbug' or 'feelings of ceremony', as they respectively and typically put it. When Byron had passed into his Italian burlesque phase some of the most frequent moral stric-tures concerned salaciousness, attacks on the virtue of chastity, general cynicism, and cold-blooded facetiousness. These two last criticisms sometimes take the form of resentment at his habit of joking at human misery, and flinging back laughter at the reader's sympathy. Even Leigh Hunt was willing to allow that this sort of criticism had some validity. Some critics even debited Byron with an intention to corrupt the youth of the country.

The kinds of moral attack that were made on Shelley's work were generally rather different. He was only occasionally accused of misanthropy or of egotism, though he was often accused of self-assurance. Nor was he criticized for trying to make criminals or unsavoury people seem attractive. Some critics even objected that he made Count Cenci appear far worse than anyone could possibly have been. Nor did Shelley seem to the critics to be unfair to women. On the other hand, he was seen as an apostle of free love, and even a defender of incest, and for these positions he was, indeed, violently assailed. In this and other matters Shelley's general ideas seemed to threaten the social institutions on which the very existence of morality appeared to depend, and this

169

outraged his attackers. Again, unlike Byron, Shelley did not seem to the critics (except in *The Cenci*) to express an attitude of cynicism or despair. If anything, he seemed to them to have too trusting a faith in what human beings would be likely to do if they were not carefully controlled by strong and firm institutions. On the other hand, he did seem to a number of critics to have shown— particularly in *The Cenci* but also at times elsewhere—an unhealthy penchant for wallowing in horrors. On the whole, however, it was Shelley's intellectual convictions, rather than his imagery or the moods he expressed or depicted or the characters he portrayed, that revolted moral opinion.

As for Keats, the chief moral condemnations he incurred were for vanity, pretentiousness, and pruriency; though most of the reviews of his work are virtually or even entirely free from moral strictures. Apart from these criticisms, however, Keats was warned by Conder in his review of the 1817 *Poems* that the true dignity of poetry lay in being 'a vehicle for noble thoughts and feelings'— that aesthetic merit, even if achieved, would not be enough.

As for aesthetic criticisms themselves, Byron was subjected to less of these than the other two poets. Fault was occasionally found with *Childe Harold* for lack of unity, and the same kind of criticism was made against *Don Juan*. Monotony of subject was more often the accusation levelled against the earlier poems, especially in connexion with the moral stricture against egotism. The characters of the tales were sometimes ridiculed as inconsistent, or even as virtually unreal. The word 'doggerel' was sometimes fired against the verse of *Don Juan*. A few somewhat insensitive or disingenuous critics thought or affected to think that the *Don* was 'dull', but the falsity of this criticism was transparent. Even taking this perverted attack into account, however, the quantum of aesthetic strictures against Byron's work was remarkably small. The vast majority of the adverse comments on it were religious, political, or moral.

Aesthetic criticisms of Shelley were mainly for obscurity, vagueness, unintelligibility, nonsense, confusion, incongruity, extravagance, wildness, and ridiculous 'sublimity'. Sometimes it was admitted that the words and images he used were often admirable, sometimes even brilliant, in themselves, but uncoordinated and confused in combination. His poetic talents were often recognized in such attacks, but considered to be wasted through lack of discipline. Other main charges were that his

170

subjects were remote and lacking in human interest, and that he was too inclined to indulge in metaphysics. He was also sometimes censured for monotony of imagery and for vagaries of versification.

Keats was also attacked for unintelligibility, and for loose versification; and his attackers did not so often recognize transcendent talent. The most violent attacks on Keats, moreover, showed contempt for the ignorance and lack of education shown in his work, particularly in *Endymion*; and these critics regarded him as a mere unskilful imitator, whose slipshod versification and rhymes, and outrageous word-coinages and linguistic affectations, were merely derivative (and poorly derivative at that) from the upstart, vulgar, and ignorant Hunt. It is also interesting to find the term 'laborious' occurring as a black mark for Keats. There is a sense that some of his critics thought that he was *working hard* to be original; and this one seldom finds in criticism of Shelley, though curiously enough the *Quarterly* review of *Prometheus* uses the very same term 'laborious' about that poem. Keats's ignorance comes in for particular criticism in regard to his treatment of Greek mythology. The classical scholars were not willing to have their legends played about with by a young man so uninitiated as Johnny Keats. Again, the prolixity and 'interminable wanderings' of *Endymion*, though forgiven by some critics, were too much for others. The mere thought of them was enough to prevent Peacock from accepting Shelley's advice to read *Hyperion*! By his adverse critics Keats was certainly credited with far less poetic talent than either Byron or Shelley were by theirs.

It is time, however, to turn to the positive side, and summarize what the poets were praised for.

In the religious sphere not much was said in Byron's favour. Even *The Examiner* and *Literary Examiner* did not go further than to defend *Don Juan*, not very convincingly, as 'not profane', and to appreciate the 'deep sceptical ponderings' of that poem. Byron had not evolved a firmly conceived religion of benevolence like that which Shelley offered as a desirable alternative to a religion of faith.

Shelley's kind of religion, on the other hand, commanded Hunt's enthusiastic support; and Hunt was not entirely alone among critics, as can be seen from Gold's *London Magazine* and *Knight's Quarterly Magazine*.

On the other hand, the deep though vaguer religious concerns which Keats expressed in some of his work scarcely attracted any comment, and certainly no commendation.

Favourable political comment on Byron's work was by no means infrequent. A good deal came from *The Examiner*, which was outspoken about George III's 'aberration of mind', and his part in causing the American war. *The Literary Examiner*, likewise, praised Byron for cutting loose from his class and declaring 'for the many against the few'. It also praised his anti-war attitude, and his attacks on Great Britain's treatment of Napoleon, and his pungent satire both on the *grand monde* of London, and also on the Ministers and civil servants. Support on political grounds also came from other periodicals, radical and liberal alike, such as *The Monthly Magazine*, Constable's *Edinburgh Magazine*, and *The Champion*. It is noteworthy that, though some of these periodicals (*e.g.*, *The Edinburgh Magazine* and *The Champion*) were not disposed to condone the impiety, blasphemy, ribaldry, and immorality of Byron's work, they all approved in some measure of its political aspects. But *The Edinburgh Magazine* drew the line at the treatment of George III, and distrusted Byron's 'cant' about political hypocrisy.

As to Shelley, he elicited less favourable response from the critics on political grounds than Byron did. Even the very radical *Monthly Magazine* had nothing to say in his favour on that score, even in respect of *Queen Mab*. Shelley was too utopian and revolutionary for some of the practical Radicals, as can be seen from the comments of Hazlitt. Indeed, apart from the political support warmly sustained by Leigh Hunt, and enthusiastically offered by Gold's *London Magazine* in its brief career, the only substantial political backing for Shelley came from purely political writers, in particular Richard Carlile, in his weekly *The Republican* (which, however, was significantly concerned only with *Queen Mab*). There is, on the other hand, evidence that at least that poem did actually acquire a sizeable audience of working-class readers during Shelley's lifetime.

The poetry of Keats only occasionally touched on politics. Where it did so it evoked adverse comment, as from *Blackwood*'s on III. 1–23 of *Endymion*, from *The British Critic* also on the start of Book III of the same poem, and even from John Scott, on the "ledger-men" stanzas in *Isabella*. The comments of the first two were straightforward Tory abuse. The last was friendly advice to Keats to be more realistic, and not to expose himself to just that kind of attack. Keats had, of course, already exposed himself to some opprobrium from several reviewers by the sonnets he had addressed to the radical Leigh Hunt.

As for morality, there was rather little praise for that aspect of Byron's poetry. There was occasional appreciation of the depth of his moral reflections, and an enlightened critic like Lockhart could praise his honesty in *Don Juan*. Byron's satire on hypocrisy evoked some approval. There were also unconvincing defences of *Don Juan* by Hunt against the charge of 'indecency', and Lockhart maintained that the poem was no more licentious than a host of other works, including the moral Richardson's *Pamela*. On the whole, however, moral commendation of Byron's work was distinctly rare.

Interestingly enough, though Shelley's work generally received little praise on moral grounds, it received more than Byron's. A great deal came from Hunt, and it was more positive and more sustained than his moral defences of Byron. He boldly contended that Shelley's gospel of Love as the solution of the world's evils was also Christ's recommendation, and he affirmed his own faith in its practicability. Hunt's thesis was that Shelley was a better Christian than his clerical traducers. The reviewer of *Prometheus* in Gold's *London Magazine* was almost equally laudatory, praising 'the spirit of fresh enthusiasm and of youngest hope' which informed the work, its condemnation of oppression and of retributive justice, and its ideal of the universal reign of Love. His only reservation regarded Shelley's wish for the immediate abolition of restraint and authority. He was entirely unreserved in his 'deep admiration' for the 'spirit of good—of gentleness, humanity, and even of religion' in that work. The same magazine a few months later warmly endorsed Shelley's religion of benevolence, his revolt against intolerance and bigotry, and the moral and political principles following from his position. Shelley's 'noble feelings' were recognized by other critics, such as one writer in *The New Monthly Magazine*, and even Hazlitt was willing to grant Shelley's sincere love of truth, nature, and humanity. The tribute by the writer in *Knight's Quarterly Magazine* is also noteworthy.

And what of Keats? What moral approval of his work was expressed by the critics? Some of the most appreciative reviews concentrate on aesthetic matters, and say very little about morality, but Hunt's review of the 1817 volume does draw attention to the 'warm and social feelings' in the Epistle to Clarke, and praises Keats's conception of "the great end of poesy"; and later Hunt approves of Keats's sympathy with the pleasures of Lamia, and admires the deep thought of *Hyperion*, shown in its 'sublime moral' and, in general, Keats's 'high feeling of humanity'. The curiously written review in Constable's *Edinburgh Magazine* noticed the 'deep tone of moral energy' in the early volume. Again, Reynolds, in his defence of *Endymion*, contrasts Byron's 'daring selfishness' with Keats's lack of it, praising the 'awe and humility' and even 'deep and almost breathless affection' with which Keats always speaks of and describes nature, and admiring the 'high mind' revealed in Keats's poetry. *The New Monthly Magazine* also notices Keats's lack of egocentricity, and P. G. Patmore commends *Endymion* for the same feature. In each case, however, little time is spent by the critic on such moral characteristics. Jeffrey makes no moral judgments at all, favourable or unfavourable, nor does the reviewer of the 1820 Poems in the *Monthly*. Indeed, even with regard to this last volume there is seldom a whiff of moral commendation from the critics. Besides Hunt's there is a touch or so from Lamb, and John Scott notes the nobility of the last two stanzas of the Nightingale Ode, and the delicacy of the scene in Madeline's bedroom. The moral value of Keats's poetry does not seem to have really come home to the reviewers, or even, in any appreciable measure, to the members of Keats's own circle.

It is now time to turn to aesthetic judgments. Byron's work was praised incomparably more on aesthetic grounds than that of either of the other two poets. It was praised, often time and again, for energy, power, spirit, freedom, boldness of thought and expression, for felicity of diction, and, indeed, prodigious mastery of language, for versatility of style, for accuracy of description, for strength of feeling, for shrewdness, for searching knowledge of human nature, for range of sensibility, for dignity, for pathos, for tenderness, for fire, for originality, for grandeur, for wit, for power to amuse, for ease and command of versification, even for the fascination of the egotism and scorn. Byron was thought and felt to be a great creative force (which indeed he was). His 'genius' was scarcely ever put in doubt, even by those who utterly execrated the uses he made of it. A penetrating critic might on occasion suggest that his gift lay rather in heightening than in inventing or imagining, and rather in eloquence or declamation than in poetry of the highest order, but that was not the general tenor of the critical reception accorded to his work.

As for Shelley, aesthetic eulogies of his work, even when accorded, were far more restricted in range. 'Depth of sentiment', 'grandeur of imagery', and a 'versification remarkably sweet, various, and noble, like the placid playing of a great organ'— these are characteristics of *The Revolt of Islam* singled out by Hunt, and there is a fair amount of praise on all these scores by some critics of Shelley's work. '*Abundance* of poetic imagery and feeling' is an expression used of *The Revolt* by *Blackwood's*. Shelley's range of sensitive response to everything, from colour, sound, and motion, through thought, to the 'heart of man' and the 'spirit of the universe', was also appreciated by Hunt, but it is rare to find such understanding appreciation at that time. John Scott comes nearest to it in his review of *The Cenci*. The *strength* of feeling, and the *strength* of imagination were, however, admired by other critics. Yet the energy of Shelley's poetry was often considered to be fitful, and to degenerate on the one side into bombast and on the other side into dulness. There was also a tendency to treat him as an immature poet, even as late as 1820, and to whisper patronizing words of advice into his ear. At the same age Byron was being treated as a poet at the height of his powers. There was, however, a large measure of agreement as to Shelley's talent as a descriptive poet of a rather imaginative kind. 'Magnificence' and 'sublimity' are also words which recur in criticism of Shelley, especially of *Prometheus*, and that work was admitted to be 'sonorous' even by the *Quarterly* reviewer, who considered a good deal of it to be nonsensical. Shelley's scholarship was also often recognized, even though critics differed about the use he had made of it. Though Shelley did receive a fair quantum of praise, however, there was much more dispute about his poetic genius than about that of Byron. Some thought him sublime, original, richly imaginative. Others thought him unintelligible, absurd in his 'inventions', and jumbled in his imagery. Jeffrey, looking back on Shelley's poetic career, was probably expressing accurately the sense of the critical reception when he called him an 'uncertain genius'.

Those who appreciated Keats's work on aesthetic grounds often praised his rich and powerful imagination, his sparkling fancy, his intensity of feeling, and his fine ear. 'Fresh', 'sensitive', 'graceful', 'delicate', 'natural', 'genuinely simple' are also typical laudatory terms; and 'originality' is a quality emphasized by a number of critics. Keats's close observation of nature, and especially of the 'beautiful' in nature, also drew admiration. Jeffrey's praise of the 'pure poetry' of *Endymion*, and his careful definition of that concept, are noteworthy, and so is his recognition of the high value of Keats's diction. Jeffrey was almost alone in seeing these features of Keats's work in historical perspective, though even Croker admitted Keats's 'powers of language', while condemning what he considered to be his disgraceful abuse of them. Some critics found Keats's treatment of classical mythology lively and original, and, with regard to *Hyperion*, several reviewers praised its 'grandeur', and Byron was not the only reader to compare it in sublimity to Aeschylus. Even some of the earlier work was sometimes found similar to that of classical writers, and it is interesting to find such a sensitive critic as John Scott writing of the Hymn to Pan as 'among the finest specimens of classical poetry in our language'. The Hymn to Pan, indeed, would naturally have appealed to readers who recognized the impassioned element in Greek poetry, and we can imagine the approval which it would eventually have elicited from Nietzsche had he known it. As to the movement and rhythms of Keats's poetry, there was enthusiastic appreciation of their 'variety' from a number of quarters. Some readers were evidently getting tired of what seemed to them the monotonous rhythms of Dryden and Pope, and particularly of their imitators. A few critics also recognized Keats's 'depth of thought', a quality perhaps on the borderline between the aesthetic and the moral. In general, however, the impression received was one of the sensory delight so strongly felt by Jeffrey and expressed by him as 'intoxication of sweetness'.

It is natural to ask what value this large bulk of criticism of the work of our three poets by their contemporaries has for us today; and the question is an especially pertinent one in the case of Keats, on whose poetry a great deal of intensive and valuable work has been done in recent years.

Any adequate answer to this question would obviously need to include an affirmation of the value of that old criticism to the modern historian of literature and literary criticism, and to those readers curious to know how the contemporaries of our three poets received their work. Yet it is necessary to admit that such historians and readers probably only form a small minority of the readers of literature, and of literary criticism, and possibly even of the poetry of Byron, Shelley, and Keats themselves. Any call on the attention of the great majority of readers of our three poets needs to be justified in terms of the permanent critical value of the reactions of those old critics. In this connexion it is noteworthy that a good deal of that criticism is evaluative, as is natural when criticism is directed towards work which has recently appeared. The evaluations are, moreover, most often not simply *pure* evaluations, but *descriptive* evaluations, making explicit or implicit use of specific criteria of value, whether aesthetic, moral, political, or religious. Now, the judgments of this kind, which we find at thousands of points in the texture of this old critical work, can often perform the valuable service of indicating to us that we could, and possibly should, also take serious account of some of those criteria in clarifying our own attitudes to the work of the poet concerned. When Scott rates Byron for his attitude to Waterloo, for instance, may this not act upon us as a salutary admonition to take more seriously aspects of Byron's work which were for the poet himself matters of burning concern, and which we may only neglect at the cost of rendering our critical attitude to the work regrettably superficial? A fair amount of that old criticism, indeed, engaged with the work under consideration as a matter of contemporary concern, whether in relation to religion, morals, politics, or literary currents and cross-currents; and what was of contemporary concern to them is sometimes of equal concern to us today. Shelley's radicalism is not a dead letter; nor are the types of reaction to it, *pro* and *contra*, which we find expressed in the contemporary reviews of his work.

It is certainly true, on the other hand, that modern criticism of our three poets offers kinds of insight not available to their contemporary critics. Research into such matters as literary, philosophical, and extra-literary artistic influences, the contemporary social, economic, and intellectual background, the lives and letters of the poets, the relations between various parts of the whole corpus of their poetic and other work, and finally (and perhaps most important of all) intensive study of the poems themselves, have enabled critics to arrive at new or more extensive interpretations of the works concerned, and fresh descriptions of the poetic output of the poets. All this has also contributed to changes in evaluation, which no doubt also owe much to the

177

complicated changes of attitude towards life and the world which have occurred in the last century and a half. Certainly a higher moral and a higher aesthetic value are now set upon the poetry of Keats than were generally accorded to it by almost all his contemporary critics. On the other hand, *Childe Harold* has now come to be underestimated, and Byron in general to be less highly valued on aesthetic grounds except for the 'comic' poems, whose aesthetic qualities are themselves more highly valued than during his lifetime; while religious, moral, and political considerations now scarcely come into critical consideration at all, and thus some awkward and even potentially disturbing problems about Byron's poetry are neglected. The work of Shelley, in contradistinction to that of the other two poets, is probably now given a valuation as mixed as that arrived at by his contemporary critics; yet again, whereas with them the criteria involved were religious, moral, political, and aesthetic, with us the considerations are largely aesthetic. The result is certainly some impoverishment of our criticism, which may be in danger of falling—not only in the case of Byron, Shelley, and Keats, but more generally, and especially in regard to the work of poets of the past—into what Nietzsche perceptively called 'Alexandrianism'. A good draught of the criticism of the work of our three poets by their contemporaries may help us to correct this tendency and to avoid that pitfall in our own critical reflections, not only on these three poets but on other work with which we may be confronted in the course of our reading.

George Gordon, Lord Byron
(1788–1824)

A Survey of Contemporary Criticism
1807–24

Byron published his first volume of poems, *Hours of Idleness* (1807), when he was nineteen. It was widely reviewed, and generally well received. More important, however, it met with facetious contempt in *The Edinburgh Review*[1]; for it was this critique that evoked Byron's vigorous counterblast in 1809, *English Bards and Scotch Reviewers*. Here Byron gave rein to his talent for satire, which had already been noticed by *The Critical Review* in its comments on *Hours of Idleness*.[2] *English Bards and Scotch Reviewers* gained Byron high praise from such connoisseurs of satire as Gifford and Sheridan; periodical reviews were generally favourable; and the poem was already in a fourth edition two years later.

Yet, as is well known, it was with a very different kind of poem, *Childe Harold I and II* (1812), that Byron first fully caught the imagination of the reading public. This poem, of course, was the fruit of a tour in 1809–11 through Portugal and Spain, and through the Balkans and Near East. It seems likely that some of the general appeal of the poem lay in its convincing portrayal of the local scenery and people in Mediterranean lands, and also in the strong-minded treatment of contemporary topical matters, such as the battle of Talavera, and Greece under Turkish rule. The power and bitterness of some of the misanthropic reflections seem also to have attracted some readers, though they repelled others. It was also far from irrelevant that Byron was a young nobleman of ancient lineage, and a promising model for a

---

[1] The review was by Brougham, but, as was customary, it was unsigned.
[2] *CR*, XII (3rd. Ser.), September 1807.

romantic figure. The poem was published in March 1812 by John Murray, a Tory, and the publisher of the recently established *Quarterly Review*. This fact may also have contributed something to the popularity of the poem, for it received a long and favourable review by George Ellis in that periodical[1]; though this did not appear until two months or so after the publication of the poem, which had already attained 'high popularity'[2] by then. Another factor, probably of considerable importance, was the warm reception accorded to the poem by Francis Jeffrey in *The Edinburgh Review* of February 1812, which was actually issued in May.[3] Jeffrey's review appears all the more generous in that Byron, mistakenly thinking that Jeffrey had written the contemptuous dismissal of *Hours of Idleness*, had attacked him by name in *English Bards and Scotch Reviewers*. The *Edinburgh* nevertheless had slight reservations about *Childe Harold I and II*, particularly about the character of the Childe, and about the gloomy reflections strewn throughout the cantos. The *Quarterly* had more reservations. It did not approve Byron's depreciation of martial fame. It detested the Childe's character, 'whose frightful gloom is only the result of disappointed selfishness', and it demurred at Byron's open rejection of the doctrine of personal immortality. Almost all other periodicals were generally favourable. Exceptions were the Tory *Anti-Jacobin*[4] and *The Scourge*,[5] which sharply censured the poem on political grounds, and the Evangelical *Christian Observer*,[6] which attacked its moral tendencies. *Childe Harold* was, however, a new *kind* of work, and a number of the critics were puzzled as to what kind of a thing it was. To most of them it certainly did not seem to correspond to Byron's titular description of it as '*A Romaunt*'. Some critics, for example Thomas Denman in *The Monthly Review*,[7] complained that it had no story. Some, for instance William Roberts in *The British Review*,[8] held that the Childe was an otiose character. Interestingly enough, the Tory and High Church periodical *The British Critic*,[9] which was to

[1] *QR*, VII, March 1812 (publ. after 9 May 1812).

[2] *MR*, LXVIII, May 1812, 74.

[3] *ER*, XIX, February 1812 (issued May). See pp. 25–6 above, and 214–16 below.

[4] *AJR*, XLII, August 1812.   [5] *Scourge*, III, April 1812.

[6] *CO*, XI, June 1812. See pp. 69–71 above.

[7] *MR*, LXVIII, May 1812. See p. 52 above.

[8] *BR*, III, June 1812. See pp. 91–3 above.

[9] *BC*, XXXIX, May 1812. See p. 60 above.

attack some of Byron's later work with intense ferocity, pronounced very favourably on this poem, though it did criticize the religious opinions expressed.

One result of Byron's success with *Childe Harold I and II* was that he was taken up by the *grand monde*. His easy manners and his attractiveness to women helped to make him the temporary darling of London society. In the same year he made a start at becoming a political figure, and created a stir by the radicalism of his maiden speech against the stern measures proposed by the Tory Government against the Nottingham frame-breakers. His political career at home did not last, but it had the effect of making critics in liberal or radical periodicals somewhat more favourable, and critics in Tory periodicals somewhat less favourable, to his poems than they might otherwise have been.

Byron followed up his literary successes with the series of narrative poems, mostly set in the Near East, and generally known, somewhat loosely, as 'the Eastern Tales'. These also sold rapidly; though they met with less enthusiasm from some of the critics, partly as immoral, partly as incredible in their characterization, partly on technical grounds, and partly as less important than *Childe Harold*. As the series went on there were also grumbles on the score of monotony. Byron's marriage (1815) and the separation which followed the next year had the inevitable effect of keeping him much in the public eye, even if—and, indeed, partly because—his moral reputation thereby declined. Murray, who had sold 10,000 copies of *The Corsair* (1814) on the day of publication, had the comparable satisfaction of disposing of 7000 copies each of *Childe Harold III* (1816) and *The Prisoner of Chillon* volume (1816) at a dinner of booksellers towards the end of that year.

Childe Harold III was generally well received by the reviewers, some of whom, however, took exception to Byron's attacks on his wife, to his political views on Waterloo and Napoleon, and to the moral character of the Childe, who was in this canto scarcely distinguishable from the poet. Byron's old friend John Cam Hobhouse had reservations about the canto's 'air of mystery and metaphysics'.[1] This feature was probably due, in part at least, to the influence of Shelley, who at the time the canto was being written had been discussing Plato with Byron, and also making

[1] John Cam Hobhouse, Lord Broughton, *Recollections of a Long Life*, ed. Lady Dorchester, 6 vols., 1909–11, II. 11.

him read large portions of Wordsworth.[1] The Wordsworthian influence was noted by many reviewers, some of whom considered the Wordsworthian passages as inferior imitations, while others thought Byron had improved on the master. Among other critics, Gifford considered the canto far and away the best work Byron had published—'the most original and interesting', and 'the most finished'.[2] The descriptive passages, and the reflections on the historical and literary associations of the places described or mentioned, also proved attractive to some critics. Opinions on *The Prisoner of Chillon* varied considerably, from *The Champion*'s verdict that it was 'forced, feeble, and imperfect',[3] to Jeffrey's reaction to it as 'very sweet and touching'.[4] The most perceptive critique of this poem was by Walter Scott, who recognized the poem's painfulness and unostentatious power.[5]

After the predominantly adverse reception of *Manfred* (1817) and the minor success of *The Lament of Tasso* (1817), Byron broke new ground with *Beppo*, written in the autumn of 1817, and published anonymously in February 1818. The immediate literary influence sparking off the new departure was the poem known as 'Whistlecraft',[6] by John Hookham Frere, but the ultimate source was the Italian burlesque tradition of Berni, Pulci, and Casti. The critics mostly realized that Byron was the author, and the great majority of them thought well of the poem, though some quite failed to realize that there was more to it than mere entertainment, and that it had, as Byron put it, 'politics and ferocity'.[7]

Beppo had been written while Byron was finishing *Childe Harold IV*, and this last canto of the longer poem was published in April 1818. Some critics, John Wilson, for instance,[8] thought it the finest of the four cantos, but others found the egotism as tiresome as ever, and the reviewer in the *Eclectic* even considered this feature especially incongruous with the majesty of the

[1] See *e.g.*, John Buxton, *Byron and Shelley* (London, 1968), Chapter 2.

[2] Letter from Murray to Byron, 12 September 1816, published in Samuel Smiles, *A Publisher and his Friends*, 2 vols. (London, 1891), I. 365–6.

[3] *Champ*, I, December 1816, 382. See p. 153 above.

[4] *ER*, XXVII, December 1816. See p. 29 above.

[5] *QR*, XVI, October 1816. See pp. 37–8 above.

[6] The real designation was *Prospectus and Specimen of an intended National Work*, by William and Robert Whistlecraft. It was published in 1817–18.

[7] Letter to Murray, 27 January 1818 (*LJ*, IV. 195).

[8] *ER*, XXX, June 1818. See pp. 30–33 above, and 229–33 below.

Roman scene.[1] Hazlitt, who had evidently liked *Beppo*,[2] roundly asserted in *The Yellow Dwarf*[3] that *Childe Harold IV* showed a 'falling off' from *I–III*. It left on him the same impression as 'a troubled dream'—'as distorted, as confused, as disjointed, as harassing, and as unprofitable'. He regarded Byron as a spoiled nobleman, contemptuous of others and disgusted at himself:

> His Lordship, in fact, makes out his own hard case to be, that he has attained all those objects that the rest of the world admire; that he has met with none of those disasters which embitter their lives; and he calls upon us to sympathize with his griefs and his despair.
> This will never do. It is more intolerable than even Mr. Wordsworth's arbitrary egotism and pampered self-sufficiency. *He* creates a factitious interest out of nothing. Lord Byron would destroy our interest in all that is. Mr. Wordsworth, to salve his own self-love, makes the merest toy of his own mind,—the most insignificant object he can meet with,—of as much importance as the universe: Lord Byron would persuade us that the universe itself is not worth his or our notice; and yet he would expect us to be occupied with him.

This is, from a somewhat uncharitable point of view, penetrating criticism of both poets. Hazlitt went on to censure the jumbling together of a series of unrelated objects, and to assert that Byron's comments were 'more dogmatical than profound, and with all their extravagance of expression, common-place'. Hazlitt was also angry at Byron's change to a hostile attitude to Napoleon now that the man was down. He also criticizes the versification and style of the canto, complaining at the running-on between stanzas, and at what he calls 'a strange mixture of stately phraseology and far-fetched metaphor, with the most affected and bald simplicity of expression and uncouthness in the rhymes'. Singling out stanzas xvii and the first four lines of xix, he comments that 'it is well that his Lordship is born so high, or all Grub-street would set him down as a plebeian for such lines'. On the other hand, Hazlitt likes stanzas i–iii, praising the thought "but nature doth not die", as 'particularly fine, and consolatory to the mind'. Hazlitt prefers the stanzas on Petrarch's tomb (xxx–xxxiv) to any others in the poem, but he also considers the ensuing apostrophe to Tasso and his patron 'written with great force, but in a different

---

[1] *Ecl. R*, X, (2nd. Ser.), July 1818. See pp. 85–6 above.
[2] *YD*, 28 March 1818. See his notice of *Beppo* reprinted on p. 226 below.
[3] *YD*, 2 May 1818.

spirit'. Contrary to many reviewers, Hazlitt thinks Byron's powers 'better suited to express the human passions than to reflect the forms of nature'. He makes an exception, however, for the description of the Cataract of the Velino (lxix ff.), asserting that Byron had not 'invoked the genius of the place in vain':

> It represents, in some measure, the workings of his own spirit,— disturbed, restless, labouring, foaming, sparkling, and now hid in labyrinths and plunging into the gloom of night.

And Hazlitt then quotes stanzas lxx (from 'how profound') to lxxii, introducing them with the words:

> The following description is obscure, tortuous, perplexed, and abortive, yet who can say that it is not beautiful, striking, and impassioned?—

and commenting after quotation:

> We'll look no more: such kind of writing is enough to turn the mind of the reader or the author. . . . There is here in every line an effort of brilliancy, and a successful effort; and yet, in the next, as if nothing has been done, the same thing is attempted to be expressed again with the same labour as before, the same success, and with as little appearance of repose or satisfaction of mind.

Hazlitt has only commented so far on a little over half the canto, but now announces:

> It is in vain to attempt a regular account of the remainder of the poem, which is a mass of discordant things, incoherent, not gross, seen 'now in glimmer and now in gloom', and 'moving wild laughter in the throat of death'.

Yet he does go on to praise lxxxi, likening Byron's poetry to Rome itself, which, however, was glorious before it became a ruin, whereas Byron's poetry 'in its irregular and gloomy magnificence' antedated its own doom, and was 'buried in a desolation of his own creation'. But Hazlitt has nevertheless great admiration for certain passages, e.g., xciii–xcv, and especially the apostrophe to the Ocean, where, he writes, Byron's 'genius resumes its beauty and its power'. It is interesting to find even Shelley, who had admired *III*, agreeing with Peacock in his sharp reaction against the contempt for humanity and the despair expressed in this final canto.[1] A number of critics took occasion to offer their impres-

[1] Peacock to Shelley, 1 November 1818. Shelley to Peacock, 17 or 18 December 1818 (*SL*, 1964, II. 57–8).

sions of the whole poem. Wilson's piece is especially good, but the reviewer in *The Monthly Review*[1] also makes some perceptive comments, and William Roberts in *The British Review* scores a few points in his patchy critique.[2]

The verse-tale *Mazeppa*, published in June 1819, came in for some censure for its violence and its theme of adultery, but was on the whole favourably received. Meanwhile, however, Byron had started on *Don Juan*, and had finished Canto I in the autumn of 1818:

> I have finished the first canto (a long one, of about 180 octaves) of a poem in the style and measure of *Beppo*, encouraged by the good success of the same. It is called *Don Juan*, and is meant to be a little quietly facetious upon every thing. But I doubt whether it is not— at least, as far as it has yet gone—too free for these very modest days. However, I shall try the experiment, anonymously; and if it don't take, it will be discontinued.[3]

A number of Byron's London friends were unanimously against publication, because of various features in the poem: the likelihood of the attacks on Byron's wife stirring up trouble again, the bawdry, the blasphemy, the onslaughts on contemporary writers, the evidence of rakish experiences which would tend to confirm current accounts of Byron's dissolute life at Venice.[4] Byron hesitated, and even at one point decided to have the poem printed for private distribution,[5] but eventually he went ahead with anonymous publication, and Cantos I and II (the latter of which he had completed in January 1819) were published in July 1819.

Neither the *Edinburgh* nor the *Quarterly* printed a review. *The Monthly Review* recognized that here was a new and great kind of poem, and though the reviewer registered a mild moral protest, delight was clearly his dominant reaction.[6] *The Champion*, on the other hand, seems to have been genuinely disturbed at what it called 'a tissue of all immoralities'.[7] Yet it acknowledged the 'power' of the cantos, especially of *II*, which it considered perhaps more powerful than anything Byron had yet written.

[1] *MR*, LXXXVII, November 1818. See pp. 54–5 above, and 246–8 below.
[2] *BR*, XII, August 1818. See pp. 101–3 above, and 233–6 below.
[3] Letter to Moore, 19 September 1818 (*LJ*, IV. 260).　　[4] *LJ*, IV. 275–6.
[5] Letter to Murray, 25 January 1819 (*LJ*, IV. 277).
[6] *MR*, LXXXIX, July 1819. See pp. 55–7 above.
[7] *Champ*, 25 July 1819, 472. See pp. 154–6 above.

It also approved, in the main, of Byron's literary and political satire.[1] *The Literary Gazette*, on the other hand, in a much finer review,[2] had called Canto I 'an exceedingly clever and entertaining poem', and a 'witty if a little licentious, and delightful if not very moral production'. It also admired *II*, in which it found 'more of powerful and genuine poetry', and it sturdily defended the mixture of farce with human miseries, vices, and crimes. It had also high praise for the virtuostic use of the *ottava rima* in both cantos. Even this reviewer was, however (inconsistently, though honestly?) shocked at the bleeding and death of Pedrillo, and disgusted at some of the details of that gruesome scene. On the other hand, like a number of other periodicals, *The Literary Gazette* admired the tenderness of the romance of Juan and Haidée, though it considered that 'the great objection to *Don Juan* must be felt to be its licentiousness'. The most violent rejection of the cantos came from *The British Critic*,[3] which condemned them outright, both morally and aesthetically, dubbing the poem 'a narrative of degrading debauchery in doggrel rhyme', and expressing the hope that 'the good sense, and the good feeling of the English nation must and will banish it from their houses'. *The Eclectic Review*'s attitude[4] was more sensitive and discriminating, and perhaps more honest. It admired the power of the poetry, but felt morally ashamed of its admiration, and so it steadily refrained from reviewing these or any of the subsequent cantos. William Roberts of *The British Review* also admired much of the poetry, but condemned it all as immoral. He refused to review *I* and *II*,[5] but he eventually reviewed *III–V* at great length,[6] condemning them utterly on moral and religious grounds. In marked contrast the equally Tory but far more mercurial *Blackwood's* gave the most emphatic statement of aesthetic admiration and moral rejection which we find in any review at the time. The reviewer or reviewers in the unsigned 'Remarks on *Don Juan*'[7] unhesitatingly prophesied the poem's

[1] The reviewer was John Thelwall, who had taken over the weekly in 1819, and was an ardent reformer.

[2] *LG*, 17 and 24 July 1819. See pp. 159–61 above.

[3] *BC*, XI (2nd. Ser.), August 1819. See pp. 64–5 above, and 251–4 below.

[4] *Ecl. R*, XII (2nd. Ser.), August 1819. See pp. 86–7 above, and 250–1 below.

[5] *BR*, XIV, August 1819. See pp. 103–4 above.

[6] *BR*, XVIII, December 1821. See pp. 104–6 above, and 281–6 below.

[7] *BM*, V, August 1819. See pp. 44–5 above.

immortality, as 'a perpetual monument of the exalted intellect, and the depraved heart, of one of the most remarkable men to whom this country has had the honour and the disgrace of giving birth'. These 'Remarks', which also attacked Byron's character and his conduct to his wife, stung him into writing a long reply, dated 15 March 1820 from Ravenna.[1] This was not published till after Byron's death. Byron thought that Wilson was the author of the 'Remarks',[2] and he was bitterly disappointed that a man whom he liked and admired (and who had lauded *Childe Harold* to the skies) should now join the pack of moral traducers of his work and character. Byron's reply was largely concerned with personal issues, but it is also of interest as a vigorous defence of the tradition of Dryden and Pope and their followers, against the Lakers and Keats.[3] Though not usually placed in such strong contrast as in the 'Remarks', moral and aesthetic judgments of *Don Juan I and II* were generally kept distinct in the periodical criticism, and the reviewers varied, as we have seen, in the respective stress they laid on the moral and the aesthetic. *The Monthly Magazine*,[4] like *The Monthly Review*, only touched the moral aspects very lightly. In contrast *The Examiner*[5] behaved almost as a polar opposite to *The British Critic*, substantially defending the poem's moral innocence as well as glorifying its literary excellence.

It is interesting to find Shelley expressing strong admiration for these cantos, especially for the knowledge of human nature shown in the writing of Julia's love-letter, and the description of the storm and the contrast between the two fathers, which he thought was hardly excelled by Dante. But he demurred at the use of the love-letter for drawing lots in the cannibal scene, and objected in general terms to 'the bitter mockery of our common nature', as not 'quite worthy' of Byron's genius, adding, however, with admirable critical insight: 'The power and the beauty and the wit, indeed, redeem all this—chiefly because they belie and refute it.'[6] For Wordsworth, in contrast, *Don Juan* was 'infamous'[7];

[1] Reprinted in *LJ*, IV. 474–95.   [2] The matter of authorship is not yet settled.
[3] See especially *LJ*, IV. 486–94.
[4] *MM*, XLVIII, August 1819. See pp. 140–1 above.
[5] *Exar*, 31 October 1819. See pp. 118 above, and 255–9 below.
[6] Letter to Byron, 26 May 1820 (*SL*, II. 198).
[7] Letter to Henry Crabb Robinson, ? January 1820. (*The Correspondence of Henry Crabb Robinson with the Wordsworth Circle*, ed. Edith J. Morley (London, 1927), II. 856–1.)

and Severn tells us that Keats on his sea-voyage to Italy threw down the book in disgust, describing the storm scene as 'one of the most diabolical attempts ever made upon our sympathies'.[1] It must be remembered, however, that Keats was very ill at the time; but he would in any case have had no reason to like Byron, who only a month later was expressing a nasty contempt for him and his work.[2]

Besides the periodical reviews *Don Juan I and II* provoked a number of apparently worthless pamphlets, attacking Byron or the poem for immorality.[3] Such pamphlets continued to appear after the issue of later cantos. In contrast with these, and towering above them, there appeared in 1821, based upon a reading of Cantos I and II, the stoutest vindication of the poem, the *Letter to the Right Hon. Lord Byron. By John Bull,* now known to have been written by Lockhart.[4] This full-blooded defence of the vitality and honesty of the work makes some of the most refreshing reading in Byron criticism.[5] Byron himself was delighted with it. Before it appeared, however, many months had elapsed since the first two Cantos had gone to press.

It was two years after the publication of *Don Juan I and II* before Cantos III–V came out. Byron had not been idle. He had been writing *The Prophecy of Dante*, translating a canto of Pulci, defending the poetry of Pope, and working on four dramas, none of which, for reasons stated above, concerns us here.[6] Moreover, his enthusiasm for *Don Juan* had been damped by the moral outcry (Byron said it had not frightened, but *hurt* him),[7] and he was also clearly affected by Teresa Guiccioli's dislike of the poem.[8] There was also the possible difficulty of protecting

[1] Sidney Colvin, *John Keats, His Life and Poetry, His Friends, Critics, and After-Fame* (London, 1917), 3rd. ed. 1920, 496.

[2] In a letter to Murray after the favourable review of *Endymion* and the *Lamia* volume by Jeffrey in the *Edinburgh*: 'Of the praises of that little dirty blackguard Keates [*sic*] in the *Edinburgh*, I shall observe as Johnson did when Sheridan the actor got a *pension*: "What! has *he* got a pension? Then it is time that I should give up *mine*!" ' (18 November 1820, *LJ*, V. 120).

[3] See the account of some of these in S. C. Chew, *Byron in England: his Fame and After-Fame* (London, 1924), Chapter II.

[4] For further details see pp. 45–6 above. For a full account see the modern edition of the *Letter* by Professor A. L. Strout, *John Bull's Letter to Lord Byron* (Norman, Oklahoma, 1947).

[5] Some extracts are reprinted on pp. 276–80 below.

[6] See pp. 6–7 above.   [7] Letter to Murray, 23 April 1820 (*LJ*, V. 16).

[8] Letter to Murray, 12 October 1820 (*LJ*, V. 96–7).

the poem against piracy, in view of its perilous standing in relation to the law.[1] In any case, however, Canto III had been started in 1819, *III* and *IV* were finished by February 1820; and all three Cantos had been completed by late in 1820. Byron himself was not very satisfied with them, especially with *III*, which he thought rather dull.[2] Nevertheless, when they were published in August 1821, without the name of either author or publisher, the sale was enormous.[3] Byron now seemed more pleased with his work, and regretted that he had in July promised *La Guiccioli* not to continue the poem beyond these cantos.[4] The periodicals were, however, generally unfavourable. *The Monthly Review*, which had received *I* and *II* enthusiastically, was bored with *III–V*, save for 'occasional passages of beauty, and striking thoughts', and for 'The Isles of Greece'.[5] *The British Critic* positively retched with disgust.[6] *The British Review*, in a more dignified vein, took the cantos to task on moral, but also still more on religious grounds; but did recognize that some passages had 'considerable merit', 'both in thought and expression'.[7] *The Investigator* mainly attacked the salaciousness.[8] Constable's *Edinburgh Magazine* thought both the 'ribaldry' and the 'blasphemy' poisonous.[9] *The Literary Gazette* considered the cantos poetically inferior to *I* and *II*, and their 'tendency to obscenity', 'of a more depraved kind'.[10] The chief defences, which were both moral and aesthetic, came from *The Monthly Magazine*[11] and *The Examiner*.[12] In October, however, Shelley wrote to Byron a glowing letter, which showed uncommon appreciation

[1] In the splendidly droll case of Southey's *Wat Tyler*, Lord Eldon, L.C. had ruled that that work could not be protected by injunction against piracy, because it was a seditious libel.

[2] Letter to Murray, 19 January 1821 (*LJ*, V. 224).

[3] R. E. Prothero in a note in *LJ*, V. 351, quoting the *Memoir of John Murray*, I. 413.

[4] Letters to Murray, 6 July 1821 (*LJ*, V. 320–1); 31 August 1821 (*ibid.*, 352); 4 September 1821 (*ibid.*, 359).

[5] *MR*, XCV, August 1821. See pp. 56–7 above.

[6] *BC*, XVI (n.s.), September 1821, See pp. 65–6 above, and 280–1 below.

[7] *BR*, XVIII, December 1821. See pp. 104–6 above, and 281–6 below.

[8] *Investigr*, III, October 1821.

[9] *Ed. M*, IX (2nd. Ser.), August 1821. See pp. 135–6 above.

[10] *LG*, 11, 18 August 1821. See p. 161 above.

[11] *MM*, LII, September 1821. See p. 141 above.

[12] *Exar*, 26 August 1821. See pp. 118–19 above.

of the *magnitude* of Byron's new achievement.[1] Moreover, much earlier (in March 1820), the arch-Tory Croker had read *III–V* in manuscript, and written to Murray in defence of *Don Juan*.[2]

In February 1822 Jeffrey broke the silence of *The Edinburgh Review* about *Don Juan*, in a critique of *Sardanapalus*, *The Two Foscari*, and *Cain*.[3] This is a well-balanced piece of criticism, exonerating Byron from any intention to corrupt the morals of the land, but contending that *Don Juan*, of which *I–V* had by then appeared, would nevertheless have a tendency to do this. Byron had 'exerted all the powers of his mind to convince his readers, both directly and indirectly, that all ennobling pursuits, and disinterested virtues, are mere deceits and illusions—hollow and despicable mockeries for the most part, and, at best, but laborious follies'. Jeffrey recognized Byron's passages of dignity and tenderness, and of 'infinite sublimity and beauty', but he censured the bold and false speculations, the indecencies, the seductive descriptions, and the heartlessness revealed in characters who had been 'transiently represented as actuated by the purest and most exalted emotions'. Jeffrey rejects the idea that this was legitimate satire against hypocrisy, and sees it rather as a nihilistic attack on humanity at large.

In July 1822 the *Quarterly* followed with a briefer, but not altogether dissimilar, attack on *Don Juan*, again in a review of the same three dramas.[4] The reviewer was Reginald Heber, who became Bishop of Calcutta the same year. He explains the silence of the *Quarterly* about *Don Juan* as follows:

> We knew not any severity of criticism which could reach the faults or purify the taste of *Don Juan*, and we trusted that its author would himself, ere long, discover, that if he continued to write such works as these, he would lose the power of producing any thing better, and that his pride, at least, if not his principle, would recall him from the island of Acrasia.

This had, in Heber's view, actually happened. The plays were morally 'unimpeachable'.

> Even the *Mystery of Cain*, wicked as it may be, is the work of a nobler and more daring wickedness than that which delights in insulting the miseries, and stimulating the evil passions, and casting a cold-blooded ridicule over all the lofty and generous feelings of

[1] See the extract on p. 204 below.   [2] See the extract on pp. 259–62 below.
[3] *ER*, XXXVI, February 1822. See the extract on pp. 286–92 below.
[4] *QR*, XXVII, July 1822 (publ. October 1822).

our nature: and it is better that Lord Byron should be a manichee or a deist,—nay, we would almost say, if the thing were possible, it is better that he should be a moral and argumentative atheist, than the professed and systematic poet of seduction, adultery and incest; the contemner of patriotism, the insulter of piety, the raker into every sink of vice and wretchedness to disgust and degrade and harden the hearts of his fellow-creatures. . . . The infidel *may*, the adversary of good morals *cannot* be, under a mistake as to the tendency of his doctrines.

Byron, who had recently resolved to confine his 'English studies' to *Galignani's Messenger*, a newspaper in English published in Paris, eventually saw part of Heber's review which had been printed there.[1] He was agreeably surprised at Heber's treatment of the dramas, and thought the strictures on *Don Juan* only to be expected:

> As I take the good in good part, I must not, nor will not, quarrel with the bad: what the writer says of *Don Juan* is harsh, but it is inevitable. He must follow, or at least not directly oppose, the opinion of a prevailing, and yet not very firmly seated, party: a review may and will direct or 'turn awry' the Currents of opinion, but it must not directly oppose them. *Don Juan* will be known by and bye, for what it is intended,—a *Satire* on Abuses of the present states of Society, and not a eulogy of vice: it may be now and then voluptuous: I can't help that. Ariosto is worse; Smollett . . . ten times worse; and Fielding no better. No girl will ever be seduced by reading *D.J.*:—no, no; no, no; she will go to Little's poems and Rousseau's romans for that: they will encourage her, and not the Don, who laughs at that, and—and—most other things.[2]

It was through Shelley that Byron proposed to Leigh Hunt in 1822 that he should come out to Italy and join them in conducting a periodical.[3] This project was realized in *The Liberal*, a quarterly which petered out in 1823 after only four numbers.[4] Shelley had died before the publication of the first number, which is in any case our only concern here. It contained Byron's *The Vision of Judgment*. The number appeared on 15 October 1822. It was published in London by Leigh Hunt's brother John.

[1] Letter to Murray, 25 October 1822 (*LJ*, VI. 155).
[2] *Loc. cit.*, 155–6.
[3] Shelley, Letter to Leigh Hunt, 26 August 1821 (*SL*, II. 343–4).
[4] See the excellent study of the whole project by Professor William H. Marshall, *Byron, Shelley, Hunt, and 'The Liberal'* (University of Pennsylvania Press, Philadelphia, 1960).

Murray, to whom Byron had originally sent the poem and its Preface, had withheld the latter from John Hunt, and so the poem was printed without the Preface, with the result that readers would often not have been aware of Byron's reasons for the savagery of the poem's attack on Southey. Southey himself wrote to his brother expressing apparently detached contempt for the attack and for the whole journal.[1] The newspapers and periodicals mostly concentrated on expressing in pretty strong terms their view that *The Vision of Judgment* was impious and morally disgusting, but some thought it also a rather poor literary performance. *The Literary Gazette*, for instance, considered that Southey's absurd *A Vision of Judgment* could have been far more effectively attacked and ridiculed than it had been by Byron—an opinion with which the writer of the present work heartily agrees.[2] A good deal of the periodical criticism of the poem, however, laid its main stress on the depravity of the attacks on the dead King, and the poisonous profanity. *The Literary Chronicle and Weekly Review* suggested that some passages in the poem were 'more deserving the notice of the Attorney General than the critic'.[3] There was hardly any favourable comment on the poem in the other weeklies, except, of course, *The Examiner*.[4] Of the monthlies *The New European Magazine*, like *The Literary Gazette*, found the poem 'dull'.[5] Constable's *Edinburgh Magazine* also considered that Byron had produced 'the most commonplace drivelling and impotency'.[6] *Blackwood's* thought the poem 'vastly inferior to *Beppo*, to say nothing of the exquisite *Don Juan*', though the periodical saw hope for Byron if he could break away from the Hunts.[7] The next month *Blackwood's* again expressed the view that the poem was a poor effort, 'a jest that does not excite a smile, drawled out through nine-and-thirty pages'.[8] *The Monthly Magazine*, sympathetic to *Don Juan*, regarded *The Vision*'s abuse even of the 'malignant turncoat' Southey as a sorry business.[9]

[1] *Selections from the Letters of Robert Southey*, ed. J. W. Warter, 4 vols. (London, 1856), III. 40.

[2] *LG*, 19, 26 October, 2 November 1822. See pp. 161–2 above.

[3] *LC*, 19, 26 October 1822.

[4] *Exar*, 13 October 1822. See pp. 120–1 above.

[5] *NEM*, I, October 1822.

[6] *Ed. M*, XI (2nd. Ser.), November 1822. See pp. 136–7 above, and 292 below.

[7] *BM*, XII, December 1822, 695–709.

[8] *BM*, XIII, January 1823, 108–24.   [9] *MM*, LIV, December 1822.

The first number of *The Liberal* even evoked some pamphlets solely devoted to criticizing the poem.[1] As criticism of the poem these are barely worth mention, save for a rather amusing parody called 'The Vision of Parnassus. By Andrew Mucklegrin', printed in *The London Liberal* in 1823.[2] Meanwhile, late in 1822, the Constitutional Association had brought a charge against John Hunt, and he was indicted by the Grand Jury in Middlesex in December 1822 for publishing in *The Liberal* 'a certain false, scandalous, malicious, and defamatory libel, of and concerning his late Majesty, and also of and concerning his reign, death, and burial'. Passages of *The Vision of Judgment* were cited to support the charges. In January 1823 Hunt printed a second edition of the first number of *The Liberal* including the Preface to the poem. This did not, however, impede the process of law, or, consequently, prevent piracy of the poem, against which John Hunt could not now hope for an injunction. Ultimately, in January 1824, John Hunt was brought to trial in the Court of King's Bench,[3] found guilty by a Special Jury, and sentenced in June to pay a fine of £100 (which might be about £800–£1000 in present money). Periodicals were politically aligned about the justice of the trial and the conviction.[4] Byron, on hearing of the *conviction*, had written to his friend Kinnaird saying he intended to pay Hunt's fine,[5] but Byron had already died by the time the *sentence* was passed.

We must now take a look at the critical reception of the remaining cantos (*VI–XVI*) of *Don Juan*. These were issued in cheap pamphlets by John Hunt.

Cantos VI–VIII were published in July 1823. Byron wrote a Preface to them in which he lashed out at the hypocrisy and degeneracy of objectors to the previous cantos, and fiercely attacked the political character of Castlereagh, who had recently committed suicide. This seems to have angered some of the critics. *The Literary Examiner*, however, also published by John Hunt, puffed the cantos by previews.[6] The reviews themselves were almost all unfavourable, in varying degrees. Even the Whig

[1] For a description of many of these see S. C. Chew, *Byron in England: His Fame and After-Fame.*

[2] The poem consists of sixty-eight stanzas. The author is not known. The first sixteen stanzas are reprinted by W. H. Marshall, *op. cit.*, Appx. II.

[3] See Marshall, *op. cit.*, 205 ff. [4] *Ibid.*, 207 ff.

[5] Byron, *Correspondence*, ed. John Murray, 2 vols. (London, 1922), II. 290.

[6] *Lit. Exar.* 5, 12 July 1823. See pp. 122 above, and 294–6 below.

Monthly Review gave no support.[1] *The Literary Gazette* was contemptuous, both morally and aesthetically.[2] *The British Critic* scornfully referred to the pamphlet as a 'shilling's worth of ribaldry', but then went on to show more concern at the radicalism of the cantos.[3] Constable's *Edinburgh Magazine* made some distinctions.[4] It attacked the Preface as 'cant' designed to disguise Byron's real intention to sap the foundations of religion and morality. It also censured the indecency of *VI*; but it admired the powerful description in *VII* and *VIII*, and supported Byron's political stand for liberty. *Blackwood's*, on the other hand, dubbed the cantos 'garbage', and placed them below the worst of Southey and Gifford.[5] *The Gentleman's Magazine* dismissed the cantos as 'incomparably the most abominable in spirit, and wretched in execution, of all the writings of the author'.[6] *The British Magazine* thought *VI–VIII* united the indecency of *I–II* with the dulness of *III–V*.[7] More favourable notices, however, appeared. *The Monthly Magazine* was one of the few periodicals to recognize the serious purpose behind Byron's apparent levity towards misery.[8] *The Portfolio*, while regretting Byron's use of his talents, praises the 'keen but unpolished wit', and the occasional 'beautiful poetry', and attacks critics who had condemned the poem on political or religious grounds.[9]

Cantos IX–XI were published in August 1823, only a month after *VI–VIII*. *The Literary Examiner* had given these cantos a longer puff than *VI–VIII*,[10] but the critical reception was again predominantly hostile. A notable exception, however, was the Letter from ODoherty in *Blackwood's*,[11] now known to have been written by Lockhart, and following a very similar line to that of his *Letter from John Bull* which had appeared two years before. Constable's *Edinburgh Magazine*, on the other hand, thought three

[1] *MR*, CI, July 1823.   [2] *LG*, 19 July 1823. See p. 162 above.
[3] *BC*, XX (n.s.), August 1823. See pp. 66–7 above.
[4] *Ed. M*, XIII (2nd. Ser.), August 1823. See pp. 137–8 above.
[5] *BM*, XIV, July 1823.   [6] *GM*, XCIII, September 1823.
[7] *Brit. Mag*, I, August 1823.
[8] *MM*, LVI, September 1823. See pp. 142–3 above.
[9] *Portfolio*, I, nos. xxi–xxii, 1823. This review was brought to my attention by P. G. Trueblood's *The Flowering of Byron's Genius* (Stanford University Press, 1945), where it is more fully described on pp. 55–6.
[10] *Lit. Exar*, 2, 9, 16, 23 August 1823. See pp. 124–5 above, and 296–7 below.
[11] *BM*, XIV, September 1823. See pp. 47–8 above, and 297–301 below.

cantos a month 'a jot too much', and *IX–XI* a great comedown.[1]
The fiercest attack on these cantos, however, came from *The
Literary Gazette*, which expressed its conviction that the poet was
insane, and the cantos devoid of any evidence of talent.[2] Other
journals[3] professed to see that Byron had become dull as well as
wicked. *The Monthly Review* expressed its usual lack of interest.[4]
The British Critic, which had utterly condemned *I* and *II*, now
disingenuously alleged that it had found them 'highly talented',
and that Byron's latest work had mercifully ceased to be attractive.
This review also sharply attacks what it considered to be Byron's
radicalism.[5] *The Monthly Magazine*, on the other hand, gave the
cantos quite a deal of praise, both on political and on aesthetic
grounds.[6]

Cantos XII–XIV came out in December 1823, again after a
period of preview in *The Literary Examiner*.[7] These cantos were
not so widely reviewed as earlier ones, but the reviews were
distinctly more favourable. Even *The British Critic*[8] had a word
to say in praise of the description of Norman Abbey, and found
the cantos at least free from indecency, blasphemy, and scurrility.
The Literary Gazette, too, generally so scornful of *Don Juan*,
thought these cantos 'very entertaining', and praised both the
description of Norman Abbey and the characterization of the
participants in the house party.[9]

Cantos XV–XVI, which appeared in March 1824, were hardly
reviewed at all. *The Examiner* gave a favourable preview and
review.[10] *The Monthly Review* simply indicated the topics of the
cantos, and shrugged off 'this interminable poem'.[11] *The Literary
Gazette* considered the cantos so weak that it thought they were
certainly not Byron's.[12]

Byron died on 19 April. His letters written during the last few
months do not show much concern for the poem or its fate. He

[1] *Ed. M*, XIII, September 1823. See p. 138 above.

[2] *LG*, 6 September 1823. See pp. 162–3 above.

[3] E.g., *The British Magazine*, I, September 1823; *The Gentleman's Magazine*,
XCIII–ii, September 1823.   [4] *MR*, CII, October 1823.

[5] *BC*, XX (n.s.), September 1823. See p. 67 above.

[6] *MM*, LVI, December 1823. See pp. 143 above, and 301–2 below.

[7] *Lit. Exar*, 8, 15, 22, 29 November 1823. See pp. 125–6 above, and 301–2
below.

[8] *BC*, XX (n.s.), December 1823. See pp. 67–8 above.

[9] *LG*, 6 December 1823. See p. 163 above.

[10] *Exar*, 14, 21 March 1824.   [11] *MR*, CIII, April 1824.

[12] *LG*, 3 April 1824.

was occupied with other matters. But two years before, in a letter to his friend Douglas Kinnaird,[1] he had expressed faith in his 'present productions', by which phrase he was clearly referring at least *inter alia* to *Don Juan*:

My object is not *immediate* popularity in my present productions, which are written on a different system from the rage of the day. But *mark what I say*; that the time will come when these will be preferred to any I have before written:—it is not from the cry or hubbub of a month that these things are to be decided upon.

The effect of Byron's death upon his poetic reputation is another story, which lies beyond the scope of this book.

On the other hand, it is worth adding something further about the opinions expressed on Byron's work during his lifetime outside the periodical reviews, which contain, however, as already mentioned, by far the most important detailed criticism of all our three poets.

Wordsworth's attitude to Byron's work was predominantly hostile, and this hostility grew sharper as time went on.

In 1812, soon after the appearance of *Childe Harold I and II*, Wordsworth, in conversation with Crabb Robinson, 'allowed' Byron 'power', but 'denied his style to be English'. He shared Crabb Robinson's low opinion of Byron's 'moral qualities', pointed out that there was insanity in Byron's family, and said he believed Byron to be 'somewhat cracked'. On the same occasion Crabb Robinson read Wordsworth some of the poems of Blake, and Wordsworth told him that he considered that Blake had 'the elements of poetry a thousand times more than either Byron or Scott'.[2] Later the same year Wordsworth, again talking to Crabb Robinson, contrasted Byron's passage on Solitude in *Childe Harold II*[3] unfavourably with some lines from *Tintern Abbey*.[4]

In May 1814, when *The Excursion* was about to be published, Wordsworth wrote to Samuel Rogers to announce it, and said he would be content if the publication paid its expenses, 'for Mr Scott and your friend Lord Byron flourishing at the rate they do, how can an honest *Poet* hope to thrive?'[5] Later the same year,

---

[1] Letter to Kinnaird, 25 February 1822 (*LJ*, VI. 25).
[2] Crabb Robinson, *Diary*, 24 May 1812 (*HCRBW*, I. 85; *D*, 20).
[3] *CH II*. xxv–xxvi.
[4] Crabb Robinson, *Diary*, 3 June 1812 (*HCRBW*, I. 93; *D*, 24–25).
[5] *The Letters of William and Dorothy Wordsworth. The Middle Years*, ed. E. de Selincourt, 2 vols. (Oxford, 1937), II. 597.

writing to R. P. Gillies, Wordsworth refers to Byron as 'a bad writer', *tout court*.[1] And there was evidently another letter, written possibly in 1815, to a Mrs Bryan of Bristol, in which Wordsworth wrote of a poet who had 'degraded his talents to immoral and vicious purposes',[2] and in which he also said that the only two popular poets of the day were men one of whom had no feeling, and the other of whom had none but perverted feelings. Rogers told Wordsworth that the letter had been betrayed to Byron, who was much incensed, and gave it as his justification for attacking Wordsworth in *Don Juan*.[3]

Early in 1816 Wordsworth wrote a letter to John Scott, in which he referred to the 'bold bad Bard Baron B.',[4] and two months later, again writing to John Scott, he launched into a virulent attack, calling Byron 'insane', and stating that he had never thought him anything else 'since his first appearance in public'. Byron's poems on his private affairs excited in Wordsworth 'less indignation than pity'. He also refers to the Ode to Napoleon as 'contemptible as a work of Art', and criticizes John Scott himself for appearing 'to labour under some delusion as to the merits of Lord Byron's Poetry'. His own prescription is as follows:

> It avails nothing to attempt to heap up indignation upon the heads of those whose talents are extolled in the same breath. The true way of dealing with these men is to shew that they want genuine power. That talents they have, but that these talents are of a *mean* order; and that their productions have no solid basis to rest upon. Allow them to be men of high genius, and they have gained their point and will go on triumphing in their iniquity; demonstrate them to be what in truth they are, in all essentials, Dunces, and I will not say that you will reform them; but by abating their pride you will strip their wickedness of the principal charm in their own eyes.[5]

Wordsworth's advice, it will be seen, is identical with what was the policy of such periodicals as *The British Critic*. Now, such a policy, whatever its pragmatic value, had the grave disadvantage of denying a genius that existed, and it therefore fell into the category of 'humbug', so effectively pilloried by Lockhart.

[1] *Ibid.*, II. 610.

[2] See Mary Moorman, *William Wordsworth. A Biography. The Later Years* (London, 1965), 211, n. 3.

[3] Crabb Robinson, *Diary*, 17 June 1833 (*HCRBW*, I. 428–9; *D*, 127).

[4] 25 February 1816. *Letters. Middle Years*, II. 712.

[5] 18 April 1816. *Ibid.*, II. 734.

Over a year later, in a letter to R. P. Gillies,[1] Wordsworth returns to the consideration of Byron's lines on Solitude. Gillies had sent him one of his poems, and Wordsworth praises some of the lines, questioning whether there was anything comparable in Byron, and comparing the language favourably to most of Byron's, but adding that 'the sentiment' was somewhat in Byron's style. Wordsworth then goes on to comment on an essay which Gillies had also sent him, in which Gillies had evidently quoted Byron's passage on Solitude. Wordsworth takes the opportunity to make the kind of comparison with *Tintern Abbey* that Crabb Robinson had briefly referred to :

> The famous passage on Solitude which you quote from Lord Byron does not deserve the notice that has been bestowed upon it. As *composition* it is bad—particularly the line (Minions of grandeur shrinking from distress)[2] which in defiance of all syntax is foisted in for the sake of the rhyme. But the sentiment by being expressed in an *antithetical* manner, is taken out of the Region of high and imaginative feeling, to be placed in that of point and epigram. To illustrate my meaning and for no other purpose I refer to my own Lines on the Wye, where you will find the same sentiment not formally put as it is here, but ejaculated as it were fortuitously in the musical succession of preconceived feeling. Compare the passage ending 'How often has my spirit turned to thee' and the one where occur the lines
>
> > And greetings where no kindness is and all
> > The dreary intercourse of daily life,
>
> with the lines of Lord Byron—and you will perceive the difference. *You* will give me credit for writing for the sake of truth, and not from so disgusting a motive as self commendation at the expense of a man of Genius. Indeed if I had not known you so well, I would rather have suppressed the truth, than incurred the risk of such an imputation.

This is fine-grained criticism; but it is noticeable that Wordsworth here seems to concede Byron's genius, which renders all the more reprehensible his previous recommendation not to give the devil his due.

All this was, of course, written before the appearance of any of the cantos of *Don Juan*. In January 1820, however, when the first two cantos of the *Don* had appeared, but before the publica-

[1] 9 June 1817. *Letters. Middle Years*, II. 789–90.
[2] Wordsworth misquotes 'splendour' as 'grandeur'.

tion of Byron's attacks on Wordsworth in Canto III, Wordsworth wrote a letter, evidently to Crabb Robinson,[1] in which he asked Robinson to urge Gifford to have the poem attacked in the *Quarterly*:

As I purpose, if possible, to go to Switzerland this summer, my journey to London will be deferred till May; so that I cannot hope for the pleasure of accompanying you. You will probably see Gifford, the Editor of the Quarterly Review; tell him from me, if you think proper, that every true-born Englishman will regard the pretensions of the Review to the character of a faithful defender of the institutions of the country, as *hollow*, while it leaves that infamous publication Don Juan unbranded; I do not mean by a formal Critique, for it is not worth it; it would also tend to keep it in memory; but by some decisive words of reprobation, both as to the damnable tendency of such works, and as to the despicable quality of the powers requisite for their production. What avails it to hunt down Shelley, whom few read, and leave Byron untouched?

There is also evidence that during the Byron–Southey conflict, in 1821–2, Wordsworth published an article in a London newspaper, presumably taking Southey's side, but this article has not yet been identified.[2]

Even when, in 1824, Wordsworth heard the news of Byron's death, he still commented on the baneful character of Byron's influence. Wordsworth was walking at the time in the cloisters of Nevile's Court, Trinity, where it is probable that Byron had had his rooms when an undergraduate;[3] and, though he expressed himself 'shocked' by the news, he foretold that Byron's spirit would now walk abroad, 'to do some good I hope, but a plaguey deal of mischief'.[4]

Coleridge remarked at the end of 1822 that to his ear there was 'a sad want of harmony' in Byron's verses, and he also expressed the familiar complaint that it was 'unnatural to be always connecting very great intellectual power with utter depravity',

[1] *The Correspondence of Henry Crabb Robinson with the Wordsworth Circle*, II. 850–1. The letter was supplied and annotated by Sir Charles Firth, whose argument for the date and addressee is entirely convincing.

[2] Letter to Daniel Stuart, 17 May 1838. *Letters. Later Years*, II. 942; and see Moorman, *op. cit.*, 211.

[3] Of the three candidates suggested by various authorities as the location of Byron's rooms by far the most likely is the set I. 1, Nevile's Court.

[4] Letter to Samuel Rogers, 21 January 1825. *Letters. Later Years*, I. 175; quoted Moorman, *op. cit.*, 450, n. 2.

questioning whether such a combination does often exist *in rerum natura*. There is, however, very little reference to Byron in anything Coleridge wrote before Byron's death.

Hazlitt included some criticism of Byron in 1818 in Lecture VIII of his Lectures on the English Poets at the Surrey Institution, which were published the same year. He made the rather interesting remark that Byron, in contrast with Moore, 'might be thought to have suffered too much to be a truly great poet'. He considered Byron's poetry as 'morbid' as Moore's was 'careless and dissipated':

> He has more depth of passion, more force and impetuosity, but the passion is always of the same unaccountable character, at once violent and sullen, fierce and gloomy. It is not the passion of a mind struggling with misfortune, or the hopelessness of its desires, but of a mind preying upon itself, and disgusted with, or indifferent to all other things. There is nothing less poetical than this sort of unaccommodating selfishness. There is nothing more repulsive than this sort of ideal absorption of all the interests of others, of the good and ills of life, in the ruling passion and moody abstraction of a single mind, as if it would make itself the centre of the universe, and there was nothing worth cherishing but its intellectual diseases. It is like a cancer, eating into the heart of poetry.

Yet Hazlitt's attitude was sharply ambivalent. He was impressed with the intensity and consistency of Byron's work:

> But still there is power; and power rivets attention and forces admiration. 'He hath a demon': and that is the next thing to being full of the God. His brow collects the scattered gloom: his eye flashes livid fire that withers and consumes. But still we watch the progress of the scathing bolt with interest, and mark the ruin it leaves behind with awe. Within the contracted range of his imagination he has great unity and truth of keeping. . . . In vigour of style and force of conception, he in one sense surpasses every writer of the present day. His indignant apophthegms are like oracles of misanthropy. He who wishes for 'a curse to kill with', may find it in Lord Byron's writings.

But Hazlitt also conceded that there was an underlying tenderness:

Yet he has beauty lurking underneath his strength, tenderness sometimes joined with the frenzy of despair. A flash of golden light follows from the stroke of his pencil, like a falling meteor. The flowers that adorn his poetry bloom over charnel-houses and the grave.

It must, of course, be remembered that all this was said before Byron had started on his work in the Italian burlesque tradition.

In 1820[1] Hazlitt wrote an article in *The London Magazine* on drama, in the course of which he passes the opinion that Byron was no dramatist, and suggests why:

> Lord Byron's patrician haughtiness and monastic seclusion are, we think, no less hostile than the levelling spirit of Mr. Wordsworth's muse, to the endless gradations, variety, and complicated ideas or *mixed modes* of this sort of composition.

Still later Hazlitt in *Table Talk* (1821) has a passage which offers an acute account of the effect of Byron's peerage on his poetic reputation:

> He towers above his fellows by all the height of the peerage. If the poet lends a grace to the nobleman, the nobleman pays it back to the poet with interest. What a fine addition is ten thousand a year and a title to the flaunting pretensions of a modern rhapsodist! His name so accompanied becomes the mouth well: it is repeated thousands of times, instead of hundreds, because the reader in being familiar with the Poet's works seems to claim acquaintance with the Lord.
>
> > 'Let but a lord once own the happy lines:
> > How the wit brightens, and the style refines!'
>
> He smiles at the high-flown praise or petty cavils of little men. Does he make a slip in decorum, which Milton declares to be the principal thing? His proud crest and armorial bearings support him:—no bend-sinister slurs his proud escutcheon! Is he dull, or does he put off some trashy production on the public? It is not charged to his account, as a deficiency which he must make good at the peril of his admirers. His Lordship is not answerable for the negligence or extravagances of his Muse. He 'bears a charmed reputation, which must not yield' like one of vulgar birth. The noble Bard is for this reason scarcely vulnerable to the critics. The double barrier of his pretensions baffles their puny, timid efforts. Strip off some of his tarnished laurels, and the coronet appears glittering beneath: restore them, and it still shines through with keener lustre. In fact, his Lordship's blaze of reputation culminates from his rank and place in society. He sustains two lofty and imposing characters; and in order to simplify the process of our admiration, and 'leave no rubs or botches in the way', we equalise his pretensions, and take it for granted that he must be as superior to other men in genius as he is in birth. Or, to give a more familiar solution of the enigma, the Poet

---

[1] *LM*, I, April 1820, 'The Drama. No. IV'.

and the Peer agree to honour each other's acceptances on the bank of Fame, and sometimes cozen the town to some tune between them.[1]

Hazlitt's most important pronouncement on Byron's work, however, is in *The Spirit of the Age*. Almost all that essay was written before Byron's death, and it therefore falls within the scope of our study. The essay is readily available in many collections, and I am therefore confining the extract in the anthology to the passage on *Don Juan*.[2] The whole essay is perhaps one of Hazlitt's best pieces of criticism.

It is also, however, worth mentioning the brief characterization of Byron's work in his *Select British Poets* (1824):

> Lord Byron's distinguishing quality is intensity of conception and expression. He *wills* to be sublime or pathetic. He has great wildness of invention, brilliant and elegant fancy, caustic wit, but no humour. Gray's description of the poetical character—'Thoughts that glow, and words that burn' applies to him more than to any of his contemporaries.[3]

Among other good criticism of Byron I have already mentioned the admirable *Letter from John Bull*, and the observations by Croker in letters to John Murray. I shall shortly mention more fully the sympathetic reactions of Shelley. Meanwhile, however, I want to indicate the attitude of Keats.

Keats's antipathy to the storm scene in *Don Juan II* has already been mentioned above.[4] Keats had, however, all along had a certain hostility to Byron both as a figure and as a poet. We find him quite early contrasting Byron as a 'superfine rich or noble poet' with himself as a 'common' one.[5] Later he groups Byron with Scott as a 'literary King',[6] and, still later, makes the following distinction between Byron's work and his own:

> He describes what he sees—I describe what I imagine—Mine is the hardest task. You see the immense difference.[7]

Earlier the same year he had made a disparaging distinction, not unrelated to this one, between Byron and Shakespeare:

[1] Hazlitt, *Complete Works*, ed. P. P. Howe (London and Toronto, 1932), VIII. 209–10.

[2] See p. 303 below.

[3] Hazlitt, *Works*, ed. Howe, IX. 244.   [4] See p. 188 above.

[5] Keats, Letter to C. W. Dilke, 20, 21 September 1818 (*KL*, I. 368).

[6] Letter to George and Georgiana Keats, 29 (?) December 1818 (*ibid.*, II. 16).

[7] Letter to George and Georgiana Keats, 20 September 1819 (*ibid.*, II. 200).

A Man's life of any worth is a continual allegory—and very few eyes can see the Mystery of his life—a life like the scriptures, figurative—which such people can no more make out than they can the hebrew Bible. Lord Byron cuts a figure—but he is not figurative—Shakespeare led a life of Allegory; his works are the comments on it—[1]

Shelley, on the other hand, had a tremendous, almost awestruck, admiration for Byron's poetic gifts, though he was far from being blind to his defects as a man. Shelley was particularly attracted by *Childe Harold III*, which is not surprising, since he had been in Byron's company during part of the time when it was being written, and had, indeed, influenced it directly and indirectly. He read the canto in manuscript, and thought that it 'infinitely' surpassed any poem Byron had so far published.[2] He was not attracted by Byron's indulgence in 'despair' in the Eastern Tales.[3] And though Shelley greatly liked the apostrophe to Ocean in *Childe Harold IV*, he agreed with Peacock in violently disapproving of the spirit expressed in the canto—'if insane, the most wicked and mischievous insanity that ever was given forth'. Shelley attributed it to Byron's dissipated life in Venice.[4] Equally interestingly, however, and perhaps somewhat unexpectedly, Shelley warmly welcomed *Don Juan I and II*, and concurrently appealed to Byron to write his great poem 'containing within itself the germs of a permanent relation to the present, and to all succeeding ages!'[5] As mentioned above, he admired the 'strange and terrible storm' in *II*, and particularly the passage about the two fathers, commenting that Dante hardly exceeded it. As to Julia's letter in *I*, it is worth quoting more fully from Shelley's letter to Byron already referred to[6]:

> The love letter and the account of its being written, is altogether a masterpiece of portraiture; of human nature laid with the eternal colours of the feelings of humanity. Where did you learn all these secrets? I should like to go to school there. I cannot say I equally approve of the service to which this letter was appropriated; or that I altogether think the bitter mockery of our common nature, of which this is one of the expressions, quite worthy of your genius. The power and the beauty and the wit, indeed, redeem all this—

[1] Letter to George and Georgiana Keats, 19 February 1819 (*ibid.*, II. 67).
[2] Shelley, Letter to Hogg, 18 July 1816 (*SL*, I. 493).
[3] Letter to Byron, 9 July 1817 (*ibid.*, I. 547).
[4] Letter to Peacock, [17 or 18] December 1818 (*ibid.*, II. 57–8).
[5] Letter to Byron, 16 [or 17] April 1821 (*ibid.*, II. 284).
[6] See p. 187 above.

chiefly because they belie and refute it. Perhaps it is foolish to wish that there had been nothing to redeem.

When Byron sent him *III–V* Shelley was still more enthusiastic[1]:

> Nothing has ever been written like it in English—nor if I may venture to prophesy, will there be; without carrying upon it the mark of a secondary or borrowed light.—You unveil and present in its true deformity what is worst in human nature, and this is what the witlings of the age murmur at, conscious of their want of power to endure the scrutiny of such a light.—We are damned to the knowledge of good and evil, and it is well for us to know what we should avoid no less than what we should seek.—The character of Lambro —his return—the merriment of his daughter's guests made as it were in celebration of his funeral—the meeting with the lovers—and the death of Haidee—are circumstances combined and developed in a manner that I seek elsewhere in vain. The fifth canto, which some of your pet Zoili in Albemarle St. said was *dull*, gathers instead of loses, splendour and energy—the language in which the whole is clothed—a sort of chameleon under the changing sky of the spirit that kindles it—is such as these lisping days could not have expected,—and are, believe me, in spite of the approbation which you wrest from them—little pleased to hear. One can hardly judge from recitation and it was not until I read it in print that I have been able to do it justice.—This sort of writing on a great plan and perhaps in a more compact form is what I wished you to do when I made my vows for an epic.—But I am content—You are building up a drama, such as England has not yet seen, and the task is sufficiently noble and worthy of you.

Shelley had already thought that Canto V—which Byron read to him at Ravenna—set the latter 'not above but far above all the poets of the day', and that 'every word' had 'the stamp of immortality'.[2]

Crabb Robinson wrote some interesting things about Byron's work in his *Diary*. In November 1816 he describes his reactions on first reading *Childe Harold III*[3]:

> This I read with more interest than any other of Lord Byron's works. Whether it is that knowing more about them I am more interested in his personalities, or that his sentiments are become more humane, I cannot tell. He certainly presents himself as an

---

[1] Letter to Byron, 21 October 1821 (*SL*, II. 397–8).
[2] Letter to Mary Shelley, 10 August 1821 (*SL*, II. 323).
[3] *Diary*, 20 November 1816 (*HCRBW*, I. 198).

object of compassion in these poetical confessions. He does not obtrude his worn-out sensibilities, his unpatriotic contempt of his country, his disregard of all that is beautiful in courage and religion, etc. I know not that there is more poetry in this work, but there is more humanity.

Shortly afterwards he read *The Prisoner of Chillon* volume. He thought the title-poem 'feeble', but considered *The Dream* to be 'a pathetic and interesting composition', even though it exhibited Byron 'in a most unfortunate point of view—thinking of his first love when at the altar marrying his wife whom he is still represented loving'. *Darkness* impressed him greatly—'a powerful picture of all nature suffering under the horror of darkness— famine and murder being its accompaniments'. The incantation against the governess also caught his attention. He comments in conclusion:

> Certainly Lord Byron has the elements of poetry in him and his style is singularly changing. He has grossly and palpably imitated Wordsworth in his latter works, but his imitations are by no means happy.[1]

Several years later Crabb Robinson tells of a meeting he had with a certain Mr Mulock, 'a lecturer in English Literature at Geneva and Lausanne'. Mulock was apparently an 'ultra-Calvinist' who thought 'all declamations about God as recognized in the beauties and wonders of nature were mystical nonsense'. Mulock believed Wordsworth's religious poetry to be 'atheism', but 'avowed the highest admiration' for Byron, whom he considered 'a greater poet than Shakespeare'. Mulock saw in Byron's works 'the profoundest views of the depravity of human nature—not indeed spiritual views, but though not spiritually-minded', Byron had 'developed the human heart', and 'the intense truth of all his poetry' was its 'great excellence'. Crabb Robinson drily comments:

> I admitted that Lord Byron's works do exhibit a most depraved and corrupt heart, but observed that he shares this merit with Voltaire, Lord Rochester, and all the obscene and profligate writers of Italy and France. Mr. Mulock did not feel the observation.[2]

Just over a year later we find Crabb Robinson reading *Don Juan III–V*. He was 'amused by parts', and thought the 'gaiety'

[1] *Ibid.*, 1 December 1816 (*HCRBW*, I. 198–9).
[2] *Diary*, 20 September 1820 (*HCRBW*, I, 246–7; *D*, 65–66).

was 'agreeable enough' when 'playful and ironical', and considered it 'less malignant' here than on other occasions. 'The gross violations of decorum and morality' he felt used to, and he did not resent the lines on *The Excursion* or the 'affected contempt' towards Wordsworth which Byron always obtruded. Crabb Robinson admired the 'beautiful hymn to Greece', and thought the cantos also contained 'one or two powerful descriptions'.

On the other hand, Crabb Robinson was by no means attracted by *The Vision of Judgment*, calling it 'as dull as it is profligate':

> He offends the moral feelings of men and does not bribe their taste. This trash is not redeemed by a single passage of poetry, sense, or wit.[1]

Crabb Robinson changed his mind when he read the poem to Goethe seven years later; but I believe his first reaction was a sounder one.

Perhaps, however, it is well to end this survey on a more favourable note, by mentioning the comprehensive tribute to *Don Juan* by Sir Walter Scott in *The Edinburgh Weekly Journal* for 19 May 1824, where he wrote that in that poem Byron had 'combined every topic of human life, and sounded every string of the divine harp, from its slightest to its most powerful and heart-astounding tones'.

[1] *Ibid.*, 20 October 1822 (*HCRBW*, I. 286).

An Anthology of Contemporary Criticism
1807–24

From the unsigned review by George Edward Griffiths of *Hours of Idleness* (1807) in *The Monthly Review*, November 1807.

Indications of early capacity and bias, whether directed towards literature or the arts, should never be despised nor neglected; since nature thus points out the road which she seems to intend the youth to travel in his journey through life, and in which she will afford him more potent aid than he would derive from other sources in different pursuits. . . .

These compositions are generally of a plaintive or an amatory cast, with an occasional mixture of satire; and they display both ease and strength, both pathos and fire. They sometimes convey the strains of sorrow, occasioned by illness and the *crosses in love* of the too susceptible youth; and in one instance he laments his own lot, in being denied the solace of the nearest and dearest society,—of parent, of brother, and of sister,—with a tenderness and a feeling that are highly creditable. . . .

We discern in Lord Byron a degree of mental power, and a turn of mental disposition, which render us solicitous that both should be well cultivated and wisely directed, in his career of life. He has received talents, and is accountable for the use of them. We trust that he will render them beneficial to man, and a source of real gratification to himself in declining age.

The unsigned review by Henry Brougham of *Hours of Idleness* in *The Edinburgh Review*, January 1808.

The poesy of this young lord belongs to the class which neither gods nor men are said to permit. Indeed, we do not recollect to have seen a quantity of verse with so few deviations in either direction from that exact standard. His effusions are spread over a dead flat, and can no more get above or below the level, than if they were so much stagnant water. As an extenuation of this offence, the noble author is peculiarly forward in pleading minority. We have it in the title-page, and on the very back of the volume; it follows his name like a favourite part of his *style*. Much stress is laid upon it in the preface, and the poems are connected with this general statement of his case, by particular dates, substantiating the age at which each was written. Now, the law upon the point of minority, we hold to be perfectly clear. It is a plea available only to the defendant; no plaintiff can offer it as a supplementary ground of action. Thus, if any suit could be brought against Lord Byron, for the purpose of compelling him to put into court a certain quantity of poetry; and if judgement were given against him; it is highly probable that an exception would be taken, were he to deliver *for poetry*, the contents of this volume. To this he might plead *minority*; but as he now makes voluntary tender of the article, he hath no right to sue, on that ground, for the price in good current praise, should the goods be unmarketable. This is our view of the law on the point, and we dare to say, so will it be ruled. Perhaps however, in reality, all that he tells us about his youth, is rather with a view to increase our wonder, than to soften our censures. He possibly means to say, 'See how a minor can write! This poem was actually composed by a young man of eighteen, and this by one of only sixteen!'—But, alas, we all remember the poetry of Cowley at ten, and Pope at twelve; and so far from hearing, with any degree of surprise, that very poor verses were written by a youth from his leaving school to his leaving college, inclusive, we really believe this to be the most common of all occurrences; that it happens in the life of nine men in ten who are educated in England; and that the tenth man writes better verse than Lord Byron.

His other plea of privilege, our author rather brings forward in order to wave it. He certainly, however, does allude frequently to his family and ancestors—sometimes in poetry, sometimes in notes; and while giving up his claim on the score of rank, he takes care to remember us of Dr Johnson's saying, that when a nobleman appears as an author, his merit should be handsomely acknowledged. In truth, it is this consideration only, that induces us to give Lord Byron's poems a place in our review, beside our desire to counsel him, that he do forthwith abandon poetry, and turn his talents, which are considerable, and his opportunities, which are great, to better account.

With this view, we must beg leave seriously to assure him, that the mere rhyming of the final syllable, even when accompanied by the presence of a certain number of feet; nay, although (which does not always happen) those feet should scan regularly, and have been all counted accurately upon the fingers,—is not the whole art of poetry. We would entreat him to believe, that a certain portion of liveliness, somewhat of fancy, is necessary to constitute a poem; and that a poem in the present day, to be read, must contain at least one thought, either in a little degree different from the ideas of former writers, or differently expressed. We put it to his candour, whether there is any thing so deserving the name of poetry in verses like the following, written in 1806, and whether, if a youth of eighteen could say any thing so uninteresting to his ancestors, a youth of nineteen should publish it.

> 'Shades of heroes, farewell! your descendant, departing
>   From the seat of his ancestors, bids you, adieu!
> Abroad, or at home, your remembrance imparting
>   New courage, he'll think upon glory, and you.
>
> Though a tear dim his eye, at this sad separation,
>   'Tis nature, not fear, that excites his regret:
> Far distant he goes, with the same emulation;
>   The fame of his fathers he ne'er can forget.
>
> That fame, and that memory, still will he cherish,
>   He vows, that he ne'er will disgrace your renown;
> Like you will he live, or like you will he perish;
>   When decay'd, may he mingle his dust with your own.'
>   [*On leaving Newstead Abbey*, sts. 6–8]

Now we positively do assert, that there is nothing better than these stanzas in the whole compass of the noble minor's volume.

Lord Byron should also have a care of attempting what the greatest poets have done before him, for comparisons (as he must have had occasion to see at his writing master's) are odious.—Gray's Ode on Eton College, should really have kept out the ten hobbling stanzas 'on a distant view of the village and school of Harrow.'

> 'Where fancy, yet, joys to retrace the resemblance,
>   Of comrades, in friendship and mischief allied;
> How welcome to me, your ne'er fading remembrance,
>   Which rests in the bosom, though hope is deny'd.'
>   [*On a Distant View of Harrow* . . . *1806*, st. 2]

In like manner, the exquisite lines of Mr Rogers, '*On a Tear*,' might have warned the noble author off those premises, and spared us a whole dozen such stanzas as the following.

> 'Mild Charity's glow,
> To us mortals below,
> Shows the soul from barbarity clear;
> Compassion will melt,

209

Where this virtue is felt,
And its dew is diffus'd in a Tear.

The man doom'd to fail,
With the blast of the gale,
Through billows Atlantic to steer,
As he bends o'er the wave,
Which may soon be his grave,
The green sparkles bright with a Tear.'

[*The Tear*, sts. 3–4]

And so of instances in which former poets had failed. Thus, we do not think Lord Byron was made for translating, during his non-age, Adrian's Address to his Soul, when Pope succeeded so indifferently in the attempt. If our readers, however, are of another opinion, they may look at it.

'Ah! gentle, fleeting, wav'ring sprite,
Friend and associate of this clay!
To what unknown region borne,
Wilt thou, now, wing thy distant flight?
No more, with wonted humour gay,
But pallid, cheerless, and forlorn.'

However, be this as it may, we fear his translations and imitations are great favourites with Lord Byron. We have them of all kinds, from Anacreon to Ossian; and, viewing them as school exercises, they may pass. Only, why print them after they have had their day and served their turn? And why call the thing in p. 79. a translation, where *two* words (θελω λεγειν) of the original are expanded into four lines, and the other thing in p. 81, where μεσονυκτιοις ποθ' ὁ ραις,[1] is rendered by means of six hobbling verses?—As to his Ossianic poesy, we are not very good judges, being, in truth, so moderately skilled in that species of composition, that we should, in all probability, be criticizing some bit of the genuine Macpherson itself, were we to express our opinion of Lord Byron's raphsodies [*sic*]. *If*, then, the following beginning of a 'Song of bards,' is by his Lordship, we venture to object to it, as far as we can comprehend it. 'What form rises on the roar of clouds, whose dark ghost gleams on the red stream of tempests? His voice rolls on the thunder; 'tis Orla, the brown chief of Otihona. He was,' &c. After detaining this 'brown chief' some time, the bards conclude by giving him their advice to 'raise his fair locks;' then to 'spread them on the arch of the rainbow;' and 'to smile through the tears of the storm.' Of this kind of thing

[1] Incorrect Greek for the *Anacreontea*'s μεσονυκτίοις ποθ' ὥραις (xxx. 1) —Ed.

there are no less than *nine* pages; and we can so far venture an opinion in their favour, that they look very like Macpherson; and we are positive they are pretty nearly as stupid and tiresome.

It is a sort of privilege of poets to be egotists; but they should 'use it as not abusing it;' and particularly one who piques himself (though indeed at the ripe age of nineteen), of being 'an infant bard,'—('The artless Helicon I boast is youth;')—should either not know, or should seem not to know, so much about his own ancestry. Besides a poem above cited on the family seat of the Byrons, we have another of eleven pages, on the self-same subject, introduced with an apology, 'he certainly had no intention of inserting it;' but really, 'the particular request of some friends,' &c. &c. It concludes with five stanzas on himself, 'the last and youngest of a noble line.' There is a good deal also about his maternal ancestors, in a poem on Lachin-y-gair, a mountain where he spent part of his youth, and might have learnt that *pibroch* is not a bagpipe, any more than duet means a fiddle.

As the author has dedicated so large a part of his volume to immortalize his employments at school and college, we cannot possibly dismiss it without presenting the reader with a specimen of these ingenious effusions. In an ode with a Greek motto, called Granta, we have the following magnificent stanzas.

> 'There, in apartments small and damp,
>   The candidate for college prizes,
> Sits poring by the midnight lamp,
>   Goes late to bed, yet early rises.

[Here the reviewer omits to quote two stanzas]

> 'Who reads false quantities in Sele,
>   Or puzzles o'er the deep triangle;
> Depriv'd of many a wholesome meal,
>   In barbarous Latin, doom'd to wrangle,
>
> Renouncing every pleasing page,
>   From authors of historic use;
> Preferring to the lettered sage,
>   The square of the hypothenuse.
>
> Still harmless are these occupations,
>   That hurt none but the hapless student,
> Compar'd with other recreations,
>   Which bring together the imprudent.'

> *[Granta, a Medley*, sts. 8, 11–13]

We are sorry to hear so bad an account of the college psalmody as is contained in the following Attic stanzas.

'Our choir would scarcely be excus'd,
    Even as a band of raw beginners;
All mercy, now, must be refus'd
    To such a set of croaking sinners.

If David, when his toils were ended,
    Had heard these blockheads sing before him,
To us, his psalms had ne'er descended;
    In furious mood, he would have tore 'em.'

                          [*Ibid.*, sts. 20–1]

But whatever judgment may be passed on the poems of this noble minor, it seems we must take them as we find them, and be content; for they are the last we shall ever have from him. He is at best, he says, but an intruder into the groves of Parnassus; he never lived in a garret, like thorough-bred poets; and 'though he once roved a careless mountaineer in the Highlands of Scotland,' he has not of late enjoyed this advantage. Moreover, he expects no profit from his publication; and whether it succeeds or not, 'it is highly improbable, from his situation and pursuits hereafter,' that he should again condescend to become an author. Therefore, let us take what we get and be thankful. What right have we poor devils to be nice? We are well off to have got so much from a man of this Lord's station, who does not live in a garret, but 'has the sway' of Newstead Abbey. Again, we say, let us be thankful; and, with honest Sancho, bid God bless the giver, nor look the gift horse in the mouth.

From the review of *English Bards and Scotch Reviewers* (1809) in *The Eclectic Review*, May 1809.

We understand this poem has already attained a large circulation; a circumstance by no means surprising, when we consider its high seasoning of invective and sarcasm, its humour and spirited versification, and the peculiarity of its subject and its occasion, combined with the rank of its reputed author. The world is said to be indebted for this effusion of "the milk of human kindness" to no less a personage than Lord Byron, on no less an occasion than the discipline bestowed on the said Lord, for certain 'Hours of Idleness,' by the Busby hands of the Edinburgh Reviewers. This is just as it should be. For equitable discrimination, for devotedness to truth, for gentlemanly deportment, and the genuine Christian spirit of candour, amenity, forgiveness of injuries, and reluctance to inflict pain, the combatants are pretty fairly matched. The literary *canaille* will gaze on this game-cock spectacle with a delight, which happily need not be diminished by any compunction for the cause, or apprehension for the consequences. If, however, the noble lord, and the learned advocate, have the courage requisite to sustain their mutual insults, we shall probably soon hear the explosions of another kind of *paper*-war, after the fashion of the ever-memorable duel which the latter is said to have fought, or seemed to fight, with 'Little Moore'. We confess there is sufficient provocation, if not in the critique, at least in the satire, to urge a 'man of honour' to defy his assailant to mortal combat, and perhaps to warrant a man of law to *declare* war in Westminster-Hall. Of this, no doubt, we shall hear more in due time. The lines we principally allude to are these;—from the opening hemistich, which seems to have been copied from the celebrated 'Epistle to Warburton,' though the acknowledgement of the imitation is *accidentally* omitted, we should guess that the noble lord has been for some time under training for this attack, and has both strengthened and encouraged his stomach for fighting by a course of *Churchill*; and we must confess he does credit to his feeding. . . .

The sheer folly of the author's criticisms on many of our living poets will very much defeat the effect of those strictures, in his poem, which are both spirited and just. There is so little discretion and taste in many of his decisions, such total insensibility to indisputable merit in others, such unmitigated and arrogant reprobation when there was only need for partial and judicious reproof, that he will be regarded, not as a severe and indignant Censor, but as a petulant school-boy, smarting and exasperated almost to madness with his flagellation, blind with rage and anguish, and dealing out his indiscriminate revenge in kicks and blows preposterously excessive in malice and deficient in power. The influence of this satire will be no less diminished by the absurdity of the praise, which the angry nobleman, for no imaginable reason, condescends in some instances to bestow. What will any considerate man care for the opinions, decrees, or censures of a writer, who can extol Macneil as a genuine son of Poesy, while he degrades Southey and Scott to the dust, and can find nothing but vulgar ridicule to requite the sublimity of Coleridge or the pathos and vivid painting of Grahame! His premature *requiem* over the 'lost works' of Montgomery, whose genius he nevertheless acknowledges, and whose fame both lives and flourishes, is equally childish.

The utmost we can promise the noble lord is, that his wrath will be very entertaining to the public for several weeks to come; by the end of that period, the same public will perhaps be called upon to deplore his fall in the field of honour, and it may be our melancholy office to criticise elegies on his untimely fate.

From Francis Jeffrey's unsigned review of *Childe Harold I and II*
(1812) in *The Edinburgh Review*, February 1812 (publ. May).

Lord Byron has improved marvellously since his last appearance
at our tribunal;—and this, though it bear a very affected title, is
really a volume of very considerable power, spirit and originality—
which not only atones for the evil works of his nonage, but gives
promise of a further excellence hereafter; to which it is quite comfortable to look forward.

The most surprising thing about the present work, indeed, is,
that it should please and interest so much as it does, with so few of
the ordinary ingredients of interest or poetical delight. There is no
story or adventure—and, indeed, no incident of any kind; the whole
poem—to give a very short account of it—consisting of a series of
reflections made in travelling through a part of Spain and Portugal,
and in sailing up the Mediterranean to the shores of Greece. These
reflections, too, and the descriptions out of which they arise, are
presented without any regular order or connexion—being sometimes
strung upon the slender thread of Childe Harold's Pilgrimage, and
sometimes held together by the still slighter tie of the author's local
situation at the time of writing. As there are no incidents, there cannot well be any characters;—and accordingly, with the exception of a
few national sketches, which form part of the landscape of his
pilgrimage, that of the hero himself is the only delineation of the
kind that is offered to the reader of this volume;—and this hero,
we must say, appears to us as oddly chosen as he is imperfectly employed. Childe Harold is a sated epicure—sickened with the very
fulness of prosperity—oppressed with ennui, and stung with occasional remorse;—his heart hardened by a long course of sensual
indulgence, and his opinion of mankind degraded by his acquaintance with the baser part of them. In this state he wanders over the
fairest and most interesting parts of Europe, in the vain hope of
stimulating his palsied sensibility by novelty, or at least of occasionally forgetting his mental anguish in the toils and perils of his
journey. Like Milton's fiend, however, he 'sees undelighted all
delight,' and passes on through the great wilderness of the world
with a heart shut to all human sympathy,—sullenly despising the stir
both of its business and its pleasures—but hating and despising
himself most of all, for beholding it with so little emotion.

Lord Byron takes the trouble to caution his readers against
supposing that he meant to shadow out his own character under the
dark and repulsive traits of that which we have just exhibited; a
caution which was surely unnecessary—though it is impossible
not to observe, that the mind of the noble author has been so far
tinged by his strong conception of this Satanic personage, that the

sentiments and reflections which he delivers in his own name, have all received a shade of the same gloomy and misanthropic colouring which invests those of his imaginary hero. The general strain of those sentiments, too, is such as we should have thought very little likely to attract popularity, in the present temper of this country. They are not only complexionally dark and disdainful, but run directly counter to very many of our national passions, and most favoured propensities. Lord Byron speaks with the most unbounded contempt of the Portuguese—with despondence of Spain—and in a very slighting and sarcastic manner of wars, and victories, and military heroes in general. Neither are his religious opinions more orthodox, we apprehend, than his politics; for he not only speaks without any respect of priests, and creeds, and dogmas of all de-scriptions, but doubts very freely of the immortality of the soul, and other points as fundamental.

Such are some of the disadvantages under which this poem lays claim to the public favour; and it will be readily understood that we think it has no ordinary merit, when we say, that we have little doubt that it will find favour, in spite of these disadvantages. Its chief excellence is a singular freedom and boldness, both of thought and expression, and a great occasional force and felicity of diction, which is the more pleasing that it does not appear to be the result either of long labour or humble imitation. There is, indeed, a tone of self-willed independence and originality about the whole com-position—a certain plain manliness and strength of manner, which is infinitely refreshing after the sickly affectations of so many modern writers; and reconciles us not only to the asperity into which it sometimes degenerates, but even in some degree to the unamiable-ness upon which it constantly borders. We do not know, indeed, whether there is not something *piquant* in the very novelty and singularity of that cast of misanthropy and universal scorn, which we have already noticed as among the repulsive features of the composition. It excites a kind of curiosity, at least, to see how objects, which have been usually presented under so different an aspect, appear through so dark a medium; and undoubtedly gives great effect to the flashes of emotion and suppressed sensibility that occasionally burst through the gloom. The best parts of the poem, accordingly, are those which embody those stern and disdainful reflexions, to which the author seems to recur with unfeigned cordiality and eagerness—and through which we think we can sometimes discern the strugglings of a gentler feeling, to which he is afraid to abandon himself. There is much strength, in short, and some impetuous feeling in this poem—but very little softness; some pity for mankind —but very little affection; and no enthusiasm in the cause of any living men, or admiration of their talents or virtues. The author's inspiration does not appear to have brought him any beatific visions, nor to have peopled his fancy with any forms of loveliness; and though his lays are often both loud and lofty, they neither 'lap us in Elysium,' nor give us any idea that it was in Elysium that they were framed.

The descriptions are often exceedingly good; and the diction, though unequal and frequently faulty, has on the whole a freedom, copiousness and vigour, which we are not sure that we could match in any cotemporary poet. Scott alone, we think, possesses a style equally strong and natural; but Scott's is more made up of imitations, and indeed is frequently a mere cento of other writers— while Lord Byron's has often a nervous simplicity and manly freshness which reminds us of Dryden, and an occasional force and compression, in some of the smaller pieces especially, which afford no unfavourable resemblance of Crabbe.

The versification is in the stanza of Spencer; and none of all the imitators of that venerable bard have availed themselves more extensively of the great range of tones and manners in which his example entitles them to indulge. Lord Byron has accordingly given us descriptions in all their extremes;—sometimes compressing into one stanza the whole characteristic features of a country, and sometimes expanding into twenty the details of a familiar transaction;— condescending, for pages together, to expatiate in minute and ludicrous representations,—and mingling long apostrophes, execrations, and the expression of personal emotion, with the miscellaneous picture which it is his main business to trace on the imagination of his readers. Not satisfied even with this license of variety, he has passed at will, and entirely, from the style of Spencer, to that of his own age,—and intermingled various lyrical pieces with the solemn stanza of his general measure.

A letter about *Childe Harold III* (1816) from John Wilson Croker to John Murray, 18 September 1816.

Admiralty, September 18th, 1816.

My dear Murray,

I have read with great pleasure the poem you lent me. It is written with great vigour, and all the descriptive part is peculiarly to my taste, for I am fond of realities, even to the extent of being fond of localities. A spot of ground a yard square, a rock, a hillock, on which some great achievement has been performed, or to which any recollections of interest attach, excite my feelings more than all the monuments of art. Pictures fade, and statues moulder, and forests decay, and cities perish, but the sod of Marathon is immortal, and he who has had the good fortune to stand on that sacred spot has identified himself with Athenian story in a way which all the historians, painters, and poets of the world could not have accomplished for him. Shakespeare, whom nothing escaped, very justly hints that one of the highest offices of good poetry is to connect our ideas with some "local habitation." It is an old and highly absurd phrase to say that poetry deals in fiction; alas, *history*, I fear, deals in fiction, but good poetry is concerned only with *realities*, either of visible or moral nature; and so much for local poetry. But I did not read with equal pleasure a note or two which reflects on the Bourbon family. What has a poet who writes for immortality, to do with the little temporary passions of political parties? Such notes are like Pope's "flies in amber." I wish you could persuade Lord Byron to leave out these two or three lines of prose, which will make thousands dissatisfied with his glorious poetry. For my own part I am not a man of rank and family, and have not, therefore, such motives for respecting rank and family as Lord Byron has, yet I own (however I may disapprove and lament much of what is going on in France) that I could not bring myself to speak irreverently of the children of St. Louis, of assuredly the most ancient and splendid family of the civilised world, of a house which is connected with the whole system of European policy, European literature, European refinement, and, I will add, European glory. My love of realities comes in here again, and I say to myself, when I see Louis XVIII., overlooking all his personal qualities, here is the lineal descendant of fifty kings, all famous, many illustrious; men who have held in their hands from age to age the destinies of millions; some of whom have been the benefactors of mankind, and others (and this part of the recollection is not the least *interesting*) who have astonished and afflicted the world by their crimes. No; pray use your influence on this point. As to the poem itself, except a word or two suggested by Mr. Giffard [*sic*], I do not think anything can be altered for the better.

Yours faithfully,

J. W. CROKER.

From Francis Jeffrey's unsigned review of *Childe Harold III* in *The Edinburgh Review*, December 1816.

The most considerable of these [Byron's most recent publications] is the Third Canto of Childe Harold, a work which has the disadvantage of all continuations in admitting of little absolute novelty in the plan of the work, or the cast of its character, and must, besides, remind all Lord Byron's readers of the extraordinary effect produced by the sudden blazing forth of his genius upon their first introduction to that title. In spite of all this, however, we are persuaded that this Third Part of the poem will not be pronounced inferior to either of the former; and, we think, will probably be ranked above them by those who have been most delighted with the whole. The great success of this singular production, indeed, has always appeared to us an extraordinary proof of its merits; for, with all its genius, it does not belong to a sort of poetry that rises easily to popularity.—It has no story or action—very little variety of character—and a great deal of reasoning and reflection of no very attractive tenor. It is substantially a contemplative and ethical work, diversified with fine description, and adorned or overshaded by one emphatic person, who is sometimes the author, and sometimes the object of the reflections on which the interest is chiefly rested. It required, no doubt, great force of writing, and a decided tone of originality to recommend a performance of this sort so powerfully as this has been recommended to public notice and admiration—and those high characteristics belong perhaps still more eminently to the part that is now before us, than to any of the former. There is the same stern and lofty disdain of mankind, and their ordinary pursuits and enjoyments, with the same bright gaze on nature, and the same magic power of giving interest and effect to her delineations—but mixed up, we think, with deeper and more matured reflections, and a more intense sensibility to all that is grand or lovely in the external world.—Harold, in short, is somewhat older since he last appeared upon the scene—and while the vigour of his intellect has been confirmed, and his confidence in his own opinions increased, his mind has also become more sensitive; and his misanthropy, thus softened over by habits of calmer contemplation, appears less active and impatient, even although more deeply rooted than before. Undoubtedly the finest parts of the poem before us, are those which thus embody the weight of his moral sentiments, or disclose the lofty sympathy which binds the despiser of Man to the glorious aspects of Nature. It is in these, we think, that the great attractions of the work consist, and the strength of the author's genius is seen. The narrative and description are of far inferior interest. With reference to the sentiments and opinions, however, which thus give its distinguishing character to the piece, we must say, that it seems no longer possible to ascribe them to the ideal person whose name it bears, or to any other than the author himself.—Lord Byron, we think, has formerly complained of those who identified him with his hero, or supposed that Harold was but the expositor of his own feelings and opinions;—and in noticing the former portions of the work, we thought it unbecoming to give any countenance to such a supposition.—In this last part, however, it is really impracticable to distinguish them.—Not only do the author and his hero travel and reflect together—but, in truth, we scarcely ever have any notice to which of them the sentiments so energetically expressed are to be ascribed; and in those which are unequivocally given as those of the Noble author himself, there is the very same tone of misanthropy, sadness and scorn, which we were formerly willing to regard as a part of the assumed costume of the Childe. We are far from supposing, indeed, that Lord Byron would disavow any of these sentiments; and though there are some which we must ever think it most unfortunate to entertain, and others which it appears improper to have published, the greater part are admirable, and cannot be perused without emotion even by those to whom they may appear erroneous. . . .

There can be no more remarkable proof of the greatness of Lord Byron's genius than the spirit and interest he has contrived to communicate to his picture of the often drawn and difficult scene of the breaking up from Brussels before the great battle. It is a trite remark, that poets generally fail in the representation of great events, when the interest is recent, and the particulars are consequently clearly and commonly known: and the reason is obvious; for as it is the object of poetry to make us feel for distant or imaginary occurrences nearly as strongly as if they were present and real, it is plain that there is no scope for her enchantments, where the impressive reality, with all its vast preponderance of interest, is already before us, and where the concern we take in the gazette far outgoes any emotion that can be conjured up in us by the help of fine descriptions. It is natural, however, for the sensitive tribe of poets, to mistake the common interest which they then share with the unpoetical part of their countrymen, for a vocation to versify; and so they proceed to pour out the lukewarm distillations of their fantasies upon the unchecked effervescence of public feeling. All our bards, accordingly, great and small, and of all sexes, ages, and professions, from Scott and Southey down to hundreds without names or additions, have adventured upon this theme—and failed in the management of it; and while they yielded to the patriotic impulse, as if they had all caught the inspiring summons—

Let those rhyme now who never rhymed before,
And those who always rhyme, rhyme now the more—

the result has been, that scarcely a line to be remembered had been produced on a subject which probably was thought, of itself, a secure passport to immortality. It required some courage to venture on a theme beset with so many dangers, and deformed with the wrecks of so many former adventurers;—and a theme, too, which, in its general conception, appeared alien to the prevailing tone of Lord Byron's poetry. See, however, with what easy strength he enters upon it, and with how much grace he gradually finds his way back to his own peculiar vein of sentiment and diction.

[Quotes stanza xxi: "There was a sound of revelry by night", and some of the following stanzas]

. . . .

This [the apostrophe to Napoleon in stanzas xxxix–xlv] is splendidly written, no doubt—but we trust it is not true;—and as it is delivered with much more than poetical earnestness, and recurs, indeed, in other forms in various parts of the volume, we must really be allowed to enter our dissent somewhat at large. With regard to conquerors, we wish with all our hearts that the case were as the Noble author represents it: But we greatly fear they are neither half so unhappy, nor half so much hated as they should be. On the contrary, it seems plain enough that they are very commonly idolized and admired, even by those on whom they trample; and we suspect, moreover, that in general they pass their time rather agreeably, and derive considerable satisfaction from the ruin and desolation of the world. From Macedonia's Madman to the Swede—from Nimrod to Bonaparte, the hunters of men have pursued their sport with as much gaiety, and as little remorse, as the hunters of other animals—and have lived as cheerily in their days of action, and as comfortably in their repose, as the followers of better pursuits. For this, and for the fame which they have generally enjoyed, they are obviously indebted to the great interests connected with their employment, and the mental excitement which belongs to its hopes and hazards. It would be strange, therefore, if the other active, but more innocent spirits whom Lord Byron has here placed in the same predicament, and who share all their sources of enjoyment, without the guilt and the hardness which they cannot fail of contracting, should be more miserable or more unfriended than those splendid curses of their kind—and it would be *passing strange*, and pitiful, if the most precious gifts of Providence should produce only unhappiness, and mankind regard with hostility their greatest benefactors. We do not believe in any such prodigies. Great vanity and ambition may indeed lead to feverish and restless efforts—to jealousies, to hate and to mortification—but these are only their effects when united to inferior abilities. It is not those, in short, who actually surpass mankind, that are unhappy, but those who struggle in vain to surpass them; and this moody temper, which eats into itself from within, and provokes fair and unfair opposition from without, is generally the result of pretensions which outgo the merits by which they are supported—and disappointments, that may be clearly traced, not to the excess of genius, but its defect.

It will be found, we believe, accordingly, that the master spirits of their age have always escaped the unhappiness which is here supposed to be the inevitable lot of extraordinary talents; and that this strange tax upon genius has only been levied upon those who held the secondary shares of it. Men of truly great powers of mind have generally been cheerful, social, and indulgent;—while a tendency to sentimental whining, or fierce intolerance, may be ranked among the surest symptoms of little souls and inferior intellects. In the whole list of our English poets, we can only remember Shenstone and Savage—two, certainly, of the lowest—who were querulous and discontented. Cowley, indeed, used to call himself melancholy;—but he was full of conceits and affectations, and has nothing to make us proud of him. Shakespeare, the greatest of them all, was evidently of a free and joyous temperament;—and so was Chaucer, their common master. The same disposition appears to have predominated in Fletcher, Johnson [*sic*], and their great contemporaries. The genius of Milton partook something of the austerity of the party to which he belonged, and of the controversies in which he was involved; but even when fallen on evil days and evil tongues, his spirit seems to have retained its serenity as well as its dignity;—and in his private life, as well as in his poetry, the majesty of a high character is tempered with great sweetness and practical wisdom. In the succeeding age, our poets were but too gay; and though we forbear to speak of living authors, we know enough of them to say with confidence, that to be miserable or to be hated is not now, any more than heretofore, the common lot of those who excel.

If this, however, be the case with poets, confessedly the most irritable and fantastic of all men of genius—and of poets, too, bred and born in the gloomy climate of England, it is not likely that those who have surpassed their fellows in other ways, or in other regions, have been more distinguished for unhappiness. Were Socrates and Plato, the greatest philosophers of antiquity, remarkable for unsocial or gloomy tempers?—was Bacon, the greatest in modern times?—was Sir Thomas More—or Erasmus—or Hume—or Voltaire? —was Newton—or Fenelon?—was Henry IV., the paragon of kings and conquerors?—was Fox, the most ardent, and, in the vulgar sense, the least successful of statesmen? These, and men like these, are undoubtedly the lights and the boast of the world. Yet there was no alloy of misanthropy or gloom in their genius. They did not disdain the men they had surpassed; and neither feared nor

221

experienced their hostility. Some detractors they might have, from envy or misapprehension; but, beyond all doubt, the prevailing sentiments in respect to them have always been those of gratitude and admiration; and the error of public judgment, where it has erred, has much oftener been to overrate than to undervalue the merits of those who had claims on their good opinion. On the whole, we are far from thinking that eminent men are happier than those who glide through life in peaceful obscurity; but it is their eminence, and the consequences of it, rather than the mental superiority by which it is obtained, that interferes with their enjoyment. Distinction, however won, usually leads to a passion for more distinction; and is apt to engage us in laborious efforts and anxious undertakings: and those, even when successful, seldom repay, in our judgment at least, the ease, the leisure and tranquillity, of which they require the sacrifice:—But it really passes our imagination to conceive, that the very highest degrees of intellectual vigour, or fancy, or sensibility, should of themselves be productive either of unhappiness or general dislike.

From the review of *Childe Harold III* and *The Prisoner of Chillon and other Poems* (1816) in *The British Critic*, December 1816.

The first publication of the noble Lord which claims our attention is the third part of Childe Harold. As the first and second parts of this poem appeared before we commenced our critical labours, we shall pass no opinion upon their merits, except that they were too generally over-rated by the fashion of the day. The poem before us is much more likely to find its level. The noble Lord has made such draughts upon public partiality, that little is now left him but the dregs of a cup which he once fondly thought to be inexhaustible. The hero of the poem is, as usual, himself: for he has now so unequivocally identified himself with his fictitious hero, that even in his most querulous moods, he cannot complain of our impertinence in tracing the resemblance. We really wish that the noble Lord would suppose that there was some other being in the world besides himself, and employ his imagination in tracing the lineament of some other character than his own. One would have imagined that in twelve several and successive efforts of his muse, something a little newer than this same inexhaustible self might have been invented. Wherever we turn, the same portrait meets our eye. We see it now glaring in oils, now sobered in fresco, now dim in transparency. Sometimes it frowns in the turban of the Turk, sometimes it struts in the buskins and cloak of the Spaniard, and sometimes it descends to fret in its native costume; but frown, strut or fret where it will, the face is still but one, and the features are still the same. "Mungo here, Mungo there, Mungo every where." We are ever ready to listen with all due patience to a long story, provided it be not too often repeated, but there is really a limit beyond which human patience ceases to be a virtue. We must come at last to the question, What is Lord Byron to us, and what have we to do either with his sublimity or his sulks? It is his poetical not his personal character which is the subject of our criticism, and when the latter is so needlessly and so unsparingly obtruded upon our attention, it betrays at once poverty of invention and lack of discretion. The noble Lord is ever informing us how vastly superior both he and his genius are to the common herd of mankind; that he is a being of another and a higher order, whose scowl is sublimity, and whose frown is majesty. We have the noble Lord's word for this and for a great deal more, and if he would have been content with telling us so not more than half a dozen times, to please him, we would have believed it. But he has pressed us so unmercifully, that we now begin to call for proof, and all the proof we can find is in his own assertion. The noble Lord has written a few very fine, and a few very pretty verses, which may be selected from a heap of crude, harsh, unpoetical strains; farther than this we neither know nor wish to know of his Lordship's fame. His Lordship's style, by a fortunate hit, caught the favourable moment in the turn of the public taste; his gall was mistaken for spirit, his affectation for feeling, and his harshness for originality. The world are now growing tired of their luminary, and wait only for the rise of some new meteor, to transfer their admiration and applause. The noble Lord had talents, which if they had been duly husbanded, might have ensured him a more permanent place in their estimation. His Lordship never could have been a Milton, a Dryden, a Pope, or a Gray, but he might have been a star of the third or fourth magnitude, whose beams would have shone even upon posterity with no contemptible lustre. As the matter stands, he will now be too late convinced that he whose theme is only self, will find at last that self his only audience.

From William Roberts's unsigned review of *Childe Harold III* in *The British Review*, February 1817.

Upon the whole, with respect to the execution of this third Canto of the poem, so unmeaningly called "Childe Harold's Pilgrimage," we think it quite equal to the former parts of the work; and of consequence greatly superior to the smaller poems of the same author, of which we have in former numbers spoken as we have thought they deserved. The loose and luxuriant harmony of the stanza in which this his principal poem is written has afforded room enough for that expansion of thought in which he seems to delight, and has allowed him to interweave sentiment and description into one continuous and complex idea; and the necessity which this structure imposes of filling out the dimensions of each stanza with a single subject, which to minds less abundant would be felt as an inconvenience, has greatly favoured the play and pliability of Lord Byron's genius. Each stanza, being a whole, made up of parts mutually conspiring to one general impression, acts with a collective force upon the imagination; and when the necessary amplification does not dilute but accumulate the strength of the general idea, there is no form of versification more powerfully pleasing. Lord Byron has many harsh lines, some proceeding from inadvertence and some perhaps from affectation, but in general he is a great master of this form of verse; less monotonous than either Thomson or Beattie, and as rich as either of them in poetical combinations; nor does Lord Byron come much behind them in the higher qualities of the poet. The one may excel him in magnificence, and the other in pathos, but in variety of description, boldness of imagery, and a certain opulence of expression derived from native resources, Lord Byron is inferior to none, Spencer perhaps alone excepted, who have gone before him in the same path of poetry. The difficulty arising from the necessary repetition of the rhymes, Lord Byron has overcome with as little appearance of struggle, or sacrifice of the proprieties of language, as any of his predecessors: his victory has been easy, and his triumph complete. He has also avoided the argumentative, the allegorical, and the pedantic manner. His figures are natural, short, and perspicuous, and his pictures warm and bright, without gaudiness or deceptious ornament. But still it must be confessed that there is in this poem neither the elevation of thought nor strength of delineation which are found in the Castle of Indolence, nor that picturesque display of character, and delicacy of touch in moral painting, by which the Minstrel is distinguished, wherein is described the early call of the poet of nature to the fulfilment of his destiny, with the vigour and vivacity of conscious genius, and with the intelligence of an initiated votary, to whom the mysteries of poetic inspiration were known by experience.

From Francis Jeffrey's unsigned review of *Beppo* (1818) in *The Edinburgh Review*, February 1818.

Though there is as little serious meaning or interest in this extraordinary performance, as can easily be imagined, we think it well entitled to a place in our fastidious Journal—and that, not merely because it is extremely clever and amusing, but because it affords a very curious and complete specimen of a kind of diction and composition of which our English literature has hitherto afforded very few examples. It is, in itself, absolutely a thing of nothing—without story, characters, sentiments, or intelligible object;—a mere piece of lively and loquacious prattling, in short, upon all kinds of frivolous subjects,—a sort of gay and desultory babbling about Italy and England, Turks, balls, literature and fish sauces. But still there is something very engaging in the uniform gayety, politeness, and good humour of the author—and something still more striking and admirable in the matchless facility with which he has cast into regular, and even difficult versification, the unmingled, unconstrained, and unselected language of the most light, familiar, and ordinary conversation. The French have always had a great deal of this sort of poetry—though with a very severe regard to the purity of the diction—and the Italians also, in a looser and more extravagant tone; but, in England, it seems never to have been naturalized. The nearest approach to it is to be found in some of the tales and lighter pieces of Prior—a few stanzas here and there among the trash and burlesque of Peter Pindar—and in several passages of Mr Moore, and the author of the facetious miscellany, entitled, the Twopenny Post Bag. Chaucer and Shakespeare had ease and gayety enough for the style of which we are speaking—but it belongs intrinsically to the silver, and not to the golden age of poetry; and implies the existence of certain habits of dissipation, derision, and intelligence in general society, and of a sort of conventional language, for the expression of those things, which were still to be formed in the days of these great masters.—It is scarcely necessary to add, except for our duller readers, that this same familiar, lively, conversational poetry, is perfectly distinct both from the witty, epigrammatic and satirical vein, in which Pope will never be surpassed—or equalled; and from the burlesque, humorous and distorted style which attained its greatest height in Hudibras, and has been copied abundantly enough by humbler imitators. The style of which we are speaking is, no doubt, occasionally satirical and witty and humorous —but it is, on the whole, far more gay than poignant, and is characterized, exactly as good conversation is, rather by its constant ease and amenity, than by any traits either of extraordinary brilliancy, or of strong and ludicrous effect. There must be a certain allowance of sense and sagacity—and little flying traits of picturesque description —and small flights of imagination—and sallies of naïveté and humour—but nothing very powerful, and nothing very long. The great charm is in the simplicity and naturalness of the language—the free but guarded use of all polite idioms, and even of all phrases of temporary currency that have the stamp of good company upon them,—with the exclusion of all scholastic or ambitious eloquence, all profound views, and all deep emotions.

The unknown writer before us has accomplished all these objects with great skill and felicity; and, in particular, has furnished us with an example, unique we rather think in our language, of about one hundred stanzas of good verse, entirely composed of common words, in their common places; never presenting us with one sprig of what is called poetical diction, or even making use of a single inversion, either to raise the style or assist the rhyme—but running on in an inexhaustible series of good easy colloquial phrases, and finding them fall into verse by some unaccountable and happy fatality. In this great and characteristic quality it is almost invariably excellent. In some other respects it is more unequal. About one half is as good as possible, in the style to which it belongs; the other half bears perhaps too many marks of that haste with which we take it for granted that such a work must necessarily be written. Some passages are rather too foolish, some too snappish, and some run too much on the cheap and rather plebeian humour of out-of-the-way rhymes and strange sounding words and epithets. But the greater part is very pleasant, amiable, and gentleman-like.

Hazlitt's brief notice of *Beppo* in *The Yellow Dwarf*, 28 March 1818.

This is a trifling story, if story it can be called, of a Venetian woman, who, in the absence of her husband, who has been kept in slavery in Turkey, and who afterwards has turned pirate, forms a connection with a coxcombical Count. It is made the means of conveying a humorous description of Italian manners, and some touches of severe satire, all in eight-line stanzas, with a playful profusion of double rhimes [*sic*], which remind us of some parts of Sir John Harington's *Ariosto*. It is attributed to Lord Byron, and certainly must be the production of some one who has great power and practice in versification.

From William Roberts's unsigned review of *Beppo* in *The British Review*, May 1818.

Put feeling, and virtue, and the interests of human happiness, out of the question; assume the hypothesis of a world without souls; level man to the consideration of brutes; take him out of his moral state; set him at large the vagrant son of nature in full physical freedom to indulge his temperament; suppose all the enclosures of civilized life laid open, and family ties, and "relations dear," and "all the charities—of father, son, and brother" fairly out of the way, and then this little poem of Beppo, which it is said, but which we are slow to believe, Lord Byron, an English nobleman, an English husband, and an English father, hath sent reeking from the stews of Venice, is a production of great humour and unquestionable excellence. There is throughout the performance an evident care taken to make the ridicule fall not on the manner, or the sentiment, or the principles of Lord Byron's poems, but upon poor unrespected virtuous love, and woman's honour, and rustic shame, and household joys, and hum-drum human happiness. We are quite sure that many a maiden and many a mother, British-born and British-bred, will rise from the perusal of this little delightful display of Italian manners, this light and sportive raillery on the marriage vow, with many troublesome prejudices removed, an encreased dread of being righteous over-much, and a resolution, in spite of a prying and censorious world, to live in charity with her neighbours of the other sex, though it should be called facility or levity.

In all seriousness, then, we mean to say, that the way in which the writer of this bantering poem has treated the sin of adultery, and all the sanctions by which marriage is made holy and happy, desig-nates it as the product of a mind careless, cold, and callous: for who but a man of such a mind could, at a distance from his country and home, with a full knowledge of what makes that country great and prosperous, her families honourable, her sons manly and true, and her daughters the objects of delicate and respectful love, send among us a tale of pollution, dipped in the deepest die of Italian debauchery, relieved and recommended by a vivacity and grace of colouring that takes from the mischief its apparent turpitude, and disarms the vigilance of virtue.

From the review of *Childe Harold IV* (1818) in Constable's *Edinburgh Magazine*, May 1818.

We are clearly of opinion, that, notwithstanding all the praises which have been lavished upon Lord Byron's poetry by his contemporaries, the deep feeling of the power of his genius is reserved as a luxury for after ages; and that, when the attention of mankind ceases to be distracted by the conflicting claims of those rival poets who now, so honourably for the age, are contending for immortality, the works of Lord Byron will be perused with an admiration which those of no other living writer will be able to awaken. The truth is, that the poetry of this author is not only of a cast superior to most of that of which the present age has been so prolific, but is also of a species quite new and unexampled. In former times, a line that awakened any of the deeper feelings of our nature, and, in the calm of their closets, made mankind alive to those powerful sympathies which relate only to the more extraordinary events of life, was valued as a gem which gave interest and worth to the whole composition of which it formed a part. It was retained in the memory, and enthusi-astically repeated whenever the romantic and the tender happened to meet; and that author was supposed to have attained the highest felicity in his art who could adorn his pages by even a scanty portion of such "pearls of price." It has been reserved for Lord Byron to produce whole poems replete with sentiments of this nature. Trained in the discipline of ardent passion, he has been able to look with a steady eye upon those terrible wonders of our common nature, of which other minds have only had some faint and occasional perceptions; and, gifted at the same time with a courage and an openness, which led him fearlessly to attempt the task assigned him, he has trod in the highest sphere of his art, with a majesty and a glory which have eclipsed the splendours of all contemporary genius.

We are persuaded that the perusal of the fourth and last Canto of Childe Harold must awaken many interesting reflections in the minds of those who recollect the progress of the author's mind, and can compare the varying tones of feeling by which the different parts of that work are characterized. The fact is, that Lord Byron is, in one sense, of all poets perhaps that ever lived, the most complete and fearless egotist,—and his works have uniformly borne the exact impression of the feelings that prevailed in his heart at the moment of composition. When the first two cantos of Childe Harold appeared, we accordingly found them most profusely replenished with the indications of a mind that searched anxiously through life for some form of beauty of which it vainly hoped to discover the reality, and that dwelt upon the past as upon some celestial dream that had given place to substantial and hopeless misery. In his various works which appeared between this period and the publication of the third canto of Childe Harold, the feelings of the author were evidently in some degree quieted,—and pathetic lamentations over the wrecks of antiquity, or gloomy delineations of love and crime, employed the powers of a mind which must ever feel its highest gratification in the indulgence of great and overpowering emotions. No reader can forget the terrible tone of anguish which broke forth in the magic sounds of the third canto,—nor will those who are best able to judge of what is exquisite in poetry ever be able to separate the recollection of the sublime description of an Alpine thunder-storm, from the idea of a mind that found a solace for its own mighty struggles in the tremendous uproar of the elements of Nature. We apprehend it will be equally clear to most readers, that the concluding canto, which is now before us, is characterized by a tone decidedly more subdued; and those who love the poet for his lay, will hail the symptoms which this volume discovers, as the harbingers of feelings infinitely more suitable to our nature, and honourable to the author himself, than the utmost splendour which it is possible to associate with the dark or sceptical propensities of our hearts.

We by no means intend it to be believed, from any thing we have now said, that Lord Byron has entirely given up that powerful vein of pathetic description, or that terrible energy of indignant denunciation which every reader must have recognized as the peculiar characteristic of all his Lordship's former writings. . . .

We have not stopped to point out particularly the faults of this work,—partly because it is the privilege of transcendant genius to mock the "carping of the critic's toil,"—and partly because the extraordinary popularity of Lord Byron's poetry has rendered every reader acquainted with his peculiarities and defects. Yet it is not proper that great transgressions should ever be completely hidden by their accompaniments,—and we may therefore remind our readers, that, in this, as in all the previous works of the same author, they will have to make a large allowance for the obtrusive egotism, which has yet had the advantage of concentrating our sympathies upon a real character, rather than upon a mere creature of fancy;—for that bitter scorn of the whole human race, which has yet given a kind of Satanic grandeur to the author's courage;—for those gloomy views of the destinies of our nature, which have only been rendered tolerable by the evidence afforded of their own falsity in the sublime talent which their description has developed; and lastly, for much occasional harshness in the structure of the verse, and in the present work, particularly, for a too frequent straggling of one stanza into one or more which follow it. With all these defects, however,—and had they occurred in the case of any other author, they would have sunk his work "down to the centre,"—we have yet hailed the accomplishment of this poem with a feeling in no ordinary degree resembling that with which we imagine the author himself must have been impressed at its close;—and amidst the many works of doubtful destiny, though of high talent, which are daily appearing, we have learned from this performance what is that singular feeling with which we naturally contemplate the completion of a work, which, by the infallible signs that every eye can read, is plainly destined to live for ever.

From John Wilson's unsigned review of *Childe Harold IV* in *The Edinburgh Review*, June 1818.

The Pilgrimage of Childe Harold has now been brought to its close; and of his character there remains nothing more to be laid open to our view. It is impossible to reflect on the years which have elapsed since this mysterious stranger was first introduced to our acquaintance, without feeling that our own spirits have undergone in that time many mighty changes—sorrowful in some it may be, in others happy changes. Neither can we be surprised, knowing as we well do who Childe Harold is, that he also has been changed. He represented himself, from the beginning, as a ruin; and when we first gazed upon him, we saw indeed in abundance the black traces of recent violence and convulsion. The edifice has not been rebuilt; but its hues have been sobered by the passing wings of time, and the calm slow ivy has had leisure to wreathe the soft green of its melancholy among the fragments of the decay. In so far, the Pilgrim has become wiser. He seems to think more of others, and with a greater spirit of humanity. There was something tremendous, and almost fiendish, in the air with which he surveyed the first scenes of his wanderings; and no proof of the strength of genius was ever exhibited so strong and unquestionable, as the sudden and entire possession of the minds of Englishmen by such a being as he then appeared to be. He looked upon a bull-fight, and a field of battle, with no variety of emotion. Brutes and men were, in his eyes, the same blind, stupid victims of the savage lust of power. He seemed to shut his eyes to every thing of that citizenship and patriotism which ennobles the spirit of the soldier, and to delight in scattering the dust and ashes of his derision over all the most sacred resting-places of the soul of man.

Even then, we must allow, the original spirit of the Englishman and the poet broke triumphantly, at times, through the chilling mist in which it had been spontaneously enveloped. In Greece, above all, the contemplation of Athens, Salamis, Marathon, Thermopylæ, and Platæa, subdued the prejudices of him who had gazed unmoved upon the recent glories of Trafalgar and Talavera. The nobility of manhood appeared to delight this moody visitant; and he accorded, without reluctance, to the shades of long-departed heroes that reverent homage, which, in the strange mixture of envy and scorn wherewith the contemplative so often regard active men, he had refused to the living, or to the newly dead.

At all times, however, the sympathy and respect of Childe Harold —when these have been excited by any circumstances external to himself—have been given almost exclusively to the intellectual, and refused to the moral greatness of his species. There is certainly less of this in his last Canto. Yet we think that the ruins of Rome might have excited within him not a few glorious recollections, quite apart from those vague lamentations and worshippings of imperial power, which occupy so great a part of the conclusion of his Pilgrimage. The stern purity and simplicity of domestic manners—the devotion of male and female bosoms—the very names of Lucretia, Valeria, and the mother of the Gracchi, have a charm about them at least as enduring as any others, and a thousand times more delightful than all the iron memories of conquerors and consuls.—But the mind must have something to admire—some breathing-place of veneration—some idol, whether of demon or of divinity, before which it is its pride to bow. Byron has chosen too often to be the undoubting adorer of Power. The idea of tyrannic and unquestioned sway seems to be the secret delight of his spirit. He would pretend, indeed, to be a republican,—but his heroes are all stamped with the leaden signet of despotism; and we sometimes see the most cold, secluded, immitigable tyrant of the whole, lurking beneath the 'scallop-shell and sandal-shoon' of the Pilgrim itself.

In every mien and gesture of this dark being, we discover the traces of one that has known the delights, and sympathized with the possessors of intellectual power; but too seldom any vestiges of a mind that delights in the luxuries of quiet virtue, or that could repose itself in the serenity of home. The very possession of purity would sometimes almost seem to degrade, in his eyes, the intellectual greatness with which it has been sometimes allied. He speaks of Pompey with less reverence than Cæsar; and, in spite of many passing visitings of anger and of scorn, it is easy to see that, of all cotemporary beings, there is ONE only with whom he is willing to acknowledge mental sympathy—one only whom he looks upon with real reverence—one only whose fortunes touch the inmost sanctuaries of his proud soul—and that this one is no other than that powerful, unintelligible, unrivalled spirit, who, had he possessed either private virtue or public moderation, might still have been in a situation to despise the offerings of even such a worshipper as Harold.

But there would be no end of descanting on the character of the Pilgrim, nor of the moral reflections which it awakens. Of the Poet himself, the completion of this wonderful performance inspires us with lofty and magnificent hopes. It is most assuredly in his power to build up a work that shall endure among the most august fabrics of the genius of England. Indeed, the impression which the collective poetry of our own age makes upon our minds is, that it contains great promise of the future; and that, splendid as many of its achievements have been, some of our living poets seem destined still higher to exalt the imaginative character of their countrymen. When we look back and compare the languid, faint, cold delineations of the very justest and finest subjects of inspiration, in the poetry of the first half of the last century, with the warm, life-flushed and life-breathing pictures of our own, we feel that a great accession has been made to the literature of our day,—an accession not only of delight, but of power. We cannot resist the persuasion, that if literature, in any great degree, impresses and nourishes the character of a people,—then this literature of ours, pregnant as it is with living impressions,—gathered from Nature in all her varieties of awfulness and beauty,—gathered too from those high and dread

Passions of men, which our ordinary life scarcely shows, and indeed could scarcely bear, but which, nevertheless, have belonged, and do belong, to our human life,—and held up in the powerful representations of the poets to our consciousness at times, when the deadening pressure of the days that are going by might bereave us of all genial hope and all dignified pride,—we say it is impossible for us to resist the belief that such pregnant, glowing, powerful poetry, must carry influences into the heart of this generation, even like those which are breathed from the heart of nature herself,—or like those which lofty passions leave behind them in bosoms which they have once possessed. The same spirit of poetical passion which so uniformly marks the works of all our living poets, must exist very widely among those who do not aspire to the name of genius; it must be very widely diffused throughout the age, and, as we think, must very materially influence the reality of life. Yet highly as we estimate the merits of our modern poetry, it is certain, that the age has not yet produced any one great epic or tragic performance. Vivid and just delineations of passion there are in abundance,—but of moments of passions—fragments of representation. The giant grasp of thought, which conceives, and brings into full and perfect life, full and perfect passion—passion pervading alike action and character, through a majestic series of events, and at the same time cast in the mould of grand imagination,—this seems not to be of our age. In the delineation of external nature, which, in a poet's soul, requires rather moral beauty than intellectual strength, this age has excelled. But it has produced no poem gloriously illustrative of the agencies, existences, and events, of the complex life of man. It has no Lear— no Macbeth—no Othello. Some such glory as this Byron may yet live to bring over his own generation. His being has in it all the elements of the highest poetry. And that being he enjoys in all the strength of its prime. We might almost say, that he needs but to exercise his will to construct a great poem. There is, however, much for him to alter in what may be called, his Theory of Imagination respecting Human Life. Some idols of his own setting-up he has himself overthrown. There are yet some others, partly of gold, and partly of clay, which should be dashed against the floor of the sanctuary. We have already spoken of his personal character, as it shines forth in his poetry. This personal character exists in the nature of his imagination, and may therefore be modified—purified— dignified by his own will. His imagination does, to his own eyes, invest him with an unreal character. Purposes, passions, loves, deeds, events, may seem great and paramount in imagination, which have yet no power to constrain to action; and those which perhaps may govern our actions, vanish altogether from our imagination. There is a region—a world—a sphere of being in imagination, which, to our real life, is no more than the world of a dream; yet, long as we are held in it by the transport of our delusion, we live, not in delight only, but in the conscious exaltation of our nature. It is in this world that the spirit of Byron must work a reformation for itself. He knows, far better than we can tell him, what have been the most hallowed objects of love and of passion to the souls of great poets in the most splendid eras of poetry,—and he also knows well, that those objects, if worshipped by him with becoming and steadfast reverence, will repay the worship which they receive, by the more fervent and divine inspiration which they kindle.

From William Roberts's unsigned review of *Childe Harold IV* in *The British Review*, August 1818.

The most important part of a poem like this, is doubtless the sentimental part. The descriptive part is its dress, and this may satisfy superficial tastes. But those who look for profounder pleasure decide by severer tests. They feel that the value of poetry, and the pledge of its immortality, consist in its tone of thought, and in the spirit of its expression; in that deep-stirring impulse which is felt in the recesses of the heart; that here its power, its virtue, its vitality resides: that it is the part in which it is most emphatically and spiritually efficacious for good or for bad; and that if poetry fail in this part of its office and character, the defect is punished by the retributive hand of time, which sweeps it into the limbo of oblivion with other vanities, that, after their day of mischief and delusion, retire to make way for their successors. Lord Byron's poetry in the descriptive part is admirable; it fails in the sentimental altogether. In this his greatest work there is no consistent line of thought; the poem has no argument, no purpose, no principle, neither harmony of character, nor identity of plan; an ill-assorted variety of vague impressions are made upon the hearer, having only a common character of discontent to unite them, and reconciled only in their equal distance from truth and utility. . . .

One of the most general and obvious faults of this poem of Childe Harold is, that it is altogether without design or arrangement. It is also too long for so desultory a performance. Without something to lead attention forward, some progressive chain of interest, a reader is apt to become languid even amidst vigour and variety. But for the most part, in compositions of this loose texture, the languor of the reader is justified by the repetitions of the writer. When a man is rambling without ultimate purpose or destination, it is natural, and hardly avoidable, for him to re-tread his steps; and Lord Byron was the more in danger of so doing from the morbid bias of his mind.

So long a poem, without integrity of plan, or progress of action, with no development of any leading idea, without point, and without moral, maintains but a feeble hold upon the attention, and has no power of engrossing the reader. Indeed, his Lordship seems utterly incapable of all scheme and design in poetry; his strength seems to lie in talking of himself, except where the local magic of the scenery dilates his thoughts, and relieves him from the oppression of self, and the prison of his own mind. But even on these occasions the scene may rather be said to be full of Lord Byron, than Lord Byron of the scene. His descriptions are often mere expansions of himself; and of this we complain; for though it may be permitted to an author to transfuse something of the colouring of his own mind into his representations of natural objects, it is beyond the privilege of any poet, still borrowing our image from the painter's art, to present himself in the foreground of every landscape. We should enjoy Lord Byron's poetry much more if it were not for Lord Byron himself: he obstructs others and himself also: he stands full in his own light, we will not say, by turning his back upon heaven, but certainly by placing himself in a wrong position for seeing or displaying the truth.

Of the melancholy of this poem, we have said enough, as far as it arises out of the circumstances of the poet. Where it is suggested by the locality and features of the scene described, it is still neither a sublime nor a moral melancholy. It is far from that spiritual mood

"Which wings the soul and points her to the skies."

The feelings which it incorporates are more like the stings of an unrepentant conscience than the depressions of benevolent sensibility. It seems to be of a sort, that, if it wins us from ourselves, brings us no nearer to God: it leaves us bleeding from the rupture of the ligament which associates us to the world, without carrying us where alone the balsam is supplied that can cure the wound.

The taste of this poem is classical, and sufficiently informed by learning, without being disfigured by pedantry; and though we have it upon his own confession, that the poet suffered the time spent at school to pass without much profit, yet it appears sufficiently clear that he has so availed himself of subsequent opportunities, as to make up for his early neglect. His descriptions of the Venus and Apollo, those purest and most perfect remains of ancient sculpture, glow with the fervours of classic enthusiasm, and leave behind, in the general vigour of the sketch, however exceptionable on certain grounds some parts of it may be thought, all the tributes which we have seen paid by poetry to its sister art. The broken piles and scattered fragments of the *eternal* city, her rivers, and sites, and hills,— all that remains to remind us of what once was deemed imperishable, and now has nothing but a name, or a trace, and that dubious, Lord Byron has touched with such admirable force and feeling, as to leave us nothing to wish, except that he would wake for ever from the feverish dreams of a morbid temperament, and consign his faculties to subjects more agreeable to the lofty vocation of his genius.

Of the harmony of the verse we cannot help observing that it suffers but too often either from an incorrectness of ear, or from a strange affectation in the poet. We have said much, in our former reviews, of the advantages and disadvantages of the Spenser stanza, of its loose and luxuriant harmony, and the play it allows for the dilatation of thought and imagery, as well as its tendency to debilitating expansion; but there is a difficulty in the structure and modulation of this verse which has scarcely been enough noticed. The flow of the lines must have a certain briskness imparted to them, or they will be continually settling into prose; and whenever they assume this heavy and interrupted motion, there is no style which poetry can assume more disagreeable in its effect on the ear. Lord Byron is occasionally, and not unfrequently, entirely negligent of measure, and this neglect is oftenest shown in the concluding line, in which the thought is finished and condensed, and which therefore requires the greatest assistance from majesty of sound. A pretty strong illustration of this remark occurs in the 12th stanza, which runs as follows:

> "The Suabian sued, and now the Austrian reigns—
> An Emperor tramples where an Emperor knelt;
> Kingdoms are shrunk to provinces, and chains
> Clank over sceptred cities; nations melt
> From power's high pinnacle, when they have felt
> The sunshine for a while, and downward go
> Like lauwine loosen'd from the mountain's belt;
> Oh for one hour of blind old Dandolo!
> Th' octogenarian chief, Byzantium's conquering foe."

The two last lines of the stanza just cited are in the worst possible taste, and surely the recollection of the exclamation of the Highlander, "Oh for an hour of old Dundee!" affords no apology, as the learned commentator appears to think in the note in page 118, to these two miserable lines. The 31st stanza ends thus:

> "Than if a pyramid form'd his monumental fame."

And the 139th as follows:

> "Both are but theatres where the chief actors rot;"

which is again immediately followed by a line still more impracticable:

> "I see before me the gladiator lie."

235

The 19th stanza thus begins:

"I can re-people with the past—and of."

Some few vulgarisms occasionally occur, as "Awake thou shalt and must." Again,

"But France got drunk with blood to vomit crime."

In aiming at strength it is not uncommon to drop into vulgarity; but as the attempt is laudable, criticism ought not to be severe; we shall therefore exhibit no more of these failures, which are not numerous enough to affect the general character of the poem. Upon the whole, though we do not think that after a few years shall have passed, this greatest work of Lord Byron will often be taken down from the shelf, yet we have no doubt of its having obtained that immortality for the poet which sometimes, alas! is the poet's supreme and solitary hope.

From Walter Scott's unsigned review of *Childe Harold IV* in *The Quarterly Review*, April 1818 (publ. September).

'Farewell! a word that must be, and hath been—
A sound which makes us linger;—yet—farewell!
Ye! who have traced the Pilgrim to the scene
Which is his last, if in your memories dwell
A thought which once was his, if on ye swell
A single recollection, not in vain
He wore his sandal-shoon, and scallop-shell;
Farewell! with *him* alone may rest the pain,
If such there were—with *you*, the moral of his strain!'

This solemn valediction, the concluding stanza of Lord Byron's poem, forms at once a natural and an impressive motto to our essay. 'There are few things,' says the moralist, 'not purely evil, of which we can say, without some emotion of uneasiness, *this is the last*. Those who could never agree together shed tears when mutual discontent has determined them to final separation, and of a place that has been frequently visited, though without pleasure, the last look is taken with heaviness of heart.' When we resume, therefore, our task of criticism, and are aware that we are exerting it for the last time upon this extraordinary work, we feel no small share of reluctance to part with the Pilgrim, whose wanderings have so often beguiled our labours, and diversified our pages. We part from 'Childe Harold' as from the pleasant and gifted companion of an interesting tour, whose occasional waywardness, obstinacy and caprice are forgotten in the depth of thought with which he commented upon subjects of interest as they passed before us, and in the brilliancy with which he coloured such scenery as addressed itself to the imagination. His faults, if we at all remember them, are recollected only with pity, as affecting himself indeed, but no longer a concern of ours:—his merits acquire double value in our eyes when we call to mind that we may perhaps never more profit by them. The scallop-shell and staff are now laid aside, the pilgrimage is accomplished, and Lord Byron, in his assumed character, is no longer to delight us with the display of his wondrous talents, or provoke us by the use he sometimes condescends to make of them,—an use which at times has reminded us of his own powerful simile,

'It was as is a new-dug grave,
Closing o'er one we sought to save.'

Before we part, however, we feel ourselves impelled to resume a consideration of his 'Pilgrimage,' not as consisting of detached accounts of foreign scenery and of the emotions suggested by them, but as a whole poem, written in the same general spirit, and pervaded by the same cast of poetry. In doing this, we are conscious we must repeat much which has perhaps been better said by others, and even be guilty of the yet more unpardonable crime of repeating ourselves. But if we are not new we will at least be brief, and the occasion seems to us peculiarly favourable for placing before our readers the circumstances which secured to the Pilgrimage of Childe Harold a reception so generally popular. The extrinsic circumstances, which refer rather to the state of the public taste than to the genius and talent of the author, claim precedence in order because, though they are not those on which the fame of the poet must ultimately rest, they are unquestionably the scaffolding by means of which the edifice was first raised which now stands independent of them.

Originality, as it is the highest and rarest property of genius, is also that which has most charms for the public. Not that originality is always necessary, for the world will be contented, in the poverty of its mental resources, with mere novelty or singularity, and must therefore be enchanted with a work that exhibits both qualities. The vulgar author is usually distinguished by his treading, or attempting to tread, in the steps of the reigning favourite of the day. He is didactic, sentimental, romantic, epic, pastoral, according to the taste of the moment, and his 'fancies and delights,' like those of Master Justice Shallow, are sure to be adapted to the tunes *which the carmen whistle*. The consequence is, not that the herd of imitators gain their object, but that the melody which they have profaned becomes degraded in the sated ears of the public—its original richness, wildness and novelty are forgotten when it is made manifest how easily the leading notes can be caught and parodied, and whatever its intrinsic merit may have been, it becomes, for the time, stale and fulsome. If the composition which has been thus hunted down possesses intrinsic merit, it may—indeed it will—eventually revive and claim its proper place amid the poetical galaxy; deprived, indeed, of the adventitious value which it may at first have acquired from its novelty, but at the same time no longer over-shaded and incumbered by the croud of satellites now consigned to chaos and primæval night. When the success of Burns, writing in his native dialect with unequalled vigour and sweetness, had called from their flails an hundred peasants to cudgel their brains for rhymes, we can well remember that even the bard of Coila was somewhat injured in the common estimation—as a masterpiece of painting is degraded by being placed amid the flaring colours and ill-drawn figures of imitative daubers. The true poet attempts the very reverse of the imitator. He plunges into the stream of public opinion even when its tide is running strongest, crosses its direction, and bears his crown of laurel as Cæsar did his imperial mantle, triumphant above the waves. Such a phenomenon seldom fails at first to divide and at length to alter the reigning taste of the period, and if the bold adventurer has successfully buffeted the ebbing tide which bore up his competitor, he soon has the benefit of the flood in his own favour.

In applying these general remarks to Lord Byron's gravest and most serious performance, we must recal to the reader's recollection that since the time of Cowper he has been the first poet who, either in his own person, or covered by no very thick disguise, has directly appeared before the public, an actual living man expressing his own sentiments, thoughts, hopes and fears. Almost all the poets of our day, who have possessed a considerable portion of public attention, are personally little known to the reader, and can only be judged from the passions and feelings assigned by them to persons totally fictitious. Childe Harold appeared—we must not say in the character of *the* author—but certainly in that of a real existing person, with whose feelings as such the public were disposed to associate those of Lord Byron. Whether the reader acted right or otherwise in persisting to neglect the shades of distinction which the author endeavoured to point out betwixt his pilgrim and himself, it is certain that no little power over the public attention was gained from their being identified. Childe Harold may not be, nor do we believe he is, Lord Byron's very self, but he is Lord Byron's picture, sketched by Lord Byron himself, arrayed in a fancy dress, and disguised perhaps by some extrinsic attributes, but still bearing a sufficient resemblance to the original to warrant the conclusion that we have drawn. This identity is so far acknowledged in the preface to the Canto now before us, where Lord Byron thus expresses himself.

'The poem also, or the pilgrim, or both, have accompanied me from first to last; and perhaps it may be a pardonable vanity which induces me to reflect with complacency on a composition which in some degree connects me with the spot where it was produced, and the objects it would fain describe; and however unworthy it may be deemed of those magical and memorable abodes, however short it may fall of our distant conceptions and immediate impressions, yet as a mark of respect for what is venerable, and of feeling for what is glorious, it has been to me a source of pleasure in the production, and I part with it with a kind of regret, which I hardly suspected that events could have left me for imaginary objects.'

But besides the pleasing novelty of a traveller and a poet, throwing before the reader his reflections and opinions, his loves and his hates, his raptures and his sorrows; besides the novelty and pride which the public felt, upon being called as it were into familiarity with a mind so powerful, and invited to witness and partake of its deep emotions; the feelings themselves were of a character which struck with awe those to whom the noble pilgrim thus exposed the sanctuary of his bosom. They were introduced into no Teian paradise of lutes and maidens, were placed in no hall resounding with music and dazzling with many-coloured lights, and called upon to gaze on those gay forms that flutter in the muse's beam. The banquet had ceased, and it was the pleasure of its melancholy lord that his guests should witness that gloominess, which seems most dismal when it succeeds to exuberant and unrestrained gaiety. The emptied wine-cup lay on the ground, the withered garland was flung aside and trodden under foot, the instruments of music were silent, or waked but those few and emphatic chords which express sorrow; while, amid the ruins of what had once been the palace of pleasure, the stern pilgrim stalked from desolation to desolation, spurning from him the implements of former luxury, and repelling with equal scorn the more valuable substitutes which wisdom and philosophy offered to supply their place. The reader felt as it were in the presence of a superior being, when, instead of his judgment being consulted, his imagination excited or soothed, his taste flattered or conciliated in order to bespeak his applause, he was told, in strains of the most sublime poetry, that neither he, the courteous reader, nor aught the earth had to shew, was worthy the attention of the noble traveller.—All countries he traversed with a heart for entertaining the beauties of nature, and an eye for observing the crimes and follies of mankind; and from all he drew subjects of sorrow, of indignation, of contempt. From Dan to Beersheba all was barrenness. To despise the ordinary sources of happiness, to turn with scorn from the pleasures which captivate others, and to endure, as it were voluntarily, evils which others are most anxious to shun, is a path to ambition; for the monarch is scarcely more respected for possessing, than the anchoret for contemning the means of power and of pleasure. A mind like that of Harold, apparently indifferent to the usual enjoyments of life, and which entertains, or at least exhibits, such contempt for its usual pursuits, has the same ready road to the respect of the mass of mankind, who judge that to be superior to humanity which can look down upon its common habits, tastes, and pleasures.

This fashion of thinking and writing of course had its imitators, and those right many. But the humorous sadness which sat so gracefully on the original made but a poor and awkward appearance on those who

> —— wrapp'd themselves in Harold's inky cloak,
> To show the world how 'Byron' did *not* 'write.'

Their affected melancholy shewed like the cynicism of Apemantus contrasted with the real misanthropy of Timon. And, to say the truth, we are not sorry that the fashion has latterly lost ground. This species of general contempt of intellectual pleasures, and worldly employment, is more closely connected with the Epicurean philosophy than may be at first supposed. If philosophy be but a pursuit of words, and the revolutions of empires inevitable returns of the same cycle of fearful transitions; if our earliest and best affections 'run to waste, and water but the desert,' the want of worthier motives to action gives a tremendous and destructive impulse to the dangerous *Carpe diem* of the Garden—that most seductive argument of sensual pleasure. This doctrine of the nothingness of human pursuits, not as contrasted with those of religion and virtue, (to which they are indeed as nothing,) but absolutely and in themselves, is too apt to send its pupils in despair to those pleasures which promise a real gratification, however short and gross. Thus do thoughts and opinions, in themselves the most melancholy, become incitements to the pursuit of the most degrading pleasures; as the Egyptians placed skulls upon their banqueting tables, and as the fools of Holy Writ made the daring and fearful association of imminent fate and present revelling—*Let us eat and drink, for to-morrow we die.*

If we treat the humour less gravely, and consider it as a posture of the mind assumed for the nonce, still this enumeration of the vain pursuits, the indulged yet unsatiated passions of humanity, is apt to weary our spirits if not our patience, and the discourse terminates in a manner as edifying as the dialogue in Prior's Alma:—

> ' "Tired with these thoughts"—"Less tired than I,"
> Quoth Dick, "with your philosophy—

That people live and die I knew,
An hour ago as well as you;
What need of books those truths to tell,
Which folks perceive who cannot spell;
And must we spectacles apply,
To view what hurts our naked eye?
If to be sad is to be wise,
I do most heartily despise
Whatever Socrates has said,
Or Tully wrote, or Wanley read."
   'Dear Drift! to set our matters right,
Remove these papers from my sight,
Burn Mat's Des-carte and Aristotle—
Here, Jonathan, your master's bottle.'

But it was not merely to the novelty of an author speaking in his own person, and in a tone which arrogated a contempt of all the ordinary pursuits of life, that 'Childe Harold' owed its extensive popularity: these formed but the point or sharp edge of the wedge by which the work was enabled to insinuate its way into that venerable block, the British public. The high claims inferred at once in the direct appeal to general attention, and scorn of general feeling, were supported by powers equal to such pretensions. He who despised the world intimated that he had the talents and genius necessary to win it if he had thought it worth while. There was a strain of poetry in which the sense predominated over the sound; there was the eye keen to behold nature, and the pen powerful to trace her varied graces of beauty or terror; there was the heart ardent at the call of freedom or of generous feeling, and belying every moment the frozen shrine in which false philosophy had incased it, glowing like the intense and concentrated alcohol, which remains one single but burning drop in the centre of the ice which its more watery particles have formed. In despite of the character which he had assumed, it was impossible not to see in the Pilgrim what nature designed him to be, and what, in spite of bad metaphysics and worse politics, he may yet be, a person whose high talents the wise and virtuous may enjoy without a qualifying sigh or frown. Should that day arrive, and if time be granted, it will arrive, we who have ventured upon the precarious task of prophecy—we who have been censured for not mingling the faults of genius with its talents—we shall claim our hour of heartfelt exultation. He himself, while deprecating censure on the ashes of another great but self-neglected genius, has well pleaded the common cause of those who, placed high above the croud, have their errors and their follies rendered more conspicuous by their elevation.

'Hard is his fate on whom the public gaze
Is fix'd for ever to detract or praise;
Repose denies her requiem to his name,
And Folly loves the martydom of Fame:
The secret enemy, whose sleepless eye
Stands sentinel, accuser, judge, and spy;
Her for the fool, the jealous, and the vain,
The envious, who but breath in others' pain:
Behold the host delighting to deprave,
Who track the steps of Glory to the grave.'

For ourselves, amid the various attendants on the triumph of genius, we would far rather be the soldier who, pacing by the side of his general, mixes, with military frankness, censure amid his songs of praise, than the slave in the chariot to flatter his vanity by low adulation, or exasperate his feelings by virulent invective. In entering our protest therefore against the justice and the moral tendency of that strain of dissatisfaction and despondency, that cold and sceptical philosophy which clouds our prospects on earth, and closes those beyond it, we willingly render to this extraordinary poem the full praise that genius in its happiest efforts can demand from us.

The plan, if it can be termed so, hovers between that of a descriptive and a philosophical poem. The Pilgrim passes from land to land, alternately describing, musing, meditating, exclaiming, and moralizing; and the reader, partaking of his enthusiasm, becomes almost the partner of his journey. The first and second Cantos were occupied by Spain and Greece—the former, the stage upon which those incidents were then passing which were to decide, in their consequence, the fate of existing Europe; the latter, the country whose sun, so long set, has yet left on the horizon of the world such a blaze of splendour. It is scarcely necessary to say, that in both countries, but especially in the last, the pilgrim found *room for meditation even to madness*. The third Canto saw Childe Harold once more upon the main, and traced him from Belgium to Switzerland, through scenes distinguished by natural graces, and rendered memorable by late events. Through this ample field we accompanied the Pilgrim, and the strains which describe the beauties of the Rhine and the magnificence of the Leman lake, are still glowing in our ears. . . .

[Scott then runs through the canto, with plentiful quotations]

From the copious specimens which we have given, the reader will be enabled to judge how well the last part of this great poem has sustained Lord Byron's high reputation. Yet we think it possible to trace a marked difference, though none in the tone of thought and expression, betwixt this canto and the first three. There is less of

242

passion, more of deep thought and sentiment, at once collected and general. The stream which in its earlier course bounds over cataracts and rages through narrow and rocky defiles, deepens, expands, and becomes less turbid as it rolls on, losing the aspect of terror and gaining that of sublimity. Eight years have passed between the appearance of the first volume and the present which concludes the work, a lapse of time which, joined with other circumstances, may have contributed somewhat to moderate the tone of Childe Harold's quarrel with the world, and, if not to reconcile him to his lot, to give him, at least, the firmness which endures it without loud complaint.—To return, however, to the proposition with which we opened our criticism, certain it is, that whether as Harold or as Lord Byron no author has ever fixed upon himself personally so intense a share of the public attention. His descriptions of present and existing scenes however striking and beautiful, his recurrence to past actions however important and however powerfully described, become interesting chiefly from the tincture which they receive from the mind of the author. The grot of Egeria, the ruins of the Palatine, are but a theme for his musings, always deep and powerful though sometimes gloomy even to sullenness. This cast of solemnity may not perhaps be justly attributed to the native disposition of the author, which is reported to be as lively as, judging from this single poem at least, we might pronounce it to be grave. But our ideas of happiness are chiefly caught by reflection from the minds of others, and hence it may be observed that those enjoy the most uniform train of good spirits who are thinking much of others and little of themselves. The contemplation of our minds, however salutary for the purposes of self-examination and humiliation, must always be a solemn task, since the best will find enough for remorse, the wisest for regret, the most fortunate for sorrow. And to this influence more than to any natural disposition to melancholy, to the pain which necessarily follows this anatomizing of his own thoughts and feelings which is so decidedly and peculiarly the characteristic of the Pilgrimage, we are disposed in a great measure to ascribe that sombre tint which pervades the poem. The poetry which treats of the actions and sentiments of others may be grave or gay according to the light in which the author chuses to view his subject, but he who shall mine long and deeply for materials in his own bosom will encounter abysses at the depth of which he must necessarily tremble. This moral truth appears to us to afford, in a great measure, a key to the peculiar tone of Lord Byron. How then, will the reader ask, is our proposition to be reconciled to that which preceded it? If the necessary result of an inquiry into our own thoughts be the conviction that all is vanity and vexation of spirit, why should we object to a style of writing, whatever its consequences may be, which involves in it truths as certain as they are melancholy? If the study of our own enjoyments leads us to doubt the reality of all except the indisputable pleasures of sense, and inclines us therefore towards the Epicurean system,—it is nature, it may be said, and not the poet which urges us upon the fatal conclusion. But this is not so. Nature, when she created man a social being, gave him the capacity of drawing that happiness from his relations with the rest of his race, which he is doomed to seek in vain in his own bosom. These relations cannot be the source of happiness to us if we despise or hate the kind with whom it is their office to unite us more closely. If the earth be a den of fools and knaves, from whom the man of genius differs by the more mercurial and exalted character of his intellect, it is natural that he should look down with pitiless scorn on creatures so inferior. But if, as we believe, each man, in his own degree, possesses a portion of the ethereal flame, however smothered by unfavourable circumstances, it is or should be enough to secure the most mean from the scorn of genius as well as from the oppression of power, and such being the case, the relations which we hold with society through all their gradations are channels through which the better affections of the loftiest may, without degradation, extend themselves to the lowest. Farther, it is not only our social connections which are assigned us in order to qualify that contempt of mankind, which too deeply indulged tends only to intense selfishness; we have other and higher motives for enduring the lot of humanity—sorrow, and pain, and trouble—with patience of our own griefs and commiseration for those of others. The wisest and the best of all ages have agreed that our present life is a state of trial not of enjoyment, and that we now suffer sorrow that we may hereafter be partakers of happiness. If this be true, and it has seldom been long, or at least ultimately, doubted by those who have turned their attention to so serious an investigation, other and worthier motives of action and endurance must necessarily occur to the mind than philosophy can teach or human pride supply. It is not our intention to do more than merely indicate so ample a topic for consideration. But we cannot forbear to add, that the vanishing of Lord Byron's Pilgrim strongly reminded us of the close of another work, the delight of our childhood. Childe Harold, a prominent character in the first volume of the Pilgrimage, fades gradually from the scene like the spectre associate who performed the first stages of his journey with a knight-errant, bearing all the appearance of a living man, but who lessened to the sight by degrees, and became at length totally invisible when they approached the cavern where his mortal remains were deposited.

CLXIV.

'But where is he, the Pilgrim of my song,
The being who upheld it through the past?
Methinks he cometh late and tarries long.
He is no more—these breathings are his last;
His wanderings done, his visions ebbing fast
And he himself as nothing:—if he was
Aught but a phantasy, and could be class'd
With forms which live and suffer—let that pass—
His shadow fades away into Destruction's mass.'—

In the corresponding passage of the Tales of the Genii, Ridley, the amiable author or compiler of the collection, expresses himself to the following purport, for we have not the book at hand to do justice to his precise words,—'Reader, the Genii are no more, and Horam, but the phantom of my mind, fiction himself and fiction all that he seemed to write, speaks not again. But lament not their loss, since if desirous to see virtue guarded by miracles, Religion can display before you scenes tremendous, wonderful, and great, more worthy of your sight than aught that human fancy can conceive— the moral veil rent in twain and the Sun of Righteousness arising from the thick clouds of heathen darkness.' In the sincere spirit of admiration for Lord Byron's talents, and regard for his character which has dictated the rest of our criticism, we here close our analysis of Childe Harold.

Our task respecting Lord Byron's poetry is finished, when we have mentioned the subject, quoted passages of superior merit, or which their position renders most capable of being detached from the body of the poem. For the character of his style and versification once distinctly traced, (and we have had repeated occasion to consider it,) cannot again be dwelt on without repetition. The harmony of verse, and the power of numbers, nay, the selection and arrangement of expressions, are all so subordinate to the thought and sentiment, as to become comparatively light in the scale. His poetry is like the oratory which hurries the hearers along without permitting them to pause on its solecisms or singularities. Its general structure is bold, severe, and as it were Doric, admitting few ornaments but those immediately suggested by the glowing imagination of the author, rising and sinking with the tones of his enthusiasm, roughening into argument, or softening into the melody of feeling and sentiment, as if the language fit for either were alike at the command of the poet, and the numbers not only came uncalled, but arranged themselves with little care on his part into the varied modulation which the subject requires. Many of the stanzas, considered separately from the rest, might be objected to as involved, harsh, and

245

overflowing into each other beyond the usual license of the Spenserian stanza. But considering the various matter of which the poet had to treat—considering the monotony of a long-continued smoothness of sound, and accurate division of the sense according to the stanzas—considering also that the effect of the general harmony is, as in music, improved by the judicious introduction of discords wherewith it is contrasted, we cannot join with those who state this occasional harshness as an objection to Lord Byron's poetry. If the line sometimes 'labours and the words move slow,' it is in passages where the sense is correspondent to these laborious movements. A highly finished strain of versification resembles a dressed pleasure ground, elegant—even beautiful—but tame and insipid compared to the majesty and interest of a woodland chase, where scenes of natural loveliness are rendered sweeter and more interesting by the contrast of irregularity and wildness.

From the concluding section of the review of *Childe Harold IV* in *The Monthly Review*, November 1818.

After having said thus much of the fourth canto, it may be expected from us to give our opinion on the general character of the pilgrim- age of Childe Harold, now that it is complete. It is a descriptive poem, written in a sort of epic language: without story, progression of passions, or gradation of incidents. The same solitary person stalks about; sometimes, in fits of sullen misanthropy, investing even the beautiful objects of nature with his perverted feelings; sometimes lulled by the charms of external nature into a momentary forgetful- ness of the world of man, and won from the empire of his own mor- bid humours into a reverie on all that is lovely and fair. Of his style of moralizing, we think that his night-thoughts on contemplation and solitude, early in the second canto, are sufficiently characteristic to be recognized as those of Lord Byron, and at the same time are written in his freest and happiest manner. His mere descriptions are composed with great truth, but occasionally with a minuteness, with an indiscriminate and mechanical exactness, which must impair their interest. How tiresome a description may be rendered by such exactness, any person who has looked into Crabbe's productions will easily apprehend.—Of simple and pleasing reflection, inter- spersed amid views of scenery, nothing can be more interesting or lovely than a great part of the third canto, and that passage on Egeria which we have extracted from the fourth. Of grand and elevated sentiments, we have some specimens in the second canto; as in the invocation of the spirit of antient Greece:—but the remark made on Collins may be applied, we think, with great justice to Lord Byron, that sublimity is rather the character of his inclination than of his genius. On many grand occasions, he exhibits a great restlessness and gasping; a struggle, as it were, towards some higher range of thought, which often ends in a repetition of the same idea in different terms, or in mere bombast and tumour of phrase. Even in that noble passage near the close of the fourth canto, part of which we have extracted, his fancy seems to be principally impressed with the hugeness and the might of the ocean, as if it were some untameable and savage monster that played with human power as a bauble: rather than as an element which, from an immensity of years, has been rolling its fathomless billows in obedience to some superior laws, and in harmony with the rest of the creation; and which, in its wildest buffetings, amid its loudest and most tempestuous uproar, still listens to some more than human voice whose sovereign influence wields its vastness and quells its fury.

Of the style of composition in this poem, it may be remarked that the general blemish is that it is too artificial. The account of the maid of Sarragoza in the first canto is as elaborate in structure as if it had been composed by one of those declaimers of antiquity, who for a trial of skill stationed every word in antithesis, and had all the clauses in a period balanced against each other with critical exactness. So again the reflections on a skull, which occur in another part of the same canto, are decked out in such laced and stately language, that we can scarcely recognize our favourite Hamlet's church-yard meditations in their strange disguise. Much more ease and simplicity, however, prevail in the third than in any of the other cantos: though the instances of extravagance of diction, such as 'their dust is immortality,' and the 'desert' of Italy 'surpasses other realms in fertility,' are innumerable. The author's attempts at a humourous turn, whether in his own notes, where it is more frequently introduced, or in his poetry, are not very successful: while his antiquarians crying out 'Eureka,' and his 'crown hight foolscap,' with many such phrases, may excite a smile, but surely not of approbation.

In many respects, Lord Byron may be considered as holding the same station in our national poetry which Gibbon has obtained in our prose. Their style is not according to old English directness of phrase, than which in our opinion nothing better can be substituted. With regard also to labour and research, little as such qualities might be expected from the spirited air of both these authors, we must remark that Gibbon is known to have been indefatigable; and we cannot help thinking that Lord Byron, in his closet, and in moments not much observed by others, indulges in a minuteness of investigation and of scrutiny which is not always bestowed by votaries of the muses. Few authors can be named whose trains of thought can be more directly traced to various sources than these two, and still

247

fewer who have so entirely appropriated what they have borrowed: for the native force of genius has enabled them to impart the air of novelty and originality to the entire body of their compositions. The result of long elaboration, and of a tedious fermentation of the intellect, is by both of them thrown forth in one mass of vivid conception, somewhat wrenched indeed by such Sibylline throes, but imbued with the fire of a master-spirit. Both, in their usual march and on the most ordinary occasions, support a certain degree of stateliness; and in their boldest elevations neither of them is entirely destitute of artifice and turgidity.

Diary entries about *Don Juan I and II* (1819) made in 1818–19 by John Cam Hobhouse (later Lord Broughton).

Dec. 27 [1818]. I have my doubts about *Don Juan*; the blasphemy and bawdry and the domestic facts overpower even the grand genius it displays. . . .

Dec. 29. I called on Hookham Frere, and had a long conversation with him about Byron's *Don Juan*. He was decisively against publication, and gave some excellent reasons. First, 'A friend of freedom should be a friend to morality'. Second, there was preparing a convulsion between the religionists and free-thinkers. The first would triumph and the latter be extirpated with their works. . . .

He said that Byron should not attack his wife, because she and her family forbore all attack as he could witness, having been with Sir R. and Lady Noel at Tunbridge, when they never mentioned him except once, and that *en passant* talking about *Beppo* and *Whistlecraft*.

I felt I was talking in some sort to a rival of *Don Juan*'s style, but then, as what he said was sensible, I did not care for the coincidence. Frere said of Byron's attack on Southey and others that it did not sink people already so placed, but it might sink Lord Byron. He had begun by writing a satire which he had suppressed; might he not suppress this also in time? On the whole, Frere was convincing. . . .

Jan. 2 [1819]. Called on Murray. Told him my feelings about *Don Juan*. He acquiesced, and I suppose is not sorry to be off from the violence and the attack on Bob Southey, although he tells me he dislikes Southey.

Jan. 8. I wrote a long letter to Byron advising him not to publish *Don Juan*. Sent it on Tuesday, having read it to Murray and to Kinnaird, and part to Davies. All agree with me, and Frere said stronger things to Murray than he did to me. The attacks on the wife, the bawdry and the blasphemy, as it is called, are the reasons. I trust he will listen to me. It is a very ticklish affair, and most likely

Byron will refer to Rogers or to Moore, who, being bepraised therein, will advise publication.

Feb. 1. Tom Moore breakfasted with me and read *Don Juan*. He perfectly agreed with me it could not be published, and told me to tell Byron his opinion.

Apr. 21. Byron has written to Murray resolving on publication, and to me; also a second canto of *Don Juan* sent.

May 1. *Don Juan* going through the press. I do not think it so bad or so good as I did, not so indecent or so clever.

May 14. Correcting *Don Juan* second canto, which I really do not think clever, at least not for Byron.

June 12. This day went to Murray's and found Kinnaird had just bargained to give 2,000 guineas for *Don Juan*, *Mazeppa*, and the Ode [on Venice]. Lord Byron is determined to publish, at all events anonymously. I have given the warning, and can do no more.

From a letter from John Keats to George and Georgiana Keats, 19 February 1819.

A man's life of any worth is a continual allegory—and very few eyes can see the Mystery of his life—a life like to scriptures, figurative—which such people can no more make out than they can the hebrew Bible. Lord Byron cuts a figure—but he is not figurative—Shakespeare led a life of Allegory: his works are the comments on it—

Some remarks about *Don Juan I and II* in a letter from John Wilson Croker to John Murray, 18 July 1819.

Ryde, July 18th, 1819.

Dear Murray,

I am agreeably disappointed at finding 'Don Juan' very little offensive. It is by no means worse than 'Childe Harold,' which it resembles as comedy does tragedy. There is a prodigious power of versification in it, and a great deal of very good pleasantry. There is also some magnificent poetry, and the shipwreck, though too long, and in parts very disgusting, is on the whole finely described. In short, I think it will not lose him any character as a poet, and, on the score of morality, I confess it seems to me a more innocent production than 'Childe Harold.' What 'Don Juan' may become by-and-bye I cannot foresee, but at present I had rather a son of mine were Don Juan than, I think, any other of Lord Byron's heroes. Heaven grant he may never resemble any of them. . . .

Some remarks on *Don Juan I and II* from a review of *Mazeppa* in *The Eclectic Review*, August 1819.

There are cases in which it is equally impossible to relax into laughter or to soften into pity, without feeling that an immoral concession is made to vice. The Author of the following stanzas might seem to invite our compassionate sympathy.

> 'No more—no more—Oh! never more on me
>   The freshness of the heart can fall like dew,
> Which out of all the lovely things we see
>   Extracts emotions beautiful and new,
> Hived in our bosoms like the bag o' the bee;
>   Thinkest thou the honey with those objects grew?
> Alas! 'twas not in them, but in thy power
> To double even the sweetness of a flower.'

> 'No more—no more—Oh! never more my heart,
>   Canst thou be my sole world, my universe!
> Once all in all, but now a thing apart,
>   Thou canst not be my blessing or my curse:
> The illusion's gone for ever, and thou art
>   Insensible, I trust, but none the worse,
> And in thy stead I've got a deal of judgement,
> Though heaven knows how it ever find [found] a lodgment.'

> 'Ambition was my idol, which was broken
>   Before the shrines of Sorrow and of Pleasure;
> And the two last have left me many a token
>   O'er which reflection may be made at leisure.
> 'Now like Friar Bacon's brazen head, I've spoken,
>   "Time is, Time was, Time's past," a chymic treasure
> In [Is] glittering youth, which I have spent betimes—
> My heart in passion, and my head on rhymes.'

[*I.* ccxiv, ccxv, ccxvii]

These lines, which we wish to redeem from the profane ribaldry of their context, are exceedingly touching, and they have that character of truth which distinguishes Lord Byron's poetry. He writes like a man who has that clear perception of the truth of things, which is the result of the guilty knowledge of good and evil, and who by the light of that knowledge, has deliberately preferred the evil, with a proud malignity of purpose which would seem to leave little for the last consummating change to accomplish. When he calculates that the reader is on the verge of pitying him, he takes care to throw him back the defiance of laughter, as if to let him know that all the

Poet's pathos is but the sentimentalism of the drunkard between his cups, or the relenting softness of the courtesan, who the next moment resumes the bad boldness of her degraded character. With such a man who would wish either to laugh or to weep? And yet, who that reads him, can refrain alternately from either?

From the review of *Don Juan I and II* in *The British Critic*, August 1819.

If Don Juan then be not a satire—what is it? A more perplexing question could not be put to the critical squad. Of the four hundred and odd stanzas which the two Cantos contain, not a tittle could, even in the utmost latitude of interpretation, be dignified by the name of poetry. It has not wit enough to be comic; it has not spirit enough to make it lyric; nor is it didactic of any thing but mischief. The versification and morality are about upon a par; as far therefore as we are enabled to give it any character at all, we should pronounce it a narrative of degrading debauchery in doggrel rhyme.

But putting morality out of the question, the style which the Noble Lord has adopted is tedious and wearisome to a most insufferable degree. We are perfectly aware that it is not his own, but that it is borrowed from poets of high authority in ancient days. It is not, however, our intention to enter into any comparison of the imitation with the original, but simply to remark that no authority can justify what is radically tiresome and irrational. In the didactic, an easy flowing negligence of versification, is often peculiarly successful. But the hand of a master is even here especially required to check the licentiousness of indolence, and to prevent the familiar and the unnatural from degenerating into the vapid and the vulgar. The satires of Horace, and the Religio Laici of Dryden, cost them each as much or more trouble and care, than their more florid and elevated compositions; the former, indeed, appears anxious to repel the imputation either of carelessness or of haste, and the latter expressly declares, that the language of a poem designed for instruction "ought to be plain and natural, and yet majestic." The same characteristics should appear with but little variation in the satirical or the comic narration. The Absalom and Archithophel [*sic*] of Dryden, and the tales of Prior, though different in their subject and their style, are yet each in their way examples of the highest excellence in this department of poetry. We would not degrade them by drawing a comparison between them and the work before us.

Hudibras, indeed, is grossly familiar, but Hudibras is a burlesque; yet still, with all vigour of fancy and variety of learning, which adorn its inimitable author, Hudibras, as a whole, cannot be read without fatigue. Don Juan is no burlesque, nor mock heroic: it consists of the common adventures of a common man ill conceived, tediously told, and poorly illustrated. The Broad Grins of the facetious Colman, are tales somewhat in the style of our author: but amidst much vulgar ribaldry and licentious indecency, there is a broad and boisterous humour, both in his incidents and his character, which is quite irresistible: and in spite of our better sense, provokes a free and hearty laugh. Now certainly in the present thick and heavy quarto, containing upwards of four hundred doggrel stanzas, there are not a dozen places that even in the merriest mood could raise a smile. It is true that we may be very dull dogs, and as little able to comprehend the wit of his Lordship, as to construe his poetry.

In the second canto, the Noble Lord has presented us with a shipwreck. The vessel goes to the bottom, the crew are set adrift upon the ocean in an open boat, their provisions are exhausted, they draw lots who shall be immolated to satisfy the hunger of the remainder. These are circumstances which are drawn from the very depths of human woe. They are such as not only make the good and tender heart to melt, but even the most hardened to shudder. In these fearful narrations, pain and misery are not presented to our view merely in an embodied form; they are dissected and anatomized, as it were, before our eyes. There is a variety, there is a length, there is an endurance of evil which bows down our spirits while we read. In the scenes of confusion and agony attending a shipwreck, in the struggles for self-preservation, in the loss of so many souls, perhaps but too unprepared for their great account, in tracing the protracted sufferings of those whose lot is still to linger on in desperation drearier than death, in viewing a company of fellow-creatures on the wide ocean, devouring their last morsel, in witnessing hunger and thirst increasing upon them, the cannibal passions beginning to rise, the casting of lots for destruction, the self-immolation, the feast upon human blood, the frantic feeling of satiety—surely in bringing all these things home to our hearts, we can ill endure a full-born jest. Much less can we tolerate the mixing up these fearful events with low doggrel, and vapid absurdity. The poverty of a man's wit is never so conspicious, as when he is driven to a joke upon human misery.

XLIII.

"Then came the carpenter, at last, with tears
  In his rough eyes, and told the captain, he
Could do no more; he was a man in years,
  And long had voyaged through many a stormy sea,
And if he wept at length, they were not fears
  That made his eyelids as a woman's be,
But he, poor fellow, had a wife and children,
Two things for dying people quite bewildering.

XLIV.

"The ship was evidently settling now
  Fast by the head; and, all distinction gone,
Some went to prayers again, and made a vow
  Of candles to their saints—but there were none
To pay them with; and some look'd o'er the bow;
  Some hoisted out the boats; and there was one
That begg'd Pedrillo for an absolution,
Who told him to be damn'd—in his confusion."

This specimen of the taste, the feeling, and the wit of the Noble Lord, will fully suffice. We will not, cannot follow him through the remainder of his disgusting melange. "*Sunt lacrymæ rerum, et mentem mortalia tangunt*" will ever be the honest, the tender feeling of the British nation. Notwithstanding his Lordship, and a few exotic dandies, who wear black stocks, and fancy that they look like his Lordship, may be of another notion, and another heart.

This is not

"Moody madness laughing wild
Amid severest woe."

In madness there is not a callous insensibility to human woe. In madness there is an excess of acute and irritable feeling. If in madness there is a quick perception of the ludicrous, there is a rapid, and almost electrical return to the serious. Even in the humour of a madman there is an acute apprehension of reality, which finds its way to the heart. But in the flippant doggrel of the Noble Lord, we can discover neither madness, nor its genius. All is calculating, vapid, and heartless. It is not mad, but bad—bad in expression, worse in taste, and worst of all in feeling and in heart.

Upon the indecency, and the blasphemy which this volume contains, a very few words will suffice. The adventures which it recounts are of such a nature, and described in such language, as to forbid its entrance within the doors of any modest woman, or decent man. Nor is it a history only, but a manual of profligacy. Its tendency is not only to excite the passions, but to point out the readiest means and method of their indulgence. Vice is here represented not merely in that grosser form which carries with it its own shame, and almost its own destruction, but in that alluring and sentimental shape, which at once captivates and corrupts. If without knowing the name of the poet, or the history of the work, our opinion had been required of the intention of the canto, we should have answered—that it was a calm and deliberate design to palliate and recommend the crime of adultery, to work up the passions of the young to its commission, and to afford them the most practical hints for its consummation. But it is not, we trust, by the maudlin and meritricious [*sic*] cant of the lascivious Little, nor by the doggrel narrations of his friend and admirer, the author of the poem before us, that the British nation is to be tricked out of that main bulwark of its national strength, its sturdy and unbending morality.

Of the blasphemous sneers, so liberally scattered through the present volume, it is our intention to say but little. He that has no regard for the feelings of human misery, or for the claims of public morality, has not (and we should be sorry if he had) the slightest respect for public religion. The assaults of such a man are true Religion's best defence. Nor is it to be wondered, that the man who can so laboriously inculcate the breach of one commandment, should furnish a parody, *a la* Hone, of all the ten. A parody indeed it is, but so miserable and poor, that it is really difficult to say whether the bad principle, or the bad poetry, most predominates. It certainly has not the sin of recommending itself by its wit. . . .

Reports from without, and evidence from within, fix this composition upon Lord Byron. His name indeed is not upon the title-page; but this is not the first time that his Lordship has played off that piece of coquetry with the public. Should however his Lordship be tempted in reality to disavow it, we shall be among the first to hail the disavowal, and to give it the publicity which it deserves, accompanying it with our sincere apology for having in common with the whole English nation, fixed upon his Lordship the stain of so flippant, dull and disgraceful a publication.

Some further remarks on *Don Juan I and II* in a letter from John Wilson Croker to John Murray, 15 September 1819.

I told you from the first moment that I read 'Don Juan,' that your fears had exaggerated its danger. I say nothing about what may have been suppressed; but if you had published 'Don Juan' without hesitation or asterisks, nobody would have ever thought worse of it than as a larger Beppo, gay and lively and a little loose. Some persons would have seen a strain of satire running beneath the gay surface, and might have been vexed or pleased according to their temper; but there would have been no outcry either against the publisher or author.

Yours, &c.,
J. W. C.

From a letter from John Keats to George and Georgiana Keats, 17/27 September 1819.

You speak of Lord Byron and me—There is this great difference between us. He describes what he sees—I describe what I imagine. Mine is the hardest task. You see the immense difference.

From Leigh Hunt's unsigned review of *Don Juan I and II* in *The Examiner*, 31 October 1819.

Some persons consider this the finest work of Lord Byron,—or at least that in which he displays most power. It is at all events the most extraordinary that he has yet published. His other poems, with the exception of that amusing satire—*Beppo*, are written for the most part with one sustained serious feeling throughout,—either of pathos, or grandeur, or passion, or all united. But *Don Juan* contains specimens of all the author's modes of writing, which are mingled together and push one another about in a strange way. The ground-work (if we may so speak of a stile) is the satirical and humourous; but you are sometimes surprised and moved by a touching piece of human nature, and again startled and pained by the sudden transition from loveliness or grandeur to ridicule or the mock-heroic. The delicious and deep descriptions of love, and youth, and hope, came upon us like the "young beams" of the sun breaking through the morning dew, and the terrific pictures of the misery of man and his most appalling sensations, like awful flashes of lightning;—but when the author reverses this change, he trifles too much with our feelings, and occasionally goes on, turning to ridicule or hopelessness all the fine ideas he has excited, with a recklessness that becomes extremely unpleasant and mortifying. What, for instance, can be more beautiful and at the same time true to nature than where,—just after a very anti-pathetic description of the confusion of *Julia* at her husband's sudden appearance, and her contrivances and lovers' falsehoods to elude his search for the beloved youth, he says (speaking of their alarm at the expected return of the old gentleman)—

> Julia did not speak,
> But pressed her bloodless lip to Juan's cheek.

> He turn'd his lip to hers, and with his hand
> Call'd back the tangles of her wandering hair;
> Even then their love they could not all command,
> And half forgot their danger and despair.
>
> [*I.* clxix–clxx]

What more calculated to "harrow up one's soul" than the following stanzas, which come in the very midst of some careless jests on the abstract ludicrousness of the wretched shifts of starving sailors in a becalmed boat, surrounded by a boundless prospect of the ocean? The Italics are our own.

255

The seventh day, and no wind—the burning sun
    Blister'd and scorch'd; and, stagnant on the sea,
They lay like carcases! and hope was none,
    Save in the breeze which came not: *savagely*
They glared upon each other—all was done,
    Water, and wine, and food,—and you might see
The *longings of the cannibal arise*,
(*Although they spoke not*) in their *wolfish* eyes.

At length one whispered his companion, who
    Whispered another, and thus it went round,
And then into a *hoarser murmur* grew,
    An ominous and wild and desperate sound;
And when his comrade's thought each sufferer knew,
    'Twas but his own, suppress'd till now, he found:
And *out they spoke* of lots for flesh and blood,
And who should die to be his fellow's food.

                    [*II*. lxxii–lxxiii]

Then, immediately following this awful passage, comes an affected delicacy at the tearing up of *Julia's* letter to *Juan* to make the lots ("materials which must shock the muse"), and a *sang froid* account of the division of the body: shortly after follow some terrific lines relating the dreadful consequences of this gorging of human flesh; and a little farther on there is a laughable description of *Juan's* dislike to feed on "poor Pedrillo," and his preference for "chewing a piece of bamboo and some lead," the stanza ending with the irresistible fact, that

    At length they caught two boobies and a noddy,
    And then they left off eating the dead body.

                    [lxxxii]

    It is not difficult to account for this heterogeneous mixture,—for the bard has furnished us with the key to his own mind. His early hopes were blighted, and his disappointment vents itself in satirizing absurdities which rouse his indignation; and indeed a good deal of bitterness may be found at the bottom of much of this satire. But his genius is not naturally satirical; he breaks out therefore into those frequent veins of passion and true feeling of which we have just given specimens, and goes on with them till his memory is no longer able to bear the images conjured up by his fine genius; and it is to get rid of such painful and "thick-coming" recollections, that he dashes away and relieves himself by getting into another train of ideas, however incongruous or violently contrasted with the former. This solution will, we think, be borne out by the following affecting description of the poet's feelings. Observe in particular the remarkable parenthesis after the first line, whose pregnant meaning seems to have compelled him to take refuge in a lighter and more humourous idea:—

But now at thirty years my hair is grey—
  (I wonder what it will be like at forty?
I thought of a peruke the other day)—
    My heart is not much greener; and, in short, I
Have squandered my whole summer while 'twas May,
    And feel no more the spirit to retort; I
Have spent my life, both interest and principal,
And deem not, what I deem'd, my soul invincible.

No more—no more—Oh! never more on me
  The freshness of the heart can fall like dew,
Which out of all the lovely things we see
    Extracts emotions beautiful and new,
Hived in our bosoms like the bag o' the bee:
    Think'st thou the honey with those objects grew?
Alas! 'twas not in them, but in thy power
To double even the sweetness of a flower.

No more—no more—Oh! never more, my heart,
  Canst thou be my sole world—my universe!
Once all in all, but now a thing apart
    Thou canst not be my blessing or my curse.
                        [*I.* ccxiii ff.]

Here is some evidence that the poet is not without the milk of human kindness, and to our minds there is much more in the rest of the volume. His bent is not, as we have said, satirical, nor is he naturally disposed to be ill-natured with respect to the faults and vices of his fellow-creatures. There is an evident struggle throughout these two cantos in the feelings of the writer, and it is very fine to see him, as he gets on, growing more interested in his fiction, and pouring out at the conclusion in a much less interrupted strain of rich and deep beauty. . . .

Don Juan is accused of being an "immoral" work, which we cannot at all discover. We suppose that this charge more particularly alludes to the first canto. Let us see then on what foundation it rests. The son of a Spanish patrician, educated in the most prudish manner by a licentious, yet affectedly virtuous mother, falls in love with the young wife of an old man. She returns his affection, and their passion being favoured by opportunity, she gives way to her natural feelings, and is unfaithful to her marriage vows, the example (observe) being set her by this very husband's intrigues with *Juan's* mother. Now Lord Byron speaks lightly of the effect of any scruples of conscience upon her, and of her infidelity; and this, it is said, has tendency to corrupt the minds of "us youth," and to make us *think* lightly of breaking the matrimonial contract. But if to do this be immoral, we can only say that Nature is immoral. Lord Byron does no more than relate the consequences of certain absurdities. If he speaks slightingly of the ties between a girl and a husband old enough for her father, it is because the ties themselves *are* slight.

He does not ridicule the bonds of marriage generally, or where they are formed as they should be: he merely shows the folly and wickedness of setting forms and opinions against nature. If stupid and selfish parents will make up matches between persons whom difference of age or disposition disqualifies for mutual affection, they must take the consequences:—but we do not think it fair that a poet should be exclaimed against as a promoter of nuptial infidelity because he tells them what those consequences are. In this particular case, too, the author does not omit some painful consequences to those who have sinned according to "nature's law." *Julia*, the victim of selfishness and "damned custom," is shut up in a convent, where no consolation remains to her but the remembrance of her entire and hapless love; but even that was perhaps pleasanter to her than living in the constant irksomeness of feigning an affection she could not feel.

There are a set of prudish and very suspicious moralists who endeavour to make vice appear to inexperienced eyes much more hateful than it really is. They would correct Nature:—and they always over-reach themselves. Nature has made vice to a certain degree pleasurable, though its painful consequences outweigh its present gratification. Now the said prudes, in their lectures and sermons and moral discourses (for they are chiefly priests) are constantly declaiming on the *deformity* of vice, and its almost total want of attraction. The consequence is, that when they are found to have deceived (as they always are) and immoral indulgence is discovered to be not without its charms,—the minds of young persons are apt to confound their true with their false maxims, and to think the threats of future pain and repentance mere fables invented to deter them from their rightful enjoyments. Which then, we would ask, are the immoral writings,—those which, by misrepresenting the laws of nature, lead to false views of morality and consequent licentiousness?—or those, which ridicule and point out the effects of absurd contradictions of human feelings and passions, and help to bring about a reformation of such practises.

Of the story in the second canto it is unnecessary to say much, for these remarks will apply to both. We suppose there has been some sermonizing on the description of the delight arising from the "illicit intercourse" of *Juan* and *Haidee*. People who talk in this way can perceive no distinctions. It certainly is not to be inculcated, that every handsome young man and woman will find their account in giving way to all their impulses, because the very violent breaking through the habits and forms of society would create a great deal of unhappiness, both to the individuals, and to others. But what is there to blame in a beautiful and affectionate girl who gives way to a passion for a young shipwrecked human creature, bound to her by gratitude as well as love? She exacts no promises, says the bard, because she fears no inconstancy. Her father had exposed her to the first temptation that comes across her, because he had not provided against it by allowing her to know more of mankind. And does she not receive, as well as bestow, more real pleasure (for that is the question) in the enjoyment of a first and deep passion, than in becoming the wife of some brother in iniquity to whom her pirating father would have trucked her for lucre?

The fact is, at the bottom of all these questions, that many things are made vicious, which are not so by nature; and many things made virtuous, which are only so by calling and agreement: and it is on the horns of this self-created dilemma, that society is continually writhing and getting desperate.

From a letter from Robert Southey to Walter Savage Landor, 20 February 1820.

A fashion of poetry has been imported which has had a great run, and is in a fair way of being worn out. It is of Italian growth—an adaptation of the manner of Pulci, Berni, and Ariosto in his sportive mood. Frere began it. What he produced was too good in itself and too inoffensive to become popular; for it attacked nothing and nobody; and it had the fault of his Italian models, that the transition from what is serious to what is burlesque was capricious. Lord Byron immediately followed; first with his *Beppo*, which implied the profligacy of the writer, and, lastly, with his *Don Juan*, which is a foul blot on the literature of his country, an act of high treason on English poetry.

A letter concerning *Don Juan III and IV* (1821) from John Wilson Croker to John Murray, 26 March 1820.

Dear Murray,

I have to thank you for letting me see your two new cantos [*III* and *IV*], which I return. What sublimity! what levity! what boldness! what tenderness! what majesty! what trifling! what variety! what *tediousness*!—for tedious to a strange degree, it must be confessed that whole passages are, particularly the earlier stanzas of the fourth canto. I know no man of such general powers of intellect as Brougham, yet I think *him* insufferably tedious; and I fancy the reason to be that he has such *facility* of expression that he is never recalled to a *selection* of his thoughts. A more costive orator would be obliged to choose, and a man of his talents could not fail to choose the best; but the power of uttering all and everything which passes across his mind, tempts him to say all. He goes on without thought—I should rather say, without pause. His speeches are poor from their richness, and dull from their infinite variety. An impediment in his speech would make him a perfect Demosthenes. Something of the same kind, and with something of the same effect, is Lord Byron's wonderful fertility of thought and facility of expression; and the Protean style of *Don Juan*, instead of checking (as the fetters of rhythm generally do) his natural activity, not only gives him wider limits to range in, but even generates a more roving disposition. I dare swear, if the truth were known, that his digressions and repetitions generate one another, and that the happy jingle of some of his comical rhymes has led him on to episodes of which he never originally thought; and thus it is that, with the most extraordinary merit, *merit of all kinds*, these two cantos have been to *me*, in several points, tedious and even obscure.

As to the PRINCIPLES, all the world, and you, Mr. Murray, *first of all*, have done this poem great injustice. There are levities here and there, more than good taste approves, but nothing to make such a terrible rout about—nothing so bad as *Tom Jones*, nor within a hundred degrees of *Count Fathom*. I know that it is no justification of one fault to produce a greater, neither am I justifying Lord Byron. I have acquaintance none, or next to none, with him, and of course no interest beyond what we must all take in a poet who, on the whole, is one of the first, if not the very first, of our age; but I direct my observations against you and those whom you deferred to. If you print and sell *Tom Jones* and *Peregrine Pickle*, why did you start at *Don Juan?* Why smuggle it into the world and, as it were, pronounce it illegitimate in its birth, and induce so many of the learned rabble, when they could find so little specific offence in it, to refer to its supposed original state as one of original sin? If instead of this you had touched the right string and in the right place, Lord Byron's own good taste and good nature would have revised and corrected some phrases in his poem which in reality disparage it more than its imputed looseness of principle; I mean some expressions of political and personal feelings which, I believe, he, in fact, never felt, and threw in wantonly and *de gaieté de cœur*, and which he would have omitted, advisedly and *de bonté de cœur*, if he had not been goaded by indiscreet, contradictory, and urgent *criticisms*, which, in some cases, were dark enough to be called *calumnies*. But these are blowing over, if not blown over; and I cannot but think that if Mr. Gifford, or some friend in whose taste and disinterestedness Lord Byron could rely, were to point out to him the cruelty to individuals, the injury to the national character, the offence to public taste, and the injury to his own reputation, of such passages as those about Southey and Waterloo and the British Government and the head of that Government, I cannot but hope and believe that these blemishes in the first cantos would be wiped away in the next edition; and that some that occur in the two cantos (which you sent me) would never see the light. What interest can Lord Byron have in being the poet of a party in politics, or of a party in morals, or of a party in religion? Why should he wish to throw away the suffrages (you see the times infect my dialect) of more than half the nation? He has no interest in that direction, and, I believe, has no feeling of that kind. In politics, he cannot be what he appears, or rather what Messrs. Hobhouse and Leigh Hunt wish to make him appear. A man of his birth, a man of his taste, a man of his talents, a man of his habits, can have nothing in common with such miserable creatures as we now call *Radicals*, of whom I know not that I can better express the illiterate and blind ignorance and vulgarity than by saying that the best informed of them have probably never heard of Lord Byron. No, no, Lord Byron may be indulgent to these jackal followers of his; he may connive at their use of his name—nay, it is not to be denied that he has given them too, too much countenance—but he never can, I should think, now that he sees not only the road but the rate they are going, continue to take a part so contrary to all his own interests and feelings, and to the feelings and interests of all the respectable part of his country. And yet it was only yesterday at dinner that somebody said that he had read or seen a letter of Lord Byron's to somebody, saying that if the Radicals only made a little progress and showed some real force, he would hasten over and get on horseback to head them. This is evidently either a gross lie altogether, or a grosser misconstruction of some epistolary pleasantry; because if the proposition were serious, the letter never would have been shown. Yet see how a bad name is given. We were twelve at dinner, all (except myself) people of note, and yet (except Walter Scott and myself again) every human being will repeat the story to twelve others—and so on. But what is to be the end of all this rigmarole of mine? To conclude, this—to advise you, for your own sake as a tradesman, for Lord Byron's sake as a poet, for the sake of good literature and good principles, which ought to be united, to take such measures as you may be able to venture upon to get Lord Byron to revise these two cantos, and not to make another step in the odious path which Hobhouse beckons him to pursue. There is little, very little, of this offensive nature in these cantos; the omission, I think, of five stanzas out of 215,[1] would do all I should ask on this point; but I confess that I think it would be much better for his fame and your profit if the two cantos were thrown into one,[2] and brought to a proper length by the retrenchment of the many careless, obscure, and idle passages which *incuria fudit*. I think Tacitus says that the Germans formed their plans when drunk and matured them when sober. I know not how this might answer in public affairs, but in poetry I should think it an excellent plan—to pour out, as Lord Byron says, his whole mind in the intoxication of the moment, but to revise and condense in the sobriety of the morrow. One word more: experience shows that the Pulcian style is very easily written. Frere, Blackwood's Magaziners, Rose, Cornwall, all write it with ease and success; it therefore behoves Lord Byron to distinguish his use of this measure by superior and peculiar beauties. He should refine and polish; and by the *limae labor et mora*, attain the perfection of ease. A vulgar epigram says that '*easy writing is damned hard reading*;' and it is one of the eternal and general rules by which heaven warns us, at every step and at every look, that this is a mere transitory life; that what costs no trouble soon perishes; that what grows freely dies early; and that nothing endures but in some degree of proportion with the time and labour it has cost to create. Use these hints if you can, but not my name.

Yours ever,

J. W. Croker.

From John Scott's unsigned article 'Lord Byron' in the series 'Living Authors' in *The London Magazine*, January 1821.

Lord Byron's compositions do not entitle him to be called the best of our present poets; but his personal character, and the history of his life have clearly rendered him the most interesting and remarkable of the persons who now write poetry. If he is not, as we have said of another, "the author we would most wish to be," he is certainly the living author who is chiefly "the marvel, and the show" of our day and generation—leaving the word "boast" out of the quotation, as leading to premature discussion.—Whatever general

[1] Byron later brought the number up to 228.
[2] Byron himself thought of splitting Canto III into two (see *III*. cxi)!

judgment we may pronounce on his qualities as a writer, guiding ourselves by the rules of criticism, there can be no doubt of his standing a towering object in the moral and intellectual horizon of his age; and he is destined so to endure, and to captivate and astonish the eye of posterity, when all that is common of our possessions is forgotten, and all that is weak and little is crumbled into dust; when the outline of that busy and crowded portion of space and time which is so much to us, will be traced, like that of an ancient city, by a few single, elevated, and imperishable monuments.

It does seem scarcely possible to pay too much for the glorious assurance of so enduring, to be so hereafter regarded;—yet, by Lord Byron, it has been purchased at a most serious, and even appalling expense in more than one kind of earthly good. Never,—in our opinion at least,—has that which is properly called *notoriety* been so intimately united with the more noble essence of true *fame*, as it is in the case of this writer; and, what strikes us as more strange still, he even reconciles those dubious and questionable qualities, which fall under the head of empirical, with the acquirement of sterling renown.—The personal interest, we believe, has always been above the poetical in Lord Byron's compositions; and, what is much worse, they appear to have been, in almost every instance, studiously calculated to produce this effect. It is true, the noble author has never distinctly offered us a professed portrait of himself in any of his heroes; but his plan, we think, has been a more objectionable one. While he has introduced, in most of them, features so odious and anti-social, that self-exposure in such a light might be regarded as an unnatural offence, and one more directly insulting to moral feeling than the bare practice of vice,—he has boldly and bare-facedly coupled the histories of his bravoes and villains with the incidents of his own life; mingled their feelings with even affectedly open disclosures of his own;—nay, he has sketched from the most sacred recesses of his own privacy, to the injury of other sensibility than his own, accompaniments to the scenes of debauchery, despair, and violence of which he has chiefly formed his poetical representations. Rousseau's confessions were avowedly of himself: whatever may be their absolute truth, they are most curiously true as an exhibition of character: their minute moral anatomy is as stupendous as the system of the blood-vessels and capillary tubes of the body; and, though indecent and offensive as a piece of self-exposure, they are coupled, all the way through, with so much evidence of actual personal responsibility, that the fancy is kept in subordination to the moral judgment of the reader, and the usual rules of social intercourse and human duty are not respited in his mind. Lord Byron's creations, however, are addressed to the poetical sympathies of his readers, while their main interest is derived from awakening a recollection of some fact of the author's life, or a conviction of an analogy to the author's own character. A confusion is thus occasioned in the breast of him whose attention is captivated by the productions in question, unfavourable altogether to right and pure feeling. The impression left on the mind, is neither strictly that of a work of art, to be pronounced upon according to the rules applicable to art,—nor of a matter-of-fact, appealing to the principles of sound judgment in such cases;—but what is striking in poetry is made a set-off against what is objectionable in morals,—while that which would be condemned as false, theatrical, or inconsistent, according to the laws of poetical criticism, is often rendered the most taking part of the whole composition by its evident connection with real and private circumstances, that are of a nature to tickle the idle, impertinent, and most unpoetical curiosity of the public. This sort of balancing system is not fair:—Lord Byron should either give us Childe Harold, Conrad, &c. as what painters call historical portraits of himself, or he should leave us free to judge of them as we would judge of a statue, or of a picture, or of any strictly poetical personage. As it is, the literary imperfections of the Childe, &c. merge in the personal peculiarities of the author;—and again, where it might be useful to hold the latter to answer personally for certain licences, rendered stimulating and seductive by irregular and unfit allusions, he escapes from this responsibility into the fictitious hero—after perhaps mortally corrupting principle by touching the sensibility with traits that derive all their force from his own history. The unsoundness of this style of composition, is of a double nature: it depraves the taste as well as taints the purity of the moral feeling.

A personal interest of this nature by no means enters legitimately amongst the qualities that form poetical power and beauty: if the reflection of the author's character must be seen in such compositions as profess to be imaginative, it too should take an imaginative hue, and lie deep and dim in the heart of the strain, going, shadow-like, with all the variations of its current. Lord Byron's egotism, therefore, we consider to be one of those properties displayed in his works, which we alluded to at the commencement as partaking of an empirical nature. Its effect is to give a prodigious interest to his compositions with the common run of the readers and buyers of books: it forms admirable matter for *table-talk*—not such as that in the LONDON MAGAZINE, but such as is to be heard about the west-end of the town—to be enabled, on his lordship's own authority, to discuss his lordship's remorse, and misanthropy, and withered feelings, and youthful disappointments, and faded hopes!—Lord

Byron's genius should be above supplying matter for such heartless gossip:—if he really have (as we earnestly hope he has not) genuine cause for melancholy reminiscences, approaching to the horror of despair, he should "*instruct his sorrows to be proud*;" otherwise his own fine verse tells against himself—

> The rock, the vulture, and the chain,
> *All that the proud can feel of pain,*
> *The agony they do not show,*
> The suffocating sense of woe
>   Which speaks but in its loneliness,
>   And then is jealous lest the sky
>   Should have a listener, nor will sigh
>   Until its voice is echoless.[1]

Griefs revolting in their cause, and poisonous and cureless in their effects, ought to be kept as secret as a mortal cancer,—which no one who pines under it ever thinks of displaying to company, to have its gangrenous colours admired, and made a theme for the exclamations of silly wonder. Sufferings calculated to excite deep commiseration and kind pity, when sustained with dignity, and expressed with reserve, are justly regarded as public nuisances when they court display and are obtruded on our senses,—not merely as offensive spectacles, but as dangerous causes of the deformity of others by operating on susceptible dispositions with their diseased and monstrous influence. Besides, there is but too much reason for suspecting, that there is more of trick than calamity in many of these exhibitions: the seemingly infirm object, who painfully limps on crutches before the passengers in the street, calling their attention to his old, but unhealed wounds; his festering sores which he must carry about with him to his dying day,—is often known to join the merry dance in the evening, with other active cripples, and healthful bed-ridden! In the pauses of the fiddle they count the gains which they owe to their afflictions,—and chirp over their cups on the strength of the supply which their agonies have procured to them.

Is there no ground for suspicion that Lord Byron's grief, and despair,—which are for ever at the end of his pen, except when he is writing notes to his poems, and those New Moralities, Beppo and Don Juan,—are in a good measure *feelings of ceremony*. They are certainly excellent prompters of phrase; they supply solemn poetical apparel for public occasions; and invest the person of the author, in the imaginations of the daughters of noblemen, and the wives of tradesmen, with the charm of a melancholy air,—set off by a

---

[1] Lines 7–14 of *Prometheus*, published in the *Prisoner of Chillon* volume (1816). The italics are Scott's.

cap-and-feather look of desperation, and gestures of gentlemanly
ferocity. . . .

> Seared in heart, and lone, and blighted—
> More than this, *I scarce can die*:—[1]

thus concludes Lord Byron's Farewell, on the occasion of his
leaving England, and we have had good reason since to admire the
strength of the vivacious principle in his breast. His subsequent
productions have seemed to intimate that dying was as far from his
own thoughts, as his death is far from the wishes of booksellers, and
book-readers, and the admirers of genius, and they who desire to
see one of England's most distinguished children restored to her
under circumstances in every way satisfactory. But it absolutely
makes one angry, in the midst of high-toned strains of energetic
feeling, sounding a requiem over departed glory, or a celebration of
immortal genius, or a hymn to natural beauty, glowing and en-
kindling as the rays of morning, to have our touched sympathies
interrupted by the stage-trick of a displayed pocket-handkerchief,
or the strut of theatrical magnanimity in martyrdom.

> Meantime *I seek no sympathies, nor need*;
> The thorns which I have reaped are of the tree
> I planted: they have torn me,—and I bleed;
> I should have known what fruit would spring from such a seed.
> > *Childe Harold, Canto* 4.
> > [st. x; Scott's italics]

This is weak if sincere, and weak if affected. Indeed, affected it is,
whether it be sincere or not. What we chiefly object to, is the
mawkishness of such passages: their decency as confessions, and
their consistency with self-respect, and the respect of others, in the
mouth of a fashionable nobleman of these days, who writes elsewhere
of "lobster sallad" and "champaign punch," are matters we leave
to his lordship's own reflection. If Lord Byron has ever appeared in
Rotten-row on horseback, he seems to us precluded from talking,
even in his own poetry, in such a strange ranting sort of way of his
sorrows and errors. His station in society, and his manners as an
English gentleman, turn the laugh against his sombre heroics. We
dare say he has done nothing sufficiently worse than other people,
if all were known, to justify, or even render excusable, his rhymed
remorse. . . .

His frequent allusions to his own private history; his almost constant appeals to sickly sensibility by tricked-out representations of
disreputable and garrulous sorrow and suffering; and the false and
inconsistent character of many of his heroes, in whom strong effect

[1] The last two lines of 'Fare thee well!' (1816). The italics are again Scott's.

266

is purchased at the expense of propriety of every kind, constitute faults in Lord Byron's style of composition, palpable to an eye of any discernment. But, more unfortunately, they are hurtfully seductive to inexperienced and uninstructed taste, and most mischievously calculated to give ascendancy to the heterodox judgments, generated in the heat and rankness of fashionable manners. It is the popularity of these faults that has made us feel it necessary to commence our observations by noticing them. We should not have deemed ourselves free to give full vent to our admiration of the marvellous powers of this remarkable intellect, if we had not at the outset entered a protest against its various heresies. That Lord Byron irradiates the literature of the day by his genius, is incontestable; but that it can be said of him, that he elevates the general reputation of the literature of his country, we doubt. The truth is, he mingles up many questions that are not literary, but of a more serious and important nature, with the consideration of his literary merits. It is his misfortune to have done this; for not only, we apprehend, must a verdict be given against him whenever the inquiry is directed towards moral tendency, personal fairness, and public decency, but the worst faults of his style are, we think, clearly traceable to that looseness of feeling which is the unhappy source of so much irregularity of another nature staining his works—often demanding indulgence, and often forbidding it altogether. Lord Byron's last work is avowedly licentious;—it is a satire on decency, on fine feeling, on the rules of conduct necessary to the conservation of society, and on some of his own near connections. Having said this, we need say no more on its character independently of literary considerations: he would himself, we are sure, allow it to be all we now say; his publisher has done so by scrupling to put his name in the title-page.—The only questions, agreeably to the known frankness of his disposition, which it is probable he would think of discussing, would be the degree of mischief it is likely to do; and whether jokes on the inconsistencies of human professions and practice, and exposures of the ridiculous side of social institutions and domestic observances, have not before been ventured, quite as pointed as Don Juan, without incurring on their parents the heavy charge of being arrayed in hostility against the best interests of their fellow men.—We would be disposed to concede a good deal to his lordship on these points: the world has by this time been pretty-well accustomed to see the vivacity of talent employed in raising a laugh against things which do honour to conduct, and passing as pleasantry what is discreditable. Man, in fact, is at once a laughing animal, and a laughable one; he is not, and cannot be, consistent. His nature is made up of absurdities, as they now appear,—which are probably only enigmas, the solution of which is reserved for another state of being. Hence, very considerable freedom has always been taken with the stricter doctrines of the moralist, and the most essential regulations of social intercourse, in the vivacity of penetrating intellects, seeing through disguises, and solemn hypocrisies,—and necessary, but unreal pretensions, and all the solemn masquerade of serious life. The temptation to irreverent mirth and dangerous ridicule is so great, that we are obliged to seek securities against their effects, rather than to prohibit or severely condemn their exercise. It is now pretty well understood, what these poetical licences are worth; their language may introduce impure terms and images into breasts that would otherwise have remained, for some time longer at least, unsullied: so far they are mischievous and reprehensible; but as to actually furnishing grounds of conduct, or leading to the formation of false principles, we do not think that these evident caricatures of manners are likely to do this. They pass as exaggerations, or caprices on their side: they are considered to be intentionally wide of the truth: their authors are supposed to be prepared to say with Prior,

Gadzooks, who would swear to the truth of a song!

In our view of the matter, Lord Byron's serious poetry is of a much more deleterious tendency than his late compositions professing levity of purpose. The former is calculated to introduce disease into the heart through admiration excited in favour of false and hateful qualities of character: the latter address themselves only to the unscrupulous, and the experienced. To regard what is improper in them with approbation, would bespeak previous corruption. But the first ruin taste, infect feeling, and unsettle principle: what is showy in them wins and perverts; what is pathetic softens towards temptation; what is horrible familiarizes with evil, and misrepresents nature.

Still, however, it must be admitted, that Lord Byron has carried the licence of his levities farther than we have been accustomed to see men of his powers of mind care to commit themselves in such irregularities; and it is to be deplored, for his sake, as well as for ours, that, with such undoubted possession of genius as he certainly has, he should only vary his style of writing to make a new trespass. Much, too, do we regret, that a very suspicious circumstance attends the variation: the qualities that are objectionable in both his styles, *equally belong to the class of expedients for cheaply gaining popularity*: they are equally included within the set of resources which grovelling souls have recourse to, in the absence of talent, to realize their selfish schemes. Indecency is saleable; so are lampoons; so are pieces of overcharged colouring and staring effect; so are affected confidences, and allusions to domestic discords, private errors, and mental horrors. All of these present baneful stimuli to depraved appetites:—it is lucky for Lord Byron's reputation as a poet, that he has mingled much of the celestial fire, and of glowing feeling of that which is inspiring in the noblest terrestrial objects, with these baser materials of composition: he has done this to a degree quite sufficient to exculpate him from having sought to shelter his weakness by pandering to the baser desires: but what we have stated,— the candour of which we are sure cannot be denied by any reader of his works,—fully bears out what we affirmed of him at the commencement of this article;—viz. that he strangely *reconciles those dubious and questionable qualities which fall under the head of empirical, with the acquirement of sterling renown.* His pieces are indeed of a "mingled yarn:" the coarse is mixed with the fine; the subtlest texture with the veriest botch-work.—We would point out to his lordship's serious reflection, if we had any assurance of being honoured by his notice, as the features most degrading to the character of the author in his last compositions, those which are calculated to throw doubt altogether on the sincerity of his emotions, and the healthiness of his heart, putting joke and levity out of the question. Vivacious allusions to certain practical irregularities are things which it is to be supposed innocence is strong enough to resist,—otherwise, the commerce of the world forbids hope of its long-life. But the quick alternation of pathos and profaneness,—of serious and moving sentiment and indecent ribaldry,—of afflicting, soul-rending pictures of human distress, rendered keen by the most pure and hallowed sympathies of the human breast, and absolute jeering of human nature, and general mockery of creation, destiny, and heaven itself,— this is a sort of violence, the effect of which is either to sear or to disgust the mind of the reader—and which cannot be fairly characterized but as an insult and outrage. This is not an English fault; for it affects the sincerity of the writer's design, and the honour of his intentions. Some bad specimens of it exist in foreign literature,— but that of our own country has not hitherto been so contaminated. —Our writers have composed burlesque, and grossness, and caricature, and indecency; but they have not insulted the very principle of goodness, the image of God in the soul of man, by exciting the best affections of the spirit, and leading it to direct communion with the powers that scatter sublimity and beauty over this sublunary scene, in order to startle and shame it, by suddenly confronting it with a Satanic laugh at some mortifying slur thrown on what is best and fairest to human eye and thought,—and dearest to human feeling! To do this is to reduce reader, author, and subject to one general level of contempt: to make us, so far as he has power over us, despise and hate ourselves, him, and all about us.—Degradation of nature is felt to be suffered, when from so exquisite, so elaborate, so painfully exact a description of parental tenderness, hanging over the mortal agonies of a beloved child, as we find in the Don Juan, we are suddenly called upon to turn our sympathies to sneering jests and cruel mirth. What is the difference between doing this in a poem, and doing it in real life?—and what should we say of the disposition of him who should turn from the death-bed of a fine boy, round which hearts are breaking, and from which hopes are departing, to crack scurril jokes on human weakness, calamity, and despair? Lord Byron would be as much shocked at this as any man; and, therefore, we must come to the conclusion, that he considers his authorship a mere piece of representation altogether, in which he is to perform the part of the moment,—now in tragedy, now in farce, as Garrick performed Hamlet and Abel Drugger in the same evening; and Kean, Othello and Harlequin. This we are pretty sure, from the general evidence of his works, is what he really does; but he ought not to do it to the injury either of personal or public feeling, or even to the perversion of taste.— . . .

We find our objections have run out to fill a larger proportion of our paper than we had anticipated,—for, when we set out, we felt chiefly our personal inclination to handle favourably the object of our intended remarks. We necessarily, however, put the volumes of this great and prolific author on the table before us, and their collected evidence has compelled us to what we have said. But how much remains to be said of a very different nature, with reference to the real poetical power displayed in these eloquent rhapsodies! We know there are critics who deny that Lord Byron is a distinguished poet,—affirming that his style is often false, and often feeble,—that his sentiments are often unnatural, his imagery tawdry, his effects forced, and in bad taste. We think so too,—and yet affirm him to be one of the greatest of poets. The mere vigour and rapidity of his course would almost be enough to constitute him a great poet, particularly when it is considered through what mighty scenery his course has been directed. He has carried a countless number of readers, with glowing, untiring ardour, over almost the whole expanse of the poetical map, as it includes the marvels of history, of art, and external creation. What traveller in prose has ever conveyed such lively ideas of what is essential and peculiar in the aspect of climes and situations which have long fed our dreams of beauty, and of wonders, and to the influence of which he has now added tenfold efficacy? Whom have we amongst us to do any thing like what follows to bring home the power of a classical land, and the enchantments of classical monuments, so as to make them bear with force on the mass

270

of public feeling, and give a general elevation to the level of fancy and thought amongst us?

[Quotes *CH I.* xli–xlii and *IV.* lxxviii–lxxix]

This may not be the very purest of all styles of poetry, (though we confess our perceptions are not open to its faults), but at least it is noble declamation, rich with splendour, and sonorous with lofty music. It enlivens the circulation of thought and feeling, and raises the port of the imagination. The principal charm of Lord Byron's poetry consists, we are willing to confess, in its scenery,—but no one we think, but himself, could have brought it to bear so point-blank on the universal sympathy. It is the glory of the places and objects themselves that beams on his page, that has intoxicated his soul, and that inspires the reader: he seems to have been rendered poetical solely by the influence of his subjects—that is to say, when his object is not to make a representation of himself, or to wound others: with these exceptions he speaks as one full of the sacred inflatus. What vivacity of observation is apparent in his descriptions, what zeal in his celebrations,—how quick, varied, and bright, the running flame of his allusions! He is justly entitled to be the most popular of poets, though he is not the best, and though he so often condescends to improper lures of popularity. But he is entitled to be so, because, more than any other modern writer whom we can name, he is the *minstrel of fame*, whose lays are best adapted to gain the common ear, and find their way to the common heart. He fills galleries, long vistas of magnificence, with images of glory, with stories of passion and suffering, with the annals of departed greatness, and the sublimities of the world that never depart: and he issues an irresistible summons to thousands, to millions, to enter these, and admire and venerate what they see, and bow before that might of destiny which, while it seems to reduce individuals to nothing, gives grandeur and importance to the race, by storing human consciousness with vast and terrible images, that,—better than all the pleasures of existence,—prove its elevation in the scale of nature. Lord Byron, it is true, marks only the stronger divisions of the great picture; he is not skilful in running those cunning, delicate, and fine gradations, which the most refined fancies chiefly delight to distinguish;—but he raises the voice of poetry, as it was wont to be raised, when the excitement of animation in assembled crowds was the minstrel's design. The voice indeed is not now the same in its accents that it was then, but, if it were, it would not have the same effect: the auditors are changed. He, however, conjures up the common inspirations of high and strong feeling: beauty, valour, danger, death, renown, and immortality; and these ideas he passes through the soul

271

like quick-following flashes of lightning. This is his talent: his reasoning is generally bad; his mere "moods of his own mind," when not closely connected with some external cause of excitement, are very bad; his conception of character is monotonous and false; his sentiments are not often profound, and very often mingle in wild inconsistency with each other: he is pensive or enthusiastic on a theme in one page, which in another he treats with sarcasm or expressions of disgust. In style he is frequently tortuous, involved, clumsy, and affected: we are often tempted to suppose he could not himself declare what his meaning was in particular passages, if they were referred to him for explanation. His metaphysics of the mind are in bad taste, and worse philosophy; and on his various offences in regard to moral tendency, and the respect which an author owes to himself, we have already too fully commented to have any occasion again to refer to them. Yet, with all these faults heaped on his writings, and staring the reader in the face, there is a principle of captivating power in them, supreme and triumphant above all faults; defying faults to lessen it; and attracting after the author, wherever he chooses to wander, a following train, formed of a nation's admiration and sympathy. He has awakened, by literary exertion, a more intense interest in his person than ever before resulted from literature. He is thought of a hundred times, in the breasts of young and old, men and women, for once that any other author is,—popular as are many of his living rivals. He casts his shadow from afar over the surface of our society; and he is talked of in book-clubs and ball-rooms as the only companion which the age has produced to the French revolution! Drawing much from deeper sources than his own, he has rendered palateable what the public taste before rejected. The most musical names of the world,—those that sound, even in the ears of the uninstructed, as equivalent to the noblest ideas and the deepest feelings, are closely associated with his; for he has repeated and celebrated them so as to redouble their empire. Athens, Arqua, Rome, and Venice, fall within the territory over which he is lord: he has visited Waterloo as a foreigner, and Thermopylæ as an Englishman; celebrated Napoleon's fall as a friend of liberty, and sung with rapture his triumphs as the bard of despotism: he has received letters from young ladies, anxious for his salvation; has been inquired after by Maria Louisa,—"proud Austria's mournful flower," in a theatre,—and, in fine, he has *swum across the Hellespont*! He who has claims to have all this engraved on his tomb-stone, need not fear becoming soon a prey to "dumb forgetfulness."

The principle of *chiaroscuro* will account for much of the strong effect of his pieces. A sombre thought or image is introduced to give high *relief* to a lovely description: this is often done with too much show of design,—but it is also sometimes done with consummate skill and feeling, of which we have an instance in the following fine stanza.

> The morn is up again, the dewy morn,
> With breath all incense, and with cheek all bloom,
> Laughing the clouds away with playful scorn,
> *And living as if earth contained no tomb,—*
> And glowing into day: we may resume
> The march of our existence: and thus I,
> Still on thy shores, fair Leman! may find room
> And food for meditation, nor pass by
> Much, that may give us pause, if pondered fittingly.
>
> [*Childe Harold, III.* xcviii; Scott's italics]

We know nothing, in the whole range of poetry, more true to experience, and at the same time more original, than the thought glanced across the mind in the line we have distinguished by Italics. It gives voice to an impression which has many a day lain on many a heart, without the consciousness being sufficiently awakened to it to define it exactly.—Again, on the other hand, how delightfully does he throw the beauty of silent ceaseless nature, over scenes of moral vicissitude, and historical melancholy!

> Where'er we tread 'tis haunted, holy ground;
> No earth of thine is lost in vulgar mould,
> But one vast realm of wonder spreads around,
> And all the Muse's tales seem truly told,
> Till the sense aches with gazing to behold
> The scenes our earliest dreams have dwelt upon:
> Each hill and dale, each deepening glen and wold
> Defies the power which crush'd thy temples gone:
> Age shakes Athena's tower, but spares gray Marathon.
>
> [*Ibid., II.* lxxxviii]

We have living poets—several—whose contemplation is more intense,—whose passion is more exclusively poetical,—whose language is more pure, and expedients more select; but none whose spirit is so active, or range of sensibility so wide. He spreads himself out over nature and history, like a bird of prey; the storm does not beat down his wing, and he sails in the calm sunshine without fainting. The best specimens of poetry which the present day has produced, lie deep and clear like lakes: Byron's verse rushes like a mountain river through many realms; carrying down to one the productions of another;—often shallow, sometimes showing dry bald spots; but usually rushing forwards with vehement impetuosity:

sometimes, too, collecting into depths equal to that of the lake—then again pouring onward, as if enlivened, excited, by the call of the roaring ocean.

Eloquence, rather than poetry, forms, perhaps, the great charm of Lord Byron's verses: like some of the loftier passages in Tasso, his finest morsels are generally declamatory;—the objects are all shown off in exhibition, but the exhibitor is evidently penetrated by their qualities; he anxiously adjusts the display, but he feels them to be worth displaying. His descriptions of scenery, and the exquisite effects of nature, are what we think he does best.

> The moon is up, and yet it is not night—
> Sunset divides the sky with her—a sea
> Of glory streams along the Alpine height
> Of blue Friuli's mountains; Heaven is free
> From clouds, but of all colours seems to be
> Melted to one vast Iris of the West,
> Where the day joins the past eternity;
> While, on the other hand, meek Dian's crest
> Floats through the azure air—an island of the blest.
>
> *Childe Harold, Canto* 4.
> [st. xxvii]

After passages of this class, the bitterness of sceptical emotion in his compositions seems most marked by energy and earnestness. As a moral philosopher, and even as a misanthrope, he is childishly inconsistent; and his inconsistency would lead us to doubt, or more than doubt, his cherishing any real sentiment corresponding with his expressions in such passages. For instance, in stanza 176, of his fourth Canto of Childe Harold, he makes it his boast that he can

> —reap from earth, sea, *joy almost as dear*
> *As if there were no man to trouble what is clear.*
>
> [Scott's italics]

This is very school-boy like; but, what is worse, it is not felt with the sincerity of the school-boy; for, in stanza 178, he tells us that he

> *Loves not man the less,* but nature more,
>
> [Scott's italics]

for these pleasures enjoyed in the "pathless woods," and "by the deep sea:" and then again, in stanza 180, we find him exulting in the idea, that his favourite, the ocean, is in the habit of sending human beings "shivering in its playful spray, and howling to their gods"—then dashing them to the earth,—"where let them lay!"—which last exclamation is bad grammar, and idle rhodomontade.—We could

274

multiply instances of these inconsistencies from all his compositions. . . .

Our author is, in short, a genuine master in his art, though his
style is false, and his resources are often unworthy of his talents.—
We have heard him called a bad poet; but if his poetry be bad, we
can only say, that we like it better than much that is allowed to be
good. Who denies that Salvator Rosa was a genuine artist,—because
signs of affectation, and false ambition, are to be discerned in his
pictures? Lord Byron's last compositions—Beppo and Don Juan—
are wonderful proofs of the versatility of his powers; but they piti-
lessly sacrifice personal consistency and dignity in the caprice of a
petulant disdain of opinion, or a distasteful avidity for notoriety as
a man and an author.

From Robert Southey's Preface to his poem *A Vision of Judgment*,
published 11 April 1821.[1]

The publication of a lascivious book is one of the worst offences
that can be committed against the well-being of society. It is a sin,
to the consequences of which no limits can be assigned, and those
consequences no after repentance in the writer can counteract.
Whatever remorse of conscience he may feel when his hour comes
(and come it must!) will be of no avail. The poignancy of a death-bed
repentance cannot cancel one copy of the thousands which are sent
abroad; and as long as it continues to be read, so long is he the pander
of posterity, and so long is he heaping up guilt upon his soul in
perpetual accumulation.

These remarks are not more severe than the offence deserves,
even when applied to those immoral writers who have not been
conscious of any evil intention in their writings, who would acknowledge a little levity, a little warmth of colouring, and so forth,
in that sort of language with which men gloss over their favourite
vices, and deceive themselves. What then should be said of those
for whom the thoughtlessness and inebriety of wanton youth can no
longer be pleaded, but who have written in sober manhood and
with deliberate purpose? . . . Men of diseased hearts and depraved
imaginations, who, by forming a system of opinions to suit their
own unhappy course of conduct, have rebelled against the holiest
ordinances of human society, and hating that revealed religion which,
with all their efforts and bravadoes, they are unable entirely to
disbelieve, labour to make others as miserable as themselves, by
infecting them with a moral virus that eats into the soul! The school

[1] It was this Preface that largely provoked Byron's savage mock-epic in
parody, in the Preface to which he refers in stinging terms to Southey's
remarks in this passage.—*Ed.*

which they have set up may properly be called the Satanic school; for though their productions breathe the spirit of Belial in their lascivious parts, and the spirit of Moloch in those loathsome images of atrocities and horrors which they delight to represent, they are more especially characterised by a Satanic spirit of pride and audacious impiety, which still betrays the wretched feeling of helplessness wherewith it is allied.

From the anonymous *Letter to the Right Honourable Lord Byron*, by John Bull (April–May 1821), now known to have been written by John Gibson Lockhart.

. . . But to return to your Lordship, (not that I am done with the stamp-master,)—all the world agrees with yourself in thinking you a great poet,—those only excepted whom the most egregious vanity hath hoodwinked, doth hoodwink, and ever will hoodwink,—and in calling you so, except those whom the most egregious envy prompts to speak the thing that is not, and the thing that they think not. And a great poet you unquestionably are; not near so great a poet as Milton or Spenser; but a much greater poet (and it is humbug to say you yourself don't think so) than Alexander Pope. You see I don't make the least allusion to Shakespeare, and I am sure, were you in my place, you would never dream of doing so any more than myself. It would be just as ridiculous to compare Milton to Shakespeare, as it would be to compare Pope to Shakespeare; and these the positive and the superlative being out of the question, what use would there be in lugging in you,—the comparative? Shakespeare stands by himself. He is not one of our race. You, Milton, and Pope, are all very clever men,—but there is not the least semblance of anything superhuman about any of you. But what, in the name of wonder, do you mean by this attempt of yours,[1] to persuade us that there is no difference of ranks among poets, except what depends on the difference of execution? This is not the point at all, my Lord, and you very well know it is not. The thing does not depend upon the nature of the execution, but on the order of the conceptions of the man. Shakespeare himself, in spite of all Schlegel's humbug, does not at all exceed all other men's excellence in the *execution* of his tragedies; and Martial does excel all other men in the *execution* of his epigrams. Tom Moore executes a song as well as Robert Burns—perhaps better,—but who except a miss dying over her harpsichord, with an ensign at her back, ever dreamt of considering Tom Moore as great a poet as Burns? The 'fact' is, that

[1] This refers to Byron's *Letter to **** ****** [John Murray], Esqre, on the Rev. W. L. Bowles's Strictures on the Life and Writings of Pope*, written in February and published in March 1821.—*Ed.*

Tom Moore, and Martial, and Pope, (I beg his pardon, however, for putting him alongside of Mr Moore,) are not poets of the highest cast, because they have not conceptions of the highest cast,—and that Burns and Byron are, because they have. This, therefore, is a piece of utter humbug on your part; and I give you no credit for it, because it is a piece of humbug that everybody will see through, just as well as myself. . . .

. . . You are a great poet, but even with your poetry you mix too much of that at present very saleable article against which I am now bestirring myself [i.e. humbug]. The whole of your misanthropy, for example, is humbug. You do not hate men, 'no, nor woman neither', but you thought it would be a fine, interesting thing for a handsome young Lord to depict himself as a dark-souled, melancholy, morbid being, and you have done so, it must be admitted, with exceeding cleverness. In spite of all your pranks, (*Beppo*, &c. *Don Juan* included,) every boarding-school in the empire still contains many devout believers in the amazing misery of the black-haired, high-browed, blue-eyed, bare-throated, Lord Byron. How melancholy you look in the prints! Oh! yes, this is the true cast of face. Now, tell me, Mrs. Goddard, now tell me, Miss Price, now tell me, dear Harriet Smith, and dear, dear Mrs. Elton, do tell me, is not this just the very look, that one would have fancied for Childe Harold? Oh! what eyes and eyebrows!—Oh! what a chin!—well, after all, who knows what may have happened? One can never know the truth of such stories. Perhaps her *Ladyship* was in the wrong after all.—I am sure if I had married such a man, I would have borne with all his little eccentricities—a man so evidently unhappy.—Poor Lord Byron! who can say how much he may have been to be pitied? I am sure I would; I bear with all Mr. E.'s eccentricities, and I am sure any woman of real sense would have done so to Lord Byron's: poor Lord Byron!—well, say what they will, I shall always pity him;—do you remember these dear lines of his—

> It is that settled ceaseless gloom,
> The fabled Hebrew wanderer bore,
> That will not look beyond the tomb,
> But cannot hope for rest before.
>
> [st. 5 of 'To Inez' in *Childe Harold I*]

—Oh! beautiful! and how beautifully you repeat them! You always repeat Lord Byron's fine passages so beautifully. What think you of that other we were talking of on Saturday evening at Miss Bates's?

> Nay, smile not at my sullen brow,
> Alas! I cannot smile again.
>
> [*Ibid.*, st. 1]

I forget the rest;—but nobody has such a memory as Mrs. E. Don't you think Captain Brown has a look of Lord Byron?

How you laugh in your sleeve when you imagine to yourself (which you have done any one half-hour these seven years) such beautiful scenes as these:—they are the triumphs of humbug: but you are not a Bowles: you ought to be (as you might well afford to be) ashamed of them. You ought to put a stop to them, if you are able; and the only plan I can point out is, that of making a vow and sticking to it, as I have done, and ever, I hope, shall do, of never writing a line more except upon the anti-humbug principle. You say you admire Pope, and I believe you: well, in this respect, I should really be at a loss to suggest a better model; do you also, my Lord, 'stoop to truth, and ⟨de⟩moralize your song.' Stick to *Don Juan*: it is the only sincere thing you have ever written; and it will live many years after all your humbug Harolds have ceased to be, in your own words,

A school-*girl's* tale—the wonder of an hour.[1]

Perhaps you will stare at this last piece of my advice: but, nevertheless, upon honour, it is as sincere as possible. I consider *Don Juan* as out of all sight the best of your works; it is by far the most spirited, the most straightforward, the most interesting, and the most poetical; and everybody thinks as I do of it, although they have not the heart to say so. . . .

I will not insult *Don Juan* by saying that his style is *not* like that of Signior Penseroso di Cornuaglia[2]; in truth, I think the great charm of its style is, that it is not much like the style of any other poem in the world. It is utter humbug to say, that it is borrowed from the style of the Italian weavers of merry *rima ottava*; their merriment is nothing, because they have nothing but their merriment; yours is every thing, because it is delightfully intermingled with and contrasted by all manner of serious things—murder and lust included. It is also mere *humbug* to accuse you of having plagiarized it from Mr. Frere's pretty and graceful little *Whistlecrafts*. The measure to be sure is the same, but then the measure is as old as the hills. But the spirit of the two poets is as different as can be. Mr. Frere writes elegantly, playfully, very like a gentleman, and a scholar, and a respectable man, and his poems never sold, nor ever will sell. Your *Don Juan* again, is written strongly, lasciviously, fiercely, laughingly—every body sees in a moment, that nobody could have written it but a man of the first order both in genius and in dissipation;—a real master of all his tools —a profligate, pernicious, irresistible, charming Devil—and, accord-

---

[1] Byron actually wrote 'school-boy's' (*Childe Harold*, II. ii. 6).
[2] Barry Cornwall, on whom see p. 433, n. 1 below.

ingly, the *Don* sells, and will sell to the end of time, whether our good friend Mr. John Murray honours it with his *imprimatur* or doth not so honour it. I will mention a book, however, from which I do think you have taken a great many hints—nay, a great many pretty full sketches for your Juan. It is one which (with a few more) one never sees mentioned in reviews, because it is a book written on the anti-humbug principle. It is—you know it excellently well—it is no other than FAUBLAS,[1] a book which contains as much good fun as *Gil Blas*, or Molière—as much good luscious description as the *Heloise*; as much fancy and imagination as all the Comedies in the English language put together—and less humbug than any one given romance that has been written since *Don Quixote*—a book which is to be found on the tables of Roués, and in the desks of divines and under the pillows of spinsters—a book, in a word, which is read universally—I wish I could add,—in the original. Your fine Spanish lady, with her black hair lying on the pillow, and the curly-headed little Juan couched under the coverlid—she is taken—every inch of her—from the *Marquise de B——*; your Greek girl (sweet creature!) is *La petite Contesse*, but she is the better, because of her wanting even the semblance of being married. You have also taken some warm touches from *Peregrine Proteus*,[2] and if you read *Peregrine* over again you will find there is still more well worth the taking.

But all this has nothing to do with the charming *style* of *Don Juan*, which is entirely and inimitably your own—the sweet, fiery, rapid, easy—beautifully easy, anti-humbug style of *Don Juan*. Ten stanzas of it are worth all your *Manfred*—and yet your *Manfred* is a noble poem too in its way; and Meinherr von Goethe has exhibited no more palpable symptom of dotage than in his attempt to persuade his *lesende publicum* that you stole it from his *Faustus*; for it is, as I have said, a noble and an original poem, and not in the least like either *Don Juan* or *Faust*, and quite inferior to both of them. I had really no idea what a very clever fellow you were till I read *Don Juan*. In my humble opinion, there is very little in the literature of the present day that will really stand the test of half a century, except the *Scotch* novels of Sir Walter Scott and *Don Juan*. *They* will do so because they are written with perfect facility and nature—because their materials are all drawn from nature—in other words, because they are neither made up of cant, like Wordsworth and Shelley, nor

---

[1] *La vie et les amours du Chevalier de Faublas*, 1786–9, by Jean-Baptiste Louvet, a Girondin who survived the Reign of Terror, was a novel about the gay aristocracy of the Ancien Régime. It had a great success, which would have been even greater but for the outbreak of the Revolution. For Louvet see J. Rivers: *Louvet* (London, 1910).
[2] *Peregrine Proteus* (1797), a novel by Wieland.

of humbug like *Childe Harold* and *The City of the Plague*, nor of Brunswick Mum, like the *Rime of the Ancient Mariner*, nor of milk and water like Mr. Barry Cornwall.

From the review of *Don Juan III–V* in *The British Critic*, September 1821.

The king of birds, in his noble and generous nature, builds his eyrie aloft, under the mid-light of heaven, and gives his callow brood full cognizance of the sun. It is the eft, and toad, and lizard on the other hand, the slimy, and creeping, and venomous tribes, which shrink from observation, and bring forth in covert. The Poem before us is one of these hole and corner deposits; not only begotten but spawned in filth and darkness. Every accoucheur of literature has refused his obstetric aid to the obscure and ditch-delivered foundling; and even its father, though he unblushingly has stamped upon it an image of himself which cannot be mistaken, forbears to give it the full title of avowed legitimacy. It is not a little to the honour of the respectable publisher who hitherto has been Lord Byron's channel to the press, that in the present instance he has refused his customary assistance; for, though in common with "all the booksellers" as the advertisement notifies, he *sells* Don Juan, no one, we are sure, who knows his character, will do him the injustice to suppose that he *publishes* any work to which he is ashamed or afraid to affix his name.

The rare merit of consistency must be granted in its very utmost extent to Lord Byron. Whatever be the masque which he assumes for the moment, whether he struts and mouths under the tinsel and pasteboard trappings of the melodramatic hero, or jingles the cap and bells of the motley jackpudding, the same "Mungo every where" peeps forth from his disguise. One pervading ὕλη, as the Aristotelians say, is cut and carved by him into numberless forms. His table is perpetually spread, like that of the old noble whose fare was so piteously bewailed by his chaplain, with "rabbits roasted and rabbits boiled;" or perhaps more like that of the Barmicede with a seeming variety of dainties, which when closely examined, resolve themselves one and all into—nothing. Now we have no quarrel with a single dish so long as it affords clean, wholesome, nutritive, substantial aliment; but when *sauce piquante* and high seasoning are called in to disguise corruption, and our ragout when stripped of its garnish turns out to be garbage, it is no wonder that our appetite fails. . . .

Of the story of these cantos we cannot be expected to present any detail. It consists of a few scenes closely imitated from Louvet and Laclos (and this does not surprize us, for vice after all is drearily monotonous,) done into rhymes, which may furnish mottos for the snuff-boxes of the Palais Royal. Besides these, there is a profusion of episodical matter, from which we collect that matrimony is still the thorn in his lordship's flesh; that though now approaching to the confines of middle age and (if we are not misinformed) inclining to *embonpoint*, he is still desirous to be thought a *beau garçon*, and well with the ladies; and that he is most sensitively jealous of the fame of all contemporary poets, excepting (neither does this surprize us) Mr. Rogers!

From William Roberts's unsigned review of *Don Juan III–V* in *The British Review*, December 1821.

It may for the most part be truly said, that the tender, elevated, and virtuous emotions of the soul can only be treated with ridicule by those who are incapable by nature of understanding, appreciating, and describing them. It is often the luxury of an obtuse capacity to make sport of our finest moral sensibilities; but where there is a full and clear cognisance of these properties of our better nature, and a power not only to apprehend, but to express and delineate them with force and accuracy, the disposition to degrade them by banter and sarcasm is an unnatural and anomalous case in the history of mind. Such a case, however, this little pernicious volume presents. It is not the semblance or pretence of virtue that is here affected to be unmasked and exposed. The author of this poem has not thought it expedient to designate it as spurious, or display it under any characteristic disadvantages of eccentricity or excess, to justify or even to colour the attack which he has made upon it. Virtue, in her most veracious form, her most honourable, happy, and holy exercise, in her domestic scenes and relations, in her softest charities, where Nature joins with her in the promotion of human happiness, is held up to the finger of unfeeling ridicule. The book has the name neither of author nor publisher, of which *suppressio veri* we can understand neither the policy nor the pretext. All that it effects is to show that the mischief is done with a full consciousness of its moral turpitude. Indeed, this is the peculiar character of the performance. "Whatsoever things are honest, whatsoever things are pure, whatsoever things are lovely, whatsoever things are of good report," are here brought into immediate contrast with their opposites, in order, as it would seem, that by the display of the one withered by the blast of infidel art, and of the other blooming in its own atmosphere of voluptuousness, the triumph of iniquity might be complete, even to the perversion of moral and natural feeling.

In characterizing a performance like that before us, we labour under no common difficulty. It offers no proper subject for criticism. There is nothing for discrimination, nothing for correction, nothing for disquisition. We can only review the work as Englishmen and Christians. All minor topics are absorbed in the consideration of its sweeping mischief. All particular censure is lost in general indignation: before the head can examine, the heart has decided. When an attack is made upon the sources of human happiness and comfort, we are in no temper for discriminating observations; it is hard, under such circumstances, to do even critical justice. The variegated skin, and graceful folds of the adder, have no beauty for him who sees its menacing approach, and apprehends its mischievous power.

We scarcely know the book from the perusal of which we have returned more dejected than from that which now lies before us. In the poems of this class we generally find the display of a blank and stupid profligacy of heart, a dullness to all the delights of innocent sensibility; but not so here; virtuous happiness and unspotted pleasures are alluded to with sufficient frequency and force, to make the general strain of the performance look rather like apostasy than an innate depravity of disposition; and our vexation is doubled by the testimonies which the work itself bears to the competency of its author to describe with much higher poetical success the qualities which adorn and illustrate, than those which disgrace and betray his fellow beings. Most unfortunately for himself and his readers he has fallen into a sort of slip-shod manner of versifying, in which his genius delights to lounge in the laxity and slovenliness of indecent and unprincipled disorder; and so fascinating does he seem to find this fallacious facility of composition, that he has laid out for himself a sempiternal theme of reprobate sing-song, in the adventures of an imaginary youthful debauchee; a "pretextatus adulter" of the grossest description: of one who carries his pollutions from place to place, living in the world as in a capacious brothel, and having no other intercourse with society than that which tends to loosen its cements, and scatter its foundations. This pretty pupil of pleasure is very carefully adorned, and recommended by as much beauty and bravery as the fancy of the poet could command, for the purpose of giving him an interest in the eyes of those who require something beyond mere animal passion to engage their sympathies. He is that same right handsome and chivalrous sort of vagrant voluptuary, who for these twenty years past has usurped so large a part of the province of poetry, improved in this instance by a certain callous effeminacy of heart, which lust and insensibility must combine to produce.

What the pleasure can be to one that claims kindred with humanity, in putting such a being forward, in colours captivating and deceptious to the weak and unwary, in attenuating his crimes by the sportiveness of wit, and in treating with humour what the honest and considerate must turn from with disgust, we find it impossible to conceive. We would willingly think that the author of this anonymous poem (the most acceptable present which has been made to the devil of any production of recent ingenuity), has not measured with a malignant forecast the whole compass of the mischief it may produce, but that from a strange apathy of soul to the soul's supreme concern, and a morbid habit, now grown irresistible, of justifying, if not indulging the lowest enjoyments of sense, he has not feared to do his part towards opening the flood-gates for vice to rush in upon the fair domains of civilized life. We would not have this anonymous author suppose that we charge him with these offences against society upon Christian grounds alone. The honest heathen, with the light of nature and his conscience for his guides, has long set the seal of his reprobation upon this mental prostitution, this gratuitous propagation of sin and misery. The principle of modesty, —the spirit of conscious shame,—the sanctity of the marriage tie, are so obviously the first constituents of society,—so plain and familiar is the deduction from history and experience, that sensuality approximates man to the brute,—that it issues in blood, and all the varieties of crime,—that it defeats the very end and purpose of the sexual passion itself,—that its tendency is to dissolve the social union into selfish and savage individuality; so necessary, in short, is its coercion as the first step in the process of civilization, that while the gross traditions of their wretched mythology filled the pagan heaven itself with pollution and scandal, the condition and exigence of the social system compelled the recognition among men of those duties and decencies to which their Jupiter and Apollo were strangers. Whatever the gods might do, man's happiness, it was early perceived, demanded another constitution of things. A scheme of ethics, bred out of the necessities of human condition, opposed itself to the examples of an unhallowed rabble of deities. It ought, indeed, to shame us to reflect what a small proportion of the works of the heathen classics were written for the purpose of inflaming the passions. They are stained with their impurities, but their impurities have often their apology in their general subject, and always in their religious ignorance: and thus far we are bold to assert concerning them, that there is scarcely a work of classic antiquity, that has come down to us, the express object of which has been to put the passions into commotion; positively none in which virtue has been ridiculed as virtue, and the πρεπον, or the decens, been attempted to be laughed out of countenance.

It is not easy to explain why wit should have any alliance with indecency; nor can we see any rational way of accounting for our being speculatively pleased with that which tends practically to bring on sorrow and suffering, unless we look for the cause in the turpitude of the natural heart of man, always disposed to rise vindictively against those restraints which curtail his pleasures, or condemn his conduct. It may be considered, that the cause of profligacy has reached its consummation of success, when the bulk of mankind are persuaded to accept at once the very appearance of virtue as the proof of hypocrisy. Under this name every form of virtue may be successfully attacked; but with respect to chastity, not even such artifice or management seems to be thought necessary. Not the appearance, but the reality is the jest; and though it be that which crowns and consecrates the marriage union, and is the grace and honour of womanhood; though it be that which makes the sexual connexion the "true source of human offspring,"—the "loyal, just, and pure" estate, from which

> Relations dear, and all the charities
> Of father, son, and brother

can alone arise, and which is therefore absolutely essential to the very being of society; yet in an age when all this is well seen and understood, it continues, from some strange perversion of sentiment, to be the best joke in the world to laugh it to scorn. It may be said, that these remarks do not apply to the book before us; that we have no right to impute to an author any meaning beyond the literal import of his expressions; and it is very true, that it is no where said explicitly in this work, that chastity, or the marriage vow, or domestic affection, or decorum of manners, or self-restraint, or virtuous forbearance, are wrong things, or ridiculous pretences; they are nowhere called laughable, but they are every where laughed at: the very humour of the composition consists in a contemptuous and reprobate banter, couched in a mock sobriety of phrase, and a degrading familiarity of manner in the treatment of truths unutterably solemn;—in ironical compliments to virtue, and such an encouraging good-humoured disapprobation of vice as must be taken in good part by the devil himself. Gibbon, as far as we know, has nowhere in his history passed a censure upon Christianity in terms; he treats it occasionally with a courtesy of diction; but we suppose it will hardly be contended that it is not the manifest aim of that performance to asperse its holy character, and invalidate the proofs of its divine origin.

One of the principal resources of wit is the vivacious and ingenious approximation of contrarieties: he, therefore, that holds in contempt whatever is most exalted, pure, and venerable, most important to the soul's peace, and man's everlasting doom, has, without doubt, a great advantage as a humourist;—he has a large inheritance in the territory of wit;—nothing to him is sacred or interdicted, nor can any thing be more infallible than his success in producing merriment, whenever it pleases him to bring into juxta-position holy and unhallowed things, or to apply the language that belongs to what is ordinary and base, to those things which the very constitution of our nature has made the objects of our habitual reverence. To treat lightly and jocosely the chastity of women, though on that attribute hangs the honour, and the grace, and the peace of society, is a very sure game for the humourist to play. Good men may abhor it, and wise men may despise it, for no doubt it is as easy as it is destructive, but the great and morbid multitude devour the joke; every vulgar, delighted fool exults in his discovery of its mischievous meaning, and every debauchee is most comfortably convinced by it that self-denial is only hypocrisy, virtue nothing but seeming; and honesty, as well as wit, entirely on the side of his own free and pleasurable course.

Of these dispositions the author of the poem under review has been very adroit in availing himself. By a skilful use of these propensities of our nature he has succeeded (to borrow the language of a very different sort of poet) in "painting damnation gay;"—in representing villany as a very facetious sort of thing; lust as a very harmless sport; and the world as a sort of moral wilderness for the wide and predatory range of the passions. In the licentious life and amatory adventures of a profligate young Spaniard, a train is laid for undermining that early conservative principle of shame, which has a spontaneous growth in tender minds, and is perhaps the only pure moral gift of nature. . . .

It has appeared to us that the most extraordinary part of the character of this poem is this, that it delights in extracting ridicule out of its own pathos. While it brings the tears of sympathy into the eyes of the reader, and this it often does, for come they must at the potent bidding of this enchanter, a heartless humour immediately succeeds, showing how little the writer participates in the emotion he excites. Skilful to play upon another's bosom, and to touch with mysterious art the finest chords of sensibility himself, he is all the while an alien to his own magical creation, frigid amidst his own fires, and without a single fibre in accordance with his own affecting melody. With a melancholy sweep of his lyre he dissolves the soul into tenderness and pity, and then, profanely sporting with the feelings he has excited, resumes, with an apparent alacrity, the levity of his habitual manner, lets his heart triumph over his imagination, and after dipping his pencil in the colours of heaven, delights to merge it again in the pollutions of his own malicious wit. There is as much bad taste in this as there is moral mischief. It is true that this existence is a medley of joy and sorrow, close upon each other's confines; and that moral and pathetic representations of life in prose or verse proceeding in correspondence with the reality, admit of being checquered by grave and gay, pensive and playful moods; but they must not be suffered to run one into another and disturb each other's impressions. Sorrow is engrossing—nor can the heart at the same time lend itself to two opposite emotions; but of all incongruities, the most irreconcilable are those which are exhibited in the noblest and the meanest parts of our moral nature; for there is a fastidiousness in our finer sympathies which makes the jar intolerable when they find themselves on a sudden in contact with unchaste allusions and coarse merriment.

[Roberts quotes *IV*. xxi–xxv as an example]

From Francis Jeffrey's discussion of *Don Juan* in his unsigned review of *Sardanapalus, The Two Foscari,* and *Cain* in *The Edinburgh Review,* February 1822.

But it is not with him,[1] or the merits of the treatment he has either given or received, that we have now any concern. We have a word or two to say on the griefs of Lord Byron himself. He complains bitterly of the detraction by which he has been assailed—and intimates that his works have been received by the public with far less cordiality and favour than he was entitled to expect. We are constrained to say that this appears to us a very extraordinary mistake. In the whole course of our experience, we cannot recollect a single author who has had so little reason to complain of his reception—to whose genius the public has been so early and so constantly just—to whose faults they have been so long and so signally indulgent. From the very first, he must have been aware that he offended the principles and shocked the prejudices of the majority, by his sentiments, as much as he delighted them by his talents. Yet there never was an author so universally and warmly applauded, so gently admonished —so kindly entreated to look more heedfully to his opinions. He took the praise, as usual, and rejected the advice. As he grew in fame and authority, he aggravated all his offences—clung more fondly to all he had been reproached with—and only took leave of Childe Harold to ally himself to Don Juan! That he has since been talked of, in public and in private, with less unmingled admiration—that his name is now mentioned as often for censure as for praise—and that the exultation with which his countrymen once hailed the

[1] Robert Southey, who had coined the phrase 'The Satanic School' to refer to such poets as Byron, and who thereafter was engaged in bitter literary and personal warfare with him.—*Ed.*

greatest of our living poets, is now alloyed by the recollection of the tendency of his writings—is matter of notoriety to all the world; but matter of surprise, we should imagine, to nobody but Lord B. himself.

He would fain persuade himself, indeed, that this decline of his popularity—or rather this stain upon its lustre—for he is still popular beyond all other example—and it is only because he is so that we feel any interest in this discussion;—he wishes to believe, that he is indebted for the censures that have reached him, not to any actual demerits of his own, but to the jealousy of those he has supplanted, the envy of those he has outshone, or the party rancour of those against whose corruptions he has testified;—while, at other times, he seems inclined to insinuate, that it is chiefly because he is a *Gentleman* and a *Nobleman* that plebeian censors have conspired to bear him down! We scarcely think, however, that these theories will pass with Lord B. himself—we are sure they will pass with no other person. They are so manifestly inconsistent as mutually to destroy each other—and so weak, as to be quite insufficient to account for the fact, even if they could be effectually combined for that purpose. *The party* that Lord B. has offended, bears no malice to Lords and Gentlemen. Against its rancour, on the contrary, these qualities have undoubtedly been his best protection; and had it not been for them, he may be assured that he would, long ere now, have been shown up in the pages of the Quarterly, with the same candour and liberality that has there been exercised towards his friend Lady Morgan. That the base and the bigotted—those whom he has darkened by his glory, spited by his talent, or mortified by his neglect—have taken advantage of the prevailing disaffection, to vent their puny malice in silly nicknames and vulgar scurrility, is natural and true. But Lord B. may depend upon it, that the dissatisfaction is not confined to them,—and, indeed, that they would never have had the courage to assail one so immeasurably their superior, if he had not at once made himself vulnerable by his errors, and alienated his natural defenders by his obstinate adherence to them. *We* are not bigots, nor rival poets. We have not been detractors from Lord Byron's fame, nor the friends of his detractors; and *we* tell him—far more in sorrow than in anger—that we verily believe the great body of the English nation—the religious, the moral, and the candid part of it—consider the tendency of his writings to be immoral and pernicious—and look upon his perseverance in that strain of composition with regret and reprehension. We ourselves are not easily startled, either by levity of temper, or boldness, or even rashness of remark; we are, moreover, most sincere admirers of Lord Byron's genius—and have always felt a pride and an interest in his fame. But we cannot dissent from the censure to which we have alluded; and shall endeavour to explain, in as few and as temperate words as possible, the grounds upon which we rest our concurrence.

He has no priestlike cant or priestlike reviling to apprehend from us. We do not charge him with being either a disciple or an apostle of Satan; nor do we describe his poetry as a mere compound of blasphemy and obscenity. On the contrary, we are inclined to believe that he wishes well to the happiness of mankind—and are glad to testify, that his poems abound with sentiments of great dignity and tenderness, as well as passages of infinite sublimity and beauty. But their general tendency we believe to be in the highest degree pernicious; and we even think that it is chiefly by means of the fine and lofty sentiments they contain, that they acquire their most fatal power of corruption. This may sound at first, perhaps, like a paradox; but we are mistaken if we shall not make it intelligible enough in the end.

We think there are indecencies and indelicacies, seductive descriptions and profligate representations, which are extremely reprehensible; and also audacious speculations, and erroneous and uncharitable assertions, equally indefensible. But if these had stood alone, and if the whole body of his works had been made up of gaudy ribaldry and flashy scepticism, the mischief, we think, would have been much less than it is. He is not more obscene, perhaps, than Dryden or Prior, and other classical and pardoned writers; nor is there any passage in the history even of Don Juan, so degrading as Tom Jones's affair with Lady Bellaston. It is no doubt a wretched apology for the indecencies of a man of genius, that equal indecencies have been forgiven to his predecessors: But the precedent of lenity might have been followed; and we might have passed both the levity and the voluptuousness—the dangerous warmth of his romantic situations, and the scandal of his cold-blooded dissipation. It might not have been so easy to get over his dogmatic scepticism— his hard-hearted maxims of misanthropy—his cold-blooded and eager expositions of the non-existence of virtue and honour. Even this, however, might have been comparatively harmless, if it had not been accompanied by that which may look, at first sight, as a palliation—the frequent presentment of the most touching pictures of tenderness, generosity, and faith.

The charge we bring against Lord B. in short is, that his writings have a tendency to destroy all belief in the reality of virtue—and to make all enthusiasm and constancy of affection ridiculous; and that this is effected, not merely by direct maxims and examples, of an imposing or seducing kind, but by the constant exhibition of the most profligate heartlessness in the persons of those who had been transiently represented as actuated by the purest and most exalted emotions—and in the lessons of that very teacher who had been, but a moment before, so beautifully pathetic in the expression of the loftiest conceptions. When a rash and gay voluptuary descants, somewhat too freely, on the intoxications of love and wine, we ascribe his excesses to the effervescence of youthful spirits, and do not consider him as seriously impeaching either the value or the reality of the severer virtues; and in the same way, when the satirist deals out his sarcasms against the sincerity of human professions, and unmasks the secret infirmities of our bosoms, we consider this as aimed at hypocrisy, and not at mankind: or, at all events, and in either case, we consider the Sensualist and the Misanthrope as wandering, each in his own delusion—and pity those who have never known the charms of a tender or generous affection. The true antidote to such seductive or revolting views of human nature, is to turn to the scenes of its nobleness and attraction; and to reconcile ourselves again to our kind, by listening to the accents of pure affection and incorruptible honour. But if those accents have flowed, in all their sweetness, from the very lips that instantly open again to mock and blaspheme them, the antidote is mingled with the poison, and the draught is the more deadly for the mixture!

The reveller may pursue his orgies, and the wanton display her enchantments with comparative safety to those around them, while they know or believe that there are purer and higher enjoyments, and teachers and followers of a happier way. But if the priest pass from the altar, with persuasive exhortations to peace and purity still trembling on his tongue, to join familiarly in the grossest and most profane debauchery—if the matron, who has charmed all hearts by the lovely sanctimonies of her conjugal and maternal endearments, glides out from the circle of her children, and gives bold and shameless way to the most abandoned and degrading vices—our notions of right and wrong are at once confounded—our confidence in virtue shaken to the foundations—and our reliance on truth and fidelity at an end for ever.

This is the charge which we bring against Lord Byron. We say that, under some strange misapprehension as to the truth, and the duty of proclaiming it, he has exerted all the powers of his powerful mind to convince his readers, both directly and indirectly, that all ennobling pursuits, and disinterested virtues, are mere deceits or illusions—hollow and despicable mockeries for the most part, and, at best, but laborious follies. Love, patriotism, valour, devotion, constancy, ambition—all are to be laughed at, disbelieved in, and despised!—and nothing is really good, so far as we can gather, but a succession of dangers to stir the blood, and of banquets and intrigues to sooth it again! If this doctrine stood alone, with its examples, it would revolt, we believe, more than it would seduce:—but the author of it has the unlucky gift of personating all those sweet and lofty illusions, and that with such grace and force and truth to nature, that it is impossible not to suppose, for the time, that he is among the most devoted of their votaries—till he casts off the character with a jerk—and, the moment after he has moved and exalted us to the very height of our conception, resumes his mockery at all things serious or sublime—and lets us down at once on some coarse joke, hard-hearted sarcasm, or fierce and relentless personality—as if on purpose to show

'Whoe'er was edified, himself was not'—

or to demonstrate practically as it were, and by example, how possible it is to have all fine and noble feelings, or their appearance, for a moment, and yet retain no particle of respect for them—or of belief in their intrinsic worth or permanent reality. Thus, we have an indelicate but very clever scene of the young Juan's concealment in the bed of an amorous matron, and of the torrent of 'rattling and audacious eloquence' with which she repels the too just suspicions of her jealous lord. All this is merely comic, and a little coarse:— But then the poet chuses to make this shameless and abandoned woman address to her young gallant, an epistle breathing the very spirit of warm, devoted, pure and unalterable love—thus profaning the holiest language of the heart, and indirectly associating it with the most hateful and degrading sensuality. In like manner, the sublime and terrific description of the Shipwreck is strangely and disgustingly broken by traits of low humour and buffoonery;— and we pass immediately from the moans of an agonizing father fainting over his famished son, to facetious stories of Juan's begging a paw of his father's dog—and refusing a slice of his tutor!—as if it were a fine thing to be hard-hearted—and pity and compassion were fit only to be laughed at. In the same spirit, the glorious Ode on the aspirations of Greece after Liberty, is instantly followed up by a strain of dull and cold-blooded ribaldry;—and we are hurried on from the distraction and death of Haidee to merry scenes of intrigue and masquerading in the seraglio. Thus all good feelings are excited only to accustom us to their speedy and complete extinction; and we are brought back, from their transient and theatrical exhibition, to the staple and substantial doctrine of the work—the non-existence of constancy in women or honour in men, and the folly of expecting to meet with any such virtues, or of cultivating them, for an un- deserving world;—and all this mixed up with so much wit and cleverness, and knowledge of human nature, as to make it irresistibly pleasant and plausible—while there is not only no antidote supplied, but every thing that might have operated in that way has been anticipated, and presented already in as strong and engaging a form as possible—but under such associations as to rob it of all efficacy, or even turn it into an auxiliary of the poison.

This is our sincere opinion of much of Lord B.'s most splendid poetry—a little exaggerated perhaps in the expression, from a desire to make our exposition clear and impressive—but, in substance, we think merited and correct. We have already said, and we deliberately repeat, that we have no notion that Lord B. had any mischievous intention in these publications—and readily acquit him of any wish to corrupt the morals, or impair the happiness of his readers. Such a wish, indeed, is in itself altogether inconceivable; but it is our duty, nevertheless, to say, that much of what he has published appears to us to have this tendency—and that we are acquainted with no writings so well calculated to extinguish in young minds all generous enthusiasm and gentle affection—all respect for themselves, and all love for their kind—to make them practise and profess hardily what it teaches them to suspect in others—and actually to persuade them that it is wise and manly and knowing, to laugh, not only at self-denial and restraint, but at all aspiring ambition, and all warm and constant affection.

How opposite to this is the system, or the temper, of the great author of Waverley—the only living individual to whom Lord Byron must submit to be ranked as inferior in genius—and still more deplorably inferior in all that makes genius either amiable in itself, or useful to society! With all his unrivalled power of invention and judgment, of pathos and pleasantry, the tenor of his sentiments is uniformly generous, indulgent, and good-humoured; and so remote from the bitterness of misanthropy, that he never indulges in sarcasm, and scarcely, in any case, carries his merriment so far as derision. But the peculiarity by which he stands most broadly and proudly distinguished from Lord Byron is, that, beginning, as he frequently does, with some ludicrous or satirical theme, he never fails to raise out of it some feelings of a generous or gentle kind, and to end by exciting our tender pity, or deep respect for those very individuals or classes of persons who seemed at first to be brought on the stage for our mere sport and amusement—thus making the ludicrous itself subservient to the cause of benevolence—and inculcating, at every turn, and as the true end and result of all his trials and experiments, the love of our kind, and the duty and delight of a cordial and genuine sympathy, with the joys and sorrows of every condition of men. It seems to be Lord Byron's way, on the contrary, never to excite a kind or a noble sentiment, without making haste to obliterate it by a torrent of unfeeling mockery or relentless abuse, and taking pains to show how well those passing fantasies may be reconciled to a system of resolute misanthropy, or so managed as even to enhance its merits, or confirm its truth. With what different sensations, accordingly, do we read the works of these two great writers!—With the one, we seem to share a gay and gorgeous banquet—with the other, a wild and dangerous intoxication. Let Lord Byron bethink him of this contrast—and its causes and effects. Though he scorns the precepts, and defies the censure of ordinary men, he may yet be moved by *the example* of his only superior!—In the mean time, we have endeavoured to point out the canker that stains the splendid flowers of his poetry—or, rather, the serpent that lurks beneath them. If it will not listen to the voice of the charmer, that brilliant garden, gay and glorious as it is, must be deserted, and its existence deplored, as a snare to the unwary.

A summary estimate of *The Vision of Judgment* (1822), from an article entitled 'Oldmixon's Account of *The Liberal*' printed in Constable's *Edinburgh Magazine*, November 1822.

As to "The Vision of Judgment" by "Quevedo Redivivus, *alias* Lord Byron," we have some doubts whether we can be justified in polluting our pages by such impious and detestable trash. The reader need not be told that the object is to ridicule the ill-starred but well-intentioned performance of a similar title, from the pen of the Laureate; nor will he be surprised to learn that the blasphemy and impurity with which it is so pregnant, are all made subservient to the master purpose—the demolition of the obnoxious Southey, whom Lord Byron appears to dread and detest nearly in equal degrees. It is in the stanza of Beppo and Don Juan; but vastly inferior to either, in every quality, save profligacy. Here there are no redeeming bursts of reluctant eloquence—no splendid, over-mastering, and subduing descriptions—no glimpses of transcendant genius or irrepressible feeling—no struggles of insulted Nature to vindicate her prerogatives, and prove that the heart of the writer is still, in *some* things, human. Even the hard-heartedness and villainy of Don Juan was sometimes forgotten, if not atoned for, in the splendid corruscations of a lofty and commanding intellect; and we believe there are few readers whose hearts have not acknowledged the almost superhuman power displayed in the description of the shipwreck, and of the death of the Austrian officer who had fallen under the stiletto of a midnight assassin. Here, however, there are no such atoning attributes or accompaniments. "The Vision of Judgment" is one blank, frozen, unvaried, and unvarnished piece of heartless atrocity and cold-blooded ruffianism, in which every generous and honourable feeling of the heart is outraged,—human nature scoffed at,—the memory of an aged Monarch insulted,—the faith of Christians derided,—and the foulest, and, let us add, the lowest abuse flung at the head of a man of amiable manners, great learning, and irreproachable life.

From a letter entitled 'Canting Slander' addressed to Rev. William Bengo Collyer, printed in *The Examiner*, 10 November 1822.

While thousands in this corrupt age (according to you) revel sensually in impure descriptions and indecent anecdotes, how can you so far forget your character as a priest and a censor, as to pander to this degrading appetite by pointing out all the sources of depraved gratification? Are you so ignorant of human nature as not to know, that all your denouncements and invective against certain publications only operate as an incentive to a passion already sufficiently strong? No work of modern days has been so cried out against as immoral and indecent as *Don Juan*; and you see the consequence:— the critics, one and all, shake their heads at it; grave old gentlemen turn up their eyes and sigh out a lamentation over the depravity of the age; all ladies of character *blush* at its very mention; no writer has yet been found hardy enough to hint a word in defence or palliation, —yet, lamentable to relate, every body reads it! *Twenty thousand copies* of the cheap editions have been sold, fifteen of which may be safely placed to the account of such prudent moralists as you and the Vice-Suppressors, and such solemn critics as those of My Grandmother's Review.

From a letter entitled 'Canting Slander' addressed to Rev. William Bengo Collyer, printed in *The Examiner*, 24 November 1822.

You cavil at the jokes and irony of *Don Juan*, as if you had found them in a sermon. But what right have you to comment on a satirical poem as if the author intended an essay on the Whole Duty of Man? The very essence of this sort of poetry is the ease and freedom with which the author indulges in the vein in which he finds himself. He passes *ad libitum*

"From grave to gay, from lively to severe."

He is not bound to be didactic or consistent. He does not seat himself in the Professor's Chair of Moral Philosophy; nor is he to assign a reason for his rhymes "upon compulsion." There are two ways of viewing most subjects—the serious and the comic; and he chuses one or the other, or combines both, as his own pleasure or

that of his readers prompts him. To charge him with not doing what
he neither pretends nor is expected to do, is about as fair and reasonable as to quarrel with an essay on geometry for not being facetious,
or with a treatise on the dry-rot for lack of merriment. The following
stanza is a fair specimen of your quotations on this score:—

> Well—well, the world must turn upon its axis—
>   And all mankind turn with it—heads or tails;
> And live and die, make love and pay our taxes,
>   And as the veering wind shifts, shift our sails;
> The king commands us, and the doctor quacks us,
>   The priest instructs—and so our life exhales—
> A little breath, love, wine, ambition, fame,
>   Fighting, devotion, dust—perhaps a name.
>
> [*Don Juan II.* iv]

Where is the offence of this? Where is the harm of a joke upon
human life? You may find the same idea, not only in satirists and
comedians, but in the gravest and most pious writers. The style of
the reflection indeed varies—some talk of "the vanity of human
wishes," of "the sinful and sorrowful world"—but the meaning of
all is the same. The difference is, that the puritans and the hypocrites
are *seriously* aiming to make their fellow-creatures as miserable and
desponding in this world, as they say most of us will be in the next;
while the object of Lord Byron and the wits is to add to our stock
of innocent laughter and amusement, to help to make us "merry and
wise."

Yet you actually quote this stanza as an evidence of the misanthropic feeling with which Lord Byron seeks to poison the sources
of human hope and joy! What can your real opinion be of the
understandings of your readers?

From the preview of *Don Juan VI–VIII* (1823) in *The Literary
Examiner*, 5 July 1823.

Of the general characteristics of *Don Juan*, it would now be almost
impertinent to dilate. We shall therefore spare ourselves all expatia-
tion upon its felicitous combination of description, humour, pathos,
and keen and pervading satire; the last of which, after all, we
apprehend is what disturbs the moral prudery of the well-dressed
mob more than those amatory scenes and glowing descriptions to
which the manifestation of the said disturbance is so greatly attributed. The first canto, for instance—Are certain people quite so
alarmed at the loves of Don Juan and Donna Julia, as at certain
tangential strokes in the delineation of the character of the hero's
grave and prudential mother, and transient glances at the infirmities

and peccadilloes of good sort of people? The same story told in another manner, they would possibly regard as a moral tale; but this air *riant*, and disturbance of composed masks and orderly decencies, are unbearable. Circumspection avails nothing in this case, and (*contra bonos mores*) the "simulars of virtue" are in as much danger as the vicious—a frightful and comprehensive calamity. To be sure, we have heard the objection urged very speciously. We do not like to be eternally put upon the weak or wicked points of our nature; and in poetry particularly, prefer more gentle portraiture,—"Alice Fell," and the "Thoughts too deep for tears." Without deciding whether some of the latter may not be found even in the stanzas of *Don Juan*, we utterly protest against this very convenient species of interdiction, which, we maintain, would foster every species of rancorous weed, by the mere absence of annoyance. It would require more time and space than the nature of this publication will allow, to enter into a comparison of the advantages to be derived from the exaltation of conspicuous virtue and the exposure of latent vice; but if both are good, Lord Byron is vindicated; and every body must allow that the latter is the most fruitful field. Sound divines (not being Court Chaplains) take both ways, we believe; an observation that drops from us in the pure spirit of orthodoxy. Again: Lord Byron *will* take up such dark-featured and reckless heroes! . . .

Virtue, define it as we may, consists chiefly in forbearance, negation, and the mastery of the passions. We may go still further, and add, that even its activity wears the aspect of self-denial, as all the self-devotion of Greek and Roman story—all that we understand of exalted virtue, from Alfred to Washington, will testify. This is well in fact, but is it so in poetry? Or, in plainer terms, is it not the force, prevalence, and violence of the passions, which supply the latter with the richest *materiel*? From the very nature of things it must be so, as Milton found out in Paradise Lost, *his* Satan being objected to on this very account; and to talk a hundred years old, that is to say, in reference to Homer and Virgil,—who prefers not, poetically speaking, the fierce and wrathful Achilles, to the *Dux Trojanus*, the pious Æneas? The lofty department of tragedy, what is its essence?— Masterless passion; the absence of which, and the poor substitution of mere poetry, make some recent efforts so very mawkish. Let us hear no more of this.

Looking at *Don Juan* as far as it has gone, it is quite obvious, that having taken up the general conception, Lord Byron has bound himself to no particular series of adventures, but writes on under the influence of his immediate impulses. Every one is aware that there is both loss and gain by this process: that something is lost in unity and consistency of object, and something gained in occasional freshness and spirit. It may be further observed, that, after all, *Don Juan* is not an epic; and that we can scarcely conceive an outline more capable of excursion *ad libitum* than the pilotage of a Don Galaor of headlong courage and boundless adventure to the gates of hell. This, however, is a secondary consideration; as we have already hinted, this conspicuous and alarming attribute of Lord Byron is an intuitive perception of the almost mathematical point which marks the confines of vice and virtue, harmlessness and innocence; and a rapid detection of the approximation of extremes, which renders him the Asmodeous or Mephistophiles of poets, a creature which penetrates into your secrets at will. This is startling to every one, but absolutely terrific to the orderly people, who, muffled up in exterior decencies, place well-doing in a mental costume. We never heard an individual express more horror at the first canto of *Don Juan* than a grave merchant, who regularly sent his clerk out of the way to take tea with his wife; or a woman more piously outraged by it than the mistress of the man who married her. These persons felt themselves detected. It is not confounding good and evil to shew the slightness of the partitions which divide them; on the contrary, the former may be guarded and secured by a dread of the rapidity of glance which can at once perceive and expose the myriads of lurking avenues by which the one can slide into the other.

From the preview of *Don Juan IX–XI* (1823) in *The Literary Examiner*, 2 August 1823.

We observed in a note to our account of the three preceding Cantos of Don Juan, that several additional volumes would soon follow. We shall endeavour in our present and succeeding numbers to convey some notion of the first of them, consisting of the Cantos enumerated in our heading. The task is difficult, for in no previous portion of this indescribable production is the sarcasm more caustic, the wit more pungent and volatile, or the general taxing more uncircumscribed. In the course of these Cantos, too, the all-conquering Juan is brought to our own best of all possible countries, and introduced to the *haut ton* and *Blues* of London—a field altogether uncultivated by the Society for the Suppression of Vice, and therefore peculiarly demanding the attention of an inflexible and *impartial* moralist like the author of *Don Juan*. Moreover, if the physician be able, the benefit is always in proportion to the docility of the patient in respect to the prescription; and notwithstanding the doubts of the Chancellor, and the pious deprecation of various less eminent personages, there is much reason to fear, that people of quality swallow doses of Don Juan with more avidity than religious tracts, or even Mr. Irving's sermons.

From the same preview, continued 16 August 1823.

In our last Number, we carried our observations upon this forthcoming publication to the close of the tenth Canto, and we are now about to enter on the eleventh, with an increasing perception of the difficulty of our task. In no preceding division is the noble author more himself, and less any body else; and all the variety of his moods, but especially the mood sarcastic, are exhibited with singular versatility and piquancy. The ease and felicity of Lord Byron's transitions from "grave to gay, from lively to severe," are without example; only as it was observed of the "Allegro" of Milton, that it was the mirth of a melancholy man, so it may be asserted of the humour of Lord Byron, that it is uniformly tinged with the hue of his Poco-curantish philosophy. Even when dwelling on the Loves and the Graces,—the pure and genuine breathings of early and unsophisticated attachment,—the noblest and least interested of human impulses, the concealed lancet will dart from the barrel of his quill, and in the midst of all manner of smilingness and complacency, as accurately breathe a given vein as Sir Ashley Cooper himself. In the direct manner of inculcating the sombre conclusion of Solomon, that all is vanity, Lord Byron may be equalled, but where is he who can so readily and playfully detect the *anguis in herbâ*—the snake in the grass—the serpent beneath the flowers— the universal condition of being—the taint of the earthly in all below the moon? It is however a fearful privilege, being necessarily alarming to fraud and hypocrisy in all its ramifications; and hence the pious horror of bigotted authority.

From the letter to 'Christopher North' signed 'M. ODOHERTY', concerning *Don Juan IX–XI*, printed in *Blackwood's Edinburgh Magazine*, September 1823. (The writer has been reliably identified as Lockhart. 'Christopher North' was, of course, John Wilson.)

DEAR NORTH,—I have a great respect both for old Tickler and yourself, but now and then you both disquiet me with little occasional bits of lapses into the crying sin of the age—*humbug*! What could possess him to write, and you to publish, that absurd critique —if indeed it be worthy of any such name—upon the penult batch of Don Juan? The ancient scribe must have read those cantos when he was crop-sick, and had snapped his fiddle-string. You must never have read them at all.

297

Call things wicked, base, vile, obscene, blasphemous; run your tackle to its last inch upon these scores, but never say that they are stupid when they are not. I cannot suffer this sort of cant from YOU. Leave it to Wordsworth to call Voltaire "a dull scoffer." Leave it to the British Review to talk of "the dotage" of Lord Byron. Depend upon it, your chief claim to merit as a critic has always been *your justice to* INTELLECT. I cannot bear to see you parting with a shred of this high reputation. It was you "that first praised Shelley as he deserved to be praised." Mr Tickler himself said so in his last admirable letter to you. It was in your pages that justice was first done to Lamb and to Coleridge—greatest of all, it was through and by you that the public opinion was first turned in regard to the poetry of Wordsworth himself.—These are things which never can be forgotten; these are your true and your most honourable triumphs. Do not, I beseech you, allow your claim to this noble distinction to be called in question. Do not let it be said, that even in one instance you have suffered any prejudices whatever, no matter on what proper feelings they may have been bottomed, to interfere with your candour as a judge of *intellectual* exertion.—Distinguish as you please: brand with the mark of your indignation whatever offends your feelings, moral, political, or religious—but "nothing extenuate." If you mention a book at all, say what it really is. Blame Don Juan; blame Faublas; blame Candide; but blame them for what really is deserving of blame. Stick to your own good old rule—abuse Wickedness, but acknowledge Wit.

In regard to such a man as Byron, this, it must be evident, is absolutely necessary—that is, if you really wish, which you have always said you do, to be of any use to him. Good heavens! Do you imagine that people will believe three cantos of DON JUAN to be unredeemedly and uniformly DULL, merely upon your saying so, without proving what you say by quotation? No such things need be expected by you, North, far less by any of your coadjutors.

I maintain, and have always maintained, that Don Juan is, without exception, the first of Lord Byron's works. It is by far the most original in point of *conception*. It is decidedly original in point of *tone*, [for to talk of the tone of Berni, &c. being in the least like this, is pitiable stuff: Any old Italian of the 15th or 16th century write in the same tone with Lord Byron! Stuff! stuff!]—it contains the finest specimens of serious poetry he has ever written; and it contains the finest specimens of ludicrous poetry that our age has witnessed. Frere may have written the stanza earlier; he may have written it more carefully, more musically if you will; but what is he to Byron? Where is the sweep, the pith, the soaring pinion, the lavish luxury, of genius revelling in strength? No, sir; Don Juan, say the canting world what it will, is destined to hold a permanent rank in the literature of our country. It will always be referred to as furnishing the most powerful picture of that vein of thought, (no matter how false and bad,) which distinguishes *a great portion of the thinking people of our time.* You and I disagree with them—we do not think so; we apprehend that to think so, is to think greenly, rashly, and wickedly; but who can deny, that many, many thousands, do think so? Who can deny, that that is valuable in a certain way which paints the prevailing sentiment of a large proportion of the people of any given age in the world? Or, who, that admits these things, can honestly hesitate to admit that Don Juan is a great work—a work that must last? I cannot.

And, after all, say the worst of Don Juan, that can with fairness be said of it, what does the thing amount to? Is it *more* obscene than Tom Jones?—Is it *more* blasphemous than Voltaire's novels? In point of fact, it is not within fifty miles of either of them: and as to obscenity, there is more of that in the pious Richardson's pious Pamela, than in all the novels and poems that have been written since.

The whole that can with justice be said of Byron, *as to these two great charges,* is, that he has practised in this age something of the licence of the age of our grandfathers. In doing so, he has acted egregiously amiss. The things were bad, nobody can doubt that, and we had got rid of them; and it did not become a man of Byron's genius to try to make his age retrograde in anything, least of all in such things as these. He also has acted most unwisely and imprudently in regard to himself. By offending the feelings of his age, in regard to points of this nature, he has undone himself as a popular writer.—I don't mean to say that he has done so for ever—Mercy and Repentance forbid! but he has done so most effectually for the present. People make excuses for Fielding and Voltaire, because they don't know in how far these men may have been acted upon by circumstances: but people will not make *such* excuses for Lord Byron, because they know, we all know, that he was educated among the same sort of people as ourselves, that he must know and feel the same things to be wrong which his neighbours know and feel to be so. He, therefore, is no longer a popular author. But,—and here I come back to my question—Is he no longer a great author? Has his genius deserted him along with his prudence? Is his Hippocrene lazy as well as impure? Has he ceased, in other words, to be Byron, or is he only Byron playing mad tricks?

The latter is my opinion, and I propose to convince you, in case you are not already of the same mind, by quoting a few passages from the other three cantos that have just appeared—and which I humbly conceive to be the very best, in so far as talent is concerned, of all that have as yet come forth. . . .

[Lockhart then quotes extensively from all three cantos]

Now, my dear North, I sincerely hope you will gratify me so far, as to put these verses in without curtailment, and that for three good and sufficient reasons, viz.—

1st, They occur in the original work in the midst of so much beastliness, gross filth, outrageous filth, abominable filth, that it is quite impossible they should have been seen by far the greater proportion of your readers. Don Juan is a sealed book to the ladies of our time, (to say no more,) and you will be doing them a great favour in thus affording a few extracts, upon the "Family Bowdler" principle, from a work, which, as a whole, they have no chance of seeing; or, if they did see it, of reading three pages in it without blushing to the back-bone. This will be a benefit.

2dly, Another great benefit will be this, that you will, by doing as I suggest, restore the line, which in former days always distinguished YOU from what Plutarch calls, "the rest of the hunters;" and which I was very sorry to see my worthy friend Timothy Tickler, of all men in the world, doing his best to erase and obliterate. You will shew the world that you are still the old Christopher—too manly to deny anything that you feel, too just to confound together two questions essentially separate and distinct—the question of *moral tendency*, and that of *intellectual power*.

3dly, By vindicating your character as to this matter, you will give your own voice a chance of being really listened to by this singular man when you happen to address him in the words of admonition. A man like Byron will feel when any one calls him a devil for a piece of blackguardism; but he will only laugh at being called a dunce for a piece of brilliancy, even by You. That there is a prodigious deal of blackguardism in these three cantos, who can deny? What can be more so than to attack THE KING, as this Lord does, with low, vile, personal buffooneries—bottomed in utter falsehood, and expressed in crawling malice? Nothing, nothing. What can be more exquisitely worthy of contempt than the savage imbecility of these eternal tirades against the Duke of Wellington? What more pitiable than the state of mind that can find any gratification in calling such a man as Southey by nicknames that one would be ashamed of applying to a coal-heaver? What can be so abject as this eternal trampling upon the dust of Castlereagh? Shame! shame! shame! Byron ought to know, that all men of all parties (for Cockneys are not men, and saloop-parties are not parties,) unite in regarding all these things, but especially the first and the last, as

300

insults to themselves, and as most miserable degradations of HIM. But he ought to be told this in a sensible manner. He ought not to be treated as if he were a driveller, or capable of being mistaken for one even for a moment; but he ought to be told plainly, distinctly, solemnly, and with a total negation of all humbug, that he is a writer of extraordinary talents—that Don Juan contains the outline of an extraordinary poem—and that he is voluntarily ruining both himself and his production.

I observe some of the Monthly idiots talk of "Don Juan" as if it were a by-job of Lord Byron's—a thing that he just takes up now and then, when he is (I must quote their own sweet words) "relaxing from the fatigues of more serious literary exertions." This I look upon as trash of the first water. It is very likely—indeed I have no doubt of it—that a canto of Don Juan costs Lord Byron much less trouble than a "Werner" or a "Cain." In like manner, I daresay, one of Voltaire's lumbering tragedies cost Voltaire ten times more fatigue than ten Zadigs, Taureau Blancs, or Princesses of Babylon, would have done. In like manner, I have no doubt Wordsworth's "Convention of Cintra" pamphlet cost him much more trouble than his "Ruth," or his "Song for Brougham Castle," or his "Hart-leap Well." In like manner, I have no doubt the Monthly List of Deaths, Marriages, Births, Bankruptcies, Patents, and Promotions, costs you more trouble than the "Leading Article." But this is not the way to judge of these things. Almost any one canto of Juan—certainly any one of these three—contains more poetry and more genius than any three of Byron's recent tragic attempts have done. The worthy I have been dishing probably opines that Lord Byron dashes off a canto of the Don after a tragedy, just as he himself *does* an article for "My Grandmother," after he has finished his sermon for next Sunday.

I shall now beg leave to "relax from the fatigue of this serious literary exertion" over a tumbler of gin-twist; and, wishing mine Editor many similar relaxations, remain his most humble servant,

Kilkenny, Sept. 12. M. ODOHERTY.

[Evidently not by Maginn, though he often used the pseudonym.— *Ed.*]

From the preview of *Don Juan XII–XIV* (1823) in *The Literary Examiner*, 8 November 1823.

It is a miserable thing, after the repeated assurances of the Literary Gazette, and similar high authorities, that as a Poet, Lord Byron is utterly defunct, that

His fire is out, his wit decay'd,
His fancy sunk, his Muse a jade:—

that not only Canto after Canto of the irreclaimable Don Juan should be published, but that people will be guilty of the insufferable crime of buying them with extreme avidity. Hypocrisy, in its variety of gradation is quite dumb-founded at this pertinacity, and having exhausted all its affectation in hyperbole in the first instance, looks upon each succeeding mass of mischief in much the same humour as honest John Bunyan describes the impotent Giant Pope, who regarded the heretics whom his paralysis would not allow him to sacrifice as heretofore, with willing but helpless malignity. The town *will not* listen, or at least *will* purchase, and the poet refuses to shake hands with the Gang, or to be negatived out of countenance by writers who prattle about Religion and Morals so like to "waiting gentlewomen." Without affecting indiscriminate approbation of all which is produced by the fertile Muse of Lord Byron, we think it matter of exultation that a writer exists, whose rank, fortune—and more than all—whose disposition, place him utterly beyond the reach of the conventional jargon with which it is sought to overlay every effusion of mind, good or bad, that will not be confined to the railway of cant, subserviency, or party spirit. What says Lord Byron in the first of the Cantos about to be published?

> My Muses do not care a pinch of rosin
>   About what's called success, or not succeeding:
> Such thoughts are quite below the strain they have chosen:
>   'Tis a "great moral lesson" they are reading.
> I thought, at setting off, about two dozen
>   Cantos would do: but at Apollo's pleading,
> If that my Pegasus should not be foundered,
> I think to canter gently through a hundred.

[XII. lv]

So much for the operation, in the way of prevention, of the literary *masquers*, who abuse the original, and supply the quotation*. "Rail on good youths," and instead of one, the number of Cantos may amount to two hundred, to the infinite exposure of the latent impurities and morbid secretions springing out of the scrophulous hypocrisy which has become the disgusting disorder of the English body-social—the mental *malaria* that is diffusing itself over every department of British intellect.

From the review of *Don Juan IX–XI* in *The Monthly Magazine*, December 1823.

Some of the *hebdomadal* critics have been merciless in their attacks upon his lordship's heinous outrages on what they conceive to be legitimate rhyme. Had these gentlemen been permitted to devote a *fortnight* to their lucubrations, they might possibly have discovered

* This is a ludicrous fact in several instances. [Reviewer's footnote.]

that these alleged violations of *rhythmus* were the effect, not of negligence, but design; they might have reflected that, since the author's powers of versification were undoubted, he had probably been influenced in the choice of his rhymes by their suitableness to the subjects introduced; and that of this he might probably be as competent a judge as any Zoilus, of the critic tribe. We wish it were practicable to put Butler's "Hudibras" into the hands of such censors, as a new publication: their strictures upon it would doubtless be highly amusing.

William Hazlitt's critique of *Don Juan* in the essay 'Lord Byron' in *The Spirit of the Age*, published in January 1825, but almost all written before Byron's death in 1824.

The *Don Juan* indeed has great power; but its power is owing to the force of the serious writing, and to the oddity of the contrast between that and the flashy passages with which it is interlarded. From the sublime to the ridiculous there is but one step. You laugh and are surprised that any one should turn round and *travestie* himself: the drollery is in the utter discontinuity of ideas and feelings. He makes virtue serve as a foil to vice; *dandyism* is (for want of any other) a variety of genius. A classical intoxication is followed by the splashing of soda-water, by frothy effusions of ordinary bile. After the lightning and the hurricane, we are introduced to the interior of the cabin and the contents of wash-hand basins. The solemn hero of tragedy plays *Scrub* in the farce. This is 'very tolerable and not to be endured.' The Noble Lord is almost the only writer who has prostituted his talents in this way. He hallows in order to desecrate; takes a pleasure in defacing the images of beauty his hands have wrought; and raises our hopes and our belief in goodness to Heaven only to dash them to the earth again, and break them in pieces the more effectually from the very height they have fallen. Our enthusiasm for genius or virtue is thus turned into a jest by the very person who has kindled it, and who thus fatally quenches the sparks of both. It is not that Lord Byron is sometimes serious and sometimes trifling, sometimes profligate, and sometimes moral—but when he is most serious and most moral, he is only preparing to mortify the unsuspecting reader by putting a pitiful *hoax* upon him. This is a most unaccountable anomaly. It is as if the eagle were to build its eyry in a common sewer, or the owl were seen soaring to the mid-day sun. Such a sight might make one laugh, but one would not wish or expect it to occur more than once.[1]

[1] This censure applies to the first cantos of *Don Juan* much more than to the last. It has been called a *Tristram Shandy* in rhyme: it is rather a poem written about itself. [Hazlitt's note.]

303

Percy Bysshe Shelley
(1792–1822)

A Survey of Contemporary Criticism, 1815–22, with an exceptional extension to cover *Posthumous Poems (1824)*

It has been clear ever since Professor Newman Ivey White's epoch-making publication in 1938 of the results of his researches into periodical criticism of Shelley's work during the poet's lifetime[1] that the old idea that Shelley was little noticed and completely misunderstood by the reviewers is no longer tenable. Though the whole corpus of criticism of Shelley's work by his contemporaries is slight in comparison with the quantum of print devoted to the work of Byron, its bulk is far from negligible.

Shelley's juvenile works before *Queen Mab* (1813) were, indeed, given scant attention; and *Queen Mab* itself (apart from a series of laudatory articles in *The Theological Inquirer* of 1815, which Shelley himself may have encouraged), only began to be reviewed in 1821, soon after the poem had been piratically republished. It was then, however, extensively discussed. The rest of Shelley's poetical works published during his lifetime, with the exception of *Epipsychidion* (1821) and *Hellas* (1822), were given considerable attention, and from 1820 onward there was also a fair amount of general comment on Shelley as a poet. The *Posthumous Poems*, published in 1824, which include so many of the poems of Shelley still read today, were also reviewed in a number of periodicals. On the whole the balance between domin-

---

[1] *The Unextinguished Hearth* (Duke University Press, Durham, N. Carolina, 1938); reprinted in 1966 by Octagon Books, Inc., New York, and published in England by Frank Cass and Co., 1966.

antly favourable and dominantly unfavourable reactions to Shelley's poetry was a distinctly adverse one, but the story is actually far more complex than that.

The *Alastor* volume, on its appearance in 1816, was adversely criticized by *The Monthly Review*,[1] *The British Critic*,[2] and *The Eclectic Review*.[3] The *Monthly*, while noting 'some beautiful imagery and poetical expressions', ridiculed the 'sublime obscurity' of the poems, and suggested that Shelley should provide 'a glossary and copious notes' with his next publication. *The British Critic* makes the same kind of criticism, ironically citing the references to a man's hair singing dirges, a boat pausing and shuddering, and a stream ascending, as among the least of Shelley's 'inventions'. Later, in a review of Leigh Hunt's *Foliage*, it dismisses Shelley as guilty of 'flagitious offence', and compares him unfavourably with Keats.[4] It offered no further review of his work. The *Eclectic* thought *Alastor* 'wild and specious, untangible and incoherent as a dream', and took it as an instance of 'the fatal tendency' of the 'morbid ascendancy of the imagination over the other faculties'. The reviewer (the editor, Josiah Conder) also noticed the absence of an indication that the author believed in immortality or, with one doubtful exception, 'in the moral government of God'. On the other hand, he recognizes 'very considerable talent for descriptive poetry'. The *Eclectic* devoted no more reviews to Shelley. (Interestingly enough, from later incidental comment on Shelley it appears that the *Eclectic* considered that, with all its faults, *Alastor* was Shelley's best work.[5]) The only favourable mention of *Alastor* in its year of publication is by implication in Leigh Hunt's article in *The Examiner* entitled 'Young Poets',[6] which introduced Shelley, John Hamilton Reynolds, and Keats to its readers, referring to Shelley as the author of *Alastor*, and calling him 'a very striking and original thinker'. The words chosen are probably significant, since this aspect of Shelley, the intellectual strength which enabled him to develop and to propound in poetry the bold beliefs and ideals which commanded Hunt's enthusiastic assent, continued to evoke his admiration throughout Shelley's literary career. It is interesting,

[1] *MR*, LXXIX, April 1816.   [2] *BC*, V (n.s.), May 1816.
[3] *Ecl. R*, VI (2nd. Ser.), October 1816. See the extract on pp. 327–9 below.
[4] *BC*, X (n.s.), July 1818.
[5] *Ecl. R*, XVIII (2nd. Ser.), November 1822. See p. 89 above.
[6] *Exar*, 1 December 1816.

in this connexion, to consider a remark made by Shelley in a letter to Peacock early in 1819:

> I consider Poetry very subordinate to moral and political science, and if I were well, certainly I should aspire to the latter.[1]

Though Hunt's brief reference was the only favourable comment on *Alastor* in a periodical at that time, three years later the Tory *Blackwood's*, which had meanwhile given a pretty kind reception to *The Revolt of Islam* (1818)[2] and to the *Rosalind and Helen* volume (1819),[3] went back to *Alastor*,[4] and gave it a substantial review, praising its power and 'sublimity', but criticizing its extravagance, vagueness, and obscurity, and censuring Shelley for being 'too fond of allegories'. Among the shorter poems in the volume the reviewer singled out the poem on Lechlade Churchyard for its 'spirit of deep, solemn, and mournful repose', and the 'strange unintelligible fragment' entitled *The Daemon of the World* as 'exceedingly beautiful'. Towards the end of the review, in a sharp onslaught on the *Quarterly's* review of *The Revolt of Islam*, the conviction is expressed that 'Mr. Shelley is a poet, almost in the very highest sense of that mysterious word'. On the other hand, the reviewer is hostile to the 'many wicked and foolish things in Mr. Shelley's creed', and hazards the view that the poet himself did not fully believe in them, and might be reclaimable. Shelley himself, however, had long ceased to think much of *Alastor*,[5] but his beliefs were more tenaciously held than *Blackwood's* seemed to think.

We must now go back, however, to an earlier time. The *Hymn to Intellectual Beauty* had appeared in January 1817,[6] and still more important, in November 1817, *Laon and Cythna*, the original version, swiftly withdrawn, of *The Revolt of Islam*. The Hymn was published in *The Examiner*, where Hunt gave it a few words of high praise. Shelley had written to him the month before telling him that the poem was 'composed under the influence of feelings which agitated' him 'even to tears'.[7] The poem did not, however, either then or when it appeared in the *Rosalind and Helen* volume in 1819, attract much attention from the critics.

---

[1] 23/24 January 1819 (*SL*, II. 71).　　[2] *BM*, IV, January 1819.

[3] *BM*, V, June 1819.

[4] *BM*, VI, November 1819. An extract appears on pp. 347–50 below.

[5] Letter to Peacock, 17 July 1816 (*SL*, I. 490); to Leigh Hunt, 8 December 1816 (*SL*, I. 517).

[6] *Exar*, 19 January 1817.

[7] 8 December 1816 (*SL*, I. 517).

About the same time that the Hymn was published there occurred the Chancery case concerning Shelley's suitability to have guardianship of his children by Harriet Westbrook, and this attracted some attention to *Queen Mab*, and, together with Shelley's connection with Leigh Hunt, exacerbated the hostility of 'establishment' opinion against him and his work. The situation was probably aggravated by the fact that Leigh Hunt addressed two sonnets to Shelley in his *Foliage* published the same year, and that he printed a passage from *Laon and Cythna* in *The Examiner* shortly before the publication of *The Revolt of Islam*.[1] Moreover, a fortnight after the publication of that poem, Hunt printed the passage describing Laon's execution (ll. 4466 ff.),[2] and followed this by three highly laudatory articles on the poem.[3] These take the poem as a 'philosophical' poem, and Hunt defends the ideas against the charges of perfectionism, wildness, and romanticism, and against the view that Christianity pins its faith on an after-life and not on the possibility of happiness in this world. Hunt's ideas here are not unlike some of those developed by Tolstoy in his later years. Hunt expresses the belief that the world is capable of moral improvement, and cites the recent abolition of the Slave Trade. Besides the ideas Shelley expresses in the poem Hunt admires the depth of feeling, grandeur of imagery, and musical versification. Yet he is critical of the obscurity, and what he considered to be the monotony and arbitrariness and gratuitousness of the imagery. Hunt laid great stress, however, on the 'humanity' of the work. Yet he warned that it would not be popular. Shelley would have to forget his 'metaphysics and sea-sides' if he wished to write a work with wide appeal. In March 1818 there came another notice, but it was only a brief dismissal. The left-wing liberal *Monthly Magazine*[4] condemned the poem as unmetrical and unmusical, showing no sense that such concepts posed any problems.

Far more important were the reviews of *The Revolt of Islam* published the next year. First came the long review in *Blackwood's*[5] whose authorship still cannot be regarded as conclusively determined. Formerly the evidence, internal and external, seemed to point to Wilson, but now it looks as if Lockhart had at least a major share in it, and may perhaps have written it all. It still seems

---

[1] *Exar*, 30 November 1817.   [2] *Exar*, 25 January 1818.
[3] *Exar*, 1, 22 February, 1 March 1818. Lengthy extracts are reprinted on pp. 329–33 below. See also pp. 127–8 above.   [4] *MM*, XLV, March 1818.
[5] *BM*, IV, January 1819. A long extract is reprinted on pp. 333–7 below.

possible, however, that De Quincey may have had some influence upon the review. However this may be, it is certainly notable in much the same way as some of Lockhart's critiques of Byron, in that it keeps a sharp distinction between aesthetic and extra-aesthetic criteria of value. While firmly repudiating what the reviewer considered 'a pernicious system of opinion concerning man and his moral government, a superficial audacity of unbelief, an overflowing abundance of uncharitableness towards almost the whole of his race, and a disagreeable measure of assurance and self-conceit', the review yet has high praise for Shelley 'as a poet', calling him 'strong, nervous, original, well entitled to take his place near to the great creative masters, whose works have shed its truest glory round the age in which we live'. Though the reviewer thought that the poem bore marks of haste, especially in the confusion, in places, of the allegories, he greatly admired the portrayal of the 'intense, overmastering, unfearing, unfading love' of Laon and Cythna. The poet had, moreover, 'poured over his narrative a very rare strength and abundance of poetic imagery', and that was the poem's great merit. He had also shown at times 'right understanding and generous feeling'. He was 'a scholar, a gentleman, and a poet', and should look for better companions than Hunt and Keats. This championship of Shelley by the Tory *Blackwood's*, and especially by Lockhart, is very remarkable, and, together with Lockhart's critiques on Byron, says a great deal for his critical intelligence, even though it may not compensate for his dastardly treatment of Keats.

The next review of the poem was a short notice by the *Monthly* in March.[1] It regarded the poem as a philosophic rhapsody springing from the French Revolution, by an immature poet who indulged in 'the strangest vagaries of versification', and did not render a just account of a single one of what were clearly his 'many poetical talents'. Far more important, however, was the adverse review published in the *Quarterly* for April 1819, which came out late, in September 1819.[2] This was by Shelley's old schoolfellow at Eton, John Taylor Coleridge, a nephew of the poet. It seems as if John Murray, the *Quarterly*'s publisher, had taken some part in arranging this. There is an undated letter from Murray, evidently written to Croker, in which Murray writes:

[1] *MR*, LXXXVIII, March 1819.
[2] *QR*, XXI, April 1819 (publ. September 1819). A long extract appears on pp. 337–47 below.

I send you a most extraordinary poem by Godwin's new Son-in-law—pray keep it under lock & key—it is an avowed defense of *Incest*—the author is the vilest wretch in existence—living with Leigh Hunt—The Book was published & he is now endeavouring to suppress it.[1]

Murray is clearly referring to the unrevised version, *Laon and Cythna*. This had, indeed, been published late in 1817 (though under the imprint 1818), but had been suppressed by the publishers, pending revision. A few copies, however, no doubt including Murray's, had got out, but they were recalled, and some, though not his, were recovered. The next summer Gifford wrote to Murray a letter[2] in which he says:

By all means let Mr. Coleridge give us a few pages on Shelley.

Coleridge wrote what he obviously considered a conclusively crushing review. Shelley was much put out by it. He wrongly attributed it first to Southey[3] and then to Milman or Gifford.[4] The review is actually a brilliant, though somewhat unscrupulous, piece of work, taking Shelley's poem seriously, allowing it poetical merit, but arguing, by no means unreasonably, against the philosophy expressed, and totally repudiating it. The shadier features of the review are that it took into account the withdrawn *Laon and Cythna*, and that it hinted at some shameful hidden behaviour in Shelley's past. Leigh Hunt came to Shelley's defence in three articles in *The Examiner*,[5] the terms of which have been outlined in the general survey above.[6] Shelley himself regarded the poem as a work of some importance, the result of ' "the agony & bloody sweat" of intellectual travail'.[7] He knew it would shock what he called 'the bigots',[8] and he was interested to see how it would be reviewed, and appreciated the praise from *Blackwood's*,[9] but he came to find many things in it that he wished to improve, and in 1821 we find him writing to his publisher

---

[1] Murray Register, Brown MS, quoted by H. and H. C. Shine, *The Quarterly Review under Gifford* (Chapel Hill, 1949).

[2] Gifford to Murray, 4 August 1818, Murray MS, also quoted by the Shines.

[3] Letter to Charles Ollier, 15 October 1819 (*SL*, II. 127).

[4] Letter to Byron, 16 July 1821 (*SL*, II. 309).

[5] *Exar*, 26 September, 3 and 10 October 1819.

[6] On pp. 128–9.

[7] Letter to Godwin, 11 December 1817 (*SL*, I. 577).

[8] Letter to Charles Ollier, 22 January 1818 (*SL*, I. 594).

[9] Letter to Charles Ollier, 15 December 1819 (*SL*, II. 162).

asking if there were any chance of a second edition. None was, however, published during his lifetime.

J. T. Coleridge had included in his review of *The Revolt of Islam* a short dismissal of *Rosalind and Helen* (1819), which Hunt had praised fulsomely in *The Examiner* earlier in the year,[1] even disproportionately placing it above *The Revolt*. This was typical of Hunt, who preferred the 'more popular style of poetry', which brought Shelley's 'humanity' closer to the reader. No doubt this entered into his inordinate admiration for *The Cenci*.

The Cenci (1820), which does not fall within the scope of our survey, nevertheless needs brief mention. It was the most accessible for the general reader of all Shelley's works of any length. Shelley himself did not place it high among his productions. Yet it was, as I have said above, reviewed more widely than any of his other works. The reception was mixed, ranging from unqualified admiration by Hunt[2] to execration by *The Literary Gazette*.[3] Favourable reviews tended to emphasize the power with which Shelley expressed the feelings of those involved in the horrible series of situations. Unfavourable reviews often stressed, in a somewhat Platonic way, the thorough unsuitability of the events for human contemplation, either on the stage or in the imagination.

In September 1820 came *Prometheus Unbound*, by which Shelley rightly set far greater store, though he realized that it would not have wide appeal.[4] It was 'written only for the elect'.[5] Shelley considered it up to then the best thing he had ever written[6] and he claimed for it a large measure of originality[7]:

> *Prometheus Unbound* is in the merest spirit of ideal Poetry, and not, as the name would indicate, a mere imitation of the Greek drama, or indeed if I have been successful, is it an imitation of anything.

In June 1820 *The London Magazine* (Baldwin's) had given a very favourable notice to the work before publication,[8] calling it 'a very noble effort of a high and commanding imagination', and comparing its view of humanity as far more 'inspiriting' and

---

[1] *Exar*, 9 May 1819. [2] *Indicr*, 26 July 1820. [3] *LG*, 1 April 1820.
[4] Letter to Charles Ollier, 6 March 1820 (*SL*, II. 174).
[5] Letter to Leigh Hunt, 26 May 1820 (*SL*, II. 219).
[6] Letter to Charles Ollier, 15 December 1819 (*SL*, II. 164).
[7] Letter to Medwin, 20 July 1820 (*SL*, II. 221).
[8] *LM*, I, June 1820. A short extract appears on p. 350 below.

'magnanimous' than that shown in *The Cenci*. The first review after publication, that in *The Literary Gazette*,[1] was, however, utterly condemnatory of the poem, both for the 'ludicrously wicked' principles it expressed, and for its nonsensical 'unintelligibility'. But the same month *Blackwood's* once again came out with a fine review,[2] in which Shelley's attitudes to kings and priests and to the institution of marriage are indeed abominated, but the eloquence, pathos, magnificence in description, and melody of versification are warmly extolled. Even more laudatory was the reception from Gold's *London Magazine*.[3] The minor pieces in the volume were briefly but highly praised for their 'strong and healthy freshness', *The Cloud* being singled out and quoted entire. As to *Prometheus*, the reviewer welcomes it as 'one of the most stupendous of those works which the daring and vigorous spirit of modern poetry and thought has created'. The reviewer even sympathizes considerably with Shelley's ideals as ultimate aims, and only dissents from his hurry to realize them by casting down restraint and authority. In this connexion the reviewer regrets the presence of the *Ode to Liberty* in the volume. As for 'literary' merits, the reviewer claims that *Prometheus* is 'replete with clear, pure, and majestical imagery, accompanied by a harmony as rich and various as that of the loftiest of our English poets'. These reviews in Gold's, and the later article there to be mentioned presently, are probably the most favourable Shelley ever received, with the possible exception of some of Leigh Hunt's. As far as I am aware, it is not yet known who wrote them. *The Monthly Review*'s reactions to the volume were far less favourable,[4] maintaining that Shelley had here mingled the sublime with the ridiculous, and the fanciful with the foolish. Gold's *London Magazine*, however, took up the tale again early in February 1821, in an admirable article 'On the Philosophy and Poetry of Shelley'[5] endorsing his religion of benevolence, the moral and political principles springing from it, and the embodiment of it in *Prometheus Unbound*. This article seems to go farther

[1] *LG*, 9 September 1820. For a detailed account of this review see pp. 164–6 above.

[2] *BM*, VII, September 1820. A long extract appears on pp. 351–5 below.

[3] *Gold's LM*, II, September and October 1820. An extract from the October review appears on pp. 355–7 below.

[4] *MR*, XCIV, February 1821. An extract is reprinted on pp. 357–9 below.

[5] *Gold's LM*, III, February 1821. A lengthy extract is reprinted on pp. 359–62 below.

than the review of *Prometheus* in October. No complaints are expressed at Shelley's reforming precipitancy, and no reservations are uttered about the 'magnificent' *Ode to Liberty*. The article also claims Shelley to be 'infinitely superior' to Byron in 'intensity of description, depth of feeling, and richness of language'. But at the end of the same year the *Quarterly* came out strongly against the volume.[1] William Sidney Walker, a Cambridge don,[2] wrote an intensely interesting review, starting by impugning Shelley's poetry for 'frequent and total want of meaning', going on to discuss its deviations from 'nature', jumbled metaphors, confusions of style, and violations of grammar, and finally turning from Shelley's 'sins against sense and taste' to his 'flagrant offences against morality and religion'. It was in this part of the review that either Walker or Gifford or somebody else tampered with some asterisks at one point in the printed text of the *Ode to Liberty* so as to make Shelley seem guilty of blasphemy. Leigh Hunt took the *Quarterly* up on this in *The Examiner* the next summer.[3]

There had been some general comment on Shelley's poetry in 1820 and 1821. There are, for example, some interesting passages in an ephemeral weekly called *The Honeycomb*,[4] which exalts Shelley far above the Cockneys, Leigh Hunt and Barry Cornwall, passing the opinion that, unlike them, he had never been duly appreciated, though adding that it was his own fault for being 'too mystical'. He seemed to nurse 'the wildness of imagination, at the expense of clearness and vigour of style'. The writer of the article had heard that Shelley actually wanted a cheap edition of *The Revolt of Islam* to be published, so as to teach 'freedom', 'patriotism', 'philanthropy', and 'toleration' to 'all classes of

[1] *QR*, XXVI, October (publ. December 1821). A long extract is reprinted on pp. 362–72 below.   [2] For details about Walker see p. 41 above.

[3] *Exar*, 16 June 1822. The lines in the *Ode to Liberty* are 211–12. Hunt writes: 'These *four* stars, which in fact imply a civil title, and not a religious word, as the allusion to "the page of fame" might evince, are silently turned by the Reviewer into *six* stars, as if implying the name of Christ'; and Hunt goes on to ridicule the possible suggestion that the alteration was not deliberate. The rough draft in the Boscombe MS reads 'KING'. Curiously enough Swinburne was eventually to conjecture, luridly but crassly, that the right reading was, after all, 'CHRIST'!

[4] *The Honeycomb*, 12 August 1820. A large part of this article is reprinted in Professor White's *The Unextinguished Hearth*. *The Champion* repeated some of *The Honeycomb*'s comments, at times verbatim, in its issue of 23 December 1821, over the signature 'J.W.'

persons', but to have reached such a wide audience, he should have 'written intelligibly to common understandings'. Yet the writer praises the versification of that poem as 'a very high effort of genius', maintaining that Shelley had 'new-modelled the Spencerian [*sic*] Stanza, and given it a beauty and power of expression which it did not possess before', managing his pauses very skilfully, and introducing double rhymes with fine effects. The opening stanzas i–iv, vii–ix, and xiv are cited as proof. Shelley's poetry is commended as free of the 'puerilities' of the Cockneys. He did not, like Barry Cornwall, 'follow the scent of strong-smelling phrases', and he knew that poetry was not 'composed of the language of common life' as Wordsworth thought, or of 'its spirit of common feelings', but was 'above the common nature of man'. He also refused 'to wear the cast-off garments of antiquity'. Moreover, unlike the Cockneys, he was continually *improving*.

Far less favourable was Hazlitt's verdict, delivered in 1821.[1] He dubbed the poet of *Prometheus* a 'philosophic fanatic', 'drawn up by irresistible levity to the regions of mere speculation and fancy':

> He puts every thing into a metaphysical crucible to judge of it himself and exhibit it to others as a subject of interesting experiment, without first making it over to the ordeal of his common sense or trying it on his heart.

For people like Shelley, Hazlitt writes, 'any thing new, any thing remote, any thing questionable' was 'sure of a cordial welcome'. Hazlitt's complaint was that of a practical reformer who sees the chances of real progress being brought to nothing by unrealizable schemes:

> The practical is with them always the antipodes of the ideal; and like other visionaries of a different stamp, they date the Millenium or New Order of Things from the Restoration of the Bourbons. Fine words butter no parsnips, says the proverb. 'While you are talking of marrying, I am thinking of hanging', says Captain Macheath. Of all people the most tormenting are those who bid you hope in the midst of despair, who, by never caring about any thing but their own sanguine, hair-brained Utopian schemes, have at no time any particular cause for embarrassment and despondency because they have never the least chance of success, and who by

[1] In his essay 'On Paradox and Commonplace', published in *Table Talk*, 1821–2.

including whatever does not hit their idle fancy, kings, priests, religion, government, public abuses or private morals, in the same sweeping clause of ban and anathema, do all they can to combine all parties in a common cause against them, and to prevent every one else from advancing one step farther in the career of practical improvement than they do in that of imaginary and unattainable perfection.

Hazlitt's reaction somewhat resembles that of Lenin to 'way-out' revolutionaries in his *Left-Wing Communism: an Infantile Disorder*.[1]

A pirated edition of the juvenile *Queen Mab* appeared in May 1821, and gave rise to a great deal of comment. Gold's *London Magazine*[2] and *John Bull's British Journal*[3] gave it favourable previews as 'poetry'. *The Literary Gazette*[4] fulminated against its views, but had high praise for the 'literary' merits of the start of the poem and of many other passages. *The Monthly Magazine*[5] condemned both the poetry and the principles; while *The Literary Chronicle*[6] also repudiated the beliefs, but acknowledged 'much powerful writing and many beautiful passages'. The pirated *Queen Mab* even evoked a small book called *A Reply to the Anti-Matrimonial Hypothesis and Supposed Atheism of Percy Bysshe Shelley as Laid Down in Queen Mab*.[7] This was published by William Clark, who had published the pirated edition. It was probably intended by Clark to protect him against the law, since he cited it in court in defence against a prosecution initiated by The Society for the Suppression of Vice, for blasphemous libel. The edition was suppressed, but later Richard Carlile, a bolder man than Clark, brought out four more pirated editions.[8] The most violent attack on the poem was that by Rev. William Bengo Collyer in *The Investigator* in the article 'Licentious Productions in High Life',[9] which also attacked a number of Byron's works

[1] Lenin, *Selected Works* (London, 1936–), Vol. X, 55–158.

[2] *Gold's LM*, III, March 1821.   [3] *JBBJ*, 11 March 1821.

[4] *LG*, 19 May 1821.   [5] *MM*, LI, June 1821.   [6] *LC*, 2 June 1821.

[7] This able piece is reprinted by Professor White in *The Unextinguished Hearth*.

[8] Carlile was editor of *The Republican* and other Radical periodicals. Carlile was a fearless, somewhat lone, Radical, who served long prison sentences for seditious and blasphemous libels. For further information on him see E. P. Thompson, *The Making of the English Working Class* (London, 1963), *passim*; and N. I. White, *op. cit.*, 95–8.

[9] *Investigr*, V, October 1822.

including *Don Juan,* and which has been mentioned above in that connexion.[1]

Epipsychidion, published in the summer of 1821, seems to have attracted little attention from the critics. A lively little weekly called *The Gossip* printed two reviews.[2] The first called the poem 'a very singular production, abounding with poetic beauties, lax morality, and wild incoherent fancies', but thought the author seemed 'a selfish being', who gave no consideration to the possible fate of his female partner when they might come to tire of each other, and return to society after their 'experiment' in free love. The reviewer makes a shrewd point:

> The author himself, we believe, would not be disposed to extend his protection under such circumstances to one so situated, and appears much too delicate to contemplate the idea of forming any attachment to one whose first love had been bestowed on another.

The other review is a sprightly letter from a 'Seraphina' living with her sister 'Clementina' in St James's Square. It contains some rather interesting practical criticism. An admirer of Clementina's had brought in a copy of *The Gossip*'s earlier review, and the three discuss the extracts from *Epipsychidion* which it contained. On the first extract (ll. 190–216) Clementina comments 'It is poetry *intoxicated*', and Seraphina 'It is poetry in *delirium*', and the admirer joins in with the revelation that it was 'a new system of poetry', which could be 'taught by a few simple rules' and when learned could be 'written by the league'. Clementina next draws attention to the number of adjectives, and their strange coupling with nouns, and her admirer rejoins with the comment:

> It is a species of poetry that excites no emotion but that of wonder— we wonder what it means! It lives without the vitality of life; it has animation but no heart; it worships nature but spurns her laws; it sinks without gravity and rises without levity. Its shadows are substances, and its substances are shadows, its odours may be felt, and its sounds may be penetrated—its frosts have the melting quality of fire, and its fire may be melted by frost. Its animate beings are inanimate things, and its local habitations have no existence. It is a system of poetry made up of adjectives, broken metaphors, and indiscriminate personifications. In this poetry everything must live, and move, and have a being, and they must live and move with intensity of action and passion, though they have their origin and their end in nothing.

[1] At p. 119.   [2] *The Gossip,* 23 June, 14 July 1821.

The friends analyse the extract further, criticizing such things as the 'new metonymy' of 'steps' (l. 197) for 'path', the idea of a 'voice' coming from 'odours deep of flowers' (ll. 201–3), and also 'from the singing of the summer birds,/And from all sounds, all silence' (ll. 208–9). Seraphina tries to defend the lines by citing a parallel from Dryden,[1] but Clementina's admirer will not have either metaphor, and suggests that before employing any figure one should always 'consider what sort of a picture it would make on canvas', a narrow-minded criterion, yet one with some valid application. Clementina, however, even objects to 'flame/Out of her looks into my vitals came' (ll. 259–60), on the ground that looks are 'a mere modality', so that one might as well say that flame came 'not from her face, but merely from its length, or its breadth'. Seraphina herself is puzzled by the 'green heart' with its 'leaves' (ll. 263–4). Clementina suggests that it means the heart of a cabbage, but her admirer points out that the heart of a cabbage is generally white, and that, in any case, this green heart would be a bad figure to paint on canvas. The letter continues in this bantering vein, sometimes scoring hits, or at least raising, as in some of these cases, the question how to distinguish between brilliant enlargement of the bounds of imagination, and falling into flagrant absurdity; but sometimes betraying a disabling timidity or conventionality of fancy on the part of the critical trio. One other comment on *Epipsychidion* is worth brief mention. A 'Letter from London' in *Blackwood's* for February 1822[2] described the poem as 'a threefold curiosity, on account of the impenetrable mysticism of its greater portion, the delicious beauty of the rest, and the object of the whole, which I take to be an endeavour to set aside the divine prohibition, that a man may not marry his own sister'. The writer was either purposely or mistakenly construing the invocations to 'Sister' in a literal sense. Nevertheless, and possibly without irony, he goes on to state that he had read the poem 'last night at the hushed and sleeping hour of twelve' and that he was 'never so enchanted as in wandering among its strange, etherial, dreamy fancies, some of which contain,

---

[1] The lines in Dryden quoted by Seraphina are:

> Yet when that flood in its own depths was drowned,
> It left behind its false and slippery ground.

Seraphina misquotes the second line, where 'its' should read 'it'. The lines are ll. 5–6 from Dryden's poem *To His Sacred Majesty: A Panegyrick on his Coronation*, 1661. [2] *BM*, XI, February 1822.

in my opinion, the very soul and essence of ideal poesy'. He quotes ll. 422–47 and 470–5, carefully omitting the obscurities, metaphysicalities, and harsh realities of ll. 448–69. He ends his comments on Shelley by quoting the 'exquisite lines' 502–7 and 514–17, again leaving out the rangingly imaginative lines 508–12, which he probably considered obscure or even nonsensical.

Keats had died in February 1821, and Shelley had written his elegy *Adonais* at Pisa early in June 1821, and had it printed there within the next few weeks. He then sent copies to London by his friend John Gisborne, for the Olliers, his London publishers, and for friends, including Peacock and Horace Smith,[1] and also a substantial part of the Pisan impression to the Olliers by freight, for sale in England. Shelley had a very high opinion of the poem, as appears from a number of letters, in which the tone varies somewhat, according to the addressee. To his friends the Gisbornes, for instance, he called it 'a highly wrought *piece of art*, perhaps better in point of composition than any thing I have written',[2] and to Claire Clairmont he wrote:

> I have lately been composing a poem on Keats: it is better than any thing that I have yet written, and worthy both of him & of me.[3]

On the other hand, to Peacock, who in any case had no high opinion of Keats, Shelley toned down somewhat his enthusiasm for the poem:

> The subject, I know, will not please you; but the composition of the poetry, & the taste in which it is written, I do not think bad. You & the enlightened public will judge.[4]

Horace Smith wrote saying he preferred the poem to anything of Shelley's except *The Cenci*, finding in it 'a great deal of fancy, feeling, and beautiful language, with none of the metaphysical abstraction, which is so apt to puzzle the uninitiated in your

---

[1] Horatio (Horace) Smith (1779–1849) was a stockbroker. He wrote a number of novels, but is best known as co-author, with his brother James (1775–1839), a solicitor, of the famous *Rejected Addresses* (1812), parodies of many of the poets of the day, published shortly after the opening of the rebuilt Drury Lane Theatre. For details of the story of publication see A. Boyle's edition, London, 1929; and, for the brothers, A. H. Beavan, *James and Horace Smith*, London, 1899. Horace Smith was a friend of both Shelley and Byron, but Keats thought him too worldly.

[2] Letter to John and Maria Gisborne, [5 June 1821] (*SL*, II. 293–4).

[3] Letter to Claire Clairmont, 8 June 1821 (*SL*, II. 296).

[4] Letter to Peacock, [? 10] August 1821 (*SL*, II. 330).

productions'.[1] Shelley was especially glad that Smith did not think the poem 'metaphysical', which Shelley himself was afraid it was. Moore was apparently also pleased with the poem.[2] Shelley for once openly showed great interest in 'the fate' of one of his creations, proudly telling Ollier that he would be surprised if *Adonais* were 'born to an immortality of oblivion'.[3]

In December 1821 *The Literary Chronicle*[4] printed the whole of *Adonais* except stanzas xix–xxiv, calling Shelley, in an accompanying note, 'a gentleman of no ordinary genius', and suggesting that 'to every poetic mind' the 'transcendent merits' of the poem 'must be apparent'. Yet they were far from apparent to *The Literary Gazette*, which a few days later launched a vitriolic attack on the poem[5] as 'altogether unconnected, interjectional, and nonsensical', and as blasphemous, both in attributing envy to God (l. 42—in quoting which the review helps its case by capitalizing Shelley's 'god' and adding two exclamation marks), and in coupling Cain and Christ (l. 306—here the review carefully omits the last half of the line, which could have made the accusation lose weight, but adds three exclamation marks for good measure!). The reviewer ridicules stanza xiii without apparently taking the least trouble to understand it (Hunt was to indicate the true sense); but in the examples of 'nonsense' he over-confidently cites he does pose some genuine problems about the limits, if any, of bold imagery. The next review came from *Blackwood's*,[6] but this time the review was entrusted to an unsympathetic reviewer, Rev. Dr George Croly, who is also known to have reviewed for *The Literary Gazette*, and whom I suspect of having written the review of *Adonais* in that periodical too. Like that review, the *Blackwood's* critique was wholly unfavourable. It starts by taking the Cockneys, and also Byron and Shelley, as a reappearance of the Della Crusca school, who affected to be "smitten with nature, and nature's love", and were 'simple down to the lowest degree of silliness'. The Della Cruscans had been destroyed by Gifford's satires, but, unlike their successors, they had at least, asserts Croly, not boasted of their impurity, or hated everything generous, true, and honourable, nor

[1] Horace Smith to Shelley, 30 August 1821 (*SL*, II. 348).
[2] Horace Smith to Shelley, 3 October 1821 (*SL*, II. 351).
[3] Letter to Charles Ollier, 11 November 1821 (*SL*, II. 365).
[4] *LC*, 1 December 1821.
[5] *LG*, 8 December 1821. A substantial extract appears on pp. 377–81 below.
[6] *BM*, X, December 1821.

had they been guilty of any 'daring and fiendlike insult to feeling, moral ties, and Christian principle'. Both they and their successors, however, 'summoned' the public 'to take in every thing belonging to their own triviality', and thought 'all within their enchanted ring was perfection'. The New School had therefore puffed up Keats's vanity, and they now declared that he had been 'slaughtered' by the review in the *Quarterly*. The review continues as reprinted below in the anthology, punctuated by a mock elegy for the city marshal who had broken his leg on the last Lord Mayor's day, and by some contemptuous comments on some passages in *The Cenci*. It will be seen that the review endorses the *Quarterly*'s review of *Endymion*, and condemns Shelley's attack on the review, not only as unjustified and unintelligible, but as 'malignant, and peevishly personal', and execrates him as 'the only verseman of the day, who has dared, in a Christian country, to work out for himself the character of direct ATHEISM!'

In January 1822 Shelley wrote dolefully to Hunt from Pisa[1]:

> If *Adonais* had no success & excited no interest what incentive can I have to write?

and the next day to Gisborne[2]:

> You know I don't think much about Reviews nor of the fame they give nor of that they take away—It is absurd in any review to criticize *Adonais*, & still more to pretend that the verses are bad. *Prometheus* was never intended for more than 5 or 6 persons

[implying that *Adonais* was intended to reach a wider public]. And Shelley reiterated the same view to Gisborne in April,[3] and in June was still lamenting that the poem had not had 'a fair chance'.[4]

It was left to Leigh Hunt to provide the only effective counterattack on the adverse reviewers. This he did in July 1822.[5] He recognized that *Adonais* was no more likely to be popular than *Prometheus*, because it was 'too abstract and subtle' for that; but he knew that it would 'delight the few, to whom Mr. Shelley is accustomed to address himself'. Hunt defends the elaborate 'poetical abstractions' of the elegy, contending that they were

[1] 25 January 1822 (*SL*, II. 382). [2] 26 January 1822 (*SL*, II. 388).
[3] 10 April 1822 (*SL*, II. 406).
[4] Letter to Gisborne, 18 June 1822 (*SL*, II. 434).
[5] *Exar*, 7 July 1822. A long extract appears on pp. 383–8 below.

entirely compatible with sincerity. He emphasizes that Shelley only spent a 'few hours' with Keats, and that those were passed almost entirely in poetical concerns. As will be seen, the review contains some valuable detailed criticism. Towards the end of it, moreover, Hunt tilts at the *Quarterly* for not daring to review or even to hint at the existence of the poem, though they had presumed to offer a review of 'a poem which appeared to them the least calculated for their readers' understandings'.[1] Hunt also taunts the *Quarterly* for its omission to mention the 'majestic tragedy' of *The Cenci*, or to take any notice of Keats's 'beautiful' *Lamia* volume. The reason in each case was probably, Hunt suggests, that the words of *Adonais* would not have been ' "unintelligible" to the dullest *Quarterly* peruser'.

At the start of 1822 Hunt had also launched a series of 'Letters to the readers of *The Examiner*' attacking the *Quarterly*. The first was a general attack.[2] The second concerned the *Quarterly*'s treatment of radicals.[3] The third and fourth were specifically about the *Quarterly*'s review of the *Prometheus* volume.[4] Hunt starts the third by accusing the reviewer of not discussing the doctrines put forward in *Prometheus*. He hazards the guess that the reviewer was 'some assistant clergyman, who is accustomed to beg the question in the pulpit, and who thinks that his under-toned breath of malignity will be mistaken for Christian decorum'. The reviewer had, says Hunt, collected passages to prove Shelley's enmity to Christianity, but Shelley always took care to confine his enmity 'to the violent consequences of faith as contrasted with practice, there being in the latter sense no truer Christian than himself'. It is at this point that Hunt exposes the reviewer's trick with the asterisks in the text of the *Ode to Liberty*.[5] Hunt gives another instance of disingenuousness. The reviewer had referred to Shelley's description of Christ on the cross (*Prometheus*, I. 540 ff.) as introduced merely to intimate that Christianity was the great cause of misery and vice, and he had quoted Prometheus' words:

It hath become a curse.

Thy name I will not speak,

as another instance of blasphemy. Hunt rightly points out that Shelley had used the words here in a passage whose intention was

[1] I.e., *Prometheus*.   [2] *Exar*, 20 January 1822.   [3] *Exar*, 9 June 1822.
[4] *Exar*, 16 and 23 June 1822. An extract from the latter is reprinted on pp. 381–3 below.
[5] See p. 312 above.

to instance Christ as having undergone 'the fate of benevolent reformers':

All that he meant in short is this,—that as Christ's benevolence subjected him to the torments he endured, so the uncharitable dogmas produced by those who make a *sine qua non* of the Christian *faith* have hitherto done more harm than good to mankind; and all the rest of his poem may be said to be occupied in shewing, that it is benevolence, as opposed to faith, which will survive these horrible consequences of its associate, and make more than amends for them.

And Hunt goes on to quote the whole context from l. 578 to l. 634. He continues by conceding that Shelley often painted 'the state of mankind' in too dark colours, but maintains that his descriptions were fairly applicable. Hunt also concedes that Shelley's poetry was often too 'abstract and metaphysical', and apt to be 'too wilful and gratuitous in its metaphors', but he leaves the reader to judge from the passage quoted whether it was all 'nonsense'.

In the fourth 'letter' (from which a large extract is printed below[1]) Hunt takes the reviewer up for trying to prove his charge of 'nonsense' by printing a difficult passage of *Prometheus* as prose. Hunt does the same thing with a passage from Cary's Dante to show what a shallow trick that was.

Shelley came in for both abuse and commendation for his share in the projection of *The Liberal*, but he had died before No. 1 came out, and his only contribution to it was his translation of the 'May-day Night' scene from Goethe's *Faust*. His *Defence of Poetry* was intended for No. 2, but was eventually not included; and all that appeared of him there was 'Song, Written for an Indian Air'. In No. 3 there was just 'Lines to a Critic', and in No. 4 nothing.

News of Shelley's death gave rise to very varied reactions; but these are not our concern. On the other hand, it seems reasonable to take account of the critical reception of the edition of Shelley's *Posthumous Poems* published by Mary Shelley in 1824, since that volume contained so many of the poems of Shelley which are still widely read today.

A short notice of the volume appeared in *The Examiner* in June 1824,[2] possibly by Albany Fonblanque, who eventually became editor of the periodical. It has scarcely any critical value. It

---

[1] On pp. 381–3.   [2] *Exar*, 13 June 1824.

affirms a faith in the permanent recognition of Shelley's superior position as a poet, and singles out from the newly published work *The Triumph of Life* as 'one of the most elaborate' of his 'finished productions', and praises *all* the poems as abounding with 'elegant and reflective beauty'! *The Literary Gazette*,[1] on the other hand, though taking up the volume in forgiving mood, yet finds in it the same blend of 'beauty and blasphemy, trash by the side of some fine poetry' as in Shelley's other work:

> In short, we can but liken his genius to some African river,—there is gold in its waters, but it is embedded in sand, mud, slime, and filth.

The reviewer picks out *The Witch of Atlas* as 'a good specimen' of Shelley's 'style', 'wild, imaginative, revelling in dreams of unreal beauty'. But he decides to quote *Ginevra* entire, 'as the fittest specimen, both from its negative merit of having in it nothing to offend, and also for its great sweetness and pathos'. He goes on to pass the opinion that, though perhaps excusable, Mrs Shelley's estimate, in her Preface, of the value of 'the very rubbish which loads almost every page' had to be denied; and in support of his view the reviewer quotes the first six lines of stanzas i and ii of *Arethusa*, as 'trash' which was a rather favourable sample of nine-tenths of the volume.

Far more interesting than either of these pieces is Hazlitt's review in the *Edinburgh*.[2] Its main criticism of Shelley is substantially that his poetry was not close enough to reality. It was too much of a wilful and arbitrary creation out of nothing. On the other hand, Hazlitt recognizes Shelley's honesty and humanity and love of nature. Yet he thought him too confident in his own intellectual explorations, and too scornful of the weight of tried opinion. This played into the hands of those who were 'wedded to all existing abuses':

> By flying to the extremes of scepticism, we make others shrink back, and shut themselves up in the strongholds of bigotry and superstition—by mixing up doubtful or offensive matters with salutary and demonstrable truths, we bring the whole into question, fly-blow the cause, risk the principle, and give a handle and a pretext to the enemy to treat all philosophy and all reform as a compost of crude, chaotic and monstrous absurdities.

It is the same point that Hazlitt made earlier in his review of

[1] *LG*, 17 July 1824.
[2] *ER*, XL, July 1824. A long extract is printed below on pp. 388–96.

Prometheus.[1] In his remarks on specific poems in the new volume, Hazlitt is particularly interesting on *Julian and Maddalo*, which Shelley had intended to be one of a series of poems about 'dreadful or beautiful realities' set in various Italian cities, and which he had deliberately written in a familiar style (in which he was 'not yet sure of himself'), so utterly opposed to the 'idealism' of the style of *Prometheus* that he would not allow his publisher to print them in the same volume.[2] That Hazlitt should find the poem 'in Mr. Shelley's best and least mannered manner' is consistent with his wish for more realism. It is also of interest to find Hazlitt reacting negatively to what he thought the chaos of *The Witch of Atlas, The Triumph of Life*, and *Marianne's Dream*. Also worth noting is his preference of *The Witch* to the 'dreary and lamentable' 'execution' of *Alastor*. Hazlitt is, moreover, making a shrewd remark when he indicates how 'pointed and intelligible' Shelley's writing becomes when he is moved by indignation. This is certainly true of *The Masque of Anarchy*, the powerful satire on 'Peterloo', which was too plain and too scarifying for even Hunt to dare to print it at the time, and which was only published (by him) in 1832. Hazlitt's general admiration for the shorter poems and translations is also fully justified, and his view, with respect to *Ginevra* and the *Dirge*, that modern writers were prone to sprawl, gloom, and excessive expressions of personality, is a salutary reaction to Romantic excesses.

The review in Constable's *Edinburgh Magazine*[3] is far less able, but not without interest. It sees in the volume the old characteristics, 'solemnity', 'obscurity', 'perfection of poetical expression' (in which it thinks Shelley superior to all other modern poets), but even more 'carelessness' than before. It prefers his treatment of the pleasant to his treatment of the appalling, regrets the inclusion in the volume of so much unfinished work, and generally prefers the shorter pieces, while yet finding *The Triumph of Life* 'written with very peculiar power and originality'.

Only two other reviews are worth mention, but both these are superior pieces of work. The first is that by 'E. Haselfoot' in *Knight's Quarterly Magazine*.[4] This is a well-written defence of

---

[1] See pp. 313–14 above.
[2] Letters to Charles Ollier, 15 December 1819 and 14 May 1820 (*SL*, II. 164, 196). [3] *Ed. M*, XV (2nd. Ser.), July 1824.
[4] *KQM*, III, August 1824. It is reprinted below on pp. 399–405. The late Professor White writes in *The Unextinguished Hearth*, p. 240, that W. S.

Shelley's poetry in general, rather than specifically a critique of the volume. It proceeds by excluding all considerations except the works themselves. Its moderate but firm tone, and its excellent choice of references, give it an effect of authority. As will be seen, the defence is conducted both on aesthetic and on moral grounds; and it makes certain well-judged concessions in both fields. The result is a weighty vindication. On the other hand, the review is less convincing when it goes on to maintain that Shelley's opinions in politics and theology are mere 'excrescences on the surface' of the poems, rather than 'interwoven' with their 'texture'. On the whole, however, this must be considered one of the ablest reviews that Shelley's work ever received.

The other review of the *Posthumous Poems* is that by Leigh Hunt. This was apparently written early in 1825. It was evidently sent off to London in March for publication in *The Westminster Review*, but was ultimately not published there. Most of the review appeared in revised form in 1828 in Leigh Hunt's book *Lord Byron and Some of his Contemporaries*. The first part concerns Shelley's life and character, the second part is about the poetry. This forms an answer to Hazlitt's review, and is printed below.[1] As will be seen, Hunt repudiates some of Hazlitt's accusations as 'caricature of an imaginary original', especially the idea that Shelley was simply out to shock by novelty and paradox. It is interesting to find Hunt even maintaining that Shelley's opinions were all to be found in such writers as Plato, Epicurus, Montaigne,

Walker (the *Quarterly* reviewer of *Prometheus*) is 'known' to have written this review. He does not quote evidence, and it seems hard to believe this, not only because of the marked change of attitude, but also because this reviewer accuses the *Quarterly* reviewer of 'insensibility to whatever is poetical'. On the other hand, Walker is known to have been an unstable character, subject to hallucinations in later life, and, during his tenure of his Trinity Fellowship, he had grave religious doubts, and felt bound to resign in 1829. He is, moreover, known to have written for *Knight's Quarterly*. Therefore the possibility that he adopted a tortuous white-sheet procedure on the present occasion cannot be excluded.

[1] I have printed it in the revised form included in *Lord Byron and Some of his Contemporaries* (London, 1828). It is not known quite how much revised this part of the review is, since the manuscript of most of the literary section is not extant. Possibly this section of the manuscript (the rest of which is in the Luther A. Brewer Leigh Hunt Collection of the State University of Iowa Libraries) was detached, revised, and sent to the publisher of *Lord Byron*, as conjectured by Mr Payson G. Gates in his article 'Leigh Hunt's Review of Shelley's *Posthumous Poems*', *PBSA*, 42 (1948), 1–40.

Bacon, and Sir Thomas More (a by no means homogeneous array), and that all that was his own was 'the genius that impelled him to put philosophical speculations in the shape of poetry, and a subtle and magnificent style'. As for Hazlitt's criticism that Shelley's poetry lacks reality, Hunt is perhaps not so successful in his reference to Shelley's dream of 'mortal strife' in *The Witch of Atlas*, or in his epigram:

If fiction is his reality by day, reality will be his fiction during his slumber.

Hunt has to admit that Shelley's works are not 'calculated to be popular'. On the other hand, his ensuing description of the general character of the poetry is admirable, and he is sensible in conceding that Shelley's poetry lacks 'a proper distribution of light and shade', and that in his longer poems his imagery tends to be monotonous. Hunt's wish to divorce the philosophical speculations from the poetry, and drive them into prose, is, however, far less attractive. Some of the detailed criticism, on the other hand, is well conceived, especially the brief remarks on *Stanzas Written in Dejection near Naples*. The whole review, indeed, despite some wild statements, such as that Shelley 'ought to have written nothing but dramas, interspersed with such lyrics as' 'Music, when soft voices die', and 'Love's Philosophy', is a noble and worthy tribute to a great friend.

Apart from the reviews there seems to be little worth-while criticism of Shelley extant from our period. Coleridge is barren on the subject. Wordsworth is said by Crabb Robinson to have 'placed' Shelley above Byron.[1] Of Hazlitt's and Leigh Hunt's views we have the best record in the reviews and articles already mentioned. As for Byron, although Shelley said a good deal about his work, we have little by way of return. We know that Byron did not profess to understand *The Revolt of Islam*,[2] that he thought the *subject* of *The Cenci* '*un*dramatic', and that he was not an admirer of 'our old dramatists as *models*', though he admitted to Shelley that his play was powerful.[3] We also know that he thought very highly of *Prometheus*[4]; but there is not much more. Even Keats's

---

[1] We do not know at what date Wordsworth did so. Crabb Robinson's diary entry is for 20 December 1827 (*HCRBW*, I. 351; *D*, 95).

[2] Letter to Murray, 24 November 1818 (*LJ*, IV. 273).

[3] Letter to Shelley, 26 April 1821 (*LJ*, V. 268).

[4] *LJ*, V. 339 and Shelley to Leigh Hunt, 26 August 1821 (*SL*, II. 345).

criticism of Shelley is not really very valuable. His advice to him after reading *The Cenci*,[1] to 'curb' his 'magnanimity and be more of an artist, and "load every rift"' of his subject 'with ore', besides being somewhat elusive, perhaps serves best to emphasize Keats's own procedure, and, though possibly relevant as criticism of *The Cenci*, would be of doubtful validity as a point against such a work as *Prometheus*. We might have expected some interesting detailed criticism from Peacock, for his general characterization of Shelley as Scythrop in *Nightmare Abbey* is no substitute for critical reactions to the poetry; but the pieces of comment from him that we have on individual poems are not very interesting or specific, *e.g.*,

> The poetry of your *Adonais* is very beautiful; but when you write you never think of your audience. The number who understand you, and sympathize with you, is small.[2]

There are scraps of some interest here and there in other writers, such as the entry in Crabb Robinson's *Diary* in 1821, telling us that he could not get on with *Prometheus*, and was 'quickened' in his 'purpose of throwing it aside' by the review in the *Quarterly*, which had exposed its 'want of meaning'.[3] In the same entry he also states that Godwin himself was unable to read Shelley's works. But the search for good, or even substantial, criticism, is not fruitful. Indeed, even more than with our other two poets, the most interesting criticism that survives from that period is almost entirely in the reviews.

Now, despite a certain amount of favourable reviewing, the balance was hostile, and partly for this reason Shelley's poems, except for the pirated *Queen Mab*, did not sell.[4] How then did Shelley eventually acquire a high reputation and also a pretty fair number of readers? The answer to this question, which falls outside our terms of reference, is a complex one. It has been given in some detail by the late Professor Newman Ivey White in his comprehensive study of Shelley.[5]

[1] Keats to Shelley, 16 August 1820 (*KL*, II. 322–3).

[2] Peacock to Shelley, 28 February 1822 (*Works*, ed. H. F. B. Brett-Smith and C. E. Jones, 10 vols., London and New York, 1924–34; reprd. 1968, VIII. 228).

[3] 28 December 1821 (*HCRBW* I. 279; *D*, 71).

[4] It is an interesting fact that the *Posthumous Poems*, 1824, were considered such a bad risk that three admirers of Shelley had to guarantee them (N. I. White, *Shelley*, II. 395).

[5] N. I. White, *Shelley*, II. 394–410.

An Anthology of Contemporary Criticism, 1816–22, with an exceptional extension to 1828

From Josiah Conder's unsigned review of *Alastor, and other Poems* (1816) in *The Eclectic Review*, October 1816.

It is but justice to Mr. Shelley, to let him give his own explanation of this singular production.

'The poem entitled 'ALASTOR,' may be considered as allegorical of one of the most interesting situations of the human mind. It represents a youth of uncorrupted feelings and adventurous genius led forth by an imagination inflamed and purified through familiarity with all that is excellent and majestic, to the contemplation of the universe. He drinks deep of the fountains of knowledge, and is still insatiate. The magnificence and beauty of the external world sink profoundly into the frame of his conceptions, and afford to their modifications a variety not to be exhausted. So long as it is possible for his desires to point towards objects thus infinite and unmeasured, he is joyous, and tranquil, and self-possessed. But the period arrives when these objects cease to suffice. His mind is at length suddenly awakened, and thirsts for intercourse with an intelligence similar to itself. He images to himself the Being whom he loves. Conversant with speculations of the sublimest and most perfect natures, the vision in which he embodies his own imaginations unites all of wonderful, or wise, or beautiful, which the poet, the philosopher, or the lover could depicture. The intellectual faculties, the imagination, the functions of sense, have their respective requisitions on the sympathy of corresponding powers in other human beings. The Poet is represented as uniting these requisitions, and attaching them to a single image. He seeks in vain for a prototype of his conception. Blasted by his disappointment, he descends to an untimely grave.

'The picture is not barren of instruction to actual men.' pp. iii. iv.

We fear that not even this commentary will enable ordinary readers to decipher the import of the greater part of Mr. Shelley's allegory. All is wild and specious, untangible and incoherent as a dream. We should be utterly at a loss to convey any distinct idea of the plan or purpose of the poem. It describes the adventures of a poet who 'lived' and 'died' and 'sung in solitude:'—who wanders through countries real and imaginary, in search of an unknown and undefined object; encounters perils and fatigues altogether incredible; and at length expires 'like an exhalation,' in utter solitude, leaving the world inconsolable for a loss of which it is nevertheless unconscious.

The poem is adapted to shew the dangerous, the fatal tendency of that morbid ascendency of the imagination over the other faculties, which incapacitates the mind for bestowing an adequate attention on the real objects of this 'work day' life, and for discharging the relative and social duties. It exhibits the utter uselessness of imagination, when wholly undisciplined, and selfishly employed for the mere purposes of intellectual luxury, without reference to those moral ends to which it was designed to be subservient. This could not be better illustrated, than in a poem where we have glitter without warmth, succession without progress, excitement without purpose, and a search which terminates in annihilation. It must surely be with the view of furnishing some such inference as we have supposed, that every indication of the Author's belief in a future state of existence, and in the moral government of God, is carefully avoided, unless the following be an exception.

> 'O that God,
> Profuse of poisons, would concede the chalice
> Which but one living man has drained, who now,
> Vessel of deathless wrath, a slave that feels
> No proud exemption in the blighting curse
> He bears, over the world wanders for ever,
> Lone as incarnate death!'

[ll. 675–81]

Our readers will be startled at the profanity of this strange exclamation, but we can assure them that it is the only reference to the Deity in the poem. It was, we presume, part of the Author's plan, to represent his hero as an atheist of that metaphysical school, which held that the Universe was God, and that the powers of evil constituted a sort of demonology. He speaks in his Preface of 'the poet's self centered seclusion' being 'avenged by the furies of an irresistible passion pursuing him to speedy ruin.' 'But *that power*,' he adds, 'which strikes the luminaries of the world with sudden darkness and extinction, by awakening them to too exquisite a perception of its influences, dooms to a slow and *poisonous* decay those meaner spirits which dare to abjure its dominion.' It is a pity that in his Preface Mr. S. had not avoided such jargon.

We shall enter no further into the Author's theory, nor shall we subject his poetry to minute criticism. It cannot be denied that very considerable talent for descriptive poetry is displayed in several parts. The Author has genius which might be turned to much better account; but such heartless fictions as Alastor, fail in accomplishing the legitimate purposes of poetry.

From Leigh Hunt's review of *The Revolt of Islam* (1818) in *The Examiner*, 1, 22 February, and 1 March 1818.

This is an extraordinary production. The ignorant will not understand it; the idle will not take the pains to get acquainted with it; even the intelligent will be startled at first with its air of mysticism and wildness; the livelier man of the world will shake his head at it good naturedly; the sulkier one will cry out against it; the bigot will be shocked, terrified, and enraged; and fall to proving all that is said against himself; the negatively virtuous will resent the little quarter that is given to mere custom; the slaves of bad customs or bad passions of any sort will either seize their weapons against it, trembling with rage or conscious worthlessness, or hope to let it quietly pass by, as an enthusiasm that must end in air; finally, the hopeless, if they are ill-tempered, will envy its hopefulness,—if good tempered, will sorrowfully anticipate its disappointment,—both from self-love, though of two different sorts;—but we will venture to say, that the intelligent and the good, who are yet healthy-minded, and who have not been so far blinded by fear and self-love as to confound superstition with desert, anger and hatred with firmness, or despondency with knowledge, will find themselves amply repaid by breaking through the outer shell of this production, even if it be with the single reflection, that so much ardour for the happy virtues, and so much power to recommend them, have united in the same person. To will them with hope indeed is to create them; and to extend that will is the object of the writer before us. . . .

[Hunt then outlines the poem with quotations, and also quotes extensively from Shelley's Preface]

The reader has seen the fable as well as some passages of this poem, and heard the author's own account of his intentions in extracts from the preface. It remains for us to give a general criticism upon it, interspersed with a few more specimens; and as the object of the work is decidedly philosophical, we shall begin with the philosophy.

Mr. Shelley is of opinion with many others that the world is a very beautiful one externally, but wants a good deal of mending with respect to its mind and habits; and for this purpose he would quash as many cold and selfish passions as possible, and rouse up the gentle element of Love, till it set our earth rolling more harmoniously. The answer made to a writer, who sets out with endeavours like these, is that he is idly aiming at perfection; but Mr. Shelley has no such aim, neither have nine hundred and ninety-nine out of a thousand of the persons who have ever been taunted with it. Such a charge, in truth, is only the first answer which egotism makes to any one who thinks he can go beyond its own ideas of the possible. If this however be done away, the next answer is, that you are attempting something wild and romantic,—that you will get disliked for it as well as lose your trouble,—and that you had better coquet, or rather play the prude, with things as they are. The worldly sceptic smiles, and says "Hah!"—the dull rogues wonder, or laugh out;—the disappointed egotist gives you a sneering admonition, having made up his mind about all these things because he and his friends could not alter them; the hypocrite affects to be shocked; the bigot anticipates the punishment that awaits you for daring to say that God's creation is not a vile world, nor his creatures bound to be miserable;—and even the more amiable compromiser with superstition expresses alarm for you,—does not know what you may be hazarding, though he believes nevertheless that God is all good and just,—refers you to the fate of Adam, to shew you that because he introduced the knowledge of evil, you must not attempt to do it away again,—and finally, advises you to comfort yourself with *faith*, and to secure a life in the next world because *this* is a bad business, and *that*, of course, you may find a worse. It seems forgotten all this while, that Jesus Christ himself recommended Love as the great law that was to supersede others; and recommended it too to an extreme, which has been held impracticable. How far it has been found impracticable, in consequence of his doctrines having been mixed up with contradictions and threatening dogmas, and with a system of after-life which contradicts all its principles, may be left to the consideration. Will theologians never discover, that men, in order to be good and just to each other, must either think well of a Divine Being, really and not pretendingly or not think of him at all? That they must worship Goodness and a total absence of the revengeful and malignant passions, if not Omnipotence? or else that they must act upon this quality for themselves, and agree with a devout and amiable Pagan, that "it were better men should say there was no such being as Plutarch, than that there was one Plutarch who eat his own children?" Instead of the alarms about searches after happiness being wise and salutary, when the world is confessedly discordant, they would seem, if we believed in such things, the most fatal and ingenious invention of an enemy of mankind. But it is only so much begging of the question, fatal indeed as far as it goes, and refusing in the strangest manner to look after good, because there is a necessity for it. And as to the Eastern apologue of Adam and Eve (for so many Christians as well as others have thought it), it would be merely shocking to humanity and to a sense of justice in any other light; but it is, in fact, a very deep though not wisely managed allegory, deprecating the folly of mankind in losing their simplicity and enjoyment, and in taking to those very mistakes about vice and virtue, which it is the object of such authors as the one before us to do away again. Faith! It is the very object they have in view; not indeed faiths in endless terrors and contradictions, but "a faith and hope," as Mr. Shelley says, "in something good,"—that faith in the power of men to be kinder and happier, which other faiths take so much pains, and professed pains, to render unbelievable even while they recommend it! "Have faith," says the theologian, "and bear your wretchedness, and escape the wrath to come." "*Have* faith," says the philosopher, "and begin to be happier now, and do not attribute odious qualities to any one."

People get into more inconsistencies in opposing the hopes and efforts of a philosophical enthusiasm than on any other subject. They say "use your reason, instead of your expectations;" and yet this is the reverse of what they do in their own beliefs. They say, take care how you contradict custom;—yet Milton, whom they admire, set about ridiculing it, and paying his addresses to another woman in his wife's life-time, till the latter treated him better. They say it is impossible the world should alter; and yet it has often altered. They say it is impossible, at any rate, it should mend; yet people are no longer burnt at the stake. They say, but it is too old to alter to any great purpose of happiness,—that all its experience goes to the contrary; and yet they talk at other times of the brief life and short-sighted knowledge of man, and of the nothingness of "a thousand years." The experience of a man and an ephemeris are in fact just on a par in all that regards the impossibility of change. But one man,— they say—what can one man do? Let a glorious living person answer, —let Clarkson answer; who sitting down in his youth by a road-side, thought upon the horrors of the Slave Trade, and vowed he would dedicate his life to endeavour at overthrowing it. He was laughed at; he was violently opposed; he was called presumptuous and even irreligious; he was thought out of his senses; he made a noble sacrifice of his own health and strength; and he has *lived* to see the Slave Trade, aye, even the slavery of the descendants of the "cursed" Ham, made a Felony.

We have taken up so much room in noticing these objections, that we have left ourselves none for entering into a further account of Mr. Shelley's views than he himself has given; and we have missed any more quotations at last. But we are sure that he will be much better pleased to see obstructions cleared away from the progress of such opinions as his, than the most minute account given of them in particular. It may be briefly repeated, that they are at war with injustice, violence, and selfishness of every species, however disguised;—that they represent, in a very striking light, the folly and misery of systems, either practical or theoretical, which go upon penal and resentful grounds, and add "pain to pain;" and that they would have men, instead of worshipping tyrannies and terrors of any sort, worship goodness and gladness, diminish the vices and sorrows made by custom only, encourage the virtues and enjoyments which mutual benevolence may realize; and in short, make the best and utmost of this world, as well as hope for another.

The beauties of the poem consist in depth of sentiment, in grandeur of imagery, and a versification remarkably sweet, various, and noble, like the placid playing of a great organ. If the author's genius reminds us of any other poets, it is of two very opposite ones, Lucretius and Dante. The former he resembles in the Dædalian part of it, in the boldness of his speculations, and in his love of virtue, of external nature, and of love itself. It is his gloomier or more imaginative passages that sometimes remind us of Dante. The sort of supernatural architecture in which he delights has in particular the grandeur as well as obscurity of that great genius, to whom however he presents this remarkable and instructive contrast, that superstition and pain and injustice go hand in hand even in the pleasantest parts of Dante, like the three Furies, while philosophy, pleasure, and justice, smile through the most painful passages of our author, like the three Graces.

Mr. Shelley's defects as a poet are obscurity, inartificial and yet no natural economy, violation of costume, and too great a sameness and gratuitousness of image and metaphor, and of image and metaphor too drawn from the elements, particularly the sea. The book is full of humanity; and yet it certainly does not go the best way to work of appealing to it, because it does not appeal to it through the medium of its common knowledges. It is for this reason that we must say something, which we would willingly leave unsaid, both from admiration of Mr. Shelley's genius and love of his benevolence; and this is, that the work cannot possibly become popular. It may set others thinking and writing, and we have no doubt will do so; and those who can understand and relish it, will relish it exceedingly; but the author must forget his metaphysics and sea-sides a little more in his future works, and give full effect to that nice knowledge of men and things which he otherwise really possesses to an extraordinary degree. We have no doubt he is destined to be one of the leading spirits of his age, and indeed has already fallen into his place as such; but however resolute as to his object, he will only be doing it justice to take the most effectual means in his power to forward it.

We have only to observe in conclusion, as another hint to the hopeless, that although the art of printing is not new, yet the Press in any great and true sense of the word is a modern engine in the comparison, and the changeful times of society have never yet been accompanied with so mighty a one. *Books* did what was done before; they have now a million times the range and power; and the Press, which has got hold of Superstition, and given it some irrecoverable wounds already, will, we hope and believe, finally draw it in altogether, and crush it as a steam-engine would a great serpent.

From the unsigned review (by John Gibson Lockhart and possibly John Wilson) of *The Revolt of Islam* in *Blackwood's Edinburgh Magazine*, January 1819.

A pernicious system of opinions concerning man and his moral government, a superficial audacity of unbelief, an overflowing abundance of uncharitableness towards almost the whole of his race, and a disagreeable measure of assurance and self-conceit—each of these things is bad, and the combination of the whole of them in the character of any one person might, at first sight, be considered as more than sufficient to render that one person utterly and entirely contemptible. Nor has the fact, in general, been otherwise. In every age, the sure ultimate reward of the sophistical and phantastical enemies of religion and good order among mankind, has been found in the contempt and disgust of those against whose true interests their weapons had been employed. From this doom the most exquisite elegance of wit, and of words, the most perfect keenness of intellect, the most flattering despotism over contemporary opinion—all have not been able to preserve the inimitable Voltaire. In this doom, those wretched sophists of the present day, who would fain attempt to lift the load of oppressing infamy from off the memory of Voltaire, find their own living beings already entangled, "fold above fold, inextricable coil." Well may they despair:—we can almost pardon the bitterness of their disappointed malice. Their sentence was pronounced without hesitation, almost without pity—for there was nothing in them to redeem their evil. They derived no benefit from that natural, universal, and proper feeling, which influences men to be slow in harshly, or suddenly, or irrevocably condemning intellects that bear upon them the stamp of power,—they had no part in that just spirit of respectfulness which makes men to contemplate, with an unwilling and unsteady eye, the aberrations of genius. The brand of inexpiable execration was ready in a moment to scar their fronts, and they have long wandered neglected about the earth—perhaps saved from extinction, like the fratricide, by the very mark of their ignominy.

Mr Shelly [*sic*] is devoting his mind to the same pernicious purposes which have recoiled in vengeance upon so many of his contemporaries; but he possesses the qualities of a powerful and vigorous intellect, and therefore his fate cannot be sealed so speedily as theirs. He also is of the "COCKNEY SCHOOL," so far as his opinions are concerned; but the base opinions of the sect have not as yet been able entirely to obscure in him the character, or take away from him the privileges of the genius born within him. Hunt and Keats, and some others of the School, are indeed men of considerable cleverness, but as poets, they are worthy of sheer and instant contempt, and therefore their opinions are in little danger of being widely or deeply circulated by their means. But the system, which found better champions than it deserved even in them, has now, it would appear, been taken up by one, of whom it is far more seriously, and deeply, and lamentably unworthy; and the poem before us bears unfortunately the clearest marks of its author's execrable system, but it is impressed every where with the more noble and majestic footsteps of his genius. It is to the operation of the painful feeling above alluded to, which attends the contemplation of perverted power—that we chiefly ascribe the silence observed by our professional critics, in regard to the Revolt of Islam. Some have held back in the fear that, by giving to his genius its due praise, they might only be lending the means of currency to the opinions in whose service he has unwisely enlisted its energies; while others, less able to appreciate his genius, and less likely to be anxious about suppressing his opinions, have been silent, by reason of their selfish fears—dreading, it may be, that by praising the Revolt of Islam, they might draw down upon their own heads some additional marks of that public disgust which followed their praises of Rimini.

Another cause which may be assigned for the silence of the critics should perhaps have operated more effectually upon ourselves; and this is, that the Revolt of Islam, although a fine, is, without all doubt, an obscure poem. Not that the main drift of the narrative is obscure, or even that there is any great difficulty in understanding the tendency of the under-current of its allegory—but the author has composed his poem in much haste, and he has inadvertently left many detached parts, both of his story and his allusion, to be made out as the reader best can, from very inadequate data. The swing of his inspiration may be allowed to have hurried his own eye, *pro tempore*, over many chasms; but Mr Shelly [*sic*] has no excuse for printing a very unfinished piece—an error which he does not confess,—or indeed for many minor errors which he does confess in his very arrogant preface. The unskilful manner in which the allegory is brought out, and the doubt in which the reader is every now and then left, whether or no there be any allegory at all in the case; these alone are sufficient to render the perusal of this poem painful to persons of an active and ardent turn of mind; and, great as we conceive the merits of Mr Shelly's poetry to be, these alone, we venture to prophecy [sic], will be found sufficient to prevent the Revolt of Islam from ever becoming any thing like a favourite with the multitude.

At present, having entered our general protest against the creed of the author, and sufficiently indicated to our readers of what species its errors are,—we are very willing to save ourselves the unwelcome task of dwelling at any greater length upon these disagreable [sic] parts of our subject. We are very willing to pass in silence the many faults of Mr Shelly's opinions and to attend to nothing but the vehicle in which these opinions are conveyed. As a philosopher, our author is weak and worthless;—our business is with him as a poet, and, as such, he is strong, nervous, original; well entitled to take his place near to the great creative masters, whose works have shed its [sic] truest glory around the age wherein we live. As a political and infidel treatise, the Revolt of Islam is contemptible; —happily a great part of it has no necessary connexion either with politics or with infidelity. The native splendour of Mr Shelly's faculties has been his safeguard from universal degradation, and a part, at least, of his genius, has been consecrated to themes worthy of it and of him. In truth, what he probably conceives to be the most exquisite ornaments of his poetry, appear, in our eyes, the chief deformities upon its texture; and had the whole been framed like the passages which we shall quote,—as the Revolt of Islam would have been a purer, so we have no doubt, would it have been a nobler, a loftier, a more majestic, and a more beautiful poem.

We shall pass over, then, without comment, the opening part of this work, and the confused unsatisfactory allegories with which it is chiefly filled. It is sufficient to mention, that, at the close of the first canto, the poet supposes himself to be placed for a time in the regions of eternal repose, where the good and great of mankind are represented as detailing, before the throne of the Spirit of Good, those earthly sufferings and labours which had prepared them for the possession and enjoyment of so blissful an abode. Among these are two, a man and a woman of Argolis, who, after rescuing their country for a brief space from the tyranny of the house of Othman, and accomplishing this great revolution by the force of persuasive eloquence and the sympathies of human love alone, without violence, bloodshed, or revenge,—had seen the fruit of all their toils blasted

335

by foreign invasion, and the dethroned but not insulted tyrant replaced upon his seat; and who, finally, amidst all the darkness of their country's horizon, had died, without fear, the death of heroic martyrdom, gathering consolation, in the last pangs of their expiring nature, from the hope and the confidence that their faith and example might yet raise up successors to their labours, and that they had neither lived nor died in vain.

In the persons of these martyrs, the poet has striven to embody his ideas of the power and loveliness of human affections; and, in their history, he has set forth a series of splendid pictures, illustrating the efficacy of these affections in overcoming the evils of private and of public life. It is in the pourtraying of that passionate love, which had been woven from infancy in the hearts of Laon and Cythna, and which, binding together all their impulses in one hope and one struggle, had rendered them through life no more than two different tenements for the inhabitation of the same enthusiastic spirit;— it is in the pourtraying of this intense, overmastering, unfearing, unfading love, that Mr Shelly has proved himself to be a genuine poet. Around his lovers, moreover, in the midst of all their fervours, he has shed an air of calm gracefulness, a certain majestic monumental stillness, which blends them harmoniously with the scene of their earthly existence, and realizes in them our ideas of Greeks struggling for freedom in the best spirit of their fathers.—We speak of the general effect;—there are unhappily not a few passages in which the poet quits his vantage-ground, and mars the beauty of his personifications by an intermixture of thoughts, feelings, and passions, with which, of right, they have nothing to do. . . .

We forbear from making any comments on this strange narrative; because we could not do so without entering upon other points which we have already professed our intention of waving [*sic*] for the present. It will easily be seen, indeed, that neither the main interest nor the main merit of the poet at all consists in the conception of his plot or in the arrangement of his incidents. His praise is, in our judgment, that of having poured over his narrative a very rare strength and abundance of poetic imagery and feeling—of having steeped every word in the essence of his inspiration. The Revolt of Islam contains no detached passages at all comparable with some which our readers recollect in the works of the great poets our contemporaries; but neither does it contain any such intermixture of prosaic materials as disfigure even the greatest of them. Mr Shelly has displayed his possession of a mind intensely poetical, and of an exuberance of poetic language, perpetually strong and perpetually varied. In spite, moreover, of a certain perversion in all his modes of thinking, which, unless he gets rid of it, will ever prevent him from being acceptable to any considerable or respectable body of readers, he has displayed many glimpses of right understanding and generous feeling, which must save him from the unmingled condemnation even of the most rigorous judges. His destiny is entirely in his own hands; if he acts wisely, it cannot fail to be a glorious one; if he continues to pervert his talents, by making them the instruments of a base sophistry, their splendour will only contribute to render his disgrace the more conspicuous. Mr Shelly, whatever his errors may have been, is a scholar, a gentleman, and a poet; and he must therefore despise from his soul the only eulogies to which he has hitherto been accustomed—paragraphs from the Examiner, and sonnets from Johnny Keats. He has it in his power to select better companions; and if he does so, he may very securely promise himself abundance of better praise.

From John Taylor Coleridge's unsigned review of *Laon and Cythna* and of *The Revolt of Islam* in *The Quarterly Review*, April 1819 (publ. September 1819).

[As will be seen, Coleridge knew that Shelley had withdrawn *Laon and Cythna*, and had cut out or amended the most flagrantly revolutionary and anti-Christian passages before reissuing the poem as *The Revolt of Islam*. Yet Coleridge used material from the unrevised version in his review, with the obvious intention of making Shelley's work still more obnoxious to readers]

This is one of that industrious knot of authors, the tendency of whose works we have in our late Numbers exposed to the caution of our readers—novel, poem, romance, letters, tours, critique, lecture and essay follow one another, framed to the same measure, and in subjection to the same key-note, while the sweet undersong of the weekly journal, filling up all pauses, strengthening all weaknesses, smoothing all abruptnesses, harmonizes the whole strain. Of all his brethren Mr. Shelley carries to the greatest length the doctrines of the sect. He is, for this and other reasons, by far the least pernicious of them; indeed there is a naiveté and openness in his manner of laying down the most extravagant positions, which in some measure deprives them of their venom; and when he enlarges on what certainly are but necessary results of opinions more guardedly delivered by others, he might almost be mistaken for some artful advocate of civil order and religious institutions. This benefit indeed may be drawn from his book, for there is scarcely any more persuasive argument for truth than to carry out to all their legitimate consequences the doctrines of error. But this is not Mr. Shelley's intention; he is, we are sorry to say, in sober earnest:—with perfect

337

deliberation, and the steadiest perseverance he perverts all the gifts of his nature, and does all the injury, both public and private, which his faculties enable him to perpetrate.

Laon and Cythna is the same poem with the Revolt of Islam—under the first name it exhibited some features which made 'the experiment on the temper of the public mind,' as the author calls it, somewhat too bold and hazardous. This knight-errant in the cause of 'a liberal and comprehensive morality' had already sustained some 'perilous handling' in his encounters with Prejudice and Error, and acquired in consequence of it a small portion of *the better part of valour*. Accordingly Laon and Cythna withdrew from circulation; and happy had it been for Mr. Shelley if he had been contented with his failure, and closed his experiments. But with minds of a certain class, notoriety, infamy, any thing is better than obscurity; baffled in a thousand attempts after fame, they will still make one more at whatever risk,—and they end commonly like an awkward chemist who perseveres in tampering with his ingredients, till, in an unlucky moment, they take fire, and he is blown up by the explosion.

Laon and Cythna has accordingly re-appeared with a new name, and a few slight alterations. If we could trace in these any signs of an altered spirit, we should have hailed with the sincerest pleasure the return of one whom nature intended for better things, to the ranks of virtue and religion. But Mr. Shelley is no penitent; he has re-produced the same poison, a little, and but a little, more cautiously disguised, and as it is thus intended only to do the more mischief at less personal risk to the author, our duty requires us to use his own evidence against himself, to interpret him where he is obscure now, by himself where he was plain before, and to exhibit the 'fearful consequences' to which he would bring us, as he drew them in the boldness of his first conception.

Before, however, we do this, we will discharge our duty to Mr. Shelley as poetical critics—in a case like the present, indeed, where the freight is so pernicious, it is but a secondary duty to consider the 'build' of the vessel which bears it; but it is a duty too peculiarly our own to be wholly neglected. Though we should be sorry to see the Revolt of Islam in our readers' hands, we are bound to say that it is not without beautiful passages, that the language is in general free from errors of taste, and the versification smooth and harmonious. In these respects it resembles the latter productions of Mr. Southey, though the tone is less subdued, and the copy altogether more luxuriant and ornate than the original. Mr. Shelley indeed is an unsparing imitator; and he draws largely on the rich stores of another mountain poet, to whose religious mind it must be matter, we think, of perpetual sorrow to see the philosophy which comes

338

pure and holy from his pen, degraded and perverted, as it continually is, by this miserable crew of atheists or pantheists, who have just sense enough to abuse its terms, but neither heart nor principle to comprehend its import, or follow its application. We shall cite one of the passages to which we alluded above, in support of our opinion: perhaps it is that which has pleased us more than any other in the whole poem.

[Quotes Canto II, stanzas xxi–xxiv, italicizing as faulty 'Aught' (l. 850), and 'Which' (l. 876); and indicating 'any' in brackets after 'Aught' as the correct word to use]

These, with all their imperfections, are beautiful stanzas; they are, however, of rare occurrence:—had the poem many more such, it could never, we are persuaded, become popular. Its merits and its faults equally conspire against it; it has not much ribaldry or voluptuousness for prurient imaginations, and no personal scandal for the malicious; and even those on whom it might be expected to act most dangerously by its semblance of enthusiasm, will have stout hearts to proceed beyond the first canto. As a whole, it is insupportably dull, and laboriously obscure; its absurdities are not of the kind which provoke laughter, the story is almost wholly devoid of interest, and very meagre; nor can we admire Mr. Shelley's mode of making up for this defect—as he has but one incident where he should have ten, he tells that one so intricately, that it takes the time of ten to comprehend it.

Mr. Shelley is a philosopher by the courtesy of the age, and has a theory of course respecting the government of the world; we will state in as few words as we can the general outlines of that theory, the manner in which he demonstrates it, and the practical consequences, which he proposes to deduce from it. It is to the second of these divisions that we would beg his attention; we despair of convincing him directly that he has taken up false and pernicious notions; but if he pays any deference to the common laws of reasoning, we hope to shew him that, let the goodness of his cause be what it may, his manner of advocating it is false and unsound. This may be mortifying to a teacher of mankind; but a philosopher seeks the truth, and has no vanity to be mortified.

The existence of evil, physical and moral, is the grand problem of all philosophy; the humble find it a trial, the proud make it a stumbling-block; Mr. Shelley refers it to the faults of those civil institutions and religious creeds which are designed to regulate the conduct of man here, and his hopes in a hereafter. In these he seems to make no distinction, but considers them all as bottomed upon principles pernicious to man and unworthy of God, carried into details the most cruel, and upheld only by the stupidity of the many on the one hand, and the selfish conspiracy of the few on the other. According to him the earth is a boon garden needing little care or cultivation, but pouring forth spontaneously and inexhaustibly all innocent delights and luxuries to her innumerable children; the seasons have no inclemencies, the air no pestilences for man in his proper state of wisdom and liberty; his business here is to enjoy himself, to abstain from no gratification, to repent of no sin, hate no crime, but be wise, happy and free, with plenty of 'lawless love.' This is man's natural state, the state to which Mr. Shelley will bring us, if we will but break up the 'crust of our outworn opinions,' as he calls them, and put them into his magic cauldron. But kings have introduced war, legislators crime, priests sin; the dreadful consequences have been that the earth has lost her fertility, the seasons their mildness, the air its salubrity, man his freedom and happiness. We have become a foul-feeding carnivorous race, are foolish enough to feel uncomfortable after the commission of sin; some of us even go so far as to consider vice odious; and we all groan under a multiplied burthen of crimes *merely conventional*; among which Mr. Shelley specifies with great *sang froid* the commission of *incest*!

We said that our philosopher makes no distinction in his condemnation of creeds; we should rather have said, that he makes no exception; distinction he does make, and it is to the prejudice of that which we hold. In one place indeed he assembles a number of names of the founders of religions, to treat them all with equal disrespect.

> 'And through the host contention wild befell,
> As each of his own God the wondrous works did tell;
> *And Oromaze and Christ and Mahomet,
> Moses and Buddh, Zerdusht, and Brahm and Foh,
> A tumult of strange names,' &c.

[ll. 4061–5]

[The reviewer is quoting from *Laon and Cythna*, the unrevised poem]

But in many other places he manifests a dislike to Christianity which is frantic, and would be, if in such a case any thing could be, ridiculous. When the votaries of all religions are assembled with one accord (this unanimity by the bye is in a vision of the *nineteenth* century) to stifle the first breathings of liberty, and execute the revenge of a ruthless tyrant, he selects a Christian priest to be the

---

* 'And Oromaze, Joshua and Mahomet.' *Revolt of Islam.* This is a very fair specimen of Mr. Shelley's alterations, which we see are wholly prudential, and artfully so, as the blasphemy is still preserved entire. [Reviewer's footnote.]

organ of sentiments outrageously and pre-eminently cruel. The two characteristic principles upon which Christianity may be said to be built are repentance and faith. Of repentance he speaks thus:—

> 'Reproach not thine own soul, but know thyself;
> *Nor hate another's crime, nor loathe thine own.*
> It is the dark idolatry of self
> Which, when our thoughts and actions once are gone,
> Demands that we should weep and bleed and groan;
> O vacant expiation! be at rest—
> The past is death's—the future is thine own;
> And love and joy can make the *foulest* breast
> A paradise of flowers where peace might build her nest.'
>
> [ll. 3388–96. The italics are the reviewer's.
For 'we', l. 3392, Oxford text reads 'man']

Repentance then is selfishness in an extreme which amounts to idolatry! but what is Faith? our readers can hardly be prepared for the odious accumulation of sin and sorrow which Mr. Shelley conceives under this word. 'Faith is the Python, the Ogress, the Evil Genius, the Wicked Fairy, the Giantess of our children's tales;' whenever any thing bad is to be accounted for, any hard name to be used, this convenient monosyllable fills up the blank.

> 'Beneath his feet, 'mong ghastliest forms, represt
> Lay Faith, *an obscene worm.*'
>
> [ll. 2167–8; the italics are the reviewer's]

> ——————— 'sleeping there
> With lidless eyes lie Faith, and Plague, and Slaughter,
> A ghastly brood conceived of Lethe's sullen water.'
>
> [ll. 3943–5]

> 'And underneath thy feet writhe Faith and Folly,
> Custom and Hell, and mortal Melancholy.'
>
> [ll. 2185–6]

> 'Smiled on the flowery grave, in which were lain
> Fear, Faith, and Slavery.'
>
> [ll. 3124–5]

Enough of Mr. Shelley's theory.—We proceed to examine the manner in which the argument is conducted, and this we cannot do better than by putting a case.

Let us suppose a man entertaining Mr. Shelley's opinions as to the causes of existing evil, and convinced of the necessity of a change in all the institutions of society, of his own ability to produce and conduct it, and of the excellence of that system which he would substitute in their place. These indeed are bold convictions for a young and inexperienced man, imperfectly educated, irregular in his application, and shamefully dissolute in his conduct; but let us suppose them to be sincere;—the change, if brought about at all, must be effected by a concurrent will, and that, Mr. Shelley will of course tell us, must be produced by an enlightened conviction. How then would a skilful reasoner, assured of the strength of his own ground, have proceeded in composing a tale of fiction for this purpose? Undoubtedly he would have taken the best laws, the best constitution, and the best religion in the known world; such at least as they most loved and venerated whom he was addressing; when he had put all these together, and developed their principles candidly, he would have shewn that under all favourable circumstances, and with all the best propensities of our nature to boot, still the natural effect of this combination would be to corrupt and degrade the human race. He would then have drawn a probable inference, that if the most approved systems and creeds under circumstances more advantageous than could ever be expected to concur in reality, still produced only vice and misery, the fault lay in them, or at least mankind could lose nothing by adventuring on a change. We say with confidence that a skilful combatant would and must have acted thus; not merely to make victory final, but to gain it in any shape. For if he reasons from what we acknowledge to be bad against what we believe to be good; if he puts a government confessedly despotic, a religion monstrous and false, if he places on the throne a cruel tyrant, and at the altar a bigoted and corrupt priesthood, how can his argument have any weight with those who think they live under a paternal government and a pure faith, who look up with love and gratitude to a beneficent monarch, and reverence a zealous and upright priesthood? The laws and government on which Mr. Shelley's reasoning proceeds, are the Turkish, administered by a lawless despot; his religion is the Mohammedan, maintained by servile hypocrites; and his scene for their joint operation Greece, the land full beyond all others of recollections of former glory and independence, now covered with shame and sunk in slavery. We are Englishmen, Christians, free, and independent; we ask Mr. Shelley how his case applies to *us*? or what *we* learn from it to the prejudice of our own institutions?

His residence at Oxford was a short one, and, if we mistake not, rather *abruptly* terminated; yet we should have thought that even in a freshman's term he might have learned from Aldrick not to reason from a particular to an universal; and any one of our fair readers we imagine who never heard of Aldrick, would see the absurdity of inferring that all of her own sex were the victims of the lust and tyranny of the other, from the fact, if it be a fact, that young women of Greece were carried off by force to the seraglio of Constantinople. This, however, is the sum and substance of the argument, as far as it attempts to prove the causes of existing evil. Mr. Shelley is neither a dull, nor, considering all his disadvantages, a very ignorant man; we will frankly confess, that with every disposition to judge him charitably, we find it hard to convince ourselves of his belief in his own conclusions.

We have seen how Mr. Shelley argues for the necessity of a change; we must bestow a word or two upon the manner in which he brings that change about, before we come to the consequences which he derives from it. Laon and Cythna, his hero and heroine, are the principal, indeed, almost the sole agents. The latter by her eloquence rouses all of her own sex to assert their liberty and independence; this perhaps was no difficult task; a female tongue in such a cause may be supposed to have spoken fluently at least, and to have found a willing audience; by the same instrument, however, she disarms the soldiers who are sent to seize and destroy her,—

> 'even the torturer who had bound
> Her meek calm frame, ere yet it was impaled
> Loosened her weeping then, nor could be found
> One human hand to harm her.'
>
> [ll. 1576–9]

The influence of her voice is not confined to the Golden City, it travels over the land, stirring and swaying all hearts to its purpose:—

> 'in hamlets and in towns
> The multitudes collect tumultuously,—
> Blood soon, although unwillingly, to shed.'
>
> [ll. 1617–8, 1621]

These peaceable and tender advocates for 'Universal Suffrage and *no* representation' assemble in battle-array under the walls of the Golden City, keeping night and day strict blockade (which Mr. Shelley calls 'a watch of love,') around the desperate bands who still adhere to the maintenance of the iron-hearted monarch on the throne. Why the eloquence of Cythna had no power over *them*, or how the monarch himself, who had been a slave to her beauty, and to whom this model of purity and virtue *had borne a child*, was able to resist the spell of her voice, Mr. Shelley leaves his readers to find out for themselves. In this pause of affairs Laon makes his appearance to complete the revolution; Cythna's voice had done wonders, but Laon's was still more powerful; the 'sanguine slaves' of page 96, who stabbed ten thousand in their sleep, are turned in page 99 to fraternal bands; the power of the throne crumbles into dust, and the united hosts enter the city in triumph. A good deal of mummery follows, of national fêtes, reasonable rites, altars of federation, &c. borrowed from that store-house of cast-off mummeries and abominations, the French revolution. In the mean time all the kings of the earth, pagan and christian, send more sanguine slaves, who slaughter the sons of freedom in the midst of their merrymaking; Plague and Famine come to slaughter them in return; and Laon and Cythna, who had chosen this auspicious moment in a ruined tower for the commencement of their 'reign of love,' surrender themselves to the monarch and are burnt alive.

Such is Mr. Shelley's victory, such its security, and such the means of obtaining it! These last, we confess, are calculated to throw a damp upon our spirits, for if the hopes of mankind must depend upon the exertion of super-eminent eloquence, we have the authority of one who had well considered the subject, for believing that they could scarcely depend upon any thing of more rare occurrence. Plures in omnibus rebus, quàm in dicendo admirabiles, was the remark of Cicero a great many ages ago, and the experience of all those ages has served but to confirm the truth of it.

Mr. Shelley, however, is not a man to propose a difficult remedy without suggesting the means of procuring it. If we mistake not, Laon and Cythna, and even the sage, (for there is a sort of good stupid Archimago in the poem), are already provided, and intent to begin their mission if we will but give them hearing. In short, Mr. Shelley is his own Laon: this is clear from many passages of the preface and dedication. The lady to whom the poem is addressed [Mary Shelley] is certainly the original of Cythna: we have more consideration for her than she has had for herself, and will either mortify her vanity, or spare her feelings, by not producing her before the public; it is enough for the philanthropist to know that when the season arrives, she will be forth-coming. Mr. Shelley says of himself and her, in a simile picturesque in itself, but laughable in its application,—

> 'thou and I,
> Sweet friend, can look from our tranquillity,
> Like lamps, into the world's tempestuous night—
> Two tranquil stars, while clouds are passing by
> Which wrap them from the foundering seaman's sight,
> That burn from year to year with unextinguished light.'
> [ll. 121–6]

Neither will the reader be much at a loss to discover what sapient personage is dimly shadowed out in Archimago [Godwin]; but a clue is afforded even to the uninitiate by a note in the preface, in

344

which we are told that Mr. Malthus by his last edition has reduced the Essay on Population to a commentary illustrative of the unanswerableness of *Political Justice.*

With such instruments doubtless the glorious task will be speedily accomplished—and what will be the issue? this indeed is a serious question; but, as in most schemes of reform, it is easier to say what is to be removed, and destroyed, than what is to be put in its place. Mr. Shelley would abrogate our laws—this would put an end to felonies and misdemeanours at a blow; he would abolish the rights of property, of course there could thenceforward be no violations of them, no heart-burnings between the poor and the rich, no disputed wills, no litigated inheritances, no food in short for sophistical judges, or hireling lawyers; he would overthrow the constitution, and then we should have no expensive court, no pensions or sinecures, no silken lords or corrupt commoners, no slavish and enslaving army or navy; he would pull down our churches, level our Establishment, and burn our bibles—then we should pay no tithes, be enslaved by no superstitions, abused by no priestly artifices: marriage he cannot endure, and there would at once be a stop put to the lamented increase of adulterous connections amongst us, whilst by repealing the canon of heaven against incest, he would add to the purity, and heighten the ardour of those feelings with which brother and sister now regard each other; finally, as the basis of the whole scheme, he would have us renounce our belief in our religion, extinguish, if we can, the light of conscience within us, which embitters our joys here, and drown in oblivion the hopes and fears that hang over our hereafter. This is at least intelligible; but it is not so easy to describe the structure, which Mr. Shelley would build upon this vast heap of ruins. 'Love,' he says, 'is to be the sole law which shall govern the moral world;' but Love is a wide word with many significations, and we are at a loss as to which of them he would have it now bear. We are loath to understand it in its lowest sense, though we believe that as to the issue this would be the correctest mode of interpreting it; but this at least is clear, that Mr. Shelley does not mean it in its highest sense: he does not mean that love, which is the fulfilling of the law, and which walks after the commandments, for he would erase the Decalogué, and every other code of laws; not the love which is said to be of God, and which is beautifully coupled with 'joy, peace, long suffering, gentleness, goodness, faith, meekness, temperance,' for he pre-eminently abhors that religion, which is built on that love and inculcates it as the essence of all duties, and its own fulfilment.

It is time to draw to an end.—We have examined Mr. Shelley's system slightly, but, we hope, dispassionately; there will be those, who will say that we have done so coldly. He has indeed, to the best of his ability, wounded us in the tenderest part.—As far as in him lay, he has loosened the hold of our protecting laws, and sapped the principles of our venerable polity; he has invaded the purity and chilled the unsuspecting ardour of our fireside intimacies; he has slandered, ridiculed and blasphemed our holy religion; yet these are all too sacred objects to be defended bitterly or unfairly. We have learned too, though not in Mr. Shelley's school, to discriminate between a man and his opinions, and while we shew no mercy to the sin, we can regard the sinner with allowance and pity. It is in this spirit, that we conclude with a few lines, which may serve for a warning to others, and for reproof, admonition, and even if he so pleases of encouragement to himself. We have already said what we think of his powers as a poet, and doubtless, with those powers, he might have risen to respectability in any honourable path, which he had chosen to pursue, if to his talents he had added industry, subordination, and good principles. But of Mr. Shelley much may be said with truth, which we not long since said of his friend and leader Mr. Hunt: he has not, indeed, all that is odious and contemptible in the character of that person; so far as we have seen he has never exhibited the bustling vulgarity, the ludicrous affectation, the factious flippancy, or the selfish heartlessness, which it is hard for our feelings to treat with the mere contempt they merit. Like him, however, Mr. Shelley is a very vain man; and like most very vain men, he is but half instructed in knowledge, and less than half-disciplined in his reasoning powers; his vanity, wanting the controul of the faith which he derides, has been his ruin; it has made him too impatient of applause and distinction to earn them in the fair course of labour; like a speculator in trade, he would be rich without capital and without delay, and, as might have been anticipated, his speculations have ended only in disappointments. They both began, his speculations and his disappointments, in early childhood, and even from that period he has carried about with him a soured and discontented spirit—unteachable in boyhood, unamiable in youth, querulous and unmanly in manhood,—singularly unhappy in all three. He speaks of his school as 'a world of woes,' of his masters 'as tyrants,' of his school-fellows as 'enemies,'—alas! what is this, but to bear evidence against himself? every one who knows what a public school ordinarily must be, will only trace in these lines the language of an insubordinate, a vain, a mortified spirit.

We would venture to hope that the past may suffice for the speculations in which Mr. Shelley has hitherto engaged; they have brought him neither honour abroad nor peace at home, and after so fair a trial it seems but common prudence to change them for some new venture. He is still a young man, and though his account be assuredly black and heavy, he may yet hope to redeem his time, and wipe it out. He may and he should retain all the love for his fellow-creatures, all the zeal for their improvement in virtue and happiness which he now professes, but let that zeal be armed with knowledge and regulated by judgment. Let him not be offended at our freedom, but he is really too young, too ignorant, too inexperienced, and too vicious to undertake the task of reforming any world, but the little world within his own breast; that task will be a good preparation for the difficulties which he is more anxious at once to encounter. There is a book which will help him to this preparation, which has more poetry in it than Lucretius, more interest than Godwin, and far more philosophy than both. But it is a sealed book to a proud spirit; if he would read it with effect, he must be humble where he is now vain, he must examine and doubt himself where now he boldly condemns others, and instead of relying on his own powers, he must feel and acknowledge his weakness, and pray for strength from above.

[There follows a brief, adverse critique of *Rosalind and Helen*, and the review ends with some dark hints about the enormities of Shelley's private life]

From the review of *Alastor, and other Poems* in *Blackwood's Edinburgh Magazine*, November 1819

We believe this little volume to be Mr Shelley's first publication; and such of our readers as have been struck by the power and splendour of genius displayed in the Revolt of Islam, and by the frequent tenderness and pathos of "Rosalind and Helen," will be glad to observe some of the earliest efforts of a mind destined, in our opinion, under due discipline and self-management, to achieve great things in poetry. It must be encouraging to those who, like us, cherish high hopes of this gifted but wayward young man, to see what advances his intellect has made within these few years, and to compare its powerful, though still imperfect display, in his principal poem with its first gleamings and irradiations throughout this production almost of his boyhood. In a short preface, written with all the enthusiasm and much of the presumption of youth, Mr Shelley gives a short explanation of the subject of "Alastor; or, the Spirit of Solitude," which we cannot say throws any very great light upon it, but without which, the poem would be, we suspect, al- together unintelligible to ordinary readers. Mr Shelley is too fond of allegories; and a great genius like his should scorn, now that it has reached the maturity of manhood, to adopt a species of poetry in

347

which the difficulties of the art may be so conveniently blinked, and weakness find so easy a refuge in obscurity. . . .

[The reviewer then outlines *Alastor*, with copious quotation and brief comments, and then quotes a few of the shorter poems, noting the 'dreams of death' in 'The pale, the cold, and the moony smile'; the 'spirit of deep, solemn, and mournful repose' in the poem on Lechlade Churchyard, and the extreme beauty of *The Daemon of the World*]

We beg leave, in conclusion, to say a few words about the treatment which Mr Shelley has, in his poetical character, received from the public. By our periodical critics he has either been entirely overlooked, or slightingly noticed, or grossly abused. There is not so much to find fault with in the mere silence of critics; but we do not hesitate to say, with all due respect for the general character of that journal, that Mr Shelley has been infamously and stupidly treated in the Quarterly Review. His Reviewer there, whoever he is, does not shew himself a man of such lofty principles as to entitle him to ride the high horse in company with the author of the Revolt of Islam. And when one compares the vis inertiæ of his motionless prose with the "eagle-winged raptures" of Mr Shelley's poetry, one does not think indeed of Satan reproving Sin, but one does think, we will say it in plain words and without a figure, of a dunce rating a man of genius. If that critic does not know that Mr Shelley is a poet, almost in the very highest sense of that mysterious word, then, we appeal to all those whom we have enabled to judge for themselves, if he be not unfit to speak of poetry before the people of England. If he does know that Mr Shelley is a great poet, what manner of man is he who, with such conviction, brings himself, with the utmost difficulty, to admit that there is any beauty at all in Mr Shelley's writings, and is happy to pass that admission off with an accidental and niggardly phrase of vague and valueless commendation. This is manifest and mean—glaring and gross injustice on the part of a man who comes forward as the champion of morality, truth, faith, and religion. This is being guilty of one of the very worst charges of which he accuses another; nor will any man who loves and honours genius, even though that genius may have occasionally suffered itself to be both stained and led astray, think but with contempt and indignation and scorn of a critic who, while he pretends to wield the weapons of honour, virtue, and truth, yet clothes himself in the armour of deceit, hypocrisy, and falsehood. He *exults* to calumniate Mr Shelly's moral character, but he *fears* to acknowledge his genius. And therefore do we, as the sincere though sometimes sorrowing friends of Mr Shelley, scruple not to say, even though it may expose us to the charge of personality from those from whom alone such a charge could at all affect our minds, that the critic shews himself by such conduct as far inferior to Mr Shelley as a man of worth, as the language in which he utters his falsehood and uncharitableness shews him to be inferior as a man of intellect.

In the present state of public feeling, with regard to poets and poetry, a critic cannot attempt to defraud a poet of his fame, without paying the penalty either of his ignorance or his injustice. So long as he confines the expression of his envy or stupidity to works of moderate or doubtful merit, he may escape punishment; but if he dare to insult the spirit of England by contumelious and scornful treatment of any one of her gifted sons, that contumely and that scorn will most certainly be flung back upon himself, till he be made to shrink and to shiver beneath the load. It is not in the power of all the critics alive to blind one true lover of poetry to the splendour of Mr Shelley's genius—and the reader who, from mere curiosity, should turn to the Revolt of Islam to see what sort of trash it was that so moved the wrath and the spleen and the scorn of the Reviewer, would soon feel, that to understand the greatness of the poet, and the littleness of his traducer, nothing more was necessary than to recite to his delighted sense any six successive stanzas of that poem, so full of music, imagination, intellect, and passion. We care comparatively little for injustice offered to one moving majestical in the broad day of fame—it is the injustice done to the great, while their greatness is unknown or misunderstood that a generous nature most abhors, in as much as it seems more basely wicked to wish that genius might never lift its head, than to envy the glory with which it is encircled.

There is, we firmly believe, a strong love of genius in the people of this country, and they are willing to pardon to its possessor much extravagance and error—nay, even more serious transgressions. Let both Mr Shelley and his critic think of that—let it encourage the one to walk onwards to his bright destiny, without turning into dark or doubtful or wicked ways—let it teach the other to feel a proper sense of his own insignificance, and to be ashamed, in the midst of his own weaknesses and deficiencies and meannesses, to aggravate the faults of the highly-gifted, and to gloat with a sinful satisfaction on the real or imaginary debasement of genius and intellect.

And here we ought, perhaps, to stop. But the Reviewer has dealt out a number of dark and oracular denunciations against the Poet, which the public can know nothing about, except that they imply a charge of immorality and wickedness. Let him speak out plainly, or let him hold his tongue. There are many wicked and foolish things in Mr Shelley's creed, and we have not hitherto scrupled, nor shall we henceforth scruple to expose that wickedness and that folly. But we do not think that he believes his own creed—at least, that he believes it fully and to utter conviction—and we doubt not but the scales will yet all fall from his eyes. The Reviewer, however, with a face of most laughable horror, accuses Mr Shelly in the same breath of some nameless act of atrocity, and of having been rusticated, or expelled, or warned to go away from the University of Oxford! He seems to shudder with the same holy fear at the violation of the laws of morality and the breaking of college rules. He forgets that in the world men do not wear caps and gowns as at Oriel or Exeter. He preaches not like Paul—but like a Proctor.

Once more, then we bid Mr Shelley farewell. Let him come forth from the eternal city, where, we understand, he has been sojourning, —in his strength, conquering and to conquer. Let his soul watch his soul, and listen to the voice of its own noble nature—and there is no doubt that the future will make amends for the past, whatever its errors may have been—and that the Poet may yet be good, great, and happy.

From the notice of *Prometheus Unbound* (1819–20) in Baldwin's *London Magazine*, June 1820.

Mr. Shelley's announced dramatic poem, entitled *Prometheus Unbound*, will be found to be a very noble effort of a high and commanding imagination: it is not yet published, but we have seen some parts of it which have struck us very forcibly. The poet may perhaps be accused of taking a wild view of the latent powers and future fortunes of the human race; but its tendency is one of a far more inspiriting and magnanimous nature than that of the Cenci. The soul of man, instead of being degraded by the supposition of improbable and impossible vice, is elevated to the highest point of the poetical Pisgah, from whence a land of promise, rich with blessings of every kind, is pointed out to its delighted contemplation. This poem is more completely the child of the *Time* than almost any other modern production: it seems immediately sprung from the throes of the great intellectual, moral, and political *labour* of nations. Like the Time, its parent, too, it is unsettled, irregular, but magnificent.

From a letter from Keats to Shelley, 16 August 1820.

You, I am sure, will forgive me for sincerely remarking that you might curb your magnanimity, and be more of an artist, and load every rift of your subject with ore. The thought of such discipline must fall like cold chains upon you, who perhaps never sat with your wings furled for six months together. And is not this extraordinary talk for the writer of *Endymion*, whose mind was like a pack of scattered cards? I am picked up and sorted to a pip. My imagination is a monastery, and I am its monk. I am in expectation of *Prometheus* every day. Could I have my own wish effected, you would have it still in manuscript, or be but now putting an end to the second act. I remember you advising me not to publish my first blights, on Hampstead Heath. I am returning advice upon your hands. Most of the poems in the volume I send you have been written above two years, and would never have been published but for hope of gain; so you see I am inclined enough to take your advice now. I must express once more my deep sense of your kindness, adding my sincere thanks and respects for Mrs. Shelley. In the hope of soon seeing you,

I remain most sincerely yours,

John Keats

From the unsigned review (probably mainly or wholly by Lockhart) of *Prometheus Unbound, with other Poems*, in *Blackwood's Edinburgh Magazine*, September 1820.

Whatever may be the difference of men's opinions concerning the measure of Mr Shelley's poetical power, there is one point in regard to which all must be agreed, and that is his Audacity. In the old days of the exulting genius of Greece, Æschylus dared two things which astonished all men, and which still astonish them—to exalt contemporary men into the personages of majestic tragedies—and to call down and embody into tragedy, without degradation, the elemental spirits of nature and the deeper essences of Divinity. We scarcely know whether to consider the *Persians* or the *Prometheus Bound* as the most extraordinary display of what has always been esteemed the most audacious spirit that ever expressed its workings in poetry. But what shall we say of the young English poet who has now attempted, not only a flight as high as the highest of Æschylus, but the very flight of that father of tragedy—who has dared once more to dramatise Prometheus—and, most wonderful of all, to dramatise the *deliverance* of Prometheus—which is known to have formed the subject of a lost tragedy of Æschylus no ways inferior in mystic elevation to that of the $\Delta\epsilon\sigma\mu\omega\tau\eta\varsigma$.[1]

Although a fragment of that perished master-piece be still extant in the Latin version of Attius—it is quite impossible to conjecture what were the personages introduced in the tragedy of Æschylus, or by what train of passions and events he was able to sustain himself

---

[1] I.e., the *Prometheus Bound*—Ed.

on the height of that awful scene with which his surviving *Prometheus* terminates. It is impossible, however, after reading what is left of that famous trilogy,* to suspect that the Greek poet symbolized any thing whatever by the person of Prometheus, except the native strength of human intellect itself—its strength of endurance above all others—its sublime power of patience. STRENGTH and FORCE are the two agents who appear on this darkened theatre to bind the too benevolent Titan—*Wit* and *Treachery*, under the forms of Mercury and Oceanus, endeavour to prevail upon him to make himself free by giving up his dreadful secret;—but *Strength* and *Force*, and *Wit* and *Treason*, are all alike powerless to overcome the resolution of that suffering divinity, or to win from him any acknowledgment of the new tyrant of the skies. Such was this simple and sublime allegory in the hands of Æschylus. As to what had been the original purpose of the framers of the allegory, that is a very different question, and would carry us back into the most hidden places of the history of mythology. No one, however, who compares the mythological systems of different races and countries, can fail to observe the frequent occurrence of certain great leading Ideas and leading Symbolisations of ideas too—which Christians are taught to contemplate with a knowledge that is the knowledge of reverence. Such, among others, are unquestionably the ideas of an Incarnate Divinity suffering on account of mankind—conferring benefits on mankind at the expense of his own suffering;—the general idea of vicarious atonement itself—and the idea of the dignity of suffering as an exertion of intellectual might—all of which may be found, more or less obscurely shadowed forth, in the original Μυθοσ of Prometheus the Titan, the enemy of the successful rebel and usurper Jove. We might have also mentioned the idea of a *deliverer*, waited for patiently through ages of darkness, and at last arriving in the person of the child of Io—but, in truth, there is no pleasure, and would be little propriety, in seeking to explain all this at greater length, considering, what we cannot consider without deepest pain, the very different views which have been taken of the original allegory by Mr Percy Bysshe Shelley.

It would be highly absurd to deny, that this gentleman has manifested very extraordinary powers of language and imagination in his treatment of the allegory, however grossly and miserably he may have tried to pervert its purpose and meaning. But of this more anon. In the meantime, what can be more deserving of reprobation

---

* There was another and an earlier play of Æschylus, Prometheus the Fire-Stealer, which is commonly supposed to have made part of the series; but the best critics, we think, are of opinion, that that was entirely a satirical piece. [Reviewer's footnote.]

than the course which he is allowing his intellect to take, and that too at the very time when he ought to be laying the foundations of a lasting and honourable name. There is no occasion for going round about the bush to hint what the poet himself has so unblushingly and sinfully blazoned forth in every part of his production. With him, it is quite evident that the Jupiter whose downfall has been predicted by Prometheus, means nothing more than Religion in general, that is, every human system of religious belief; and that, with the fall of this, he considers it perfectly necessary (as indeed we also believe, though with far different feelings) that every system of human government also should give way and perish. The patience of the contemplative spirit in Prometheus is to be followed by the daring of the active Demagorgon, at whose touch all "old thrones" are at once and for ever to be cast down into the dust. It appears too plainly, from the luscious pictures with which his play terminates, that Mr Shelly looks forward to an unusual relaxation of all moral *rules*—or rather, indeed, to the extinction of all moral feelings, except that of a certain mysterious indefinable *kindliness*, as the natural and necessary result of the overthrow of all civil government and religious belief. It appears, still more wonderfully, that he contemplates this state of things as the ideal SUMMUM BONUM. In short, it is quite impossible that there should exist a more pestiferous mixture of blasphemy, sedition, and sensuality, than is visible in the whole structure and strain of this poem—which, nevertheless, and notwithstanding all the detestation its principles excite, must and will be considered by all that read it attentively, as abounding in poetical beauties of the highest order—as presenting many specimens not easily to be surpassed, of the moral sublime of eloquence—as overflowing with pathos, and most magnificent in description. Where can be found a spectacle more worthy of sorrow than such a man performing and glorying in the performance of such things? His evil ambition,—from all he has yet written, but most of all, from what he has last and best written, his *Prometheus*,—appears to be no other, than that of attaining the highest place among those poets,—enemies, not friends, of their species,—who, as a great and virtuous poet has well said (putting evil consequence close after evil cause).

"Profane the God-given strength, and *mar the lofty line*."

[There follow long quotations from the drama, and from the 'magnificent' 'Vision of the Sea', and high praise of the 'melody of versification' and 'tenderness of feeling' of the short poems, from which *The Sensitive Plant* is singled out as 'the most affecting'. There follows a blast against the Cockneys, and the review then concludes as follows:]

353

Last of all, what should forbid us to announce our opinion, that Mr Shelley, as a man of genius, is not merely superior, either to Mr Hunt, or to Mr Keats, but altogether out of their sphere, and totally incapable of ever being brought into the most distant comparison with either of them. It is very possible, that Mr Shelley himself might not be inclined to place himself so high above these men as we do, but that is his affair, not ours. We are afraid that he shares, (at least with one of them) in an abominable system of belief, concerning Man and the World, the sympathy arising out of which common belief, may probably sway more than it ought to do on both sides. But the truth of the matter is this, and it is impossible to conceal it were we willing to do so, that Mr Shelley is destined to leave a great name behind him, and that we, as lovers of true genius, are most anxious that this name should ultimately be pure as well as great.

As for the principles and purposes of Mr Shelley's poetry, since we must again recur to that dark part of the subject, we think they are on the whole, more undisguisedly pernicious in this volume, than even in his Revolt of Islam. There is an Ode to Liberty at the end of the volume, which contains passages of the most splendid beauty, but which, in point of meaning, is just as wicked as any thing that ever reached the world under the name of Mr Hunt himself. It is not difficult to fill up the blank which has been left by the prudent bookseller, in one of the stanzas beginning:

> O that the free would stamp the impious name,
> Of * * * * into the dust! Or write it there
> So that this blot upon the page of fame,
> Were as a serpent's path, which the light air
> Erases, &c. &c.
>
> [*Ode to Liberty*, st. xv]

but the next speaks still more plainly,

> "O that the WISE from their bright minds would kindle
> Such lamps within the dome of this wide world,
> That the pale name of PRIEST might shrink and dwindle
> Into the HELL from which it first was hurled!"

This is exactly a versification of the foulest sentence that ever issued from the lips of Voltaire. Let us hope that Percy Bysshe Shelley is not destined to leave behind him, like that great genius, a name for ever detestable to the truly FREE and the truly WISE. He talks in his preface about MILTON, as a "Republican," and a "bold inquirer into Morals and religion." Could any thing make us despise Mr Shelley's understanding, it would be such an instance of voluntary blindness as this! Let us hope, that ere long a lamp of genuine truth may be kindled within his "bright mind;" and that he may walk in its light the path of the true demigods of English genius, having, like them, learned to "fear God and honour the king."

From the review of *Prometheus Unbound, with other Poems,* in Gold's *London Magazine,* October 1820.

This is one of the most stupendous of those works which the daring and vigorous spirit of modern poetry and thought has created. We despair of conveying to our readers, either by analysis or description, any idea of its gigantic outlines, or of its innumerable sweetnesses. It is a vast wilderness of beauty, which at first seems stretching out on all sides into infinitude, yet the boundaries of which are all cast by the poet; in which the wildest paths have a certain and a noble direction; and the strangest shapes which haunt its recesses, voices of gentleness and of wisdom. It presents us with the oldest forms of Greek mythology, informed with the spirit of fresh enthusiasm and of youngest hope; and mingles with these the creatures of a new mythology, in which earth, and the hosts of heaven, spirits of time and of eternity, are embodied and vivified, to unite in the rapturous celebration of the reign of Love over the universe.

This work is not, as the title would lead us to anticipate, a mere attempt to imitate the old tragedy of the Greeks. In the language, indeed, there is often a profusion of felicitously compounded epithets; and in the imagery, there are many of those clear and lucid shapes, which distinguish the works of Æschylus and of Sophocles. But the subject is so treated, that we lose sight of persons in principles, and soon feel that all the splendid machinery around us is but the shadow of things unseen, the outward panoply of bright expectations and theories, which appear to the author's mind instinct with eternal and eternally progressive blessings. The fate of Prometheus probably suggested, even to the heroic bard by whom it was celebrated in older time, the temporary predominance of brute force over intellect; the oppression of right by might; and the final deliverance of the spirit of humanity from the iron grasp of its foes. But, in so far as we can judge from the mighty fragment which time has spared, he was contented with exhibiting the visible picture of the magnanimous victim, and with representing his deliverance, by means of Hercules, as a mere personal event, having no symbolical meaning. In Mr. Shelley's piece, the deliverance of Prometheus, which is attended by the dethroning of Jupiter, is scarcely other than a symbol of the peaceful triumph of goodness over power; of the subjection of might to right; and the restoration of love to the full exercise of its benign and all-penetrating sympathies. To represent

355

vividly and poetically this vast moral change, is, we conceive, the design of this drama, with all its inward depths of mystical gloom, its pregnant clouds of imagination, its spiry eminences of icy splendour, and its fair regions overspread by a light "which never was by sea or land," which consecrates and harmonizes all things.

To the ultimate prospect exhibited by that philosophical system which Mr. Shelley's piece embodies, we have no objection. There is nothing pernicious in the belief that, even on earth, man is destined to attain a high degree of happiness and of virtue. The greatest and wisest have ever trusted with the most confiding faith to that nature, with whose best qualities they were so richly gifted. They have felt that in man were undeveloped capabilities of excellence; stores of greatness, suffered to lie hidden beneath basest lumber; sealed up fountains, whence a brighter day might loosen streams of fresh and ever-living joys. In the worst and most degraded minds, vestiges of goodness are not wanting; some old recollections of early virtue; some feeling of wild generosity or unconquerable love; some divine instinct; some fragments of lofty principle; some unextinguishable longings after nobleness and peace, indicate that there is good in man which can never yield to the storms of passion or the decays of time. On these divine instances of pure and holy virtue; on history; on science; on imagination; on the essences of love and hope; we may safely rest, in the expectation that a softer and tenderer light will ultimately dawn on our species. We further agree with Mr. Shelley, that Revenge is not the weapon with which men should oppose the erring and the guilty. He only speaks in accordance with every wise writer on legislation, when he deprecates the infliction of one vibration of *unnecessary* pain on the most criminal. He only echoes the feeling of every genuine Christian, when he contends for looking with deep-thoughted pity on the vicious, or regarding them tenderly as the unfortunate, and for striving "not to be overcome of evil, but to overcome evil with good." He only coincides with every friend of his species, when he deplores the obstacles which individuals and systems have too often opposed to human progress. But when he would attempt to realize in an instant his glorious visions; when he would treat men as though they were now the fit inhabitants of an earthly paradise; when he would cast down all restraint and authority as enormous evils; and would leave mankind to the guidance of passions yet unsubdued, and of desires yet unregulated, we must protest against his wishes, as tending fearfully to retard the good which he would precipitate. Happy, indeed, will be that time, of which our great philosophical poet, Wordsworth, speaks, when love shall be an "unclouded light, and joy its own security." But we shall not hasten this glorious era by destroying

356

those forms and dignities of the social state, which are essential to the restraint of the worst passions, and serviceable to the nurture of the kindliest affections. The stream of human energy is gathering strength; but it would only be scattered in vain, were we rashly to destroy the boundaries which now confine it in its deep channel; and it can only be impeded by the impatient attempt to strike the shores with its agitated waters.

Although there are some things in Mr. Shelley's philosophy against which we feel it a duty thus to protest, we must not suffer our difference of opinion to make us insensible to his genius. As a poem, the work before us is replete with clear, pure, and majestical imagery, accompanied by a harmony as rich and various as that of the loftiest of our English poets. . . .

We have left ourselves no room to expatiate on the minor Poems of this volume. The "Vision of the Sea" is one of the most awful pictures which poetry has set before us. In the "Ode to Liberty," there are passages of a political bearing, which, for the poet's sake, we heartily wish had been omitted. It is not, however, addressed to minds whom it is likely to injure. In the whole work there is a spirit of good—of gentleness, humanity, and even of religion, which has excited in us a deep admiration of its author, and a fond regret that he should ever attempt to adorn cold and dangerous paradoxes with the beauties which could only have been produced by a mind instinctively pious and reverential.

From the review of *Prometheus Unbound, with other Poems*, in *The Monthly Review*, February 1821.

There is an excess of fancy which rapidly degenerates into nonsense: if the *sublime* be closely allied to the *ridiculous*, the *fanciful* is twin-sister to the *foolish*; and really Mr. Shelley has worthily maintained the relationship. What, in the name of wonder on one side, and of common sense on the other, is the meaning of this metaphysical rhapsody about the unbinding of Prometheus? Greek plays, Mr. Shelley tells us in his preface, have been his study; and from them he has caught—what?—any thing but the tone and character of his story; which as little exhibits the distinct imaginations of the heathen mythology as it resembles the virtuous realities of the Christian faith. It is only *nonsense*, pure unmixed *nonsense*, that Mr. Shelley has derived from his various lucubrations, and combined in the laudable work before us.

We are so far from denying, that we are most ready to acknowledge, the great merit of detached passages in the *Prometheus Unbound*: but this sort of praise, we fear from expressions in his prose advertisements, the poet before us will be most unwilling to receive; for he says on one occasion, (preface to the Cenci,) 'I have avoided, *with great care*, in writing this play, the introduction of what is commonly called *mere poetry*; and I imagine there will scarcely be found *a detached simile, or a single isolated description*,'!! &c. Charming prospect, indeed! "I could find it in my heart," says Dogberry, "to bestow all my tediousness upon your Worship;" and so his anti-type, the author of *Prometheus Unbound*, (which, a punster might say, will always remain *unbound*,) studiously excludes from his play every thing like 'mere poetry,' (*merum sal*,) or a 'single isolated description.' This speaks for itself; and we should have thought that we had been reading a burlesque preface of Fielding to one of his *mock tragedies*, rather than a real introduction by a serious dramatist to one of his *tragic plays*. We may be told, however, that we must consider the Prometheus Unbound as a philosophical work. "We cry you mercy, cousin Richard!" Where are the things, then, "not dreamt of in *our* philosophy?" The '*Prometheus Unbound*' is amply stored with such things. First, there is a *wicked supreme deity*.—Secondly, there is a Demogorgon; superior, in process of time, to that *supreme wickedness*.—Thirdly, there are nymphs, naids, nereids, spirits of flood and fell, depth and height, the four elements, and fifty-four imaginary places of creation and residence.—Now, to what does all this tend? To nothing, positively to nothing. Like Dandie Dinmont's unproduceable child, the author cannot, in any part of his work, "*behave distinctly*." How should he? His Manichean absurdities, his eternally indwelling notion of a good and an evil principle fighting like furies on all occasions with their whole *posse comitatus* together, cross his clearer fancy, and lay the buildings of his better mind in glittering gorgeous ruins. Let his readers observe the manner in which he talks of death, and hope, and all the thrilling interests of man; and let us also attend to what follows:—'For my part I had rather be damned with Plato and Lord Bacon, than go to Heaven with Paley and Malthus.' Preface to Prometheus, p. 14. This appears to us to be nothing but hatred of contemporaries; not admiration of the antients. *This* "offence is rank;—it smells to Heaven."

The benevolent opposition of Prometheus to the oppressive and atrocious rule of Jupiter forms the main object, as far as it can be understood, of this generally unintelligible work; though some of it can be understood too plainly; and the passage beginning, 'A woful sight,' at page 49, and ending, 'It hath become a curse,' must be most offensive, as it too evidently seems to have been intended to be, to every sect of Christians.[1]

We must cease, however, to expostulate with Mr. Shelley, if we may hope to render him or his admirers any service; and most

---

[1] The passage is I. i. 584–604—*Ed.*

assuredly we have a sincere desire to be thus serviceable, for he has power to do good, or evil, on an extensive scale;—and whether from admiration of genius, or from a prudent wish to conciliate its efforts, we are disposed to welcome all that is good and useful in him, as well as prepared to condemn all that is the contrary.

[Quotes II. iv. 7–86, commenting on its mixture of *nonsense* with 'much benevolent feeling, beautiful language, and powerful versification'; and IV. i. 1–55 as mingling much of 'uncommon merit' with much more absurdity, and conjecturing that here and in many other passages Shelley was heartily laughing in his reader's face]

From the article 'On the Philosophy and Poetry of Shelley' in Gold's *London Magazine*, February 1821.

In differing from the religious opinions of society, Mr. Shelley is only sustaining a more elevated tone of feeling, and applying himself to the fountain head of devotion, instead of stopping to slake his thirst at the numerous streamlets that wander by the way-side. He has not bewildered himself in the folio controversies of Warburton and Lowth; or versed his mind in the learned disputes of Travis, Porson, and Co. about the credit of the three witnesses; or puzzled himself with the sage Jesuits of old, as to the startling fact of ten thousand angels dancing on the point of a needle, without jostling each other; but he has consulted his own heart; he has "held converse" with his own reason; and instead of arriving at the truth by a circumbendibus, has reached it by a straight-forward direction. His principal feeling respecting religion appears to consist in the sentiment of benevolence toward mankind, that strikes home to the heart as an immediate emanation of the Deity. His mind revolts at intolerance and bigotry; and he believes in his devotional creed as one that deserves love as well as admiration. His moral and political principles all spring from the same source, and are founded on the same dignified contempt for bigotry and the "sway of tyranny." . . .

In his dramatic poem of "Prometheus Unbound," Mr. Shelley has given us, in the portraiture of the noble-minded victim, a most "beautiful idealism of moral excellence." He has shown us Virtue, not as she is, but as she should be—magnanimous in affliction, and impatient of unauthorised tyranny. Prometheus, the friend and the champion of mankind, may be considered as a type of religion oppressed by the united powers of superstition and tyranny. He is for a time enchained, though not enfeebled, by the pressure of his misfortunes, but is finally triumphant; and by the manful assertion of his own lawful claims frees himself from his ignominious thraldom, and proves the truth of that axiom which is engraved in undying characters on the "fair front of nature"—that right shall always overcome might. This is the leading principle in Mr. Shelley; in its more trifling bearings it is occasionally inconsistent, but exhibits a noble illustration of the intuitive powers and virtues of the human mind. This is the system that he is anxious to disseminate, and a more sublime one was never yet invented. It appeals at once from nature to God, discards the petty bickerings of different creeds, and soars upward to the Throne of Grace as the lark that "sings at Heaven's gate" her matin song of thanksgiving. There may be different opinions respecting matters of taste, feeling, and metaphysics, but there can be but one respecting the holiness of benevolence, and universal philanthropy. Before this great, this important truth, all minor creeds sink into their native insignificance. It is the ladder by which man mounts to Heaven,—the faith which enables him to hear the voice of the Deity welcoming him as he ascends.

In the creed of Mr. Shelley the humanity of religion is so intimately connected with its sacred origin that it is impossible to separate them. He will not, like less humane, but more orthodox believers, condemn any one for the difference of his creed, or write long books to prove that all who disbelieve in his opinions must be eventually damned. He forms his religion on a more elevated principle,—he makes it the religion of the heart as well as of the head, and by its own virtues proves more strongly the fact of its divine origin:—

> "For modes of faith let graceless zealots fight;
> His can't be wrong, whose life is in the right."
> [Pope, *Essay on Man*, Ep. IV, ll. 305–6]

This opinion of one of England's choicest spirits, followed as it has been, and still is, by Shelley and others of the same school, is daily gaining ground in the world; and the march of intellect, which day after day is rapidly encreasing, threatens the destruction of all civil and religious prejudices.

Men can be no longer hood-winked; they now at least think for themselves; and this strenuous exertion of intellect will eventually prove fatal to fanaticism. It is not now as it was fifty years ago, when the piety of bishops was measured by their circumference, and the devotion of a minister adjudged by the comparative length and drowsiness of his sermon. The waters are out; a fearful ebullition of the human mind is already on the eve of breaking forth; the spirit of the nation heaves, as the ocean billows, from the depth of its own mightiness; and the muttering sound of the distant thunder may be even now heard in the awful pause that precedes the tempest.

"The great writers of our own age," says Mr. Shelley, "are, we have reason to suppose, the companions and forerunners of some unimagined change in our social condition, or the opinions which cement it. The cloud of mind is discharging its collected lightning, and the equilibrium between institutions and opinions is now restoring, or is about to be restored." Let us hope then, for the honor of our nature and the advancement of true religion, that the days are not far distant when the Deity shall once again be imaged in the breasts of his creation; when his worship shall be unsullied by the animosity of alarmists, and be considered as benevolence to our fellow-mortals, and love to the being that created us. Let us hope that intolerance, and all the present uncharitableness of the Protestant religion, shall be for ever banished from our creed, and that Catholic and Jew, Mahometan and Bramin, Pagan and Protestant, shall alike vie with each other in the noblest exercise of religion —in love to all around them; and meet with one common purpose, in one temple of concord, to praise the same Deity, whether he be reverenced as Jupiter, Mahomet, Bramah, Jehovah, or God!

Having advanced thus much on the philosophical opinions of Shelley, it remains to say a few words respecting his poetical qualifications. He is perhaps the most intensely sublime writer of his day, and with the exception of Wordsworth, is more highly imaginative than any other living poet. There is an air of earnestness, a tone of deep sincerity in all his productions, that give them an electrical effect. No one can read his "Prometheus Unbound," or the magnificent "Ode to Liberty," without a sensation of the deepest astonishment at the stupendous mind of their author. The mental visions of philosophy contained in them are the most gorgeous that can be conceived, and expressed in language well suited to the sentiment. They soar with an eagle's flight to the heaven of heavens, and come back laden with the treasures of humanity. But with all the combined attractions of mind and verse, we feel that Mr. Shelley can never become a popular poet. He does not sufficiently link himself with man; he is too visionary for the intellect of the generality of his readers, and is ever immersed in the clouds of religious and metaphysical speculations. His opinions are but skeletons, and he does not sufficiently embody them to render them intelligible. They are magnificent abstractions of mind,—the outpourings of a spirit "steeped to the very full" in humanity and religious enthusiasm.

In intensity of description, depth of feeling, and richness of language, Mr. Shelley is infinitely superior to Lord Byron. He has less versatility of talent, but a purer and a loftier imagination. His poetry is always adapted to the more kindly and sublime sensibilities of human nature, and enkindles in the breast of the reader a corresponding enthusiasm of benevolence. It gives him an added respect for the literature of his country, and warms his whole soul, as he marks in the writings of his contemporaries the progressive march of the human intellect[1] to the very perfection of divinity. And well indeed may we rejoice at the exalted character our country still retains in the annals of the world. The national spirit which has been so long enfeebled, is now bursting forth in all its meridian splendor; every day augments the number of our poets and literary characters; and the human mind may soon vie with the Angels of Heaven—in the purity and refinement of its intellect. Great days of light and liberty are on the eve of bursting forth with such excessive splendor, that the whole world shall bask in its cheering beams. Byron, Shelley, Godwin, Wordsworth, Hazlitt, and many other such glorious spirits, are the bows of promise that shine in the intellectual atmosphere, to predict the dispersal of gloom, and the restoration of unclouded sunshine. Their example even now produces a generous emulation in the breasts of thousands, who will disseminate their principles and their talents with the improvements that age and circumstance may suggest. In exact proportion to the progress of intellect, is the decay of prejudice and fanaticism. Literature has always the effect of enlightening and humanizing the mind, and dispersing the dense clouds that ignorance had hung around it. Thus then, the glorious example of that "bold enquirer, Shelley," will be followed, at no great lapse of time, by the enthusiasm of his votaries, who in their turn will serve as models to the exertions of others; and thus, from one little seed that was sown in good ground, shall spring up a fruitful crop destined to overshadow the face of the earth, and fatten the natural increase of the land.

From the unsigned review by Rev. Dr W. S. Walker of *Prometheus Unbound, with other Poems*, in *The Quarterly Review*, October 1821 (publ. December).

A great lawyer of the present day is said to boast of practising three different modes of writing: one which any body can read; another which only himself can read; and a third, which neither he nor any body else can read. So Mr. Shelley may plume himself upon writing in three different styles: one which can be generally understood; another which can be understood only by the author; and a third which is absolutely and intrinsically unintelligible. Whatever his command may be of the first and second of these styles, this volume is a most satisfactory testimonial of his proficiency in the last.

[1] Cf. Peacock's sceptical references in *Crotchet Castle* and *Gryll Grange* to the 'march of mind'.—*Ed.*

If we might venture to express a general opinion of what far surpasses our comprehension, we should compare the poems contained in this volume to the visions of gay colours mingled with darkness, which often in childhood, when we shut our eyes, seem to revolve at an immense distance around us. In Mr. Shelley's poetry all is brilliance, vacuity, and confusion. We are dazzled by the multitude of words which sound as if they denoted something very grand or splendid: fragments of images pass in crowds before us; but when the procession has gone by, and the tumult of it is over, not a trace of it remains upon the memory. The mind, fatigued and perplexed, is mortified by the consciousness that its labour has not been rewarded by the acquisition of a single distinct conception; the ear, too, is dissatisfied: for the rhythm of the verse is often harsh and unmusical; and both the ear and the understanding are disgusted by new and uncouth words, and by the awkward, and intricate construction of the sentences.

The predominating characteristic of Mr. Shelley's poetry, however, is its frequent and total want of meaning. Far be it from us to call for strict reasoning, or the precision of logical deductions, in poetry; but we have a right to demand clear, distinct conceptions. The colouring of the pictures may be brighter or more variegated than that of reality; elements may be combined which do not in fact exist in a state of union; but there must be no confusion in the forms presented to us. Upon a question of mere beauty, there may be a difference of taste. That may be deemed energetic or sublime, which is in fact unnatural or bombastic; and yet there may be much difficulty in making the difference sensible to those who do not preserve an habitual and exclusive intimacy with the best models of composition. But the question of meaning, or no meaning, is a matter of fact on which common sense, with common attention, is adequate to decide; and the decision to which we may come will not be impugned, whatever be the want of taste, or insensibility to poetical excellence, which it may please Mr. Shelley, or any of his coterie, to impute to us. We permit them to assume, that they alone possess all sound taste and all genuine feeling of the beauties of nature and art: still they must grant that it belongs only to the judgment to determine, whether certain passages convey any signification or none; and that, if we are in error ourselves, at least we can mislead nobody else, since the very quotations which we must adduce as examples of nonsense, will, if our charge be not well founded, prove the futility of our accusation at the very time that it is made. If, however, we should completely establish this charge, we look upon the question of Mr. Shelley's poetical merits as at an end; for he who has the trick of writing very showy verses without ideas, or without coherent ideas, can contribute to the instruction of none, and can please only those who have learned to read without having ever learned to think.

The want of meaning in Mr. Shelley's poetry takes different shapes. Sometimes it is impossible to attach any signification to his words; sometimes they hover on the verge between meaning and no meaning, so that a meaning may be obscurely conjectured by the reader, though none is expressed by the writer; and sometimes they convey ideas, which, taken separately, are sufficiently clear, but, when connected, are altogether incongruous. We shall begin with a passage which exhibits in some parts the first species of nonsense, and in others the third.

> 'Lovely apparitions, dim at first,
> Then radiant, as the mind, arising bright
> From the embrace of beauty, whence the forms
> Of which these are the phantoms, casts on them
> The gathered rays which are reality,
> Shall visit us, the immortal progeny
> Of painting, sculpture, and wrapt poesy,
> And arts, tho' unimagined, yet to be.'
>
> [III. iii. 49–56]

The verses are very sonorous; and so many fine words are played off upon us, such as, *painting, sculpture, poesy, phantoms, radiance, the embrace of beauty, immortal progeny*, &c. that a careless reader, influenced by his habit of associating such phrases with lofty or agreeable ideas, may possibly have his fancy tickled into a transient feeling of satisfaction. But let any man try to ascertain what is really said, and he will immediately discover the imposition that has been practised. From beauty, or the embrace of beauty, (we know not which, for ambiguity of phrase is a very frequent companion of nonsense,) certain forms proceed: of these forms there are phantoms; these phantoms are dim; but the mind arises from the embrace of beauty, and casts on them the gathered rays which are reality; they are then baptized by the name of the immortal progeny of the arts, and in that character proceed to visit Prometheus. This *galimatias* (for it goes far beyond simple nonsense) is rivalled by the following description of something that is done by a cloud.

> 'I am the daughter of earth and water,
>   And the nursling of the sky;
> I pass through the pores of the oceans and shores,
>   I change, but I cannot die.
> For after the rain, when with never a stain
>   The pavilion of heaven is bare,

And the winds and sunbeams with their convex gleams,
   Build up the blue dome of air,
I silently laugh at my own cenotaph,
   And out of the caverns of rain,
Like a child from the womb, like a ghost from the tomb,
   I arise, and unbuild it again.'

[*The Cloud*, ll. 73–84]

. . . Metaphors and similes can scarcely be regarded as ornaments of Mr. Shelley's compositions; for his poetry is in general a mere jumble of words and heterogeneous ideas, connected by slight and accidental associations, among which it is impossible to distinguish the principal object from the accessory. In illustrating the incoherency which prevails in his metaphors, as well as in the other ingredients of his verses, we shall take our first example, not from that great storehouse of the obscure and the unintelligible—the Prometheus, but from the opening of a poem, entitled, 'A Vision of the Sea,' which we have often heard praised as a splendid work of imagination.

'————The rags of the sail
Are flickering in ribbons within the fierce gale:
From the stark night of vapours the dim rain is driven,
And when lightning is loosed, like a deluge from heaven,
She sees the black trunks of the water-spouts spin,
And bend, as if heaven was raining in,
Which they seem'd to sustain with their terrible mass
As if ocean had sunk from beneath them: they pass
To their graves in the deep with an earthquake of sound,
And the waves and the thunders made silent around
Leave the wind to its echo.'

[ll. 1–11]

At present we say nothing of the cumbrous and uncouth style of these verses, nor do we ask who this 'she' is, who sees the water-spouts; but the funeral of the water-spouts is curious enough: 'They pass to their graves with an earthquake of sound.' The sound of an earthquake is intelligible, and we suspect that this is what Mr. Shelley meant to say: but an earthquake of sound is as difficult to comprehend as a cannon of sound, or a fiddle of sound. The same vision presents us with a battle between a tiger and a sea-snake; of course we have—

'——The whirl and the splash
As of some hideous engine, whose brazen teeth smash
The thin winds and soft waves into thunder; the screams
And hissings crawl fast o'er the smooth ocean streams,
Each sound like a centipede.'

[ll. 144–8]

The comparison of sound to a centipede would be no small addition to a cabinet of poetical monstrosities: but it sinks into tame commonplace before the engine, whose brazen teeth pound thin winds and soft waves into thunder.

Sometimes Mr. Shelley's love of the unintelligible yields to his preference for the disgusting and the impious. Thus the bodies of the dead sailors are thrown out of the ship:

'And the sharks and the dog-fish their grave-cloths unbound,
And were glutted, like Jews, with this manna rained down
From God on their wilderness.'

[ll. 56–8]

. . . Another characteristic trait of Mr. Shelley's poetry is, that in his descriptions he never describes the thing directly, but transfers it to the properties of something which he conceives to resemble it by language which is to be taken partly in a metaphorical meaning, and partly in no meaning at all. The whole of a long poem, in three parts, called 'the Sensitive Plant,' the object of which we cannot discover, is an instance of this. The first part is devoted to the description of the plants. The sensitive plant takes the lead:

'No flower ever trembled and panted with bliss,
In the garden, the field, or the wilderness,
Like a doe in the noon-tide with love's sweet want,
As the companionless sensitive plant.'

[ll. 9–12. For 'no flower' Oxford reads 'But none']

Next come the snow-drop and the violet:

'And their breath was mixed with fresh odour, sent
From the turf, *like the voice and the instrument.*'

[ll. 15–16. Reviewer's italics in quotations]

The rose, too,

'——Unveiled the depth of her glowing breast,
Till, fold after fold, *to the fainting air
The soul of her beauty and love lay bare.*'

[ll. 30–3]

The hyacinth is described in terms still more quaint and affected:

'[And] The hyacinth, purple, and white, and blue,
Which flung from *its bells a sweet peal anew,*
Of music so delicate, soft, and intense,
It was felt like an odour within the sense.'

[ll. 25–8]

It is worth while to observe the train of thought in this stanza. The

366

bells of the flower occur to the poet's mind; but ought not bells to ring a peal? Accordingly, by a metamorphosis of the odour, the bells of the hyacinth are supposed to do so: the fragrance of the flower is first converted into a peal of music, and then the peal of music is in the last line transformed back into an odour. These are the tricks of a mere poetical harlequin, amusing himself with

'The clock-work tintinnabulum of rhyme.'
[Cowper, *Table Talk*, l. 529]

In short, it is not too much to affirm, that in the whole volume there is not one original image of nature, one simple expression of human feeling, or one new association of the appearances of the moral with those of the material world.

As Mr. Shelley disdains to draw his materials from nature, it is not wonderful that his subjects should in general be widely remote from every thing that is level with the comprehension, or interesting to the heart of man. He has been pleased to call 'Prometheus Unbound' a lyrical drama, though it has neither action nor dramatic dialogue. The subject of it is the transition of Prometheus from a state of suffering to a state of happiness; together with a corresponding change in the situation of mankind. But no distinct account is given of either of these states, nor of the means by which Prometheus and the world pass from the one to the other. The Prometheus of Mr. Shelley is not the Prometheus of ancient mythology. He is a being who is neither a God nor a man, who has conferred supreme power on Jupiter. Jupiter torments him; and Demogorgon, by annihilating Jupiter's power, restores him to happiness. Asia, Panthea, and Ione, are female beings of a nature similar to that of Prometheus. Apollo, Mercury, the Furies, and a faun, make their appearance; but have not much to do in the piece. To fill up the *personæ dramatis*, we have voices of the mountains, voices of the air, voices of the springs, voices of the whirlwinds, together with several echos. Then come spirits without end: spirits of the moon, spirits of the earth, spirits of the human mind, spirits of the hours; who all attest their super-human nature by singing and saying things which no human being can comprehend. We do not find fault with this poem, because it is built on notions which no longer possess any influence over the mind, but because its basis and its materials are mere dreaming, shadowy, incoherent abstractions. It would have been quite as absurd and extravagant in the time of Æschylus, as it is now.

It may seem strange that such a volume should find readers, and still more strange that it should meet with admirers. We were ourselves surprized by the phenomenon: nothing similar to it occurred to us, till we recollected the numerous congregations which the incoherencies of an itinerant Methodist preacher attract. These preachers, without any connected train of thought, and without attempting to reason, or to attach any definite meaning to the terms which they use, pour out a deluge of sonorous words that relate to sacred objects and devout feelings. These words, connected as they are with all that is most venerable in the eyes of man, excite a multitude of pious associations in the hearer, and produce in him a species of mental intoxication. His feelings are awakened, and his heart touched, while his imagination and understanding are bewildered; and he receives temporary pleasure, sometimes even temporary improvement, at the expense of the essential and even permanent depravation of his character. In the same way, poetry like that of Mr. Shelley presents every where glittering constellations of words, which taken separately have a meaning, and either communicate some activity to the imagination, or dazzle it by their brilliance. Many of them relate to beautiful or interesting objects, and are therefore capable of imparting pleasure to us by the associations attached to them. The reader is conscious that his mind is raised from a state of stagnation, and he is willing to believe, that he is astounded and bewildered, not by the absurdity, but by the originality and sublimity of the author.

It appears to us much more surprizing, that any man of education should write such poetry as that of 'Prometheus Unbound,' than, that when written, it should find admirers. It is easy to read without attention; but it is difficult to conceive how an author, unless his intellectual habits are thoroughly depraved, should not take the trouble to observe whether his imagination has definite forms before it, or is gazing in stupid wonder on assemblages of brilliant words. Mr. Shelley tells us, that he imitates the Greek tragic poets: can he be so blinded by self-love, as not to be aware that his productions have not one feature of likeness to what have been deemed classical works, in any country or in any age? He, no doubt, possesses considerable mental activity; for without industry he could never have attained to so much facility in the art of throwing words into fantastical combinations: is it not strange that he should never have turned his attention from his verses to that which his verses are meant to express? We fear that his notions of poetry are fundamentally erroneous. It seems to be his maxim, that reason and sound thinking are aliens in the dominions of the Muses, and that, should they ever be found wandering about the foot of Parnassus, they ought to be chased away as spies sent to discover the nakedness of the land. We would wish to persuade him, if possible, that the poet is distinguished from the rest of his species, not by wanting what other men have, but by having what other men want. The reason of the poet ought to be cultivated with as much care as that of the philosopher, though the former chooses a peculiar field for its exercise, and associates with it in its labours other faculties that are not called forth in the mere investigation of truth.

But it is often said, that though the poems are bad, they at least show poetical power. Poetical power can be shown only by writing good poetry, and this Mr. Shelley has not yet done. The proofs of Mr. Shelley's genius, which his admirers allege, are the very exaggeration, copiousness of verbiage, and incoherence of ideas which we complain of as intolerable. They argue in criticism, as those men do in morals, who think debauchery and dissipation an excellent proof of a good heart. The want of meaning is called sublimity, absurdity becomes venerable under the name of originality, the jumble of metaphor is the richness of imagination, and even the rough, clumsy, confused structure of the style, with not unfrequent violations of the rules of grammar, is, forsooth, the sign and effect of a bold overflowing genius, that disdains to walk in common trammels. If the poet is one who whirls round his reader's brain, till it becomes dizzy and confused; if it is his office to envelop he knows not what in huge folds of a clumsy drapery of splendid words and showy metaphors, then, without doubt, may Mr. Shelley place the Delphic laurel on his head. But take away from him the unintelligible, the confused, the incoherent, the bombastic, the affected, the extravagant, the hideously gorgeous, and 'Prometheus,' and the poems which accompany it, will sink at once into nothing.

But great as are Mr. Shelley's sins against sense and taste, would that we had nothing more to complain of! Unfortunately, to his long list of demerits he has added the most flagrant offences against morality and religion. We should abstain from quoting instances, were it not that we think his language too gross and too disgusting to be dangerous to any but those who are corrupted beyond the hope of amendment. After a revolting description of the death of our Saviour, introduced merely for the sake of intimating, that *the religion he preached is the great source of human misery and vice*, he adds,

> —'Thy name I will not speak,
> It hath become a curse.'

[I. i. 603–4]

Will Mr. Shelley, to excuse this blasphemy against the name '*in which all the nations of the earth shall be made blessed*,' pretend, that these are the words of Prometheus, not of the poet? But the poet himself hath told us, that his Prometheus is meant to be 'the type of the highest perfection of moral and intellectual excellence.' There are other passages, in which Mr. Shelley speaks directly in his own person. In what he calls an ode to Liberty, he tells us that she did

> —'groan, not weep,
> When from its sea of death to kill and burn
> The Galilæan serpent forth did creep
> And made thy world an undistinguishable heap.'
>
> [ll. 117–20]

And after a few stanzas he adds,

[Quotes ll. 211–33 of the 'Ode to Liberty':

> 'O, that the free would stamp the impious name
> Of * * * * * * into the dust! or write it there,
> So that this blot upon the page of fame
> Were as a serpent's path, which the light air
> Erases, and that the flat sands close behind!
>
> . . .
> . . .
>
> Of its own awless soul, or of the power unknown!'

In the 1820 edition this had been printed with *four* asterisks in l. 212. The rough draft in the Boscombe MS reads 'KING']

At present we say nothing of the harshness of style and incongruity of metaphor, which these verses exhibit. We do not even ask what is or can be meant by *the kneeling of human thought before the judgment-throne of its own awless soul*: for it is a praiseworthy precaution in an author, to temper irreligion and sedition with nonsense, so that he may avail himself, if need be, of the plea of lunacy before the tribunals of his country. All that we now condemn, is the wanton gratuitous impiety thus obtruded on the world. If any one, after a serious investigation of the truth of Christianity, still doubts or disbelieves, he is to be pitied and pardoned; if he is a good man, he will himself lament that he has not come to a different conclusion; for even the enemies of our faith admit, that it is precious for the restraints which it imposes on human vices, and for the consolations which it furnishes under the evils of life. But what is to be said of a man, who, like Mr. Shelley, wantonly and unnecessarily goes out of his way, not to reason against, but to revile Christianity and its author? Let him adduce his arguments against our religion, and we shall tell him where to find them answered: but let him not presume to insult the world, and to profane the language in which he writes, by rhyming invectives against a faith of which he knows nothing but the name.

The real cause of his aversion to Christianity is easily discovered.

Christianity is the great prop of the social order of the civilized world; this social order is the object of Mr. Shelley's hatred; and, therefore, the pillar must be demolished, that the building may tumble down. His views of the nature of men and of society are expressed, we dare not say explained, in some of those *'beautiful idealisms of moral excellence,'* (we use his own words,) in which the 'Prometheus' abounds.

'The painted veil, by those who were, called life, which mimicked, as with colours idly spread, all men believed and hoped, is torn aside; the loathsome mask has fallen, the man remains sceptreless, free, uncircumscribed, but man equal, unclassed, tribeless, and nationless, exempt from awe, worship, degree, the king over himself; just, gentle, wise: but man passionless; no, yet free from guilt or pain, which were for his will made or suffered them, nor yet exempt, tho' ruling them like slaves, from chance and death, and mutability, the clogs of that which else might oversoar the loftiest star of unascended heaven, pinnacled dim in the intense inane.'

[III. iv. 190–204]

Our readers may be puzzled to find out the meaning of this paragraph; we must, therefore, inform them that it is not prose, but the conclusion of the third act of Prometheus verbatim et literatim. With this information they will cease to wonder at the absence of sense and grammar; and will probably perceive, that Mr. Shelley's poetry is, in sober sadness, *drivelling prose run mad.*

With the prophetic voice of a misgiving conscience, Mr. Shelley objects to criticism. 'If my attempt be ineffectual, (he says) let the punishment of an unaccomplished purpose have been sufficient; let none trouble themselves to heap the dust of oblivion upon my efforts.' Is there no respect due to common sense, to sound taste, to morality, to religion? Are evil spirits to be allowed to work mischief with impunity, because, forsooth, the instruments with which they work are contemptible? Mr. Shelley says, that his intentions are pure. Pure! They may be so in his vocabulary; for, (to say nothing of his having unfortunately mistaken nonsense for poetry, and blasphemy for an imperious duty,) vice and irreligion, and the subversion of society are, according to his system, pure and holy things; Christianity, and moral virtue, and social order, are alone impure. But we care not about his intentions, or by what epithet he may choose to characterize them, so long as his works exhale contagious mischief. On his own principles he must admit, that, in exposing to the public what we believe to be the character and tendency of his writings, we discharge a sacred duty. He professes to write in order to reform the world. The essence of the proposed reformation is the destruction of religion and government. Such a reformation is not to our taste; and he must, therefore, applaud us for scrutinizing the merits of works which are intended to promote so detestable a purpose. Of Mr. Shelley himself we know nothing, and desire to know nothing. Be his private qualities what they may, his poems (and it is only with his poems that we have any concern) are at war with reason, with taste, with virtue, in short, with all that dignifies man, or that man reveres.

From the unsigned review (possibly by Rev. George Croly[1]) of *Adonais* (1821), in *Blackwood's Edinburgh Magazine*, December 1821.

[All quotations are as printed in the review. They diverge markedly from readings now generally accepted]

The present story is thus:—A *Mr John Keats*, a young man who had left a decent calling for the melancholy trade of Cockney-poetry, has lately died of a consumption, after having written two or three little books of verses, much neglected by the public. His vanity was probably wrung not less than his purse; for he had it upon the authority of the Cockney Homers and Virgils, that he might become a light to their region at a future time. But all this is not necessary to help a consumption to the death of a poor sedentary man, with an unhealthy aspect, and a mind harassed by the first troubles of verse-making. The New School, however, will have it that he was slaughtered by a criticism of the Quarterly Review.—"O flesh, how art thou fishified!"—There is even an aggravation in this cruelty of the Review—for it had taken three or four years to slay its victim, the deadly blow having been inflicted at least as long since. We are not now to defend a publication so well able to defend itself. But the fact is, that the Quarterly finding before it a work at once silly and presumptuous, full of the servile *slang* that Cockaigne dictates to its servitors, and the vulgar indecorums which that Grub Street Empire rejoiceth to applaud, told the truth of the volume, and recommended a change of manners and of masters to the scribbler. Keats wrote on; but he wrote *indecently*, probably in the indulgence of his social propensities. He selected from Boccacio, and, at the feet of the Italian Priapus, supplicated for fame and farthings.

"Both halves the winds dispersed in empty air."[2]

Mr P. B. Shelly having been the person appointed by the *Pisan*

---

[1] It has been suggested that William Maginn may have been responsible for the parodies which the review contains.

[2] As Mr Roy Minton has suggested to me, this is presumably a distortion of *The Rape of the Lock*, II. 45–6.

triumvirate to canonize the name of this apprentice, "nipt in the bud," as he fondly tells us, has accordingly produced an Elegy, in which he weeps "after the manner of Moschus for Bion." The canonizer is worthy of the saint.—"*Et tu, Vitula!*"—Locke says, that the most resolute liar cannot lie more than once in every three sentences. Folly is more engrossing; for we could prove, from the present Elegy, that it is possible to write two sentences of pure nonsense out of every three. A more faithful calculation would bring us to ninety-nine out of every hundred, or,—as the present consists of only fifty-five stanzas,—leaving about five readable lines in the entire. It thus commences:—

> "O weep for Adonais—he is dead!
> O, weep for Adonais! though our tears
> *Thaw not the frost* which binds so dear a head!
> And thou, sad hour! selected from all years
> *To mourn our loss*, rouse thy obscure compeers,
> *And teach them thine own sorrow, say with me
> Died* Adonais! till the *future does
> Forget the past*. His fate and fame shall be
> *An echo and a light!!* unto eternity."[1]

Now, of this unintelligible stuff the whole fifty-five stanzas are composed. Here an hour—a *dead* hour too—is to say that Mr J. Keats died *along with it!* yet this hour has the heavy business on its hands of mourning the loss of its *fellow-defunct*, and of rousing all its *obscure compeers* to be taught its *own sorrow*, &c. Mr Shelley and his tribe have been panegyrized in their turn for power of language; and the man of "Table-talk" swears by all the gods he owns, that he has a great command of words, to which the most eloquent effusions of the Fives Court are *occasionally* inferior. But any man may have the command of every word in the vocabulary, if he will fling them like pebbles from a sack; and even in the most fortuitous flinging, they will sometimes fall in pleasing though useless forms. The art of the modern *Della Cruscan* is thus to eject every epithet that he can conglomerate in his piracy through the Lexicon, and throw them out to settle as they will. He follows his own rhymes, and shapes his subject to the close of his measure. He is a glutton of all names of colours, and flowers, and smells, and tastes, and crowds his verse with scarlet, and blue, and yellow, and green; extracts tears from every thing, and makes moss and mud hold regular conversations with him. "A goose-pye talks,"—it does more, it thinks, and has its peculiar sensibilities,—it smiles and weeps, raves to the stars,

[1] The italics, double exclamation marks and block capitals here and elsewhere are the reviewer's.

and is a listener to the western wind, as fond as the author himself.

On these principles, a hundred or a hundred thousand verses might be made, equal to the best in Adonais, without taking the pen off the paper. The subject is indifferent to us, let it be the "Golden age," or "Mother Goose,"—"Waterloo," or the "Wit of the Watch-house,"—"Tom Thumb," or "Thistlewood." We will undertake to furnish the requisite supply of blue and crimson daisies and dandelions, not with the toilsome and tardy lutulence of the puling master of verbiage in question, but with a burst and torrent that will sweep away all his weedy trophies. . . .

. . . *Percy Byshe* feels his hopelessness of poetic reputation, and therefore lifts himself on the stilts of blasphemy. He is the only verseman of the day, who has dared, in a Christian country, to work out for himself the character of direct ATHEISM! In his present poem, he talks with impious folly of "the *envious* wrath of man or GOD!" Of a

> "Branded and ensanguined brow,
> Which was like *Cain's* or CHRIST's."

Offences like these naturally come before a more effective tribunal than that of criticism. We have heard it mentioned as the only apology for the predominant irreligion and nonsense of this person's works, that his understanding is unsettled. But in his Preface, there is none of the exuberance of insanity; there is a great deal of folly, and a great deal of bitterness, but nothing of the wildness of his poetic fustian. The Bombastes Furioso of these stanzas cools into sneering in the preface; and his language against the *death-dealing* Quarterly Review, which has made such havoc in the Empire of Cockaigne, is merely malignant, mean, and peevishly personal. We give a few stanzas of this performance, taken as they occur.

> "O weep for Adonais! He is dead!
> Weep, melancholy mother, wake and weep;
> Yet *wherefore?* quench within their burning bed
> Thy *fiery* tears, and let thy *loud* heart keep
> Like his, a mute and uncomplaining sleep,
> For he is gone, where all things wise and fair
> *Descend!* Oh dream not that the *amorous* deep
> Will yet restore him to the vital air.
> Death *feeds* on his *mute voice*, and *laughs* at our despair."

The seasons and a whole host of personages, ideal and otherwise, come to lament over *Adonais*. They act in the following manner:

> "Grief made the young Spring *wild*, and she threw down
> Her kindling buds, as if she Autumn were,
> Or they dead leaves, since her delight is flown,

374

For whom should she have wak'd the sullen year?
To Phœbus was not Hyacinth so dear,
Nor to himself Narcissus, as to both,
Thou, Adonais; wan they stand, and sere,
Amid the drooping comrades of their youth,
With dew all turn'd to tears, odour to sighing ruth."

Here is left, to those whom it may concern, the pleasant perplexity, whether the lament for Mr J. Keats is shared between Phœbus and Narcissus, or Summer and Autumn. It is useless to quote those absurdities any farther *en masse*, but there are flowers of poesy thickly spread through the work, which we rescue for the sake of any future Essayist on the Bathos.

Absurdity.
The green lizard, and the golden snake,
Like *unimprison'd* flowers out of their trance awake. An hour—

. . .

Say, with me
Died Adonais, *till the Future dares*
Forget the Past—his fate and fame shall be
An *echo* and a *light* to all eternity.

. . .

Whose *tapers yet* burn there the night of Time,
For which *Suns perish'd!*

. . .

Echo,—pined away
Into a *shadow* of all *sounds!*

. . .

That mouth whence it was wont to draw the breath
Which gave it strength to pierce the guarded wit!

. . .

Comfortless!
As *silent* lighting leaves the starless night.

. . .

Live thou whose *infamy* is not thy *fame!*

. . .

Thou *noteless* blot on a remembered name!

. . .

We in mad trance *strike with our spirit's knife,*
Invulnerable nothings!

. . .

Where lofty thought
Lifts a young heart above its mortal lair,
And love, and life, contend in it—for what

375

Shall be its earthly doom—The dead live there,
And move, like *winds of light*, on dark and stormy air.
. . .

Who mourns for Adonais—oh! come forth,
Fond wretch! and know thyself and him aright,
Clasp with thy *panting* soul the *pendulous Earth!*
. . .

Dart thy spirit's light
Beyond all worlds, until its *spacious might*
Satiate the *void circumference!*
. . .

Then sink
Even to a point within our day and night,
And keep thy heart *light*, lest it make *thee sink*,
When *hope has kindled hope*, and *lured thee to the* brink.
. . .

A light is past from *the revolving year*;
And man and women, and what still is dear
Attracts to crush, repels to make thee wither.
. . .

That benediction, which th' *eclipsing curse*
Of birth can quench not, that sustaining love,
Which, through *the web of being blindly wove*,
By *man, and beast, and earth, and air, and sea!*
Burns bright or dim, as each are mirrors of
The *fire* for which all *thirst*.

Death makes, as becomes him, a great figure in this "Lament,"—
but in rather curious operations. He is alternately a person, a thing,
nothing, &c.

He is, "The coming bulk of Death,"
Then "Death feeds on the *mute voice*."

A clear sprite
Reigns over Death—

Kingly Death
Keeps his pale court.

Spreads apace
The *shadow* of *white* Death.

The damp Death
Quench'd its caress—

Death
Blush'd to annihilation!

Her distress
Roused Death. Death rose and smiled—
He lives, he wakes, 'tis Death is *dead!*

376

As this wild waste of words is altogether beyond our comprehension, we will proceed to the more gratifying office of giving a whole, unbroken specimen of the Poet's powers, exercised on a subject rather more within their sphere.

[There follows an 'Elegy on my Tomcat', which the review pretends was sent in by Shelley, but which is simply a schoolboy parody of the style of *Adonais*. This may have been by Maginn, though Croly himself could have written it easily enough. The review comments:]

This poem strikes us as an evidence of the improvement that an appropriate subject makes in a writer's style. It is incomparably less nonsensical, verbose, and inflated, than Adonais; while it retains all its knowledge of nature, vigour of colouring, and felicity of language.

The review of *Adonais* in *The Literary Gazette*, 8 December 1821.

We have already given some of our columns to this writer's merits, and we will not now repeat our convictions of his incurable absurdity. On the last occasion of our alluding to him, we were compelled to notice his horrid licentiousness and profaneness, his fearful offences to all the maxims that honorable minds are in the habit of respecting, and his plain defiance of Christianity. On the present occasion we are not met by so continued and regular a determination of insult, though there are atrocities to be found in this poem quite enough to make us caution our readers against its pages. Adonais is an elegy after *the manner of Moschus*, on a foolish young man, who, after writing some volumes of very weak, and, in the greater part, of very indecent poetry, died some time since of a consumption: the breaking down of an infirm constitution having, in all probability, been accelerated by the discarding his neckcloth, a practice of the cockney poets, who look upon it as essential to genius, inasmuch as neither Michael Angelo, Raphael nor Tasso are supposed to have worn those antispiritual incumbrances. In short, as the vigour of Sampson lay in his hair, the secret of talent with these persons lies in the neck; and what aspirations can be expected from a mind enveloped in muslin. Keats caught cold in training for a genius, and, after a lingering illness, died, to the great loss of the Independents of South America, whom he had intended to visit with an English epic poem, for the purpose of exciting them to liberty. But death, even the death of the radically presumptuous profligate, is a serious thing; and as we believe that Keats was made presumptuous chiefly by the treacherous puffing of his cockney fellow gossips, and profligate in his poems merely to make them saleable, we regret that he did not live long enough to acquire common sense, and abjure the pestilent and perfidious gang who betrayed his weakness to the grave, and are now panegyrising his memory into contempt. For what is the praise of the cockneys but disgrace, or what honourable inscription can be placed over the dead by the hands of notorious libellers, exiled adulterers, and avowed atheists.

Adonais, an Elegy, is the form in which Mr. Shelley puts forth his woes. We give a verse at random, premising that it consists of fifty-five stanzas, which are, to our seeming, altogether unconnected, interjectional, and nonsensical. We give one that we think among the most comprehensible. An address to Urania:—

Most musical of mourners, weep anew!
　　Not all to that bright station dared to climb;
And *happier they their happiness who knew,*
　　Whose tapers yet burn thro' that night of time
In which suns perish'd; others more sublime,
　　Struck by the *envious* wrath of man or God!!
Have sunk extinct in their refulgent prime;
　　And some yet live. . . .

[st. v; reviewer's italics, capital G in God
and double exclamation marks]

Now what is the meaning of this, or of any sentence of it, except indeed that horrid blasphemy which attributes crime to the Great Author of all virtue! The rest is mere empty absurdity. If it were worth our while to dilate on the folly of the production, we might find examples of every species of the ridiculous within those few pages.

Mr. Shelley summons all kinds of visions round the grave of this young man, who, if he has now any feeling of the earth, must shrink with shame and disgust from the touch of the hand that could have written that impious sentence. These he classifies under names, the greater number as new we believe to poetry as strange to common sense. Those are—

Desires and *Adorations,*
Winged *Persuasions* and veiled Destinies,
Splendours, and *Glooms,* and glimmering *Incarnations*
　　Of hopes and fears and twilight Phantasies,
And Sorrow with her family of *Sighs,*
　　And Pleasure, *blind with tears!* led by the *gleam*
Of her own *dying* SMILE instead of eyes!!

[st. xiii; reviewer's italics, block capitals, and exclamation marks]

Let our readers try to imagine these weepers, and close with "*blind* Pleasure led," by what? "by the *light* of *her own dying smile*—instead of *eyes*!!!"

We give some specimens of Mr. S.'s[1]

Nonsense—pastoral.

Lost Echo sits amid the voiceless mountains,[2]
    And feeds her grief with his remember'd lay,
    And will no more reply to winds and fountains.

Nonsense—physical.

. . . for whose disdain she (Echo) pin'd away
    Into a *shadow* of all *sounds!*

Nonsense—vermicular.

Flowers springing from the corpse
    . . . . illumine death
And *mock* the *merry* worm that wakes beneath.

Nonsense—pathetic.

Alas! that all we lov'd of him should be,
    But for our grief, as if it had not been,
And grief itself be mortal! woe is me!

Nonsense—nondescript.

In the death chamber for a moment Death,
    Blush'd to annihilation!

Nonsense—personal.

A pardlike spirit, beautiful and swift—
    A love in *desolation mask'd,*—a Power
Girt *round with weakness;*—it can scarce *uplift*
    The *weight* of the *superincumbent hour!*

We have some idea that this fragment of character is intended for Mr. Shelley himself. It closes with a passage of memorable and ferocious blasphemy:—

He with a sudden hand
Made bare his branded and ensanguin'd brow,
Which was like Cain's or CHRIST's!!!

[1] The reviewer italicizes, supplies exclamation marks, and quotes inaccurately—*Ed.*

[2] Though there is *no Echo* and the mountains are *voiceless*, the woodmen, nevertheless, in the last line of this verse hear 'A drear murmur between their Songs'!! [Reviewer's footnote.]

What can be said to the wretched person capable of this daring profanation. The name of the first murderer—the accurst of God—brought into the same aspect image with that of the Saviour of the World! We are scarcely satisfied that even to quote such passages may not be criminal. The subject is too repulsive for us to proceed even in expressing our disgust for the general folly that makes the Poem as miserable in point of authorship, as in point of principle. We know that among a certain class this outrage and this inanity meet with some attempt at palliation, under the idea that frenzy holds the pen. That any man who insults the common order of society, and denies the being of God, is essentially mad we never doubted. But for the madness, that retains enough of rationality to be wilfully mischievous, we can have no more lenity than for the appetites of a wild beast. The poetry of the work is *contemptible*—a mere collection of bloated words heaped on each other without order, harmony, or meaning; the refuse of a schoolboy's commonplace book, full of the vulgarisms of pastoral poetry, yellow gems and blue stars, bright Phoebus and rosy-fingered Aurora; and of this stuff is Keats's wretched Elegy compiled.

We might add instances of like incomprehensible folly from every stanza. A heart *keeping*, a mute *sleep*, and death *feeding* on a mute *voice*, occur in one verse (page 8); Spring in despair "throws down her *kindling* buds as if she Autumn were," a thing we never knew Autumn do with buds of any sort, the kindling kind being unknown to our botany; a *green lizard* is like an *unimprisoned flame*, *waking* out of its *trance* (page 13). In the same page the *leprous corpse* touched by the tender spirit of Spring, so as to exhale itself in flowers, is compared to *"incarnations of the stars, when splendour is changed to fragrance!!!"* Urania (page 15) *wounds* the "invisible palms of her tender feet" by treading on human hearts as she journeys to see the corpse. Page 22, somebody is asked to "clasp with panting soul the pendulous earth," an image which, we take it, exceeds that of Shakspeare, to "put a girdle about it in forty minutes."

It is so far a fortunate thing that this piece of impious and utter absurdity can have little circulation in Britain. The copy in our hands is one of some score sent to the Author's intimates from Pisa, where it has been printed in a quarto form "with the types of Didot," and two learned Epigraphs from Plato and Moschus. Solemn as the subject is, (for in truth we must grieve for the early death of any youth of literary ambition,) it is hardly possible to help laughing at the mock solemnity with which Shelley charges the Quarterly Review for having murdered his friend with . . . a critique! If Criticism killed the disciples of that school, Shelley would not have been alive to write an Elegy on another:—but the whole is most farcical from a pen which, on other occasions, has treated of the soul, the body, life and death agreeably to the opinions, the principles, and the practice of Percy Bysshe Shelley.

From Leigh Hunt's unsigned 'Letters to the readers of *The Examiner* "On the Quarterly Review"' concerning *Prometheus Unbound* and *Ode to a Skylark*, 9, 16, 23 June 1822.

As a conclusive proof of Mr. Shelley's nonsense, the Reviewer selects one of his passages which most require attention, separates it from its proper context, and turns it into prose: after which he triumphantly informs the reader that this prose is not prose, but "the conclusion of the third act of *Prometheus verbatim et literatim.*" Now poetry has often a language as well as music of its own, so distinct from prose, and so universally allowed a right to the distinction (which none are better aware of than the versifiers in the *Quarterly Review*), that secretly to decompose a poetical passage into prose, and then call for a criticism of a reader upon it, is like depriving a body of its distinguishing properties, or confounding their rights and necessities, and then asking where they are. Again, to take a passage abruptly from its context, especially when a context is more than usually necessary to its illustration, is like cutting out a piece of shade from a picture, and reproaching it for want of light. And finally, to select an obscure passage or two from an author, or even to shew that he is often obscure, and then to pretend from these specimens, that he is nothing but obscurity and nonsense, is mere dishonesty. . . .

The lines in question from Mr. Shelley's poem are as follow. A spirit is describing a mighty change that has just taken place on earth. It is the consummation of a state of things for which all the preceding part of the poem has been yearning:—

[Quotes Act III. iv. 190–204: 'The painted veil . . . Pinnacled dim in the intense inane']

That is to say,—The veil, or superficial state of things, which was called life by those who lived before us, and which had nothing but an idle resemblance to that proper state of things, which we would fain have thought it, is no longer existing. The loathsome mask is fallen; and the being who was compelled to wear it, is now what he ought to be, one of a great family who are their own rulers, just, gentle, wise, and passionless; no, not passionless, though free from guilt or pain, which were only the consequences of their former wilful mistakes; nor are they exempt, though they turn them to the best and most philosophical account, from chance, and death, and mutability; things, which are the clogs of that lofty spirit of humanity, which else might rise beyond all that we can conceive of the highest and happiest star of heaven, pinnacled, like an almost viewless atom, in the space of the universe.—*The intense inane* implies excess of emptiness, and is a phrase of Miltonian construction, like "the palpable obscure" and "the vast abrupt." Where is the unintelligible nonsense of all this? and where is the want of "grammar," with which the "pride" of the Reviewer, as *Mr. Looney M'Twoulter* says, would "come over" him?

Mr. Shelley has written a great deal of poetry equally unmetaphysical and beautiful. The whole of the tragedy of the *Cenci*, which the Reviewers do not think it to their interest to notice, is written in a style equally plain and noble. But we need not go farther than the volume before us, though, according to the Reviewer, the "whole" of it does not contain "*one* original image of nature, *one* simple expression of human feeling, or *one* new association of the appearances of the moral with those of the material world." We really must apologize to all intelligent readers who know anything of Mr. Shelley's genius, for appearing to give more notice to these absurdities than they are worth; but there are good reasons why they ought to be exposed. The *Prometheus* has already spoken for itself. Now take the following *Ode to a Skylark*, of which I will venture to say, that there is not in the whole circle of lyric poetry a piece more *full* of "original images of nature, of simple expressions of human feeling, and of the associations of the appearances of the moral with those of the material world." You shall have it entire, for it is as fitting for the season, as it is true to the musical and etherial beauty of its subject.

[Quotes *To a Skylark* entire]

I know of nothing more beautiful than this,—more choice of tones, more natural in words, more abundant in exquisite, cordial, and most poetical associations. One gets the stanzas by heart unawares, and repeats them like "snatches of old tunes." To say that nobody who writes in the *Quarterly Review* could produce any thing half as good (unless Mr. Wordsworth writes in it, which I do not believe he does) would be sorry praise. When Mr. Gifford "sings" as the phrase is, one is reminded of nothing but snarling. Mr. Southey, though the gods have made him more poetical than Mr. Gifford, is always affecting something original, and tiring one to death with common-place. "Croker," as Goldsmith says, "rhymes to joker;" and as to the chorus of priests and virgins,—of scribes and pharisees, —which make up the poetical undersong of the Review, it is worthy of the discordant mixture of worldliness and religion, of faith and bad practice, of Christianity and malignity, which finds in it something ordinary enough to merit its approbation.

From Leigh Hunt's unsigned review of *Adonais* in *The Examiner*, 7 July 1822.

Since I left London, Mr. Shelley's *Adonais, or Elegy on the Death of Mr. Keats*, has, I find, made its appearance. I have not seen the London edition; but I have an Italian one printed at Pisa, with which I must content myself at present. The other was to have had notes. It is not a poem calculated to be popular, any more than the *Prometheus Unbound*; it is of too abstract and subtle a nature for that purpose; but it will delight the few, to whom Mr. Shelley is accustomed to address himself. Spenser would be pleased with it if he were living. A mere town reader and a Quarterly Reviewer will find it *caviare*. *Adonais*, in short, is such an elegy as poet might be expected to write upon poet. The author has had before him his recollections of Lycidas, of Moschus and Bion, and of the doctrines of Plato; and in the stanza of the most poetical of poets, Spenser, has brought his own genius, in all its etherial beauty, to lead a pomp of Loves, Graces, and Intelligences, in honour of the departed.

Nor is the Elegy to be considered less sincere, because it is full of poetical abstractions. Dr. Johnson would have us believe, that *Lycidas* is not "the effusion of real passion."—"Passion," says he, in his usual conclusive tone, (as if the force of critic could no further go) "plucks no berries from the myrtle and ivy; nor calls upon Arethuse and Mincius, nor tells of rough Satyrs and Fauns with cloven heel. Where there is leisure for fiction, there is little grief." This is only a more genteel common-place, brought in to put down a vulgar one. Dr. Johnson, like most critics, had no imagination; and because he found nothing natural to his own impulses in the associations of poetry, and saw them so often abused by the practice of versifiers inferior to himself, he was willing to conclude, that on natural occasions they were always improper. But a poet's world is as real to him as the more palpable one to people in general. He spends his time in it as truly as Dr. Johnson did his in Fleet-street or at the club. Milton felt that the happiest hours he had passed with his friend had been passed in the regions of poetry. He had been accustomed to be transported with him "beyond the visible diurnal sphere" of his fire-side and supper-table, things which he could record nevertheless with a due relish. (See the *Epitaphium Damonis*.) The next step was to fancy himself again among them, missing the dear companion of his walks; and then it is that the rivers murmur complainingly, and the flowers hang their heads,—which to a truly poetical habit of mind, though to no other, they may literally be said to do, because such is the aspect which they present to an afflicted imagination. "I see nothing in the world but melancholy," is a common phrase with persons who are suffering under a great loss. With ordinary minds in this condition the phrase implies a vague feeling, but still an actual one. The poet, as in other instances, gives it a life and particularity. The practice has doubtless been abused; so much so, that even some imaginative minds may find it difficult at first to fall in with it, however beautifully managed. But the very abuse shews that it is founded in a principle in nature. And a great deal depends upon the character of the poet. What is mere frigidity and affectation in common magazine rhymers, or men of wit and fashion about town, becomes another thing in minds accustomed to live in the sphere I spoke of. It was as unreasonable in Dr. Johnson to sneer at Milton's grief in *Lycidas*, as it was reasonable in him to laugh at Prior and Congreve for comparing Chloe to Venus and Diana, and *pastoralizing* about Queen Mary. Neither the turn of their genius, nor their habits of life, included this sort of ground. We feel that Prior should have stuck to his tuckers and boddices, and Congreve appeared in his proper Court-mourning.

Milton perhaps overdid the matter a little when he personified the poetical enjoyments of his friend and himself under the character of actual shepherds. Mr. Shelley is the more natural in this respect, inasmuch as he is entirely abstract and imaginative, and recalls his lamented acquaintance to mind in no other shape than one strictly poetical. I say acquaintance, because such Mr. Keats was; and it happens, singularly enough, that the few hours which he and Mr. Shelley passed together were almost entirely of a poetical character. I recollect one evening in particular, which they spent with the writer of these letters in composing verses on a given subject. But it is not as a mere acquaintance, however poetical, that Mr. Shelley records him. It is as the intimate acquaintance of all lovely and lofty thoughts, as the nursling of the Muse, the hope of her coming days, the creator of additional Beauties and Intelligences for the adornment and inhabitation of the material world. The poet commences with calling upon Urania to weep for her favourite; and in a most beautiful stanza, the termination of which is in the depths of the human heart, informs us where he is lying. You are aware that Mr. Keats died at Rome:—

> To that high Capital, where kingly Death
> Keeps his pale court in beauty and decay,
> He came;—and bought, with price of purest breath,
> A grave among the eternal—Come away!
> Haste, while the vault of blue Italian day

Is yet his fitting charnel-roof! while still
He lies, as if in dewy sleep he lay;
Awake him not! surely he takes his fill
Of deep and liquid rest, forgetful of all ill.

"The forms of things unseen," which Mr. Keats's imagination had
turned into shape,—the "airy nothings" to which it is the high
prerogative of the poet to give "a local habitation and a name," are
then represented, in a most fanciful manner, as crowding about his
lips and body, and lamenting him who called them into being:

And others came . . . Desires and Adorations,
Winged Persuasions and veiled Destinies,
Splendours, and glooms, and glimmering Incarnations
Of hopes and fears, and twilight Phantasies;
And Sorrow, with her family of sighs;
And Pleasure, blind with tears, led by the gleam
Of her own dying smile instead of eyes.
All he had loved, and moulded into thought,
From shape, and hue, and odour, and sweet sound,
Lamented Adonais.

A phrase in the first line of the following passage would make an
admirable motto for that part of the *Literary Pocket Book*, in which
the usual lists of kings and other passing dominations are superseded by a list of Eminent Men:

And he is gathered to *the kings of thought*,
Who waged contention with their time's decay,
And of the past are all that cannot pass away.

The spot in which Mr. Keats lies buried is thus finely pointed out.
The two similes at the close are among the happiest we recollect,
especially the second:

Go thou to Rome,—at once the Paradise,
The grave, the city, and the wilderness;
And where its wrecks like shattered mountains rise,
And flowering weeds, and fragrant copses dress
The bones of Desolation's nakedness,
Pass, till the Spirit of the spot shall lead
Thy footsteps to a slope of green access,
Where, like an infant's smile, over the dead,
A light of laughing flowers along the grass is spread

And gray walls moulder round, on which dull Time
Feeds, like slow fire upon a hoary brand.

In the course of the poem some living writers are introduced; among whom Lord Byron is designated as

> The Pilgrim of Eternity, whose fame
> Over his living head like Heaven is bent
> An early but enduring monument!

The poet of Ireland is called, with equal brevity and felicity,

> The sweetest lyrist of her saddest wrong:

And among "others of less note," is modestly put one, the description of whom is strikingly calculated to excite a mixture of sympathy and admiration. The use of the Pagan mythology is supposed to have been worn out; but in fact, they who say so, or are supposed to have worn it out, never wore it [at] all. See to what a natural and noble purpose a true scholar can turn it:—

> He, as I guess,
> Had gazed on Nature's naked loveliness,
> Actaeon-like, and now he fled astray
> With feeble steps o'er the world's wilderness,
> And his own thoughts, along that rugged way,
> Pursued, like raging hounds, their father and their prey.
>
> A pard-like Spirit, beautiful and swift—
> A Love in desolation masked;—a Power
> Girt round with weakness;—it can scarce uplift
> The weight of the superincumbent hour;
> It is a dying lamp, a falling shower,
> A breaking billow;—even while we speak
> Is it not broken? On the withering flower
> The killing sun smiles brightly: on a cheek
> The life can burn in blood, even while the heart may break.
>
> Ah! te meae si partem animae rapit
> Maturior vis!

But the poet is here, I trust, as little of a prophet, as affection and a beautiful climate, and the extraordinary and most vital energy of his spirit, can make him. The singular termination of this description, and the useful reflections it is calculated to excite, I shall reserve for another subject in my next. But how is it, that even that termination could not tempt the malignant common-place of the Quarterly Reviewers to become blind to the obvious beauty of this poem, and venture upon laying some of its noble stanzas before their readers? How is it that in their late specimens of Mr. Shelley's powers they said nothing of the style and versification of the majestic tragedy of *The Cenci*, which would have been equally intelligible to the lowest, and instructive to the highest, of their readers? How is it that they have not even hinted at the existence of this *Elegy on the Death of Mr. Keats*, though immediately after the arrival of copies of it from Italy they thought proper to give a pretended review of a poem which appeared to them the least calculated for their reader's under-standings? And finally, how happens it, that Mr. Gifford has never taken any notice of Mr. Keats's *last* publication,—the beautiful volume containing *Lamia*, the Story from Boccaccio, and that magnificent fragment *Hyperion*? Perhaps the following passage of the Elegy will explain:

> Our Adonais has drunk poison!—Oh,
> What deaf and viperous murderer could crown
> Life's early cup with such a draught of woe?
> The nameless worm would now itself disown:
> It felt, yet could escape the magic tone
> Whose prelude held all envy, hate, and wrong
> But what was howling in one breast alone
> Silent with expectation, of the song,
> Whose master's hand is cold, whose silver lyre unstrung.

> Live thou, whose infamy is not thy fame!
> Live! fear no heavier chastisement from me,
> Thou noteless blot on a remembered name!
> But be thyself, and know thyself to be!
> And ever at thy season be thou free
> To spill the venom when thy fangs o'erflow:
> Remorse and Self-Contempt shall cling to thee,
> Hot Shame shall burn upon thy secret brow,
> And like a beaten hound tremble thou shalt—as now.

This, one would think, would not have been "unintelligible" to the dullest *Quarterly* peruser, who had read the review of Mr. Keats's *Endymion*. Nor would the following perhaps have been quite obscure:

> Nor let us weep that our delight is fled
> Far from these carrion kites that scream below;
> He wakes or sleeps with the enduring dead;
> Thou canst not soar where he is sitting now.
> Dust to the dust! but the pure spirit shall flow
> Back to the burning fountain whence it came,
> A portion of the Eternal, which must glow

Through time and change, unquenchably the same,
While thy cold embers choke the sordid hearth of shame.

However, if further explanation had been wanted, the Preface to the
Elegy furnishes it in an abundance, which even the meanest admirers
of Mr. Gifford could have no excuse for not understanding. Why
then did he not quote this? Why could he not venture, once in his
life, to try and look a little fair and handsome; and instead of making
all sorts of misrepresentations of his opponents, lay before his
readers something of what his opponents say of him? He only ventures to allude, in convulsive fits and starts, and then not by name,
to the *Feast of the Poets*. He dares not even allude to Mr. Hazlitt's
epistolary dissection of him. And now he, or some worthy co-
adjutor for him, would pretend that he knows nothing of Mr. Shelley's
denouncement of him, but criticises his other works out of pure
zeal for religion and morality! Oh these modern "Scribes, Pharisees,
and Hypocrites!" How exactly do they resemble their prototypes of
old!

From Hazlitt's unsigned review of Shelley's *Posthumous Poems*
(1824) in *The Edinburgh Review*, July 1824.

Mr Shelley's style is to poetry what astrology is to natural science—
a passionate dream, a straining after impossibilities, a record of fond
conjectures, a confused embodying of vague abstractions,—a fever
of the soul, thirsting and craving after what it cannot have, indulging
its love of power and novelty at the expense of truth and nature,
associating ideas by contraries, and wasting great powers by their
application to unattainable objects.

Poetry, we grant, creates a world of its own; but it creates it out
of existing materials. Mr Shelley is the maker of his own poetry—
out of nothing. Not that he is deficient in the true sources of strength
and beauty, if he had given himself fair play (the volume before us,
as well as his other productions, contains many proofs to the contrary): But, in him, fancy, will, caprice, predominated over and
absorbed the natural influences of things; and he had no respect for
any poetry that did not strain the intellect as well as fire the imagination—and was not sublimed into a high spirit of metaphysical
philosophy. Instead of giving a language to thought, or lending the
heart a tongue, he utters dark sayings, and deals in allegories and
riddles. His Muse offers her services to clothe shadowy doubts and
inscrutable difficulties in a robe of glittering words, and to turn
nature into a brilliant paradox. We thank him—but we must be
excused. Where we see the dazzling beacon-lights streaming over the
darkness of the abyss, we dread the quicksands and the rocks below.

Mr Shelley's mind was of 'too fiery a quality' to repose (for any continuance) on the probable or the true—it soared 'beyond the visible diurnal sphere,' to the strange, the improbable, and the impossible. He mistook the nature of the poet's calling, which should be guided by involuntary, not by voluntary impulses. He shook off, as an heroic and praiseworthy act, the trammels of sense, custom, and sympathy, and became the creature of his own will. He was 'all air,' disdaining the bars and ties of mortal mould. He ransacked his brain for incongruities, and believed in whatever was incredible. Almost all is effort, almost all is extravagant, almost all is quaint, incomprehensible, and abortive, from aiming to be more than it is. Epithets are applied, because they do not fit: subjects are chosen, because they are repulsive: the colours of his style, for their gaudy, changeful, startling effect, resemble the display of fire-works in the dark, and, like them, have neither durability, nor keeping, nor discriminate form. Yet Mr Shelley, with all his faults, was a man of genius; and we lament that uncontrollable violence of temperament which gave it a forced and false direction. He has single thoughts of great depth and force, single images of rare beauty, detached passages of extreme tenderness; and, in his smaller pieces, where he has attempted little, he has done most. If some casual and interesting idea touched his feelings or struck his fancy, he expressed it in pleasing and unaffected verse: but give him a larger subject, and time to reflect, and he was sure to get entangled in a system. The fumes of vanity rolled volumes of smoke, mixed with sparkles of fire, from the cloudy tabernacle of his thought. The success of his writings is therefore in general in the inverse ratio of the extent of his undertakings; inasmuch as his desire to teach, his ambition to excel, as soon as it was brought into play, encroached upon, and outstripped his powers of execution.

Mr Shelley was a remarkable man. His person was a type and shadow of his genius. His complexion, fair, golden, freckled, seemed transparent with an inward light, and his spirit within him

> ——'so divinely wrought,
> That you might almost say his body thought.'

He reminded those who saw him of some of Ovid's fables. His form, graceful and slender, drooped like a flower in the breeze. But he was crushed beneath the weight of thought which he aspired to bear, and was withered in the lightning-glare of a ruthless philosophy! He mistook the nature of his own faculties and feelings—the lowly children of the valley, by which the skylark makes its bed, and the bee murmurs, for the proud cedar or the mountain-pine, in which the eagle builds its eyry, 'and dallies with the wind, and scorns the sun.' —He wished to make of idle verse and idler prose the frame-work of the universe, and to bind all possible existence in the visionary chain of intellectual beauty—

> 'More subtle web Arachne cannot spin,
> Nor the fine nets, which oft we woven see
> Of scorched dew, do not in th' air more lightly flee.'

Perhaps some lurking sense of his own deficiencies in the lofty walk which he attempted, irritated his impatience and his desires; and urged him on, with winged hopes, to atone for past failures, by more arduous efforts, and more unavailing struggles.

With all his faults, Mr Shelley was an honest man. His unbelief and his presumption were parts of a disease, which was not combined in him either with indifference to human happiness, or contempt for human infirmities. There was neither selfishness nor malice at the bottom of his illusions. He was sincere in all his professions; and he practised what he preached—to his own sufficient cost. He followed up the letter and the spirit of his theoretical principles in his own person, and was ready to share both the benefit and the penalty with others. He thought and acted logically, and was what he professed to be, a sincere lover of truth, of nature, and of human kind. To all the rage of paradox, he united an unaccountable candour and severity of reasoning: in spite of an aristocratic education, he retained in his manners the simplicity of a primitive apostle. An Epicurean in his sentiments, he lived with the frugality and abstemiousness of an ascetick. His fault was, that he had no deference for the opinions of others, too little sympathy with their feelings (which he thought he had a right to sacrifice, as well as his own, to a grand ethical experiment)—and trusted too implicitly to the light of his own mind, and to the warmth of his own impulses. He was indeed the most striking example we remember of the two extremes described by Lord Bacon as the great impediments to human improvement, the love of Novelty, and the love of Antiquity. . . .

Considered in this point of view, his career may not be uninstructive even to those whom it most offended; and might be held up as a beacon and warning no less to the bigot than the sciolist. We wish to speak of the errors of a man of genius with tenderness. His nature was kind, and his sentiments noble; but in him the rage of free inquiry and private judgment amounted to a species of madness. Whatever was new, untried, unheard of, unauthorized, exerted a kind of fascination over his mind. The examples of the world, the opinion of others, instead of acting as a check upon him, served but to impel him forward with double velocity in his wild and hazardous career. Spurning the world of realities, he rushed into the world of nonentities and contingencies, like air into a *vacuum*. If a thing was old and established, this was with him a certain proof of its having no solid foundation to rest upon: if it was new, it was good and right. Every paradox was to him a self-evident truth; every prejudice an undoubted absurdity. The weight of authority, the sanction of ages, the common consent of mankind, were vouchers only for ignorance, error, and imposture. Whatever shocked the feelings of others, conciliated his regard; whatever was light, extravagant, and vain, was to him a proportionable relief from the dulness and stupidity of established opinions. The worst of it however was, that he thus gave great encouragement to those who believe in all received absurdities, and are wedded to all existing abuses: his extravagance seeming to sanction their grossness and selfishness, as theirs were a full justification of his folly and eccentricity. The two extremes in this way often meet, jostle,—and confirm one another. The infirmities of age are a foil to the presumption of youth; and 'there the antics sit,' mocking one another—the ape Sophistry pointing with reckless scorn at 'palsied eld,' and the bed-rid hag, Legitimacy, rattling her chains, counting her beads, dipping her hands in blood, and blessing herself from all change and from every appeal to common sense and reason! Opinion thus alternates in a round of contradictions: the impatience or obstinacy of the human mind takes part with, and flies off to one or other of the two extremes 'of affection' and leaves a horrid gap, a blank sense and feeling in the middle, which seems never likely to be filled up, without a total change in our mode of proceeding. The martello-towers with which we are to repress, if we cannot destroy, the systems of fraud and oppression should not be castles in the air, or clouds in the verge of the horizon, but the enormous and accumulated pile of abuses which have arisen out of their own continuance. The principles of sound morality, liberty and humanity, are not to be found only in a few recent writers, who have discovered the secret of the greatest happiness to the greatest numbers, but are truths as old as the creation. To be convinced of the existence of wrong, we should read history rather than poetry: the levers with which we must work out our regeneration are not the cobwebs of the brain, but the warm, palpitating fibres of the human heart. It is the collision of passions and interests, the petulance of party-spirit, and the perversities of self-will and self-opinion that have been the great obstacles to social improvement—not stupidity or ignorance; and the caricaturing one side of the question and shocking the most pardonable prejudices on the other, is not the way to allay heats or produce unanimity. By flying to the extremes of scepticism, we make others shrink back, and shut themselves up in the strongholds of bigotry and superstition—by mixing up doubtful or offensive matters with salutary and demonstrable truths, we bring the whole into question, fly-blow the cause, risk the principle, and give a handle and a pretext to the enemy to treat all philosophy and all reform as a compost of crude, chaotic, and monstrous absurdities. We thus arm the virtues as well as the vices of the community against us; we trifle with their understandings, and exasperate their self-love; we give to superstition and injustice all their old security and sanctity, as if they were the only alternatives of impiety and profligacy, and league the natural with the selfish prejudices of mankind in hostile array against us. To this consummation, it must be confessed that too many of Mr Shelley's productions pointedly tend. He makes no account of the opinions of others, or the consequences of any of his own; but proceeds—tasking his reason to the utmost to account for every thing, and discarding every thing as mystery and error for which he cannot account by an effort of mere intelligence—measuring man, providence, nature, and even his own heart, by the limits of the understanding—now hallowing high mysteries, now desecrating pure sentiments, according as they fall in with or exceeded those limits; and exalting and purifying, with Promethean heat, whatever he does not confound and debase. . . .

The volume before us is introduced by an imperfect but touching Preface by Mrs Shelley, and consists almost wholly of original pieces, with the exception of *Alastor, or the Spirit of Solitude*, which was out of print; and the admirable Translation of the *May-day Night*, from Goethe's Faustus.

Julian and Maddalo (the first Poem in the collection) is a Conversation or Tale, full of that thoughtful and romantic humanity, but rendered perplexing and unattractive by that veil of shadowy or of glittering obscurity, which distinguished Mr Shelley's writings. The depth and tenderness of his feelings seems often to have interfered with the expression of them, as the sight becomes blind with tears. A dull, waterish vapour, clouds the aspect of his philosophical poetry, like that mysterious gloom which he has himself described as hanging over the Medusa's Head of Leonardo da Vinci. The metre of this poem, too, will not be pleasing to every body. It is in the antique taste of the rhyming parts of Beaumont and Fletcher and Ben Jonson—blank verse in its freedom and unbroken flow, falling into rhymes that appear altogether accidental—very colloquial in the diction—and sometimes sufficiently prosaic. But it is easier showing than describing it. We give the introductory passage.

[Quotes *Julian and Maddalo*, ll. 1–33: 'I rode . . . spirit tame'; ll. 53–111: 'Meanwhile . . . vespers'; and ll. 132–40: 'The broad star . . . by the way']

The march of these lines is, it must be confessed, slow, solemn, sad: there is a sluggishness of feeling, a dearth of imagery, an unpleasant glare of lurid light. It appears to us, that in some poets, as well as in some painters, the organ of colour (to speak in the language of the adepts) predominates over that of form; and Mr Shelley is of the number. We have every where a profusion of dazzling hues, of glancing splendours, of floating shadows, but the objects on which they fall are bare, indistinct, and wild. There is something in the preceding extract that reminds us of the arid style and matter of Crabbe's versification, or that apes the labour and throes of parturition of Wordsworth's blank-verse. It is the preface to a story of Love and Madness—of mental anguish and philo-sophic remedies—not very intelligibly told, and left with most of its mysteries unexplained, in the true spirit of the modern metaphysical style—in which we suspect there is a due mixture of affectation and meagreness of invention.

This poem is, however, in Mr Shelley's best and *least mannered* manner. If it has less brilliancy, it has less extravagance and con-fusion. It is in his stanza-poetry, that his Muse chiefly runs riot, and baffles all pursuit of common comprehension or critical acumen. The *Witch of Atlas*, the *Triumph of Life*, and *Marianne's Dream*, are rhapsodies or allegories of this description; full of fancy and of fire, with glowing allusions and wild machinery, but which it is difficult to read through, from the disjointedness of the materials, the incongruous metaphors and violent transitions, and of which, after reading them through, it is impossible, in most instances, to guess the drift or the moral. They abound in horrible imaginings, like records of a ghastly dream;—life, death, genius, beauty, victory, earth, air, ocean, the trophies of the past, the shadows of the world to come, are huddled together in a strange and hurried dance of words, and all that appears clear, is the passion and paroxysm of thought of the poet's spirit. The poem entitled the *Triumph of Life*, is in fact a new and terrific *Dance of Death*; but it is thus Mr Shelley transposes the appellations of the commonest things, and subsists only in the violence of contrast. How little this poem is deserving of its title, how worthy it is of its author, what an example of the waste of power, and of genius 'made as flax,' and devoured by its own elementary ardours, let the reader judge from the concluding stanzas.

[Quotes ll. 480–535: 'The grove . . . As the sun shapes the clouds' with some omissions and variants as compared with the Oxford text]

Any thing more filmy, enigmatical, discontinuous, unsubstantial than this, we have not seen; nor yet more full of morbid genius and vivifying soul. We cannot help preferring *The Witch of Atlas* to *Alastor, or the Spirit of Solitude;* for, though the purport of each is equally perplexing and undefined, (both being a sort of mental voyage through the unexplored regions of space and time), the execution of the one is much less dreary and lamentable than that of the other. In the 'Witch,' he has indulged his fancy more than his melancholy, and wantoned in the felicity of embryo and crude conceits even to excess.

[Quotes ll. 161–4: 'And there lay Visions . . . bliss'; and ll. 169–176: 'And odours . . . destined minds']

We give the description of the progress of the 'Witch's' boat as a slight specimen of what we have said of Mr Shelley's involved style and imagery.

[Quotes ll. 345–52: 'And down the streams . . . unfathomably'; and ll. 377–84: 'And down . . . lampless way']

This we conceive to be the very height of wilful extravagance and mysticism. Indeed it is curious to remark every where the proneness to the marvellous and supernatural, in one who so resolutely set his face against every received mystery, and all traditional faith. Mr Shelley must have possessed, in spite of all his obnoxious and indiscreet scepticism, a large share of credulity and wondering curiosity in his composition, which he reserved from common use, and bestowed upon his own inventions and picturesque caricatures. To every other species of imposture or disguise he was inexorable; and indeed it is his only antipathy to established creeds and legitimate crowns that ever tears the veil from his *ideal* idolatries, and renders him clear and explicit. Indignation makes him pointed and intelligible enough, and breathes into his verse a spirit very different from his own boasted spirit of Love.

The *Letter to a Friend in London* shows the author in a pleasing and familiar, but somewhat prosaic light; and his *Prince Athanase, a Fragment,* is, we suspect, intended as a portrait of the writer. It is amiable, thoughtful, and not much over-charged. We had designed to give an extract, but from the apparently personal and doubtful interest attached to it, perhaps it had better be read altogether, or not at all. We rather choose to quote a part of the *Ode to Naples,* during her brief revolution,—in which immediate and strong local feelings have at once raised and pointed Mr Shelley's style, and made of 'light-winged toys of feathered cupid,' the flaming ministers of Wrath and Justice.

[Quotes ll. 52–90 *passim*: 'Naples! thou Heart of men . . . Thou shalt be great—All haill' and ll. 102–end: 'Didst thou not start . . . worship ever free!']

This Ode for Liberty, though somewhat turbid and overloaded in the diction, we regard as a fair specimen of Mr Shelley's highest powers—whose eager animation wanted only a greater sterness and solidity to be sublime. The poem is dated *September* 1820. Such were then the author's aspirations. He lived to see the result,— and yet Earth does not roll his billows over the heads of its oppressors! The reader may like to contrast with this the milder strain of the following stanzas, addressed to the same city in a softer and more desponding mood.

[Quotes *Stanzas written in Dejection, near Naples*, but without stanza 3 as printed in the Oxford text]

We pass on to some of Mr Shelley's smaller pieces and translations, which we think are in general excellent and highly interesting. His *Hymn of Pan* we do not consider equal to Mr Keats's sounding lines in the Endymion. His *Mont Blanc* is full of beauties and of defects; but it is akin to its subject, and presents a wild and gloomy desolation. GINEVRA, a fragment founded on a story in the first volume of the 'Florentine Observer,' is like a troublous dream, disjointed, painful, oppressive, or like a leaden cloud, from which the big tears fall, and the spirit of the poet mutters deep-toned thunder. We are too much subject to these voluntary inflictions, these 'moods of mind,' these effusions of 'weakness and melancholy,' in the perusal of modern poetry. It has shuffled off, no doubt, its old pedantry and formality; but has at the same time lost all shape or purpose, except that of giving vent to some morbid feeling of the moment. The writer thus discharges a fit of the spleen or a paradox, and expects the world to admire and be satisfied. We are no longer annoyed at seeing the luxuriant growth of nature and fancy clipped into arm-chairs and peacocks' tails; but there is danger of having its stately products choked with unchecked underwood, or weighed down with gloomy nightshade, or eaten up with personality, like ivy clinging round and eating into the sturdy oak! The *Dirge*, at the conclusion of this fragment, is an example of the manner in which this craving after novelty, this desire 'to elevate and surprise,' leads us to 'overstep the modesty of nature,' and the bounds of decorum.

'Ere the sun through heaven once more has roll'd,
The rats in her heart
Will have made their nest,

395

And the worms be alive in her golden hair,
While the spirit that guides the sun,
Sits throned in his flaming chair,
    She shall sleep.'

[Reviewer's italics]

The 'worms' in this stanza are the old and traditional appendages of the grave;—the 'rats' are new and unwelcome intruders; but a modern artist would rather shock, and be disgusting and extravagant, than produce no effect at all, or be charged with a want of genius and originality. In the unfinished scenes of Charles I., (a drama on which Mr Shelley was employed at his death) the *radical* humour of the author breaks forth, but 'in good set terms' and specious oratory. We regret that his premature fate has intercepted this addition to our historical drama. From the fragments before us, we are not sure that it would be fair to give any specimen.

The TRANSLATIONS from Euripides, Calderon, and Goethe in this Volume, will give great pleasure to the scholar and to the general reader. They are executed with equal fidelity and spirit.

From the review of Shelley's *Posthumous Poems* in Constable's *Edinburgh Magazine*, July 1824.

This is the last memorial of a mind singularly gifted with poetical talent, however it may have been obscured, and to many, we doubt not, absolutely eclipsed by its unhappy union with much that is revolting in principle and morality. Mr Shelley was one of those unfortunate beings in whom the imagination had been exalted and developed at the expense of the reasoning faculty; and with the confidence, or presumption, of talent, he was perpetually obtruding upon that public, whose applause he still courted, the startling principles of his religious and political creed. He naturally encountered the fate which even the highest talent cannot avert, when it sets itself systematically in array against opinions which men have been taught to believe and to venerate, and principles with which the majority of mankind are persuaded that the safety of society is connected. He was denounced as a poetical *enfant perdu* by the Quarterly, and passed over in silence by other periodical works, which, while they were loth to censure, felt that they could not dare to praise. Whether abuse of this nature may not engender, or, at all events, increase the evil it professes to cure; and whether in the case of Shelley, as in that of another great spirit of the age, his contemporary and his friend, this contempt for received opinions, at first affected, may not have been rooted and made real by the virulence with which it was assailed, is a question which it is difficult to answer. But now, when death, the great calmer of men's minds, has removed from this scene of critical warfare its unfortunate subject,—when we can turn to the many passages of pure and exquisite beauty, which brighten even the darkest and wildest of his poetical wanderings, with that impartiality which it was vain to expect while the author lived, and wrote, and raved, and reviled,—what mind of genius or poetical feeling would not wish that his errors should be buried with him in the bosom of the Mediterranean, and lament that a mind so fruitful of good as well as of evil, should have been taken from us, before its fire had been tempered by experience, and its troubled but majestic elements had subsided into calmness? . . .

This volume, which contains a republication of his "Alastor," a collection of all his smaller poems which have been scattered through different periodical works, with the addition of several unpublished poems and fragments, and some translations from the Greek and modern languages, possesses exactly the same beauties and defects which characterize his published works—the same solemnity—the same obscurity—the same, or rather greater carelessness, and the same perfection of poetical expression. It is this last quality which will always give to Shelley an original and distinct character among the poets of the age; and in this, we have little hesitation in saying, that we consider him decidedly superior to them all. Every word he uses, even though the idea he labours to express be vague, or exaggerated, or unnatural, is intensely poetical. In no writer of the age is the distinction between poetry and prose so strongly marked: deprive his verses of the rhymes, and still the exquisite beauty of the language, the harmony of the pauses, the arrangement of the sentences, is perceptible. This is in itself a talent of no ordinary kind, perfectly separate in its nature, though generally found united with that vigour of imagination which is essential to a great poet, and in Mr Shelley it overshadows even his powers of conception, which are unquestionably very great. It is by no means improbable, however, that this extreme anxiety to embody his ideas in language of a lofty and uncommon cast, may have contributed to that which is undoubtedly the besetting sin of his poetry, its extreme vagueness and obscurity, and its tendency to allegory and personification.

Hence it is in the vague, unearthly, and mysterious, that the peculiar power of his mind is displayed. Like the Goule in the Arabian Tales, he leaves the ordinary food of men, to banquet among the dead, and revels with a melancholy delight in the gloom of the churchyard and the cemetery. He is in poetry what Sir Thomas Browne is in prose, perpetually hovering on the confines of the grave, prying with a terrible curiosity into the secrets of mortality, and speculating with painful earnestness on every thing that disgusts or appals mankind.

But when, abandoning these darker themes, he yields himself to the description of the softer emotions of the heart, and the more smiling scenes of Nature, we know no poet who has felt more intensely, or described with more glowing colours the enthusiasm of love and liberty, or the varied aspects of Nature. His descriptions have a force and clearness of painting which are quite admirable; and his imagery, which he accumulates and pours forth with the prodigality of genius, is, in general, equally appropriate and original. How forcible is this Italian sunset, from the first poem in the present collection, entitled Julian and Maddalo, a piece of a very wild, and not a very agreeable cast, but rich in eloquent and fervid painting!

[Quotes ll. 68–92]
[Then praises stanzas xxxviii–xlii of *The Witch of Atlas* as 'delicately beautiful']

By far the greater number of the pieces which the present volume contains are fragments, some of them in a very unfinished state indeed; and though we approve the feeling which led the friends of Mr Shelley to collect them all, we question whether a selection, from the more finished pieces, would not have been a more prudent measure, as far as his fame is concerned. It dissolves entirely the illusion which we wish to cherish as to the intuitive inspiration—the *estro* of poetry—to be thus admitted, as it were, into the workshop of Genius, and to see its materials confused and heaped together, before they have received their last touches from the hand of the poet, and been arranged in their proper order. And it is wonderful how much the effect of the finest poem depends on an attention to minutiæ, and how much it may be injured by a harsh line, an imperfect or forced rhyme, a defective syllable, or, as is often the case here, an unfortunate [   ] occurring in the middle of a stanza. Others, however, are fortunately in a more finished state; and though even in these it is probable that much is wanting, which the last touches of the author would have given, we have no fear but that, imperfect as they are, they will bear us out in what we have said of the powers of the poet.

[Then admires the 'quiet stillness' that 'breathes over' the description of the pine forest of the Cascine, near Pisa]

We should pity any one who could peruse the following affecting lines, entitled "Stanzas written in dejection, near Naples," without the strongest sympathy for their unfortunate author.

[Quotes the poem in full]

The following lines also appear to us extremely beautiful, though, in order to preserve the full effect of the rythm, they require some management in the reading.

[Quotes 'When the lamp is shattered' entire]

The following appear to us very much in the style of our old English lyric poets of the age of Charles I.

[Gives 'Rarely, rarely, comest thou', 'Mutability', and 'Swifter far than summer's flight']

The longer poems, from which we have made no extracts, we think less interesting, though some of them, and particularly the Triumph of Life, an imitation of Petrarch's Trionfi, are written with very peculiar power and originality. Some translations are also included in this volume, of which the Scenes from Goethe's Faust, and Calderon's "Magico Prodigioso," are the most interesting.

From the review, by 'E. Haselfoot' (W. S. Walker??), of Shelley's *Posthumous Poems* in *Knight's Quarterly Magazine*, August 1824.

Amidst the crowd of feeble and tawdry writers with which we are surrounded, tantalizing us with a mere shew of power, and rendering their native baldness more disgusting by the exaggerations and distortions with which they attempt to hide it, it is refreshing to meet with a work upon which the genuine mark of intellectual greatness is stamped. Here are no misgivings, no chilling doubts, no reasoning with ourselves as to the grounds of our temporary admiration; no comparison of canons, no reference to criterions of beauty. We feel ourselves raised above criticism, to that of which criticism is only the shadow; we perceive that it is from sources like these that her rules, even where true, are exclusively derived,—servants that know not their master's will,—and we feel that we have no need of them, when all that they could teach us presents itself to us by intuition. It is a reviving feeling—a sense of deliverance and of exaltation; we are emancipated from the minute and narrowing restraints to which an habitual intercourse with petty prejudices almost insensibly subjects us; we breathe freely in the open air of enlarged thought; and we deem ourselves ennobled by our relation to a superior mind, and by the sense of our own capabilities which its grand conceptions awaken in us.

Such were the feelings—mixed, it is true, and alternating with feelings of a different kind—with which we perused the posthumous poems of Percy Shelley. We are aware that this expression of our sentiments will probably astonish some, and scandalize others. We know that public opinion (that opinion to which every one is now required to surrender the independent suggestions of his own reason and conscience, on pain of ridicule and obloquy) has doomed the name of Shelley to unmixed reprobation. We are a review-and-newpaper-ridden people; and while we contend clamorously for the right of thinking for ourselves, we yet guide ourselves unconsciously by the opinion of censors whom we know to be partial and incompetent. Shelley was a leveller in politics—this all knew; and they had been told that Shelley was an Atheist, that he was a man of flagitious character, and that his poems are nothing more than a heap of bombast and verbiage, of immorality and blasphemy. They believe implicitly what they are taught, and he who would disturb the fixed persuasion runs some danger of being himself involved in the obloquy which he would remove from another. We may be excused from ceremony in contradicting the decisions of an authority of which we do not acknowledge the legitimacy. Let it not be supposed that we are standing forth as the panegyrists of Shelley, when we state our belief that the outcry against him originated in other causes than his personal delinquency, whether literary or moral. It was not merely that he erred, but that his errors (so far as they were such) were unpopular, and that he was incapable of concealing them. Could he have truckled to the time,—could he have refrained from violating the majesty of custom,—could he have avoided collision with established interest,—could he have condescended, as many others have done, to mask his peculiar opinions under a decent guise of conformity, he might have remained undisturbed. Besides this, the extravagant lengths to which he carried his system afforded more than ordinary facilities for attack; his poetical errors, being errors of excess and not of effect, were peculiarly obnoxious to that kind of ridicule in which modern criticism delights to indulge; and, to crown all, he was the friend of Leigh Hunt and Hazlitt. Hence the critics of one party assailed him without mercy; and as the vindication of his fame was not calculated to serve any temporary purpose, the critics of the other party forbore to defend him! Blackwood's Magazine first praised him, then abused him, and then praised him again. Their laudatory critiques were acute, vigorous, and written with a true feeling of the excellence which they extolled; their attack was mere vapid banter, betraying its insincerity by its laborious feebleness. The author of the article on the Revolt of Islam in the Quarterly was, undoubtedly, a writer of a different cast from the reviewer of Keats: we believe him to have been a conscientious, and even a benevolent man, whose simplicity of mind had been impaired, as well as his natural perception of beauty deadened, by the habit of reviewing. Hence the scanty measure of cold praise doled out to a work of extraordinary beauty and still more extraordinary promise, a work saturated and glowing all over with poetry beyond example since the days of Comus; hence the harsh and captious tone of the review, so discordant with the subject; and hence the disproportionate space allotted to the confutation of his errors. His attacks on the writer's character are not to be confounded with the wanton personalities so common of late among periodical writers; they were made deliberately and on principle, under the idea (an erroneous one, as it appears to us) that Shelley's situation as promulgator of a new moral theory placed him without the pale of that courtesy which protects private character from public discussion. In the remarks of the second reviewer on Prometheus Unbound, there is some justice, as far as relates to the mysticism of the design, and the intricacy of the style; but when the reviewer asserts that Shelley has never written good poetry, he only proves his own insensibility to whatever is poetical. But we must not linger on this unpleasing subject.

Even if our respect for truth did not prevent us from insulting its dignity by a shew of deference to such assailants, it would avail little to set the public opinion right on a particular subject, unless we could at the same time eradicate the servile principle which is the endless source of errors on all subjects. Our only aim in these remarks is to impress on the reader the self-evident truth, that the intellectual as well as the moral character of Shelley's writings is to be judged of from the writings themselves. With respect then to his poetry, the question admits of a very easy decision. We might appeal to the whole series of his writings, from Alastor to Adonais; but we shall content ourselves with referring to a few passages. If the vision of Alastor in the first mentioned poem, his voyage, and death,—if the exquisite dedication to the Revolt of Islam, the storm with which the poem opens, the allegorical combat which follows, and the appearance of the mysterious Lady on the sea-shore, Laon's history of his early years in the second book, and the dream with which the third opens,—if the Æschylean opening of the Prometheus, and the choral songs at p. 72 and 94, (the latter of which the reviewer has selected, with his usual felicity, as a specimen of words without meaning,)—if the inimitable fragment beginning "How wonderful is Death!" (to which we know not whether Milton himself, at the same early age, produced any thing superior,)—if the Hymn to Intellectual Beauty, the description of the garden in the "Sensitive Plant," the lines beginning "Away! the moor is dark beneath the moon," and those written in Lechlade Church-yard*;—

---

* These two pieces ought to have formed part of the present volume, as Alastor, to which they were originally subjoined is reprinted. The former is

we have selected these as being comparatively free from the fault to which we adverted above;—if these are not poetry, we will not say poetry almost unequalled for beauty of conception, richness, and appropriateness of expression, and melody of versification; we do not insist upon this; we are content to have him degraded to the level of a second or third rate poet;—if these are denied to be poetry, the discussion is at an end; there is no common ground of argument. We are at issue with regard to the very essentials of poetry; for any definition, in which the above passages shall not be included, baffles our comprehension.

With regard to the moral tendency of Shelley's works, the same criterion must be applied. It is nothing to the purpose to say, that they must necessarily be immoral, from the nature of their subjects. Such, indeed, is the received logic—they must be so, therefore they are so: but this is a mere fallacy. It is not the subject on which an author writes, but the spirit in which he treats it, that determines the tendency of his work. It might as well be said that Professor Milman must be a moral and religious writer, because his dramas are on sacred subjects*. The true question is—what is the effect produced by Shelley's writings on the reader? Are they characterized by sentimental impurity, by high-wrought pictures of vice, with sophistical endeavours to confound the right and the wrong, with brutal jests on what is good and generous, and cold-hearted sneers at the belief in human virtue? Are they calculated to foster the sensual or the malignant passions? Are they writings to which a bad man would resort in search of food for his depraved propensities? We answer without hesitation—no. Such spirits, like Milton's builders of Babel, would quickly be "famished of breath" in that "thin clime." Even Wordsworth is scarcely worse adapted to that purpose. The tendency of his writings is uniformly elevated; they teach us, through the medium of lofty images and impassioned exhortation, to rise above petty interests, envy, vanity, and low enjoyments; to investigate and follow out the boundless capabilities of our being; to "fear ourselves, and love all human kind."

We are far, indeed, from holding him forth as a moral writer *par excellence*; though his faults were, perhaps, rather of omission than commission. There is a vagueness in his system; a want of

remarkable for its singular and exquisitely beautiful versification. [Reviewer's footnote.]

* We mean no disparagement to a man of Mr. Milman's talents and acquirements; but we can never hear his works extolled for their religious tendency, without thinking of Jemmy Twitcher in Gray;

"Besides, he repents—*for he talks about God.*"
[Reviewer's footnote.]

substantial foundation for his principles; there is a turbulence, and a feverish restlessness, too much removed from that calm in which wisdom loves to dwell; and there are a few pictures of passion which may be considered as too warmly wrought, sublimed as they are, and almost purified, by the atmosphere of noble thoughts and images with which they are surrounded. But let the reader compare the impression left on him by these poems with that resulting from the perusal of any one of those works which are universally allowed to be immoral; and let him declare, from his heart, whether he considers them writings of the same class. They inculcate truth and simplicity of heart, intellectual liberty and enlargement of thought, a passionate devotion to the graces and sublimities of nature, and above all, a love for others, fervent, deep-seated, persevering, unlimited by place or circumstance, and patient of shame, labour, and suffering, in the glorious endeavour to promote the general welfare;

> "———Overpowering strength
> By weakness, and hostility by love."

They inculcate a belief in the immutability of virtue, in the omnipotence of right intention, and in the final happiness and exaltation of human nature, to be brought about by the exertions and self-sacrifices of the good and wise;

> "Life may change, but it may fly not;
> Hope may vanish, but can die not;
> Truth be veil'd—but still it burneth;
> Love repulsed—but it returneth!"

If this is not religion, it is something not wholly unallied to it; and there are numberless passages of his works in which every worthy and generous mind may recognise, with little or no change, the echo of its own high aspirations; ennobling and consoling truths, clothed in the highest beauty of imagination.

How far, or in what sense, some of the opinions above-mentioned are well founded; whether they are not combined with errors which derogate from their effect; and, above all, how their operation is likely to be qualified by the grand deficiency above alluded to, we will not inquire. We feel our incapability to weigh in a perfect scale the truth and error of his tenets, any more than the good and evil of his life,—and we most willingly resign the solemn task to wiser heads and better hearts than our own. We may however observe, that he has himself protested against the charge of Atheism (and he was not a man to disown an obnoxious opinion); that his ideas on some other subjects appear to us to have been misrepresented; and that his peculiar opinions in politics and theology, instead of being interwoven with the texture of his poems, appear rather as excrescences on the surface, disfiguring them in parts. Were a few of his minor poems, and a small portion of each of his longer ones expunged, and the remainder published under the name of some popular writer, we venture to assert that few would be found to charge them with a mischievous tendency. It is, indeed, remarkable that the worst parts of his poems are those which are devoted to the promulgation of the controverted points; his theory hangs like a leaden weight on his fancy*.

What Shelley was, in some points at least, we have, in the above hasty and imperfect words, delivered our opinion; what he would have been, it is now vain to inquire. We can only state our belief, that he would have developed new treasures in our language, and enriched our literature with some greater and more perfect performance, something transcending all that he had before achieved; and a conjecture not altogether gratuitous, that the troubled current of his opinions would have subsided into the calmness and depth of assured belief. Let us not compromise the dignity of truth, or the sacredness of religious principle, even in favour of those who cannot reward us; but let us think of him in the wisdom of charity, and with that feeling with which a well-constituted mind cannot but regard the premature and sudden disappearance from the earth of the noblest of God's intellectual creations!

We had intended to add something like a delineation of Shelley's poetical character; but we feel that the task would demand many qualifications which we do not possess. It may suffice to say, as a general description, that his element lay in the mixture of passion and imagination—the imagery being, as it were, impregnated with the passion which brooded over it. His extraordinary sensitive power overbalanced his power of reflection; he would otherwise have been even greater than he was. He wants pliancy of genius; no first-rate poet ever possessed less variety of powers; there is not merely a want of thought, but a want of human interest in his

* Such is the case in the Revolt of Islam, in the Prometheus, and above all, in the suppressed poem of Queen Mab, in which extraordinary powers of imagination and language are thrown away on a design incurably bad. Never was there a greater mistake than when the publishers of debauchery and impiety, and their imitators in America, selected this work as calculated to promote the *good cause*. Its merits and its defects alike disqualified it for such a purpose. Shelley was a wretched reasoner—and we could select some singular specimens of logic from this work; but we remember the verdict which he himself afterwards passed on the production of his boyhood. [Reviewer's footnote.]

productions*. But no words can do justice to the mixed sublimity and sweetness of his images. It is as if the solid grandeur of Milton were combined with the thrilling vividness and overpowering sweetness of Jeremy Taylor. It is like the glory of the noontide sun, and the glory of the lightning, united in one. We have left ourselves no room to speak of his marvellous command of language, and the delicious melody of his versification; the sweetness of which would be cloying, were it not supported by a strength equally remarkable. Neither can we do much more than specify the titles of the post-humous poems now before us. They consist of Julian and Maddalo, a tale written in an ill-chosen form, but containing some powerful passages; the Witch of Atlas, a wildly luxuriant fancy-piece (the heroine of which is the prototype of our own Maïmoune;) the Triumph of Life, a Dantesque conception, and composed in the great master's own metre; translations of the Cyclops of Euripides; Homer's Hymn to Mercury, &c.; and Miscellaneous Poems, many of them fragments; besides a reprint of Alastor.

From Leigh Hunt's critique of Shelley's *Posthumous Poems* (apparently written early in 1825, later revised, and printed in this form in *Lord Byron and Some of his Contemporaries*, London, 1828).

The writer who criticised the "Posthumous Poems," in the "Edinburgh Review," does justice to the excellence of Mr. Shelley's intentions, and acknowledges him to be one of those rare persons called men of genius; but accuses him of a number of faults, which he attributes to the predominance of his will, and a scorn of every thing received and conventional. To this cause he traces the faults of his poetry, and what he conceives to be the errors of his philosophy. Furthermore, he charges Mr. Shelley with a want of reverence for antiquity, and quotes a celebrated but not unequivocal passage from Bacon, where the Philosopher, according to the advice of the Prophet, recommends us to take our stand upon the ancient ways, and see what road we are to take for progression. He says Mr. Shelley had "too little sympathy with the feelings of others, which he thought he had a right to sacrifice, as well as his own, to a grand ethical experiment;" and asserts that "if a thing were old and established, this was with him a certain proof of its having no solid foundation to rest upon: if it was new, it was good and right: every paradox was to him a self-evident truth: every prejudice an undoubted absurdity. The weight of authority, the sanction of ages, the common consent of mankind, were vouchers only for ignorance, error, and imposture. Whatever shocked the feelings of others, conciliated his

* We except that most powerful work, the Tragedy of the Cenci. [Reviewer's footnote.]

regard; whatever was light, extravagant, and vain, was to him a proportionable relief from the dulness and stupidity of established opinions." This is caricature; and caricature of an imaginary original.

Alas! Mr. Shelley was so little relieved by what was light and vain, (if I understand what the Reviewer means by those epithets,) and so little disposed to quarrel with the common consent of mankind, where it seemed reasonably founded, that at first he could not endure even the comic parts of Lord Byron's writings, because he thought they tended to produce mere volatility instead of good; and he afterwards came to relish them, because he found an accord with them in the bosoms of society. Whatever shocked the feeling of others so little conciliated his regard, that with the sole exception of matters of religion (which is a point on which the most benevolent Reformers, authors of "grand ethical experiments," in all ages, have thought themselves warranted in hazarding alarm and astonishment,) his own feelings were never more violated than by disturbances given to delicacy, to sentiment, to the affections. If ever it seemed otherwise, as in the subject of his tragedy of the Cenci, it was only out of a more intense apprehensiveness, and the right it gave him to speak. He saw, in every species of tyranny and selfish will, an image of all the rest of the generation. That a love of paradox is occasionally of use to remind commonplaces of their weakness, and to prepare the way for liberal opinions, nobody knows better or has more unequivocally shown than Mr. Shelley's critic; and yet I am not aware that Mr. Shelley was at all addicted to paradox; or that he loved any contradiction, that did not directly contradict some great and tyrannical abuse. Prejudices that he thought innocent, no man was more inclined to respect, or even to fall in with. He was prejudiced in favour of the dead languages; he had a theoretical antipathy to innovations in style; he had almost an English dislike of the French and their literature, a philosopher or two excepted: it cost him much to reconcile himself to manners that were not refined; and even with regard to the prejudices of superstition, or the more poetical sides of popular faith, where they did not interfere with the daily and waking comforts of mankind, he was for admitting them with more than a spirit of toleration. It would be hazardous to affirm that he did not believe in spirits and genii. This is not setting his face against "every received mystery, and all traditional faith." He set his face, not against a mystery nor a self-evident proposition, but against whatever he conceived to be injurious to human good, and whatever his teachers would have forced down his throat, in defiance of the inquiries they had suggested. His opposition to what was established, as I have said before, is always to be considered with reference to that feature in his disposition, and that fact in his history.

406

Of antiquity and authority he was so little a scorner, that his opinions, novel as some of them may be thought, are all to be found in writers, both ancient and modern, and those not obscure ones or empirical, but men of the greatest and wisest, and best names,— Plato and Epicurus, Montaigne, Bacon, Sir Thomas More. Nothing in him was his own, but the genius that impelled him to put philosophical speculations in the shape of poetry, and a subtle and magnificent style, abounding in Hellenisms, and by no means exempt (as he acknowledged) from a tendency to imitate whatever else he thought beautiful, in ancient or modern writers.

But Mr. Shelley was certainly definite in his object: he thought it was high time for society to come to particulars: to know what they would have. With regard to marriage, for instance, he was tired with the spectacle continually presented to his eyes, of a community always feeling sore upon that point, and cowed, like a man by his wife, from attempting some real improvement in it. There was no end, he thought, of setting up this new power, and pulling down that, if the one, to all real home purposes, proceeded just as the other did, and nothing was gained to society but a hope and a disappointment. This, in his opinion, was not the kind of will to be desired, in opposition to one with more definite objects. We must not, he thought, be eternally generalizing, shilly-shallying, and coquetting between public submission and private independence; but let a generous understanding and acknowledgment of what we are in want of, go hand in hand with our exertions in behalf of change; otherwise, when we arrive at success, we shall find success itself in hands that are but physically triumphant—hands that hold up a victory on a globe, a splendid commonplace, as a new-old thing for us to worship. This, to be sure, is standing *super vias antiquas*; but not in order to "make progression." The thing is all to be done over again. If there is "something rotten in the state of Denmark," let us mend it, and not set up Sweden or Norway, to knock down this rottenness with rottenness of their own; continually waiting for others to do our work, and finding them do it in such a manner, as to deliver us bound again into the hands of the old corruptions. We must be our own deliverers. An Essay on the Disinterestedness of Human Action is much; but twenty articles to show that the most disinterested person in the world is only a malcontent and a fanatic, can be of no service but to baffle conduct and resolution, in favour of eternal theory and the talking about it.

Mr. Shelley had no doubt a great deal of will; but the mistake of the Reviewer lies in giving it an antipathetical, instead of a sympathetic character. This may be the fault of some reformers. It may also be a fault of others to lament the want of will in their brethren

407

at one time, and the excess of it at another, but particularly the want; satirizing the sparing and fastidious conduct of the better part of the lovers of freedom, "the inconsistent, vacillating good," and bewailing the long misfortunes of the world, which a few energetic persons might put an end to by a resolute and unconditional exercise of their free agency. The writer in question is not exempt from these inconsistencies. I do not accuse him of want of sympathy. On the contrary, I think the antipathies which he has sometimes given way to so strangely, and the will which he at other times recommends, and at all times sets an example of, arise out of the impatience of his very sympathy with mankind. This it is, which together with his own extraordinary amount of talent, and the interesting evidences of it which continually appear, has for so long a time kept his friends in good blood with him, whatever mood he has happened to be in; though he has tried them, of late, pretty hard. But this it is also, which ought to have led him into a different judgment with regard to Mr. Shelley. A greater portion of will among reformers is desirable; but it does not follow that an occasional excess of it (if such) can or does do the mischief he supposes, or furnishes any excuse worth mention for the outcries and pretended arguments of the opposite party. If he will have a good deal of will, he must occasionally have an excess of it. The party in question, that is to say, all the bad systems and governments existing, with all their slaves and dependents, have an infinite will of their own, which they already make use of, with all their might, to put down every endeavour against it: and the world in general is so deafened with the noise of ordinary things, and the great working of the system which abuses it, that an occasional excess in the lifting up of a reforming voice appears to be necessary to make it listen. It requires the example of a spirit not so prostrate as its own, to make it believe that all hearts are not alike kept under, and that the hope of reformation is not everywhere given up. This is the excuse for such productions as Werter, the Stranger, and other appeals to the first principles of sympathy and disinterestedness. This is the excuse for the paradoxes of Rousseau; for the extravagances of some of the Grecian philosophers (which were necessary to call the attention to all parts of a question); and if I did not wish to avoid hazarding misconception, and hurting the feelings, however unreasonably, of any respectable body of men, I might add stronger cases in point; cases, in which principles have been pushed to their greatest and most impracticable excess, for the purpose, we are told, of securing some attention to the reasonable part of them. Mr. Shelley objected to the present state of the intercourse of the sexes, and the vulgar notions of the Supreme Being. He also held with Sir Thomas More, that a community of property was desirable; an opinion, which obtained him more ill-will, perhaps, than any other, at least in the class among which he was born. The Reviewer implies, that he put forth some of these objections alarmingly or extravagantly. Be it so. The great point is to have a question discussed. The advocates of existing systems of all sorts are strong enough to look to the defence; whereas, those who suffer by them are so much intimidated by their very sufferings, as to be afraid to move, lest they should be worse off than they are at present. They do not want to know their calamity; they know it well enough. They require to be roused, and not always to sit groaning over, or making despairing jests of their condition. If a friend's excess excites them to differ with him, they are still incited to look at the question. His sympathy moves them to be ashamed of their passiveness, and to consider what may be done. We need not fear, that it will be too much. At the very least, matters will find their level. If we are our own masters under Providence; if Nature works with us for tools, and intends amelioration through the means of our knowledge, we are roused to some purpose. If not, or if we are to go so far and no farther, no farther shall we go. The sweet or bitter waters of humanity will assuredly find where to settle.

The Reviewer, still acknowledging the genius of Mr. Shelley, and his benevolent intentions, finds the same fault with his poetry as with his philosophy, and traces it to the same causes. Of all my friend's writings, the poetical parts are those which I should least conceive to subject him to the charge of want of sympathy. Is the quarrelling with constituted authorities and received calamities, the same thing as scorning the better part of what exists? Is the quitting the real world for the ideal in search of consolation, the same thing as thrusting one's foot against it in contempt, and flying off on the wings of antipathy? And what did Mr. Shelley carry thither when he went? A perpetual consciousness of his humanity; a clinging load of the miseries of his fellow-creatures. The *Witch of Atlas*, for example, is but a personification of the imaginative faculty in its most airy abstractions; and yet the author cannot indulge himself long in that fairy region, without *dreaming* of mortal strife. If he is not in this world, he must have visions of it. If fiction is his reality by day, reality will be his fiction during his slumbers. The truth is, Mr. Shelley was in his whole being, mental and physical, of an extreme delicacy and sensibility. He felt every part of his nature intensely; and his impulse, object, and use in this world, was to remind others of some important points touching our common nature and endeavours, by affording a more than ordinary example of their effect upon himself. It may be asked, who are to be reminded? how many? To which we answer, those who have been reminded already, as well as the select portion who remain to be so; never mind how few, provided they are reminded to some purpose. Mr. Shelley's writings, it is admitted, are not calculated to be popular, however popular in their ultimate tendency, or cordial in their origin. They are, for the most part, too abstract and refined. But "fit audience though few," is the motto of the noblest ambition; and it is these audiences that go and settle the world.

Mr. Shelley's poetry is invested with a dazzling and subtle radiance, which blinds the common observer with light. Piercing beyond this, we discover that the characteristics of his poetical writings are an exceeding sympathy with the whole universe, material and intellectual; an ardent desire to benefit his species; an impatience of the tyrannies and superstitions that hold them bound; and a regret that the power of one loving and enthusiastic individual is not proportioned to his will, nor his good reception with the world at all proportioned to his love. His poetry is either made up of all these feelings united, or is an attempt to escape from their pressure into the widest fields of imagination. I say an attempt,— because, as we have seen, escape he does not; and it is curious to observe how he goes pouring forth his baffled affections upon every object he can think of, bringing out its beauties and pretensions by the light of a radiant fancy, and resolved to do the whole detail of the universe a sort of poetical justice, in default of being able to make his fellow-creatures attend to justice political. From this arises the fault of his poetry, which is a want of massiveness,—of a proper distribution of light and shade. The whole is too full of glittering points; of images touched and illustrated alike, and brought out into the same prominence. He ransacks every thing like a bee, grappling with it in the same spirit of penetration and enjoyment, till you lose sight of the field he entered upon, in following him into his subtle recesses. He is also too fond, in his larger works, of repeating the same images drawn from the material universe and the sea. When he is obliged to give up these peculiarities, and to identify his feelings and experience with those of other people, as in his dramatic poems, the fault no longer exists. His object remains,—that of increasing the wisdom and happiness of mankind: but he has laid aside his wings, and added to the weight and purpose of his body: the spiritual part of him is invested with ordinary flesh and blood. In truth, for ordinary or immediate purposes, a great deal of Mr. Shelley's poetry ought to have been written in prose. It consists of philosophical speculations, which required an introduction to the understandings of the community, and not merely, as he thought, a recommendation to their good will. The less philosophic he becomes, reverting to his own social feelings, as in some of the pathetic complaints before us; or appealing to the common ones of mankind upon matters immediately agitating them, as in the "Ode to Naples;" or giving himself fairly up to the sports of fancy, as in the "Witch of Atlas," or "The Translations from Goethe and Homer;" the more he delights and takes with him, those who did not know whether to argue, or to feel, in some of his larger works. The common reader is baffled with the perplexing mixture of passion and calmness; of the severest reasoning, and the wildest fiction; of the most startling appearances of dissent, and the most conventional calls upon sympathy. But in all his writings there is a wonderful sustained sensibility, and a language lofty and fit for it. He has the art of using the stateliest words and the most learned idioms, without incurring the charge of pedantry; so that passages of more splendid and sonorous writing are not to be selected from any writer, since the time of Milton: and yet when he descends from his ideal worlds, and comes home to us in our humbler bowers, and our yearnings after love and affection, he attunes the most natural feelings to a style so proportionate, and withal to a modulation so truly musical, that there is nothing to surpass it in the lyrics of Beaumont and Fletcher.

Let the reader, whom these pages may have rendered more desirous of knowing Mr. Shelley, turn to the volume in question, and judge for himself in what sort of spirit it was that he wrote the "Witch of Atlas," the "Letter" [to M. Gisborne] at p. 59, part of the "Ode to Naples," the "Song" ["Rarely, Rarely"], a "Lament," the "Question," "Lines to an Indian Air," "Stanzas written in dejection near Naples," Lines on a "Faded Violet," "Lines to a Critic," "Tomorrow," "Good Night," "Love's Philosophy," the "Stanzas" [Music . . .], and the "Translations from Goethe and Homer." The verses "On the Medusa's Head of Leonardo da Vinci" are perhaps as fine as any thing in the book, for power. The poetry seems sculptured and grinning, like the subject. The words are cut with a knife. But love is the great inspirer of Mr. Shelley. His very abstract ideas are in love.

> "The deep recesses of her odorous dwelling
>   Were stored with magic treasures—sounds of air,
> Which had the power all spirits of compelling,
>   Folded in cells of crystal silence there;
> Such as we hear in youth, and think the feeling
>   Will never die—yet ere we are aware,
> The feeling and the sound are fled and gone,
> And the regret they leave remains alone.

> "And there lay Visions swift, and sweet, and quaint,
>   Each in its thin sheath like a chrysalis;

411

Some eager to burst forth, some weak and faint
With the soft burthen of intensest bliss."

[*The Witch of Atlas*, stanza xiv, st. xv, ll. 1–4]

We have heard of ladies falling in love with Lord Byron, upon the strength of Don Juan. These must be ladies in towns. If ever a more sequestered heroine could become enamoured of a poet out of the mere force of sentiment, or at least desire to give him exceeding comfort and consolation, it would be such a poet as Mr. Shelley. The most physical part of the passion acquires, from his treatment of it, a grace and purity inexpressible. It is curious to see with what fearlessness, in the conscious dignity of this power, he ventures to speak of things that would defy all mention from a less ingenuous lip. The "Witch of Atlas," will be liked by none but poets, or very poetical readers. Spenser would have liked it: Sir Kenelm Digby would have written a comment upon it. Its meanings are too remote, and its imagery too wild, to be enjoyed by those who cannot put on wings of the most subtle conception, and remain in the uttermost parts of idealism. Even those who can, will think it something too dreamy and involved. They will discover the want of light and shade, which I have before noticed, and which leaves the picture without its due breadth and perspective. It is the fault of some of Mr. Shelley's poems, that they look rather like store-houses of imagery, than imagery put into proper action. We have the misty regions of wide air,

"The hills of snow, and lofts of piled thunder,—"

which Milton speaks of; but they are too much in their elementary state, as if just about to be used, and moving in their first chaos. To a friend, who pointed out to him this fault, Mr. Shelley said, that he would consider it attentively, and doubted not he should profit by the advice. He scorned advice as little as he did any other help to what was just and good. He could both give and take it with an exquisite mixture of frankness and delicacy, that formed one of the greatest evidences of his superiority to common virtue. I have mentioned before, that his temper was admirable. He was naturally irritable and violent; but had so mastered the infirmity, as to consider every body's inclinations before his own. Mr. Trelawney pronounced him to be a man absolutely without selfishness. In his intercourse with myself, nothing delighted him more than to confound the limits of our respective property, in money-matters, books, apparel, &c. He would help himself without scruple to whatever he wanted, whether a book or a waistcoat; and was never better pleased, than at finding things of his own in his friend's possession.

The way in which Mr. Shelley's eye darted "from heaven to earth,"

412

and the sort of call at which his imagination was ever ready to descend, is well exemplified in the following passage of the *Letter* at p. 59. The unhappy mass of prostitution which exists in England, contrasted with something which seems to despise it, and which, in more opinions than his, is a main cause of it, was always one of the subjects that at a moment's notice would overshadow the liveliest of his moods. The picturesque line in italics is beautifully true. The poet is writing to a friend in London.

> "Unpavilioned heaven is fair,
> Whether the moon, into her chamber gone,
> Leaves midnight to the golden stars, or wan
> Climbs with diminish'd beams the azure steep;
> Or whether clouds sail o'er the inverse deep,
> Piloted by the many-wandering blast,
> *And the rare stars rush through them, dim and fast.*
> All this is beautiful in every land.
> But what see you beside? A shabby stand
> Of hackney coaches—a brick house or wall,
> Fencing some lonely court, white with the scrawl
> Of our unhappy politics; or worse.
> A wretched woman, reeling by, whose curse
> Mix'd with the watchman's, partner of her trade,
> You must accept in place of serenade."
>
> [*Letter to Maria Gisborne*, ll. 257–71]

[All italics here and elsewhere are Hunt's; and the quotations often deviate from the modern Oxford text—*Ed.*]

These miserable women, sometimes indeed owing to the worst and most insensible qualities on their own parts, but sometimes also to the best and most guileless, are at such a dreadful disadvantage compared with those who are sleeping at such an hour in their comfortable homes, that it is difficult to pitch our imaginations among the latter, for a refuge from the thought of them. Real love, however, even if it be unhappy, provided its sorrow be without contempt and sordidness, will furnish us with a transition less startling. The following *Lines to an Indian Air*,[1] make an exquisite serenade.

> "I arise from dreams of thee
> In the first sweet sleep of night,
> When the winds are breathing low,
> And the stars are shining bright;
> I arise from dreams of thee,
> And a spirit in my feet

[1] Entitled *The Indian Serenade* in the Oxford edition of Shelley—*Ed.*

Has led me—who knows how?
To thy chamber-window, sweet!

"The wandering airs they faint
On the dark, the silent stream—
The champak odours fall,
Like sweet thoughts in a dream;
The nightingale's complaint
It dies upon her heart,
As I must upon thine,
Beloved as thou art!

"O lift me from the grass!
I die, I faint, I fail!
Let thy love in kisses rain
On my lips and eyelids pale.
My cheek is cold and white, alas!
My heart beats loud and fast;
Oh! press it close to thine again
Where it will break at last."

I know not that two main parts of Mr. Shelley's poetical genius, the
descriptive and the pathetic, ever vented themselves to more
touching purpose than in the lines *Written in Dejection near Naples.*
The brilliant yet soft picture with which they commence, introduces
the melancholy observer of it in a manner extremely affecting. He
beholds what delights others, and is willing to behold it, though it
delights him not. He even apologizes for "insulting" the bright day
he has painted so beautifully, with his "untimely moan." The stanzas
exhibit, at once, minute observation, the widest power to generalize,
exquisite power to enjoy, and admirable patience at the want of
enjoyment. This latter combination forms the height of the amiable,
as the former does of the intellectual character. The fourth stanza
will strongly move the reader of this memoir.

"The sun is warm, the sky is clear,
    The waves are dancing fast and bright,
Blue isles and snowy mountains wear
    The purple moon's transparent light

†   *   *   *   *   *   *

Around its unexpanded buds;
    Like many a voice of one delight,
The winds, the birds, the ocean floods,
    The City's voice itself is soft, like Solitude's.

† A line is wanting in the Edition. [Reviewer's footnote.]

"I see the deep's untrampled floor
    With green and purple sea-weeds strown;
I see the waves upon the shore,
    Like light dissolved in star-showers, thrown.
I sit upon the sands alone;
    The lightning of the noon-tide ocean
Is flashing round me, and a tone
    Arises from its measured motion,
How sweet! did any heart now share in my emotion.

"Alas! I have nor hope, nor health,
    Nor peace within, nor calm around,
Nor that content surpassing wealth,
    The sage in meditation found,
And walked with inward glory crowned;
    Nor fame, nor power, nor love, nor leisure.
Others I see whom these surround;
    Smiling they live, and call life pleasure;—
To me that cup has been dealt in another measure.

"Yet now despair itself is mild,
    Ev'n as the winds and waters are;
I could lie down like a tired child,
    And weep away the life of care
Which I have borne and yet must bear,
    Till death, like sleep, might steal on me,
And I might feel in the warm air
    My cheek grow cold, and hear the sea
Breathe o'er my dying brain its last monotony.

"Some might lament that I were cold,
    As I when this sweet day is done,
Which my lost heart, too soon grown old,
    Insults with this untimely moan:
They might lament, for I am one
    Whom men love not, and yet regret;
Unlike this day, which, when the sun
    Shall on its stainless glory set,
Will linger, though enjoyed, like joy in memory yet."

The pieces, that call to mind Beaumont and Fletcher, are such as the following:—

"Music, when soft voices die,
    Vibrates in the memory;

Odours, when sweet violets sicken,
Live within the sense they quicken.

"Rose-leaves, when the rose is dead,
Are heap'd for the beloved's bed;
And so thy thoughts, when thou art gone,
Love itself shall slumber on."

"*Love's Philosophy*" is another. It has been often printed; but for the same reason will bear repetition. The sentiment must be understood with reference to the delicacy as well as freedom of Mr. Shelley's opinions, and not as supplying any excuse to that heartless libertinism which no man disdained more. The poem is here quoted for its grace and lyrical sweetness.

"The fountains mingle with the river,
    And the river with the ocean;
The winds of heaven mix for ever,
    With a sweet emotion:
Nothing in the world is single;
    All things by a law divine
In one another's being mingle—[1]
    Why not I with thine?

"See the mountains kiss high heaven,
    And the waves clasp one another;
No sister flower would be forgiven,
    If it disdain'd its brother:
And the sunlight clasps the earth,
    And the moonbeams kiss the sea;
What are all these kissings worth,
    If thou kiss not me?"

Mr. Shelley ought to have written nothing but dramas, interspersed with such lyrics as these. Perhaps had he lived, he would have done so; for, after all, he was but young; and he had friends of that opinion, whom he was much inclined to agree with. The fragment of the tragedy of *Charles the First*, in this volume, makes us long for more of it. With all his republicanism, he would have done justice to Charles, as well as to Pym and Hampden. His completest production is unquestionably the tragedy of the "Cenci." The objections to the subject are, on the face of them, not altogether unfounded; but they ought not to weigh with those who have no scruple in grappling with any of the subjects of our old English

[1] An alternative version is 'In one spirit meet and mingle'—*Ed.*

drama; still less, if they are true readers of that drama, and know how to think of the great ends of poetry in a liberal and masculine manner. "Cenci" is the personification of a will, maddened, like a Roman emperor's, by the possession of impunity; deadened to all sense of right and wrong by degrading notions of a Supreme Being; and consequently subjected to the most frightful wants, and knowing no pleasure but in sensuality or malignity. The least of his actions becomes villainous, because he does it in defiance of principle. On the other hand, his death by the hand of his outraged daughter produces a different meeting of extremes, because it results, however madly, from horror at the violation of principle. The reader refuses to think that a daughter has slain a *father*, precisely because a dreadful sense of what a father ought not to have done has driven her to it, and because he sees that in any other situation she would be the most exemplary of children. This remark is made for the benefit of the curious reader, and to vindicate Mr. Shelley from having taken up a subject out of pure scorn of his feelings: a strange policy in any author, and not surely to be found in him. Considering what an excellent production the *Cenci* is, it is certainly difficult to help wishing that the subject had been of a nature to startle nobody; but it may be as truly added, that such a subject could have been handled by no other writer in a manner less offensive, or more able to suggest its own vindication.

John Keats
(1795–1821)

A Survey of Contemporary Criticism
1817–20

Of our three poets Keats received least attention from contemporary critics. This is quite understandable. Keats's creative life was appreciably shorter than those of the other two poets. Moreover, he matured very rapidly as a poet, and his last volume, *Lamia, Isabella, The Eve of St Agnes, and Other Poems* (1820), was perhaps the only one that deserved much more from the reviewers than the encouragement of promise. This volume was, however, highly praised by a number of reviewers, quite apart from Jeffrey, who may well have held back from reviewing *Endymion* in the *Edinburgh* until he could see how the wind was going to blow. Keats himself read some of the critiques of his 1820 volume before leaving England for Italy in September 1820, and remarked in a letter: 'My book has had good success among the literary people.' Among the reviews he probably saw was that by Lamb in *The New Times* of 19 July, reprinted by Leigh Hunt in *The Examiner* of 30 July, that in *The Monthly Review* for July, that by Jeffrey in August (which, however, spent most of its time on *Endymion*), and that by Hunt in *The Indicator* for 2 and 9 August. All these were favourable, and others were to come, notably that by John Scott in *The London Magazine* for September.

Even Keats's first volume (*Poems*, 1817), however, though not noticed at all by the two 'great reviews', or, until a year later, by *Blackwood's*, had quite a reasonable press. There were six critiques in 1817, and, though three were by friends (John Hamilton Reynolds in *The Champion*,[1] George Felton Mathew in *The*

[1] *Champ*, 9 March 1817.

European Magazine,[1] and Leigh Hunt in *The Examiner*[2]), three were by independent witnesses (those in *The Monthly Magazine*,[3] *The Eclectic Review*,[4] and Constable's *Edinburgh Magazine*[5]), and the first and last were distinctly favourable, especially the last, while Josiah Conder in the *Eclectic*, though critical of some aspects of the poems—*e.g.*, the narrow range of ideas and feelings expressed, and the frequently nebulous character of the meaning—recognized that Keats had poetical talent.

It was over Keats's second volume, *Endymion* (1818), that he was heavily belaboured. The poem was ridiculed by the Tory and High Church monthly, *The British Critic*,[6] and attacked, in their several ways, both in the Tory *Blackwood's*[7] and in the Tory *Quarterly*.[8] *The British Critic* (which had championed Wordsworth so handsomely) dismissed the poem in a jocularly scornful review which tried to show that Keats was nothing but an inferior imitator of Hunt. The *Blackwood's* article 'On the Cockney School of Poetry No. IV' by the notorious 'Z' (probably in this case mostly Lockhart, but partly Wilson) is a nasty piece of work, and Lockhart does not come at all well out of the story of what led up to it. 'Z' had previously attacked Leigh Hunt, who had called on the anonymous critic to reveal his identity. This the pair of cowards refused to do. Keats had said that if *Blackwood's* were to attack him he would require satisfaction; but he did not know whom he would have to call out. J. H. Christie, who wrote for *Blackwood's* and who eventually killed John Scott, editor of *The London Magazine*, in a duel, had met Keats in London and reported favourably on him to Lockhart, who promised to print a piece by Christie on Keats if he would care to write it. Not long after, however, Lockhart met Keats's friend Bailey at Bishop Gleig's in Stirling, and Lockhart wormed out of him a substantial amount of information on Keats's background as a medical student. Bailey later gave three somewhat differing accounts of the talk[9]; but it seems pretty clear that he asked Lockhart not to use the information to attack Keats in *Blackwood's*, and that Lockhart

[1] *Eur.M*, LXXI, May 1817.   [2] *Exar*, 1 June, 6, 13 July 1817.
[3] *MM*, XLIII, April 1817.   [4] *Ecl. R*, VIII (2nd. Ser.), September 1817.
[5] *Ed. M*, I (2nd. Ser.), October 1817.
[6] *BC*, IX (2nd. Ser.), June 1818. See pp. 68–9 above.
[7] *BM*, III, August 1818. See pp. 467–72 below.
[8] *QR*, XIX, April 1818 (publ. September 1818). See pp. 472–6 below.
[9] See *The Keats Circle*, ed. H. E. Rollins (Camb., Mass; London, 1965), I. 34, 243–7.

undertook that 'he' certainly would not do so (which seems to have been a miserable piece of prevarication). In August 1818 *Blackwood's* attacked not only *Endymion* but also Keats's 1817 *Poems*. The *Quarterly* attack (by J. W. Croker) in the April number, which was not published till September, was a more serious piece of criticism, and also very damaging to sales. Keats had attacked Pope in *Sleep and Poetry*. Croker was a Popean devotee. He was outraged by the freedom of Keats's couplets, and by his word-coinage, by his diffuseness, and by his unintelligibility, and clearly hoped that the review would put paid to Keats as a would-be poet, at least in his style to date. Many of Croker's criticisms were valid, but his tone was often supercilious, and he failed to give due weight to the merits of *Endymion*, and even to amplify his admission that Keats had 'powers of language, rays of fancy, and gleams of genius'.

Letters appeared in several newspapers protesting at the *Quarterly*'s treatment of *Endymion*, but they seem to have had little effect on sales. Nor had Bailey's 'letters' in *The Oxford Herald*,[1] or the very favourable notice in *The Champion*,[2] both of which had appeared by June. Nor, apparently, did the letter from 'J.S.' (? John Scott) to *The Morning Chronicle* in October,[3] or Reynolds's admirable article 'Keats and the Quarterly Review', published in *The Alfred*, and reprinted in *The Examiner*, also in October.[4] Much later, however, in April 1820, another substantial attempt was made to answer the *Quarterly* and to indicate some of the special beauties of the poem. This was a review in *The London Magazine*[5] by P. G. Patmore (father of Coventry Patmore). It must also be said that Jeffrey's belated review in August 1820 undoubtedly helped materially to influence opinion in favour of the poem. Jeffrey, like Hunt, realized with great clarity that Keats was not simply an untraditional innovator, but belonged to a tradition deriving from the poets of the reign of Elizabeth and the early seventeenth century. Moreover, Jeffrey considered that he was himself responsible to a great degree for the recent revival of interest in that earlier body of work.

Yet the most effective answer to Keats's detractors was the publication of his 1820 volume. This established Keats's poetic

---

[1] *Oxford Herald*, 30 May, 6 June 1818.   [2] *Champ*, 7 June 1818.
[3] *The Morning Chronicle*, 30 October 1818.
[4] *The Alfred*, 6 October 1818; reprd. *Exar*, 11 October 1818.
[5] *LM*, I, April 1820.

reputation once and for all. Just after the volume appeared, *The Retrospective Review* (which bore nobly on its title-page an engraving of the Great Gate of Trinity College, Cambridge) in a review of Wallace's *Various Prospects of Mankind, Nature, and Providence*,[1] wrote:

> Keats, whose *Endymion* was so cruelly treated by the critics, has just put forth a volume of poems which must effectively silence his deriders. The rich romance of his *Lamia*—the holy beauty of *St Agnes' Eve*—the pure and simple diction and intense feeling of his *Isabella*—and the rough sublimity of his *Hyperion*—cannot be laughed down, though all the periodical critics in England and Scotland were to assail them with their sneers.

The British Critic relented on the appearance of the 1820 Poems.[2] *Blackwood's* did not review them, nor did the *Quarterly*. In the latter case this may have been because Murray was too fair-minded to allow further abuse. But *Blackwood's* continued to ridicule Keats up to and for years after his death.[3] It deservedly got some rough handling from John Scott of *The London Magazine* in his stinging article 'The Mohock Magazine',[4] which gave rise to the duel with Lockhart's friend Christie, in which Scott was mortally wounded. In the course of this article Scott dismissed as hypocritical a purported apology for the 'Cockney School' article, and condemned virulently the underhand and pernicious practices of the *Blackwood's* set.

Speaking generally, the attacks on Keats were partly motivated by political distrust of his association with the radical Leigh Hunt, partly by social and intellectual snobbery but partly by genuine bewilderment at his innovations, and by a distaste for what seemed to be sensuous self-indulgence and formal indiscipline. Keats's mastery of form was, of course, only evident in a few cases in his early volume, and in a few parts of *Endymion*, and was not fully revealed until his last volume came from the press. But contemporary critics often complained that even in the 1820 volume Keats's language was 'obscure', and he was also attacked by some critics for using Ancient Greek myths, not only on the

---

[1] *RR*, August 1820. *The Retrospective Review* only actually *reviewed* works of dead authors.

[2] *BC*, XIV (2nd. Ser.), September 1820.

[3] *E.g.*, in *BM*, VII, September 1820, 613–17, 675–9; X, December 1821, 696–700; and XIV, August 1823, 'Letters of Timothy Tickler, Esq., No. 8'.

[4] *LM*, I, December 1820, 666–85.

ground that he knew hardly any Greek, but also because he gave his gods Romantic feelings. Indeed, many of the specific beauties of Keats's work remained unrealized by almost all of his contemporary critics. Its texture was too dense and rich to be easy to understand, and too unfamiliar to be readily accepted by critics and a public used to the straightforward, lucid poetry of post-Restoration tradition.[1]

It does not seem, in the light of modern scholarship, that the view that Keats was killed by the critics is tenable. On the other hand, there is plenty of evidence that some, at least, of the unfavourable reviews irritated and upset him.[2]

It is possibly interesting to consider in some detail what the more favourable reviewers saw in Keats's work. Reynolds's review of the 1817 *Poems*[3] found the volume 'filled throughout with very graceful and genuine poetry'. He considered it also as a wholesome reaction against the traditions of Boileau and Pope. But, unlike Jeffrey and Hunt, he thought of Keats as singing 'from the pure inspiration of nature'. Reynolds also writes of Keats as looking at natural objects 'with his mind' and 'not merely with his eye'. He credits Keats with 'a powerful imagination', but also with restraint, and characterizes his work as 'remarkably abstracted' yet 'never out of the reach of the mind'. Reynolds criticizes the poems for some 'faultiness of measure', and does not approve of compound epithets or 'overwrought descriptions'. He has high praise for the sonnets, which he considers, apart from Milton's and Wordsworth's, 'the most powerful ones in the whole range of English poetry'.

The reviewer in *The Monthly Magazine*[4] writes of the 'sweetness and beauty of the composition', notes that Keats had taken Elizabethan poets as his model, and considers that he had often rivalled their diction. He sums up his impressions by saying:

[1] Even his fellow Romantic, Byron, steeped in the poetry of lucidity, found it so. Leigh Hunt tells in *Lord Byron and Some of His Contemporaries* (1828) how Byron asked him 'what was the meaning of a beaker "full of the warm south" '. Hunt comments: 'It was not the word "beaker" that puzzled him. College had made him intimate enough with that. But the sort of poetry in which he excelled, was not accustomed to these poetical concentrations.'

[2] See *e.g.*, H. E. Briggs, 'Keats's Conscious and Unconscious Reactions to Criticisms of *Endymion*', *PMLA*, LX (1945), 1106–29.

[3] *Champ*, 9 March 1817. An extract appears on pp. 451–2 below.

[4] *MM*, XLIII, April 1817.

There is in his poems a rapturous glow and intoxication of the fancy
—an air of careless and profuse magnificence in his diction—a
revelry of the imagination and tenderness of feeling, that forcibly
impress themselves on the reader.

George Felton Mathew[1] notes the particular affinity of the
poems with Spenser, and he praises the 'fine ear' Keats had 'for
the grand, elaborate, and abstracted music of nature'. He finds
the volume full of 'imaginations and descriptions' which were
'delicate and elegant'. On the other hand, Mathew refuses to
regard Keats as the equal of Byron, Moore, Campbell, or Rogers
for 'maturity of thought, propriety of feeling, or felicity of style'.
He also censures Keats for seeming to believe that 'plan and
arrangement are prejudicial to natural poetry'. Mathew takes the
opportunity to tilt at Hunt, who had replaced him in Keats's
affections, and draws attention to some of Keats's earliest poems,
which he considers 'of superior versification'. He also pillories
Keats's attack on Pope, which he thought would only expose him
to 'ridicule and rebuke'. Mathew sums up his impression of the
volume by claiming that it was full of instances of the 'luxuriance'
of Keats's 'imagination', and 'the puerility of his sentiments'.
He recommends 'religion and the love of virtue', and concludes
with a purple passage:

> We consider that the specimens here presented to our readers, will
> establish our opinion of Mr. Keats's poetical imagination; but the
> mere luxuries of imagination, more especially in the possession of the
> proud egotist of diseased feelings and perverted principles, may
> become the ruin of a people—inculcate the falsest and most danger-
> ous ideas of the condition of humanity—and refine us into the
> degeneracy of butterflies that perish in the deceitful glories of a
> destructive taper. These observations might be considered imperti-
> nent, were they applied to one who had discovered any incapacity
> for loftier flights—to one who could not appreciate the energies of
> Milton or of Shakespeare—to one who could not soar to the heights
> of poesy,—and ultimately hope to bind his brows with the glorious
> sunbeams of immortality.

Leigh Hunt's review[2] was much more generally favourable,
and contained no moral or religious strictures. Hunt explicitly
rejects as 'not poetry' the work of post-Restoration poets before

[1] *Eur. M*, LXXI, May 1817.
[2] *Exar*, 1 June, 6, 13 July 1817. A long extract appears on pp. 452-9
below.

the advent of the Lake poets. Moreover, among these Wordsworth alone was a worthy 'successor of the true and abundant poets of the older time'. Now here was Keats, whose volume was 'one of the greatest evidences' that 'the Graces' of 'real poetry' were reappearing. Here was 'a young poet giving himself up to his own impressions and revelling in real poetry for its own sake'. It is evident that Hunt regarded 'real poetry' as essentially sense-fulfilling and abounding with 'beauties'. He writes of its 'rich and enchanted ground' as being 'fertile with all that English succulence could produce, bright with all that Italian sunshine could lend, and haunted with exquisite humanities'. Hunt admits faults in the volume, 'a tendency to notice every thing too indiscriminately and without an eye to natural proportion and effect', and 'a sense of the proper variety of versification without a due consideration of its principles'. The positive characteristics, on the other hand, were 'a fine ear, a fancy and imagination at will, and an intense feeling of external beauty in its most natural and least expressible simplicity'. (The last is an unclear phrase, which Hunt does not amplify.)

The strictures in Josiah Conder's review in the *Eclectic*[1] have already been alluded to, but his few favourable comments are possibly worth mention. Despite his finding little good either in the thoughts expressed or in their expression, Conder yet credited Keats with 'the requisite fancy and skill' to write good poetry. He found 'considerable taste and sprightliness' in part of 'I stood tip-toe', and sensed 'a summer's day glow' over the whole poem; whereas in *Sleep and Poetry* he thought Keats far gone 'in affectation and absurdity'. He thought the sonnets the best things in the volume.

The far more favourable review in *The Edinburgh Magazine*[2] noted the scattering of 'Spencerianisms' throughout the volume, but claimed that it also contained 'a great deal of that *picturesqueness* of fancy and licentious brilliancy of epithet which distinguish the early Italian novelists and amorous poets' (the reviewer refers specifically to Pulci and Ariosto). After quoting the start of the Epistle to Clarke the reviewer comments: 'All this is just, and brilliant too,—though rather ambitious to be kept up for any length of time in a proper and fitting strain'. The reviewer also

[1] *Ecl. R*, VIII (2nd. Ser.), 267–75. An extract is printed on pp. 459–61 below.

[2] *Ed. M*, I, October 1817. An extract appears on pp. 462–5 below.

quotes from l. 109 to the end of the same poem as 'the very pink of the smart and flowing conversational style', and characterizes it as 'truly such elegant *badinage* as should pass between scholars and gentlemen who can feel as well as judge'. But the reviewer thought Keats had 'ventured on ground very dangerous for a young poet' by adopting, like Hunt, this style—'vivacious, smart, witty, changeful, sparkling, and learned—full of bright points and flashy expressions that strike and even seem to please by sudden boldness of novelty,—rather abounding in familiarities of conception and oddnesses of manner which shew ingenuity, even though they be perverse, or common, or contemptuous'. The reviewer believes that this sort of thing would not be likely to excite more than 'a cold approbation in the long-run'. He goes on to contrast 'mannerism' and 'sickly refinement' with 'the truest strain of poetry', in which Keats could only succeed by casting off the 'uncleanness' of the school of Hunt and Hazlitt. It is clear that the reviewer wanted more simplicity and passion and less 'metaphysical wit' and 'giddy wanderings' of 'untamed imagination'. But he praises Keats's touching expression of his love of nature in the sonnets 'O Solitude' and 'To one who has been long in city pent', and the 'felicitous' character of the sonnet to Haydon ('High-mindedness, a jealousy for good'), noting its similarity to Milton, unrivalled except by Wordsworth. In these poems the reviewer found a 'deep tone of moral energy' and 'the pathos of genius'. He demurs, however, at some affectations and carelessness in the volume, but ends by noting the 'glorious and Virgilian conception' of

> The moon lifting her silver rim
> Above a cloud, and with a gradual swim
> Coming into the blue with all her light.
> ['I stood tip-toe', ll. 113–15]

As can be seen, then, the reviewers of Keats's first volume, though they varied to some extent in the features they singled out for praise, and in the weight they attached to them, all showed themselves aware that the poems were the work of a poet of striking imagination and descriptive ability, the chief objections being to the manner, or the character of the opinions expressed, or the absence of mature thinking.

The first favourable review of *Endymion* appeared in *The Literary Journal*.[1] It is largely a synopsis of parts of the story, with

[1] *Lit. J*, 17, 24 May 1818.

quotations. The reviewer thought little of the first thirty lines, but admired the 'beautiful simplicity' of I. 34–62, and thought Endymion's narration of his dream of Peona (I. 578–671) showed Keats 'to possess a vivid imagination and refined mind', though the verse was 'frequently irregular'. Again, the description of the garden, and of the subsequent meeting with Diana (II. 670–853) was 'written with a warmth of feeling, and a tenderness of expression', which were seldom exceeded 'in some of our most popular poets'. The reviewer also thought that 'the anxious desire of liberty, and almost maddening anticipation of its possession, expressed by Glaucus' (III. 234–55), were 'described with considerable spirit', and he noted that there were also 'some beautiful lines' in the description of Endymion's flight with Diana (IV. 481–512). As to the 'measure' of the poem, the reviewer considered it 'nearly allied to that of Chaucer'.

Bailey's 'letters' to the *Oxford Herald*[1] were superlatively encomiastic both about *Endymion* and about the earlier volume, in which, Bailey says in his first 'letter', he had found 'the richest promise I ever saw of an ethereal imagination maintained by vast intellectual power'. He quotes in support of that evaluation ll. 284–93 of *Sleep and Poetry*, to 'give the reader some idea of the conscious capability of real genius', and goes on to comment:

> This is no common language. It is the under-breath of a 'master-spirit'. It is the deep yearning of genius after the beautiful and fair. It is, as it were, the brooding of an earthquake.

He continues by extolling the 'extraordinary merit' of *Endymion*, and calling upon the age 'to countenance and encourage this rising genius, and not to let him pine away in neglect, lest his memory to after ages speak trumpet-tongued the disgrace of this'. Bailey had, of course, been with Keats during a fair amount of the time when he was writing *Endymion*, and may well, for all we know, have had as much insight into the poem as anyone at that time or since. On the other hand, his connexion with it may have led him to an unjustified overestimate. It is hard to tell. In his second 'letter' Bailey reaffirms his high opinion of the poem, and likens Keats to the young Milton 'panting for fame', though he expresses the view that Keats's genius was actually more like Shakespeare's than like Milton's. Bailey quotes a few short extracts from *Endymion*, praising the 'beautiful turn' Keats had

[1] *Oxford Herald*, 30 May, 6 June 1818.

426

given in Book II to the story of Adonis, and quoting the description of the procession of Bacchus in Book IV (ll. 188–267) 'to give the reader some idea of the lyrical beauty of his description'. The ending of the poem seemed to Bailey to resemble that of *Paradise Regained*. In his conclusion Bailey admits that the poem is not faultless, but holds that the faults are those of an 'ardent genius, not sufficiently curbed'; and he claims that the poems Keats had already published were 'the germs of future greatness'. Bailey's 'letters' are gallant expressions of faith in Keats's genius, but they are otherwise unremarkable as literary criticism.

The same cannot be said of the interesting review of *Endymion* in *The Champion*,[1] which has been tentatively ascribed to three writers, John Hamilton Reynolds, John Scott, and, most recently, Richard Woodhouse. Whoever wrote it was, in any case, a critic of some ability and penetration, though some of his judgments may have been misguided. The reviewer expresses the hope that Keats will be fairly treated by the most influential reviews, and also the fear that if he is not he may 'maintain those errors that have been justly objected against him, because they have been urged too far'. As to *Endymion*, the reviewer thinks it unlikely to become popular, partly because the 'passions' and 'feelings' expressed in it were not, like those of other modern poets, clearly those which the poet himself had felt, but were 'as much imaginative' as Keats's situations; and partly because the poem was, like *Venus and Adonis*, 'a *representation* and not a *description* of passion'. This was 'the excellence of dramatic poetry'; but in poetry of any other kind it was impossible to feel its 'truth and power' unless one abandoned one's 'ordinary feeling and common consciousness', and identified oneself with the scene; and few people could do that:

> to make an ordinary *reader* sensible of the excellence of a poem, he must be told what the poet felt; and he is affected by him and not by the scene. Our modern poets are the showmen of their own pictures and point out its [*sic*] beauties.

The reviewer goes on to speculate that Keats's 'very excellence' would 'tell against him'. By the 'very excellence' the reviewer evidently meant 'the immediate impress of truth and nature' that every scene bore. Now, in his opinion, what was required in addition, for the scene to be fully enjoyed, was that the poet should

[1] *Champ*, 7 June 1818. An extract appears on pp. 465–7 below.

tell us what he himself felt about it. The reviewer instances the first meeting of Endymion and Cynthia. Yet the reviewer does praise the 'necessarily abrupt breaking off of this scene of intense passion', saying that 'it is scarcely possible to conceive any thing more poetically imaginative', and he quotes II. 827–54. And he goes on to quote also the Hymn to Pan 'as among the finest specimens of classic poetry in our language'. It is evident that the reviewer regarded Keats as an objective rather than a self-regarding and expressively Romantic writer.

The dismissive reviews in *The British Critic*[1] and in *Blackwood's*[2] had not a good word to say for the poem or for Keats's poetic gifts; and Croker[3] does not follow up his admission that Keats had 'powers of language, rays of fancy, and gleams of genius'.

The next substantial review of *Endymion* that was at all favourable was that by Reynolds in *The Alfred*,[4] reprinted in *The Examiner*.[5] Like the reviewer in *The Champion*, Reynolds considers Keats's genius 'peculiarly classical'. He admits 'a few faults, which are the natural followers of youth', but holds that Keats's 'imaginations' and 'language' have 'a spirit and an intensity which we should in vain look for in the popular poets of the day'. He contrasts Byron as 'a splendid and noble egoist' always obtruding his 'gloomy and ghastly feelings' into his descriptions, with Keats whose 'feelings' were 'full, earnest, and original', and who described nature 'with an awe and a humility, but with a deep and almost breathless affection'. Reynolds also praises Keats's work as universal and not local, and contrasts his 'true pathetic' which is 'to be found in the reflections on things', with Moore's, which are 'the moods and miseries of one person'. Reynolds goes on to prophesy that none of the popular poets of his day, including Wordsworth and Coleridge, would live. He considers that Keats had not yet perfected anything, but contends that he had the power to, and appeals to readers to read the poem, where they would find 'passages of singular feeling, force, and pathos'. Reynolds even goes so far as to contend that 'the very passages which the *Quarterly Review* quotes as ridiculous, have in them the beauty that sent us to the poem itself', and he quotes the address to Sleep (I. 45–60) as 'full of repose and feeling', and

---

[1] *BC*, IX (n.s.), June 1818.   [2] *BM*, III, August 1818.
[3] *QR*, XIX, April 1818, published September 1818.
[4] *The Alfred, West of England Journal and General Advertiser*, 6 October 1818.
[5] *Exar*, 11 October 1818. A long extract appears on pp. 477–81 below.

I. 817–31 as something even 'finer', with a 'truly Shakespearian' turn; and he goes on to single out II. 195–8 as 'scarcely to be surpassed in the whole range of English poetry':

> It has all the naked and solitary vigour of old sculpture, with all the energy and life of Old Poetry.

He also quotes II. 441–9 as 'exquisitely classical lines, clear and reposing as a Grecian sky—soft and lovely as the waves of Ilyssus', and finally II. 827–39 as lines than which nothing could be 'more imaginative'. In conclusion, Reynolds stresses two features of the poem, first that Keats excelled (like Milton) in 'putting a spirit of life and novelty into the Heathen Mythology', and secondly, that 'in the structure of his verse, and the sinewy quality of his thoughts', Keats greatly resembled 'old Chapman, the nervous translator of Homer', and his mind had "thews and limbs like to its ancestors". Reynolds here shows himself sensitive to the range in *Endymion* from tenderness to grandeur, and he also perceives the 'classical' character of Keats's work, coming out in its favour more openly than the review in *The Champion* did. Reynolds's review is one of the most perceptive—perhaps, indeed, the most perceptive—that *Endymion* received.

The most elaborate defence of *Endymion* did not appear until April 1820, when P. G. Patmore reviewed it in *The London Magazine*.[1] Patmore states flatly that '*Endymion*, if it be not, technically speaking, a poem, is poetry itself', and announces that 'as a *promise*', he knew of 'nothing like it, except some things of Chatterton'. Pope's Pastorals and *Essay on Criticism* were 'proofs of an extraordinary precocity, not of genius, but of taste'; Southey's *Joan of Arc* was 'diffuse' from being 'diluted', and Campbell's *Pleasures of Hope*, though 'delightful', was a 'work' and should have been written at thirty, not twenty. *Endymion* was unlike these, and all other pieces. It was 'an ecstatic dream of poetry'. Scarcely a passage of any length in it was free of 'the most glaring faults', yet they were 'as much collateral evidences of poetical power, as the beauties themselves are direct ones'. If Keats had had 'time, or patience, or we will even say taste, to have weeded out these faults as they sprang up, he could not have possessed the power to create the beauties to which they are joined'. Patmore admitted that 'as a tale' the work was 'nothing':

---

[1] *LM*, II, April 1820. A long extract appears on pp. 482–7 below.

Almost any two parts of it might be transposed, without disadvantage to either, or to the whole. We repeat, it is not a poem, but a dream of poetry; and while many of its separate parts possess that vivid distinctness which frequently belongs to the separate parts of a dream, the impression it leaves as a whole is equally indistinct and confused.

Patmore goes on to quote a number of passages, including two from the Hymn to Pan (I. 232–46, and 279–92), directing attention in the case of these two to the imagery and rhythm. He also praises the 'melody' of the passage describing Endymion settling to sleep in Peona's favourite bower (I. 442–52), and claims that in general the 'rhythm' of the passages quoted in the review combined 'more freedom, sweetness, and variety' than were to be found in that of any long poem in heroic couplets. Patmore maintains that 'sweetness and variety of music in the versification of a young writer' are 'among the most authentic evidences of poetical power'; and that here it was natural, not systematic. Another passage (I. 682–705) he praises as 'finely passionate and natural', and yet another (I. 783–97) as 'exceedingly fine, notwithstanding some obvious faults in the diction', and as 'the very faith, the religion, of imaginative passion'. A little later in the review, after commenting on Endymion's address to the moon, Patmore draws attention to 'the great power, and even sublimity' in II. 179–98 ['Though the playful rout . . . for the morn']. Surveying the events of the poem, Patmore claims that Keats had 'raised a glittering and fantastic temple' out of the 'rich fund of materials', and that this 'fabric' was 'at least as well adapted to the airy and fanciful beings who dwell in it, as a regular Epic Palace' was 'to its kings and heroes'. Patmore devotes part of the rest of his review to quoting and commenting briefly on 'the fancies, images, and detached thoughts and similes . . . which form the mere ornaments of the building, and are scattered here and there, almost at random'. He likens a number of these to the work of painters—Salvator, Claude, Poussin, and Titian, a matter which has recently been considered far more elaborately in Dr Ian Jack's interesting study *Keats and The Mirror of Art*.[1] Patmore goes on to deplore that the *Quarterly* reviewer had failed to discover in the poem anything to redeem it from contempt. But Patmore thinks it 'difficult, if not impossible, to state its peculiar beauties as a whole, in any other than general

[1] *Keats and The Mirror of Art* (Oxford, 1967).

terms', and this, he believes, was because Keats's 'poetical character' had not yet 'taken up any tangible or determinate ground'. The distinguishing feature of *Endymion* might indeed be 'nothing more than that exuberant spirit of youth,—that transport, of imagination, fancy, and sensibility—which gushes forth from every part, in a glittering shower of words, and a confused and shadowy pomp of thoughts and images, creating and hurrying each other along like waves of the sea'. Keats could not yet control all this, but Patmore urges him never to disown this 'wild and wayward firstling'.

Jeffrey's review of *Endymion*[1] is undoubtedly one of the best. He was sympathetic because he considered Keats to be imitating the poets of the Elizabethan and Jacobean periods, and especially the dramatists, and regarded himself, quite rightly, as having given a strong impetus to this type of imitation. He thought that *Endymion* and the 1820 Poems displayed 'genius', and that 'the spirit of poetry' breathed 'through all their extravagance'. They were obviously the work of a very young man:

> They are full of extravagance and irregularity, rash attempts at originality, interminable wanderings, and excessive obscurity. They manifestly require, therefore, all the indulgence that can be claimed for a first attempt:—but we think it no less plain that they deserve it; for they are flushed all over with the rich lights of fancy, and so coloured and bestrewn with the flowers of poetry, that even while perplexed and bewildered in their labyrinths, it is impossible to resist the intoxication of their sweetness, or to shut our hearts to the enchantments they so lavishly present.

Endymion was, Jeffrey thought, modelled on Fletcher's *Faithful Shepherdess* and Jonson's *Sad Shepherd*, and Keats had 'copied' their 'exquisite metres and inspired diction' with 'great boldness and fidelity', and he had imparted to the whole poem

> that true rural and poetical air which breathes only in them and in Theocritus—which is at once homely and majestic, luxurious and rude, and sets before us the genuine sights and sounds and smells of the country, with all the magic and grace of Elysium.

Jeffrey thought, on the other hand, that the subject's being mythological was a disadvantage. He also thought the 'raised and rapturous tone' rather like that of *Comus* and *Arcades*, which the poem seemed in many places to be imitating. But in Fletcher,

[1] *ER*, XXXIV, August 1820. An extract appears on pp. 493–7 below.

Jonson, and Milton, 'imagination' was 'subordinate to reason and judgment', whereas with Keats it was 'paramount and supreme'. A good deal of the poem was written 'in the strangest and most fantastical manner that can be imagined':

> It seems as if the author had ventured everything that occurred to him in the shape of a glittering image or striking expression—taken the first word that presented itself to make up a rhyme, and then made that word the germ of a new cluster of images—a hint for a new excursion of the fancy—and so wandered on, equally forgetful whence he came, and heedless whither he was going, till he had covered his pages with an interminable arabesque of connected and incongruous figures, that multiplied as they extended, and were only harmonized by the brightness of their tints, and the graces of their forms. In this rash and headlong career he has of course many lapses and failures.

But the work was 'at least as full of genius as of absurdity', and Keats was 'deeply imbued' with the true spirit of English poetry. Jeffrey goes so far as to say that he knew 'no book which he would sooner employ as a test to ascertain whether any one had in him a native relish for poetry, and a genuine sensibility to its intrinsic charm'. Presumably by the 'book' he meant *Endymion*, though his review also, towards the end, discusses the new volume. He considered that 'the greater and more distinguished poets of our country' had other things than simply their 'poetry' by which to gratify their readers—'the interest of the stories they tell—the vivacity of the characters they delineate—the weight and force of the maxims and sentiments in which they abound—the very pathos and wit and humour they display', apart from their higher gift of 'poetry'. It was only in work where these other characteristics were lacking or only present in a weaker degree, that

> the true force of the attraction, exercised by the pure poetry with which they are so often combined, can be fairly appreciated—where, without much incident or many characters, and with little wit, wisdom, or arrangement, a number of bright pictures are presented to the imagination, and a fine feeling expressed of those mysterious relations by which visible external things are assimilated with inward thoughts and emotions, and become the images and exponents of all passions and affections.

A great part of *Endymion* was of this kind. It would seem to 'unpoetical readers' to be 'mere raving and absurdity', but, even to a fitter audience, 'the scope and substance' of Keats's poetry was 'rather too dreamy and abstracted to excite the strongest interest, or to sustain the attention through a work of any great compass or extent'. Keats and Barry Cornwall[1] had, however, treated their Pagan deities interestingly, giving them each 'an original character and distinct individuality', which had 'all the merit of invention, and all the grace and attraction of the fictions on which it' was 'engrafted'. Jeffrey thought it doubtful whether such beings would be permanently interesting to the reading public; but he considered that the way these poets managed them gave them the best chance, and that the effect was 'striking and graceful'. Jeffrey then quotes extensively from the poem, praising the choral hymn (I. 232–87), noting that the account of Endymion's wanderings was 'very fantastical', but contained 'splendid pieces of description, and a sort of wild richness on the whole'. He quotes passages from the description of the sleeping Adonis (II. 393–4, 403–14, 418–27) and the 'more classical sketch' of Cybele (II. 639–49). He describes III. 119–36 as 'abundantly extravagant', but adds that 'it comes of no ignoble lineage, nor shames its high descent'. Jeffrey's review rests on the firm basis of a historical perspective. It actually embodies some of the points made by Reynolds in *The Alfred*, but, unlike Reynolds's review, it is written from a judicial bench, and possesses both the advantages and the disadvantages of that type of criticism.

If one looks over the critiques of *Endymion* it can be seen that the favourable observations cover a considerable number of features. Some features, such as the flexibility of the rhythm or the intensity of the language, are only praised by one or two critics. But there was a fair measure of agreement that here was a poet of abundant and vivid imagination, with a great gift of fusing description with intense feelings of considerable range. But only Reynolds and the critic in *The Champion* emphasized the objective quality of Keats's work, and distinguished it from the egoistic character of the work of his contemporaries; and only Reynolds picked out the 'awe and humility' combined with 'affection' so frequent and so distinctive in Keats's approach to nature. The favourable reactions to *Endymion* are, however, creditable to

[1] 'Barry Cornwall'=Bryan Waller Procter (1787–1874), a minor poet of the time, particularly known for *A Sicilian Story* (1820), which treated the same theme as *Isabella*, and *Marcian Colonna* (1820). See R. W. Armour, *Barry Cornwall. A Biography* (Boston, 1935).

criticism. Yet the dominant weight of the most influential periodical reviewing, it must be remembered, was critical, harsh, or even dismissive.

The 1820 Poems were far more favourably received. The *Quarterly* and *Blackwood's*, as already mentioned, said nothing, and Hunt, who had not reviewed *Endymion*, wrote a lengthy and appreciative critique of the new volume.

Lamb[1] stresses the 'almost Chaucer-like painting' of *The Eve of St Agnes*, but gives his highest praise to *Isabella*, claiming that there was nothing in Dante, Chaucer, or Spenser 'more awfully simple in diction, more nakedly grand and moving in sentiment' than the description in stanzas xlvi–xlviii of Isabella's arrival at the spot where Lorenzo was buried, and her digging for his body. *Lamia*, 'more exuberantly rich in imagery and painting', he thought to be 'of as gorgeous stuff as ever romance was composed of', and he notes in passing the abundance of 'prodigal phrases' in Keats's work. While Lamb admitted that the scenes of *Lamia* were 'all that fairy land can do for us', he preferred *Isabella* on the ground that to him 'an ounce of feeling' was 'worth a pound of fancy'.

The reviewer in the *Monthly*,[2] unlike Conder, found in all that Keats wrote 'proof of deep thought and energetic reflection'. He recognized Keats as an innovator, whose work deserved to be thought over, and who in his manner ran 'boldly . . . counter to old opinions'. He was at fault in being often 'laboriously obscure', but his work exhibited 'great force and feeling'. The best of the poems was *Hyperion*, which displayed 'very great' power of 'both heart and hand', and 'less conceit than other parts of the volume'. Unlike Lamb, the reviewer thought *Isabella* the worst poem in the volume in its 'simplicity and affectation'. But Keats was 'very rich both in imagination and fancy', and there was a 'superabundance' of fancy in *To Autumn*, which brought 'the reality of nature' more before the reviewer's eyes than 'almost any description' he could remember.

Leigh Hunt's review in *The Indicator*[3] is far more elaborate. In the course of it Hunt notes Keats's capacity to 'pass to the most striking imagination from the most delicate and airy fancy', and he praises also Keats's narrative gift, as shown in *Isabella*, where

---

[1] The *New Times*, 19 July 1820; reprd. *Exar*, 30 July 1820.

[2] *MR*, XCII, July 1820. An extract appears on pp. 488–90 below.

[3] *Indicr*, 2, 9 August 1820. An extract appears on pp. 497–9 below.

he relates the story 'as happily, as if he had never written any poetry but that of the heart'. In *The Eve of St Agnes* Hunt stresses the 'union of extreme richness and good taste' in the portrait of Madeline preparing to go to bed, and considers this 'a striking specimen of the sudden and strong maturity of the author's genius'. Among the shorter poems he singles out the Nightingale Ode as containing 'that mixture . . . of real melancholy and imaginative relief, which poetry alone presents us in her "charmed cup" '. *Hyperion* Hunt called a 'gigantic' fragment, 'like a ruin in the desart, or the bones of the mastodon'. He thought it 'truly of a piece with its subject'. Hunt noted the 'very grand and deep-thoughtful cause' assigned by Oceanus for the irrecoverable character of the old gods' loss of their empire, and he maintained that 'the more imaginative parts of the poem' were 'worthy of this sublime moral'. Summing up Keats's achievement in the volume, Hunt claims that his versification was now 'perfected', and 'the exuberances of his imagination restrained', and that 'a calm power, the surest and loftiest of all power' had taken the place of 'the impatient workings of the younger god within him'; and Hunt continues:

> The character of his genius is that of energy and voluptuousness, each able at will to take leave of the other, and possessing, in their union, a high feeling of humanity not common to the best authors who can less combine them.

The ironical reviews in *The Guardian*[1] and Gold's *London Magazine*[2] do not come into consideration here, and the next review which has favourable things to say is Jeffrey's in the *Edinburgh*.[3] Jeffrey had spent most of the review discussing *Endymion*, and left little space for the new volume. He mentions the 'deep pathos' of several of the stanzas of *Isabella*, and, like Lamb, he was struck by the passage on Isabella's discovery of Lorenzo's corpse. He remarks on some lines of the Nightingale Ode (15–28; 63–70) as 'equally distinguished for harmony and feeling', and commends the 'lively lines to Fancy'. In *Hyperion*, too, though he could not 'advise' its 'completion', he conceded that there were 'passages of some force and grandeur'. And, speaking generally, he held that Keats had 'unquestionably a very beautiful imagination, and a great familiarity with the finest diction

---

[1] *Guardian*, 6 August 1820. [2] *Gold's LM*, II, August 1820.
[3] *ER*, XXXIV, August 1820. An extract appears on pp. 496–7 below.

of English poetry'. It is interesting that though Jeffrey writes of the 'harmony' and 'feeling' and 'liveliness' and 'force' and 'grandeur' of Keats's 'beautiful imagination' and fine diction, he does not mention depth of thought or value of attitude.

The reviewer in *The Edinburgh Magazine*[1] interestingly thought *Endymion* more completely in Keats's style than the 1820 volume, and that, though careless perhaps, it had 'greater freshness'. In the new volume *Lamia* seemed to the reviewer to display 'the greatest fancy'. *Isabella* he thought 'eminently beautiful', though the 'ledger-men' passage was 'in bad taste'. The best minor poem was the Nightingale Ode, which the reviewer felt inclined to prefer to all the rest in the book, stanzas iii and vii having for him 'a charm' which he would find it 'difficult to explain'. *Hyperion* did not impress him as much as some of the other poems, though it had 'an air of grandeur' and opened strikingly. He notices resemblances in that poem to other writers. The volume as a whole he thought to contain 'as much absolute poetry as the works of almost any contemporary writer'.

The *New Monthly*,[2] on the other hand, thought the *Lamia* volume 'far superior' to anything Keats had published before. These poems were not 'strong, or extravagant, or eccentric', but were 'pieces of calm beauty, or of lone and self-supported grandeur'. They had a 'fine freeness of touch', and were 'as pure, as genuine, and as lofty, as the severest critic could desire'. In *Lamia* the reviewer found 'a mingling of Greek majesty with fairy luxuriance' which he had not encountered elsewhere; and Keats told the tale of *Isabella* 'with a naked and affecting simplicity which goes irresistibly to the heart'. This reviewer, like several others, was impressed by the passage describing Isabella's visit to Lorenzo's burial place and the digging for the head, calling the passage 'as wildly intense as any thing which we can remember'. *The Eve of St Agnes* he writes of as 'a piece of consecrated fancy' in which 'a soft religious light is shed over the whole story'. The scene in Madeline's room he terms 'exquisite'. As for *Hyperion*, nothing exceeded 'in silent grandeur' the opening, and the picture of the Titans' abode was 'in the sublimest style of Aeschylus'. Keats had now chosen a 'high and pure style', and if he proceeded in it he would 'attain an exalted and a lasting station among English poets'.

[1] *Ed.M*, VII (2nd. Ser.), August and October 1820.
[2] *NMM*, XIV, September 1820.

John Scott, in *The London Magazine*,[1] takes Keats to task for his tirade against the 'ledger-men' and compares his 'flippant impatience' at 'the great phenomena of society' (presumably money, trade, and industry) with the 'more genial spirit' of Boccaccio. He wishes that to his 'picturesque imagination' Keats would add 'a more pliable, and, at the same time, a more magnanimous sensibility'. But Scott thought the 1820 volume would present Keats's poetical power 'to common understandings', in a 'more tangible and intelligible shape' than his earlier volumes had done. Scott instances the last two stanzas of the Nightingale Ode as 'distinct, noble, pathetic, and true', and the description of Madeline preparing to go to bed, 'in which we know not whether most to admire the magical delicacy of the hazardous picture, or its consummate, irresistible attraction'. He considered it to have 'an exquisite moral influence, corresponding with the picturesque effect'. He also praises the 'vast and gloomy grandeur' of *Hyperion*, and its 'huge' sorrows, and holds up to admiration the opening of Book I as giving the reader an illusion of 'entering the awful demesne of primeval solitude'.

The short review in *The Monthly Magazine*[2] notes the 'boldness of fancy' and 'classical expression of language' in Keats's work, and also recognizes that there was 'more of poetic capacity, more depth and intenseness of thought and feeling, with more classical power of expression' than in the work of Hunt or Barry Cornwall. He also considers Cornwall derivative from Shakespeare and Hunt; and Hunt from Dryden and Crabbe; whereas Keats was 'always himself', and 'as long as fair originality' would be thought 'superior to good imitation' he would always be preferred.

The British Critic, so savage to *Endymion*, thought the new volume a great improvement.[3] It did not approve of the 'morality' of 'the principal poems' in the volume, but it admired the 'richness of fancy' in *Lamia*. It thought little of *The Eve of St Agnes* and *Isabella*, but was impressed by *Hyperion*, which contained 'some very beautiful poetry', though most of the poem seemed 'not to have been executed with much success', and Keats was right to leave it unfinished. The reviewer singled out I. 1–51 and 72–92

[1] *LM*, II, September 1820. An extract appears on pp. 502–5 below.

[2] *MM*, L, September 1820. See pp. 509–10 below.

[3] *BC*, XIV (2nd. Ser.), September 1820. An extract appears on pp. 499–502 below.

for special praise. Keats clearly had 'poetical powers'. He should avoid the ridiculous affectations he had learned from Hunt.

The *Eclectic*[1] was disappointed with the new volume. Keats had not paid enough attention to the *Eclectic*'s critique of the 1817 *Poems*, and *Endymion*, 'that matchless tissue of sparkling and delicious nonsense', had then 'had the good fortune to fall into the hands of critics who rarely deal in either half-praise or half-censure'. Yet the publishers of that poem had included in the present volume 'an unfinished poem in the same strain'. Nevertheless, this volume did contain 'something much better'. The reviewer quotes *To Autumn* in full, lines 1–66 of *Fancy*, and *Robin Hood* in full, and commends *Lamia* as 'decidedly the best' of the longer pieces; but, though the story as given by Burton had a moral, Keats had not made use of it. The review contains no further critical observations on *Lamia*, and only accords brief mention to *Isabella*. It simply recounts the plot of *The Eve of St Agnes*, and quotes nine stanzas of the poem without comment. This lack of comment was deliberate. The reviewer wished to give Keats 'the full benefit of pleading his own cause'. He then passes to some general comments on Keats as a poet. He thinks it amply evident that Keats was 'a young man' who had 'an elegant fancy, a warm and lively imagination, and something above the average talents of persons who take to writing poetry'. But Keats had exclusively cultivated his imagination, and this was 'always attended by a dwindling or contraction of the other powers of the mind'. It was also 'the true source of affectation and eccentricity'. His treatment of Greek mythology was childish. In *Endymion* he had beaten out 'the gold of ancient fable into leaf thin enough to cover four long cantos of incoherent verse'; and now there was '*Hyperion*, books one, two, and three!' That poem did show 'a respectable degree of inventive skill and liveliness of fancy', but they were 'most miserably misapplied'. Seemingly, Keats could think or write 'scarcely any thing else than the "happy pieties" of Paganism'. And the reviewer goes on to ridicule the oracular utterance of the Grecian urn, commenting drily:

That is, all that Mr. Keats knows or cares to know—But till he knows much more than this, he will never write verses fit to live.

[1] *Ecl. R*, XIV (2nd. Ser.), September 1820. An extract appears on pp. 505–9 below.

Yet the reviewer found less affectation in this volume than in Keats's earlier poems, though there were still violent linguistic innovations. Moreover, Keats had talent, but his work had something sickly about it, and there was not 'a single reference' that the reviewer could recollect in the present volume 'to any one object of *real* interest, a single burst of virtuous affection or enlightened sentiment, a single reference, even of the most general kind, to the Supreme Being, or the slenderest indication that the Author' was 'allied by any one tie to his family, his country, or his kind'. This review, then, is largely negative, but it does express a belief in Keats's talent, and it does quote passages of which the reviewer seems to have approved. The objections he raises are mainly religious and moral, though there is also criticism of the affectations of diction. The reviewer seems, however, to have required a morality closely allied to religion, and probably deriving from it, and he fails to give Keats credit for such positive moral influences as Lamb and John Scott had noticed in *The Eve of St Agnes*.

When one considers the corpus of periodical criticism of Keats's last volume one has perforce to admit that it is, in general, disappointing; and, indeed, I believe one can say that the contemporary periodical criticism of Keats's work is not, on the whole, of such a high standard as that of Byron's or Shelley's work. Moreover, the negative criticism of Keats seems to be generally rather better, and more detailed, than that which is laudatory; though there are exceptions, such as Reynolds's and Hunt's reviews of the 1817 *Poems*, and Reynolds's, Patmore's and Jeffrey's of *Endymion*. To put the matter another way, it would be valid, I think, to say that the faults, or possible faults, in Keats's work were generally better indicated than the merits, some of which were not realized, or not clearly realized, by his contemporaries at all.

Aside from the reviews the recorded reactions of readers of Keats's poems, whether members of Keats's own circle or contemporaries outside it, are scattered and sketchy. Even so, it is of some interest to consider some of these, especially the opinions expressed by famous creative writers of the day. The record of Wordsworth's reactions is not only sparse but elusive. We have from Keats's painter friend Haydon the story of Keats reading the Ode to Pan from *Endymion* to Wordsworth, and Wordsworth only 'drily' commenting: 'a very pretty piece of paganism', which, according to Haydon, Keats 'felt very deeply'.[1] But it is by no means certain how Wordsworth pronounced the words or what he meant by them; and Keats saw Wordsworth several times in London during the next couple of weeks, and, much later, on his Northern tour, we find Keats excited about making an impromptu visit to Rydal to call on Wordsworth, who was unfortunately out.[2] Wordsworth does, in any case, seem (at least eventually) to have recognized that Keats had real talent. He asks Haydon in the last year of Keats's life: 'How is Keates [*sic*]?', adding, 'He is a youth of too great promise for the sorry company he keeps'[3]; and, in the same year, Wordsworth included in the Duddon volume some lines which echo Keats, especially, as Mrs Moorman has pointed out, in some words in one sonnet,[4] which seem like a deliberate tribute ('The Fancy, too industrious Elf'). But these are only stray reactions, and we should have liked to know a good deal more of what Wordsworth thought of any of Keats's work he may have read. The same goes for Coleridge, the accounts of whose famous chance meeting and walk with Keats on Hampstead Heath[5] are little consolation for the lack of record of his opinions on Keats's poetry. As to Byron, he began[6] by seignorially scorning the author of *Sleep and Poetry* as 'a tadpole of the Lakes, a young disciple of six or seven new schools' who had dared to attack Pope. When Murray sent him the 1820 Poems, he wrote insultingly protesting at their being sent to him,[7] and seems not to have bothered to read them[8]; and, in September 1820, outraged by Jeffrey's praise of 'Jack Keats or Ketch, or whatever his names are', he writes: 'why, his is the Onanism of Poetry', and refers to him as 'this miserable Self-polluter of the human

[1] Letter from Haydon to ? Edward Moxon, 29 November 1845, reprinted by C. L. Finney in *The Evolution of Keats's Poetry*, I. 328.

[2] See W. J. Bate, *John Keats* (Cambridge, Mass., 1965; London, 1967), 267–9, 349 ff.

[3] Letter from Wordsworth to Haydon, 16 January 1820, *Letters of William and Dorothy Wordsworth*, II. ii. 578.

[4] Mary Moorman, *William Wordsworth: A Biography*, 2 vols. (London, 1965), II. 377–8. The words occur in *The River Duddon*, sonnet xxiv, l. 10.

[5] Coleridge, *Table Talk*, 14 August 1832; and see also Bate, *op. cit.*, 468.

[6] In the 'Observations upon an Article in *Blackwood's Magazine*', written 15 March 1820, but not published in Byron's lifetime (*LJ*, IV. 493; and see p. 187 above).

[7] Letter to Murray, 12 October 1820 (*LJ*, V. 93).

[8] Marchand, *Byron*, 873.

mind'[1]; and he repeats his opinion a few days later, referring to Keats's poetry as 'a sort of mental masturbation', and adding:

> I don't mean he is *indecent*, but viciously soliciting his own ideas into a state which is neither poetry nor any thing else but a Bedlam vision produced by raw pork and opium.[2]

When Shelley wrote to him of Keats's death, however, Byron, assuming the truth of Shelley's account that Keats had died 'in paroxysms of despair at the contemptuous attack on his book in the *Quarterly Review*', wrote in reply[3]:

> I did not think criticism had been so killing. Though I differ from you essentially in your estimate of his performances, I so much abhor all unnecessary pain, that I would rather he had been seated on the highest peak of Parnassus than have perished in such a manner. Poor fellow! though with such inordinate self-love he would probably have not been very happy. I read the review of *Endymion* in the *Quarterly*. It was severe,—but surely not so severe as many reviews in that and other journals upon others.

Moreover, three months later he asked Murray to omit everything he had written about Keats in any manuscript or publication, adding 'His *Hyperion* is a fine monument, and will keep his name.'[4] Later the same year he wrote a note on the passage attacking Keats in his manuscript Observations on *Blackwood's* 'Remarks on *Don Juan*'. This note included the following recantation:

> My indignation at Mr. Keats's depreciation of Pope has hardly permitted me to do justice to his own genius, which, malgré all the fantastic fopperies of his style, was undoubtedly of great promise. His fragment of *Hyperion* seems actually inspired by the Titans, and is as sublime as Æschylus. He is a loss to our literature; and the more so, as he himself before his death, is said to have been persuaded that he had not taken the right line, and was reforming his style upon the more classical models of the language.[5]

Yet Byron could not refrain from including a mixed comment on Keats in his pageant (in *Don Juan XI*) of possible successors to Byron himself as 'the Napoleon of the realms of rhyme':

[1] Letter to Murray, 4 November 1820 (*LJ*, V. 109). See Marchand, *Byron*, n. on 886, l. 20, re T. J. Wise's supply of the omissions as printed in *LJ*.

[2] Letter to Murray, 9 November 1820 (*LJ*, V. 117); and see Marchand, *Byron*, n. on 886, l. 27, indicating British Museum Ashley MS 5161 as the source of the full text as printed by Marchand, supplying the omissions in the letter as printed in *LJ*.

[3] Letter to Shelley, 26 April 1821 (*LJ*, V. 267).

[4] Letter to Murray, 30 July 1821 (*LJ*, V. 331).   [5] *LJ*, IV, 491 n.

John Keats, who was kill'd off by one critique,
  Just as he really promised something great,
If not intelligible, without Greek
  Contrived to talk about the Gods of late,
Much as they might have been supposed to speak.
  Poor fellow! His was an untoward fate;
'Tis strange the mind, that very fiery particle,
Should let itself be snuff'd out by an article.[1]

Shelley's attitude to Keats's work was far more sympathetic, though by no means without reservations. He had met Keats in December 1816, and soon afterwards we find him advising the younger poet not to be in a hurry to publish.[2] Keats was nettled, since he had already arranged to do precisely that the following March. After the 1817 *Poems* appeared Keats's resentment seems to come out in an episode recounted by Haydon[3]:

> Keats said to me today as we were walking along 'Byron, Scott, Southey, and Shelley think they are to lead the age, but . . . . . [4] This was said with all the consciousness of Genius; his face reddened.

On the other hand, we know that Shelley had visited the printer of Keats's first volume, and told him to take special care.[5] But we have no record of Shelley's detailed views on those 1817 *Poems*, though we can gather by implication that he thought that Keats was at that stage 'entangled in the cold vanity of systems',[6] by which it seems that Shelley meant *literary* systems, systems of diction, sentence structure, and versification. He did, however, also credit Keats with a 'fine imagination', and thought that he 'ought to become something excellent'. When *Endymion* appeared Shelley considered 'much praise' due to himself for getting through it; but he also thought it 'full of some of the highest and finest gleams of poetry', adding

> indeed every thing seems to be viewed by the mind of a poet which is described in it. I think if he had printed about 50 pages of fragments from it I should have been led to admire Keats as a poet more than I ought, of which there is now no danger.[7]

---

[1] *Don Juan XI.* lx.   [2] Bate, *op. cit.*, 119–20.

[3] Haydon, diary entry for 7 April 1817, *Diary*, ed. W. B. Pope, 2 vols. (Cambridge, Mass., 1960–3), II. 106–7.

[4] Unfortunately, the rest of the sentence has been erased in the MS.

[5] Bate, *op. cit.*, 145.

[6] Letter to Charles Ollier, 16 August 1818 (*SL*, II. 31).

[7] Letter to Charles Ollier, 6 September 1818 (*ibid.*, 117).

Shelley passed the same sort of opinion, though in gentler terms, in a letter to Keats himself in July 1820[1]:

I have lately read your Endymion again and ever with a new sense of the treasures of poetry it contains, though treasures poured forth with indistinct profusion. This, people in general will not endure, and that is the cause of the comparatively few copies which have been sold. I feel persuaded that you are capable of the greatest things, so you but will.

After the publication of the 1820 Poems Shelley wrote a letter (apparently never sent) to Gifford, Editor of the *Quarterly*,[2] protesting at its review of *Endymion* and claiming that that poem 'with all its faults' was 'a very remarkable production for a man of Keats's age' and that 'the promise of ultimate excellence' was 'such as has rarely been afforded even by such as have afterwards attained high literary eminence'. Shelley draws attention to II. 893 ff., III. 113–20 ff. and 193 ff., adding

why it should have been reviewed at all, excepting for the purpose of bringing its excellencies into notice I cannot conceive, for it was very little read, and there was no danger that it should become a model to the age of that false taste with which I confess that it is replenished—

Shelley goes on to allege that the first effects of the review on Keats 'resembled insanity', and that he became suicidal, that the 'agony of his sufferings' caused the rupture of a blood vessel in his lungs, and that consumption began. Shelley then switches attention to the new volume, praising the *Hyperion* fragment as in great part 'in the very highest style of poetry', adding

I speak impartially, for the canons of taste to which Keats has conformed in his other compositions are the very reverse of my own.

One would have liked Shelley to have amplified this teasing remark. He had already commended *Hyperion* highly in a letter to Marianne Hunt (Leigh Hunt's wife),[3] contrasting Keats's 'other things' as 'imperfect enough, and what is worse written in the bad sort of style which is becoming fashionable among those who fancy that they are imitating Hunt and Wordsworth', and he

---

[1] *SL*, II. 221.   [2] *Ibid.*, II. 251–3.
[3] Letter to Marianne Hunt, 29 October 1820 (*SL*, II. 239).

expresses a similar opinion to Peacock[1] and to Byron.[2] Shelley, then, may well have still thought of Keats as a poet of promise rather than of achievement. Shelley, indeed, was evidently keen on the idea of educating Keats when he came to Italy by teaching him Spanish and Greek; but it is worth bearing in mind that he expressed his awareness that in doing so he would be 'nourishing a rival' who would 'far surpass' him.[3] It is also worth remembering not only the tribute of *Adonais* but also that Shelley had a copy of the *Lamia* volume open in his pocket when he was drowned.[4]

Shelley's friend Peacock, on the other hand, had little use for the 'amorous mythology' of the Cockney School, and he made no significant distinctions among them. To Shelley's suggestion that he should read *Hyperion*, 'an astonishing piece of writing',[5] Peacock drily rejoined:

> If I should live to the age of Methusalem, and have uninterrupted literary leisure, I should not find time to read Keats's *Hyperion*.[6]

Peacock's astringent reaction was based on his experience of *Endymion*, which seems to have offended him mightily by its unfaithfulness to the *facts* of Greek mythology.[7]

Far more sympathetic to Keats was Henry Crabb Robinson. Robinson did read *Hyperion*, and he recorded in his *Diary* his opinion both of that poem and of Keats's work in general:

> *Dec. 8th.* I read a little of Keats's poems to the Aders. The beginning of the *Hyperion*—really a piece of great promise. There is a force, wildness, and originality in the works of this young poet which, if his perilous journey to Italy does not destroy him, promise to place him at the head of the next generation of poets. Lamb places him next to Wordsworth—not meaning any comparison, for they are dissimilar.[8]

A week later he comments briefly on *Isabella* and again on Keats's status as a poet:

[1] Letter to Peacock, 8 November 1820 (*ibid.*, II. 244); 15 February 1821 (*ibid.*, II. 262).

[2] Letter to Byron, 4 May 1821 (*ibid.*, II. 290).

[3] Letter to Marianne Hunt, 29 October 1820 (*ibid.*, II. 240).

[4] Letter from Leigh Hunt to Horace Smith, 25 June 1822, in Ashley MSS, first printed (not quite entire) in *The Morning Chronicle*, 12 August 1822; first printed entire in T. J. Wise, *A Shelley Library* (London, 1924).

[5] Letter to Peacock, 8 November 1820 (*SL*, II. 244).

[6] Letter to Shelley, 4 December 1820 (*Works*, Halliford edn., VIII. 219–20).

[7] See Robert Buchanan, *A Poet's Sketchbook* (London, 1883), 107, quoted C. Dawson, *His Fine Wit* (London, 1970), 98.

[8] *Diary*, 8 December 1820 (*HCRBW*, I. 58; *D*, 66).

Dec. 15th. I read Keats's *Pot of Basil*—a pathetic tale delightfully told. I afterwards read the story in Boccaccio, each in his way excellent. I am greatly mistaken if Keats do not very soon take a high place among our poets. There is great feeling and a powerful imagination in this little volume.[1]

The terms Crabb Robinson employs are fairly typical of the commendations Keats's poetry received from its contemporary admirers.

Among Keats's own particular circle his work was probably discussed quite extensively, but what survives in written form, apart from the periodical reviews by John Hamilton Reynolds, and whoever wrote the review of *Endymion* in *The Champion* (if that was a member of Keats's circle other than Reynolds), is, on the whole, somewhat disappointing. The most interesting critical remarks are those in the notes and letters of Richard Woodhouse, though some of the things said by Benjamin Bailey and by John Taylor, Keats's publisher, are probably worth brief mention.

In October 1818 Woodhouse wrote some notes on the critiques of *Endymion* in the *Quarterly* and *Blackwood's*.[2] The notes on the *Quarterly*'s review contain one or two quite interesting points. Commenting on Croker's stricture that the rhymes in *Endymion* suggested the ideas, Woodhouse rejoins that, even if that were so, it would not be a fault, and that in any case the objection was unfounded, for, if one changed the final words of the lines, the 'sense & picture of the descriptions &c' remained. Woodhouse also repudiated Croker's attack on Keats's compound words, maintaining that these had been in use from Chaucer onwards. And to Croker's accusation that Keats had coined certain words Woodhouse replies that the majority were to be found in Shakespeare or Spenser. This last defence seems valid, but Woodhouse's choice of Chaucer as a compounder of words seems rather odd.

In the same month Woodhouse wrote a long letter to Keats,[3] in which he recalls a conversation they had had at Hessey's,[4] in which Woodhouse understood Keats to say that he intended not to write any more, because there was 'nothing original to be

[1] *Ibid.*, 15 December 1820 (*HCRBW*, I. 259; *D* 67).
[2] Printed in *The Keats Circle*, ed. H. E. Rollins, 1965, I. 44–5.
[3] 21 October 1818, *ibid.*, 46–52.
[4] James Augustus Hessey, partner in Taylor and Hessey, the publishers of *Endymion* and of the *Lamia* volume.

written in poetry'. Woodhouse expresses the contrary belief, that the wealth of poetry was inexhaustible, and he supports this philosophically by arguing that the ideas from each of the various senses taken singly and in combination 'store the mind with endless images of beauty and perfection', and that the 'passions' add 'life and motion', and 'reflection and the moral sense' give 'order relish unity and harmony' [sic] to 'this mighty world of inanimate matter', and Poetry consists 'in the gleaning of the highest, the truest and the sweetest of these ideas, in the orderly grouping of them, and arraying them in the garb of exquisite Numbers'. The true poet 'need never fear that the treasury he draws on can be exhausted, nor despair of being always able to make an original selection'. The rest of the letter is substantially an expression of Woodhouse's conviction that Keats was just such a true poet.

A few days later Woodhouse affirms his belief that such a genius as Keats had not appeared since Shakespeare and Milton[1]; and he even claims that *Endymion* contained 'more beauties (and that of a higher order) less conceit and bad taste' and 'much more promise of excellence' than were to be found in *Venus and Adonis*, which Shakespeare had written at about the same age. Woodhouse does, however, go on to admit that Keats's work had great faults; but he holds that these were 'more than counter-balanced' by its 'beauties'. Was it to be expected that poets were to be 'given to the world, as our first parents were, in a state of maturity'? And later in the same letter Woodhouse expresses his firm belief that if Keats were to live a normal span of life, and not to be stifled by the critics before full maturity, he would 'rank on a level with the best of the last or of the present generation', and after his death 'take his place at their head'. It is to be borne in mind that Woodhouse wrote this not far short of two years before the publication of the 1820 Poems.

A further few days later, Woodhouse wrote some notes on Keats's reply to his letter of 21 October.[2] He reflects carefully on Keats's idea of the 'poetical Character' which has 'no character'; and he recognizes that, besides Keats, Shakespeare alone was a poet of that kind. Byron was not. He could certainly 'conceive and describe a dark accomplished vilain [sic] in love—and a female tender and kind who loves him. Or a sated and palled Sensualist Misanthrope and Deist'—but there his power ended.

[1] Letter to Mary Frogley, 25 October 1818, *ibid.*, I. 54–7.   [2] *Ibid.*, 57–60.

The true poet's 'imaginative faculty' was not limited but fully universal. These thoughts are probably largely a reflection of Keats's own, but they seem to be a true and perceptive one.

In or about August 1819 we find Woodhouse, who was transcribing *Isabella* for the fourth time, affirming his belief that it was 'a noble poem' or else his judgment was 'not worth the tythe of a fig'.[1] More interesting than this bare evaluation, however, is Woodhouse's account of a conversation he had with Keats when Keats came to breakfast with him one morning in September 1819 and stayed with him until he boarded the coach for Weymouth at three in the afternoon.[2] Woodhouse says that he believed Keats wanted to publish *The Eve of St Agnes* and *Lamia* immediately, but that Keats never mentioned *Isabella*. Woodhouse says that he assured Keats that 'it would please more than *The Eve of St Agnes*', but that Keats said he 'could not bear' *Isabella* 'now'. It seemed to him 'mawkish'. Woodhouse thought this simply a natural revulsion of a writer on 'sobered' reflection. The feeling of mawkishness seemed to Woodhouse to be what came over one when anything 'of great tenderness and excessive simplicity' was met with when one was not 'in a sufficiently tender and simple frame of mind to bear it', and he did not believe there was anything 'in the most passionate parts of *Isabella* to excite this feeling'. He admitted that it might, like *Lear*, 'leave the reader far behind', but held that it had 'none of that sugar and butter sentiment, that cloys and disgusts'. He also mentions that Keats had made some 'trifling alterations' in *The Eve of St Agnes*, including a change in the last three lines so as 'to leave on the reader a sense of pettish disgust, by bringing Old Angela in dead stiff and ugly'. Woodhouse feared that Keats 'had a fancy for trying his hand at an attempt to play with his reader, and fling him off at last'. He suspected Keats of affecting 'the "Don Juan" style of mingling up sentiment and sneering'; but he gathered that Keats had probably not seen the poem at the time he made the alteration. This is a teasing point, and it is hard to be sure that Keats had not. A more serious change that Keats had made, indeed, was to represent Porphyro as acting 'all the acts of a bonâ fide husband' as soon as Madeline had confessed her love. Woodhouse writes that he 'abused' this change for "a full hour by the *Temple* clock", telling Keats that it would 'render the poem unfit for ladies', but that

---

[1] Letter to John Taylor, ? August 1819, *ibid.*, 78–81.
[2] Letter to John Taylor, 19, 20 September 1819, *ibid.*, 89–95.

Keats had retorted that he did not want ladies to read his poetry, and 'that he should despise a man who would be such an eunuch in sentiment as to leave a maid, with that character about her, in such a situation: and should despise himself to write about it, etc., etc., etc.' Keats then read *Lamia* to Woodhouse, who was 'much pleased with it', despite the fact that Keats was so bad at reading his own poetry, and despite Woodhouse's own slowness in catching even the sense of poetry read by the best reader for the first time. And Woodhouse remarks pertinently that Keats's poetry 'really must be studied to be properly appretiated [*sic*]'. Woodhouse recounts the plot of the poem to Taylor, and comments: 'You may suppose all these events have given Keats ample scope for some beautiful poetry: which even in this cursory hearing of it came every now and then upon me, and made me "start, as tho' a Sea Nymph quired".' Woodhouse agreed with Keats on the appropriateness of the 'Drydenian heroic' metre, with its triplets and alexandrines, and thought Keats had 'a fine feeling when and where he may use poetical licences with effect'. Woodhouse also later[1] made some observations on the second quatrain of the sonnet 'When I have fears that I may cease to be', showing that he had well understood Keats's creative process of 'culling' from a 'redundancy of images', which came to him when he was 'full of ideas'.

As to Bailey, the first things of interest that he says appear in the letter to John Taylor in which he mentions for the first time his fateful meeting with Lockhart.[2] Bailey stoutly maintains that 'as a *man of genius*' Keats was 'defensible, let him be abused as he may'; but he feels that he could not defend the '*moral* part' of *Endymion*. There were 'two great blotches in it in this respect'. The first was 'indelicacy'; and Bailey regrets that he did not 'represent' that 'very strongly' to Keats before the poem went to press, but he adds by way of excuse that Book II had been concluded before he met Keats. The second 'blotch' was its 'approaching inclination' to that 'abominable principle of *Shelley's*— that *Sensual Love* is the principle of *things*'. Nearly two years later Bailey, again in a letter to Taylor,[3] expresses the hope that Keats's new volume will succeed, but the fear that it may not. There were 'some principles' which Keats had 'taken up', which had been 'adopted by many of similar powers of mind, and under similar

[1] In ? July 1820, *ibid.*, 128–30. [2] 29 August 1818, *ibid.*, 31–6.
[3] 27 July 1820, *ibid.*, 125–7.

circumstances', which Bailey sincerely lamented, and could 'make allowances for'. Keats had 'abundant power, but little knowledge'. He had 'good dispositions and noble qualities of heart', but had not 'kept the best society for one of his character and constitution'. 'Many of his moral principles' were 'consequently loose', and his 'moral conduct not very exact'; and 'the Phantom of Honor' was 'substituted for the truth and substance of *Religion*'. Bailey feared that 'these traits' were certain to appear in Keats's book, and he was convinced, after careful reflection, that those causes would 'operate to his great hindrance throughout his career in the literary world and as a moral agent'. This is perhaps the sort of criticism Keats could have expected from *The British Review* or *The Christian Observer* had they taken any notice of him.

John Taylor's surviving critical observations on Keats's work are about as few as Bailey's. In reply to Woodhouse's letter mentioning the changes Keats had made in *The Eve of St Agnes*, Taylor condemns the changes outright[1]: 'This Folly of Keats is the most stupid piece of Folly I can conceive.' Taylor was not prepared (and he thought his partner Hessey would not be prepared either) to be 'accessary . . . towards publishing any thing which' could 'only be read by Men', since 'even on their Minds a bad effect must follow the Encouragement of those Thoughts which cannot be rased [*sic*] without Impropriety'. Had it been natural to Keats to conduct the story in that way, Taylor would still not have encouraged him, but then Keats would have been 'personally perhaps excusable', but, as it was, 'the flying in the Face of all Decency and Discretion' was 'doubly offensive from its being accompanied with so preposterous a Conceit on his part of being able to overcome the best founded Habits of our Nature'. Also, had Keats realized what the 'Society' and 'Suffrages' of women were worth, 'he would never have thought of depriving himself of them'. Taylor again states his refusal to print unless the passage be left as it was before; but then he hesitates, and promises to suspend judgment until he sees or hears more. He goes on to express surprise that Keats had taken such a dislike to *Isabella*, on which he shared Woodhouse's opinion, and which he thought he would prefer to *Lamia*, from what he had seen of that poem. Taylor did not care for fairy tales, or 'perceive true Poetry', except when it was 'in Conjunction with good Sentiment', and possibly for one or other of these reasons,

[1] 25 September 1819, *ibid.*, 95–8.

did not think he was likely to be pleased by *Lamia*. In a later letter, to Hessey,[1] Taylor tells of a call paid on him by William Blackwood, during which Taylor expostulated with Blackwood about the treatment Keats had received in his magazine. This is interesting, but not literary criticism. And what I have extracted from the records of the Keats circle is virtually all the literary criticism of interest that has survived in writing, apart from what they wrote in periodicals. It is a matter for regret that we have no record of the conversations they had, during which much of critical interest may well have been said about Keats's work.

Speaking more generally, the harvest of literary criticism of Keats's poetry by his contemporaries, apart from the periodical criticism, though sporadically of considerable value, is on the whole meagre. Indeed, as I have already suggested, it is probably valid to say that the contemporary criticism of Keats's work, even including that in the periodicals, is with few exceptions less impressive than that written on the work of Byron and Shelley.

[1] 31 August 1820, *ibid.*, 133–7.

An Anthology of Contemporary Criticism
1817–20

From the unsigned review of Keats's *Poems* (1817) by John Hamilton Reynolds in *The Champion*, 9 March 1817.

Here is a little volume filled throughout with very graceful and genuine poetry. The author is a very young man, and one, as we augur from the present work, that is likely to make a great addition to those who would overthrow that artificial taste which French criticism has long planted amongst us. At a time when nothing is talked of but the power and the passion of Lord Byron, and the playful and elegant fancy of Moore, and the correctness of Rogers, and the sublimity and pathos of Campbell (these terms we should conceive are kept ready composed in the Edinburgh Review-shop) a young man starts suddenly before us, with a genius that is likely to eclipse them all. He comes fresh from nature,—and the originals of his images are to be found in her keeping. Young writers are in general in their early productions imitators of their favorite poet; like young birds that in their first songs, mock the notes of those warblers, they hear the most, and love the best: but this youthful poet appears to have tuned his voice in solitudes,—to have sung from the pure inspiration of nature. In the simple meadows he has proved that he can

> '————See shapes of light, aerial lymning,
> And catch soft floating from a faint heard hymning.'

We find in his poetry the glorious effect of summer days and leafy spots on rich feelings, which are in themselves a summer. He relies directly and wholly on nature. He marries poesy to genuine simplicity. He makes her artless,—yet abstains carefully from giving her an uncomely homeliness:—that is, he shows one can be familiar with nature, yet perfectly strange to the habits of common life. Mr. Keats is fated, or 'we have no judgment in an honest face;' to look at natural objects with his mind, as Shakespeare and Chaucer did,— and not merely with his eye as nearly all modern poets do;—to

451

clothe his poetry with a grand intellectual light,—and to lay his
name in the lap of immortality. . . . It will be seen how familiar he
is with all that is green, light, and beautiful in nature;—and with
what an originality his mind dwells on all great or graceful objects.
His imagination is very powerful,—and one thing we have observed
with pleasure, that it never attempts to soar on undue occasions. The
imagination, like the eagle on the rock, should keep its eye constantly on the sun,—and should never be started heavenward, unless
something magnificent marred its solitude. Again, though Mr.
Keats' poetry is remarkably abstracted, it is never out of reach of the
mind; there are one or two established writers of this day who think
that mystery is the soul of poetry—that artlessness is a vice—and
that nothing can be graceful that is not metaphysical;—and even
young writers have sunk into this error, and endeavoured to
puzzle the world with a confused sensibility.

[There follows a detailed account of the volume, with ample
quotation, and especial praise for the sonnets and for *Sleep and
Poetry*. The reviewer summarizes his critique as follows:]

We conclude with earnestly recommending the work to all our
readers. It is not without defects, which may be easily mentioned,
and as easily rectified. The author, from his natural freedom of
versification, at times passes to an absolute faultiness of measure:
—This he should avoid. He should also abstain from the use of
compound epithets as much as possible. He has a few faults which
youth must have;—he is apt occasionally to make his descriptions
overwrought,—but on the whole we never saw a book which had so
little reason to plead youth as its excuse. The best poets of the day
might not blush to own it.

From Leigh Hunt's unsigned review of *Poems* (1817) in *The
Examiner*, 6 and 13 July 1817.

This is the production of the young writer whom we had the pleasure
of announcing to the public a short time since, and several of whose
Sonnets have appeared meanwhile in the "Examiner" with the
signature of J. K. From these and stronger evidences in the book
itself, the readers will conclude that the author and his critic are
personal friends; and they are so—made however, in the first instance, by nothing but his poetry, and at no greater distance of
time than the announcement above-mentioned. We had published
one of his Sonnets in our paper, without knowing more of him
than any other anonymous correspondent; but at the period in
question, a friend brought us one morning some copies of verses,

which he said were from the pen of a youth. We had not been led, generally speaking, by a good deal of experience in these matters, to expect pleasure from introductions of the kind, so much as pain; but we had not read more than a dozen lines, when we recognised "a young poet indeed."

It is no longer a new observation, that poetry has of late years undergone a very great change, or rather, to speak properly, poetry has undergone no change, but something which was not poetry has made way for the return of something which is. The school which existed till lately since the restoration of Charles the 2d, was rather a school of wit and ethics in verse, than anything else; nor was the verse, with the exception of Dryden's, of the best order. The authors, it is true, are to be held in great honour. Great wit there certainly was, excellent satire, excellent sense, pithy sayings; and Pope distilled as much real poetry as could be got from the drawing-room world in which the art then lived,—from the flowers and luxuries of artificial life,—into that exquisite little toilet-bottle of essence, the *Rape of the Lock*. But there was little imagination, of a higher order, no intense feeling of nature, no sentiment, no real music or variety. Even the writers who gave evidences meanwhile of a truer poetical faculty, Gray, Thomson, Akenside, and Collins himself, were content with a great deal of second-hand workmanship, and with false styles made up of other languages and a certain kind of inverted cant. It has been thought that Cowper was the first poet who re-opened the true way to nature and a natural style; but we hold this to be a mistake, arising merely from certain negations on the part of that amiable but by no means powerful writer. Cowper's style is for the most part as inverted and artificial as that of the others; and we look upon him to have been by nature not so great a poet as Pope: but Pope, from certain infirmities on his part, was thrown into the world, and thus had to get what he could out of an artificial sphere: Cowper, from other and distressing infirmities (which by the way the wretched superstition that undertook to heal, only burnt in upon him), was confined to a still smaller though more natural sphere, and in truth did not much with it, though quite as much perhaps as was to be expected from an organisation too sore almost to come in contact with any thing.

It was the Lake Poets in our opinion (however grudgingly we say it, on some accounts) that were the first to revive a true taste for nature; and like most Revolutionists, especially of the cast which they have since turned out to be, they went to an extreme, calculated rather at first to make the readers of poetry disgusted with originality and adhere with contempt and resentment to their magazine commonplaces. This had a bad effect also in the way of re-action; and none of those writers have ever since been able to free themselves from certain stubborn affectations, which having been ignorantly confounded by others with the better part of them, have been retained by their self-love with a still less pardonable want of wisdom. The greater part indeed of the poetry of Mr. Southey, a weak man in all respects, is really made up of little else. Mr. Coleridge still trifles with his poetical as he has done with his metaphysical talent. Mr. Lamb, in our opinion, has a more real tact of humanity, a modester, Shakespearean wisdom, than any of them; and had he written more, might have delivered the school victoriously from all its defects. But it is Mr. Wordsworth who has advanced it the most, and who in spite of some morbidities as well as mistaken theories in other respects, has opened upon us a fund of thinking and imagination, that ranks him as the successor of the true and abundant poets of the older time. Poetry, like Plenty, should be represented with a cornucopia, but it should be a real one; not swelled out and insidiously *optimized* at the top, like Mr. Southey's stale strawberry baskets, but fine and full to the depth, like a heap from the vintage. Yet from the time of Milton till lately, scarcely a tree had been planted that could be called a poet's own. People got shoots from France, that ended in nothing but a little barren wood, from which they made flutes for young gentlemen and fan-sticks for ladies. The rich and enchanted ground of real poetry, fertile with all that English succulence could produce, bright with all that Italian sunshine could lend, and haunted with exquisite humanities, had become invisible to mortal eyes like the garden of Eden:

"And from that time those Graces were not seen."

These Graces, however, are re-appearing; and one of the greatest evidences is the little volume before us; for the work is not one of mere imitation, or a compilation of ingenious and promising things that merely announce better, and that after all might only help to keep up a bad system; but here is a young poet giving himself up to his own impressions, and revelling in real poetry for its own sake. He has had his advantages, because others have cleared the way into those happy bowers; but it shews the strength of his natural tendency, that he has not been turned aside by the lingering enticements of a former system, and by the self-love which interests others in enforcing them. We do not, of course, mean to say that Mr. Keats has as much talent as he will have ten years hence, or that there are no imitations in his book, or that he does not make mistakes common to inexperience; the reverse is inevitable at his time of life. In proportion to our ideas, or impressions of the images of things, must be our acquaintance with the things themselves. But our author has all the sensitiveness of temperament requisite to receive these impressions; and wherever he has turned hitherto, he has evidently felt them deeply.

The very faults indeed of Mr. Keats arise from a passion for beauties, and a young impatience to vindicate them; and as we have mentioned these, we shall refer to them at once. They may be comprised in two; first, a tendency to notice every thing too indiscriminately and without an eye to natural proportion and effect; and second, a sense of the proper variety of versification without a due consideration of its principles.

The former error is visible in several parts of the book, but chiefly though mixed with great beauties in the Epistles, and more between pages 28 and 47, where are collected the author's earliest pieces, some of which, we think, might have been omitted, especially the string of magistrate-interrogatories about a shell and a copy of verses.[1] See also (p. 61) a comparison of wine poured out in heaven to the appearance of a falling star, and (p. 62) the sight of far-seen fountains in the same region to "silver streaks across a dolphin's fin."[2] It was by thus giving way to every idea that came across him, that Marino, a man of real poetical fancy, but no judgment, corrupted the poetry of Italy; a catastrophe, which however we by no means anticipate in our author, who with regard to this point is much more deficient in age than in good taste. We shall presently have to notice passages of a reverse nature, and these are by far the most numerous. But we warn him against a fault, which is the more tempting to a young writer of genius, inasmuch as it involves something so opposite to the contented commonplace and vague generalities of the late school of poetry. There is a superabundance of detail, which, though not so wanting, of course, in power of perception, is as faulty and unseasonable sometimes as common-place. It depends upon circumstances, whether we are to consider ourselves near enough, as it were, to the subject we are describing to grow microscopical upon it. A person basking in a landscape, for instance, and a person riding through it, are in two very different situations for the exercise of their eyesight; and even where the license is most allowable, care must be taken not to give to small things and great, to nice detail and to general feeling, the same proportion of effect. Errors of this kind in poetry answer to a want of perspective in painting, and of a due distribution of light and shade. . . .

Mr. Keats' other fault, the one in his versification, arises from a similar cause, that of contradicting over-zealously the fault on the opposite side. It is this which provokes him now and then into mere

[1] On receiving a Curious Shell—Ed.
[2] To my brother George, ll. 41–2, 50—Ed.

roughness and discords for their own sake, not for that of variety and contrasted harmony. We can manage, by substituting a greater feeling for a smaller, a line like the following:

I shall roll on the grass with two-fold ease;
[*To Charles Cowden Clarke*, l. 79]

but by no contrivance of any sort can we prevent this from jumping out of the heroic measure into mere rhythmicality,

How many bards gild the lapses of time!
[*Sonnet IV*]

We come now however to the beauties; and the reader will easily perceive that they not only outnumber the faults a hundred fold, but that they are of a nature decidedly opposed to what is false and inharmonious. Their characteristics indeed are a fine ear, a fancy and imagination at will, and an intense feeling of external beauty in its most natural and least expressible simplicity.

We shall give some specimens of the least beauty first, and conclude with a noble extract or two that will shew the second, as well as the powers of our young poet in general. The harmony of his verses will appear throughout.

The first poem consists of a piece of luxury in a rural spot, ending with an allusion to the story of Endymion and to the origin of other lovely tales of mythology, on the ground suggested by Mr. Wordsworth in a beautiful passage of his *Excursion*. Here, and in the other largest poem, which closes the book, Mr. Keats is seen to his best advantage, and displays all that fertile power of association and imagery which constitutes the abstract poetical faculty as distinguished from every other. He wants age for a greater knowledge of humanity, but evidences of this also bud forth here and there. To come however to our specimens:

The first page of the book presents us with a fancy, founded, as all beautiful fancies are, on a strong sense of what really exists or occurs. He is speaking of

A gentle Air in Solitude

There crept
A little noiseless noise among the leaves,
Born of the very sigh that silence heaves.
['I stood tip-toe', ll. 10–12]

456

Young Trees

There too should be
The frequent chequer of a youngling tree,
That with a score of light green brethren shoots
From the quaint mossiness of aged roots;
Round which is heard a spring-head of clear waters.

[*Ibid.*, ll. 37–41]

Any body who has seen a throng of young beeches, furnishing those natural clumpy seats at the root, must recognise the truth and grace of this description. The remainder of this part of the poem, especially from

Open afresh your round of starry folds,
Ye ardent marigolds!

[ll. 47 ff.]

down to the bottom of page 5, affords an exquisite proof of close observation of nature as well as the most luxuriant fancy.

The Moon

Lifting her silver rim
Above a cloud, and with a gradual swim
Coming into the blue with all her light.

[ll. 113–15]

Fir Trees

Fir trees grow around,
Aye dropping their hard fruit upon the ground.

[*Calidore*, ll. 40–1]

This last line is in the taste of the Greek simplicity.

A starry Sky

The dark silent blue
With all its diamonds trembling through and through.

[*To my brother George*, ll. 57–8]

Sound of a Pipe

And some are hearing eagerly the wild
Thrilling liquidity of dewy piping.

[*Sleep and Poetry*, ll. 370–1]

The *Specimen of an Induction to a Poem*, and the fragment of the Poem itself entitled *Calidore*, contain some very natural touches on

457

the human side of things; as when speaking of a lady who is anxiously looking out on the top of a tower for her defender, he describes her as one

> Who cannot feel for cold her tender feet;
>
> *[Specimen of an Induction to a Poem*, l. 14]

and when Calidore has fallen into a fit of amorous abstraction, he says that

> —The kind voice of good Sir Clerimond
> Came to his ear, as [like] something from beyond
> His present being.
>
> *[Calidore*, ll. 99–101]

The Epistles, the Sonnets, and indeed the whole of the book, contain strong evidences of warm and social feelings, but particularly the Epistle to Charles Cowden Clarke, and the Sonnet to his own Brothers, in which the "faint cracklings" of the coal-fire are said to be

> Like whispers of the household gods that keep
> A gentle empire o'er fraternal souls.
>
> *[To my Brothers*, ll. 3–4]

The Epistle to Mr. Clarke is very amiable as well as poetical, and equally honourable to both parties,—to the young writer who can be so grateful towards his teacher, and to the teacher who had the sense to perceive his genius, and the qualities to call forth his affection. . . .

The following passage in one of the Sonnets passes, with great happiness, from the mention of physical associations to mental; and concludes with a feeling which must have struck many a contemplative mind, that has found the sea-shore like a border, as it were, of existence. He is speaking of

The Ocean

> The Ocean with its vastness, its blue green,
> Its ships, its rocks, its caves,—its hopes, its fears,—
> Its voice mysterious, which whoso hears
> Must think on what will be, and what has been. . . .
>
> *[To my brother George*, ll. 5–8]

. . . The best poem is certainly the last and longest, entitled *Sleep and Poetry*. It originated in sleeping in a room adorned with busts and pictures, and is a striking specimen of the restlessness of the young poetical appetite, obtaining its food by the very desire of it, and glancing for fit subjects of creation "from earth to heaven." Nor do we like it the less for an impatient, and as it may be thought by some, irreverent assault upon the late French school of criticism and monotony, which has held poetry chained long enough to render it somewhat indignant when it got free. . . .

Upon the whole, Mr. Keats's book cannot be better described than in a couplet written by Milton when he too was young, and in which he evidently alludes to himself. It is a little luxuriant heap of

> Such sights as youthful poets dream
> On summer eves by haunted stream.
>
> [*L'Allegro*, ll. 129–30]

From Josiah Conder's unsigned review of *Poems* (1817) in *The Eclectic Review*, September 1817.

. . . We have no hesitation in pronouncing the Author of these Poems, to be capable of writing good poetry, for he has the requisite fancy and skill which constitute the talent. We cannot, however, accept this volume as any thing more than an immature promise of possible excellence. There is, indeed, little in it that is positively good, as to the quality of either the thoughts or the expressions. Unless Mr. Keats has designedly kept back the best part of his mind, we must take the narrow range of ideas and feelings in these Poems, as an indication of his not having yet entered in earnest on the business of intellectual acquirement, or attained the full development of his moral faculties. To this account we are disposed to place the deficiencies in point of sentiment sometimes bordering upon childishness, and the nebulous character of the meaning in many passages which occur in the present volume. Mr. Keats dedicates his volume to Mr. Leigh Hunt, in a sonnet which, as possibly originating in the warmth of gratitude, may be pardoned its extravagance; and he has obviously been seduced by the same partiality, to take him as his model in the subsequent poem, to which is affixed a motto from the "Story of Rimini." To Mr. Hunt's poetical genius we have repeatedly borne testimony, but the affectation which vitiates his style must needs be aggravated to a ridiculous excess in the copyist. Mr. Hunt is sometimes a successful imitator of the manner of our elder poets, but this imitation will not do at second hand, for ceasing then to remind us of those originals, it becomes simply unpleasing. . . .

[Quotes ll. 1–60 of 'I stood tip-toe'—*i.e.*, up to 'To bind them all about with tiny rings']

There is certainly considerable taste and sprightliness in some parts of this description, and the whole poem has a sort of summer's day glow diffused over it, but it shuts up in mist and obscurity.

After a 'specimen of an induction to a poem,' we have next a fragment, entitled Calidore, which, in the same indistinct and dreamy style, describes the romantic adventure of a Sir Somebody, who is introduced 'paddling o'er a lake,' edged with easy slopes and 'swelling leafiness,' and who comes to a castle gloomy and grand, with halls and corridor, where he finds 'sweet-lipped ladies,' and so forth; and all this is told with an air of mystery that holds out continually to the reader the promise of something interesting just about to be told, when, on turning the leaf, the Will o' the Wisp vanishes, and leaves him in darkness. However ingenious such a trick of skill may be, when the writer is too indolent, or feels incompetent to pursue his story, the production cannot claim to be read a second time; and it may therefore be questioned, without captiousness, whether it was worth printing for the sake of a few good lines which ambitiously aspired to overleap the portfolio.

The 'epistles' are much in the same style, *all about* poetry, and seem to be the first efflorescence of the unpruned fancy, which must pass away before any thing like genuine excellence can be produced. The sonnets are perhaps the best things in the volume. We subjoin one addressed 'To my brother George.'

[Quotes the sonnet 'Many the wonders . . .']

The 'strange assay' entitled Sleep and Poetry, if its forming the closing poem indicates that it is to be taken as the result of the Author's latest efforts, would seem to shew that he is indeed far gone, beyond the reach of the efficacy either of praise or censure, in affectation and absurdity. We must indulge the reader with a specimen.

[Quotes ll. 270–93 'Will not some say . . . The end and aim of Poesy']

We must be allowed, however, to express a doubt whether its nature [the nature of poetry] has been as clearly perceived by the Author, or he surely would never have been able to impose even upon himself as poetry the precious nonsense which he has here decked out in rhyme. . . .

Mr. Keats has satirized certain *pseudo* poets, who,

> 'With a puling infant's force,
> Sway'd about upon a rocking horse,
> And thought it Pegasus.'
>
> [*Sleep and Poetry*, ll. 185–8]

Satire is a two-edged weapon: the lines brought irresistibly to our imagination the Author of these poems in the very attitude he describes. Seriously, however, we regret that a young man of vivid imagination and fine talents, should have fallen into so bad hands, as to have been flattered into the resolution to publish verses, of which a few years hence he will be glad to escape from the remembrance. The lash of a critic is the thing the least to be dreaded, as the penalty of premature publication. To have committed one's self in the character of a versifier, is often a formidable obstacle to be surmounted in after-life, when other aims require that we should obtain credit for different, and what a vulgar prejudice deems opposite qualifications. No species of authorship is attended by equal inconvenience in this respect. When a man has established his character in any useful sphere of exertion, the fame of the poet may be safely sought as a finish to his reputation. When he has shewn that he can do something else besides writing poetry, then, and not till then, may he safely trust the public with his secret. But the sound of a violin from a barrister's chamber, is not a more fatal augury than the poet's lyre strummed by a youth whose odes are as yet all addressed to Hope and Fortune.

But perhaps the chief danger respects the individual character, a danger which equally attends the alternative of success or failure. Should a young man of fine genius, but of half-furnished mind, succeed in conciliating applause by his first productions, it is a fearful chance that his energies are not dwarfed by the intoxication of vanity, or that he does not give himself up to the indolent day-dream of some splendid achievement never to be realized. Poetical fame, when conceded to early productions, is, if deserved, seldom the fruit of that patient self-cultivation and pains-taking, which in every department of worthy exertion are the only means of excellence; and it is but the natural consequence of this easy acquisition of gratification, that it induces a distaste for severer mental labour. Should, however, this fatal success be denied, the tetchy aspirant after fame is sometimes driven to seek compensation to his mortified vanity, in the plaudits of some worthless coterie, whose friendship consists in mutual flattery, or in community in crime, or, it may be, to vent his rancour in the satire of envy, or in the malignity of *patriotism*. . . .

Mr. Keats has, however, a claim to leave upon our readers the full impression of his poetry; and we shall therefore give insertion to another of his sonnets, which we have selected as simple and pleasing.

[Quotes the sonnet 'Happy is England!']

461

From the review of *Poems* (1817) in Constable's *Edinburgh Magazine*, October 1817.

Of the author of this small volume we know nothing more than that he is said to be a very young man, and a particular friend of the Messrs Hunt, the editors of the Examiner, and of Mr Hazlitt. His youth accounts well enough for some injudicious luxuriancies and other faults in his poems; and his intimacy with two of the wittiest writers of their day, sufficiently vouches both for his intellect and his taste. Going altogether out of the road of high raised passion and romantic enterprise, into which many ordinary versifiers have been drawn after the example of the famous poets of our time, he has attached himself to a model more pure than some of these, we imagine; and, at the same time, as poetical as the best of them. "Sage, serious" *Spencer*, the most melodious and mildly fanciful of our old English poets, is Mr Keats's favourite. He takes his motto from him, —puts his head on his title-page,—and writes one of his most luxurious descriptions of nature in his measure. We find, indeed, *Spencerianisms* scattered through all his other verses, of whatsoever measure or character. But, though these things sufficiently point out where Mr K. has caught his inspiration, they by no means determine the general character of his manner, which partakes a great deal of that *picturesqueness* of fancy and licentious brilliancy of epithet which distinguish the early Italian novelists and amorous poets. For instance, those who know the careless, sketchy, capricious, and yet archly-thoughtful manner of *Pulci* and *Ariosto*, will understand what we mean from the following specimens, better than from any laboured or specific assertion of ours.

[Quotes ll. 61–106 of 'I stood tip-toe': 'Linger . . . auburne'; and ll. 110–end of the *Epistle to my brother George*: 'Could I, at once, . . . to you!']

This is so easy, and so like the ardent fancies of an aspiring and poetical spirit, that we have a real pleasure in quoting, for the benefit of our readers, another fragment of one of Mr Keats's *epistles*:

[Quotes ll. 1–14 of the *Epistle to Charles Cowden Clarke*]

All this is just, and brilliant too,—though rather ambitious to be kept up for any length of time in a proper and fitting strain. What follows appears to us the very pink of the smart and flowing conversational style. It is truly such elegant *badinage* as should pass between scholars and gentlemen who can feel as well as judge.

[Quotes ll. 109– end of the same poem: 'But many days . . . good night']

These specimens will be enough to shew that Mr K. has ventured on ground very dangerous for a young poet;—calculated, we think, to fatigue his ingenuity, and try his resources of fancy, without producing any permanent effect adequate to the expenditure of either. He seems to have formed his poetical predilections in exactly the same direction as Mr Hunt; and to write, from personal choice, as well as emulation, at all times, in that strain which can be most recommended to the favour of the general readers of poetry, only by the critical ingenuity and peculiar refinements of Mr Hazlitt. That style is vivacious, smart, witty, changeful, sparkling, and learned— full of bright points and flashy expressions that strike and even seem to please by a sudden boldness of novelty,—rather abounding in familiarities of conception and oddnesses of manner which shew ingenuity, even though they be perverse, or common, or contemptuous. The writers themselves seem to be persons of considerable taste, and of comfortable pretensions, who really appear as much alive to the socialities and sensual enjoyments of life, as to the contemplative beauties of nature. In addition to their familiarity, though, —they appear to be too full of conceits and sparkling points, ever to excite any thing more than a cold approbation at the long-run— and too fond, even in their favourite descriptions of nature, of a reference to the factitious resemblances of society, ever to touch the heart. Their verse is straggling and uneven, without the lengthened flow of blank verse, or the pointed connection of couplets. They aim laudably enough at force and freshness, but are not so careful of the inlets of vulgarity, nor so self-denying to the temptations of indolence, as to make their force a merit. . . .

If Mr Keats does not forthwith cast off the uncleannesses of this school, he will never make his way to the truest strain of poetry in which, taking him by himself, it appears he might succeed. We are not afraid to say before the good among our readers, that we think this true strain dwells on features of manly singleness of heart, or feminine simplicity and constancy of affection,—mixed up with feelings of rational devotion, and impressions of independence spread over pictures of domestic happiness and social kindness,— more than on the fiery and resolute, the proud and repulsive aspects of misnamed humanity. It is something which bears, in fact, the direct impress of natural passion,—which depends for its effect on the shadowings of unsophisticated emotion, and takes no merit from the refinements of a metaphysical wit, or the giddy wanderings of an untamed imagination,—but is content with the glory of stimulating, rather than of oppressing, the sluggishness of ordinary conceptions.

It would be cold and contemptible not to hope well of one who has expressed his love of nature so touchingly as Mr K. has done in the following sonnets:

[Quotes the sonnets 'O solitude!' and 'To one who has been long in city pent']

Another sonnet, addressed to Mr Haydon the painter, appears to us very felicitous. *The thought*, indeed, of the first eight lines is altogether admirable; and the whole has a veritable air of Milton about it which has not been given, in the same extent, to any other poet except Wordsworth.

[Quotes the sonnet 'Highmindedness . . .']

We are sorry that we can quote no more of these sweet verses which have in them so deep a tone of moral energy, and such a zest of the pathos of genius. We are loth to part with this poet of promise, and are vexed that critical justice requires us to mention some passages of considerable affectation, and marks of offensive haste, which he has permitted to go forth into his volume. "Leafy luxury," "jaunty streams," "lawny slope," "the moon-beamy air," "a sun-beamy tale;" these, if not namby-pamby, are, at least, the "holiday and lady terms" of those poor affected creatures who write verses "in spite of nature and their stars."—

> "*A little noiseless noise among the leaves,*
> *Born of the very sigh that silence heaves.*"

This is worthy only of the Rosa Matildas whom the strong-handed Gifford put down.

> "To possess but a span of the hour of leisure."
>   . . .
> "No sooner had I stepped into these pleasures."

These are two of the most unpoetical of Mr K.'s lines,—but they are not single. We cannot part, however, on bad terms with the author of such a glorious and Virgilian conception as this:

> "The moon lifting her silver rim
> Above a cloud, and with a gradual swim
> Coming into the blue with all her light."
>   ['I stood tip-toe', ll. 113–15]

A striking natural vicissitude has hardly been expressed better by Virgil himself,—though the severe simpleness of his age, and the

464

compact structure of its language, do so much for him in every instance:

> *"Ipse Pater*, mediâ nimborum in nocte, *coruscâ*
> *Fulmina molitur dextra."*

[*Georgics*, I. 328–9]

From a letter from Benjamin Bailey to John Taylor, 9 April 1818.

I am glad Endymion is so near the commencement of his Pilgrimage into & through the world of letters. . . . I have now and then a few & far-between-angel-like visits of poetical feelings I once possessed, which, I own with sadness & humility, a long series of bodily sickness, *heart*-sickness, utter disappointments of golden hopes has almost effaced from my mind. Yet there is something so etherial in Keats's Poetry that it pierces the cloud. It no longer mantles my spirits when I am in his fairy world. Nothing but the finest poetry can now touch me, but that *does* touch me in the most secret springs, the "resting-places calm & deep", of my soul. Keats's is of this power.

From the review of *Endymion* (1818) in *The Champion*, 7 June 1818.

It is ever hazardous to predict the fate of a great original work; and of *Endymion*, all we dare venture in this way is an opinion, that an inferior poem is likely to excite a more general interest. The secret of the success of our modern poets, is their universal presence in their poems—they give to every thing the colouring of their own feeling; and what a man has felt intensely—the impressions of actual existence—he is likely to describe powerfully: what he has felt we can easily sympathize with. But Mr. Keats goes out of himself into a world of abstractions:—his passions, feelings, are all as much imaginative as his situations. Neither is it the mere outward signs of passions that are given: there seems ever present some being that was equally conscious of its internal and most secret imaginings. There is another objection to its ever becoming popular, that it is, as the *Venus and Adonis* of Shakespeare, a *representation* and not a *description* of passion. Both these poems would, we think, be more generally admired had the poets been only veiled instead of concealed from us. Mr. Keats conceives the scene before him, and represents it as it appears. This is the excellence of dramatic poetry; but to feel its truth and power in any other, we must abandon our ordinary feeling and common consciousness, and identify ourselves with the scene. Few people can do this. In representation, which is the ultimate purpose of dramatic poetry, we should feel something of sympathy though we could merely observe the scene, or

465

the gesticulation, and no sound could reach us: but to make an ordinary *reader* sensible of the excellence of a poem, he must be told what the poet felt; and he is affected by him and not by the scene. Our modern poets are the showmen of their own pictures, and point out its [*sic*] beauties.

Mr. Keats's very excellence, we fear, will tell against him. Each scene bears so actually the immediate impress of truth and nature, that it may be said to be local and peculiar, and to require some extrinsic feeling for its full enjoyment:—perhaps we are not clear in what we say. Every man then, according to his particular habit of mind, not only gives a correspondent colouring to all that surrounds him, but seeks to surround himself with corresponding objects, in which he has more than other people's enjoyment. In every thing then that art or nature may present to man, though gratifying to all, each man's gratification and sympathy will be regulated by the disposition and bent of his mind. Look at Milton's Sonnets. With what a deep and bitter feeling would a persecuted religious enthusiast select and dwell on 'On the late Massacre in Piedmont'. . . . What is common to humanity we are all readily sensible of, and all men proportioned to their intelligence, will receive pleasure on reading that on his birth day:—it wants nothing exclusive either in persons or age:—but would not a young and fearful lover find a thousand beauties in his address to the nightingale that must for ever escape the majority? In further illustration, we would adduce the first meeting of Endymion and Cynthia in the poem before us; which, though wonderfully told, we do not think most likely to be generally liked. It is so true to imagination, that passion absorbs every thing. Now, as we have observed, to transfer the mind to the situation of another, to feel as he feels, requires an enthusiasm, and an abstraction, beyond the power or the habit of most people. It is in this way eloquence differs from poetry, and the same speech on delivery affects people that, on an after reading, would appear tame and unimpassioned. We have certain sympathies with the person addressing us, and what he feels we feel in an inferior degree; but he is afterwards to describe to us his passion; to make us feel by *telling us what he felt*: and this is to be done by calculating on the effect of *others'* feelings, and not by abandoning ourselves to our own. If Mr. Keats can do this, he has not done it. When he writes of passion, it seems to have possessed him. This, however, is what Shakespeare did, and if *Endymion* bears any general resemblance to any other poem in the language, it is to *Venus and Adonis* on this very account. In the necessarily abrupt breaking off of this scene of intense passion, however, we think he has exceeded even his ordinary power. It is scarcely possible to conceive any thing more poetically imaginative;

and though it may be brought in rather abruptly, we cannot refuse ourselves the pleasure of immediately extracting it.

[Quotes II. 827–54: 'Ye who have yearn'd . . . . . . Now turn we to our former chroniclers.—']

The objection we have here stated is equally applicable to the proper and full appreciation of many other beautiful scenes in this poem; but having acknowledged this, we shall extract the hymn to Pan, that our readers may be satisfied there are others to which universal assent must be given as among the finest specimens of classic poetry in our language.

[Quotes almost all of Hymn to Pan from Bk. I]

We shall trespass a little beyond the poem itself, and must then postpone our further observations.

[Quotes lines immediately succeeding Hymn to Pan, up to l. 319, 'But in old marbles ever beautiful'.]

This last line is as fine as that in Shakespeare's Sonnet,

  'And beauty making beautiful old rhyme':

and there are not a dozen finer in Shakespeare's poems.

From the article (No. 4) by 'Z' (probably John Gibson Lockhart and John Wilson) on 'The Cockney School of Poetry' in *Blackwood's Edinburgh Magazine*, August 1818.

————————OF KEATS,
THE MUSES' SON OF PROMISE, AND WHAT FEATS
HE YET MAY DO, &c.

       CORNELIUS WEBB

Of all the manias of this mad age, the most incurable, as well as the most common, seems to be no other than the *Metromanie*. The just celebrity of Robert Burns and Miss Baillie has had the melancholy effect of turning the heads of we know not how many farm-servants and unmarried ladies; our very footmen compose tragedies, and there is scarcely a superannuated governess in the island that does not leave a roll of lyrics behind her in her band-box. To witness the disease of any human understanding, however feeble, is distressing; but the spectacle of an able mind reduced to a state of insanity is of course ten times more afflicting. It is with such sorrow as this that we have contemplated the case of Mr John Keats. This young man appears to have received from nature talents of an excellent, perhaps even of a superior order—talents which, devoted to the purposes of any useful profession, must have rendered him a respectable, if not an eminent citizen. His friends, we understand, destined him to the career of medicine, and he was bound apprentice some years ago to a worthy apothecary in town. But all has been undone by a sudden attack of the malady to which we have alluded. Whether Mr John had been sent home with a diuretic or composing draught to some patient far gone in the poetical mania, we have not heard. This much is certain, that he has caught the infection, and that thoroughly. For some time we were in hopes, that he might get off with a violent fit or two; but of late the symptoms are terrible. The phrenzy of the "Poems" was bad enough in its way; but it did not alarm us half so seriously as the calm, settled, imperturbable drivelling idiocy of "Endymion." We hope, however, that in so young a person, and with a constitution originally so good, even now the disease is not utterly incurable. Time, firm treatment, and rational restraint, do much for many apparently hopeless invalids; and if Mr Keats should happen, at some interval of reason, to cast his eye upon our pages, he may perhaps be convinced of the existence of his malady, which, in such cases, is often all that is necessary to put the patient in a fair way of being cured.

The readers of the Examiner newspaper were informed, some time ago, by a solemn paragraph, in Mr Hunt's best style, of the appearance of two new stars of glorious magnitude and splendour in the poetical horizon of the land of Cockaigne. One of these turned out, by and by, to be no other than Mr John Keats. This precocious adulation confirmed the wavering apprentice in his desire to quit the gallipots, and at the same time excited in his too susceptible mind a fatal admiration for the character and talents of the most worthless and affected of all the versifiers of our time. One of his first productions was the following sonnet, "*written on the day when Mr Leigh Hunt left prison.*" It will be recollected, that the cause of Hunt's confinement was a series of libels against his sovereign, and that its fruit was the odious and incestuous "Story of Rimini."

['Z' then quotes the sonnet]

The absurdity of the thought in this sonnet is, however, if possible, surpassed in another, "*addressed to Haydon*" the painter, that clever, but most affected artist, who as little resembles Raphael in genius as he does in person, notwithstanding the foppery of having his hair curled over his shoulders in the old Italian fashion. In this exquisite piece it will be observed, that Mr Keats classes together WORDS-WORTH, HUNT, and HAYDON, as the three greatest spirits of the age, and that he alludes to himself, and some others of the rising brood of Cockneys, as likely to attain hereafter an equally honourable elevation. Wordsworth and Hunt! what a juxta-position! The purest, the loftiest, and, we do not fear to say it, the most classical of living English poets, joined together in the same compliment with the meanest, the filthiest, and the most vulgar of Cockney poetasters. No wonder that he who could be guilty of this should class Haydon with Raphael, and himself with Spencer.

['Z' then quotes the sonnet 'Great spirits now on earth . . .']

The nations are to listen and be dumb! and why, good Johnny Keats? because Leigh Hunt is editor of the Examiner, and Haydon has painted the judgment of Solomon, and you and Cornelius Webb, and a few more city sparks, are pleased to look upon yourselves as so many future Shakspeares and Miltons! The world has really some reason to look to its foundations! Here is a *tempestas in matulâ* with a vengeance. At the period when these sonnets were published, Mr Keats had no hesitation in saying, that he looked on himself as "*not yet* a glorious denizen of the wide heaven of poetry," but he had many fine soothing visions of coming greatness, and many rare plans of study to prepare him for it. The following we think is very pretty raving.

[Quotes *Sleep and Poetry*, ll. 89–121: 'Why so sad a moan . . . In the recesses of a pearly shell']

Having cooled a little from this "fine passion," our youthful poet passes very naturally into a long strain of foaming abuse against a certain class of English Poets, whom, with Pope at their head, it is much the fashion with the ignorant unsettled pretenders of the present time to undervalue. Begging these gentlemens' pardon, although Pope was not a poet of the same high order with some who are now living, yet, to deny his genius, is just about as absurd as to dispute that of Wordsworth, or to believe in that of Hunt. Above all things, it is most pitiably ridiculous to hear men, of whom their country will always have reason to be proud, reviled by uneducated and flimsy striplings, who are not capable of understanding either their merits, or those of any other *men of power*— fanciful dreaming tea-drinkers, who, without logic enough to analyse a single idea, or imagination enough to form one original image, or learning enough to distinguish between the written language of Englishmen and the spoken jargon of Cockneys, presume to talk with contempt of some of the most exquisite spirits the world ever produced, merely because they did not happen to exert their faculties in laborious affected descriptions of flowers seen in window-pots, or cascades heard at Vauxhall; in short, because they chose to be wits, philosophers, patriots, and poets, rather than to found the Cockney school of versification, morality, and politics, a century before its time. After blaspheming himself into a fury against Boileau, &c. Mr Keats comforts himself and his readers with a view of the present more promising aspect of affairs; above all, with the ripened glories of the poet of Rimini. Addressing the manes of the departed chiefs of English poetry, he informs them, in the following clear and touching manner, of the existence of "him of the Rose," &c.

> "From a thick brake,
> Nested and quiet in a valley mild,
> Bubbles a pipe; fine sounds are floating wild
> About the earth. Happy are ye and glad."

From this he diverges into a view of "things in general." We smile when we think to ourselves how little most of our readers will understand of what follows.

[Quotes *Sleep and Poetry*, ll. 248–76: 'Yet I rejoice . . . In the very fane, the light of Poesy']

From some verses addressed to various amiable individuals of the other sex, it appears, notwithstanding all this gossamer-work, that Johnny's affections are not entirely confined to objects purely etherial. Take, by way of specimen, the following prurient and vulgar lines, evidently meant for some young lady east of Temple-bar.

[Quotes 'Hadst thou liv'd in days of old', ll. 23–40: 'Add too, the sweetness . . . Will I call the Graces four']

So much for the opening bud; now for the expanded flower. It is time to pass from the juvenile "Poems," to the mature and elaborate "Endymion, a Poetic Romance." The old story of the moon falling in love with a shepherd, so prettily told by a Roman Classic, and so exquisitely enlarged and adorned by one of the most elegant of German poets, has been seized upon by Mr John Keats, to be done with as might seem good unto the sickly fancy of one who never read a single line either of Ovid or of Wieland. If the quantity, not the quality, of the verses dedicated to the story is to be taken into account, there can be no doubt that Mr John Keats may now claim Endymion entirely to himself. To say the truth, we do not suppose either the Latin or the German poet would be very anxious to dispute about the property of the hero of the "Poetic Romance."

Mr Keats has thoroughly appropriated the character, if not the name. His Endymion is not a Greek shepherd, loved by a Grecian goddess; he is merely a young Cockney rhymester, dreaming a phantastic dream at the full of the moon. Costume, were it worth while to notice such a trifle, is violated in every page of this goodly octavo. From his prototype Hunt, John Keats has acquired a sort of vague idea, that the Greeks were a most tasteful people, and that no mythology can be so finely adapted for the purposes of poetry as theirs. It is amusing to see what a hand the two Cockneys make of this mythology; the one confesses that he never read the Greek Tragedians, and the other knows Homer only from Chapman; and both of them write about Apollo, Pan, Nymphs, Muses, and Mysteries, as might be expected from persons of their education. We shall not, however, enlarge at present upon this subject, as we mean to dedicate an entire paper to the classical attainments and attempts of the Cockney poets. As for Mr Keats' "Endymion," it has just as much to do with Greece as it has with "old Tartary the fierce;" no man, whose mind has ever been imbued with the smallest knowledge or feeling of classical poetry or classical history, could have stooped to profane and vulgarise every association in the manner which has been adopted by this "son of promise." Before giving any extracts, we must inform our readers, that this romance is meant to be written in English heroic rhyme. To those who have read any of Hunt's poems, this hint might indeed be needless. Mr Keats has adopted the loose, nerveless versification, and Cockney rhymes of the poet of Rimini; but in fairness to that gentleman, we must add, that the defects of the system are tenfold more conspicuous in his disciple's work than in his own. Mr Hunt is a small poet, but he is a clever man. Mr Keats is a still smaller poet, and he is only a boy of pretty abilities, which he has done every thing in his power to spoil.

['Z' then outlines the poem, with long quotations and brief mocking comments]

We had almost forgot to mention, that Keats belongs to the Cockney School of Politics, as well as the Cockney School of Poetry.

It is fit that he who holds Rimini to be the first poem, should believe the Examiner to be the first politician of the day. We admire consistency, even in folly. Hear how their bantling has already learned to lisp sedition.

[Quotes *Endymion*, III. 1-23]

And now, good-morrow to "the Muses' son of Promise;" as for "the feats he yet may do," as we do not pretend to say, like himself,

471

"Muse of my native land am I inspired," we shall adhere to the safe old rule of *pauca verba*. We venture to make one small prophecy, that his bookseller will not a second time venture £50 upon any thing he can write. It is a better and a wiser thing to be a starved apothecary than a starved poet; so back to the shop Mr John, back to "plasters, pills, and ointment boxes," &c. But, for Heaven's sake, young Sangrado, be a little more sparing of extenuatives and soporifics in your practice than you have been in your poetry.   Z.

From a letter from Benjamin Bailey to John Taylor, 29 August 1818.

As a *man of Genius* I know Keats is defensible, let him be abused as he may. And I hope they may attack him in this point. But the quarter I *fear*, & cannot defend, is the *moral* part of it. There are two great blotches in it in this respect. The first must offend *every* one of proper feelings: and indelicacy is not to be borne; & I greatly reproach myself that I did not represent this very strongly to him before it was sent to the Press—not that I apprehend it would have had any great effect; but it would have been more *self*-satisfaction. The *second* book, however, was concluded before I knew Keats. The second fault I allude to I think we have noticed—The approaching inclination it has to that abominable principle of *Shelley's*—that *Sensual Love* is the principle of *things*. Of this I believe him to be unconscious, & can see how by a process of imagination he might arrive at so false, delusive, & dangerous conclusion—which may be called "a most lame & impotent conclusion". If he be attacked on these points, & on the *first* he assuredly will, he is *not* defensible.

John Wilson Croker's unsigned review of *Endymion* in *The Quarterly Review*, April 1818 (but actually published in September 1818).

Reviewers have been sometimes accused of not reading the works which they affected to criticise. On the present occasion we shall anticipate the author's complaint, and honestly confess that we have not read his work. Not that we have been wanting in our duty— far from it—indeed, we have made efforts almost as superhuman as the story itself appears to be, to get through it; but with the fullest stretch of our perseverance, we are forced to confess that we have not been able to struggle beyond the first of the four books of which this Poetic Romance consists. We should extremely lament this want of energy, or whatever it may be, on our parts, were it not for one consolation—namely, that we are no better acquainted with the meaning of the book through which we have so painfully toiled,

472

than we are with that of the three which we have not looked into.

It is not that Mr. Keats, (if that be his real name, for we almost doubt that any man in his senses would put his real name to such a rhapsody,) it is not, we say, that the author has not powers of language, rays of fancy, and gleams of genius—he has all these; but he is unhappily a disciple of the new school of what has been somewhere called Cockney poetry; which may be defined to consist of the most incongruous ideas in the most uncouth language.

Of this school, Mr. Leigh Hunt, as we observed in a former Number, aspires to be the hierophant. Our readers will recollect the pleasant recipes for harmonious and sublime poetry which he gave us in his preface to 'Rimini,' and the still more facetious instances of his harmony and sublimity in the verses themselves; and they will recollect above all the contempt of Pope, Johnson, and such like poetasters and pseudo-critics, which so forcibly contrasted itself with Mr. Leigh Hunt's self-complacent approbation of

> ——'all the things itself had wrote,
> Of special merit though of little note.'

This author is a copyist of Mr. Hunt; but he is more unintelligible, almost as rugged, twice as diffuse, and ten times more tiresome and absurd than his prototype, who, though he impudently presumed to seat himself in the chair of criticism, and to measure his own poetry by his own standard, yet generally had a meaning. But Mr. Keats had advanced no dogmas which he was bound to support by examples; his nonsense therefore is quite gratuitous; he writes it for its own sake, and, being bitten by Mr. Leigh Hunt's insane criticism, more than rivals the insanity of his poetry.

Mr. Keats's preface hints that his poem was produced under peculiar circumstances.

'Knowing within myself (he says) the manner in which this Poem has been produced, it is not without a feeling of regret that I make it public.—What manner I mean, will be *quite clear* to the reader, who must soon perceive great inexperience, immaturity, and every error denoting a feverish attempt, rather than a deed accomplished.'— *Preface*, p. vii.

We humbly beg his pardon, but this does not appear to us to be *quite so clear*—we really do not know what he means—but the next passage is more intelligible.

'The two first books, and indeed the two last, I feel sensible are not of such completion as to warrant their passing the press.'— *Preface*, p. vii.

473

Thus 'the two first books' are, even in his own judgment, unfit to appear, and 'the two last' are, it seems, in the same condition—and as two and two make four, and as that is the whole number of books, we have a clear and, we believe, a very just estimate of the entire work.

Mr. Keats, however, deprecates criticism on this 'immature and feverish work' in terms which are themselves sufficiently feverish; and we confess that we should have abstained from inflicting upon him any of the tortures of the *'fierce hell'* of criticism, which terrify his imagination, if he had not begged to be spared in order that he might write more; if we had not observed in him a certain degree of talent which deserves to be put in the right way, or which, at least, ought to be warned of the wrong; and if, finally, he had not told us that he is of an age and temper which imperiously require mental discipline.

Of the story we have been able to make out but little; it seems to be mythological, and probably relates to the loves of Diana and Endymion; but of this, as the scope of the work has altogether escaped us, we cannot speak with any degree of certainty; and must therefore content ourselves with giving some instances of its diction and versification:—and here again we are perplexed and puzzled. —At first it appeared to us, that Mr. Keats had been amusing himself and wearying his readers with an immeasurable game at *bouts-rimés*; but, if we recollect rightly, it is an indispensable condition at this play, that the rhymes when filled up shall have a meaning; and our author, as we have already hinted, has no meaning. He seems to us to write a line at random, and then he follows not the thought excited by this line, but that suggested by the *rhyme* with which it concludes. There is hardly a complete couplet inclosing a complete idea in the whole book. He wanders from one subject to another, from the association, not of ideas but of sounds, and the work is composed of hemistichs which, it is quite evident, have forced themselves upon the author by the mere force of the catchwords on which they turn.

We shall select, not as the most striking instance, but as that least liable to suspicion, a passage from the opening of the poem.

> ———'Such the sun, the moon,
> Trees old and young, sprouting a shady boon
> For simple sheep; and such are daffodils
> With the green world they live in; and clear rills
> That for themselves a cooling covert make
> 'Gainst the hot season; the mid forest brake,
> Rich with a sprinkling of fair musk-rose blooms:
> And such too is the grandeur of the dooms
> We have imagined for the mighty dead; &c. &c.'
>
> [I. 13–21]

Here it is clear that the word, and not the idea, *moon* produces the simple sheep and their shady *boon*, and that 'the *dooms* of the mighty dead' would never have intruded themselves but for the '*fair musk-rose blooms.*'

Again.

> 'For 'twas the morn: Apollo's upward fire
> Made every eastern cloud a silvery pyre
> Of brightness so unsullied, that therein
> A melancholy spirit well might win
> Oblivion, and melt out his essence fine
> Into the winds: rain-scented eglantine
> Gave temperate sweets to that well-wooing sun;
> The lark was lost in him; cold springs had run
> To warm their chilliest bubbles in the grass;
> Man's voice was on the mountains; and the mass
> Of nature's lives and wonders puls'd tenfold,
> To feel this sun-rise and its glories old.'
>
> [I. 95–106]

Here Apollo's *fire* produces a *pyre*, a silvery pyre of clouds, *wherein* a spirit might *win* oblivion and melt his essence *fine*, and scented *eglantine* gives sweets to the *sun*, and cold springs had *run* into the *grass*, and then the pulse of the *mass* pulsed *tenfold* to feel the glories *old* of the new-born day, &c.

One example more.

> 'Be still the unimaginable lodge
> For solitary thinkings; such as dodge
> Conception to the very bourne of heaven,
> Then leave the naked brain: be still the leaven,
> That spreading in this dull and clodded earth
> Gives it a touch ethereal—a new birth.'
>
> [I. 293–8]

Lodge, dodge—heaven, leaven—earth, birth; such, in six words, is the sum and substance of six lines.

We come now to the author's taste in versification. He cannot indeed write a sentence, but perhaps he may be able to spin a line. Let us see. The following are specimens of his prosodial notions of our English heroic metre.

> 'Dear as the temple's self, so does the moon,
> The passion poesy, glories infinite.' [I. 28–9]
> 'So plenteously all weed-hidden roots.' [I. 65]
> 'Of some strange history, potent to send.' [I. 324]

475

'Before the deep intoxication.' [I. 502]

'Her scarf into a fluttering pavilion.' [I. 628]

'The stubborn canvass for my voyage prepared——.' [I. 772]

' "Endymion! the cave is secreter
Than the isle of Delos. Echo hence shall stir
No sighs but sigh-warm kisses, or light noise
Of thy combing hand, the while it travelling cloys
And trembles through my labyrinthine hair." ' [I. 965–9]

By this time our readers must be pretty well satisfied as to the meaning of his sentences and the structure of his lines; we now present them with some of the new words with which, in imitation of Mr. Leigh Hunt, he adorns our language.

We are told that 'turtles *passion* their voices,' [I. 247–8]; that 'an arbour was *nested*,' [I. 431]; and a lady's locks '*gordian'd* up,' [I. 614]; and to supply the place of the nouns thus verbalized Mr. Keats, with great fecundity, spawns new ones; such as 'men-slugs and human *serpentry*,' [I. 821]; the '*honey-feel* of bliss,' [I. 903]; 'wives prepare *needments*,' [I. 208]—and so forth.

Then he has formed new verbs by the process of cutting off their natural tails, the adverbs, and affixing them to their foreheads; thus, 'the wine out-sparkled,' [I. 154]; the 'multitude up-followed,' [I. 164]; and 'night up-took,' [I. 561]. 'The wind up-blows,' [I. 627, but the line reads 'out-blows']; and the 'hours are down-sunken,' [I. 708].

But if he sinks some adverbs in the verbs he compensates the language with adverbs and adjectives which he separates from the parent stock. Thus, a lady 'whispers *pantingly* and close,' makes '*hushing* signs,' and steers her skiff into a '*ripply* cove,' [I. 407, 409, 430]; a shower falls '*refreshfully*,' [I. 898]; and a vulture has a '*spreaded* tail,' [I. 867].

But enough of Mr. Leigh Hunt and his simple neophyte.—If any one should be bold enough to purchase this 'Poetic Romance,' and so much more patient, than ourselves, as to get beyond the first book, and so much more fortunate as to find a meaning, we entreat him to make us acquainted with his success; we shall then return to the task which we now abandon in despair, and endeavour to make all due amends to Mr. Keats and to our readers.

From Richard Woodhouse's 'Notes on the Critiques on *Endymion* in *The Quarterly Review* and *Blackwood's Edinburgh Magazine*', October 1818.

In the Quarterly review for April (publish^d about the 27 Sep^r) 1818 is a most unjust & illiberal criticism upon Endymion—The

476

critic first objects that the work is not written in couplets—This objection can require no answer, tho' it is very natural that one, who has been all his poetical life employed in tagging couplets together, should be unable to conceive a poem to be good, that is written otherwise.—He next makes a ridiculous objection about the rhymes suggesting the ideas: which, if true, would be no fault in the poem, but which may be shewn to be unfounded by the simple process of changing the final words of the lines, so as to destroy the rhyme; notwithstanding which, the sense & picture of the descriptions &c remain—He then finds fault with the versification, in such a manner as to shew he is quite ignorant of the very grounds & rudiments of English heroic verse—He next objects to certain compound words which have been in use with every bard that ever rhymed in our language—from Chaucer down to himself—And he ends with accusing Keats of coining several specified words—the majority of which are found in Shakespeare or Spencer.—To crown the whole, he professes to have read only the Ist Canto.—

In Blackwood's Edinburgh Magazine, a work as infamous in Character as the man whose name it bears, are a series of attacks upon nearly all the English poets of the day, (apparently with a view of leaving the Scotch in possession of the field of fame) & upon Keats among the number. There is nothing worth notice in it.

From the unsigned article by John Hamilton Reynolds in *The Alfred*, 6 October 1818, on the treatment of *Endymion* by *The Quarterly Review*.

We have met with a singular instance, in the last number of the Quarterly Review, of that unfeeling arrogance, and cold ignorance, which so strangely marked the minds and hearts of Government sychophants and Government writers. The Poem of a young man of genius, which evinces more natural power than any other work of this day, is abused and cried down, in terms which would disgrace any other pens than those used in the defence of an Oliver or a Castles.[1] We have read the Poetic Romance of Endymion (the book in question) with no little delight; and could hardly believe that it was written by so young a man as the preface infers. Mr. Keats, the author of it, is a genius of the highest order; and no one but a Lottery Commissioner and Government Pensioner (both of which Mr. William Gifford, the Editor of the Quarterly Review, is) could, with a false and remorseless pen, have striven to frustrate hopes and aims, so youthful and so high as this young Poet nurses. The Monthly Reviewers, it will be remembered, endeavoured, some few years

---

[1] Two Government spies.

back, to crush the rising heart of young Kirk White; and indeed they in part generated that melancholy which ultimately destroyed him; but the world saw the cruelty, and, with one voice, hailed the genius which malignity would have repressed, and lifted it to fame. Reviewers are creatures "that stab men in the dark:"—young and enthusiastic spirits are their dearest prey. Our readers will not easily forget the brutality with which the Quarterly Reviewers, in a late number of their ministerial book, commented on the work of an intelligent and patriotic woman, whose ardour and independence happened to be high enough to make them her enemies.[1] The language used by these Government critics, was lower than man would dare to utter to female ears; but Party knows no distinctions, —no proprieties,—and a woman is the best prey for its malignity, because it is the gentlest and the most undefended. We certainly think that Criticism might vent its petty passions on other subjects; that it might chuse its objects from the vain, the dangerous, and the powerful, and not from the young and the unprotected.

> It should strike hearts of age and care,
> And spare the youthful and the fair.

The cause of the unmerciful condemnation which has been passed on Mr. Keats, is pretty apparent to all who have watched the intrigues of literature, and the wily and unsparing contrivances of political parties. This young and powerful writer was noticed, some little time back, in the Examiner; and pointed out, by its Editor, as one who was likely to revive the early vigour of English poetry. Such a prediction was a fine, but dangerous compliment, to Mr. Keats: it exposed him instantly to the malice of the Quarterly Review. Certain it is, that hundreds of fashionable and flippant readers, will henceforth set down this young Poet as a pitiable and nonsensical writer, merely on the assertions of some single heartless critic, who has just energy enough to despise what is good, because it would militate against his pleasantry, if he were to praise it.

The genius of Mr. Keats is peculiarly classical; and, with the exception of a few faults, which are the natural followers of youth, his imaginations and his language have a spirit and an intensity which we should in vain look for in half the popular poets of the day. Lord Byron is a splendid and noble egotist.—He visits Classical shores; roams over romantic lands, and wanders through magnificent forests; courses the dark and restless waves of the sea, and rocks his spirit on the midnight lakes; but no spot is conveyed to our minds, that is not peopled by the gloomy and ghastly feelings of one proud

[1] Lady Morgan (? 1783–1859), a liberal who had been attacked by the *Quarterly* for her views on the French Revolution.

478

and solitary man. It is as if he and the world were the only two things which the air clothed.—His lines are majestic vanities;—his poetry always is marked with a haughty selfishness;—he writes loftily, because he is the spirit of an ancient family;—he is liked by most of his readers, because he is a Lord. If a common man were to dare to be as moody, as contemptuous, and as misanthropical, the world would laugh at him. There must be a coronet marked on all his little pieces of poetical insolence, or the world would not countenance them. Mr. Keats has none of this egotism—this daring selfishness, which is a stain on the robe of poesy—His feelings are full, earnest, and original, as those of the olden writers were and are; they are made for all time, not for the drawing-room and the moment. Mr. Keats always speaks of, and describes nature, with an awe and a humility, but with a deep and almost breathless affection.—He knows that Nature is better and older than he is, and he does not put himself on an equality with her. You do not see him, when you see her. The moon, and the mountainous foliage of the woods, and the azure sky, and the ruined and magic temple; the rock, the desert, and the sea; the leaf of the forest, and the embossed foam of the most living ocean, are the spirits of his poetry; but he does not bring them in his own hand, or obtrude his person before you, when you are looking at them. Poetry is a thing of generalities—a wanderer amid persons and things—not a pauser over one thing, or with one person. The mind of Mr. Keats, like the minds of our older poets, goes round the universe in its speculations and its dreams. It does not set itself a task. The manners of the world, the fictions and the wonders of other worlds, are its subjects; not the pleasures of hope, or the pleasures of memory. The true poet confines his imagination to no one thing—his soul is an invisible ode to the passions —He does not make a home for his mind in one land—its productions are an universal story, not an eastern tale. The fancies of Moore are exquisitely beautiful, as fancies, but they are always of one colour;— his feelings are pathetic, but they are "still harping on my daughter." The true pathetic is to be found in the reflections on things, not in the moods and miseries of one person. There is not one poet of the present day, that enjoys any popularity that will live; each writes for his booksellers and the ladies of fashion, and not for the voice of centuries. Time is a lover of old books, and he suffers few new ones to become old. Posterity is a difficult mark to hit, and few minds can send the arrow full home. Wordsworth might have safely cleared the rapids in the stream of time, but he lost himself by looking at his own image in the waters. Coleridge stands bewildered in the cross-road of fame;—his genius will commit suicide, and be buried in it. Southey is Poet Laureate, "so there is no heed to be taken of him."

Campbell has relied on two stools, "The Pleasures of Hope," and "Gertrude of Wyoming," but he will come to the ground, after the fashion of the old proverb. The journey of fame is an endless one; and does Mr. Rogers think that pumps and silk stockings (which his genius wears) will last him the whole way? Poetry is the coyest creature that ever was wooed by man: she has something of the coquette in her; for she flirts with many, and seldom loves one.

Mr. Keats has certainly not perfected anything yet; but he has the power, we think, within him, and it is in consequence of such an opinion that we have written these few hasty observations. If he should ever see this, he will not regret to find that all the country is not made up of Quarterly Reviewers. All that we wish is, that our Readers could read the Poem, as we have done, before they assent to its condemnation—they will find passages of singular feeling, force, and pathos. We have the highest hopes of this young Poet. We are obscure men, it is true, and not gifted with that perilous power of mind, and truth of judgment which are possessed by Mr. Croker, Mr. Canning, Mr. Barrow, or Mr. Gifford, (all "honourable men," and writers in the Quarterly Review). We live far from the world of letters,—out of the pale of fashionable criticism,—aloof from the atmosphere of a Court; but we are surrounded by a beautiful country, and love Poetry, which we read out of doors, as well as in. We think we see glimpses of a high mind in this young man, and surely the feeling is better that urges us to nourish its strength, than that which prompts the Quarterly Reviewer to crush it in its youth, and for ever. If however, the mind of Mr. Keats be of the quality we think it to be of, it will not be cast down by this wanton and empty attack. Malice is a thing of the scorpion kind—It drives the sting into its own heart. The very passages which the Quarterly Review quotes as ridiculous, have in them the beauty that sent us to the Poem itself. We shall close these observations with a few extracts from the romance itself:—If our Readers do not see the spirit and beauty in them to justify our remarks, we confess ourselves bad judges, and never more worthy to be trusted.

The following address to Sleep, is full of repose and feeling:—

[Quotes I. 453–60: 'O magic sleep! . . . And moonlight!']

This is beautiful—but there is something finer,

[Quotes I. 817–31: '—That men, . . . dark-grey hood']

The turn of this is truly Shakesperian, which Mr. Keats will feel to be the highest compliment we can pay him, if we know any thing of his mind. We cannot refrain from giving the following short passage,

which appears to us scarcely to be surpassed in the whole range of
English Poetry. It has all the naked and solitary vigour of old
sculpture, with all the energy and life of Old Poetry:—

> —At this, with madden'd stare,
> And lifted hands, and trembling lips he stood,
> Like old Deucalion mounted [mountain'd] o'er the flood,
> Or blind Orion hungry for the morn.
>
> [II. 195–8]

Again, we give some exquisitely classical lines, clear and reposing
as a Grecian sky—soft and lovely as the waves of Ilyssus.

[Quotes II. 441–9: '—Here is wine, . . . the boy Jupiter']

This is the very fruit of poetry.—A melting repast for the imagination. We can only give one more extract—our limits are reached.
Mr. Keats is speaking of the story of Endymion itself. Nothing can
be more imaginative than what follows:—

[Quotes II. 827–39: '—Ye who have yearn'd . . . universal freedom']

We have no more room for extracts. Does the author of such
poetry as this deserve to be made the sport of so servile a dolt as a
Quarterly Reviewer?— No. Two things have struck us on the perusal
of this singular poem. The first is, that Mr. Keats excels, in what
Milton excelled—the power of putting a spirit of life and novelty
into the Heathen Mythology. The second is, that in the structure of
his verse, and the sinewy quality of his thoughts, Mr. Keats greatly
resembles old Chapman, the nervous translator of Homer. His mind
has "thews and limbs like to its ancestors." Mr. Gifford, who knows
something of the old dramatists, ought to have paused before he
sanctioned the abuse of a spirit kindred with them. If he could not
feel, he ought to know better.

From a letter from Richard Woodhouse to Mary Frogley, 23
October 1818.

You were so flattering as to say the other day, you wished I had
been in a company where you were, to defend Keats.—In all places,
& at all times, & before all persons, I would express, and as far as
I am able, support, my high opinion of his poetical merits—Such a
genius, I verily believe, has not appeared since Shakespeare and
Milton: and I may assert without fear of contradiction from any one
competent to Judge, that if his Endymion be compared with Shakespeare's earliest work (his Venus & Adonis) written about the same
age, Keats's poem will be found to contain more beauties, more

481

poetry (and that of a higher order) less conceit & bad taste and in a word much more promise of excellence than are to be found in Shakespeare's work—This is a deliberate opinion; nor is it merely my own—The Justice of which, however, can only be demonstrated to another upon a full review of the parts & of the whole of each work. I sh^d not shrink from the task of doing it to one whose candour I was acquainted with, and whose Judgment I respected.

But in our Common conversation upon his merits, we should always bear in mind that his fame may be more hurt by indiscriminate praise than by wholesale censure. I would at once admit that he has great faults—enough indeed to sink another writer. But they are more than counterbalanced by his beauties.

From P. G. Patmore's unsigned review of *Endymion* in Baldwin's *London Magazine*, April 1820.

Endymion, if it be not, technically speaking, a poem, is poetry itself. As a *promise*, we know of nothing like it, except some things of Chatterton. . . . It is an ecstatic dream of poetry—a flush—a fever—a burning light—an involuntary out-pouring of the spirit of poetry—that will not be controuled. Its movements are the starts and boundings of the young horse before it has felt the bitt—the first flights of the young bird, feeling and exulting in the powers with which it is gifted, but not yet acquainted with their use or their extent. It is the wanderings of the butterfly in the first hour of its birth; not as yet knowing one flower from another, but only that all *are* flowers. Its similitudes come crowding upon us from all delightful things. It is the May-day of poetry—the flush of blossoms and weeds that start up at the first voice of spring. It is the sky-lark's hymn to the day-break, involuntarily gushing forth as he mounts upward to look for the fountain of that light which has awakened him. It is as if the muses had steeped their child in the waters of Castaly, and we beheld him emerging from them, with his eyes sparkling and his limbs quivering with the delicious intoxication, and the precious drops scattered from him into the air at every motion, glittering in the sunshine, and casting the colours of the rainbow on all things around.

Almost entirely unknown as this poem is to general readers, it will perhaps be better to reserve what we have further to say of its characteristics, till we have given some specimens of it. We should premise this, however, by saying, that our examples will probably exhibit almost as many faults as beauties. But the reader will have anticipated this from the nature of the opinion we have already given —at least if we have succeeded in expressing what we intended to express. In fact, there is scarcely a passage of any length in the whole work, which does not exhibit the most glaring faults—faults that in many instances amount almost to the ludicrous: yet positive and palpable as they are, it may be said of them generally, that they are as much collateral evidences of poetical power, as the beauties themselves are direct ones. If the poet had had time, or patience, or we will even say taste, to have weeded out these faults as they sprang up, he could not have possessed the power to create the beauties to which they are joined. If he had waited to make the first half dozen pages of his work faultless, the fever—the ferment of mind in which the whole was composed would have subsided for ever. Or if he had attempted to pick out those faults afterwards, the beauties must inevitably have gone with them—for they are inextricably linked together. . . .

It is not part of our plan to follow the poet and his hero—for they go hand in hand together—through their adventures; for, as a tale, this work is nothing. There is no connecting interest to bind one part of it to another. Almost any two parts of it might be transposed, without disadvantage to either, or to the whole. We repeat, it is not a poem, but a dream of poetry; and while many of its separate parts possess that vivid distinctness which frequently belongs to the separate parts of a dream, the impression it leaves as a whole is equally indistinct and confused.—

[Then quotes a number of passages, including parts of the Hymn to Pan, directing attention in that case to the imagery and rhythm. Then quotes the passage in which Endymion settles to sleep in Peona's favourite bower (Bk. I, 442–52: 'Soon was he quieted . . . all be heard')]

Nothing can be more exquisitely beautiful than this—nothing more lulling-sweet than the melody of it.—And let us here, once for all, direct the readers' attention to the r[h]ythm of the various extracts we lay before them; and add that, upon the whole, it combines more freedom, sweetness, and variety than are to be found in that of any other long poem written in the same measure, without any exception whatever. In the course of more than four thousand lines it never cloys by sameness, and never flags. To judge of the comparative extent of this praise, turn at random to Pope's Homer, or even Dryden's Virgil, and read two or three pages. Sweetness and variety of music in the versification of a young writer, are among the most authentic evidences of poetical power. These qualities are peculiarly conspicuous in Shakspeare's early poems of Lucrece, and Venus and Adonis. It should be mentioned, however, that in the work before us, these qualities seem to result from—what shall we say?—a fine natural ear?—from any thing, however, rather than system—for the verse frequently runs riot, and loses itself in air. It is the music of the happy wild-bird in the woods—not of the poor caged piping-bullfinch.

[Patmore then praises as 'finely passionate and natural' the description of the impression Endymion receives on waking from his Elysian dream of love (I. 682–705: 'For lo! the poppies hung . . . The disappointment')]

The following strikes us as being exceedingly fine, notwithstanding some obvious faults in the diction.—It is the very faith, the religion, of imaginative passion.

> ————————Hist, when the airy stress
> Of music's kiss impregnates the free winds,
> And with a sympathetic touch unbinds
> Eolian magic from their lucid wombs:
> Then old songs waken from enclouded tombs;
> Old ditties sigh above their father's grave;
> Ghosts of melodious prophecyings rave
> Round every spot where trod Apollo's foot;
> Bronze clarions awake, and faintly bruit,
> Where long ago a giant battle was;
> And, from the turf, a lullaby doth pass
> In every place where infant Orpheus slept.
> Feel we these things?—that moment have we stept
> Into a sort of oneness, and our state
> Is like a floating spirit's.
>
> [I. 783–97]

They who do not find poetry in this, may be assured that they will look for it in vain elsewhere.

[After a number of further illustrations Patmore comments]

It will be seen that here is a rich fund of materials, fitted for almost every variety and degree of poetical power to work upon. And if the young builder before us has not erected from them a regular fabric, which will bear to be examined by a professional surveyor, with his square and rule and plumb-line,—he has at least raised a glittering and fantastic temple, where we may wander about, and delightedly lose ourselves while gazing on the exquisite pictures which every here and there hang on its sunbright walls—the statues and flower-vases which ornament its painted niches—the delicious prospects opening upon us from its arabesque windows—and the sweet airs and romantic music which come about us when we mount upon its pleasant battlements. And it cannot be denied that

484

the fabric is at least as well adapted to the airy and fanciful beings who dwell in it, as a regular Epic Palace—with its grand geometrical staircases, its long dreary galleries, its lofty state apartments, and its numerous *sleeping-rooms*—is to its kings and heroes.

The whole of the foregoing extracts are taken from the first and the beginning of the second book. We had marked numerous others through the rest of the work; but the little space that we have left for quotations must be given to a few of the fancies, images, and detached thoughts and similes—the pictures, statues, flowers, &c.—which form the mere ornaments of the building, and are scattered here and there, almost at random.

[Further quotations follow, comparing Keats's descriptions with the work of the painters Salvator, Poussin, and Titian; and indicating 'clusters of beautiful thoughts, fancies and images meeting together'. Patmore finally quotes from 'O sorrow,/ Why dost borrow . . .' (IV. 146 ff.), calling it 'very touching and pathetic'. He then concludes:]

We cannot refrain from asking, Is it credible that the foregoing extracts are taken, almost at random, from a work in which a writer in the most popular—we will say *deservedly* the most popular—critical journal of the day, has been unable to discover any thing worthy to redeem it from mere contempt? Those who have the most respect for the Quarterly Review will feel most pain at seeing its pages disgraced by such an article as that to which we allude. Almost anywhere else it would have been harmless, and unworthy of particular notice; but *there* it cannot fail to gain a certain degree of credit from the company which it keeps. It would be foolish to doubt or to deny the extensive effect which such an article is likely to produce, appearing as it does in a work which is read by tens of thousands, nine-tenths of whom are not able to judge for themselves, and half of the other tenth will not take the trouble of doing so. Its chief mischief, however, is likely to take effect on the poet himself, whose work is the subject of it. Next to the necessity of pouring forth that which is within him, the strongest active principle in the mind of a young poet is the love of fame. Not fame weighed and meted out by the scales of strict justice. Not fame, properly so called. But *mere* fame—mere praise and distinction. He loves it for itself alone. During a certain period, this love exists almost in the form of an instinct in a poet's nature; and seems to be given him for the purpose of urging or leading him on to that "hereafter" which is to follow. If it is not the food and support of his poetical life, it is at least the *stimulus* without which that life would be but too apt to flag and faulter in its appointed course. Woe to the lovers of poetry, when poets are content merely to *deserve* fame! Let that pest of the literary republic, the mere versifier, be derided and put down as a common nuisance. But let us, even for our own sakes, beware of withholding from youthful poets the fame which they covet;—let us beware of heaping ridicule even upon their faults; lest, in revenge, they learn to keep to themselves the gift which was bestowed on them for the benefit of their fellow-beings, and be satisfied with finding in poetry "its own reward." But we willingly return to our more immediate subject. We at first intended to have accompanied the foregoing extracts by a few of a contrary description, shewing the peculiar faults and deficiencies of the work before us. But as, in the present instance, we disclaim any intention of writing a regular criticism, we feel that this would be superfluous. It is not our object to give a distinct idea of the work as a whole; and we repeat, it is not a fit one to be judged of by rules and axioms. We only wish to call the public notice to the great and remarkable powers which it indicates,—at the same time giving encouragement—as far as our sincere suffrage is of any value—to the poet himself; and bespeaking,—not favour,—but attention,—to any thing that he may produce hereafter. It is, therefore, surely sufficient—for it is saying a great deal—to confess that Endymion is as full of faults as of beauties. And it is the less needful to point out those faults, as they are exactly of such a description that any one who has a relish for the amusement may readily discover them for himself. They will not hide themselves from his search. He need only open a page at random, and they will look him boldly, but not impudently, in the face—for their parent is, as yet, too inexperienced himself to know how to teach them better.

The same reasons which make it unnecessary to point out the peculiar faults of this work, make it difficult, if not impossible to state its peculiar beauties as a whole, in any other than general terms. And, even so, we may exhaust all the common-places of criticism in talking about the writer's active and fertile imagination, his rich and lively fancy, his strong and acute sensibility, and so forth,—without advancing one step towards characterising the work which all these together have produced: because, though the writer possesses all these qualities in an eminent degree, his poetical character has not yet taken up any tangible or determinate ground. So that, though we know of no poetical work which differs from all others more than Endymion does, yet its distinguishing feature is perhaps nothing more than that exuberant spirit of youth,—that transport of imagination, fancy, and sensibility—which gushes forth from every part, in a glittering shower of words, and a confused and shadowy pomp of thoughts and images, creating and hurrying

486

each other along like waves of the sea. And there is no egotism in all this, and no affectation. The poet offers himself up a willing sacrifice to the power which he serves: not fretting under, but exulting and glorying in his bondage. He plunges into the ocean of Poetry before he has learned to stem and grapple with the waves; but they "bound beneath him as a steed that knows its rider;" and will not let him sink. Still, however, while they bear him along triumphantly, it is, evidently, at *their* will and pleasure, not at his. He "rides on the whirlwind" safely; but he cannot yet "direct the storm."

We have spoken of this work as being richer in promise than any other that we are acquainted with, except those of Chatterton. It by no means follows that we confidently anticipate the fulfilment of that promise to its utmost extent. We are not without our fears that it may be like that flush of April blossoms which our fine soil almost always sends forth, but which our cloudy and uncertain skies as often prevent from arriving at maturity. Notwithstanding the many living poets that we possess, the times in which we live are essentially unpoetical; and powerful and resolute indeed must that spirit be, which, even in its youth, can escape their influence. When the transports of enthusiasm are gone by, it can hardly dare hope to do so. It must submit to let "the years bring on the inevitable yoke." This has been one strong inducement for us to notice the young writer before us; and we cannot conclude these slight and desultory remarks without entreating him not to be cast down or turned aside from the course which nature has marked out for him. He is and must be a poet—and he may be a great one. But let him never be tempted to disregard this first evidence of that power which at present rules over him—much less affect to do so: and least of all let him wish or attempt to make it any thing but what it is. Nothing can ever tame and polish this wild and wayward firstling, and make it fit to be introduced to "mixed company;" but let him not therefore be ashamed to cherish and claim it for his own. He may live to see himself surrounded by a flourishing family, endowed with all sorts of polite accomplishments, and able not only to make their own way in the world, but to further *his* fortunes too. But *this*—the first-born of his hopes—the child of his youth—whatever he may say or think to the contrary—must ever be the favourite. He may admire those which are to come, and pride himself upon them; but he will never love them as he has loved this; he will never again watch over the infancy and growth of another with such full and unmixed delight: for *this* was born while his muse was his mistress, and he her rapturous lover. He will marry her by and bye—or perhaps he has already—and then he may chance to love her *better* than ever; but he will cease to be *her lover*.

From the review of *Lamia, Isabella, The Eve of St Agnes, and other Poems* (1820), in *The Monthly Review*, July 1820.

This little volume must and ought to attract attention, for it displays the ore of true poetic genius, though mingled with a large portion of dross. Mr. Keats is a very bold author, bold perhaps because (as we learn) he has yet but little more than touched the "years of discretion;" and he has carried his peculiarities both of thought and manner to an extreme which, at the first view, will to many persons be very displeasing. Yet, whatever may be his faults, he is no *Della Crusca* poet; for, though he is frequently involved in ambiguity, and dressed in the affectation of quaint phrases, we are yet sure of finding in all that he writes the proof of deep thought and energetic reflection. Poetry is now become so antient an art, and antiquity has furnished such a store-house of expression and feeling, that we daily meet with new worshippers of the Muse who are content to repeat for the thousandth time her prescriptive language. If any one would deviate from this beaten track, and from those great landmarks which have so long been the guides of the world in all matters of taste and literary excellence, he will find that it requires no timid foot to strike into new paths, and must deem himself fortunate if he be not lost amid the intricacies of a region with which he is unacquainted. Yet, even should this be partially the case, the wild and beautiful scenery, which such an excursion is frequently the means of developing, is a fair remuneration for the inequalities and obstructions which he may chance to experience on his ramble. We must add that only by attempts like these can we discover the path of true excellence; and that, in checking such efforts by illiberal and ill-timed discouragement, we shut out the prospect of all improvement. Innovations of every kind, more especially in matters of taste, are at first beheld with dislike and jealousy, and it is only by time and usage that we can appreciate their claims to adoption.

Very few persons, probably, will admire Mr. Keats on a short acquaintance; and the light and the frivolous never will. If we would enjoy his poetry, we must think over it; and on this very account, which is perhaps the surest proof of its merit, we are afraid that it will be slighted. Unfortunately, Mr. Keats may blame himself for much of this neglect; since he might have conceded something to established taste, or (if he will) established prejudice, without derogating from his own originality of thought and spirit. On the contrary, he seems to have written directly in despite of our preconceived notions of the *manner* in which a poet ought to write; and he is continually shocking our ideas of poetical decorum, at the very time when we are acknowleging the hand of genius. In thus boldly running counter to old opinions, however, we cannot conceive that

488

Mr. Keats merits either contempt or ridicule; the weapons which are too frequently employed when liberal discussion and argument would be unsuccessful. At all events, let him not be pre-judged without a candid examination of his claims.—A former work by this very young poet, (*Endymion,*) which escaped our notice, cannot certainly be said to have had a fair trial before the public; and now that an opportunity is afforded for correcting that injustice, we trust that the candour of all readers will take advantage of it.

For ourselves, we think that Mr. Keats is very faulty. He is often laboriously obscure; and he sometimes indulges in such strange intricacies of thought, and peculiarities of expression, that we find considerable difficulty in discovering his meaning. Most unluckily for him, he is a disciple in a school in which these peculiarities are virtues: but the praises of this small *coterie* will hardly compensate for the disapprobation of the rest of the literary world. Holding, as we do, a high opinion of his talents, especially considering his youth and few advantages, we regret to see him sowing the seeds of disappointment where the fruit should be honour and distinction. If his writings were the dull common-places of an every-day versifier, we should pass them by with indifference or contempt: but, as they exhibit great force and feeling, we have only to regret that such powers are misdirected.

The wild and high imaginations of antient mythology, the mysterious being and awful histories of the deities of Greece and Rome, form subjects which Mr. Keats evidently conceives to be suited to his own powers: but, though boldly and skilfully sketched, his delineations of the immortals give a faint idea of the nature which the poets of Greece attributed to them. The only modern writer, by whom this spirit has been completely preserved, is Lord Byron, in his poem of "Prometheus." In this mould, too, the character of Milton's Satan is cast.

The fragment of *Hyperion,* the last poem in the volume before us, we consider as decidedly the best of Mr. Keats's productions; and the power of both heart and hand which it displays is very great. We think, too, that it has less conceit than other parts of the volume. It is the fable of the antient gods dethroned by the younger.

[Quotes about 30 lines from the opening, and also the descriptions of Saturn's appearance among the Titans, and of Hyperion, praising both highly]

The story of Isabella, or the Pot of Basil, from Boccaccio, is the worst part of the volume; and Mr. Barry Cornwall's versification of this fable in his *Sicilian Story* is in some respects superior to Mr. Keats's attempt. The latter gentleman seems inclined, in this poem, to shew us at once the extent of his simplicity and his affectation; witness the following *tirade* against the mercantile pride of the brothers of Isabella:

[Quotes the stanza 'Why were they proud? . . .']

Mr. Keats displays no great nicety in his selection of images. According to the tenets of that school of poetry to which he belongs, he thinks that any thing or object in nature is a fit material on which the poet may work; forgetting that poetry has a nature of its own, and that it is the destruction of its essence to level its high being with the triteness of every-day life. Can there be a more pointed *concetto* than this address to the Piping Shepherds on a Grecian Urn?

> 'Heard melodies are sweet, but those *unheard*
>   Are sweeter; therefore, ye soft pipes, play on;
> Not to the sensual ear, but, more endear'd,
>   Pipe to the spirit *ditties of no tone*:'
>
>   [Reviewer's italics]

but it would be irksome to point out all the instances of this kind which are to be found in Mr. K.'s compositions.

Still, we repeat, this writer is very rich both in imagination and fancy; and even a superabundance of the latter faculty is displayed in his lines 'On Autumn,' which bring the reality of nature more before our eyes than almost any description that we remember.

[Quotes the Ode in full]

If we did not fear that, young as is Mr. K., his peculiarities are fixed beyond all the power of criticism to remove, we would exhort him to become somewhat less strikingly original,—to be less fond of the folly of too new or too old phrases,—and to believe that poetry does not consist in either the one or the other. We could then venture to promise him a double portion of readers, and a reputation which, if he persist in his errors, he will never obtain. Be this as it may, his writings present us with so many fine and striking ideas, or passages, that we shall always read his poems with much pleasure.

From the review of *Endymion* in Constable's *Edinburgh Magazine*, August 1820.

Mr Keats is a poet of high and undoubted powers. He has evident peculiarities, which some of the London critics, who are averse to his

490

style, have seized upon and produced as fair specimens of his writings; and this has operated, of course, to his disadvantage with the public, who have scarcely had an opportunity of judging what his powers really are. Some of his friends, indeed, have put in a word or two of praise, but it has been nearly unqualified; and this, when viewed at the same time with the criticism produced in an opposite spirit, has tended very much to confirm the objections made to his poetry.

Mr Keats has produced three volumes of verse: the first is very inferior in power to the two others, but containing very delightful passages, and some sonnets of great beauty. The second volume consists of the old mythological story of Endymion, and over which is scattered a multitude of thoughts and images, conceived and produced in the highest spirit of poetry. Perhaps the "Endymion," though it contains more positive faults than the last book [the *Lamia* volume], is more completely in Mr Keats's own style; and we think that it contains, at least, as many beauties. It is more careless, perhaps, but there is a greater freshness about it than about the last book, which (in "Hyperion" at least) reminds us occasionally of other writers, but which we must not be understood to speak of otherwise than in terms of the sincerest admiration.

The poem of Endymion contains about 4000 lines, and the story of the hero is not, perhaps, very interesting in itself; indeed, it is scarcely possible to endure, with a lively interest, a tale so slight and shadowy as that of the Loves of Diana and the Shepherd of Latmos. While this is stated, however, great praise must be ceded to the author, who, by force of poetry alone, can claim and compel the attention of the reader, for any length of time, to so bare (although graceful) a subject.

[The reviewer then starts to outline the poem, quoting in particular the Hymn to Pan, which he calls 'worthy of any of the gods']

We hope that our readers begin to feel that there are some (not ordinary) beauties in the volumes of Mr Keats. He is, perhaps, the poet, above all others, that we should refer to, in case we were challenged to produce *single* lines of extraordinary merit. He is very unequal in his earlier volumes certainly, (and what poet is not?) but there are beauties which might redeem ten times the amount of any defects that they may contain.

Speaking of Zephyr, before sunrise, he says, he

Fondles the flower amid the sobbing rain.

[I. 331; all italics are the reviewer's]

491

This seems to us very charming, and it is quite in the spirit of that mythology which has invested the west wind and the flowers with such delicate personifications. Again, speaking of Peona, the sister of Endymion, who sits by him while he sleeps, he says,

> ——————————————*as a willow keeps*
> *A patient watch over the stream that creeps*
> *Windingly by it,* so the quiet maid
> Held her in peace: so that a whispering blade
> Of grass,

[I. 446–9]

or any other trivial thing, might be heard. . . .
Look at the effect of a single word,—

> ——————————————————Sometimes
> A scent of violets, and blossoming limes,
> *Loiter'd* around us.

[I. 666–8]

The following lines were quoted against the author, in a London Review. They are irregular, perhaps, but still very beautiful, we think.

> Endymion! the cave is secreter
> Than the isle of Delos. Echo hence shall stir
> No sighs, but sigh-warm kisses, or *light noise*
> *Of thy combing hand, the while it travelling cloys*
> *And trembles thro' my labyrinthine hair.*

[I. 965–9]

Endymion wanders for many days

> Thro' wilderness and woods of mossed oaks,
> Counting his woe-worn minutes, by the strokes
> Of the lone wood-cutter.

[II. 49–51]

A butterfly is sent to guide him: he follows it

> Thro' the green evening quiet in the sun,
> O'er many a heath, and many a woodland dun,
> *Thro' buried paths, where sleepy twilight dreams*
> *The summer time away.*

[II. 71–4]

If this be not poetry, we do not know what is; but we must, perforce, leave Endymion, begging our readers to refer to it without more ado, both for their sakes and our own.

492

From Francis Jeffrey's unsigned review of *Endymion* and of *Lamia, Isabella, The Eve of St Agnes, and other Poems* in *The Edinburgh Review*, August 1820.

We had never happened to see either of these volumes till very lately—and have been exceedingly struck with the genius they display, and the spirit of poetry which breathes through all their extravagance. That imitation of our older writers, and especially of our older dramatists, to which we cannot help flattering ourselves that we have somewhat contributed, has brought on, as it were, a second spring in our poetry;—and few of its blossoms are either more profuse of sweetness or richer in promise, than this which is now before us. Mr Keats, we understand, is still a very.young man; and his whole works, indeed, bear evidence enough of the fact. They are full of extravagance and irregularity, rash attempts at originality, interminable wanderings, and excessive obscurity. They manifestly require, therefore, all the indulgence that can be claimed for a first attempt:—but we think it no less plain that they deserve it; for they are flushed all over with the rich lights of fancy, and so coloured and bestrewn with the flowers of poetry, that even while perplexed and bewildered in their labyrinths, it is impossible to resist the intoxication of their sweetness, or to shut our hearts to the enchantments they so lavishly present. The models upon which he has formed himself, in the Endymion, the earliest and by much the most considerable of his poems, are obviously the Faithful Shepherdess of Fletcher, and the Sad Shepherd of Ben Jonson;—the exquisite metres and inspired diction of which he has copied with great boldness and fidelity—and, like his great originals, has also contrived to impart to the whole piece that true rural and poetical air which breathes only in them and in Theocritus—which is at once homely and majestic, luxurious and rude, and sets before us the genuine sights and sounds and smells of the country, with all the magic and grace of Elysium. His subject has the disadvantage of being mythological; and in this respect, as well as on account of the raised and rapturous tone it consequently assumes, his poetry may be better compared perhaps to the Comus and the Arcades of Milton, of which, also, there are many traces of imitation. The great distinction, however, between him and these divine authors, is, that imagination in them is subordinate to reason and judgment, while, with him, it is paramount and supreme—that their ornaments and images are employed to embellish and recommend just sentiments, engaging incidents, and natural characters, while his are poured out without measure or restraint, and with no apparent design but to unburden the breast of the author, and give vent to the overflowing vein of his fancy. The thin and scanty tissue of his story is merely the light frame work on which his florid wreaths are suspended; and while his imaginations go rambling and entangling themselves everywhere, like wild honeysuckles, all idea of sober reason, and plan, and consistency, is utterly forgotten, and are 'strangled in their waste fertility'. A great part of the work indeed, is written in the strangest and most fantastical manner that can be imagined. It seems as if the author had ventured everything that occurred to him in the shape of a glittering image or striking expression—taken the first word that presented itself to make up a rhyme, and then made that word the germ of a new cluster of images—a hint for a new excursion of the fancy—and so wandered on, equally forgetful whence he came, and heedless whither he was going, till he had covered his pages with an interminable arabesque of connected and incongruous figures, that multiplied as they extended, and were only harmonized by the brightness of their tints, and the graces of their forms. In this rash and headlong career he has of course many lapses and failures. There is no work, accordingly, from which a malicious critic could call more matter for ridicule, or select more obscure, unnatural, or absurd passages. But we do not take *that* to be our office;—and just beg leave, on the contrary, to say, that any one who, on this account, would represent the whole poem as despicable, must either have no notion of poetry, or no regard to truth.

It is, in truth, at least as full of genius as of absurdity; and he who does not find a great deal in it to admire and to give delight, cannot in his heart see much beauty in the two exquisite dramas to which we have already alluded, or find any great pleasure in some of the finest creations of Milton and Shakespeare. There are very many such persons, we verily believe, even among the reading and judicious part of the community—correct scholars we have no doubt many of them, and, it may be, very classical composers in prose and in verse—but utterly ignorant of the true genius of English poetry, and incapable of estimating its appropriate and most exquisite beauties. With that spirit we have no hesitation in saying that Mr K. is deeply imbued—and of those beauties he has presented us with many striking examples. We are very much inclined indeed to add that we do not know any book which we would sooner employ as a test to ascertain whether any one had in him a native relish for poetry, and a genuine sensibility to its intrinsic charm. The greater and more distinguished poets of our country have so much else in them to gratify other tastes and propensities, that they are pretty sure to captivate and amuse those to whom their poetry is but an hindrance and obstruction, as well as those to whom it constitutes their chief attraction. The interest of the stories they tell—the vivacity of the characters they delineate—the weight and force of the maxims and sentiments in which they abound—the very pathos and wit and humour they display, which may all and each of them exist apart from their poetry and independent of it, are quite sufficient to account for their popularity, without referring much to that still higher gift, by which they subdue to their enchantments those whose souls are attuned to the finer impulses of poetry. It is only where those other recommendations are wanting, or exist in a weaker degree, that the true force of the attraction, exercised by the pure poetry with which they are so often combined, can be fairly appreciated—where, without much incident or many characters, and with little wit, wisdom, or arrangement, a number of bright pictures are presented to the imagination, and a fine feeling expressed of those mysterious relations by which visible external things are assimilated with inward thoughts and emotions, and become the images and exponents of all passions and affections. To an unpoetical reader such passages always appear mere raving and absurdity—and to this censure a very great part of the volume before us will certainly be exposed, with this class of readers. Even in the judgment of a fitter audience, however, it must, we fear, be admitted, that, besides the riot and extravagance of his fancy, the scope and substance of Mr K.'s poetry is rather too dreary and abstracted to excite the strongest interest, or to sustain the attention through a work of any great compass or extent. He deals too much with shadowy and incomprehensible beings, and is too constantly rapt into an extra-mundane Elysium, to command a lasting interest with ordinary mortals—and must employ the agency of more varied and coarser emotions, if he wishes to take rank with the seducing poets of this or of former generations. There is something very curious too, we think, in the way in which he, and Mr Barry Cornwall also, have dealt with the Pagan mythology, of which they have made so much use in their poetry. Instead of presenting its imaginary persons under the trite and vulgar traits that belong to them in the ordinary systems, little more is borrowed from these than the general conception of their conditions and relations; and an original character and distinct individuality is bestowed upon them, which has all the merit of invention, and all the grace and attraction of the fictions on which it is engrafted. The antients, though they probably did not stand in any great awe of their deities, have yet abstained very much from any minute or dramatic representation of their feelings and affections. In Hesiod and Homer, they are coarsely delineated by some of their actions and adventures, and introduced to us merely as the agents in those particular transactions; while in the Hymns, from those ascribed to Orpheus and

495

Homer, down to those of Callimachus, we have little but pompous epithets and invocations, with a flattering commemoration of their most famous exploits—and are never allowed to enter into their bosoms, or follow out the train of their feelings, with the presumption of our human sympathy. Except the love-song of the Cyclops to his Sea Nymph in Theocritus—the Lamentation of Venus for Adonis in Moschus—and the more recent Legend of Apuleius, we scarcely recollect a passage in all the writings of antiquity in which the passions of an immortal are fairly disclosed to the scrutiny and observation of men. The author before us, however, and some of his contemporaries, have dealt differently with the subject;—and, sheltering the violence of the fiction under the ancient traditionary fable, have created and imagined an entire new set of characters, and brought closely and minutely before us the loves and sorrows and perplexities of beings, with whose names and supernatural attributes we had long been familiar, without any sense or feeling of their personal character. We have more than doubts of the fitness of such personages to maintain a permanent interest with the modern public; —but the way in which they are here managed, certainly gives them the best chance that now remains for them; and, at all events, it cannot be denied that the effect is striking and graceful. But we must now proceed to our extracts.

The first of the volumes before us is occupied with the loves of Endymion and Diana—which it would not be very easy, and which we do not at all intend to analyze in detail.

[Jeffrey outlines the poem, with copious quotations and short laudatory comments]

We have left ourselves room to say but little of the second volume, which is of a more miscellaneous character. Lamia is a Greek antique story, in the measure and taste of Endymion. Isabella is a paraphrase of the same tale of Boccacio, which Mr Cornwall has also imitated under the title of 'a Sicilian Story.' It would be worth while to compare the two imitations; but we have no longer time for such a task. Mr K. has followed his original more closely, and has given a deep pathos to several of his stanzas. The widowed bride's discovery of the murdered body is very strikingly given.

[Quotes *Isabella*, stanzas xlvii–xlviii and li: 'Soon she turn'd . . . Sweet Basil, which her tears kept ever wet']

The following lines from an ode to a Nightingale, are equally distinguished for harmony and feeling.

[Quotes ll. 15–28 and 63–70]

We must close our extracts with the following lively lines to Fancy.

[Quotes *Fancy*, ll. 9–24 and 39–66]

There is a fragment of a projected Epic, entitled 'Hyperion,' on the expulsion of Saturn and the Titanian deities by Jupiter and his younger adherents, of which we cannot advise the completion: For, though there are passages of some force and grandeur, it is sufficiently obvious, from the specimen before us, that the subject is too far removed from all the sources of human interest, to be successfully treated by any modern author. Mr Keats has unquestionably a very beautiful imagination, and a great familiarity with the finest diction of English poetry; but he must learn not to misuse or misapply these advantages; and neither to waste the good gifts of nature and study on intractable themes, nor to luxuriate too recklessly on such as are more suitable.

From Leigh Hunt's unsigned review of *Lamia, Isabella, The Eve of St Agnes, and other Poems* in *The Indicator*, 2 and 9 August 1820.

Mr. Keats has departed as much from common-place in the character and moral of this story, as he has in the poetry of it. He would see fair play to the serpent, and makes the power of the philosopher an ill-natured and disturbing thing. Lamia though liable to be turned into painful shapes had a soul of humanity; and the poet does not see why she should not have her pleasures accordingly, merely because a philosopher saw that she was not a mathematical truth. This is fine and good. It is vindicating the greater philosophy of poetry. At the same time, we wish that for the purpose of his story he had not appeared to give in to the common-place of supposing that Apollonius's sophistry must always prevail, and that modern experiment has done a deadly thing to poetry by discovering the nature of the rainbow, the air, etc.: that is to say, that the knowledge of natural history and physics, by shewing us the nature of things, does away the imaginations that once adorned them. This is a condescension to a learned vulgarism, which so excellent a poet as Mr. Keats ought not to have made. The world will always have fine poetry, as long as it has events, passions, affections, and a philosophy that sees deeper than this philosophy. There will be a poetry of the heart, as long as there are tears and smiles: there will be a poetry of the imagination, as long as the first causes of things remain a mystery. A man who is no poet, may think he is none, as soon as he finds out the physical cause of the rainbow; but he need not alarm himself; he was none before. The true poet will go deeper. He will ask himself what is the cause of that physical cause; whether truths to the senses are after all to be taken as truths to the imagination; and whether there is not room and mystery enough in the universe for the creation of infinite things, when the poor matter-of-fact philosopher has come to the end of his own vision. It is remarkable that an age of poetry has grown up with the progress of experiment; and that the very poets, who seem to countenance these notions, accompany them by some of their finest effusions. Even if there were nothing new to be created, if philosophy, with its line and rule, could even score the ground, and say to poetry "Thou shalt go no further," she would look back to the old world, and still find it inexhaustible. The crops from its fertility are endless. But these alarms are altogether idle. The essence of poetical enjoyment does not consist in belief, but in a voluntary power to imagine. . . .

The Eve of St. Agnes, which is rather a picture than a story, may be analysed in a few words. It is an account of a young beauty, who going to bed on the eve in question to dream of her lover, while her rich kinsmen, the opposers of his love, are keeping holiday in the rest of the house, finds herself waked by him in the night, and in the hurry of the moment agrees to elope with him. The portrait of the heroine, preparing to go to bed, is remarkable for its union of extreme richness and good taste; not that those two properties of description are naturally distinct; but that they are too often separated by very good poets, and that the passage affords a striking specimen of the sudden and strong maturity of the author's genius. When he wrote Endymion he could not have resisted doing too much. To the description before us, it would be a great injury either to add or diminish. It falls at once gorgeously and delicately upon us, like the colours of the painted glass. Nor is Madeline hurt by all her encrusting jewelry and rustling silks. Her gentle, unsophisticated heart is in the midst, and turns them into so many ministrants to her loveliness. . . .

As a specimen of the Poems, which are all lyrical, we must indulge ourselves in quoting entire the Ode to a Nightingale. There is that mixture in it of real melancholy and imaginative relief, which poetry alone presents us in her "charmed cup," and which some over-rational critics have undertaken to find wrong because it is not true. It does not follow that what is not true to them, is not true to others. If the relief is real, the mixture is good and sufficing. A poet finds refreshment in his imaginary wine, as other men do in their real; nor have we the least doubt, that Milton found his grief for the loss of his friend King, more solaced by the allegorical recollections of Lycidas, (which were exercises of his mind, and recollections of a friend who would have admired them) than if he could have anticipated Dr. Johnson's objections, and mourned in nothing but broadcloth and matter of fact. He yearned after the poetical as well as social part of his friend's nature; and had as much right to fancy it straying, in the wilds and oceans of romance, where it had strayed, as in the avenues of Christ's College where his body had walked. In the same spirit the imagination of Mr. Keats betakes itself, like the wind, "where it listeth," and is as truly there, as if his feet could follow it. The poem will be the more striking to the reader, when he understands what we take a friend's liberty in telling him, that the author's powerful mind has for some time past been inhabiting a sickened and shaken body, and that in the mean while it has had to contend with feelings that make a fine nature ache for its species, even when it would disdain to do so for itself; we mean, critical malignity—that unhappy envy, which would wreak its own tortures upon others, especially upon those that really feel for it already.

[Quotes the *Ode to a Nightingale*]

The Hyperion is a fragment—a gigantic one, like a ruin in the desert, or the bones of the mastodon. It is truly of a piece with its subject, which is the downfall of the elder gods. . . .

Mr. Keats's versification sometimes reminds us of Milton in his blank verse, and sometimes of Chapman both in his blank verse and rhyme; but his faculties, essentially speaking, though partaking of the unearthly aspirations and abstract yearnings of both these poets, are altogether his own. They are ambitious, but less directly so. They are more social, and in the finer sense of the word, sensual, than either. They are more coloured by the modern philosophy of sympathy and natural justice. Endymion, with all its extraordinary powers, partook of the faults of youth, though the best ones; but the reader of Hyperion and these other stories would never guess that they were written at twenty.[1] The author's versification is now perfected, the exuberances of his imagination restrained, and a calm power, the surest and loftiest of all power, takes place of the impatient workings of the younger god within him. The character of his genius is that of energy and voluptuousness, each able at will to take leave of the other, and possessing, in their union, a high feeling of humanity not common to the best authors who can less combine them. Mr. Keats undoubtedly takes his seat with the oldest and best of our living poets.

From the review of *Lamia, Isabella, The Eve of St Agnes, and other Poems* in *The British Critic*, September 1820.

If there be one person in the present day, for whom we feel an especial contempt, it is Mr. Examiner Hunt; and we confess that it is

[1] They were not. Keats wrote them when he was twenty-two—*Ed.*

not easy for us to bring our minds to entertain respect for any one whose taste, whether in morals, in poetry, or politics, is so exceedingly corrupt as that person's must be supposed to be, who is willing to take such a man for his model. It was for this reason that Mr. Keats fell under our lash, so severely, upon the occasion of his poem of Endymion. Upon recurring to the poem, we are not unwilling to admit, that it possesses more merit, than upon a first perusal of it we were able to perceive, or rather than we were in a frame of mind to appreciate. We can hardly doubt as to that poem having been corrected by our modern Malvolio, and projected by his advice and under his superintendence;—so full was it, of all the peculiarities of that ingenious gentleman's ideas. The effect of this upon Mr. Keats's poetry, was like an infusion of ipecacuanha powder in a dish of marmalade. It created such a sickness and nausea, that the mind felt little inclination to analyse the mixture produced, and to consider, whether after all, the dose might not have been mixed with some ingredients that were in themselves agreeable. In the poems before us, the same obstacle to a dispassionate judgment, is still to be encountered—not perhaps to so great a degree, as upon the former occasion, but still in such a degree, as to reflect great praise, we think, upon our impartiality for the commendation which we feel willing to bestow.

We cannot approve of the morality of the principal poems in this little collection. One of them is from Boccacio, and the others upon exactly the same sort of subjects as the Florentine too generally choose[s]. However, there is nothing in the details of either poem, that would appear calculated to wound delicacy, and this, in cases whether the temptation to the contrary may be supposed to have existed, is certainly deserving of praise.

The first tale is in two parts, and called Lamia. The subject of it is taken from the following passage in Burton's "Anatomy of Melancholy;" and we extract it as conveying a very agreeable fiction, and which loses none of its merit in the hands of Mr. Keats.

[Quotes the Burton passage]

We shall now present our readers with some specimens of the manner in which our poet has dressed up the materials here afforded him; and we think those which we shall give, will prove that Mr. Keats is really a person of no ordinary genius; and that if he will only have the good sense to take advice, making Spenser or Milton his model of poetical diction, instead of Mr. Leigh Hunt, he need not despair of attaining to a very high and enviable place in the public esteem.

[Outlines the poem, with copious quotations, but no criticism except that the poem loses in interest after Lamia leaves with Lycius for Corinth]

The next tale is from Boccacio, and possesses less merit; nor is there much to admire in the "Eve of St. Agnes;" but the last poem, which is unfinished, and is called "Hyperion," contains some very beautiful poetry, although the greater part of it appears not to have been executed with much success; nor do we think that Mr. Keats has evinced any want of taste in leaving it incomplete; for it is plainly projected upon principles that would infallibly lead to failure, even supposing the subject were not, which we think it is, somewhat above the pitch of Mr. Keats' peculiar genius, which lies altogether in the region of fancy and description.

[Starts to outline the poem, praising the opening as 'very beautiful indeed' and the 'green-rob'd senators' passage as 'strikingly-fine', but then breaks off, and concludes the review]

We think that the specimens which we have now given of Mr. Keats' talents, are quite decisive as to his poetical powers. That a man who can write so well, should produce such absurd lines, and fall into such ridiculous modes of expression, as are to be met with in almost every page, is really lamentable. An example or two will be sufficient to convince our readers of the forbearance which we have exerted, in giving these poems the praise which is their due; for if we were to strike a balance between their beauties and absurdities, many would probably be disposed to doubt as to which side the scale inclined.

Thus we are told that

"——————charmed God
Began an *oath*, and through the serpent's ears it ran
Warm, tremulous, devout, psalterian."

[I. 112–14]¹

[Reviewer's italics here and below]

In another place the Lamia, as we are told,

"Writh'd about, convuls'd with *scarlet* pain:
A deep *volcanian* yellow took the place
Of all her *milder-mooned* body's grace."

[I. 154–6]

¹ The reviewer has displaced 'Began' from the end of l. 112.

501

We hear also of "a clear pool, wherein she *passioned*, to see herself escaped." [I. 182–3.] And likewise of this same person's pacing about "in a pale contented sort of discontent." [II. 135.] In another poem, we have the following exquisite nonsense to describe a kiss:

> "So said, his erewhile timid lips grew bold,
> And *poesied* with her's in *dewy rhyme*."
>
> [*Isabella*, ix. 69–70]

Thus likewise we hear of *pleasuring* a thing, and *mirroring* a thing; of doing a thing *fearingly* and *fairily*; or *leafits*; of walking "*silken* hush'd and *chaste*;" and innumerable other such follies, which are really too contemptible to criticise. If all this nonsense is mere youthful affectation, perhaps as Mr. Keats gets more sense, he will learn to see it in its true light; such innovations in language are despicable in themselves, and disgusting to the imagination of every man of virtue and taste, from having been originally *conceited*, as Mr. Keats would say, in the brain of one of the most profligate and wretched scribblers that we can remember to have ever either heard or read of.

From John Scott's unsigned review of *Lamia, Isabella, The Eve of St Agnes, and other Poems* in *The London Magazine*, September 1820.

The injustice which has been done to our author's works, in estimating their poetical merit, rendered us doubly anxious, on opening his last volume, to find it likely to seize fast hold of general sympathy, and thus turn an overwhelming power against the paltry traducers of a talent, more eminently promising in many respects, than any that the present age has been called upon to encourage. We have not found it to be quite all that we wished in this respect—and it would have been very extraordinary if we had, for our wishes went far beyond reasonable expectations. But we have found it of a nature to present to common understandings the poetical power with which the author's mind is gifted, in a more tangible and intelligible shape than that in which it has appeared in any of his former compositions. It is, therefore, calculated to throw shame on the lying, vulgar spirit, in which this young worshipper in the temple of the Muses has been cried-down; whatever questions it may still leave to be settled as to the kind and degree of his poetical merits. Take for instance, as a proof of the justice of our praise, the following passage from an Ode to the Nightingale:—it is distinct, noble, pathetic, and true: the thoughts have all chords of direct communication with naturally-constituted hearts: the echoes of the strain linger about the depths of human bosoms.

[Quotes last two stanzas of *Ode to a Nightingale*]

Let us take also a passage of another sort altogether—the description of a young beauty preparing for her nightly rest, overlooked by a concealed lover, in which we know not whether most to admire the magical delicacy of the hazardous picture, or its consummate, irresistible attraction. "How sweet the moonlight sleeps upon this bank," says Shakspeare; and sweetly indeed does it fall on the half undressed form of Madeline:—it has an exquisite moral influence, corresponding with the picturesque effect.

[Quotes stanzas xxiii and xxv–xxviii of *The Eve of St Agnes*: 'Out went . . . dell; Full on this casement . . . How fast she slept!']

One more extract,—again varying entirely the style of the composition. It shall be taken from a piece called Hyperion; one of the most extraordinary creations of any modern imagination. Its "woods are ruthless, dreadful, deaf, and dull:" the soul of dim antiquity hovers, like a mountain-cloud, over its vast and gloomy grandeur: it carries us back in spirit beyond the classical age; earlier than "the gods of the Greeks;" when the powers of creation were to be met with visible about the young earth, shouldering the mountains, and with their huge forms filling the vallies. The sorrows of this piece are "huge;" its utterance "large;" its tears "big."—Alas, centuries have brought littleness since then,—otherwise a crawling, reptile of office, with just strength enough to leave its slimy traces on the pages of a fashionable Review, could never have done a real mischief to the poet of the Titans! It is but a fragment we have of Hyperion: an advertisement tells us that "the poem was intended to have been of equal length with Endymion, *but the reception given to that work discouraged the author from proceeding*." Let Mr. Croker read the following sublime and gorgeous personification of Asia, and be proud of the information thus given him—and of that superior encouragement to which it is owing that we have his Talavera in a complete state!

[Quotes *Hyperion*, II. 52–63: 'Nearest him . . . elephants']

This is not the extract, however, which we were about to make: it was the opening of the poem we thought of. The dethronement of Saturn by Jupiter, and the later gods taking the places of the early powers of heaven and earth, form its subject. We seem entering the awful demesne of primeval solitude as the poet commences:

[Quotes *Hyperion*, I. 1–71: 'Deep in the shady sadness . . . while at thy feet I weep" ']

503

Will not our readers feel it as a disgrace attaching to the character of the period, that a dastardly attempt should have been made to assassinate a poet of power equal to these passages: that one should come like a thief to steal his "precious diadem;"—a murder and a robbery "most foul and horrible?" Cold-blooded conscious dishonesty, we have no hesitation to say, must have directed the pen of the critic of Endymion in the Quarterly Review: making every allowance for the callousness of a worldly spirit, it is impossible to conceive a total insensibility to the vast beauties scattered profusely over that disordered, ill-digested work. The author provokes opposition, as we have already fully said: not unfrequently he even suggests angry censure. We cannot help applying the word *insolent*, in a literary sense, to some instances of his neglectfulness, to the random swagger of occasional expressions, to the bravado style of many of his sentiments. But, coupling these great faults with his still greater poetical merits, what a fine, what an interesting subject did he offer for perspicacious, honourable criticism! But he was beset by a very dog-kennel; and he must be more than human if he has not had his erroneous tendencies hardened in him in consequence.

What strike us as the principal faults of his poetry, impeding his popularity, we would venture thus to specify.

1. His frequent obscurity and confusion of language. As an instance of the latter, we may mention, that he attaches the epithet of "*leaden-eyed*," to despair, considered as a quality or sentiment. Were it a personification of despair, the compound would be as finely applied, as, under the actual circumstances, it is erroneously so. There are many, many passages too, in his last volume, as well as in his earlier ones, from which we are not able, after taking some pains to understand them, to derive any distinct notion or meaning whatever.

2. He is too fond of running out glimmerings of thoughts, and indicating distant shadowy fancies: he shows, also, a fondness for dwelling on features which are not naturally the most important or prominent. His imagination coquets with, and mocks the reader in this respect; and plain earnest minds turn away from such tricks with disgust. The greatest poets have always chiefly availed themselves of the plainest and most palpable materials.

3. He affects, in bad taste, a quaint strangeness of phrase; as some folks affect an odd manner of arranging their neckcloths, &c. This "shows a most pitiful ambition." We wish Mr. Keats would not talk of *cutting mercy with a sharp knife to the bone*; we cannot contemplate the *skeleton* of mercy. Nor can we familiarize ourselves pleasantly with the *dainties made to still an infant's cries*:—the latter is indeed a very round about way of expression,—and not very complimentary either, we think. Young ladies, who know, of course, little or

nothing of the economy of the nursery, will be apt, we imagine, to pout at this periphrasis, which puts their charms on a level with baby-corals!

But we are by this time tired of criticism; as we hope our readers are:—let us then all turn together to the book itself. We have said here what we have deemed it our duty to say: we shall there find what it will be our delight to enjoy.

From the review of *Lamia, Isabella, The Eve of St Agnes, and other Poems* in *The Eclectic Review*, September 1820.

It is just three years since we were called upon to review Mr. Keats's first production. We then gave it as our opinion, that he was not incapable of writing good poetry, that he possessed both the requisite fancy and skill; but we regretted that a young man of his vivid imagination and promising talents should have been flattered into the resolution to publish verses of which he would probably be glad a few years after to escape from the remembrance. It is our practice, when a young writer appears for the first time as a candidate for public favour, to look to the indications of ability which are to be detected in his performance, rather than to its intrinsic merits. There is a wasteful efflorescence that must be thrown off before the intellect attains its maturity. The mind is then at a critical period: there is equal danger of its lavishing all its strength in the abortive promise of excellence, and of its being blighted by unjust discouragement. Such appeared to us to be then the situation of Mr. Keats; and in the spirit of candour and of kindness, we made those remarks on his volume which were designed at once to guide and to excite his future exertions, but for which he manfully disdained to be the wiser. His next production had the good fortune to fall into the hands of critics who rarely deal in either half-praise or half-censure, and whose severity of censure can at least confer notoriety upon the offender. According to his own account, the Author of Endymion must, while smarting under their unsparing lash, have claimed pity almost equally on account of his mortified feelings and his infidel creed; for, in the preface to that 'feverish attempt,' he avows his conviction 'that there is not a fiercer hell than the failure in a great object.' How complete was his failure in that matchless tissue of sparkling and delicious nonsense, his Publishers frankly confess in an Advertisement prefixed to the present volume, wherein they take upon themselves the responsibility of printing an unfinished poem in the same strain, from proceeding with which the Author was discouraged by the reception given to that poem. And yet, under the sanction, we presume, of the same advisers, Mr. Keats has ventured to proclaim himself in his title-page as the unfortunate 'Author of

Endymion.' Are we to gather from this, that he is vain and foolish enough to wish that production not to be forgotten?

The present volume, however, we have been assured, contains something much better. Startled as we were at the appearance of the ghost of Endymion in the title, we endeavoured, on renewing our acquaintance with its Author, to banish from our recollection the unpropitious circumstances under which we had last met, and, as it is now too late to expect that he will exhibit any material change as the result of further intellectual growth, to take a fresh and final estimate of his talents and pretensions as they may be judged of from the volume before us. The evidence on which our opinion is formed, shall now be laid before our readers. One naturally turns first to the shorter pieces, in order to taste the flavour of the poetry. The following ode to Autumn is no unfavourable specimen.

[Quotes the Ode in full]

Fancy has again and again been hymned in lays Pindaric or Anacreontic, but not often in more pleasing and spirited numbers than the following.

[Quotes *Fancy* , ll. 1–66]

The lines addressed to a friend, on Robin Hood, are in the same light and sportive style.

[Quotes *Robin Hood* in full]

Of the longer pieces, Lamia is decidedly the best.

[The reviewer then gives the story as recounted in Burton, and comments that that story has a moral which Keats does not make use of. The reviewer then runs through the poem, with quotations, and later briefly mentions *Isabella* and *The Eve of St Agnes*, from which he quotes stanzas xxv, xxvii–xxviii, xxxiii–xxxv, and xl–xlii]

We have laid before our readers these copious extracts from Mr. Keats's present volume, without any comment, in order that he might have the full benefit of pleading his own cause: there they are, and they can be made to speak neither more nor less in his favour than they have already testified.

Mr. Keats, it will be sufficiently evident, is a young man—whatever be his age, we must consider him as still but a young man,—possessed of an elegant fancy, a warm and lively imagination, and something above the average talents of persons who take to writing poetry. Poetry is his mistress,—we were going to say, his *Lamia*, for we suspect that she has proved a syren, that her wine is drugged, and that her treasures will be found to be like the gold of Tantalus. Mr. Keats has given his whole soul to 'plotting and fitting himself for verses fit to live;' and the consequence is, that he has produced verses which, if we mistake not, will not live very long, though they will live as long as they deserve. The exclusive cultivation of the imagination is always attended by a dwindling or contraction of the other powers of the mind. This effect has often been remarked upon: it is the penalty which second-rate genius pays for the distinction purchased by the exhaustion of its whole strength in that one direction, or upon that one object, that has seized upon the fancy; and it is the true source of affectation and eccentricity. In no other way can we account for the imbecility of judgement, the want of sober calculation, the intense enthusiasm about mean or trivial objects, and the real emptiness of mind, which are sometimes found connected with distinguishing talents. Poetry, after all, if pursued as an end, is but child's play; and no wonder that those who seem not to have any higher object than to be poets, should sometimes be very childish. What better name can we bestow on the nonsense that Mr. Keats, and Mr. Leigh Hunt, and Mr. Percy Bysshe Shelley, and some other poets about town, have been talking of 'the beautiful mythology of Greece?' To some persons, although we would by no means place Mr. Keats among the number, that mythology comes recommended chiefly by its grossness—its alliance to the sensitive pleasures which belong to the animal. With our Author, this fondness for it proceeds, we very believe, from nothing worse than a school boy taste for the stories of the Pantheon and Ovid's Metamorphoses, and the fascination of the word *classical*. Had he passed through the higher forms of a liberal education, he would have *shed* all these puerilities; his mind would have received the rich alluvial deposite of such studies; but this would only have formed the soil for its native fancies; and he would have known that the last use which a full-grown scholar thinks of making of his classical acquirements, is to make a parade of them either in prose or verse. There is nothing gives a greater richness to poetry, we admit, than classical allusions, if they are not of a common-place kind; but they will generally be found to please in proportion to their slightness and remoteness: it is as illustrations, sometimes highly picturesque illustrations of the subject, not as distinct objects of thought,—it is as metaphor, never in the broad and palpable shape of simile, that they please. It was reserved for the Author of Endymion to beat out the gold of ancient fable into leaf thin enough to cover four long cantos of incoherent verse. And now, in the present volume, we

507

have Hyperion, books one, two, and three! We do not mean to deny that there is a respectable degree of inventive skill and liveliness of fancy displayed in this last poem, but they are most miserably misapplied; nor should we have imagined that any person would have thrown away his time in attempting such a theme, unless it were some lad with his fancy half full of Homer and half full of Milton, who might, as a school exercise, try to frame something out of the compound ideas of the Titan and the Demon, of Olympus and Pandemonium. But Mr. Keats, seemingly, can think or write of scarcely any thing else than the 'happy pieties' of Paganism. A Grecian Urn throws him into an ecstasy: its 'silent form,' he says, 'doth tease us out of thought as doth Eternity,'—a very happy description of the bewildering effect which such subjects have at least had upon his own mind; and his fancy having thus got the better of his reason, we are the less surprised at the oracle which the Urn is made to utter:

> ' "Beauty is truth, truth beauty,"—that is all
> Ye know on earth, and all ye need to know.'

That is, all that Mr. Keats knows or cares to know.—But till he knows much more than this, he will never write verses fit to live.

We wish to say little of the affectation which still frequently disfigures Mr. Keats's phraseology, because there is very much less of it in the present volume than in his former poems. We are glad to notice this indication of *growth*. An imperfect acquaintance with the genuine resources of the language, or an impatience of its poverty and weakness as a vehicle for his teeming fancies, is still occasionally discernible in the violence he lays upon words and syllables forced to become such: *e.g.* 'rubious-argent?' 'milder-moon'd;' 'frail-strung heart;' a 'tithe' of eye-sight,—

> '——With eye-lids closed,
> Saving a tythe which love still open kept.'

(N.B. An American Keats would have said, '*a balance*,')

'trembled blossoms;' 'honey'd middle of the night;' and other splendid novelties.

We would, however, be the last persons to lay great stress on such *minutiæ*, in estimating the merits of a writer; but we feel it our duty to warn off all persons who are for breaking down the fences which language interposes between sense and nonsense.

The true cause of Mr. Keats's failure is, not the want of talent, but the misdirection of it; and this circumstance presents the only chance there is that some day or other he will produce something better: whether he ever does or not, is a matter of extreme insignificance to the public, for we have surely poets enough; but it would seem to be not so to himself. At present, there is a sickliness about his productions, which shews there is a mischief at the core. He has with singular ingenuousness and correctness described his own case in the preface to Endymion: 'The imagination of a boy,' he says, 'is healthy, and the *mature* [reviewer's italics] imagination of a man is healthy; but there is a space of life between, in which the soul is in a ferment, the character undecided, the way of life uncertain, the ambition thick-sighted: thence proceeds mawkishness.' The diagnosis of the complaint is well laid down; his is a diseased state of feeling, arising from the want of a sufficient and worthy object of hope and enterprise, and of the regulating principle of religion. Can a more unequivocal proof of this be given, than that there does not occur, if our recollection serves us, throughout his present volume, a single reference to any one object of *real* interest, a single burst of virtuous affection or enlightened sentiment, a single reference, even of the most general kind, to the Supreme Being, or the slenderest indication that the Author is allied by any one tie to his family, his country, or his kind? Mr. Keats, we doubt not, *has* attachments and virtuous feelings, and we would fain hope, notwithstanding the silly expressions which would justify a presumption to the contrary, that he is a Christian: if he is not, it will matter very little to him in a few years what else he may or may not be. We will, however, take it for granted that he is an amiable and well principled young man; and then we have but one piece of advice to offer him on parting, namely, to let it appear in his future productions.

The review of *Lamia, Isabella, The Eve of St Agnes, and other Poems* in *The Monthly Magazine*, September 1820.

We have read with pleasure a volume of *Poems*, lately published by Mr KEATS, the author of Endymion. There is a boldness of fancy and a classical expression of language in the poetry of this gentleman, which, we think, entitle him to stand equally high in the estimation of poetic opinion, as the author of Rimini, or as he (Barry Cornwall) of the Dramatic Scenes. Our pleasure, however, was not unmingled with sentiments of extreme disapprobation. The faults characteristic of his school, are still held up to view with as much affectation, by Mr. K. as if he were fearful of not coming in for his due share of singularity, obscurity, and conceit. But though of the same genus, his poetic labours are specifically different from those of his fellow labourers in the same vineyard.—There is more reach of poetic capacity, more depth and intenseness of thought and feeling, with more classical power of expression, than what we discover in the writings of his master, or of his fellow pupil Mr. Cornwall. It is

509

likewise more original poetry than theirs. Mr. C. is compounded of imitation—of Shakespeare, and of Mr. Leigh Hunt. Mr. H. is a familiar copier of Dryden, with the manner, only a more sparkling one, but without the pathos, of Crabbe. Mr. K., on the contrary, is always himself, and as long as *fair* originality shall be thought superior to good imitation, he will always be preferred. The Poems consist of various Tales, *Lamia, Isabella, The Eve of St. Agnes,* of which we think the first is the best. *Hyperion,* however, is the most powerful.

From John Scott's article 'The Mohock Magazine' printed in *The London Magazine* for December 1820.

In the number of Blackwood containing the *Horæ Scandicæ,* we find the following very candid and amiable declaration:

'We have no personal acquaintance with any of these men (Hunt, Keats, and Hazlitt,) and *no personal* feelings in regard to any one of them, good or bad. We never even saw any one of their faces. As for Mr. Keats, we are informed that he is in a very bad state of health, and that his friends attribute a great deal of it to the pain he has suffered from the critical castigation his Endymion drew down on him in this magazine. If it be so, we are most heartily sorry for it, and have no hesitation in saying, that had we suspected that young author of being so delicately nerved, we should have administered our reproof in a much more lenient shape and style. The truth is, we from the beginning saw marks of feeling and power in Mr. Keats' verses, which made us think it very likely, he might become a real poet of England, provided he could be persuaded to give up all the tricks of Cockneyism, and forswear for ever the thin potations of Mr. Leigh Hunt. We, therefore, rated him as roundly as we *decently could do,* for the flagrant affectations of those early productions of his.'

They have no "personal feelings," then, it seems, in regard to Mr. Keats: they are sorry to have *unnecessarily* hurt his feelings: but they have only "rated him as roundly as they *decently* could do for his flagrant affectations:"—and they afterwards ask, very reasonably, no doubt, "what is there should prevent us from expressing a simple, undisguised, impartial opinion on the merits and demerits of men we never saw, or thought of for one moment, otherwise than as in their capacities of authors?"—What, indeed? *Horæ Scandicæ* is in the *same Number* with this moderate, fair, gentlemanly appeal;—let us turn to it, and observe how decently, as well as roundly, they rate Mr. Keats for his affectations; how carefully they avoid trespassing on any thing belonging to the man, but *his capacity of author*; how obvious they make it, that they are actuated by no personal feelings towards him: in short, how strictly legitimate is their criticism on his writings,—"how pure a thing,—how free from mortal taint," as Mr. Keats says of his Beauty of St. Agnes.

> Here's Corny Webb, and this other, an please ye,
> Is *Johnny Keats*—how it *smells of magnesia!*
>
> *Horæ Scandicæ.*

A fine specimen this of their round and *decent* manner! Magnesia has much to do with "Hyperion," and the "Ode to the Nightingale!"

> We, from the hands of a *Cockney Apothecary*,
> Brought off this pestle, with which he was capering,
> Swearing and swaggering, rhyming and vapouring;
> Seized with a fit of poetical fury,
> (I thought he was drunk, my good Sir, I assure ye)
> With this he was scattering, all through the whole house,
> *Gallipot, glisterbag, cataplasm, bolus;*
> While the poor 'prentices at him were staring,
> Or perhaps in their minds a strait waistcoat preparing,
> Loud he exclaimed, "Behold here's my truncheon;
> I'm the Marshal of poets—I'll flatten your nuncheon.
> *Pitch physic to hell, you rascals, for damn ye, a—*
> *I'll physic you all with a clyster of Lamia!*"
>
> *Horæ Scandicæ.*

This is their mode of expressing their *"undisguised and impartial opinion,"* &c. &c. of Mr. Keats in his capacity of author! This is to prove that "they are most heartily sorry" for having hurt his feelings, and that they sympathise, as they conscientiously declare, with his friends who deplore his bad health!

Select Bibliography

(in addition to the material from which extracts have been drawn for this volume)

Abbreviations

BUSE	*Boston University Studies in English*
EC	*Essays in Criticism*
ELH	*The Journal of English Literary History*
ER	*The Edinburgh Review*
JEGP	*The Journal of English and Germanic Philology*
K-SJ	*The Keats-Shelley Journal*
MLN	*Modern Language Notes*
MLQ	*The Modern Language Quarterly*
MLR	*The Modern Language Review*
MP	*Modern Philology*
N&Q	*Notes and Queries*
PBSA	*Papers of the Bibliographical Society of America*
PMLA	*Publications of the Modern Language Association of America*
PQ	*The Philological Quarterly*
RES	*The Review of English Studies*
SAQ	*The South Atlantic Quarterly*
SP	*Studies in Philology*
TLS	*The Times Literary Supplement*

I. General Books and Articles

ABRAMS, M. H.: *The Mirror and the Lamp: Romantic Theory and the Critical Tradition* (London; New York, 1953). Reprd. London, 1960.

ALTICK, R. D.: *The English Common Reader: A Social History of the Mass Reading Public, 1800–1900* (Chicago; London, 1957).

AMARASINGHE, U.: *Dryden and Pope in the Early Nineteenth Century* (Cambridge, 1962).

ANDREWS, A.: *A History of British Journalism*, 2 vols. (London, 1859).

ASPINALL, A.: *Politics and the Press, c. 1780–1850* (London, 1949).

513

BATE, W. J.: *From Classic to Romantic* (Cambridge, Mass.; London, 1946).

BOURNE, H. R. Fox: *English Newspapers. Chapters in the History of Journalism*, 2 vols. (London, 1887).

BRIGGS, ASA: *The Age of Improvement, 1784–1867* (London, 1959; reprd. 1967).

BRINTON, CRANE: *The Political Ideas of the English Romanticists* (London, 1926; New York, 1962).

BROWN, FORD K.: *Fathers of the Victorians: the Age of Wilberforce* (Cambridge, 1961).

BUSH, D.: *Mythology and the Romantic Tradition in English Poetry* (Cambridge, Mass.; London, 1937).

CAINE, T. HALL: *Cobwebs of Criticism* (London, 1883).

COCKBURN, HENRY, LORD: *Memorials of His Time* (London, 1856).

COLLINS, A. S.: *The Profession of Letters, 1780–1832* (London, 1928).

Cox, R. G.: 'The Great Reviews', *Scrutiny*, VI (1937), 2–20, 155–75.

——: *Nineteenth Century Periodical Criticism*, unpubl. Cambridge Ph.D. Dissertation, 1939.

CRUSE, AMY: *The Englishman and his Books in the Early Nineteenth Century* (London, 1930).

CURWEN, H.: *A History of Booksellers: the Old and the New* (London, 1874).

DOWDEN, E.: *The French Revolution and English Literature* (London, 1897).

ELLIOTT, A. R. D.: 'Reviews and Magazines in the Early Years of the Nineteenth Century', ch. vi of Vol. XII in *The Cambridge History of English Literature*, ed. A. W. Ward and A. R. Waller (Cambridge, 1915).

ELTON, O.: *A Survey of English Literature, 1780–1830*, 2 vols. (London, 1912).

FAIRCHILD, H. N.: *Religious Trends in English Poetry (Romantic Faith, 1780–1830)* (New York, Columb. Univ. Press; London, 1949).

GATES, L. E.: *Three Studies in Literature* (London and New York, 1899).

GRAHAM, W.: *English Literary Periodicals* (New York, 1930). Reprd. New York and London, 1966.

HALÉVY, E.: *England in 1815*, tr. E. I. Watkin and D. A. Barker, from 1st Fr. edn., 1913 (London, 1924). 2nd edn., 1949.

——: *The Liberal Awakening, 1815–1830*, tr. E. I. Watkin (London, 1926). 2nd edn., 1949.

HAYDEN, J. O.: *The Romantic Reviewers, 1802–1824* (London and Chicago, 1969).

JACK, IAN: *English Literature, 1815–1832* (Vol. X of *The Oxford History of English Literature*, ed. F. P. Wilson and Bonamy Dobrée) (Oxford, 1963).
JOYCE, MICHAEL: *Edinburgh, The Golden Age, 1769–1832* (London, 1951).

KITSON CLARK, G. S. R.: *The English Inheritance* (London, 1950).
——: *The Making of Victorian England* (London, 1962; University Paperbacks, 1965).

LEAVIS, F. R.: *The Relationship of Journalism to Literature*, unpubl. Cambridge Ph.D. Dissertation, 1925.

MACCOBY, S.: *English Radicalism, 1786–1832* (London, 1955).
MACKINTOSH, R. J., ed.: *Memoirs of the Life of the Rt. Hon. Sir James Mackintosh*, 2 vols. (London, 1835).
MINEKA, F. E.: *The Dissidence of Dissent* (Chapel Hill: Univ. of North Carolina; London, 1944).

OVERTON, J. H.: *The English Church in the Nineteenth Century, 1800–1833* (London, 1894).

PERKIN, H.: *The Origins of Modern English Society, 1780–1880* (London and Toronto, 1969).

QUINLAN, M. J.: *Victorian Prelude: a History of English Manners, 1700–1830* (New York, 1941).

RODWAY, A.: *The Romantic Conflict* (London, 1963).

SOLOWAY, R. A.: *Prelates and People, Ecclesiastical Social Thought in England, 1783–1852* (London, 1969).

THOMPSON, E. P.: *The Making of the English Working Class* (London, 1964).
TREVELYAN, G. M.: *British History in the Nineteenth Century and After, 1782–1919* (London, 1937) (2nd edn. of *British History in the Nineteenth Century, 1782–1901*, London, 1922).

WAIN, J., ed.: *Contemporary Reviews of Romantic Poetry* (London, 1953).
WARD, W. S.: 'Some Aspects of the Conservative Attitude toward Poetry in English Criticism, 1798–1820', *PMLA*, LX (1945), 586–98.
WAUGH, A.: 'The English Reviewers. A Sketch of their History and Principles', *The Critic*, XI (1901), 26–37.

WELKER, J. J.: 'The Position of the Quarterlies on Some Classical Dogmas', *SP*, XXXVII (1940), 542–62.

WELLEK, R.: 'The Concept of Romanticism in Literary History', *Comparative Literature*, I (1949), 1–23; 147–72.

——: *A History of Modern Criticism, 1750–1950* (New Haven: Yale Univ. Press; London, 1955–65).

WHITE, R. J.: *From Waterloo to Peterloo* (Cambridge, 1957).

WICKWAR, W. H.: *The Struggle for the Freedom of the Press, 1819–1832* (London, 1928).

WOODWARD, E. L. (SIR LLEWELLYN): *The Age of Reform, 1815–1870* (Oxford, 1938). 2nd edn., 1962.

II. On particular periodicals

Blackwood's Edinburgh Magazine

GILLIES, R. P.: *Memoirs of a Literary Veteran*, 3 vols. (London, 1851).

OLIPHANT, MARGARET O. W.: *Annals of a Publishing House*, 2 vols. (Edinburgh, 1897).

STROUT, A. L.: *A Bibliography of Articles in Blackwood's Magazine, 1817–25* (Lubbock, Texas, 1959).

——: 'Hunt, Hazlitt, and "Maga" ', *ELH*, IV (1937), 151–9.

——: ' "Maga", Champion of Shelley', *SP*, XXIX (1932), 95–119.

TREDREY, F. D.: *The House of Blackwood, 1804–1954* (Edinburgh, 1954).
See also under items on LOCKHART and WILSON in III, below.

The British Critic

BELOE, W.: *The Sexagenarian, or, The Recollections of a Literary Life*, ed. Thos. Rennell, 2 vols. (London, 1817).

CHURTON, E.: *A Memoir of Joshua Watson*, 2 vols. (London, 1861).

HODGSON, J. T.: *A Memoir of Francis Hodgson*, 2 vols. (London, 1878).

LE BAS, C. W.: *The Life of T. F. Middleton*, 2 vols. (London, 1831).

OVERTON, J. H.: *The English Church in the Nineteenth Century (1800–1833)* (London, 1894).

REES, T.: *Reminiscences of Literary London from 1779 to 1853* (London, 1896).

RIVINGTON, S.: *The Publishing House of Rivington* (London, 1894).

——: *The Publishing Family of Rivington* (London, 1919).

STEVENS, W.: *A Short Account of the Life and Writings of the Rev. William Jones* (London, 1801).

The British Review

ROBERTS, A.: *The Life, Letters, and Opinions of William Roberts* (London, 1850).

WARD, W. S.: 'Lord Byron and "My Grandmother's Review" ', *MLN*, LXIV (1949), 25–9.

The Champion

TURNBULL, J. M.: 'Keats, Reynolds, and *The Champion*', in *London Mercury*, XIX (1929), 584–94.
    See also REYNOLDS, and SCOTT, J., in III, below.

The Christian Observer

JONES, M. G.: *Hannah More* (London, 1952).
KNUTSFORD, VISCOUNTESS: *Life and Letters of Zachary Macaulay* (London, 1900).
PEARSON, J.: *The Life of William Hey, Esq., FRS*, 2 vols. (London, 1822). 2nd edn., 1823.
PRATT, J. H.: *Eclectic Notes* (London, 1865).
ROBERTS, W.: *Memoirs of the life and correspondence of Mrs. Hannah More* (London, 1834). 2nd edn., 1834.
    See also BROWN, and MINEKA, in I, above.

The Eclectic Review

CONDER, E. R.: *Josiah Conder, A Memoir* (London, 1857).
EVERTS, W. W.: *John Foster: life and thoughts* (New York, 1883).
FOSTER, J.: *Contributions, Biographical, Literary, and Philosophical to The Eclectic Review*, 2 vols. (London, 1844).
HOLLAND, J. and EVERETT, J.: *Memoirs of the Life and Writings of James Montgomery*, 7 vols. (London, 1854–6).
RYLAND, J. E. (ed.): *The Life and Correspondence of John Foster*, 2 vols. (London, 1846).
    See also MINEKA, in I, above.

The Edinburgh Magazine (Constable's)

CONSTABLE, T.: *Archibald Constable and his Literary Correspondents*, 3 vols. (Edinburgh, 1873).

The Edinburgh Review

ANON.: '*The Edinburgh Review* (1802–1902)', *ER*, CXLV, July 1902, 275–318.
BAGEHOT, W.: 'The First Edinburgh Reviewers', in *Literary Studies*, 2 vols. (London, 1878–9), ed. R. H. Hutton.

CLIVE, J.: *Scotch Reviewers: The Edinburgh Review 1802–1815* (London, 1957).

——: '*The Edinburgh Review*: 150 Years After', *History Today*, II (1952), 844–50.

COPINGER, W. A.: *On the Authorship of the First Hundred Numbers of the 'Edinburgh Review'* (Manchester, 1895).

CRAWFORD, T.: *The Edinburgh Review and Romantic Poetry (1802–29)*, Auckland University College Bulletin No. 47, English Series No. 8, 1955.

CROSS, M.: *Selections from The Edinburgh Review*, 4 vols. (London, 1833).

HOLLAND, LADY: *A Memoir of the Rev. Sydney Smith*, 2 vols. (London, 1855).

HORNER, L., ed.: *Memoirs and Correspondence of Francis Horner*, 2 vols. (London, 1853).

SCHNEIDER, E., GRIGGS, I., KERN, J. D.: 'Early Edinburgh Reviewers: A New List', *MP*, XLIII (1946), 192–210.

SMITH, N. C., ed.: *The Letters of Sydney Smith*, 2 vols. (Oxford, 1953).

STEPHEN, SIR LESLIE: 'The First Edinburgh Reviewers', in *Hours in a Library*, 3 vols. (London, 1874–9). Several times revised and enlarged.

    See also BROUGHAM, HAZLITT, JEFFREY, in III, below.

The Examiner

BLUNDEN, E.: *Leigh Hunt's 'Examiner' Examined* (London, 1928).

DE FONBLANQUE, E. B.: *The Life and Labours of Albany Fonblanque* (London, 1874).

GRAHAM, W.: 'Shelley's Debt to Leigh Hunt and *The Examiner*', *PMLA*, XL (1925), 185–92.

    See also LEIGH HUNT in III, below.

The Indicator

    See L. LANDRÉ, *Leigh Hunt*, under LEIGH HUNT, in III, below.

Knight's Quarterly Magazine

KNIGHT, C.: *Passages of a Working Life*, 3 vols. (London, 1863–5).

The Liberal

MARSHALL, W. H.: *Byron, Shelley, Hunt, and 'The Liberal'* (Philadelphia and London, 1960).

The Literary Examiner

STOUT, G. D.: 'The "Literary Examiner" and "The Inquisitor"',
TLS (1925), 521.
  See also L. LANDRÉ under LEIGH HUNT in III, below.

The Literary Gazette

DUNCAN, R. W.: 'Byron and the London *Literary Gazette*', *BUSE*, II
(1956), 240–50.
JERDAN, W.: *Autobiography*, 4 vols. (London, 1852–3).
MARCHAND, L. A.: *The Athenaeum: A Mirror of Victorian Culture*
(Chapel Hill: Univ. of N. Carolina, 1941).
RANSOM, H.: 'William Jerdan, Editor and Literary Agent', *Studies in
English*, XXVII (1948), 68–74.
WATTS, A. A.: *Alaric Watts: A Narrative of his Life*, 2 vols. (London,
1844).

The London Magazine (Baldwin's)

BAUER, JOSEPHINE: *The London Magazine, 1820–29* (Copenhagen, 1953).
BROOKS, E. L.: 'Byron and *The London Magazine*', *K-SJ*, V (1956),
49–67.
BUTTERWORTH, S.: 'The Old *London Magazine*', *The Bookman*, LXIII,
October 1922, 12–17.
HUGHES, T. R.: '*The London Magazine*', unpubl. D.Phil. Dissertation,
Oxford, 1931.
PATMORE, P. G.: *My Friends and Acquaintances*, 3 vols. (London, 1854).
TAVE, S. M.: '*The London Magazine*, 1820–29', *MP*, LII (1954), 139–41.
  See also SCOTT, J., in III, below.

The Monthly Magazine

ANON.: *Memoirs of the Public and Private Life of Sir Richard Phillips*
(London, 1808).
BOYLE, A.: 'The Publisher—Sir Richard Phillips', *N&Q*, CXCVI
(1951), 361–6.
CARNALL, G.: '*The Monthly Magazine*', *RES*, V, n.s. (1954), 158–64.
ROBBERDS, J. W.: *A Memoir of the Life and Writings of the late William
Taylor, of Norwich*, 2 vols. (London, 1843).

The Monthly Review

ARNOULD, J.: *A Memoir of Thomas, First Lord Denman*, 2 vols. (London, 1873).

HODGSON, J. T.: *A Memoir of Francis Hodgson*, 2 vols. (London, 1878).

NANGLE, B. C.: '*The Monthly Review*': *2nd Series, 1790–1815: Indexes of Contributors and Articles* (Oxford, 1955).

ROBBERDS, J. W., ed.: *A Memoir of the Life and Writings of the late William Taylor, of Norwich*, 2 vols. (London, 1843).

The New Monthly Magazine

BEATTIE, W.: *The Life and Letters of Thomas Campbell*, 3 vols. (London, 1849). 2nd edn., 1850.

PATMORE, P. G.: *My Friends and Acquaintances*, 3 vols. (London, 1854).

REDDING, C.: *Literary Reminiscences and Memoirs of Thomas Campbell*, 2 vols. (London, 1860).

——: *Fifty Years' Recollections, Literary and Personal*, 3 vols. (London, 1858).

WATTS, A. A.: *Alaric Watts: A Narrative of his Life*, 2 vols. (London, 1884).

The Quarterly Review

ANON.: 'The Centenary of "The Quarterly Review" ', *QR*, CCX (1909), 731–84; CCXI (1909), 279–324.

BAGOT, J.: *George Canning and his Friends*, 2 vols. (London, 1909).

BARROW, SIR JOHN: *An Autobiographical Memoir of Sir John Barrow* (London, 1847).

CLARK, R. B.: *William Gifford: Tory Satirist, Critic and Editor* (New York, 1930).

ELWIN, M.: 'The Founder of "The Quarterly Review"—John Murray II', *QR*, CCLXXXI (1943), 1–15.

GRAHAM, W.: *Tory Criticism in The Quarterly Review, 1809–1853* (New York: Columbia University Press, 1921).

——: 'Some Infamous Tory Reviews', *SP*, XXII (1925), 500–17.

HOLLOWAY, O. E.: 'George Ellis, *The Anti-Jacobin* and *The Quarterly Review*', *RES*, X (1934), 55–66.

LANE-POOLE, S.: *The Life of the Rt. Hon. Stratford Canning, Viscount Stratford de Redcliffe*, 2 vols. (London, 1888).

MARRIOTT, J. A. R.: *George Canning and his Times: a Political Study* (London, 1903),

REDE, L. T.: *Memoir of the Rt. Hon. George Canning*, 2 vols. (London, 1827).

SMILES, S.: *A Publisher and his Friends. Memoir and Correspondence of the late John Murray*, 2 vols. (London, 1891).

 See also CROKER; SCOTT, WALTER; SOUTHEY, in III, below.

The Scots Magazine

See *The Edinburgh Magazine* (Constable's), above.

The Yellow Dwarf

HOWE, P. P.: *The Life of William Hazlitt* (London, 1947).

III. On individual critics

Brougham

ATKINSON, R. H. M. B. and JOHNSON, G. A.: *Brougham and His Early Friends*, 3 vols. (London, 1908).

BROUGHAM, H.: *The Life and Times of Henry, Lord Brougham, Written by Himself*, 3 vols. (Edinburgh and London, 1871).

NEW, C.: *The Life of Henry Brougham to 1830* (London, 1961).

SCHNEIDER, E. W., GRIGGS, I., KERN, J. D.: 'Brougham's Early Contributions to *The Edinburgh Review*: A New List', *MP*, XLII (1945), 152–73.

Croker

BRIGHTFIELD, M. F.: *John Wilson Croker* (Berkeley: Univ. of Calif. Press, 1940).

JENNINGS, L. J., ed.: *The Croker Papers*, 3 vols. (London, 1884). Revd. edn., 1885.

Denman

ARNOULD, J.: *Memoir of Thomas, First Lord Denman*, 2 vols. (London, 1873).

Ellis

HOLLOWAY, O. E.: 'George Ellis, *The Anti-Jacobin*, and *The Quarterly Review*', *RES*, X (1934), 55–66.

Gifford

LONGAKER, J.: *The Della Cruscans and William Gifford* (Univ. of Philadelphia, 1924).

See also *The Quarterly Review* in II, above.

Hazlitt

BAKER, H.: *William Hazlitt* (Cambridge, Mass.: Harvard Univ. Press; London, 1962).

CARVER, P. L.: 'Hazlitt's Contributions to *The Edinburgh Review*', *RES*, IV (1928), 385–93.

HOWE, P. P.: *The Life of William Hazlitt* (London, 1922). Revd., 1928, 1947.

KLINGOPOULOS, G. D.: 'Hazlitt as Critic', *EC*, VI (1956), 386–403.
SCHNEIDER, ELISABETH W.: *The Aesthetics of William Hazlitt* (Philadelphia: Univ. of Penn. Press; London, 1933). 2nd imprn., 1952.

Heber, Reginald
SMITH, G.: *Bishop Heber: Poet and Chief Missionary to the East (1783–1826)* (London, 1895).
SMYTH, T. S.: *The Character and Religious Doctrines of Bishop Heber* (London, 1831).

Hobhouse
BORST, W. A.: *Lord Byron's First Pilgrimage* (New Haven, Conn.: Yale Univ. Press, 1948).
JOYCE, M.: *My Friend H* (London, 1948).
RUTHERFORD, A.: 'The Influence of Hobhouse on Childe Harold's Pilgrimage, Canto IV', *RES*, n.s., XII (1961), 391–7.
VINCENT, E. R.: *Byron, Hobhouse and Foscolo* (London, 1949).

Hunt, Leigh
BLUNDEN, E.: *Leigh Hunt: A Biography* (London, 1930).
HOUTCHENS, L. H. and C. W., eds.: *Leigh Hunt's Literary Criticism* (New York: Columb. Univ. Press, 1956).
JOHNSON, R. B., ed.: *Shelley—Leigh Hunt: How Friendship made History* (London, 1928).
LANDRÉ, L.: *Leigh Hunt: Contribution à l'histoire du Romantisme anglais*, 2 vols. (Paris, 1936).
MARSH, G. L.: 'Louis Landré's Leigh Hunt', *MP*, XXXV (1937), 92–5.
WHEELER, P. L.: 'The Great Quarterlies of the Early Nineteenth Century and Leigh Hunt', *SAQ*, XXIX (1930), 282–303.
See also *The Examiner* in II, above, and BYRON, SHELLEY, and KEATS in IV, below.

Jeffrey
BALD, R. C.: 'Francis Jeffrey as a Literary Critic', *The Nineteenth Century and After*, XCVII (1925), 201–5.
COCKBURN, HENRY, LORD: *The Life of Lord Jeffrey with a Selection from his Correspondence*, 2 vols. (Edinburgh, 1852).
GATES, L. E., ed.: *Selections from the Essays of Francis Jeffrey* (Boston, 1894).
GREIG, J. A.: *Francis Jeffrey of The Edinburgh Review* (Edinburgh, 1948).
GUYER, B.: 'The Philosophy of Jeffrey', *MLQ*, XI (1950), 17–26.
HUGHES, M. Y.: 'The Humanism of Francis Jeffrey', *MLR*, XVI (1921), 243–51.

Jeffrey, Lord: *Contributions to The Edinburgh Review*, 4 vols. (London, 1844); 3 vols., 1846, 1853.
Smith, D. Nichol, ed.: *Jeffrey's Literary Criticism* (London, 1910).
Stephen, Sir Leslie: *Hours in a Library* (London, 1874–9).

Lamb
Blunden, E.: *Charles Lamb and his Contemporaries* (London, 1933).
Lucas, E. V.: *The Life of Charles Lamb*, 2 vols. (London, 1905). Revd. edn., 1 vol., 1921.
Tillyard, E. M. W., ed.: *Lamb's Criticism* (London, 1923).

Lockhart
Hildyard, M. C.: *Lockhart's Literary Criticism* (Oxford: Blackwell, 1931).
Lang, A.: *The Life and Letters of John Gibson Lockhart*, 2 vols. (London, 1897).
Lochhead, Marion C.: *John Gibson Lockhart* (London, 1954).
Macbeth, G.: *John Gibson Lockhart: A Critical Study* (Urbana: Univ. of Illinois, 1935).
Strout, A. L.: *John Bull's Letter to Lord Byron* (Norman: Univ. of Oklahoma Press, 1947).
——: 'Lockhart, Champion of Shelley', *TLS* (1955), 468.
Woolf, Virginia: 'Lockhart's Criticism', in *The Moment and Other Essays* (London, 1947).

Maginn
Lockhart, J. G.: 'The Doctor', *Fraser's Magazine*, January 1831.
Miscellanies: Prose and Verse, ed. R. W. Montagu, with a Memoir (London, 1885).
Thrall, Miriam M. H.: *Rebellious Fraser's* (New York: Columb. Univ. Press; London, 1934).

Peacock
Dawson, C.: *His Fine Wit: A Study of Thomas Love Peacock* (London, 1970).
Mayoux, J.-J.: *Un Épicurien anglais: Thomas Love Peacock* (Paris, 1933).
Mills, H.: *Peacock, his Circle and his Age* (Cambridge, 1969).

Reynolds, J. H.
Jones, L. M., ed.: *Selected Prose of John Hamilton Reynolds* (Cambridge, Mass.: Harvard Univ. Press; London, 1966).
Marsh, G. L.: 'The Writings of Keats's Friend Reynolds', *SP*, **XXV** (1928), 491–510.
——, ed.: *John Hamilton Reynolds: Poetry and Prose* (London, 1928).
See also *The Champion* in II, above.

Roberts, William
See *The British Review* in II, above.

Robinson, Henry Crabb
HUDSON, D., ed.: *The Diary of Henry Crabb Robinson: An Abridgement* (London, 1967).
MORLEY, EDITH J.: *The Life and Times of Henry Crabb Robinson* (London, 1935).
——, ed.: *Henry Crabb Robinson on Books and their Writers*, 3 vols. London, 1938).
SADLER, T.: *The Diary, Reminiscences, and Correspondence of Henry Crabb Robinson*, 3 vols., 1869; 2 vols., 1872.

Scott, John
HUGHES, T. R.: 'John Scott: Author, Editor and Critic', *London Mercury*, XXI (1930), 518–28.
PATMORE, P. G.: *My Friends and Acquaintances*, 3 vols. (London, 1855).
SMITH, HORACE: Memoir of Scott in *NMM*, LXXXI, 1847, 415–18.
ZEITLIN, J.: 'The Editor of *The London Magazine*', *JEGP*, XX (1921), 328–54.
See also *The London Magazine* in II, above.

Scott, Sir Walter
BALL, MARGARET: *Sir Walter Scott as a Critic of Literature* (New York, 1907).
GRIERSON, H. J. C.: *Sir Walter Scott, Bart.* (London, 1938).
— —, ed.: *The Letters of Sir Walter Scott*, 12 vols. (1932–7).
LOCKHART, J. G.: *Memoirs of the Life of Sir Walter Scott, Bart.*, 7 vols., 1837–8; revd. edn., 10 vols., 1839.

Watts, Alaric
See *The Literary Gazette* in II, above.

Wilson
GORDON, MARY: *Christopher North: A Memoir*, 2 vols. (Edinburgh, 1862).
SWANN, ELSIE: *Christopher North (John Wilson)* (Edinburgh, 1934).

IV. On criticism of the individual poets by their contemporaries

On Byron
CHEW, S. C.: *Byron in England: His Fame and After-Fame* (London, 1924).
COLERIDGE, E. H., ed.: *The Works of Lord Byron: Poetry*, 7 vols. (London, 1898–1904), *passim*.

ESCARPIT, R.: *Lord Byron: un tempérament littéraire* (Paris, 1955–7).

JOHNSON, E. D. H.: 'Don Juan in England', *ELH*, XI (1944), 135–53.

MARCHAND, L. A.: *Byron: A Biography* (London, 1957), *passim*.

PROTHERO, R. E., ed.: *The Works of Lord Byron: Letters and Journals*, 6 vols. (London, 1898–1901), *passim*.

RUTHERFORD, A.: *Byron: The Critical Heritage* (London, 1970).

———: *Byron: A Critical Study* (Edinburgh and London, 1961), *passim*.

STEFFAN, T. G. and PRATT, W. W., ed., in Vol. IV of *Don Juan*, 4 vols. (Austin, Texas, 1957).

STROUT, A. L., ed.: *John Bull's Letter to Lord Byron* (Norman, Oklahoma, 1947).

TRUEBLOOD, P. G.: *The Flowering of Byron's Genius: Studies in Byron's 'Don Juan'* (Stanford University Press; London, 1945; New York, 1962).

WALKER, KEITH: *Byron's Readers: A study of attitudes towards Byron, 1812–1832*, unpubl. Cambridge Ph.D. Dissertation, 1966.

See also SMILES, S., in II, *The Quarterly Review*, above.

On Shelley

BLUNDEN, E.: *Shelley and Keats: as they struck their Contemporaries* (London, 1925).

MARSH, G. L.: 'The Early Reviews of Shelley', *MP*, XXVII (1929), 73–95.

NORMAN, SYLVA: *Flight of the Skylark* (London, 1954).

WHITE, N. I.: *The Unextinguished Hearth* (Durham, North Carolina, 1938). Reprd. New York and London, 1966.

———: *Shelley*, 2 vols. (New York, 1940); 'corrected', 2 vols. (London, 1947), *passim*.

On Keats

BATE, W. J.: *John Keats* (Cambridge, Mass.: Harvard Univ. Press; London, 1963), *passim*.

BLUNDEN, E.: *Shelley and Keats: as they struck their Contemporaries* (London, 1925).

COLVIN, SIR SIDNEY: *John Keats: His Life and Poetry, His Friends, Critics, and After-Fame* (London, 1917, many times reprd.), *passim*.

FINNEY, C. L.: *The Evolution of Keats's Poetry* (Cambridge, Mass.: Harvard Univ. Press; Oxford, 1936), *passim*.

GITTINGS, R.: *John Keats* (London, 1968), *passim*.

HEWLETT, DOROTHY: *Adonais: A Life of John Keats* (London, 1937). Revd. edn., *A Life of John Keats*, 1949; 3rd edn., 1970.

MACGILLIVRAY, J. R.: *John Keats: A Bibliography and Reference Guide* (Toronto, 1949).

MARSH, G. L. and WHITE, N. I.: 'Keats and the Periodicals of his Time', *MP*, XXXII (1934), 37–53.
MATTHEWS, G. M.: *Keats: The Critical Heritage* (London, 1971).
WARD, AILEEN: *John Keats: The Making of a Poet* (London, 1963), *passim*.

For criticism of all three poets see also
ALDEN, R. M., ed.: *Critical Essays of the Early Nineteenth Cntury* (New York, 1921).
DAVIES, H. SYKES, ed.: Vol. II of *The Poets and their Critics* (London, 1962).
HAYDEN, J. O., ed.: *Romantic Bards and British Reviewers* (London, 1971).
WAIN, J., ed.: *Contemporary Reviews of Romantic Poetry* (London, 1953).

Index of Names

ABERDEEN, 111*n*.1
Achilles, 145, 295
Achitophel (Dryden's), 23
Acrasia, 190
Adam, 330, 331
Addison, Joseph, 25
Adeline, 126
Adonais, 373, 374, 385, 387
Adonis, 427, 433, 496
Æneas, 295
Æschylus, 50, 151, 176, 351, 352, 355, 367, 436, 441
Akenside, Mark, 453
Aldrich, Henry, 342
Alpinula, Julia, 98, 135
Alps, 74
American War, 172
Amundeville, 126
Anacreon, 55, 210
Anglicans, 23
Apemantus, 240
Apollo, 133, 234, 283, 367, 471, 475, 484
Apollo Belvedere, 63
Arachne, 390
Archimago (=Wm. Godwin), 344
Aretino, Pietro, 66
Ariadne, 56
Ariosto, Ludovico, 191, 259, 424
Aristophanes, 55
Aristotle, 55
Armour, R. W., 433*n*.1
Arqua, 272
Athena's tower, 273
Athens, 230, 272
Atherstone, Edwin, 34
Attius, 351
Attorney-General, 154
Augusta (Leigh), 74
Augustans, 25

Babel, 119

Bacchus, 427
Bacon, Francis, 105, 221, 325, 358, 390, 405, 407
Bacon, Friar, 250
Bailey, Benjamin, 420, 426, 427, 445, 448, 449, 465, 472
Baillie, Joanna, 467
Baldwin, Robert, 151
Balkans, the, 179
Barrow, Isaac, 480
Barton, Bernard, 89
Bate, W. J., 440, 442
Beatrice (in The Cenci), 107
Beattie, James, 80, 92
Beaumont, Sir Francis, 392, 411, 415
Beavan, A. H., 317*n*.1
Beersheba, 239
Belgium, 96, 242
Belial, 276
Bellaston, Lady, 288
Beloe, William, 59
Bentham, Jeremy, 46
Berni, Francesco, 182, 259, 298
Bethlehem, 102
Beyer, W. W., 161*n*.2
Bible, the, 99, 128, 249
Bion, 383
Blackwood, William, 42, 49*n*.1, 450
Blake, William, 22, 196
Blunden, Edmund, 131*n*.3, 132*n*.1
Boccaccio, Giovanni, 114, 372, 437, 445, 489, 496, 500, 501
Boileau, Nicolas, 422, 470
Bonaparte (see also Napoleon), 96, 97
Bond St. Reading Room, 104
Boon, General, 123
Bowles, Rev. W. L., 276*n*.1
Brenta, the, 32
Brett-Smith, H. F. B., 326*n*.2
Brewer, Luther A., 324*n*.1
Briggs, Harold E., 42*n*.1
British Museum, the, 59

Brougham, Henry (later Lord Brougham), 7, 25, 179*n*.1, 201, 260
Brown, Charles Armitage, 116*n*.3
Browne, Sir Thomas, 397
Bryan, Mrs, 197
Buchanan, Robert, 444*n*.7
Buckingham, Duke of, 123
'Bull, John' (=J. G. Lockhart), 45, 47, 48, 276
Bull, John (=Englishmen), 87
Bulwer, Edward (Edward G. E. Bulwer-Lytton), 150*n*.
Bunyan, John, 302
Burns, Robert, 238, 276, 467
Burton, Robert, 132, 438, 500, 506
Butler, Joseph, 93
Buxton, John, 182*n*.1
Byron, George Gordon, Lord, *passim* throughout; on Byron, 185, 189, 191, 196; on Keats, 168, 187, 188, 440, 441, 442; on Shelley, 325
Byzantium, 235

CAECILIA METELLA, 54
Caesar, Julius, 231, 238
Cain, 55, 123, 318, 374
Calderón, Pedro, 396
Caliban, 71
Caligula, 67
Callimachus, 496
Campbell, Thomas, 148, 161, 423, 429, 451, 480
Canning, George, 21, 128, 157*n*.3, 480
Carlile, Richard, 172, 314
Cary, H. F. (tr. of Dante), 321
Cascine, the, 398
Casti, Giovanni Battista, 182
Castlereagh, Robert Stewart, Viscount, 21, 121, 162, 168, 193, 300
Catherine, Empress of Russia, 124
Cenci, Count, 107, 112, 169, 350
Chapman, George, 133, 429, 499
Charles I, 416
Charles II, 453
Charlotte, Princess, 55, 63, 102, 147, 159
Chatterton, Thomas, 113, 429, 482, 487
Chaucer, Geoffrey, 139, 221, 225, 426, 434, 445, 451, 477
Chaworth, Mary, 60
Chew, S. C., 188*n*.3, 193*n*.1
Childe Harold, 72, 73, 145, 214, 230,
238, 242, 243, 244, 246, 264, 277, 286,
Childe, the (=Childe Harold), 63, 70, 72, 73, 79, 85, 92, 94, 101, 148, 180, 181, 219, 264
Chinnery, Mr, 63
Christ, 71, 76, 127, 128, 173, 318, 320, 321, 330, 369, 374
Christian doctrine, 22, 127
Christianity, 58, 72, 73, 76, 128, 162, 168, 284, 307, 320, 321, 340, 341, 370, 371, 377, 383
Christie, J. H., 108, 419, 421
Church of England, 59
Churchill, Charles, 79
Cicero, 25, 344
Cintra, 70
Clairmont, Claire, 317
Clark, William, 314
Clarke, Charles Cowden, 132, 424, 456, 458, 462
Clarkson, Thomas, 331
Claude Lorraine, 113, 430
Claudio (in *Measure for Measure*), 71
'Clementina', 315–16
Clitumnus, the, 39, 54, 63, 103
Cockaigne, 372, 374, 468
Cockney, 50, 51, 68, 139, 300, 312, 313, 318, 353, 372, 469, 471, 511
Cockney School, the, 51, 116, 334, 421, 444, 470, 473, 510
Colburn, Henry, 134, 149*n*.2
Coleridge, Samuel Taylor, 9, 22, 59, 134, 153, 161*n*.2, 199, 200, 213, 298, 309, 325, 428, 440, 454, 479
Coleridge, John Taylor, 35, 40, 308, 310, 337
Coliseum, 32, 63
Collins, William, 246, 453
Collyer, Rev. William Bengo, 119, 293, 314
Colman, George, 252
Colvin, Sidney, 188*n*.1
Conder, Josiah, 77, 78, 81, 82, 83, 84, 85, 86, 88, 89, 90, 170, 305, 327, 419, 424, 434, 459
Condorcet, Marquis de, 22, 128
Congregationalists, 23
Congreve, William, 384
Conrad (in *The Corsair*), 264
Constantinople, 343
Constitutional Association, the, 122*n*.4
Constitutional Society, the, 123
Cooper, Sir Ashley, 297

Corinth, 501
Cornuaglia (=Cornwall), Signore Penseroso di (='Barry Cornwall', *q.v.*), 278
'Cornwall, Barry' (=Bryan Waller Procter), 138, 262, 278*n*.2, 280, 312, 313, 433, 437, 489, 495, 496, 509
Corsair, the, 145
Corunna, 157*n*.3
Cossacks, 124
Cowley, Abraham, 208, 221
Cowper, William, 38, 71, 96, 128, 238, 367, 453
Crabbe, George, 22, 76, 216, 246, 393, 437, 510
Croker, John Wilson, 35, 39, 40, 41, 51, 115, 128, 176, 190, 202, 216, 217, 249, 254, 259, 262, 308, 382, 420, 428, 472, 445, 480, 503
Croly, Rev. Dr George, 43*n*.3, 50, 125, 318, 372, 377
Cromwell, Oliver, 32
Cunningham, Rev. J. W., 71-2
Cybele, 151, 433
Cyclops, 496
Cynthia, 428, 466

DAN, 239
Dandolo, Andrea, Doge of Venice, 235
Dante Alighieri, 128, 157, 187, 203, 332, 405, 434
David, 212
Davies, Scrope, 248
Dawson, C., 444*n*.7
Della Crusca, 50, 318, 488
Delos, 492
Democritus, 163
Demogorgon, 353, 358, 367
Demosthenes, 260
Denman, Thomas (afterwards Lord Denman, L.C.J.), 52, 180
De Quincey, Thomas, 108
Diana, 426, 474, 491, 496
Dido, 56
Digby, Sir Kenelm, 412
Dilke, C. W., 202*n*.5
Diogenes, 71
Dissenters, 23, 77
Don Juan, 57, 66, 87, 118, 126, 249, 286, 288, 294, 412
Don, the (=Don Juan), 56
Don Quixote, 126
Dorchester, Lady, 181*n*.1

Drachenfels, the, 53, 74, 135
Drugger, Abel, 270
Dryden, John, 23, 25, 61, 176, 187, 216, 223, 251, 288, 316, 437, 453, 483, 510

EDINBURGH UNIVERSITY, 42
Egeria, 55, 243, 246
Egerian Grot, 32
Elizabeth I, 420
Elizabethan drama, 58
Elizabethan literature, 59
Elizabethan poets, 422, 431
Elizabethans, 25, 35
Ellis, George, 36, 37, 180
Elysium, 216, 493, 495
Encyclopaedists, the French, 23
Endymion, 426, 428, 430, 433, 465, 466, 471, 474, 483, 484, 491, 496
Epicureanism, 38
Epicurus, 94, 324, 407
Erasmus, Desiderius, 221
Eton, 40, 308
'Ettrick Shepherd, The' (=James Hogg), 42
Euripides, 50, 396, 405
Europe, 62, 96
Euxine, the, 57
Evangelicals, 23, 73
Eve, 331

'F', 77
Faustus (Goethe's), 392
Fénelon, François, 221
Fielding, Henry, 181, 299, 358
Finney, C. L., 440*n*.1
Firth, Sir Charles, 199*n*.1
Fletcher, John, 221, 392, 411, 415, 431, 493
Florence, 32
Fonblanque, Albany, 120, 321
Foster, John, 77
Fox, Charles James, 221
French Revolution, the, 21, 23, 32, 57, 168, 272, 308, 344, 478*n*.1
Frere, John Hookham, 157*n*.3, 182, 248, 259, 262, 268
Frogley, Mary, 446*n*.1
Fry, Mrs, 125

GARRICK, DAVID, 270
Gates, Payson G. 324*n*.1
Geneva, Lake, 28, 62, 135
George III (*see also* 'King, the'), 21, 121, 136, 168, 172

Giaour, the, 94, 145
Gibbon, Edward, 28, 53, 62, 91, 99, 135, 247, 284
Gifford, William, 35, 41, 50, 60. 128, 179, 182, 194, 199, 217, 261, 309, 312, 382, 387, 388, 443, 464, 477, 480
Gillies, R. P., 197–8
Gisborne, John, 317, 319
Gisborne, Maria, 411
Glasgow University, 42
Glaucus, 426
God, 94, 105, 106, 205, 234, 269, 318, 328, 330, 339, 345, 360, 366, 378, 380, 404
Godwin, William, 22, 309, 326, 344, 347, 362
Goethe, J. W. von, 31, 139, 206, 279, 321, 392, 396
Gracchi, the, 230
Grahame, James, 213
Gray, Thomas, 61, 202, 209, 223, 402, 453

Hudibras, 225, 251, 303
Hume, David, 22, 23, 221
Hunt, John, 122, 192, 193
Hunt, Leigh, 50, 64, 66, 68, 77, 89, 111, 112, 117, 122, 127, 128, 129, 130, 131, 132, 133, 134, 152, 168, 169, 171, 172, 173, 174, 175, 191, 192, 255, 261, 305, 306, 307, 309, 310, 311, 312, 318, 319, 320, 321, 323, 324, 329, 334, 346, 354, 381, 383, 400, 413, 418, 419, 420, 421, 422, 423, 424, 425, 434, 435, 437, 439, 444n.4, 452, 459, 462, 463, 468, 469, 471, 473, 476, 497, 499, 500, 507, 510
Hunt brothers (John and Leigh Hunt, q.v.), 66n.2, 122
Hunt, Henry Leigh, 122
Hunt, Marianne, 443, 444n.3
Hyperion, 489

Inez, Donna, 56
Ingram, W. G., 9
Irving, Edward, 297
Irving, Washington, 46
Isabella, 133, 151, 435, 436, 489
Ismail, siege of, 123, 124, 138, 142
d'Israeli, Isaac, 46
Italy, 39, 45, 75, 101, 158, 188, 191, 225, 247, 418, 444

'J. W.', 156, 312n.4
Jack, Ian, 430
Jacobean poets, 431
Jacobinism, 21
James, Louis, 167n.1
Jeffrey, Francis, 24, 25, 26, 27, 28, 29, 30, 33, 34, 35, 37, 43, 115, 124, 143, 161n.2, 174, 175, 176, 180, 182, 188n.2, 190, 214, 217, 224, 286, 418, 420, 422, 431, 432, 433, 435, 436, 439, 440, 493, 496
Jennings, Louis, 40n.1
Jerdan, William, 134
Jesus, 102 (see also Christ)
Jews, 119, 366
Jones, C. E., 326n.2
Jones, Sir William, 106
Johnson (character in Don Juan), 66
Johnson, Samuel, 188n.2, 208, 383, 384, 473, 498
Jonson, Ben, 221, 392, 431, 432, 493
Jove, 102, 352
Juan, 56, 66, 118, 119, 124, 125, 154, 160, 255, 256, 259, 279, 290, 296
Julia, Donna, 56, 148, 154, 159, 187, 203, 255, 256, 258, 296
Junius, 47
Junta, Spanish, 157n.3
Jupiter, 49, 283, 353, 355, 358, 367, 497, 503
Juvenal, 138

Kean, Edmund, 270
Keats, George and Georgiana, 34, 202n.6, 203n.1, 249, 254
Keats, George and Tom, 131n.1
Keats, John, passim throughout; on Byron, 188, 202, 249, 254; on Keats, 254; on Shelley, 325, 326, 337, 350, 351
King, Edward, 498
King, the (see also George III), 47, 121, 192, 300
Kinnaird, Douglas, 193, 196, 248, 249
Kirke White, 34, 73, 478

Lachin-y-Gair, 211
Laclos, Choderlos de, 280
Lake Poets, 132, 424, 453
Lake School, 29, 38, 141, 187
Lamb, Charles, 108, 114, 132, 134, 150n., 174, 298, 434, 435, 439, 444, 454
Lambro, 105, 118, 161

Lamia, 174, 497, 500, 501
Lance, 38
Landor, Walter Savage, 259
Landré, Louis, 122n.2
Laocoön, 54, 63
Laon, 307
Laon and Cythna, 48, 308, 336, 343, 344
Laura, 54
Leavis, F. R., 107n.2
Lechlade Churchyard, 306, 348, 401
Leila, 124
Leman, Lake (see also Lake Geneva), 75, 242, 273
Lenin, 314n.1
Ligny, 28
Lisbon, 70, 93, 157n.3
Little (= Thomas Moore), 191, 254
Liverpool, Lord, 21
Locke, John, 105
Lockhart, John Gibson, 35, 42, 43, 44, 46, 47, 48, 49, 51n.4, 108, 152, 169, 173, 188, 197, 276, 297, 300, 307, 308, 333, 351, 419, 421, 448, 467
London, 124
Lorenzo, 132, 151, 434, 436
Louis XVIII, 125
Louvet, Jean-Baptiste, 279n.1, 280
Lowth, Robert, 359
Lucrecia, 230
Lucretius, 127, 128, 332, 347
Lyall, Rev. William Rowe, 59
Lycidas, 383, 498
Lycius, 501

MACAULAY, THOMAS BABINGTON, 33
Macaulay, Zachary, 69, 72
Macbeth, 232
Mackintosh, Sir James, 34
Macneil[l], Hector, 213
Macpherson, James, 210, 211
Madeline, 115, 133, 174, 435, 436, 437, 447, 498, 503
Madrid, 157n.3
Maginn, William, 45 and n.2, 47, 301, 372n.1, 377
Malta, 157n.3
Malthus, Rev. T. R., 358
Marathon, 230, 273
Marceau, François-Severin, 97
Marchand, Louis A., 110n.1, 440n.8, 441n.1
Maria Louisa, Empress, 272
Marmion, 145

Marshall, William H., 191n.4, 193n.2
Martial, 276, 277
Mathew, G. F., 418, 423
Matthews, G. M., 9, 131n.3, 132n.1
Matthews, John, 46
Mediterranean, 27
Medwin, Thomas, 310n.7
Merivale, J. H., 45
Methodists, 23
'Metrodorus' (J. H. Merivale), 45
Michelangelo, 377
Middleton, Thomas (later Bishop of Calcutta), 59
Mildert, William van (later Bishop of Durham), 59
Milman, Rev. H. H., 125, 309, 402
Milton, John, 61, 71, 105, 133, 139, 145, 165, 201, 214, 221, 223, 276, 295, 297, 331, 354, 383, 384, 401, 402, 411, 422, 423, 425, 426, 429, 432, 446, 454, 459, 464, 469, 481, 489, 493, 494, 498, 499, 500, 508
Mineka, F. E., 69n.2
Minton, R. R., 9, 121n.3, 372n.2
Mohammed, 76
Molière (J. B. Poquelin), 279
Moloch, 276
Montaigne, Michel de, 324, 407
Montgomery, James, 77, 83, 95, 213
Moore, Sir John, 157n.3
Moore, Thomas, 33, 100, 148, 161, 185n.3, 200, 225, 249, 276, 277, 318, 423, 428, 451, 479
Moorman, Mary, 197n.2, 199n.2, 440n.4
More, Hannah, 69, 91
More, Sir Thomas, 221, 325, 407
Morgan, Lady, 287, 478n.1
Morley, Edith J., 187n.7
Moschus, 380, 383, 496
Moxon, Edward, 150n., 440n.1
'Mucklegrin, Andrew', 193
Mulock, Thomas, 205
'Mungo', 62, 65, 222, 280
Murray, John (I), 36, 40, 103n.2, 180, 181, 182nn.2,7, 185n.5, 188nn.2,8, 191n.1, 192, 193n.5, 202, 216, 248, 249, 254, 259, 260, 279, 308, 309, 325n.2, 421, 440, 441

NAPOLEON (see also Bonaparte), 21, 22, 28, 32, 37, 38, 62, 97, 125, 135, 159, 168, 172, 181, 183, 197, 220, 272

Narcissus, 82
Nares, Robert, 59
National Library of Scotland, 49*n*.1
Nemesis, 55
Nemi, Lake of, 55
Newgate, 125
New School, the, 319, 372
Newstead Abbey, 212
Newton, Sir Isaac, 105, 221
Nietzsche, Friedrich, 176, 178
Noncomformists, 78
Norman Abbey, 68, 126, 163, 195
'North, Christopher' (=, generally, John Wilson), 42, 46, 47, 50, 297, 298, 300
Noyes, A., 29*n*.1

ODOHERTY, M., 47, 194, 297, 301
'Oldmixon', 292
Ollier, Charles, 309*nn*.3,8,9, 310*nn*.4, 6, 318, 318*n*.3, 442*nn*.6,7
Ollier, Charles and James, *q.v.*, 317
Ollier, James, 150*n*.
Olympus, 508
Orientalism, 102
Orpheus, 495
'Ossian', 161, 210
Othello, 232, 270
Ovid, 389, 470, 507
Oxford, 42, 59, 350

PALATINE HILL, 54, 243
Paley, Rev. William, 96, 358
Pandemonium, 508
Pantheon, the, 54; stories of, 507
Paris, 97, 108, 191
Parken, Daniel, 77
Parnassus, 93, 158, 212, 368, 441
Pascal, Blaise, 105
Patmore, Coventry, 108, 113*n*.1, 420
Patmore, P. G., 108, 113, 114, 174, 420, 429, 430, 431, 439, 482, 484
Paul, St, 76
Peacock, T. L., 25*n*.3, 46, 184, 203, 306, 317, 326, 263*n*.1, 444
Pedrillo, 136, 160, 186, 253, 256
Peel, Sir Robert, 21
Peona, 426, 430, 483, 492
Perceval, Spencer, 21
Petrarch, 32, 54, 183
Pinchbeck, Lady, 126
'Pindar, Peter', 50, 225
Pisa, 127, 317, 319, 383, 398
Pitt, William, The Younger, 21
Plataea, 230

Plato, 128, 181, 221, 324, 358, 380, 383, 407
Plutarch, 300
Polidori, J. W., 104
Pollok, Robert, 34
Pompey, 231
Pope, Alexander, 25, 61, 119, 176, 187, 188, 208, 210, 217, 223, 225, 276, 277, 360, 420, 422, 423, 429, 440, 441, 453, 469, 473, 483
Pope, W. B., 442*n*.3
Porphyro, 447
Portland, the Duke of, 21
Portugal, 179, 214
Portuguese, 26, 215
Poussin, Nicolas, 113, 430, 485
Pratt, Sir Joseph, 69
'Presbyter Anglicanus', 43
Prior, Matthew, 225, 240, 251, 268, 288, 384
Procter, Bryan Waller ('Barry Cornwall'), 433*n*.1
Prometheus (character), 351, 352, 353, 355, 357, 367, 369
Prometheus (myth), 49
Pulci, Luigi, 66, 157*n*.3, 182, 188, 259, 424, 462
Pym, John, 416

QUATRE BRAS, 28, 38
'Quevedo Redivivus', 121, 292
Quevedo y Villegas, Francisco Gomez de, 121*n*.1

RADCLIFFE, MRS, 161
Radicalism, 21, 67
Radicals, 22, 77*n*.1, 172
Raphael, 377, 468, 469
Ravenna, 187, 204
Redding, Cyrus, 150
Reform Act (1832), 24
Regent, Prince, 64
Restoration, the, 25
Reynolds, John Hamilton, 130, 131, 156, 174, 305, 418, 420, 422, 427, 428, 429, 433, 439, 445, 451, 477
Rhine, the, 62, 97, 135, 242
Richardson, Samuel, 173, 299
Richmond, Duchess of, 61
Ridley, James, 245
Ridotto, the, 158
Rivers, J., 279*n*.1
Roberts, William, 91, 92, 93, 94, 95, 96, 97, 98, 99, 100, 101, 102, 103, 104, 105, 106, 111, 112, 113, 141,

180, 185, 186, 223, 226, 233, 281, 286
Robinson, Henry Crabb, 187*n*.7, 196, 197*n*.3, 198, 199, 204, 205, 206, 325, 444, 445
Rochester, John Wilmot, Earl of, 123, 205
Rogers, Samuel, 196, 197, 199*n*.4, 209, 249, 281, 423, 451, 480
Rollins, H. E., 419*n*.4
Romans, the, 165
Rome, 32, 39, 54, 63, 86, 103, 159, 184, 230, 272, 384, 385, 489
Rosa, Salvator, 113, 144, 275, 430, 485
Rose, William Stewart, 262
Rousseau, Jean-Jacques, 23, 28, 30, 53, 71, 75, 76, 82, 99, 135, 191, 263, 408
Royal Society, the, 59
Russell, Clare, 10
Rutherford, Andrew, 8

St James's Reading Room, 104
St Peter's, Rome, 55, 63
Saint-Pierre, Bernardin de, 74
Salamis, 230
Sancho Panza, 212
Saragossa, the Maid of, 52, 247
Satan, 123, 288
Saturn, 151, 489, 497, 503
Savage, Richard, 221
Schiller, Johann von, 31
Schlegel, August Wilhelm von, 276
Scotland, 124
Scott, John, 108, 109, 110, 111, 112, 113, 114, 115, 116, 134, 169, 174, 175, 176, 197, 262, 265*n*.1, 266*n*.1, 273, 274, 418, 419, 420, 421, 427, 437, 439, 502, 510
Scott, Sir Walter, 35, 36, 37, 38, 39, 70, 90, 147, 161, 177, 182, 196, 202, 206, 213, 216, 219, 236, 242, 261, 279, 442
Scythrop, 326
Selincourt, E. de, 196*n*.5
'Seraphina', 315, 316
Severn, Joseph, 188
Shaftesbury, first Earl of, 22
Shaftesbury, second Earl of, 22, 23
Shakespeare, William, 41*n*.2, 68, 120, 144, 202, 203, 217, 225, 249, 276, 380, 423, 437, 445, 446, 451, 465, 466, 467, 469, 477, 480, 481, 482, 483, 494, 503, 510
Shallow, Master Justice, 237

Sheldonian Theatre, the, 63
Shelley, Mary, 204*n*.2, 321, 322, 344, 392
Shelley, Percy Bysshe, *passim* throughout; on Keats, 130, 372, 373, 384, 385, 442, 443, 444; on Byron, 184*n*., 187, 189, 190, 203, 204, 386; on Shelley, 306, 309, 310, 317, 318, 319
Shenstone, William, 221
Sheridan, R. B., 179
Sheridan, Thomas (the actor), 188*n*.2
Shine, H. and H. C., 41*n*.2, 309*n*.1
Sidmouth, Viscount, 21
'Silurensis' (John Matthews), 46
Sion, 119
Slave Trade, 307, 331
Smiles, Samuel, 40*n*.2, 182*n*.2
Smith, Horace, 108, 317, 318, 444*n*.4
Smith, James, 317*n*.1
Smollett, Tobias, 78, 191
Socrates, 221
Solomon, 76, 297
Sophocles, 355
Sotheby, William, 161
Southey, Robert, 35, 47, 76, 88, 120, 121, 137, 141, 192, 194, 199, 213, 248, 259, 261, 275, 286*n*.1, 292, 300, 309, 338, 382, 429, 442, 454, 479
Spain, 26, 56, 70, 80, 93, 179, 214, 215, 242
Spaniards, 37
Spenser, Edmund, 27, 36, 70, 216, 224, 276, 383, 412, 434, 445, 469, 477, 500
Spenserian stanza, 27, 39, 52, 70, 79, 93, 235, 246, 313
Staël, Madame de, 100, 161
Stoddart, Sir John, 59
Strout, Alan Lang, 46, 49*n*.1, 188*n*.4
Stuart, Daniel, 199*n*.2
Suliotes, 52
Suppression of Vice, Society for the, 124, 154, 293, 296, 314
Suvorov (Suwarrow), Marshal Aleksandr, 66
Swann, Elsie, 42*n*.2
Swift, Jonathan, 25, 78, 141
Swinburne, A. C., 312*n*.3
Switzerland, 62, 199, 242

Tacitus, 262
Talavera, 52, 179, 230, 503
Talfourd, Thomas Noon, 108, 149*n*.2, 150*n*.

Tartar Khan, the, 124
Tasso, Torquato, 158, 183, 274, 377
Tassoni, Alessandro, 117*n*.2
Taylor, Jeremy, 405
Taylor, John, 34, 445, 447*n*.1, 448, 449, 450, 465, 472
Tennyson, Alfred, Lord, 51
Thelwall, John, 134, 154, 155, 156, 186*n*.1
Theocritus, 496
Thermopylae, 230, 272
Thersites, 71
Thompson, E. P., 314*n*.8
Thompson, James, 453
'Tickler' (=Lockhart), 47, 51*n*.2, 297, 298, 300, 421*n*.3
Timon, 84, 163, 240
Titan, 352, 508
Titans, 133, 151, 489, 497, 503
Titian, 113, 430, 485
Tolstoy, Count Leo, 90, 307
Tories, 67
Toussaint l'Ouverture, Pierre, 97
Trafalgar, 230
Trasimene, Lake, 32, 54
Trelawney, E. J., 412
Trueblood, P. G., 194*n*.9

UGOLINO, COUNT, 136
Utopians, 57

VALERIA, 230
Velino, Cataract of, 32, 54, 103, 159, 184
Venice, 32, 39, 54, 62, 185, 203, 226, 272
Venus, 159, 235
Venus de' Medici, 54, 146
Vinci, Leonardo da, 392
Virgil, 25, 143, 161*n*.2, 165, 295, 464
Voltaire, 22, 23, 28, 53, 62, 99, 135, 137, 160, 162, 205, 221, 298, 299, 301, 333, 354

'W.C.', 149
Walker, Keith, 9, 40*n*.1, 72, 76*n*.1, 78*n*.2, 167*n*.1

Walker, Rev. Dr William Sidney, 40, 41, 312, 324*n*., 362, 399
Wallace, Robert, 421
Walton, Izaak, 126
War Office, the, 108
Warburton, William, Bishop of Gloucester, 359
Warter, J. W., 192*n*.1
Waterloo, 28, 61, 73, 76, 84, 95, 177, 181, 261, 272
Watts, Alaric, 161
Webb, Cornelius, 469
Wellington, Duke of, 22, 37, 62, 68, 122*n*.4, 168, 300
Westbrook, Harriet, 307
Weyland, John, 91
Wharton, Philip, Lord, 123
Whigs, 67
'Whistlecraft, William and Robert', 182*n*.6
White, Newman Ivey, 6, 49*n*.1, 150*n*., 167*n*.2, 304, 312*n*.4, 314*n*.7, 323*n*.4, 326
Wieland, C. M., 161*n*.2, 279*n*.2, 470
Wiffen, J. H., 148
Wilberforce, William, 69, 91, 124*n*.2
Wilkes, Rev. J. C., 69
Wilson, John, 30, 31, 32, 33, 42, 43, 45, 46, 47, 48, 49*n*.4 50, 161*n*.2, 182, 185, 229, 297, 333, 419, 467
Wise, T. J., 440*n*.9
Woburn, 148
Woodhouse, Richard, 427, 445, 446, 447, 448, 449, 476
Wordsworth, William, 9, 22, 29*n*.1, 59, 83, 84, 89, 108, 123, 152, 153, 182, 183, 187, 196, 197, 198, 199, 201, 205, 279, 298, 301, 313, 325, 356, 361, 362, 393, 402, 422, 424, 425, 428, 439, 440, 440*n*.3, 443, 444, 454, 456, 464, 468, 469, 479
Wrangham, Rev. Francis, 59

YOUNG, EDWARD, 161

'Z', 50, 145, 419, 469, 471, 472
Zephyr, 491

Index of Poems

Note: References in italics indicate subordinate importance.

POEMS BY BYRON

Age of Bronze, The: 117 (*Exar*)

Beppo: 7, 30 (ER, Jeffrey), 36 (*QR*, no rev.), 43 (BM), 47, 53–4 (MR), 62 (BC), 68 (BC), 84 (*Ecl*. R, 86 (*Ecl*.R), Conder), 100–1 (BR, Roberts), 117 (*Exar*, no rev.), 135 (*SM*), 140 (*MM*), 153–4 (*Champ*), 157–8 (*LG*), 182, 183 (*YD*, Hazlitt). **Anthology**: 224–6 (ER, Jeffrey), 226 (*YD*, Hazlitt), 226–7 (BR, Roberts), 254 (Croker), *255* (*Exar*, L. Hunt), 259 (Southey), 265 (J. Scott), 277 (Lockhart), 292 (Ed. M)

Bride of Abydos, The: 27 (ER, Jeffrey), 36 (*QR*, Ellis), 52–3 (MR, J. Hodgson), 80 (*Ecl*. R), 93–4 (BR, Roberts)

Cain: 33 (ER, Jeffrey), 88 (*Ecl*. R), 190 (ER, Jeffrey; *QR*, Reginald Heber)

Childe Harold's Pilgrimage: 7, 33 (ER, Wilson, Jeffrey), 35 (*QR*), 43 (Wilson, Jeffrey), 46–7 (BM, J. Matthews), 55 (MR, 62 (BC), 63 (BC), 69 (CO), 80–1 (*Ecl*. R), 91–2 (BR, Roberts), 103 (BR, Roberts), 110–11 (LM, J. Scott), 117 (*Exar* no review), 148 (NMM), *153* (*Champ*), *170*, *181*, 184–5 (ER, Wilson; MR; BR, Roberts). **Anthology**: 228–9 (Ed. M), 229–33 (ER, Wilson), 233–6 (BR, Roberts), 236–46 (*QR*, W. Scott), 246–7 (MR), 249 (Croker), *266–74* (LM, J. Scott).

    Cantos I and II: 26–7 (ER, Jeffrey), *28* (Jeffrey), *30* (ER, Wilson), 36 (*QR*, Ellis), *39* (*QR*, W. Scott), 52 (MR, Denman), 60 (BC), *61* (BC), 69–71 (CO), *71–2* (CO, J. W. Cunningham), 79–80 (*Ecl*. R), 91–3 (BR, Roberts), *92* (*Ecl*. R), 179–80, 180–1 (*QR*, ER, *AJR, Scourge*, CO, MR, BR, BC), *183* (*YD*, Hazlitt), 196 (Wordsworth), 198 (Wordsworth). **Anthology**: 214–15 (ER, Jeffrey), 277–8 (*John Bull's Letter*, Lockhart)

    Canto III: 28–9 (ER, Jeffrey), *30* (ER, Wilson), 37–8 (*QR*, W. Scott), *39* (*QR*, W. Scott), *40* (Croker), *43* (BM, Wilson), 53 (MR), 61–2 (BC), 72–6 (CO), 81–4 (*Ecl*. R, Conder), 88 (CO), 94–100 (BR, Roberts), 135 (*SM*), 140 (*MM*), 153 (*Champ*), 181–2, *181* (Hobhouse), *182* (Gifford), *183* (*YD*, Hazlitt), *184* (Shelley), *203* (Shelley), 204–5 (Crabb Robinson). **Anthology**: 216–17 (Croker), 217–222 (ER, Jeffrey), 222–3 (BC), 223–224 (BR, Roberts, *266–74* (LM, J. Scott)

    Canto IV: 30–3 (ER, Wilson), *37* (*QR*), 38–9 (*QR*, W. Scott), 43 (BM, Wilson), 54–5 (MR), 62–3 (BC), *85–6* (*Ecl*. R, Conder), 101–3 (BR, Roberts), *135* (Ed. M), 140 (*MM*), 145–7 (NMM), 158–9 (*LG*), *182* (ER, Wilson), 183–4 (*YD*, Hazlitt), *203* (Shelley, Peacock). **Anthology**: 227–9 (Ed. M), 229–233 (ER, Wilson), 233–6 (BR, Roberts), 236–46 (*QR*, W. Scott), 246–7 (MR), *266–74* (LM, J. Scott)

Churchill's Grave: 62 (BC)

Corsair, The: 27–8 (ER, Jeffrey), *36* (*QR*, Ellis), 52–3 (MR, J. Hodgson), 60 (BC), *69* (CO), *72* (CO), *80–1* (*Ecl*. R), *94* (BR, Roberts)

Darkness: 29 (ER, Jeffrey), 53 (MR), 62 (BC), 205 (Crabb Robinson)

Don Juan: 7, *33* (Jeffrey on why no review in ER), *36* (QR, no review), 40 (Croker), 44 (BM), 45 (BM, J. H. Merivale), 46 (*John Bull's Letter*, Lockhart), 46–7 (BM, J. Matthews), 47, 47–8 (BM, QR, Lockhart), *52* (MR), 55–7 (MR), 66–9 (BC), *78* (BC, *Ecl. R*), 86–8 (*Ecl. R*), *87* (BC), 103 (BR, Roberts), *110–11* (LM, J. Scott), 117 (*Exar*, L. Hunt), 119 (*Exar*), *123* (*Lit. Exar*). 135–6 (*Ed. M*), *138* (*Ed. M*), *169*, 170, *171* (*Exar* and *Lit. Exar*), *173* (Lockhart, L. Hunt), 185, 188, 190–1 (ER, Jeffrey; QR, Reginald Heber), 196, *197*, 198–9 (Wordsworth), 202 (Hazlitt), 203–4 (Shelley), 206 (Sir Walter Scott). **Anthology**: 259–62 (Croker), 267 (LM, J. Scott), 270 (LM, J. Scott), 275 (Southey), 276–80 (*John Bull's Letter*, Lockhart), 286–92 (ER, Jeffrey), *292* (*Ed. M*), 293–4 (*Exar*), 303 (Hazlitt)

   Cantos I and II: 44 (BM), *45* (BM, Maginn; Merivale), 55–6 (MR), 64–5 (BC), *76–7* (CO), 86–7 (*Ecl. R*), 103–4 (BR, Roberts), *111* (LM, J. Scott), 117–18 (*Exar*, Hunt), *136* (*Ed. M*), 140–1 (MM), 148–9 (NMM), *148* (MM), *153* (*Champ*), 154–6 (*Champ*, Thelwall), 159–61 (LG), 185, 185–7 (ER, QR no reviews; MR, *Champ*, LG, BC, *Ecl. R*, BR, BM, MM, *Exar*), 187–188 (Shelley, Wordsworth, Keats), 188 (*John Bull's Letter*, Lockhart), *189* (MR, LG), *194* (*Brit. Mag*), *195* (BC), 198–9 (Wordsworth), *202* (Keats), 203–4 (Shelley). **Anthology**: 248–9 (Hobhouse, Frere, Moore, and others), 249 (Croker), 250–1 (*Ecl. R*), 251–4 (BC), 254 (Croker), 255–9 (*Exar*), *259* (Southey), 276–80 (*John Bull's Letter*, Lockhart)

   Cantos III–V: 56–7 (MR), 65–6 (BC), 104–6 (BR, Roberts), 118–19 (*Exar*), *136* (*Ed. M*), 141–2 (MM), 161 (LG), *188*, 189 (MR, BC, BR, *Investigr, Ed. M, LG, MM, Exar*), 189–90 (Shelley), 190 (Croker), 204 (Shelley), 205–6 (Crabb Robinson).

Anthology: 259–62 (Croker), 280–281 (BC), 281–6 (BR, Roberts)

   Cantos VI–VIII: *57* (MR), 66–7 (BC), *119* (*Lit. Exar*), 122–4 (*Lit. Exar*), 136–8 (*Ed. M*), 142–3 (MM), 162 (LG), 193–4 (*Lit. Exar*, MR, LG, BC, *Ed. M*, BM, GM, *Brit. Mag, MM, Portfolio*). **Anthology**: 294–6 (*Lit. Exar*)

   Cantos IX–XI: 47–8 (BM, Lockhart), *57* (MR), 67 (BC), *119* (*Lit. Exar*), 124–5 (*Lit. Exar*), 138 (*Ed. M*), *141* (MM), 144 (MM), 162–3 (LG), 194–5 (*Lit. Exar, BM, Ed. M, LG, Brit. Mag, GM, MR, BC, MM*), **Anthology**: 296–7 (*Lit. Exar*), 297–301 (BM, Lockhart), 302–3 (MM)

   Cantos XII–XIV: *57* (MR), 67–68 (BC), *119* (*Lit. Exar*), 125–6 (*Lit. Exar*), 163 (LG), 195 (*Lit. Exar, BC, LG*). **Anthology**: 301–2 (*Lit. Exar*)

   Cantos XV–XVI: *52* (MR), *119* (*Exar*), *127* (*Exar*), 163–4 (LG), 195 (*Exar, MR, LG*)

Dream, The: 29 (ER, Jeffrey), 62 (BC), 205 (Crabb Robinson)

Eastern Tales: 7, *33* (ER, Jeffrey), *35* (QR), *43* (Wilson, Jeffrey), 60 (BC), *80* (*Ecl. R*), *117* (*Exar*, L. Hunt), 181, 203 (Shelley)

English Bards and Scotch Reviewers: 7, 26 (ER no review), *52* (MR no review), 60 (BC), 79 (*Ecl. R*), *92* (BR, Roberts), 179, *180*. **Anthology**: 212–13 (*Ecl. R*)

'Fare thee well!': 265–6 (LM, J. Scott)

Giaour, The: 27 (ER, Jeffrey), *36* (QR, Ellis), *52* (MR, Denman), 69 (CO), 71–2 (CO, J. W. Cunningham), 80–81 (*Ecl. R*), *93–4* (BR, Roberts)

Hebrew Melodies: 69 (CO)

Hours of Idleness: 7, 25 (ER, Brougham), *52* (MR Griffiths), 60 (BC), 78 (*Ecl. R*), *92* (BR Roberts), *148* (NMM), 179 (ER, Brougham; CR), *180*. **Anthology**: 207 (MR, Griffiths), 207–12 (ER, Brougham)

Island, The: 117 (*Exar*)

'Isles of Greece, The': *57* (MR), *161* (LG), *189* (MR)

Lament of Tasso, The: *43* (BM), *157* (LG), *182*

Lara: *35 (Q*R), *36 (Q*R, Ellis), *61*
(*BC*), *72 (CO* no review), 81 (*Ecl. R*,
Conder)
Manfred: *43 (BM)*, *48(Q*R, Lockhart),
62 (BC), *153 (Champ)*, *157 (LG)*,
182. **Anthology**: *279 (John Bull's
Letter*, Lockhart)
Marino Faliero: *33* (ER, Jeffrey)
Morgante Maggiore, Il (transln of
Canto I): 157, 188
Ode to Napoleon Buonaparte: *197*
(Wordsworth)
Parisina: 53 (MR), *72* (CO), 81 (*Ecl.
R*, Conder)
Plays: 7, *33* (ER, Jeffrey), *39 (Q*R,
Reginald Heber), *87–8 (Ecl. R)*,
117 (Exar)
Poems on His Domestic Circumstances:
72 (CO)
Prisoner of Chillon, The: 7, 28–30 (ER,
Jeffrey), 37–8 (*Q*R, W. Scott), 53
(MR), 62 (BC), 82–4 (*Ecl. R*, Con-
der), 153 (*Champ*), 181, 182
(*Champ*, ER, *Q*R), 205 (Crabb
Robinson)
Prometheus: **Anthology**: *265* (J.
Prophecy of Dante, The: *33* (ER,
Jeffrey)
Sardanapalus: *33* (ER, Jeffrey), *48*
(*Q*R, Lockhart), *190* (ER, Jeffrey;
*Q*R, Heber)
Siege of Corinth, The: *53* (MR), *61*
(BC), *72* (CO), *81 (Ecl. R*, Conder),
81 (BC)
Two Foscari, The: *33* (ER, Jeffrey),
190 (ER, Jeffrey; *Q*R, Heber)
Vision of Judgment, The (and refs. to
The Liberal No. 1): 7, 47 (BM), 67
(BC), 77 (CO), 117 (*Exar*), 120–1
(*Exar*), 120 (? A. Fonblanque), 122
(*Lit. Exar*), 136–7 (*Ed. M*), 161–2
(LG), 191–3 (Southey, LG, LC,
Exar, NEM, *Ed. M*, BM, MM),
206 (Crabb Robinson). **Anthology**:
292–3 (Ed. M)

POEMS BY SHELLEY

Adonais: 41, 50 (BM, ? Rev. G.
Croly), 130 (*Exar*, L. Hunt), 166
(LG), 317–18 (Shelley, Horace
Smith, Moore), 318–20 (LC, LG,
BM, Shelley, *Exar*, L. Hunt), *326*
(Peacock). **Anthology**: *372–7 (BM*,

? G. Croly), 377–81 (LG), 383–8
(*Exar*, L. Hunt)
Alastor, and other Poems: 49 (BM,
Lockhart and ? Wilson), 57 (MR),
68 (BC), 88 (*Ecl. R*, Conder), 89
(*Ecl. R*), 305–6 (MR, BC, *Ecl. R*,
Exar, BM), *323* (ER, Hazlitt).
Anthology: *327–9 (Ecl. R*, Con-
der), *347–50 (BM)*, *392* (ER, Haz-
litt), *397 (Ed. M)*, *405 (KQM*, 'E.
Haselfoot')
Arethusa: *322 (LG)*
Cenci, The: 58 (MR), 106–7 (BR), 111–
113 (LM, J. Scott), 112–13 (*Exar*,
L. Hunt), 129 (*Indicr*, L. Hunt), 143
(MM), 164 (LG), 169–70, 175 (LM,
J. Scott), 310 (*Exar*, L. Hunt; *LG*),
311 (LM), *319* (BM), *319 (Q*R), 320
(*Exar*, L. Hunt), *325* (Byron), *326*
(Keats). **Anthology**: *350* (LM,)
386–7 (*Exar*, L. Hunt), *405–6* (L.
Hunt), 416–17 (L. Hunt)
Charles the First: **Anthology**: *416* (L.
Hunt)
Cloud, The: 41 (*Q*R, W. S. Walker),
311 (*Q*R). **Anthology**: 364–5 (*Q*R,
W. S. Walker)
Daemon of the World, The: *306, 348*
(BM)
Dirge, The [in Ginevra]: *323* (ER,
Hazlitt). **Anthology**: *395–6* (ER,
Hazlitt)
Dramas: *325* (L. Hunt). **Anthology**:
416 (L. Hunt)
Epipsychidion: 304, 315–16 (*The
Gossip*), 316–17 (BM)
Faded Violet, On a: **Anthology**: *411*
(L. Hunt)
Ginevra: 322 (LG), *323* (ER, Hazlitt).
Anthology: *395–6* (ER, Hazlitt)
Good-night: **Anthology**: *411* (L.
Hunt)
Hellas: 304
Hymn to Intellectual Beauty: 227 (*Exar*),
306–7. **Anthology**: *401* (KQM,
'E. Haselfoot')
Hymn to Pan: **Anthology**: *395* (ER,
Hazlitt)
Julian and Maddalo: 323 (Shelley; ER,
Hazlitt). **Anthology**: *392–3* (ER,
Hazlitt), *398 (Ed. M)*, *405 (KQM*,
'E. Haselfoot')
Lament, A: **Anthology**: *411* (L.
Hunt)
Laon and Cythna: *127* (*Exar*), 307

(*Exar*), 309 (*QR*, J. T. Coleridge;
Exar, L. Hunt). **Anthology**: 337–
347(*QR*, J. T. Coleridge)
Letter to a Friend in London [*Letter to
Maria Gisborne*]: **Anthology**: *394*
(ER, Hazlitt), *411* (L. Hunt), 412–
413 (L. Hunt)
Lines to a Critic: *321*, *411* (L. Hunt)
Lines written among the Euganean Hills:
129 (*Exar*, L. Hunt)
Love's Philosophy: *325* (L. Hunt).
Anthology: *411* (L. Hunt), 416
(L. Hunt)
Marianne's Dream: *323* (ER, Hazlitt).
Anthology: *393* (ER, Hazlitt)
Masque of Anarchy, The: *323*
Medusa of Leonardo da Vinci, On the:
Anthology: *411* (L. Hunt)
Mont Blanc: **Anthology**: *395* (ER,
Hazlitt)
'Music, when soft voices die': *325*
(L. Hunt). **Anthology**: *411* (L.
Hunt), *415–16* (L. Hunt)
Mutability: **Anthology**: *399* (*Ed. M*)
Ode to Liberty: 50 (BM, probably
mainly Lockhart), 129 (*Indicr*, L.
Hunt), 129–30 (*Indicr*, L. Hunt),
311(*QR*, W. S. Walker), *311* (*Gold's
LM*), 312 (*QR*, *Exar*), *320* (*Exar*
on *QR*). **Anthology**: 354–5 (BM,
probably mainly Lockhart), 357
(*Gold's LM*), 370–1 (*QR*, W. S.
Walker), 395 (ER, Hazlitt)
Ode to Naples: **Anthology**: 394–5
(ER, Hazlitt), *411* (L. Hunt)
Ode to a Skylark: 50 (BM, probably
mainly Lockhart). **Anthology**:
381–3 (*Exar*, L. Hunt on *QR*)
Ode to the West Wind: 50 (BM, prob-
ably mainly Lockhart)
Ozymandias: *127* (*Exar*)
Pine Forest of the Cascine near Pisa, The:
Anthology: *398* (*Ed. M*)
Posthumous Poems: 34 (ER, Hazlitt),
40 (*KQM*, 'E. Haselfoot'), 304,
321–5 (*Exar*, ? A. Fonblanque;
LG; ER, Hazlitt; *Ed. M*; *KQM*,
'E. Haselfoot'; L. Hunt), *326*.
Anthology: 388–96 (ER, Hazlitt),
396–9 (*Ed. M*), 399–404 (*KQM*, 'E.
Haselfoot'), 405–17 (L. Hunt)
Prince Athanase, A Fragment: **An-
thology**: *394* (ER, Hazlitt)
Prometheus Unbound, with other Poems:
40–1 (*QR*, W. S. Walker), 49–50

(BM, probably mainly Lockhart),
58 (MR), *129* (*Exar*, no review but
see *Indicr*), 129–30 (*Indicr*, L. Hunt),
151–2 (*Gold's LM*), 164–6 (*LG*),
171 (*QR*), 173 (*Gold's LM*), 175,
310–12 (*LM*, *LG*, *BM*, *MR*, *Gold*',
LM, *QR*), 313 (Hazlitt), *319*
(Shelley; *Exar*, L. Hunt), 320–1
(*Exar*, L. Hunt on *QR*), *323* (ER.
Hazlitt; Shelley), *324* (*QR*, W. S.
Walker), *325* (Byron), *326* (Crabb
Robinson; *QR*). **Anthology**: 350
(*LM*), *351* (Keats), 351–5 (BM,
probably mainly Lockhart), 355–7
(*Gold's LM*), 357–9 (MR), 381–3
(*Exar*, L. Hunt on *QR*), 401 (*KQM*,
401 (*KQM*, 'E. Haselfoot' on *QR*),
404 (*KQM*)
Queen Mab: *139* (*Ed. M*), *143* (*MM*),
172, *304*, *307*, 314 (*Gold's LM*,
JBBJ, *LG*, *MM*, *LC*; *Investigr*,
W. B. Collyer), *326*. **Anthology**:
404(*KQM*)
Question, The: **Anthology**: *411* (L.
Hunt)
'Rarely, rarely, comest thou': **An-
thology**: *399*(*Ed. M*), *411*(L. Hunt)
Revolt of Islam, The: 35 (*QR*, J. T.
Coleridge), 40 (*QR*, J. T. Cole-
ridge), 48–9 (*BM*, Lockhart and
? Wilson), 57 (MR), 127–9 (*Exar*,
L. Hunt) 143 (*MM*), 175 (*Exar*, L.
Hunt; *BM*, Lockhart and ? Wil-
son), *306* (BM, *QR*), *306*, 307
(*Exar*, L. Hunt; *MM*), 307–8 (*BM*,
Lockhart and ? Wilson), 308 (MR),
308–9 (*QR*, J. T. Coleridge), 309
(*Exar*, L. Hunt; *BM*, Lockhart and
? Wilson), 312–13 (*The Honeycomb*),
325 (Byron). **Anthology**: 329–33
(*Exar*, L. Hunt), 333–7 (*BM*, Lock-
hart and ? Wilson), 337–47 (*QR*,
J. T. Coleridge), 400–1 (*KQM*, 'E.
Haselfoot' on *QR*), *404*(*KQM*)
Rosalind and Helen: 49 (*BM*, Lockhart
and ? Wilson), 58 (MR), 129 (*Exar*.
L. Hunt), *306*(BM), *310*(*QR*, J. T.
Coleridge; *Exar*, L. Hunt). **An-
thology**: *347*(*QR*, J. T. Coleridge)
Sensitive Plant, The: 41 (*QR*, W. S.
Walker), 50 (BM, probably mainly
Lockhart). **Anthology**: *353* (*BM*,
probably mainly Lockhart), 366–7
(*QR*, W. S. Walker), *401* (*KQM*,
'E. Haselfoot')

Song, written for an Indian Air [*The Indian Serenade*]: *321*. **Anthology**: *411* (L. Hunt), 413–14 (L. Hunt)

Stanzas written in Dejection near Naples: *325* (L. Hunt). **Anthology**: *395* (ER, Hazlitt), 398 (*Ed. M*), *411* (L. Hunt), 414–15 (L. Hunt)

Summer Evening Churchyard, A [*Lechlade, Gloucestershire*]: **Anthology**: *348* (BM), *401* (KQM, 'E. Haselfoot')

'Swifter far than summer's flight' [*Remembrance*]: *399* (*Ed. M*)

To-morrow: **Anthology**: *411* (L. Hunt)

Translations: *321*. **Anthology**: *392* (ER, Hazlitt), *396* (ER, Hazlitt), *399* (*Ed. M*), *405* (KQM, 'E. Haselfoot'), *411* (L. Hunt)

Triumph of Life, The: 322 (*Exar*, ? A. Fonblanque), *323* (ER, Hazlitt), *323* (*Ed. M*). **Anthology**: 393–4 (ER, Hazlitt), *399* (*Ed. M*), *405* (KQM, 'E. Haselfoot')

Vision of the Sea, A: 50 (BM, probably mainly Lockhart). **Anthology**: *353* (BM, probably mainly Lockhart), *357* (*Gold's LM*), 365–6 (QR, W. S. Walker)

'When the lamp is shattered': **Anthology**: 399 (*Ed. M*)

Witch of Atlas, The: *322* (LG), *323* (ER, Hazlitt), *325* (L. Hunt). **Anthology**: 393–4 (ER, Hazlitt), 398 (*Ed. M*), *405* (KQM, 'E. Haselfoot'), 409 (L. Hunt), 411–12 (L. Hunt)

POEMS BY KEATS

Autumn, To: *58* (MR), *139* (*Ed. M*), *434* (MR), *438* (*Ecl. R*). **Anthology**: *506* (*Ecl. R*)

Calidore. A Fragment: **Anthology**: *457–8* (*Exar*, L. Hunt), 460 (*Ecl. R*, Conder)

Endymion: *23*, 34–5 (ER, Jeffrey; Keats, Croker), 41–2(QR, Croker), *51* (QR, Croker), 68–9 (BC), *90* (*Ecl. R*), 113–14 (LM, P. G. Patmore; QR), *115* (LM, J. Scott on Croker on), *130* (*Chester Guardian* reprd *Exar*; *The Alfred*, J. H. Reynolds, reprd *Exar*), 130–1 (L.

Hunt), *152* (*Gold's LM* on QR and LM on), *153* (*Gold's LM*), *156* (*Champ*), 171, 172 (BM, BC), *174* (*Champ*; LM, P. G. Patmore), *176* (ER, Jeffrey; QR, Croker), *387* (*Exar*, L. Hunt on QR, Croker), *400* (KQM, 'E. Haselfoot' on QR, Croker), 419–20 (BC, BM; QR, Croker; *The Oxford Herald*, Bailey; *Champ*, *The Morning Chronicle*; *The Alfred*, J. H. Reynolds, reprd *Exar*; LM, P. G. Patmore; ER, Jeffrey), *421* (*The Retrospective Review*), 425–34 (*Lit. J*; *The Oxford Herald*, Bailey; *Champ*, BC; BM, probably Lockhart and Wilson; *The Alfred*, J. H. Reynolds (reprd *Exar*; LM, P. G. Patmore; ER, Jeffrey), *430* (LM, P. G. Patmore on QR, Croker), *433* (*The Alfred*, J. H. Reynolds; *Champ*), *436* (*Ed. M*), *438* (*Ecl. R*), *439* (*The Alfred*, J. H. Reynolds; LM, P. G. Patmore; ER, Jeffrey), *441* (Byron on QR on), 442–3 (Shelley), *444* (Peacock), *445* (*Champ*), 445–6 (R. Woodhouse), 448 (Bailey). **Anthology**: *465* (Bailey), 465–7 (*Champ*), 470–2 (BM, probably Lockhart and Wilson), 472 (Bailey), 472–6 (QR, Croker), 476–7 (R. Woodhouse on QR and BM on), 477–81 (*The Alfred*, J. H. Reynolds), 481–2 (R. Woodhouse), 482–7 (LM, P. G. Patmore), *489* (MR), 490–2 (*Ed. M*), 492–6 (ER, Jeffrey), (*Indicr*, L. Hunt), 500 (BC), *503–4* (LM, J. Scott on QR on), *507* (*Ecl. R*), *508* (*Ecl. R* on Pref.)

Epistles: **Anthology**: *458* (*Exar*, L. Hunt, 460 (*Ecl. R*, Conder)

To Charles Cowden Clarke: *132* (*Exar*, L. Hunt). **Anthology**: *456*, *458* (*Exar*, L. Hunt), 462 (*Ed. M*)

To my Brother George: **Anthology**: *455–6* (*Exar*, L. Hunt), 462 (*Ed. M*)

Eve of St. Agnes, The: 115 (LM, J. Scott), *133* (*Indicr*, L. Hunt), *139* (*Ed. M*), *151* (NMM), *174* (LM, J. Scott), *434* (*The New Times*, Lamb), 435 (*Indicr*, L. Hunt), *436* (NMM), *437* (BC), *438* (*Ecl. R*), *439* (*The New Times*, Lamb; LM, J. Scott),

447–8 (R. Woodhouse), 449 (J. Taylor). **Anthology:** 498 (*Indicr,* L. Hunt), *501–2* (*BC*), 603 (*LM,* J. Scott), *505–6* (*Ecl. R*), *510* (*MM*)
Fancy: 139 (*Ed. M*), *438* (*Ecl. R*). **Anthology:** *497* (*ER,* Jeffrey), *506* (*Ecl. R*)
'Hadst thou liv'd in days of old': **Anthology:** *456* (*Exar,* L. Hunt)
'Hymn to Pan' (in *Endymion*): *176* (*LM,* J. Scott), *439–40* (Wordsworth). **Anthology:** *467* (*Champ*)
Hyperion: 58 (*MR*), 115 (*LM* J. Scott), 133 (*Indicr,* L. Hunt), *139* (*Ed. M*), 151 (*NMM*), *174* (*Indicr,* L. Hunt), *176* (Byron), *434* (*MR*), 435 (*Indicr,* L. Hunt), *436* (*Ed. M, NMM*), *437–8* (*LM,* J. Scott; *BC, Ecl. R*), 441 (Byron), 443–4 (Shelley), *444* (Crabb Robinson). **Anthology:** *489* (*MR*), 497 (*ER,* Jeffrey), 499 (*Indicr,* L. Hunt), 501 (*BC*), 503–4 (*LM,* J. Scott), 508 (*Ecl. R*), *510* (*MM*), *511* (*LM,* J. Scott)
'I stood tip-toe': **Anthology:** *456–7* (*Exar,* L. Hunt). *459* (*Ecl. R,* Conder), *462, 464* (*Ed. M*)
Isabella: 58 (*MR*), 114 (*LM,* J. Scott), 132–3 (*Indicr,* L. Hunt; *The New Times,* Lamb), *151* (*NMM*), *152* (*Gold's LM*), 172–3 (*LM,* J. Scott), *372* (*BM,* ? G. Croly), *387* (*Exar,* L. Hunt), 434 (*The New Times,* Lamb; *MR; Indicr,* L. Hunt), *435* (*ER,* Jeffrey), *436* (*Ed. M, NMM*), *437* (*LM,* J. Scott; *BC*), *438* (*Ecl. R*), *444* (Crabb Robinson), 447 (R. Woodhouse), *506* (*Ecl. R*), *510* (*MM*)
La Belle Dame sans Merci: 132 (*Indicr,* L. Hunt)
Lamia: 132 (*Indicr,* L. Hunt), *139* (*Ed. M*), *151* (*NMM*), *152* (*Gold's LM*), *153* (*Gold's LM*), *174* (*Indicr,* L. Hunt), *387* (*Exar,* L. Hunt), 434 (*The New Times,* Lamb), *436* (*Ed. M, NMM*), *437* (*BC*), *438* (*Ecl. R*), 448 (R. Woodhouse), *449–50* (J. Taylor). **Anthology:** *496* (*ER,* Jeffrey), 497–8 (*Indicr,* L. Hunt), 500–2 (*BC*), 506 (*Ecl. R*), *510* (*MM*)
Ode on a Grecian Urn: **Anthology:** 490 (*MR*), *508* (*Ecl. R*)
Ode to a Nightingale: 115 (*LM,* J.

Scott), *133* (*Indicr,* L. Hunt), *139* (*Ed. M*), *174* (*LM,* J. Scott), *422* (Byron), *435* (*ER,* Jeffrey), *436* (*Ed. M*), *437* (*LM,* J. Scott). **Anthology:** 496 (*ER,* Jeffrey), 498–9 (*Indicr,* L. Hunt), 502–4 (*LM,* J. Scott), *511* (*LM,* J. Scott)
On receiving a Curious Shell: *455* (*Exar,* L. Hunt)
Poems (1817): 89–90 (*Ecl. R,* Conder), 89 (*MM, Ed. M*), *130* (*Exar,* L. Hunt), 131–2 (*Indicr,* L. Hunt), *139* (*Ed. M*), *144* (*MM*), *156* (*Champ,* J. H. Reynolds), *170* (*Ecl. R,* Conder), 173–4 (*Exar,* L. Hunt), *174* (*Ed. M*), 418–19 (*ER, QR* no reviews; *BM; Champ,* J. H. Reynolds; *Eur. Mag,* G. F. Mathew; *Exar,* L. Hunt; *MM; Ecl. R,* Conder; *Ed. M*), 420 (*BM,* probably Lockhart and Wilson), 422–5 (*Champ,* J. H. Reynolds; *MM; Eur. Mag,* G. F. Mathew; *Exar,* L. Hunt; *Ecl. R,* Conder; *Ed. M*), *438* (*Ecl. R*), *439* (*Champ,* J. H. Reynolds; *Exar,* L. Hunt), *440* (Byron). **Anthology:** *451–2* (*Champ,* J. H. Reynolds), 452–9 (*Exar,* L. Hunt), 459–61 (*Ecl. R,* Conder), 462–5 (*Ed. M*), 467–70 (*BM,* probably Lockhart and Wilson)
Poems (1820) (the *Lamia* volume): *35*, 58 (*MR*), *69* (*BC*), 90–1 (*Ecl. R*), 114–16 (*LM,* J. Scott), *130* (*Indicr,* L. Hunt), 132–4 (*Indicr,* L. Hunt), 139 (*Ed. M*), *144* (*MM*), 150–1 (*NMM*), 152–3 (*Gold's LM*), *174* (*MR*), *387* (*Exar,* L. Hunt), 418 (*The New Times,* Lamb, reprd *Exar; MR; ER,* Jeffrey; *Indicr,* L. Hunt; *LM,* J. Scott), 421 (*The Retrospective Review, BC*), 434–9 (*QR, BM* no reviews; *The New Times,* Lamb; *MR; Indicr,* L. Hunt; *The Guardian, Gold's LM; ER,* Jeffrey; *Ed. M, NMM; LM,* J. Scott; *MM, BC, Ecl. R*). **Anthology:** 488–90 (*MR*), *491* (*Ed. M*), 493–7 (*ER,* Jeffrey), 497–9 (*Indicr,* L. Hunt), 499–502 (*BC*), 502–5 (*LM,* J. Scott), 509 (*MM*)
Robin Hood: 139 (*Ed. M*), *438* (*Ecl. R*). **Anthology:** *506* (*Ecl. R*)
Sleep and Poetry: 42, 132 (*Exar,* L.

540

Hunt), *420, 440.* **Anthology:** *452* (*Champ,* J. H. Reynolds), *457–8* (*Exar,* L. Hunt), 460–1 (*Ecl.* R, Conder), *469–70* (*BM,* probably Lockhart and Wilson)

Sonnets: **Anthology:** *452* (*Champ,* J. H. Reynolds), *452, 458* (*Exar,* L. Hunt), *460* (*Ecl.* R, Conder)

To my Brother George: **Anthology:** *458* (*Exar,* L. Hunt), *460* (*Ecl.* R, Conder)

Written on the day that Mr. Leigh Hunt left prison: **Anthology:** *468* (*BM,* probably Lockhart and Wilson)

'How many bards gild the lapses of time!': **Anthology:** *456* (*Exar,* L. Hunt)

'O Solitude!': **Anthology:** *464* (*Ed. M*)

To my Brothers: **Anthology:** *458*

(*Exar,* L. Hunt)

'To one who has been long in city pent': **Anthology:** *464* (*Ed. M*)

On first looking into Chapman's Homer: 131 (*Exar,* L. Hunt)

Addressed to Haydon ('High-mindedness, a jealousy for good'): **Anthology:** *464* (*Ed. M*), *468* (*BM,* probably Lockhart and Wilson); ('Great spirits now on earth are sojourning'): **Anthology:** *468* (*BM,* probably Lockhart and Wilson)

'Happy is England!': **Anthology:** *461* (*Ecl.* R, Conder)

'When I have fears': *448* (R. Woodhouse)

Specimen of an Induction to a Poem: **Anthology:** *457–8* (*Exar,* L. Hunt)

Index of Periodicals, Newspapers, and Anonymous Critical Publications

Note: References to pages up to 178 are to the General Survey.

The Alfred, West of England Journal and General Advertiser: 130 (on Keats). Keats Survey: 420, 428–9, 433. Keats Anthology: 477–81

The Anti-Jacobin Review and Magazine (1798–1821): Byron: 180

Blackwood's Edinburgh Magazine (1817–): 8, 24, 41, 42–3, 43–8 (on Byron), 43–8 (on Shelley), 50–1 (on Keats), 109, 114, 116, 145, 172 (on Keats), 175 (on Shelley). Byron Survey: 186–7, 192, 194. Byron Anthology: 297–301. Shelley Survey: 306, 307–8, 309, 311, 316–17, 318–19. Shelley Anthology: 333–7, 347–9, 351–5, 372–7, 401. Keats Survey: 418, 419–20, 421, 428, 434, 441, 445, 450. Keats Anthology: 467–72, 476–477

The British Critic (1793–1826): 24, 59, 60–8 (on Byron), 68 (on Shelley), 68–69 (on Keats), 81 (on Byron), 87–8 (on Byron), 111 (on Byron), 155 (on Byron), 172 (on Keats). Byron Survey: 180–1, 186, 187, 189, 194–5, 197. Byron Anthology: 222–3, 251–4. Shelley Survey: 305. Keats Survey: 419, 421, 428, 437–8. Keats Anthology: 499–502

The British Magazine or Miscellany of Polite Literature (1823): Byron: 194

The British Review (1811–25): 24, 91, 91–106 (on Byron), 106–7 (on Shelley), 107 (ignores Keats), 111 (on Byron). Byron Survey: 180, 185, 186, 189. Byron Anthology: 223–4,

233–6, 281–6. Keats Survey: 449

The Champion (1814–22): 84 (on Byron), 108, 134, 153–6 (on Byron), 156 (on Shelley), 156 (on Keats), 172 (on Byron). Byron Survey: 182, 185. Shelley Survey: 312. Keats Survey: 418, 420, 422, 427–8, 433. Keats Anthology: 451–2, 465–7

The Chester Guardian: 130 (on Keats)

The Christian Observer (1802–74): 24, 69, 69–77 (on Byron), 77 (ignores Shelley and Keats), 88 (on Byron). Byron Survey: 80. Keats Survey: 449

The Courier (1792–1842): 121

The Critical Review (1756–1817): 45. Byron Survey: 179

The Eclectic Review (1805–68: 24, 77–78, 78–88 (on Byron), 88–9 (on Shelley), 89–91 (on Keats), 92 (on Byron). Byron Survey: 182–3, 186. Byron Anthology: 212–13, 150–1. Shelley Survey: 305. Shelley Anthology: 327–9. Keats Survey: 419, 424, 434, 438–9. Keats Anthology: 459–61, 462, 505–9

The Edinburgh Magazine (Constable's) (1817–26) (successor to *The Scots Magazine*, *q.v.*): 89 (on Keats), 134, 135–8 (on Byron), 138–9 (on Shelley), 139 (on Keats), 172 (on Byron), 174 (on Keats). Byron Survey: 189, 192, 194–5. Byron Anthology: 227–9, 292–3. Shelley Survey: 323. Shelley Anthology: 396–9. Keats Survey:

419, 424–5, 436. Keats Anthology: 461–5, 490–2

The Edinburgh Review (1802–1929): 8, 24–5, 25–33 (on Byron), 33–4 (on Shelley), 34–5 (on Keats), 42, 51, 148 (on Byron), 173 (on Shelley), 174 (on Keats), 175 (on Shelley). Byron Survey: 179, 180, 182, 185, 188, 190. Byron Anthology: 207–12, 214–16, 217–22, 224–6, 229–233, 286–92. Shelley Survey: 322–3. Shelley Anthology: 388–9, 405–9. Keats Survey: 418, 420, 431–3, 435–436. Keats Anthology: 493–7

The Edinburgh Weekly Journal (1798–1848): Byron Survey: 206

The European Magazine and London Review (1782–1826): Keats Survey: 418–19, 423

The Examiner (1808–81): 24, 33 (on Shelley), 112–13 (on Shelley), 116–17, 117–21 (on Byron), 127 (on Byron), 127–30 (on Shelley), 130–2 (on Keats), 171 (on Byron), 172 (on Byron), 173–4 (on Keats), 175 (on Shelley). Byron Survey: 187, 189, 192, 195. Byron Anthology: 255–9, 293–4. Shelley Survey: 305, 306–7, 309, 310, 312, 319–22. Shelley Anthology: 329–33, 337, 381–8. Keats Survey: 418, 419, 420, 423–4, 428. Keats Anthology: 452–9

The Gentleman's Magazine (1731–1868): Byron Survey: 194

The Gossip (1821): Shelley Survey: 315–16

The Guardian (1819–24): Keats Survey: 435

The Honeycomb (1820): Shelley Survey: 312–13

The Indicator (1819–21): 24, 116–17, 129 (on Shelley), 130 (on Keats), 132–134 (on Keats), 174 (on Keats). Keats Survey: 418, 434–5. Keats Anthology: 497–9

The Investigator (1820–24): 119–20 (on Byron). Byron Survey: 189. Shelley Survey: 314–15

John Bull (1820–92): 24

John Bull's British Journal (1821): 24. Shelley Survey: 314

Knight's Quarterly Magazine (1823–4): 40–1 (on Shelley), 171 (on Shelley), 173 (on Shelley). Shelley Survey: 323–4. Shelley Anthology: 399–405

A Letter to the Rt. Hon. Lord Byron. By John Bull (1821): 45–6 (on Byron), 47–8 (on Byron). Byron Survey: 188, 202. Byron Anthology: 276–80

The Liberal (1822–3): 47, 67, 77, 117, 122, 139, 161–2. Byron Survey: 191–193. Shelley Survey: 321

The Literary Chronicle and Weekly Review (1819–20): Byron Survey: 192. Shelley Survey: 314, 318

The Literary Examiner (1823): 24, 116–17, 119 (on Byron), 122–7 (on Byron), 171 (on Byron), 172 (on Byron). Byron Survey: 193–5. Byron Anthology: 294–7, 301–2

The Literary Gazette (1817–62): 50, 134, 142 (on Byron), 157–64 (on Byron), 164–6 (on Shelley; neglects Keats). Byron Survey: 186, 189, 192, 194–5. Byron Anthology: 301: Shelley Survey: 310, 311, 314, 318, 322, 377–81

The Literary Journal and General Miscellany (1818–19): Keats Survey: 425–426

The London Magazine (Baldwin's) (1820–9): 24, 108, 108–11 (on Byron), 111–13 (on Shelley), 113–16 (on Keats), 134, 152 (on Keats), 172 (on Keats), 174 (on Keats), 175 (on Shelley). Byron Survey: 201. Byron Anthology: 262–75. Shelley Survey: 310–11, 350. Keats Survey: 419, 420, 421, 429–31, 437, 439. Keats Anthology: 482–7, 502–5, 510–11

The London Magazine; and Monthly Critical and Dramatic Review (Gold's) (1820–1): 24, 108, 134, 151 (neglects Byron), 151–2 (on Shelley), 152–3 (on Keats), 171–3 (on Shelley). Shelley Survey: 311–12, 314. Shelley Anthology: 355–7, 359–62. Keats Survey: 435

The Mirror of Literature (1823–47): 167

The Monthly Magazine (1796–1825): 89 (on Keats), 134, 140–3 (on Byron), 143 (on Shelley), 144 (on Keats), 148 (on Byron), 172 (on Byron), 172 (on Shelley). Byron Survey: 187, 189, 192, 194–5. Byron Anthology: 302–303, 307. Keats Survey: 419, 422–3, 437, 509–10

The Monthly Review (1749–1845): 24, 45, 51–2, 52–7 (on Byron), 57–8 (on Shelley), 58–9 (on Keats), 174 (on Keats). Byron Survey: 180, 185, 187, 189, 194–5. Byron Anthology: 207, 246–8. Shelley Survey: 305, 308, 311. Shelley Anthology: 357–9. Keats Survey: 418, 434. Keats Anthology: 488–90

The Morning Chronicle (1769–1865): Keats Survey: 420

The New European Magazine (1822–4): Byron Survey: 192

The New Monthly Magazine (1814–36): 113, 134, 144–9 (on Byron), 149–50 (on Shelley), 150–1 (on Keats), 173 (on Shelley), 174 (on Keats). Keats Survey: 436

The New Times (1819–20): 132 (on Keats), 174 (on Keats). Keats Survey: 418, 434, 439

The Oxford Herald: Keats Survey: 420, 426–7

The Portfolio (1823–30): Byron Survey: 194

The Quarterly Review (1809–   ): 8, 24, 33 (on Shelley), 35, 35–40 (on Byron), 40–1 (on Shelley), 41–2 (on Keats), 42, 43 (on Byron), 59, 113 (on Keats), 114, 128–31 (on Shelley), 152 (on Keats), 171 (on Shelley), 175 (on Shelley), 177 (on Byron). Byron Survey: 180, 182, 185, 190–1, 199. Byron Anthology: 236–46. Shelley Survey: 306, 308–9, 312, 319, 320–1, 323–4, 326. Shelley Anthology: 337–347, 347–9, 362–72, 381, 387, 400–2. Keats Survey: 419–20, 421, 428, 434, 441, 443, 445. Keats Anthology: 472–6, 476–7, 477–81, 504

A Reply to the Anti-Matrimonial Hypothesis and Supposed Atheism of Percy Bysshe Shelley as Laid Down in Queen Mab (1821): Shelley Survey: 314

The Republican (1819–26): 172 (on Shelley). Shelley Survey: 314

The Retrospective Review (1820–8): 150. Keats Survey: 421

The Scots Magazine (1739–1817; became from 1817 *The Edinburgh Magazine, q.v.*): 42, 134, 135 (on Byron)

The Scourge (1811–16): Byron Survey: 180

The Theological Inquirer, or Polemical Magazine (1815): Shelley Survey: 304

The Westminster Review (1824–36, and later, under various names, till 1914): Shelley Survey: 324

The Yellow Dwarf (1818): Byron Survey: 183–4. Byron Anthology: 226

DATE DUE

MAR 2 1977			
APR 1 0 1992			